W9-BTO-826

MICHAEL W. MAHER
University of California–Davis

CLYDE P. STICKNEY
Dartmouth College

ROMAN L. WEIL
University of Chicago

Managerial Accounting

AN INTRODUCTION TO
Concepts, Methods, and Uses

9th Edition

THOMSON
™
SOUTH-WESTERN

Australia · Canada · Mexico · Singapore · Spain · United Kingdom · United States

THOMSON
━━━━━★━━━━━ ™
SOUTH-WESTERN

Managerial Accounting: An Introduction to Concepts, Methods, and Uses, Ninth Edition
Michael W. Maher, Clyde P. Stickney, and Roman L. Weil

VP/Editorial Director:
Jack W. Calhoun

Publisher:
Rob Dewey

Acquisitions Editor:
Keith Chasse

Developmental Editor:
Allison Rolfes

Marketing Manager:
Keith Chasse

Production Editor:
Margaret M. Bril

Manager of Technology, Editorial:
Vicky True

Technology Project Editor:
Sally Nieman

Web Coordinator:
Scott Cook

Manufacturing Coordinator:
Doug Wilke

Production House:
Lachina Publishing Services

Printer:
Thomson/West
Eagan, Minnesota

Art Director:
Chris Miller

Internal Designer:
Beckmeyer Design

Cover Designer:
Beckmeyer Design

COPYRIGHT © 2006
Thomson South-Western, a part
of The Thomson Corporation.
Thomson, the Star logo, and
South-Western are trademarks used
herein under license.

Printed in the United States of America
1 2 3 4 5   08 07 06 05

ISBN: 0-324-22722-1

ALL RIGHTS RESERVED.
No part of this work covered by the
copyright hereon may be reproduced
or used in any form or by any means—
graphic, electronic, or mechanical,
including photocopying, recording,
taping, Web distribution or information
storage and retrieval systems, or in
any other manner—without the written
permission of the publisher.

For permission to use material
from this text or product, submit
a request online at
http://www.thomsonrights.com

Library of Congress Control Number:
2004116545

For more information about our
products, contact us at:

Thomson Learning Academic
Resource Center

1-800-423-0563

Thomson Higher Education
5191 Natorp Boulevard
Mason, OH 45040
USA

Asia (including India)
Thomson Learning
5 Shenton Way
#01-01 UIC Building
Singapore 068808

Australia/New Zealand
Thomson Learning Australia
102 Dodds Street
Southbank, Victoria 3006
Australia

Canada
Thomson Nelson
1120 Birchmount Road
Toronto, Ontario
M1K 5G4
Canada

Latin America
Thomson Learning
Seneca, 53
Colonia Polanco
11560 Mexico
D.F.Mexico

UK/Europe/Middle East/Africa
Thomson Learning
High Holborn House
50/51 Bedford Row
London WC1R 4LR
United Kingdom

Spain (including Portugal)
Thomson Paraninfo
Calle Magallanes, 25
28015 Madrid, Spain

For

KATHLEEN, KRISTA, ANDREA

For

**LEXIE, LACEY, SANDY,
GRETA, ISABELLA, LILY, AND
CHARLIE PARKER**

AND KATHY

With Thanks

For Our Students

Whatever be the detail with which you cram your students, the chance of their meeting in after-life exactly that detail is infinitesimal; and if they do meet it, they will probably have forgotten what you taught them about it. The really useful training yields a comprehension of a few general principles with a thorough grounding in the way they apply to a variety of concrete details. In subsequent practice the students will have forgotten your particular details; but they will remember by an unconscious common sense how to apply principles to immediate circumstances.

Alfred North Whitehead
The Aims of Education and Other Essays

WITH THANKS

Preface

We three authors have reached a combined 100 years of teaching accounting. We remain convinced that our primary job as educators is to teach problem-solving skills as well as the organizational (and social) context in which students will as managers conduct economic activities. An increasing number of employers ask that business school graduates seek out ways to add value to organizations, not just work competently on projects that superiors assign to them. Focusing on problem-solving skills and the organizational context of decisions will serve current and future students well in responding to employers' expectations.

Management accounting should not primarily concern making computations. Students should aim to understand the organization's business issues that created a need for implementing such concepts as activity-based costing and the balanced scorecard. And students should view the success or failure of these methods and concepts in the context of the organization's operating and business environment. We know many examples in which thoughtful practitioners developed complex activity-based costing, balanced scorecard, and other management accounting methods only to have them fail in implementation. These methods did not fail because of errors in computations; they failed because their developers did not sufficiently understand the problems that the organization needed to solve. Or they failed because these practitioners could not gain agreement on goals and strategies from both top management and the people who would later implement the methods. In other words, understanding business concepts and real incentives for decisions is more valuable than mere proficiency with accounting tools.

As educators, and as authors, we aim to help students develop lifelong problem-solving skills and understand the organizational and social context in which the organization's members make decisions. Students educated in this manner can add value to organizations and society, whether they work in accounting or some other field.

The Ninth Edition continues to reflect our philosophy in every respect. We emphasize conceptual and analytical thinking over training in procedures. The following three examples demonstrate how we apply that philosophy:

- Much of the book focuses on decision making (Chapters 4–8) because we want students in management accounting courses to focus on business problem solving and the business context in which they use accounting information.
- We devote an entire chapter (Chapter 12) to incentive issues beyond the conventional profit and investment center material because students should be aware that these issues drive management decision making to a large degree.
- We provide answers to even-numbered exercises in addition to the usual self-study problems so students can get immediate feedback on the basic ideas that the chapter presents. By enabling students to get immediate feedback on each chapter's basic ideas, we provide opportunity for instructors to explore the big concepts and to integrate ideas from different chapters.

Themes of the Revision   We wrote this book for students who expect to become managers, whether in marketing, finance, IT, or some other area. Previous editions have taught readers how to use accounting information to add value to their organizations and have emphasized concepts over procedures. The Ninth Edition continues these themes and improves on their application, as the list of chapter changes makes clear. Further, we expanded our discussions of globalization, reflecting the reality of international business and the need for managers to understand how cultural differences affect their decisions. We have also increased our coverage of ethics, which has been a historical focus of the text. In today's business climate, management faces increased scrutiny from investors, boards of directors, and regulators. Students should be armed with the ability to make their business decisions ethical ones.

We have sharpened the exposition, updated subject matter and revised assignment materials throughout the book. We also combined two chapters on decision making, Chapters 7 and 8 from the Eighth Edition into one comprehensive chapter (Chapter 7 in the Ninth Edition). We combined these chapters in response to reviewers and our own experience in teaching this material, where we learned that the material flows better if taught in one chapter instead of two. For the same reasons, we combined two chapters on cost variances and cost center performance evaluation (Chapters 11 and 12 in the Eighth Edition) into one chapter (Chapter 10) in the Ninth Edition.

The Organization and Use of this Book
We divide the book into three major parts, which allows maximum flexibility for instructors' teaching preferences.

Part One, "Overview and Basic Concepts" (Chapters 1–3)
Part Two, "Managerial Decision Making" (Chapters 4–8)
Part Three, "Motivating Managers to Make Good Decisions" (Chapters 9–13)

Part One covers fundamental concepts, including activity-based management, and provides an overview of managerial accounting. After Part One, instructors may cover Parts Two and Three in whichever order they prefer.

Part Two discusses concepts and methods useful for managerial decision making. Chapter 4 covers strategic management of costs, quality, and time. Chapter 5 discusses cost behavior and methods of estimating cost driver rates. Chapter 6 discusses financial modeling, with cost volume profit treated as a simple example. Chapter 7 discusses differential cost and revenue analysis. Chapter 8 discusses long-run decision making involving capital budgeting.

Part Three concentrates on managerial planning and performance evaluation. Chapter 9 provides an overview of planning and control, and discusses development of budgets as tools for planning and control. Chapter 10 discusses profit and cost center performance evaluation, including profit variance analysis, cost variance analysis, variance investigation, and the use of nonfinancial performance measures. Chapter 11 focuses on performance evaluation in investment centers, including transfer pricing and EVA®. Chapter 12 discusses incentive issues, including use of the balanced scorecard and ethical problems related to incentive systems, such as financial fraud. Chapter 13 discusses cost allocation, which can be taught at any point after Chapter 2.

Appendix The Appendix to the book discusses compound interest calculations used in discounted cash flow analysis. It provides concepts of the time value of money useful to management accountants.

Glossary The Glossary defines comprehensively the concepts and terms used by managers and management accountants. It is one of the most comprehensive and informative glossaries that students might ever find.

Major Features of the Ninth Edition

Enhances Critical Thinking Skills
Users of previous editions and reviewers have always described this book as requiring critical thinking. A critical thinking approach views accounting as a process of reporting information for people to use, as opposed to a view of accounting as a set of rules or procedures to follow. We have encouraged the development of critical thinking skills since the First Edition. In short, we are preparing the next generation of managers and managerial accountants to think through specific situations for themselves using the concepts explored in this book.

To enhance instructors' ability to get students into a critical thinking mode, we include in each chapter a section of assignment materials called Critical Analysis and Discussion Questions. We have found these questions particularly useful for in-class assignments to groups of students, who discuss the issues and report the results of their discussion. These questions make good take-home group or individual writing assignments.

Conceptual Approach   This edition, like those before it, emphasizes concepts over procedures. We believe students in MBA managerial accounting classes should understand the fundamental concepts and see the "big picture," leaving more detailed procedures to cost accounting classes and on-the-job training. Although a minority of students taking managerial accounting classes will become accountants, all will use managerial accounting concepts during their careers. We intend this book to give them a solid grounding in those concepts.

Variety of End-of-Chapter Assignment Materials   Accounting instructors know the value of interesting and accurate assignment materials. We have written exercises and problems to reflect the new material. We have extensively class-tested the assignment material and worked every question, exercise, problem, and case many times in preparing this edition.

The variety and quantity of end-of-chapter assignment materials make the book suitable for various approaches to the MBA managerial course. To help the instructor assign homework and select items for class presentation, we have divided the assignment materials into five categories: Review Questions, Critical Analysis and Discussion Questions, Exercises, Problems, and Cases.

- **Review Questions** are straightforward questions about key concepts in the chapter.
- **Critical Analysis and Discussion Questions** are thought-provoking questions about the challenging issues that managers and accountants face. These questions are particularly good for written essays and class discussions.
- **Exercises** reinforce key concepts in the chapter, often referring the student to a particular illustration. Exercises typically deal with a single topic and are particularly useful for classroom demonstration. To enhance the self-learning dimension of the book, we include fully worked-out solutions at the end of the chapter to the even-numbered exercises. (For convenience, we also place these solutions in the Solutions Manual.)
- **Problems** challenge the student to apply and interpret the material in the chapter, many with thought-provoking discussion or essay questions.
- **Cases** encourage students to apply concepts from multiple chapters and their other courses to deal with complex managerial issues. These are particularly good for advanced students and graduate students with some previous background in managerial accounting.

Self-Study Problems with Full Solutions   Better and more motivated students take every opportunity to test their understanding. Students who find managerial accounting at the MBA level to be more challenging need additional resources for self-help. We have designed this book to make it easy for students to learn the basic concepts on their own, thereby making more class time available for discussion. Like most managerial accounting textbooks, this one includes **Self-Study Problems** placed at key points in each chapter. (Their answers appear at the end of the chapter.) In addition, the worked-out solutions to half of the exercises in each chapter give students ample opportunity to test their knowledge of the basic concepts. Ideally, they will come to class with a solid understanding of the basic ideas, and instructors can devote class time to provocative discussion.

Managerial Applications   Students are more motivated to learn the material if they see its application to real-world problems, particularly ones they believe they will face. This book contains **Managerial Applications** that are similar to sidebars in news magazines. These allow the student to explore company practices that illustrate concepts discussed in the text without disrupting the flow of study. See the table of contents for a list of Managerial Applications.

Supplements Accompanying the Text

Instructor's Manual   The Instructor's Manual (by P. N. Saksena, Indiana University, South Bend) includes chapter overviews, learning objectives, lecture notes with teaching suggestions, and suggestions for group discussion, all focusing on the needs of MBA instructors.

Test Bank   The Test Bank (by Peter Ben Ezra, George Washington University) includes a mix of questions and problems tuned to the lasting needs of MBA instructors.

Solutions Manual   The Solutions Manual, by the text authors, contains responses to questions and solutions to all exercises, problems, and cases.

Instructor's Resource CD with ExamView®   This CD contains the Solutions Manual, Instructor's Manual, Test Bank files in Word, ExamView®, and PowerPoint slides.

Lectures in PowerPoint   Accompanying the Ninth Edition are PowerPoint slides (by Michael Blue, Bloomsburg University), available by download to students and instructors for use in preparing and displaying material for lectures. The PowerPoint slides may be found on the product Web site and on the Instructor's Resource CD.

Product Support Web Site   Instructors and students may turn to *http://maher.swlearning.com/* for resources geared to the MBA managerial course such as PowerPoint lectures, spreadsheets, instructor supplements, and quizzes.

Management Templates   This supplement, downloadable from the product Web site, gives students experience in solving selected management accounting problems from the end-of-chapter assignments using spreadsheets.

ExamView®   The test bank, available in ExamView on the Instructor's Resource CD, contains computerized test item files. This program is easy-to-use test creation software compatible with Microsoft® Windows. Instructors can add or edit questions, instructions, and answers, and select questions (randomly or numerically) by previewing them on the screen. Instructors can also create and administer quizzes online, whether over the Internet, a local area network (LAN), or a wide area network (WAN).

Acknowledgments   We are grateful to a number of people for their comments, criticisms, and suggestions, among them Peter Ben Ezra (George Washington University), P. N. Saksena (Indiana University, South Bend), Felix Amenkhienan (Radford University), Frank LaMarra (Wayne State University), Dan Law (Gonzaga University), James Bierstaker (University of Massachusetts-Boston), Laurie McWhorter (University of North Carolina-Charlotte), Jay Holmen (University of Wisconsin-Eau Claire), and Myung-Ho Yoon (Northeastern Illinois University).

We are grateful to Kathleen Donelan-Knox (University of Notre Dame), Andrea Maher, Katherine Xenophon-Rybowiak, and Barbi Wiggins for their comments, criticisms and contributions to this book. We wish to thank acquisitions editor Keith Chasse, associate developmental editor Allison Rolfes, marketing manager Keith Chasse, production editor Marge Bril, designer Chris Miller, project manager Sheila McGill with Lachina Publishing Services, and Executive MarComm Manager Brian Chaffee, among others, for their efforts. We especially appreciate their patience and dedication to publishing excellence.

M. W. M.
C. P. S.
R. L. W.

Brief Contents

Contents

xii Contents

Part Two *Managerial Decision Making* 109

Chapter 4 **Strategic Management of Costs, Quality, and Time 110**

Why Is Quality Important? 111 | Traditional versus Quality-Based View 112 | Quality According to the Customer 112 | Quality Control 113 | Costs of Failing to Control and Improve Quality 114 | Trading Off Quality Control and Failure Costs 114 | Problem 4.1 for Self-Study 116 | Measuring the Cost of Quality in a Nonmanufacturing Setting 116 | Does Quality Really Have a Cost? 117 | **Managerial Application: Firestone Blows It 117** | Identifying Quality Problems 117 | Just-in-Time and Total Quality Management 119 | The Importance of Time in a Competitive Environment 119 | **Managerial Application: Reducing Delivery Time to Gain a Competitive Advantage 121** | Using Activity-Based Management to Improve Customer Response Time 121 | Using the Balanced Scorecard to Measure Performance 122 | Traditional Managerial Accounting Systems Can Limit the Impact of Total Quality Management 123 | Summary 124 | Key Terms and Concepts 125 | Solution to Self-Study Problem 125 | Questions, Exercises, and Problems 126 | Suggested Solutions to Even-Numbered Exercises 131

Chapter 5 **Cost Drivers and Cost Behavior 134**

The Nature of Fixed and Variable Costs 135 | Types of Fixed Costs 139 | Other Cost Behavior Patterns 139 | Problem 5.1 for Self-Study 142 | Problem 5.2 for Self-Study 144 | Cost Estimation Methods 144 | Estimating Costs Using Historical Data 144 | Problem 5.3 for Self-Study 151 | Data Problems 152 | Ethical Issues in Data Analysis 152 | **Managerial Application: United Airlines Uses Regression to Estimate Cost Behavior 153** | Strengths and Weaknesses of Cost Estimation Methods 153 | Problem 5.4 for Self-Study 155 | Summary 155 | Key Terms and Concepts 156 | Solutions to Self-Study Problems 157 | Appendix 5.1: Deriving Learning Curves 159 | Appendix 5.2: Interpreting Regression Analysis Output 160 | Questions, Exercises, and Problems 162 | Suggested Solutions to Even-Numbered Exercises 174

Chapter 6 **Financial Modeling for Short-Term Decision-Making 176**

What Is Financial Modeling? 177 | The Cost-Volume-Profit Model 178 | Applications of Financial Modeling 182 | Problem 6.1 for Self-Study 183 | Problem 6.2 for Self-Study 184 | Using Sales Dollars as a Measure of Volume 186 | Income Taxes 187 | **Managerial Application: Calculating Break-Even Points for a Brewpub 188** | Multiple Product Financial Modeling 189 | Problem 6.3 for Self-Study 192 | Simplifications and Assumptions 193 | Financial Modeling and ABC's Multiple-Cost Drivers 193 | Summary 196 | Key Terms and Concepts 197 | Solutions to Self-Study Problems 197 | Questions, Exercises, Problems, and Cases 199 | Suggested Solutions to Even-Numbered Exercises 209

Chapter 7 **Differential Cost Analysis for Operating Decisions 214**

The Differential Principle 215 | Major Influences on Pricing 217 | Short-Run versus Long-Run Pricing Decisions 218 | Differential Approach to Pricing 219 | Problem 7.1 for Self-Study 219 | Long-Run Pricing Decisions 220 | **Managerial Application: Pricing Practices in Various Countries 220** | Life-Cycle Product Costing and Pricing 221 | Using Target Prices to Set Target Costs 221 | Legal Issues Relating Costs to Prices 222 | Customer Profitability and Differential Analysis 222 | Problem 7.2 for Self-Study 224 | Product Choice Decisions 224 | Theory of Constraints and Throughput Contribution Analysis 226 | Make-or-Buy Decisions 228 | **Managerial Application: Cost Management in Action: Why Hewlett-Packard Now Manages Suppliers Instead of Overhead 228** | Problem 7.3 for Self-Study 229 | Joint Products: Sell or Process Further 230 | Problem 7.4 for Self-Study 231 | Adding and Dropping Parts of Operations 231 |

MACMU9

Part One

Overview *and* Basic Concepts

1

The noted management writer Peter Drucker calls accounting the most intellectually challenging and turbulent area in the field of management. Whatever your career plans, the ideas in this book will help you meet those challenges.
  Chapters 1–3 lay the foundation for the rest of the book. Chapter 1 discusses important managerial accounting concepts that we use throughout the book. Chapter 2 shows you how cost systems work, focusing on accounting for direct materials and direct labor. Chapter 3 extends Chapter 2 to focus on accounting for overhead costs. Both Chapters 2 and 3 emphasize the importance of managing costs, not just accounting for them.

Fundamental Concepts

Learning Objectives

1. Distinguish between managerial and financial accounting.

2. Understand how managers can use accounting information to implement strategies.

3. Identify the key financial players in the organization.

4. Understand managerial accountants' professional environment and ethical responsibilities.

5. Master the concept of *cost*.

6. Compare and contrast income statements prepared for managerial use and those prepared for external reporting.

7. Understand the concepts useful for managing costs.

8. Describe how managerial accounting supports modern production environments.

9. Understand the importance of effective communication between accountants and users of managerial accounting information.

10. Understand the ethical standards that make up the Institute of Management Accountants' Code of Ethics (Appendix 1.1).

1

Managers must equip themselves with the tools and insights to act strategically about business opportunities. This book discusses how managers can use information—both financial and non-financial—to implement strategic plans and improve the process of providing goods and services to people. Organizational success typically requires intelligent use of information. About 80 percent of new businesses fail within five years after opening their doors, often because management does not use information to make good decisions, plan for growth, and forecast cash needs. For example, the Managerial Application "Why Managers Need Cost Information" tells of the early days of Domino's Pizza, when the company nearly went bankrupt because of poor information. Organizations with poor information systems also have difficulty obtaining financing from banks, venture capitalists, and shareholders.

User Orientation

Even if you are not planning a career in finance or accounting, you will be using managerial accounting information. Here are just a few examples.

- Marketing managers use financial information to help price products and assess their profitability. Using product cost information, marketing managers ascertain how low they can drop prices and still be profitable.
- Production managers use financial and non-financial information to manage quality and costs and to assure on-time delivery.
- General managers use financial information to measure employee performance and create incentives.

We take a user's perspective of accounting in this book. We want you to understand managerial accounting so that you can effectively use the information that accountants provide.

Managerial Application

Why Managers Need Cost Information

Domino's Pizza (http://www.dominos.com) nearly went bankrupt before the owner discovered that the company was losing money on 6-inch pizzas. The company dropped the product line and went on to become a multibillion-dollar company. Many hospitals that thrived when insurers fully reimbursed health-care costs now face large deficits. Many airlines, successful under prior stringent regulations, have gone bankrupt since regulations have eased.

What do these stories all have in common? They represent situations in which better management of costs would have helped, or did help, the organization to succeed. In general, an organization's ability to manage its costs becomes more important as the environment becomes more competitive. Hospitals, airlines, banks, audit firms, and other organizations face increasingly stiff competition, driving them to seek better ways to measure productivity and costs. Perhaps you know of organizations that have struggled because they did not use cost information to manage costs. (One such organization is the U.S. government.)

Comparing Financial and Managerial Accounting

University educators usually divide accounting courses into financial accounting and managerial accounting. **Financial accounting** deals with reporting to people *outside* an organization. The users of financial accounting reports include shareholders (owners) of a corporation, creditors (those who lend money to a business), financial analysts, labor unions, and government regulators.

Managerial accounting deals with activities *inside* the organization. (Most companies call this *finance* or *corporate finance*.) Managerial accounting has no rules and regulations, such as generally accepted accounting principles. Unlike financial accounting, which must use historical data, managerial accounting can and does use projections about the future. After all, managers make decisions for the future, not the past.

Like all else in business, managerial accounting information must meet a managerial cost-benefit test. To justify providing managerial accounting information, the benefit from providing the information must exceed the cost of obtaining the information. New managerial accounting initiatives such as activity-based costing and the balanced scorecard (both discussed in later chapters), for example, must pass the cost-benefit test to be worth undertaking.

Problem 1.1 for Self-Study

Differences between Financial and Managerial Accounting. What are the differences between financial and managerial accounting?

The solution to this self-study problem is at the end of this chapter on page 22.

Implementing Strategies

A good managerial accounting system takes into account the economics of the industries in which the organization operates and the organization's strategy. For example, suppose managers of a company called e-whatever.com realize that their industry has low barriers to entry; and the organization has competitors, both in "bricks" and in "clicks." Furthermore, the company's product is essentially a *commodity* (a product that is difficult to differentiate from those of competitors) despite the managers' having spent millions of dollars to build brand equity. To compete effectively, the organization must excel at order fulfillment and manage costs both to keep prices competitive and to make a reasonable return on shareholders' investment.

E-whatever.com's managerial accounting system must provide managers with cost information to help them assess product profitability given the competitive market the company faces. It also must highlight problem areas in order fulfillment, such as delays in shipping and unexpectedly high purchase returns. In addition, the managerial accounting system must measure pricing and order fulfillment performance so that managers can reward people for doing well on such critical performance factors.

Consider another type of strategic advantage, the learning phenomenon. Assume General Electric produces a complex navigational device for spacecraft. While other companies could produce it, General Electric has developed a strategic advantage because of the learning phenomenon. The learning phenomenon, which we discuss in detail in Chapter 5, means that General Electric's labor costs per unit go down as it produces more of the navigational devices. By the time it produces the 40th navigational device, General Electric's labor costs might be only a fraction of the costs of a new market entrant that is producing its first navigational device.

General Electric's managerial accounting system should track costs that are potentially subject to the learning phenomenon. It should inform managers how the learning phenomenon affects costs and helps managers predict product costs. The managerial accounting system should also help managers budget costs of production that are subject to the learning phenomenon.

Shelter-Us is a nonprofit organization that operates a shelter for homeless people and provides transition housing for victims of domestic violence. The shelter receives donations from businesses and from private individuals, and it receives grants from various government agencies. The organization aims to provide adequate shelter at minimum cost. Its managers must consider the cost of various types of housing. For example, should the shelter build its own housing units or outsource housing to a local motel?

The managerial accounting system for Shelter-Us should provide information about the costs of various types of shelter. Because the organization receives donations and grants, it should provide information about specific uses of monies received. For example, it should not use funds from a grant earmarked for victims of spousal abuse to provide meals for homeless people.

These examples illustrate that the managerial accounting system should help managers implement an organization's strategy. The system must be adapted to each organization's objectives, strategy, and environment.

Misuses of Accounting Information

Managers and other users of accounting information often mistakenly use data for one purpose that are intended for another. For example, many companies compute various inventory costs and depreciation costs for tax purposes; this information does not usually provide data suitable for managerial uses.

Further, most managerial decisions require more detailed data than external financial reports provide. For instance, Amazon.com's (http://www.amazon.com) external financial statements present a single amount for inventory valuation and a single amount for cost of goods sold expense summarized for all product lines. For decision-making purposes, however, management wants aggregated data about the cost of each of several hundred products, such as paperback books and jazz CDs.

Managers sometimes believe that they must use the same accounting data for their decision making, planning, and other managerial activities as they present in tax returns and financial statements. That is not correct. In fact, many companies develop managerial accounting systems independent of financial accounting. Some regulated companies, such as Cinergy, have a third accounting system designed to accumulate data to show the regulators, who, to a degree, control the prices Cinergy can charge some of its customers.

Many organizations have tried simply to take their financial accounting systems as given and modify them a little for managerial uses. The results are often disastrous, because managers do not get the information they need for decision making.

Managers must realize that different uses of accounting information require different types of accounting information. "One size fits all" does not apply to managerial accounting. For example, consider a used laptop computer that you own. Think about how the data you'd want to know would differ as the question you ask changes:

1. What can I sell it for?
2. What will it fetch if I trade it in with cash for a new one?
3. What value does this old machine have as a backup if I buy a new one but keep the old one?
4. What did the old computer cost new?
5. What is the computer's book value—original cost reduced by accumulated depreciation?
6. What is the cost basis for tax reporting purposes?

Managerial accounting information would be relevant for items 1 through 3, whereas financial accounting or tax information would be relevant for items 4 through 6.

EXHIBIT 1.1   **Partial Organization Chart**

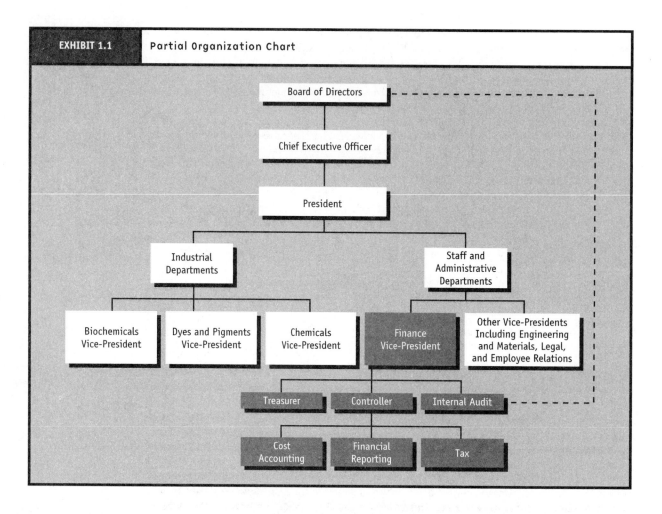

Key Financial Players in the Organization

As managers, you should know the key financial players in organizations. Who in the organization will help you get the information you need to manage the company? Exhibit 1.1 shows a typical organization chart—an abbreviated version of DuPont's. The shaded boxes represent the financial managers at the corporate level.

Financial Vice-President

The top financial person is usually a senior vice-president in the company, the **financial vice-president** (often called chief financial officer—CFO). This person is in charge of the entire accounting and finance function and is typically one of the three most influential people in the company. (The other two are the chief executive officer and the president.)

Controller

The **controller** manages cost and managerial accounting in most organizations. The name *controller* sounds like someone who "controls things." In fact, the controller's staff works in planning, decision making, designing information systems, designing incentive systems, and helping managers make operating decisions, among other things. If you have a career in marketing, production, or general management, you will have frequent interactions with controllers.

Treasurer

The corporate **treasurer** manages cash flows and raises cash for operations. The treasurer normally handles relations with banks and other lending or financing sources, including public issues of shares or debt.

Cost Accountants/Managers

Cost accountants and **cost managers** analyze and manage costs. They also work on cross-functional teams, including marketing-oriented teams, to decide whether to keep or drop products because of product profitability, and operations-oriented teams, to find ways to redesign products to save costs.

Internal Audit

The **internal audit** department provides a variety of auditing and consulting services. Internal auditors often help managers in that they provide an independent perspective on managers' problems. Internal auditors frequently act as watchdogs who find internal fraud. For example, the internal auditors at WorldCom "blew the whistle" on top executives by uncovering a substantial accounting misstatement of several billion dollars.

Internal auditors who focus on operations as well as finance are particularly helpful to managers. Such auditors are called *operational auditors*. In some companies, such as General Electric, internal auditing is an important training ground for managers. Federal legislation affecting corporate governance—the Sarbanes-Oxley Act of 2002—has increased the interaction between internal auditors and the audit committee of the board of directors. The prestige of internal auditing has increased. Likely, the audit committee not only will receive reports directly from the internal auditors but also set compensation for them.

Notice in Exhibit 1.1 that at DuPont, as at many other companies, the internal audit manager reports to the controller's superior. The controller is in charge of the accounting systems audited by the internal auditor. If internal auditors report to the controller, then internal auditors are reporting to their own boss. The dotted line between Internal Audit and the Board of Directors indicates that internal auditors can communicate directly with the audit committee of the board of directors. That allows internal auditors to blow the whistle on anybody in the company—even the president—if they believe it's necessary.

Institute of Management Accountants

The **Institute of Management Accountants (IMA)** (http://www.imanet.org) has thousands of members who work in management accounting. It publishes a journal called *Strategic Finance,* numerous policy statements, and research studies on accounting issues. It also sponsors the Certified Management Accountant (CMA) and Certified in Financial Management programs, which are the major certifications for managerial accountants.

Certified Management Accountant

The **Certified Management Accountant (CMA)** designation recognizes educational achievement and professional competence in management accounting. The examination, educational requirements, and experience requirements are similar to those for a CPA, but they aim at the professional in management and cost accounting. We have included questions from CMA examinations in this book.

Certified Public Accountant

The designation **Certified Public Accountant (CPA)** indicates that an individual has qualified to be registered or licensed by passing a written examination and, in some states, satisfying audit experience requirements. The CPA examination includes questions on managerial accounting.

Cost Accounting Standards Board

If you work in the defense industry, you will hear about the **Cost Accounting Standards Board (CASB).** The U.S. Congress established the board in 1970 to set accounting standards for contracts between the U.S. government and defense contractors, such as Boeing, Honeywell, and General Dynamics. Accountants apply CASB standards to many transactions between defense contractors and the U.S. government.

Canadian Certifications

Two Canadian organizations provide designations similar to the CPA designation in the United States. The Canadian Institute of Chartered Accountants provides the Chartered Accountant

(CA) designation, and the Certified General Accountants' Association of Canada gives the Certified General Accountant (CGA) designation. The Society of Management Accountants in Canada gives a Certified Management Accountant (CMA) designation similar to the CMA in the United States.

Ethical Issues

During your career, you may face ethical issues related to appropriate marketing tactics, environmental standards, labor relations and conditions, and financial reporting. Companies that do not meet high ethical standards not only create social messes for others to clean up but also are frequently in dire straits in the long run. Enron is a classic example.

Ethical issues arise in many places in the managerial accounting domain. Some have to do with costs. For example, a manager might ask the following questions:

- What are the differential costs of bringing an existing site in Thailand up to international labor and environmental standards?
- How do we budget for unforeseen environmental cleanup?
- How do we design performance evaluation systems that motivate managers to behave ethically?

Managers who receive compensation based on their business unit's profits may wish to record sales that have not yet occurred in order to boost the bottom line and their own pay. This premature revenue recognition usually occurs just before the end of the reporting period, say, in late December for a company using a December 31 fiscal year-end. Management may have rationalized the early revenue recognition because the firm would probably make the sale in January anyway; this practice just moves next year's sale (and profit) into this year. This is unethical and, in a public company, illegal. Also, financial accountants might use the information to generate external reports, thus exposing the company to charges of fraudulent reporting.

We include discussions of ethical issues throughout this book. We hope these discussions will help alert you to potential problems that you and your colleagues will face in your careers. Many accountants and businesspeople have found themselves in serious trouble because they did several small things, none of which appeared seriously wrong, only to find that these small things added up to a major problem.[1] If you know the warning signs of potential ethical problems, you will have a chance to protect yourself and set the proper ethical tone of your workplace at the same time.

Code of Conduct

The Institute of Management Accountants has developed a code of conduct, called "Standards of Ethical Conduct for Management Accountants." We have reproduced it in the appendix to this chapter. The IMA code mandates that management accountants have a responsibility to maintain the highest levels of ethical conduct.[2] The IMA standards recommend that people faced with ethical conflicts take the following steps:

1. Follow the company's established procedures that deal with such conflicts. These procedures include talking to an ombudsman, who keeps the names of those involved confidential.
2. If step (1) does not resolve the conflict, people should consider discussing the matter with superiors, potentially as high as the audit committee or the board of directors.
3. In extreme cases, people may have no alternative but to resign.

While desirable first steps, the IMA's Code of Conduct would have done little to uncover the major accounting scandals that came to light in the early years of this decade because top man-

---

[1]This phenomenon has a name in logic: the fallacy of composition. This fallacy states that an aggregation of items with a particular property does not necessarily have that same property. For example, if you were to stand up at a football game, you would be able to see the field more easily. If everyone stood up, everyone would not see more easily. Closer to home: An aggregate of individual items, each of which is unimportant, can be important.

[2]See *Standards of Ethical Conduct for Management Accountants* (Montvale, N.J.: National Association of Accountants [now called the Institute of Management Accountants], June 1, 1983).

agers and members of the board of directors either were involved in the scandals or were not actively engaged in corporate governance.

Nearly all large organizations have a corporate code of conduct. If you are considering taking a job at a particular company, you should first read the company's code of conduct to get a sense of top management's values. For example, the Johnson & Johnson code of conduct, summarized in the Managerial Application "J & J's Credo," discusses the company's primary responsibilities as being to customers, to the medical profession, to employees, and to the community. Responsibility to shareholders comes after these primary responsibilities.

In addition to reading the corporate code of conduct, learn whether the company's managers and workers take it seriously. In many situations, the code of conduct is only window dressing. Also, observe top managers' behavior. Do top managers look the other way or try to conceal unethical behavior in the organization? Do they say, "Don't tell me how you get the results, just get them"? If you observe such behavior, then top managers are not setting an ethical tone in the company. (Students of corporate ethics call this behavior "setting the tone at the top.")

Codes of conduct can benefit companies by communicating to customers, employees, shareholders, and suppliers that companies are trustworthy. As Kenneth Arrow states, "A close look reveals that a great deal of economic life depends for its viability on a certain limited degree of ethical commitment."[3] If managers adhere to a company's code of conduct that promises honest business practices, then those who do business with the company can trust it. Trust in business transactions reduces the need for monitoring, legal contracting, and similar transaction costs that occur in distrustful business relations. Simply stated, deals done with a handshake cost less than deals done with advocates working for each party to the transaction.

Managerial Application

J & J's Credo

If you walk into the office of a manager at the Johnson & Johnson health products company, you will likely see a document titled "Our Credo" on the wall. If you log on to the Johnson & Johnson Web site (http://www.jnj.com), you will see a link to "Our Credo" on the first page. This credo is Johnson & Johnson's code of conduct to guide managers in setting priorities. Many times, managers have relied on the Credo to guide their actions, the most famous being the Tylenol incident, during which somebody inserted toxic material into Tylenol capsules. The company's management could have resisted taking responsibility (particularly since the company was not at fault), but management ordered all Tylenol removed from all retail outlets. It then developed new tamper-resistant bottles and produced tamper-proof caplets in place of capsules. Johnson & Johnson's actions in that incident earned universal praise from business commentators. Management did not have much time to formulate its policy when it first learned of the tampering. The Credo helped managers make decisions on company principles, already stated and studied, not worked out at the moment of crisis.

Understanding Basic Cost Concepts

We now turn to the nuts and bolts concepts important in managerial accounting. This section defines and discusses basic cost concepts. You will find a glossary of accounting terms and concepts at the back of this book. See especially the cost definitions under *cost terminology*.

What Is a Cost?

In principle, a **cost** is a sacrifice of resources. For example, if you purchased an automobile for a cash payment of $12,000, the cost to purchase the automobile would be $12,000.

Although this concept is simple, it can be difficult to apply. For example, what are the costs for an individual to obtain a college education? A student sacrifices cash to pay for tuition and

---

[3]Kenneth Arrow, "Business Codes and Economic Efficiency," in Tom L. Beauchamp and Norman E. Bowie, *Ethical Theory and Business,* 6th edition, Upper Saddle River, N.J.: Prentice-Hall, 2001, p. 112.

books, clearly a cost. What about cash paid for living costs? If the student would have to pay these costs even if she or he did not attend college, one should not count them as costs of getting a college education.

Students sacrifice not only cash. They also sacrifice their time. Should one count the earnings a student forgoes by attending college? Yes, but placing a value on that time is difficult; it depends on the best forgone alternative use of the time. For students who sacrifice high-paying jobs to attend college, the total cost of college is greater than for students who do not sacrifice high-paying jobs.

The word *cost* has meaning only in context. To say "the cost of this building is $1 million" has the following meanings at various places in accounting and economics:

- the original price the current owner paid, or
- the price that the owner would pay to replace it new, or
- the price to replace it today in its current condition, or
- the annual rental fee paid to occupy the building, or
- the cash forgone from not selling it, or
- the original price paid minus accumulated depreciation.

You need to know the context for the word *cost* to know its meaning.

Many disputes arise over the definition of cost. We devote much of the remainder of this chapter to describing how different contexts affect the meaning of costs.

Opportunity Costs

The definition of a cost as a "sacrifice" leads directly to the **opportunity cost** concept. An opportunity cost is the *forgone* income from using an asset in its best alternative. If a firm uses an asset for one purpose, the opportunity cost of using it for that purpose is the return forgone from its best alternative use.

The opportunity cost of a college education includes forgone earnings during the time in school. Some other illustrations of the meaning of opportunity cost follow:

- The opportunity cost of funds invested in a government bond is the interest that an investor could earn on a bank certificate of deposit (adjusted for differences in risk).
- Proprietors of small businesses often take a salary. But the opportunity cost of their time may exceed the nominal salary recorded on the books. A proprietor can work for someone else and earn a wage. The highest such wage (adjusting for differences in risk and nonpecuniary costs or benefits of being a proprietor) is the opportunity cost of being a proprietor. Entrepreneurs such as Bill Gates at Microsoft and Phil Knight at Nike have become wealthy by developing their enterprises. They might also have become wealthy as executives in established companies.

Example   John Pavilla is an engineer at Edison International earning a salary of $61,000 per year. John is trying to decide whether he should go back to school to earn an MBA degree. If he goes to school, he would quit his job and not take on part-time work. He currently lives in an apartment for which he pays rent of $2,000 per month. John has already been accepted to Bigtime University and estimates that tuition, books, and supplies would cost $28,000 per year for two years. Housing would cost the same as what he is paying now. In this example, the opportunity cost to John is his forgone salary. His total costs of obtaining the education are his forgone salary plus the $28,000 outlay per year for tuition, books, and supplies. We do not consider the housing, meals, and other living costs to be incremental to obtaining an education; John incurs those costs whether he gets an education or not.

Opportunity versus Outlay Costs

Behavioral scientists have shown that many people have a tendency to treat opportunity and outlay costs differently. One study asked people whether they would pay $1,000 for a ticket to the Super Bowl. Most people responded that they would not. Many of the same people said, however, that they would not sell the Super Bowl ticket for $1,000 if they were given the ticket free of charge. These people refused to incur the $1,000 out-of-pocket cost of buying the Super Bowl ticket, but they were willing to incur the $1,000 opportunity cost of keeping a ticket that they already had.

Costs versus Expenses

We distinguish *cost,* as used in managerial accounting, from *expense,* as used in financial accounting. A cost is a sacrifice of resources. Period. Sometimes the sacrifice of cash leads to another resource taking its place. When a firm buys inventory for $1,000, we say the inventory has a cost of $1,000 because the firm sacrificed $1,000 cash. Inventory took the place of cash on the balance sheet. When we spend $1,000 on salary for the corporate accountant, that, too, is a sacrifice, but it is also an expense, a gone asset. The definition of expense relates to its use in financial accounting. An expense measures the outflow of assets, not merely of cash, or the increase in liabilities, such as accounts payable. All expenses are costs, but not all costs are expenses in the period of incurrence, even though they will become expenses in some later period.

Managerial accounting deals primarily with costs, not expenses. Generally accepted accounting principles and regulations such as the income-tax laws specify when the firm can or must treat costs as expenses to be deducted from revenues. We reserve the term *expense* to refer to expenses for external financial reporting as defined by generally accepted accounting principles.

Timing distinguishes costs from expenses. For instance, a firm purchases goods for resale in the amount of $2,000, sells $1,500 of the goods during the first period, and sells the remaining $500 of goods during the next period. For managerial accountants, the cost of goods acquired during the first period is $2,000 and zero in the second period. For financial accountants, the expense is $1,500 in the first period and $500 in the second, because under generally accepted accounting principles expense is recognized upon sale.

Another distinction between cost and expense results from expenses, by definition, being recorded in accounting records, while not all costs appear in accounting records. For example, the opportunity cost of an action almost never appears in the accounting records. Consider, again, the wages you forgo by going to school; this opportunity cost would not appear in your personal financial statements even though you should consider it in making the decision to go to school. Another example is the cost of equity capital in a business—the opportunity cost to the investors of providing that equity. Organizations do not record the opportunity cost of invested equity capital, so it does not appear as an expense in financial reports, even though the interest expense on borrowed funds does appear.

Direct versus Indirect Costs

A **cost object** is any item for which the manager wishes to measure cost. Costs that relate directly to a cost object are its **direct costs.** Those that do not are its **indirect costs.** Departments, stores, divisions, product lines, or units produced are typical cost objects. The cost object establishes the context for labeling a cost as direct or indirect. A cost can be direct for one cost object while simultaneously being indirect for another.

Example Starbucks Coffee produces and sells coffee products and other goodies. It buys ingredients from outside suppliers, produces coffee products, and sells the products. Assume that a particular Starbucks restaurant leases its building space. If the cost object is a cup of coffee, the ingredients and labor that the firm traces directly to the production of each cup of coffee are *direct costs* of the cup of coffee. Starbucks cannot, however, directly trace the costs of leasing the building to a particular cup of coffee, so building-lease costs are *indirect costs* of producing and selling cups of coffee.

Now suppose that the cost object is the entire restaurant because top management wishes to compare performance at two of its locations for a particular month. In that case, the cost object is each entire store, not a cup of coffee, so factory rent would be a direct cost. The lease cost for the building is direct to the restaurant but indirect to a particular cup of coffee. The distinction between direct and indirect costs is meaningful only when applied to a particular cost object.

Variable versus Fixed Costs

Variable costs are those costs that change *in total* as the level of activity changes. By contrast, **fixed costs** do not change *in total* with changes in the level of activity. Suppose you pay a monthly lease for an automobile. If the lease amount is fixed regardless of the number of miles driven, then the lease is a fixed cost during the term of the lease. If the lease requires you to pay an amount per mile, then the lease would be a variable cost because the more miles you drive, the more you pay.

Examples of variable costs include materials to make products and energy to run machines. Examples of fixed costs include rent on building space (assuming the tenant pays for an agreed term on a time basis, not a volume-of-activity basis) and salaries of top company officials. Many costs do not fit neatly into fixed and variable categories. We try to be clear in our examples as to whether you should assume a cost is fixed or variable.

The distinction between fixed and variable costs affects strategic decision making and recurs throughout this book. You will see it discussed at length starting in Chapter 5.

Contrasting Income Statements for Managerial Use to Those for External Reporting

Income statements for *managerial use* reflect this distinction between variable and fixed costs. Income statements for *external reporting* do not. Exhibit 1.2 shows a simplified income statement for external reporting. Note that it does not report which costs are fixed and which are variable. Pick up any company's income statement. You will nearly always find the income statement does not report which of the company's costs are variable and which are fixed.

Exhibit 1.2 shows the income statement for external reporting for Sherwood Travel, Inc., a travel agency that offers online travel services and consulting advice for exotic trips. Note the statement combines fixed and variable expenses into one lump sum for cost of sales and one lump sum for marketing and administrative expenses. This statement complies with income tax regulations and generally accepted accounting principles, but it aggregates data too much for managerial use.

The income statement for managerial use has two benefits. First, it demonstrates which costs are fixed and which are variable. Second, it can break down revenues and costs in a number of ways to meet the needs of managers (for example, by product line, customer, or division).

Note the difference between the gross margin and the contribution margin, as shown in Exhibits 1.2 and 1.3. The gross margin is the difference between revenue and cost of sales, whereas the contribution margin is the difference between revenue and variable costs, including variable marketing and administrative costs.

We use the term *operating profit* at the bottom of income statements prepared for managerial use to distinguish it from net income used in external reporting.

EXHIBIT 1.2	SHERWOOD TRAVEL, INC. Income Statement for External Financial Reporting for the Month Ending February 28

Sales Revenue	$400,000
Less Cost of Sales	210,000[a]
Gross Margin	$190,000
Less Marketing and Administrative Expenses	80,000[b]
Net Income before Taxes	$110,000

[a]$210,000 = $160,000 Variable + $50,000 Fixed.
[b]$80,000 = $8,000 Variable + $72,000 Fixed.

EXHIBIT 1.3	SHERWOOD TRAVEL, INC. Income Statement for Managerial Decision Making: Contribution Margin Format for the Month Ending February 28

Sales Revenue		$400,000
Less Variable Costs:		
Variable Cost of Sales	$160,000[a]	
Variable Marketing and Administrative Costs	8,000[a]	
Total Variable Costs		168,000
Contribution Margin		$232,000
Less Fixed Costs:		
Fixed Cost of Sales	$ 50,000[a]	
Fixed Marketing and Administrative Costs	72,000[a]	
Total Fixed Costs		122,000
Operating Profit		$110,000

[a]See footnotes to Exhibit 1.2.

Problem 1.2 for Self-Study

Match the concept with the definition.

Concept	Definition
Cost	a. Costs directly related to a cost object
Opportunity cost	b. A sacrifice of resources
Expense	c. Costs not directly related to a cost object
Cost object	d. Any item for which a manager wants to measure a cost
Direct costs	e. A cost charged against revenue in an accounting period
Indirect costs	f. The return that could be realized from the best forgone alternative use of a resource

The solution to this self-study problem is at the end of this chapter on page 22.

Managing Costs

Understanding What Causes Costs

Managerial accounting requires that we identify cost behavior (variable versus fixed) and present these costs in a way that displays how costs behave (as shown in Exhibit 1.3). In addition, for planning and decision-making purposes, understanding what causes costs is important.

Effective cost control requires managers to understand how producing a product requires activities and how activities, in turn, generate costs. **Activity-based management (ABM)** studies the need for activities and whether they are operating efficiently. Cost control requires activity-based management.

Consider the activities of a company facing a financial crisis. In an ineffective system, top management tells each department to reduce costs. Department heads usually respond by reducing the number of people and supplies, as these are the only cost items that they can control in the short run. Then, they ask everyone to work harder. This produces only temporary gains, however, as the workers cannot sustain the pace in the long run. If they could sustain it, departmental managers would have already reduced the size of the workforce and the amount of supplies used.

Under activity-based management, the company reduces costs by studying the activities it conducts and develops plans to eliminate non–value-added activities and to improve the efficiency of value-added activities. Eliminating activities that do not create customer value cuts costs effectively. For example, spending $100 to train an employee to avoid common mistakes will pay off many times over by reducing customer ill will caused by those mistakes.

Value-Added and Non–Value-Added Activities

A **value-added activity** is an activity that increases the product's service to the customer. For instance, purchasing the raw materials to make a product is a value-added activity. Without the purchase of raw materials, the organization would be unable to make the product. Sanding and varnishing a wooden chair are value-added activities because customers don't want splinters. Management evaluates value-added activities by how they contribute to the final product's service, quality, and cost.

Good management involves finding and, if possible, eliminating non–value-added activities. **Non–value-added activities** are activities that when eliminated reduce costs without reducing the product's service potential to the customer. In many organizations poor facility layout requires labor to move around the work in process or to store it temporarily during production. For example, a Midwestern steel company that we studied had more than 100 miles of railroad track to move things back and forth in a poorly designed facility. Moving work around a factory, an office, or a store does not usually add value for the customer.

Value Chain

We use the value chain concept throughout the book to demonstrate how to use managerial accounting to add value to organizations. The **value chain** describes the linked set of activities that increase the usefulness (or value) of the products or services of an organization (value-added activities). Management evaluates activities by how they contribute to the final product's service, quality, and cost. In general, the business functions include the following (see Exhibit 1.4):

1. *Research and development:* the creation and development of ideas related to new products, services, or processes
2. *Design:* the detailed development and engineering of products, services, or processes
3. *Production:* the collection and assembly of resources to produce a product or deliver a service
4. *Marketing:* the process that informs potential customers about the attributes of products or services, and leads to the purchase of those products or services
5. *Distribution:* the process established to deliver products or services to customers
6. *Customer service:* product- or service-support activities provided to customers

Several administrative functions span all the business activities described. Human resource management, for example, potentially affects every step of the value chain.

Global Strategies

The Internet and World Wide Web generate information about markets and products almost instantly. This provides great business opportunities, but it also means that customers can cheaply search for products. Successful companies will have lower prices than in a bricks and mortar environment.

A successful approach to gaining a cost advantage identifies where on the value chain your company has a strategic advantage. Many software companies, for example, look at foreign markets to capitalize on their prior investment in research and development. Their reservoir of intellectual capital gives these firms an advantage over competitors in foreign countries who have not yet developed such expertise. The local competitors in foreign markets would face research and development costs already incurred by established companies, making it difficult for the local competitors to charge competitive prices and still make a profit.

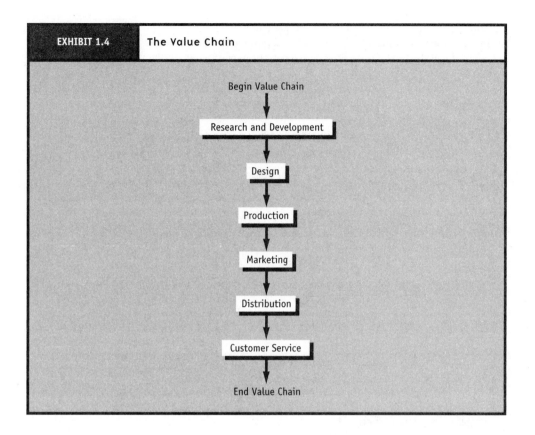

EXHIBIT 1.4   The Value Chain

Begin Value Chain

Research and Development

Design

Production

Marketing

Distribution

Customer Service

End Value Chain

Strategic Cost Analysis

Companies can identify strategic advantages in the marketplace by analyzing the value chain and information about the costs of activities. A company that eliminates non–value-added activities reduces costs without reducing the value of the product to customers. With reduced costs, the company can reduce the price it charges customers, thus giving the company a cost advantage over its competitors. Or the company can use the resources saved from eliminating non–value-added activities to provide greater service to customers. For example, by eliminating non–value-added activities, Southwest Airlines has reduced airplane turnaround time at the gate. Reduced turnaround means that Southwest can fly more flights and passengers in a given time period, which increases the company's profitability.

The idea here is simple. Look for activities that are not on the value chain. If your company can safely eliminate non–value-added activities, then it should do so. By identifying and cutting them, you will save the company money and make it more competitive.

Combining the Value Chain and Strategic Cost Analysis

Which parts of the value chain generate the most profits? The answer to this question enables companies strategically to place their business where it will earn the most profits. The following example, based on actual information from the wine industry, demonstrates how to analyze the most profitable parts of the value chain.

Example: Lone Tree Winery

After computing last year's return on investment for the winery and vineyard, Maria Fernandez, chief financial officer of Lone Tree Winery, observed, "It's the same old story. We make the wine and the distributors make the money." She wondered whether and how Lone Tree Winery could get a piece of the distributors' action, perhaps by increasing sales at the winery and using the Internet for more effective direct sales to consumers. First, though, she wanted to get her facts correct. Of the total profits earned on a case of wine throughout the value chain, how much went to the winery and vineyard, and how much to the downstream segments of the value chain?

Lone Tree Winery owned both vineyards and a winery. For her analysis, Fernandez studied the production and sale of a medium quality Chardonnay that sold retail for $150 per case. Last year, Lone Tree Winery had harvested sufficient grapes to produce 14,000 cases of this Chardonnay. The winery had produced 14,000 cases and sold them to a large distributor in the region.

To compute profitability of each segment of the value chain—vineyard, winery, distributor, and retailer—Fernandez started with her own company's data for the vineyard and winery. Computing profits for a typical distributor and retailer took a bit of digging through published financial statements and industry magazines, plus some thoughtful estimating. Fernandez summarized her findings as follows:

Vineyard All data refer to the production of enough grapes to produce 14,000 cases of Chardonnay. First, Fernandez estimated the market value of vineyard assets to be $507,000 at the beginning of the year and $493,000 at the end of the year. Second, she used the vineyard's weighted-average cost of capital of 10 percent in the cost of capital computations. Third, using these data plus data from the accounting records, she prepared the following managerial accounting income statement:

	Total	Per Case
Revenues, if grapes were sold in the market	$210,000	$15.00
Less:		
Operating costs, excluding depreciation	160,000	11.43
Economic depreciation, computed as the decline in economic value of the vineyard assets	14,000	1.00
Cost of capital (see discussion in text following)	50,000	3.57
Economic loss from the vineyard	$(14,000)	$(1.00)

The vineyard loses $14,000 from the production of 14,000 cases for an average loss of $1 per case. These results confirm Fernandez's concern—that the vineyard incurs losses on wine production.

Economic Depreciation

Note that Fernandez used an economic measure of depreciation, not a book or historical cost measure. **Economic depreciation** measures the decline in the value of assets during a period using either the sales value of assets or their replacement costs as the measure of value, whichever analysts think is appropriate for the business and for the use of the information. In general, if there is a ready market for the assets, as in the case of vineyards, aircraft, trucks, and most building space, then analysts generally compute economic depreciation as the decrease in the market or sales values of assets during the period.

Economic depreciation better measures the decline in asset value than book depreciation, which actually only allocates the original cost of some assets over their estimated lives. Land, for example, can suffer economic loss without book depreciation. In this case, the owners of Lone Tree Winery could have sold the vineyard for $14,000 more at the beginning of the year than at the end of the year. Consequently, one of their costs of operating the vineyard instead of selling it at the beginning of the year is the $14,000 lost value of the vineyard. Fernandez's estimate of economic depreciation, $14,000, considers changes in the value of the land, the vines, and the farm equipment.

Cost of Capital

Fernandez appropriately included the cost of the capital employed in the vineyard in her computations. The cost of capital is a real one—the amount a firm could earn on its assets by putting them to their best alternative use—even if the financial accounting statements do not include the cost of equity capital. The rate should be the weighted-average cost of capital appropriate for the vineyard, measured from the weighted average of the costs of the firm's sources of funds. The weighted-average cost of capital takes into account both debt and equity sources of capital.[4] In this case, Fernandez used a 10 percent weighted-average cost of capital and the average market value of vineyard assets during the year of $500,000 [= ($507,000 + $493,000)/2] to compute the $50,000 (= 10% × $500,000) cost of capital.

Winery All data are for the sale of 14,000 cases of Chardonnay to Lone Tree Winery's distributor. Fernandez estimated the market value of the winery to be $1,845,000 and $1,755,000 at the beginning and end of the year, respectively. Using a 10 percent weighted-average cost of capital, again, and data from the accounting records, she prepared the following managerial accounting income statement:

	Total	Per Case
Revenue from sale of wine to distributor	$1,120,000	$80.00
Less:		
Cost of grapes (see sales from Vineyard)	210,000	15.00
Operating costs, excluding depreciation	710,000	50.71
Depreciation, computed as the change in economic value of the winery assets	90,000	6.43
Cost of capital, using a 10 percent rate (10 percent × $1,800,000)	180,000	12.86
Economic loss from the winery	$ (70,000)	$(5.00)

Note that the cost of capital is computed using the average market value of assets—$1,800,000 [= ($1,845,000 + $1,755,000)/2].

The winery showed an economic loss of $5 per case, further confirming Fernandez's opinion that Lone Tree Winery incurred losses on its winemaking operations.

To compute the economic profit or loss for the distributor and retailer, Fernandez relied on information in trade publications. Based on that information, she computed the following amounts per case for Lone Tree Chardonnay.

Distributor All data are for 14,000 cases of Lone Tree Chardonnay sold by distributors to wine specialty retailers.

	Per Case
Revenues	$115
Less cost of goods sold (see sales from Winery)	80
Gross margin	$ 35
Less operating costs, including economic depreciation	20
Less cost of capital	5
Economic profit to the distributor	$ 10

Retailer All data are for 14,000 cases of Lone Tree Chardonnay sold by specialty retailers to their customers.

	Per Case
Revenues	$150
Less cost of goods sold (see sales from Distributor)	115
Gross margin	$ 35
Less operating costs, including economic depreciation	30
Less cost of capital	4
Economic profit to the retailer	$ 1

[4]Textbooks in finance describe how to compute the weighted-average cost of capital. See, for example, Eugene F. Brigham and Michael C. Ehrhardt, *Financial Management: Theory and Practice,* 10th ed., Cincinnati, Ohio: South-Western, 2002.

Just as Fernandez suspected, the vineyard and winery had economic losses while the distributor and retailer had economic profits. Based on this analysis of the value chain, Fernandez and her colleagues at Lone Tree Winery began developing a strategic plan that would give Lone Tree Winery more of the profits from the distribution and retail of wine. This example demonstrates how strategic cost analysis can help managers decide where to direct the organization's resources. For example, does Lone Tree Winery sell its wine to the distributor for less than other wineries? If so, it will consider raising its prices. If not, the owners might consider selling the vineyards and winery to a starry-eyed investor who wants the status of owning a winery.

Managerial Accounting in Modern Production Environments

Over the past two decades, new technologies and management philosophies have changed the face of managerial accounting in many companies. Following are key developments that have reshaped the discipline.

Integrated Information Systems

Integrated information systems, such as the Enterprise Resource Planning Systems (ERPS) produced by Oracle (http://www.oracle.com) and SAP (http://www.sap.com), provide integrated information systems that tie together managerial accounting, financial reporting, customer databases, supply chain management, and other databases. Conventional accounting systems were stand-alone information systems. With ERPS, accounting and other databases are integrated with numerous applications such as managing the supply chain, making general ledger entries, and reporting to top management. Integrated information systems imply that accountants no longer control a particular information domain. Accountants are no longer the source of accounting information because managers and staff can directly access accounting information in integrated information systems. With integrated information systems, managerial accountants serve as financial consultants on cross-functional teams that make strategic and tactical decisions. Helpful managerial accountants understand more than just the financial information and also have a good knowledge of other data, such as production and marketing data.

Web Hosting

Many companies outsource substantial portions of their information systems by using Web hosting. Web hosting enables a company to focus on its core competencies while taking advantage of the host's server and bandwidth capabilities. For example, Wells Fargo Bank (http://www.wellsfargo.com) provides a Web site to handle payment processing for small businesses.[5] Web hosting reduces the need for in-house information technology people as well as for transaction and systems managers. (They still require smart people who understand managerial accounting and who make good decisions.)

Just-in-Time and Lean Production

Just-in-time (JIT) production is part of a "lean production" philosophy that has been credited for the success of many Japanese companies and such U.S. companies as General Electric, Lincoln Electric, and Harley-Davidson. Lean production eliminates inventory between production departments, making the quality and efficiency of production the highest priority. Lean production requires the flexibility to change quickly from one product to another. It emphasizes employee training and participation in decision making.

The development of just-in-time production and purchasing methods also affects cost-accounting systems. Firms using just-in-time methods keep inventories to a minimum. If inventories are low, accountants can spend less time on inventory valuation for external reporting.

For example, a Hewlett-Packard plant eliminated 100,000 journal entries per month after installing just-in-time production methods and adapting the cost-accounting system to this new production method. Accounting/finance people were then free to work on managerial problems instead of record accounting data.

---

[5]See Gregory Dalton, "Wells Fargo Turns to Web Hosting," *Informationweek,* September 20, 1999, p. 32.

Total Quality Management

One successful recent managerial innovation is total quality management. **Total quality management (TQM)** means the organization focuses on excelling in all dimensions. Customers ultimately define quality. Customers determine the company's performance standards by their own wishes and needs (not necessarily by the wishes of product engineers, accountants, or marketing people). This exciting and sensible idea affects accounting performance measures. Under TQM, performance measures likely include product reliability and service delivery, as well as such traditional measures as profitability. Chapter 4 focuses on total quality management.

Theory of Constraints

Every profit-making enterprise must have at least one constraint. Without constraints, the enterprise could produce an infinite amount of its goal (for example, profits). The **theory of constraints (TOC)** views a business as a linked sequence of processes that transforms inputs into saleable outputs, like a chain. To strengthen the chain, a TOC company identifies the weakest link, the constraint. That link limits the scope of the rest of the process, so the company concentrates improvement efforts on that weakest link. When the efforts succeed so that link is no longer the weakest, the company changes focus to the new weakest link. TOC improves operations and has much potential for helping certain kinds of companies.

Benchmarking and Continuous Improvement

The themes of benchmarking and continuous improvement recur in modern management. **Benchmarking** is the continuous process of measuring one's own products, services, and activities against the best levels of performance. One might find these best levels of performance, the benchmarks, either inside one's own organization or in other organizations.

Toyota Motor Company gets much of the credit for applying the concept of benchmarking and continuous improvement, but many other companies have used these themes successfully. These include Daimler-Chrysler and Xerox. When U.S. managers at Xerox compared performance measures with its Fuji-Xerox subsidiary in Japan, the results shocked them. Some call benchmarking and continuous improvement "the race with no finish" because managers and employees avoid complacency with a particular performance level by seeking ongoing improvement. Organizations that adopt this philosophy find they are able to achieve performance levels previously thought unattainable.

Fads

This is an exciting time to be in management. New books, management gurus, and consulting firms prepared to save industry (or government) from great peril present themselves to students of business practices. Some of these offer sensible old ideas repackaged as new ideas. Some are fads. Others are frauds. Still others are "useful frauds" in that they don't do what they claim but they get people thinking about the problem.[6] Generally, we find that

1. no matter how good an idea, sometimes it doesn't work;
2. bad ideas often teach useful lessons; and
3. common sense goes a long way in figuring out which ideas will work in your unique situation.

Problem 1.3 for Self-Study

How have advancements in production methods affected managerial accounting?

The solution to this self-study problem is at the end of this chapter on page 22.

---

[6]An idea called "zero-base budgeting" was popular in the 1970s. Management gurus and President Jimmy Carter touted it as a way to improve efficiency and effectiveness in business and government. Complex organizations could not implement zero-base budgeting because of the time and effort it required. Nevertheless, zero-base budgeting was a reasonable concept that created opportunities to control costs. We expect to see it reinvented someday under a different name.

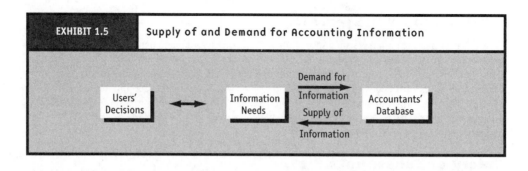

EXHIBIT 1.5	Supply of and Demand for Accounting Information

Costs and Benefits of Accounting

A steel company installed an accounting system that cost several million dollars. A public utility recently spent $20 million to develop a new accounting system. How did the managers justify such an expenditure? They believed better information would result in improved cost control and efficiency that would save the company enough to justify the cost of the system.

In practice, neither users of information nor accountants can independently assess both the costs and benefits of information. Users learn, through experience, the benefits of information, whereas accountants measure its costs. Exhibit 1.5 shows that users identify their needs based on the decisions they make and then request data from accountants, who develop systems to supply information when a cost-benefit criterion justifies it. If accountants and users interact, they eventually settle on a cost-benefit–justified supply of accounting data that meets users' needs.

The Value of Information for Particular Decisions

The costs and benefits of information interact with various managerial decisions. For example, should the firm undertake an additional marketing study that involves customer sampling of a new product? Or should the company discontinue its marketing tests and proceed immediately to full-scale production? Should a doctor order laboratory tests before taking action in an emergency situation? Should a production manager stop production to test a sample of products for defects or allow production to continue? Managers solve such problems conceptually by comparing the cost of information with the benefits of better-informed decisions.

Both users and accountants recognize that information is not free. Management must take into account the costs and benefits of information in deciding how much accounting is optimal.

The Makeup of the Book

We have organized this book into three parts.

1. Part One (Chapters 1 through 3) provides building blocks for studying managerial accounting.
2. Part Two (Chapters 4 through 9) discusses how to obtain and use information to make managerial decisions that maximize the organization's value.
3. Part Three (Chapters 10 through 15) discusses how to obtain and use information to evaluate managers' performance and motivate them to make good decisions.

Summary

The following paragraphs correspond to the learning objectives presented at the beginning of the chapter.

1. **Distinguish between managerial and financial accounting.** Managerial accounting provides information used by managers inside the organization. To that end, it does not comply

with generally accepted accounting principles. It uses cost-benefit analysis to determine the amount of detail presented and uses historical data and future estimates for planning, decision making, and performance evaluation. Financial accounting prepares general-purpose reports for people outside an organization and presents summary historical data in compliance with generally accepted accounting principles.

2. **Understand how managers can use accounting information to implement strategies.** Managers use accounting information to help project the consequences of various courses of action in the decision-making and planning process.

3. **Identify the key financial players in the organization.** The top financial person is the financial vice-president (or chief financial officer), who is in charge of the entire accounting and finance function. The controller, the chief accounting officer, oversees providing information to managers. The corporate treasurer is the manager in charge of raising cash for operations and managing cash and near-cash assets. The internal audit department provides a variety of auditing and consulting services.

4. **Understand managerial accountants' professional environment and ethical responsibilities.** Companies hold managers accountable for achieving financial performance targets. Because many firms base compensation on these targets, all managers have an ethical responsibility to report accurately even when their own compensation suffers.

5. **Master the concept of *cost*.** A cost is a sacrifice of resources. An expense is the historical cost of goods or services used. An opportunity cost is the sacrifice of forgoing the return from the best alternative use of an asset.

6. **Compare and contrast income statements prepared for managerial use and those prepared for external reporting.** Income statements for *managerial use* show the distinction between variable and fixed costs. This presentation helps planning and decision making. Income statements for *external reporting* do not show variable and fixed costs, and the firm prepares these in accordance with generally accepted accounting principles for external users.

7. **Understand the concepts useful for managing costs.** Several concepts help managers manage costs more effectively. These concepts include activity-based management, value-added and non–value-added activities, and the value chain.

8. **Describe how managerial accounting supports modern production environments.** *Integrated information systems* tie together various databases and applications. *Web hosting* enables companies to outsource their information technology requirements and take advantage of the host's bandwidth and servers. *Just-in-time production* strives to eliminate inventory and increase efficiency and quality. *Total quality management* focuses on increasing quality as perceived and defined by the customer. The *theory of constraints* emphasizes strengthening the weakest link (or constraint) of the company to improve operations. *Benchmarking* measures a company's products, services, and activities against other more efficient and effective divisions or businesses.

9. **Understand the importance of effective communication between accountants and users of managerial accounting information.** A cost-benefit analysis determines the amount of accounting information generated for managerial purposes. Such analysis requires effective communication and cooperation between users and accountants.

10. **Understand the ethical standards that make up the Institute of Management Accountants' Code of Ethics (Appendix 1.1).** Management accountants should maintain competence, confidentiality, integrity, and objectivity.

Key Terms and Concepts

Activity-based management (ABM)	Cost
Benchmarking	Cost accountants and managers
Certified Management Accountant (CMA)	Cost Accounting Standards Board (CASB)
Certified Public Accountant (CPA)	Cost object
Controller	Direct costs

Economic depreciation
Financial accounting
Financial vice-president
Fixed costs
Indirect costs
Institute of Management Accountants (IMA)
Internal audit
Just-in-time (JIT)
Managerial accounting

Non–value-added activity
Opportunity cost
Theory of constraints (TOC)
Total quality management (TQM)
Treasurer
Value-added activity
Value chain
Variable costs

Solutions to Self-Study Problems

SUGGESTED SOLUTION TO PROBLEM 1.1 FOR SELF-STUDY

Managerial accounting is the preparation of accounting information for managers' use within organizations in making decisions and evaluating performance. Financial accounting is the preparation of accounting information for use by outsiders, such as investors and creditors.

SUGGESTED SOLUTION TO PROBLEM 1.2 FOR SELF-STUDY

Concept	Definition
Cost	**b.** A sacrifice of resources
Opportunity cost	**f.** The return that could be realized from the best forgone alternative use of a resource
Expense	**e.** A cost charged against revenue in an accounting period
Cost object	**d.** Any item for which a manager wants to measure cost
Direct costs	**a.** Costs directly related to a cost object
Indirect costs	**c.** Costs not directly related to a cost object

SUGGESTED SOLUTION TO PROBLEM 1.3 FOR SELF-STUDY

The new production environment has had the following effects on accounting:

- Accounting has become more computerized, thus reducing manual bookkeeping.
- Increased competition in many industries, including e-commerce, automobile, and electronic equipment, has increased management's interest in managing costs.
- Deregulation in industries such as banking, air travel, and health care has also increased management's interest in managing costs.
- Development of more highly technical production processes has reduced emphasis on labor and increased emphasis on overhead cost control.
- Developments in new management techniques have affected accounting. For example, by reducing inventory levels, just-in-time (JIT) methods have reduced the need to compute costs of inventory. Total quality management (TQM), which strives for excellence in business, requires new measurements of performance as defined by the customers. Activity-based management (ABM) assigns indirect costs to products on the basis of the activities that caused the cost and the amount of the activity that the product consumed.

Appendix 1.1: Standards of Ethical Conduct for Management Accountants[7]

Management accountants have an obligation to the organizations they serve, their profession, the public, and themselves to maintain the highest standards of ethical conduct. In recognition of

---

[7]**Source:** Statement on Management Accounting, *Standards of Ethical Conduct for Management Accountants* (Montvale, N.J.: Institute of Management Accountants, 1983).

this obligation, the Institute of Management Accountants promulgated the following standards of ethical conduct for management accountants. Achieving the Objectives of Management Accounting requires adherence to these standards. Management accountants shall not commit acts contrary to these standards, nor shall they condone the commission of such acts by others within their organization.

COMPETENCE

Management accountants have a responsibility to do the following:

- Maintain an appropriate level of professional competence by ongoing development of their knowledge and skills.
- Perform their professional duties in accordance with relevant laws, regulations, and technical standards.
- Prepare complete and clear reports and recommendations after appropriate analyses of relevant and reliable information.

CONFIDENTIALITY

Management accountants have a responsibility to do the following:

- Refrain from disclosing confidential information acquired in the course of their work except when authorized, unless legally obligated to do so.
- Inform subordinates as appropriate regarding the confidentiality of information acquired in the course of their work and monitor their activities to assure the maintenance of that confidentiality.
- Refrain from using or appearing to use confidential information acquired in the course of their work for unethical or illegal advantage either personally or through third parties.

INTEGRITY

Management accountants have a responsibility to do the following:

- Avoid actual or apparent conflicts of interest and advise all appropriate parties of any potential conflict.
- Refrain from engaging in any activity that would prejudice their ability to carry out their duties ethically.
- Refuse any gift, favor, or hospitality that would influence or would appear to influence their actions.
- Refrain from either actively or passively subverting the attainment of the organization's legitimate and ethical objectives.
- Recognize and communicate professional limitations or other constraints that would preclude responsible judgment or successful performance of an activity.
- Communicate unfavorable as well as favorable information and professional judgments or opinions.
- Refrain from engaging in or supporting any activity that would discredit the profession.

OBJECTIVITY

Management accountants have a responsibility to do the following:

- Communicate information fairly and objectively.
- Disclose fully all relevant information that could reasonably be expected to influence an intended user's understanding of the reports, comments, and recommendations presented.

RESOLUTION OF ETHICAL CONFLICT

In applying the standards of ethical conduct, management accountants may encounter problems in identifying unethical behavior or in resolving an ethical conflict. When faced with significant ethical issues, management accountants should follow the established policies of the organization bearing on the resolution of such conflict. If these policies do not resolve the ethical conflict, management accountants should consider the following courses of action:

- Discuss such problems with the immediate superior except when it appears that the superior is involved, in which case the problem should be presented initially to the next higher managerial level. If satisfactory resolution cannot be achieved when the problem is initially presented, submit the issues to the next higher managerial level.
- If the immediate superior is the chief executive officer or equivalent, the acceptable reviewing authority may be a group such as the audit committee, executive committee, board of directors, board of trustees, or owners. Contact with levels above the immediate superior should be initiated only with the superior's knowledge, assuming the superior is not involved.
- Clarify relevant concepts by confidential discussion with an objective advisor to obtain an understanding of possible courses of action.
- If the ethical conflict still exists after exhausting all levels of internal review, the management accountant may have no other recourse on significant matters than to resign from the organization and to submit an informative memorandum to an appropriate representative of the organization.

Except where legally prescribed, communication of such problems to authorities or individuals not employed or engaged by the organization is not considered appropriate.

Questions, Exercises, Problems, and Cases

REVIEW QUESTIONS

1. Review the meaning of the concepts and terms listed in Key Terms and Concepts.
2. Who in the organization is generally in charge of managerial accounting?
3. What are two major uses of managerial accounting information?
4. What is meant by total quality management (TQM)? What performance measures are likely to be included under TQM?
5. An accounting employee notices that an employee in purchasing has been accepting tickets to sporting events from a company supplier, which is against company policy. According to the Institute of Management Accountants' code of conduct (Appendix 1.1), what steps should the accounting employee take to stop the practice?
6. Managerial accounting is used for
   a. decision making.
   b. planning.
   c. control.
   d. all of the above.
7. The controller oversees
   a. production processes.
   b. the management of cash.
   c. providing accounting information to managers.
8. Zappa, a mechanic, left his $25,000-a-year job at Joe's Garage to start his own body shop. Zappa now draws an annual salary of $15,000. Identify his opportunity costs.
9. People often use *expenses* and *costs* interchangeably, yet the terms do not always mean the same thing. Distinguish between the two terms.
10. What do managerial accountants mean when they speak of cost behavior? Why is it important in managerial decision making?

CRITICAL ANALYSIS AND DISCUSSION QUESTIONS

11. "Managerial accountants should understand the uses of accounting data, and users of data should understand accounting. Only in this way can accountants provide the appropriate accounting data for the correct uses." Do you agree with this statement? Why or why not?
12. "The best management accounting system provides managers with all the information they would like to have." Do you agree with this statement? Why or why not?
13. What is just-in-time (JIT)? How does JIT help accountants serve managers better?

14. Incentives for managers to record sales early include
    a. an effective code of conduct.
    b. being held responsible for financial performance.
    c. compensation based on sales performance.
    d. both **b.** and **c.**
15. "Nonprofit organizations, such as agencies of the federal government and nonprofit hospitals, do not need managerial accounting because they do not have to earn a profit." Do you agree with this statement? Why or why not?
16. Students planning a career in marketing ask why they should learn about accounting. How would you respond?
17. "The cost of my trip to Hawaii was $3,000." Using the concept of cost developed in this chapter, explain why this statement is ambiguous.
18. Give three examples of variable costs and three examples of fixed costs in a fast-food restaurant.
19. "Fixed costs are really variable. The more you produce, the smaller the unit cost of production." Is this statement correct? Why or why not?

EXERCISES

Solutions to even-numbered exercises are at the end of the chapter.

20. **Opportunity cost analysis.** Cliff Lawrence owns an ice-skating rink that accommodates 200 people. Cliff charges $10 per hour to skate. Attendants receive $100 per day to staff the entrance booth at CL Skating. Utilities and other fixed costs average $2,000 per month.

    Recently, the manager of an out-of-town hockey team approached Cliff concerning renting the rink for a full day of practice on an upcoming Sunday for the lump sum of $1,000. Attendants would not be needed. CL's normal operating hours on Sunday are 10 AM to 7 PM, and the average attendance is 10 skaters per hour. What is the opportunity cost of accepting the offer?

21. **Opportunity cost analysis.** Susan Ortiz operates a covered parking structure that can accommodate up to 600 cars. Susan charges $6 per hour for parking. Parking attendants receive $12 per hour to staff the cashier's booth at Susan's Parking. Utilities and other fixed costs average $4,000 per month.

    Recently, the manager of a nearby Sheraton Hotel approached Susan concerning the reservation of 100 spots over an upcoming weekend for a lump sum of $3,600. This particular weekend will be a football weekend, and the structure would be full for only the six hours surrounding the game. Other than those six hours, the structure would have more than 100 empty spots available. What is the opportunity cost of accepting the offer?

22. **Variable and fixed costs.** Intel is one of the world's largest producers of microprocessors for computers. Find its most recent annual report or 10K report (filed with the federal government) on the Internet (http://www.intel.com), and review the financial statements for Intel. Which production costs are likely to be fixed and which are likely to be variable (assuming that the product is the cost object)?

23. **Direct and indirect costs.** Starbucks is a fast-growing retail and service company that provides coffee and coffee-related products. Find its most recent annual report or 10K report (filed with the federal government) on the Internet (http://www.starbucks.com), and review the financial statements for Starbucks. Which costs are likely to be direct and which are likely to be indirect (assuming that each retail store is the cost object)?

24. **Just-in-time production.** Ford Motor Company provides automotive products and services. Find its most recent annual report or 10K report (filed with the federal government) on the Internet (http://www.ford.com), and review the financial statements for Ford. How might Ford be able to improve its financial position (balance sheet) and financial results (income statement) by increasing its use of just-in-time production?

PROBLEMS AND SHORT CASES

25. **The value chain and strategic cost analysis.** Green Products raises trees, cuts the trees into logs, and processes the logs into paper. Green Products sells the paper to a distributor, who then sells the paper to printers. Assume that a weighted-average cost of capital of 10 percent is appropriate for timber and paper processing. Here are the costs and revenues of each stage of the value chain. All data are for the production of enough timber to produce 20,000 tons of paper.

Timber   The estimated market value of timber assets at the beginning of the year is $5,100,000 and at the end of the year is $4,900,000. Revenues, if the timber were sold in the market, would equal $2,100,000. Operating costs total $1,500,000, excluding depreciation.

Paper Processing   The estimated market value of paper-processing assets at the beginning of the year is $15,000,000 and $13,000,000 at the end of the year. Revenues, if the paper were sold in the market, would be $12,000,000. Operating costs total $9,000,000, including all costs of materials but excluding depreciation.

Distributor   The distributor sells the paper for $800 per ton. The cost of the paper to the distributor (cost of goods sold) can be found by reviewing the sales from paper processing. Operating costs total $135 per ton, including economic depreciation. The cost of capital for the distributor is $50 per ton.

Retailer   The retailer sells the paper for $850 per ton. The cost of the paper to the retailer (cost of goods sold) can be found by reviewing the sales from the distributor. Operating costs total $25 per ton, including economic depreciation. The cost of capital for the retailer is $18 per ton.

   a. Compute the profits of each stage of the value chain. Show amounts in total (for 20,000 tons) and per ton.

   b. Assume you are advising a loan approval committee in a bank. Write a short memo to the loan approval committee in which you evaluate the profitability of each part of the value chain.

26. The value chain and strategic cost analysis. Bike Products, Inc., produces bike parts (for example, wheels, frames, tires, and sprockets) and uses these parts to assemble bikes. Bike Products sells the bikes to a distributor that sells the bikes to retailers. Assume that a weighted-average cost of capital of 12 percent is appropriate for Bike Products. Here are the costs and revenues of each stage of the value chain. All data are for the production of enough bike parts to produce 10,000 bikes.

Bike Part Production   The estimated market value of production assets at the beginning of the year is $1,025,000 and at the end of the year is $975,000. Revenues, if the parts were sold in the market, would be $300,000. Operating costs total $100,000, excluding depreciation.

Bike Assembly   The estimated market value of bike assembly assets at the beginning of the year is $600,000 and $400,000 at the end of the year. Revenues, if the bikes were sold in the market, would be $1,500,000. Operating costs total $1,250,000, excluding depreciation.

Distributor   The distributor sells the bikes for $175 per bike. The cost of the bike to the distributor (cost of goods sold) can be found by reviewing the sales from bike assembly. Operating costs total $5 per bike, including economic depreciation. The cost of capital for the distributor is $12 per bike.

Retailer   The retailer sells the bikes for $250 per bike. The cost of the bike to the retailer (cost of goods sold) can be found by reviewing the sales from the distributor. Operating costs total $33 per bike, including economic depreciation. The cost of capital for the retailer is $4 per bike.

   a. Compute the profits of each stage of the value chain. Show amounts in total (for 10,000 bikes) and per bike.

   b. Assume you are advising a loan approval committee in a bank. Write a short memo to the loan approval committee in which you evaluate the profitability of the company.

27. **Ethics and altering the books** (adapted from CMA exam). QT Investments, a closely held investment services group, has been successful for the past three years. Bonuses for top management have ranged from 50 percent to 100 percent of base salary. Top management, however, holds only 35 percent of the common stock, and recent industry news indicates that a major corporation may try to acquire QT. Top management fears that they might lose their bonuses, not to mention their employment, if the takeover occurs. Management has told Bob Evans, QT's controller, to make a few changes to several accounting policies and practices, thus making QT a much less attractive acquisition. Bob knows that these "changes" are not in accordance with generally accepted accounting principles. Bob has

also been told not to mention these changes to anyone outside the top-management group.

   a. What are Bob Evans's responsibilities?

   b. What steps should he take to resolve this problem?

28. **Value chain.** HP Computer Company incurs the following costs:

   a. Transportation costs for shipping computers to retail stores

   b. Utilities costs incurred by the facility assembling HP computers

   c. Salaries for personnel developing the next line of computers

   d. Cost of HP employee's visit to a major customer to illustrate computer capabilities

   e. Cost of president's salary

   f. Cost of advertising

   Assign each of these cost items to the appropriate part of the value chain shown in Exhibit 1.4.

29. **Value chain.** Schering Pharmaceuticals incurs the following costs:

   a. Cost of redesigning blister packs to make drug containers more tamper-proof

   b. Cost of videos sent to doctors to promote sales of a new drug

   c. Equipment purchased by a scientist to conduct experiments on drugs yet to be approved by the federal government

   d. Cost of fees paid to members of Schering's board of directors

   e. Cost of Federal Express courier service to deliver drugs to hospitals

   Assign each of these cost items to the appropriate part of the value chain shown in Exhibit 1.4.

30. **Responsibility for ethical action** (adapted from CMA exam). Emily Johnson recently joined Growth Chemicals, Inc., as assistant controller. Growth Chemicals, Inc., processes chemicals for use in fertilizers. During her first month on the job, Emily spent most of her time getting better acquainted with those responsible for plant operations. Emily asked the plant supervisor what the procedure was for the disposal of chemicals. The response was that he (the plant supervisor) was not involved in the disposal of waste and that Emily would be wise to ignore the issue. Of course, this only drove Emily to investigate the matter further. Emily soon discovered that Growth Chemicals, Inc., was dumping toxic waste in a nearby public landfill late at night. Further, she discovered that several members of management were involved in arranging for this dumping. Emily was, however, unable to determine whether her superior, the controller, was involved. Emily considered three possible courses of action. She could discuss the matter with her controller, anonymously release the information to the local newspaper, or discuss the situation with an outside member of the board of directors whom she knows personally.

   a. Does Emily have an ethical responsibility to take a course of action?

   b. Of the three possible courses of action, which are appropriate and which are inappropriate?

31. **Ethics and inventory obsolescence** (adapted from CMA exam). The external auditors of Heart Scientific are currently performing their annual audit of the company with the help of assistant controller Tino Mariano. Several years ago Heart Scientific developed a unique balloon technique for opening obstructed arteries in the heart. The technique utilizes an expensive component that Heart Scientific produces. Until last year, Heart Scientific maintained a monopoly in this field.

   During the past year, however, a major competitor developed a technically superior product that uses an innovative, less costly component. The competitor was granted FDA approval, and it is expected that Heart Scientific will lose market share as a result. Heart Scientific currently has several years' worth of expensive components essential for the manufacture of its balloon product. Tino Mariano knows that these components will decrease in value due to the introduction of the competitor's product. He also knows that his boss, the controller, is aware of the situation. The controller, however, has informed the chief financial officer that there is no obsolete inventory nor any need for reductions of inventories to market values. Tino is aware that the chief financial officer's bonus plan is tied directly to the corporate profits, which depend on ending inventory valuations.

   In signing the auditor's representation letter, the chief financial officer acknowledges that all relevant information has been disclosed to the auditors and that all accounting procedures have been followed according to generally accepted accounting principles. Tino knows that the external auditors are unaware of the inventory problem, and he is unsure of what to do.

   a. Has the controller behaved unethically?

   b. How should Tino Mariano resolve this problem? Should he report this inventory overvaluation to the external auditors?

32. **Value-added and non–value-added activities.** Consider a plant producing widgets and dyes. The raw materials are purchased in bulk and delivered from the supplier to be placed in a warehouse until requested by the production departments.

    The warehouse has 24-hour security guards and one full-time maintenance person. The materials are then delivered to the departments three miles away by truck, where they are used in the production of widgets and dyes. During production the pieces are inspected twice. After production the finished product is stored in another warehouse until it is shipped to customers.

    Identify the value-added and non–value-added activities.

33. **Value of information: nonbusiness setting.** Consider the value of the following information in a medical context. Suppose that a patient visits a doctor's office and that the doctor decides on the basis of the signs that the patient's appendix should be removed immediately. Meanwhile, the doctor orders a white blood cell count. The doctor decides that the appendix must be removed no matter what the blood count happens to be.

    a. What is the value to the doctor of the information (in the cost-benefit sense discussed in this chapter) about the blood cell count?

    b. Why might the doctor order the test anyway?

34. **Value chain.** For a product with which you are familiar, do a value chain analysis like that done for Lone Tree Winery on pages 15 to 18. You might know the relevant financial data from your experience. If not, consult published financial statements, the Web, and your library for information. You may make intelligent estimates if precise data are not available.

Suggested Solutions to Even-Numbered Exercises

20. **Opportunity cost analysis.** On Sundays, the opportunity cost is:

    $$(10 \text{ skaters} \times 9 \text{ hours} \times \$10) - \$100 \text{ for the attendants} = \$800.$$

    Financially, Cliff is better off to take the hockey team's offer. However, he should also consider the loss in customer satisfaction and possible future lost business if the facility is not open on Sunday as usual.

22. **Variable and fixed costs.** Answers will vary. The balance sheet will show significant investments in property, plant, and equipment. The costs associated with depreciating, maintaining, financing, and/or leasing these assets is typically a fixed cost. Variable costs include materials, purchased parts, and some labor costs.

24. **Just-in-time production.** Answers will vary. JIT should reduce inventory and its related financing, insuring, and storing costs.

chapter 2

Measuring Product Costs

$\mathcal{2}$

This chapter shows how the accounting system records and reports the flow of costs in organizations. The accounting system records costs to help managers answer questions such as these:

- What is the cost of a job at Kinko's copy shop or at the Deloitte & Touche public accounting firm?
- What cost does Levi Strauss incur to make a denim jacket? How does that cost compare with management's expectations?
- What cost does DaimlerChrysler Corporation incur to make the Jeep Grand Cherokee?
- What cost does the state of New York incur to provide an undergraduate education at the State University of New York at Buffalo?

Companies using a low-cost leadership strategy have a particular need for this information. If a company tries to provide excellent service at the lowest possible cost to the company, then success requires accurately tracing costs by job or by customer. Some companies make decisions regarding which services or products to offer (or eliminate) based on the past profitability of those products or services. Most companies need accurately recorded costs.

Product Costs in Manufacturing Companies

Recording costs for a manufacturing company requires more complexity than does recording costs for a retail, wholesale, or service company. Whereas the retailer or wholesaler *purchases* goods for sale, the manufacturer *makes* them. The manufacturer purchases materials (for example, unassembled parts for a bicycle: rims, tires, handlebars, etc.), hires workers to convert the materials to a finished product, and then offers the product for sale. Manufacturing costs divide into three major categories:

1. **Direct materials,** easily traced directly to a product. Materials not easily traced to a product (for example, cleaning supplies) are manufacturing overhead (category 3 below).
2. **Direct labor** of workers who transform the materials into a finished product. Labor not easily traced to a product (for example, supervisors overseeing production of several products) is manufacturing overhead (category 3 below).
3. **Manufacturing overhead,** or all other costs of transforming the materials to a finished product. Examples include materials and labor not easily traced to a product and other manufacturing costs (excluding direct materials and direct labor) such as depreciation and insurance for the factory building, heat, light, power, and similar expenses incurred to keep the factory operating.

Although we use the term *manufacturing overhead,* common synonyms include *factory burden, factory overhead,* and simply *overhead* (a common term used by service companies).

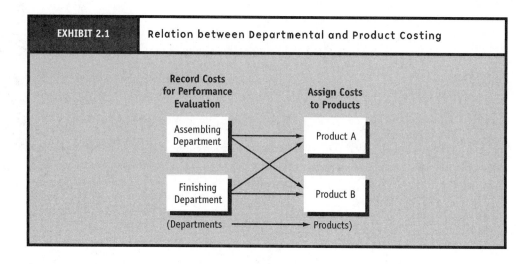

EXHIBIT 2.1 | **Relation between Departmental and Product Costing**

Recording Costs by Department and Assigning Costs to Products

Experts design managerial accounting systems to serve several purposes. For purposes of planning and performance evaluation, accountants record costs by department or other *responsibility centers*. (A responsibility center is any organizational unit with its own manager or managers.) Divisions, territories, plants, and departments all exemplify responsibility centers.

Exhibit 2.1 shows the relation between recording costs by departments and assigning costs to products for a firm with two manufacturing departments, Assembling and Finishing. The accounting system records the costs of direct materials, direct labor, and manufacturing overhead incurred in production. It uses three separate accounts in each of the manufacturing departments, in Assembly and in Finishing. Management then compares these costs with the standard or budgeted amounts and investigates significant variations, called *variances*. In recording costs by departments, the accounting system has served its function of providing data for departmental performance evaluation. The accounting system also assigns costs to products for managerial decision making, such as evaluating a product's profitability.

Nonmanufacturing Applications

You will find this relation between recording costs by category and departments and assigning costs to products (or customers) also in nonmanufacturing settings. For example, accountants record the costs of performing surgery on a patient by department (for example, the Surgery and the Recovery Room departments). They then assign these costs to a particular patient. Attorneys often track costs by department (for example, Corporate Transactions and Litigation) and then assign the costs to particular clients. Internet consultants may track costs by type of organization (for example, corporate and government), and then assign the costs to particular clients. Accountants assign the costs because managers wish to use them for billing purposes and to measure customer profitability. In general, for the accounting system to provide product or customer cost information, it must assign costs to products or customers from responsibility centers.

Fundamental Accounting Model of Cost Flows

Exhibit 2.2 shows how firms transform materials into finished goods. Note that the Work-in-Process account both *describes* the transformation of inputs into outputs in a company and *accounts* for the costs incurred in the process. Accounting systems for *service* companies resemble those for manufacturing, but with two exceptions. First, service companies use no direct materials, or almost none, because they do not manufacture a product. Service companies do, however, use supplies and include their costs as part of overhead. Second, accounting systems of service companies often allocate costs to customers rather than to units.

| EXHIBIT 2.2 | Flow of Costs through Accounts and Departments |

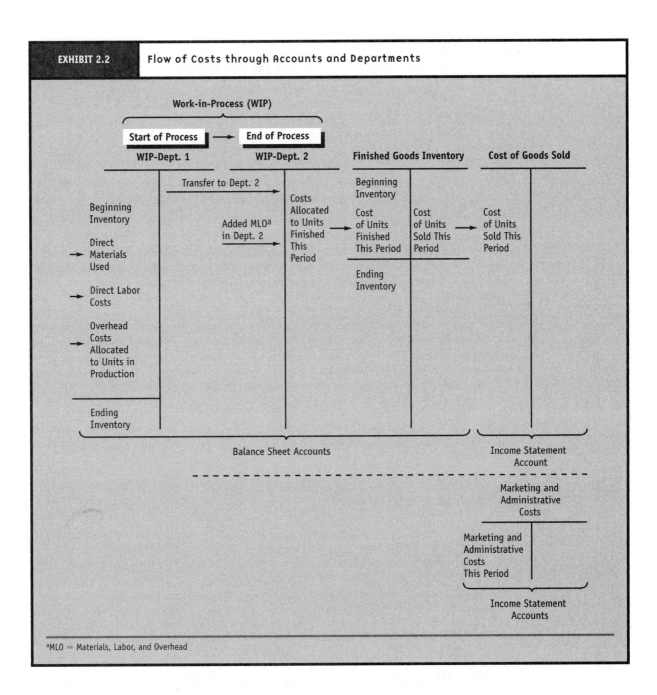

ᵃMLO = Materials, Labor, and Overhead

In most companies, each department controls its costs (for example, the Assembly Department or the Finishing Department). Thus each department has a separate Work-in-Process account, as Exhibit 2.2 shows, which accumulates departmental costs. Management holds department managers accountable for the costs accumulated in their departments.

Companies that operate in competitive markets have little direct control over prices paid for materials or prices received for finished goods. Thus, to succeed, a company must control the conversion costs (that is, direct labor and overhead), which it monitors in the Work-in-Process Inventory account.

In sum, the accounting system serves two purposes in manufacturing and service companies:

1. to record costs by responsibility center (department) for performance evaluation and cost control, and

2. to assign manufacturing costs to units produced (or customers served) for product (or customer) costing.

Basic Cost Flow Equation

Accounting systems all use the following basic **cost flow equation:**

$$\text{Beginning Balance} + \text{Transfers In} = \text{Transfers Out} + \text{Ending Balance}$$

or in symbols:

$$BB + TI = TO + EB$$

You may recall this fundamental equality in accounting from your financial accounting studies in a different form:

$$\text{Beginning Balance} + \text{Additions} - \text{Withdrawals} = \text{Ending Balance}$$

Transfers In to Work-in-Process represent the materials, labor, and overhead used in production. In merchandising, Transfers In to the inventory accounts represent the goods purchased.

Independent auditors often use the cost flow equation to perform reasonableness checks on the data they receive from clients. For example, if a client reports ending inventory of $850,000 based on a physical count of inventory, but the cost flow equation shows inventory should be $1,000,000 (i.e., $BB + TI - TO = \$1,000,000$), the auditor knows something is wrong.

Companies often use the cost flow equation periodically themselves to check that the amount of inventory recorded on the books matches the physical count of inventory. In this context, the cost flow equation becomes an internal control because it can catch errors made in recording inventory transactions. Because most companies carry significant amounts of inventory, they need accurate inventory information.

Discrepancies between physical inventory counts and the amount calculated using the cost flow equation typically result from errors made in the process of recording inventory transactions. These discrepancies sometimes, however, signal theft or financial frauds. The Managerial Application "Using the Basic Cost Flow Equation to Detect Fraud" describes a case in which the basic cost flow equation helped management discover fraudulent inventory reporting in one of its divisions.

Problem 2.1 for Self-Study

Using the basic cost flow equation, fill in the missing item for each of the following inventory accounts:

	A	B	C
Beginning Balance	$40,000	?	$35,000
Ending Balance	32,000	$16,000	27,000
Transferred In	?	8,000	8,000
Transferred Out	61,000	11,000	?

The solution to this self-study problem is at the end of this chapter on page 51.

Managerial Application

Using the Basic Cost Flow Equation to Detect Fraud

A top manager at Doughties Foods became curious about the high levels of inventory reported on the divisional financial statements of the Gravins Division. The amount of ending inventory at the Gravins Division seemed high compared with those of other divisions in the company.

Overstating the ending balance of inventory understates Cost of Goods Sold, which overstates Gross Margin and profits. In equation form,

$$BB + TI - (EB + \text{Fraud}) = TO - \text{Fraud},$$

where EB is the correct ending inventory amount and TO is the correct transfer out of inventory, which is also the correct Cost of Goods Sold. Fraud results in understating the reported Cost of Goods Sold and overstating the Ending Inventory by the same amount. One can more easily observe differences between the book and physical amounts for Ending Inventory than one can observe the differences between the book and physical amounts for Cost of Goods Sold.

As the manager of the Gravins Division discovered to his dismay, the Ending Inventory for Period 1 is the beginning inventory for Period 2. Thus, the beginning inventory on the books carried an overstated amount, which had to be matched by an equal amount of overstatement at the end of Period 2 if he were to maintain low reported Cost of Goods Sold and high income. All accounting frauds require repeated misrepresentation period after period or else the overstatement of income in one period causes a lower income in a subsequent period.

The Gravins Division kept some of its food inventory in freezers. The company's independent auditors did not like to go into the freezer, so the manager of the Gravins Division could get away with overstating his inventory by overstating the number of items in the freezer. As time passed, the Gravins Division manager continued to increase the amount of overstated inventory. Eventually the books said the freezer contained more inventory than top management thought plausible. When confronted with the high inventory numbers, the Gravins Division manager confessed to the inventory overstatement, and handed over a notebook containing records of the overstated amounts. Then he resigned.

The Securities and Exchange Commission filed charges alleging financial fraud against the manager of the Gravins Division and filed charges against the auditors for not complying with Generally Accepted Auditing Standards in conducting their audit.

Source: Based on the authors' research into Securities and Exchange Commission documents.

Cost Measure: Actual or Normal Costing

This section describes a commonly used method for assigning cost to products known as **normal costing.** Normal costing assigns to products actual direct material and direct labor costs plus an amount representing "normal" manufacturing overhead.

Under normal costing, a firm derives a rate for applying overhead to units produced before the production period, often a year, begins. The firm uses this rate in applying overhead to each unit as the firm produces it throughout the year. We first discuss the rationale for using normal manufacturing overhead costs; then we show how normal costing works.

An alternative to assigning "normal" overhead to products is to assign the actual overhead costs incurred. Assigning normal overhead costs to products has advantages over assigning actual costs. Actual total manufacturing overhead costs may fluctuate because of seasonality (the cost of utilities, for example) or for other reasons not related directly to activity levels. Also, if production is seasonal and total overhead costs remain unchanged, the per-unit costs in low-volume months will exceed the per-unit costs in high-volume months, as the following example shows:

	Production	Total Monthly Fixed Manufacturing Overhead	Per-Unit Overhead Cost
January	500 Units	$20,000	$40
July	4,000 Units	20,000	5

Normal costs enable companies to smooth out, or normalize, these fluctuations. Accountants could report equal per-unit overhead costs throughout the year, regardless of month-to-month fluctuations in actual costs and activity levels.

Accounting systems can provide actual direct material and direct labor cost information quickly. In contrast, it may take a month or more to learn about the actual overhead costs for the same units. For example, often two weeks to a month will elapse after the end of an accounting period before the firm receives utility bills. To get data quicker, firms frequently use a **predetermined overhead rate** to estimate the cost before they know the actual cost. For our discussion, we assume firms using normal costing use an overhead rate predetermined for the entire year.

Applying Overhead Costs to Production

Normal costing works like this: Accountants apply overhead costs to production using the following four steps (note that the four steps establish individual overhead rates for both fixed and variable overhead costs):

1. Select a **cost driver,** or **allocation base,** for applying overhead to production. Cost drivers cause an activity's costs. For example, machine hours could be one cause of energy and maintenance costs for a machine. For an automobile, miles driven would be a cost driver because as miles driven increases, so do some costs.
2. Estimate the dollar amount of overhead and the level of activity for the period (for example, one year).
3. Compute the predetermined (that is, normal) overhead rate from the following formula:

$$\text{Predetermined Manufacturing Overhead Rate} = \frac{\text{Estimated Manufacturing Overhead}}{\text{Normal (or Estimated) Activity Level}}$$

4. Apply overhead to production by multiplying the predetermined rate, computed in step **(3)**, times the actual activity (for example, the actual machine hours used to produce a product).

The first three steps take place before the beginning of the period. For example, a firm could complete these steps in November of Year 1 if it plans to use the predetermined rate for Year 2. Step 4 is done during Year 2.

Next we discuss these steps in more detail and show how a firm might apply them.

Example   Plantimum Builders builds mobile homes. In the previous year, Plantimum's total variable manufacturing overhead cost was $100,000 and the activity level was 50,000 direct labor hours. The company expects the same level of activity and costs for this year. Therefore, the company's accountants compute the predetermined rate to be $2.00 per direct labor hour, as follows:

$$\frac{\text{Predetermined Variable}}{\text{Manufacturing Overhead Rate}} = \frac{\$100,000}{50,000 \text{ Labor Hours}} = \$2.00 \text{ per Direct Labor Hour}$$

We compute the fixed manufacturing overhead rate in a similar fashion. Plantimum estimates fixed manufacturing overhead costs to be $50,000 for this year and the activity level to be 50,000 direct labor hours. The company's accountants computed the following rate:

$$\frac{\text{Predetermined Fixed}}{\text{Manufacturing Overhead Rate}} = \frac{\$50,000}{50,000 \text{ Labor Hours}} = \$1.00 \text{ per Direct Labor Hour}$$

The predetermined overhead rates mean that for each direct labor hour spent working on houses, the accountants charge (that is, add to the cost recorded for) the houses with $2.00 for variable manufacturing overhead cost and $1.00 for fixed manufacturing overhead.

Assume that Plantimum actually used 4,500 direct labor hours for the month. Plantimum applied the following overhead to production:

Variable Manufacturing Overhead	4,500 Hours at $2.00	$9,000
Fixed Manufacturing Overhead	4,500 Hours at $1.00	4,500

TERMINOLOGY NOTE

The word *charge* means, simply, debit. To charge an account means to debit that account. When we write "charge the houses with overhead costs," we mean to debit the account accumulating costs for the houses, increasing that amount of recorded costs.

Problem 2.2 for Self-Study

Normal costing. Pete Petezah, manager of the local Pizza Shack, has asked for your advice about product costs. Pete wants you to compute predetermined overhead rates for the Pizza Shack. Pete provides the following information to you.

Late last year, Pete made the following estimates for the Pizza Shack for this year:

(1) Estimated Variable Overhead	$108,000
(2) Estimated Fixed Overhead	$120,000
(3) Estimated Labor Hours	12,000 hours
(4) Estimated Labor Dollars per Hour	$20
(5) Estimated Output	120,000 pizzas

Compute the predetermined overhead rate for (1) variable overhead and (2) fixed overhead using each of the following cost drivers:

- Labor hours
- Labor dollars
- Units of output

The solution to this self-study problem is at the end of this chapter on page 52.

Choosing the Right Cost System

Different types of companies use different types of cost systems. An effective cost system must have all of the following three characteristics:

- *Decision focus.* It meets the needs of decision makers.
- *Different costs for different purposes.* It can provide different cost information for different purposes. For example, it provides variable costs for decision making and full absorption costs for external reporting.
- *Cost-benefit test.* It must meet a cost-benefit test. The benefits from the cost system must exceed its costs.

The selection of a cost system depends largely on the company. Exhibit 2.3 shows how production methods vary across organizations, depending on the type of product. Companies that produce **jobs** include print shops, such as Kinko's and R. R. Donnelley; custom construction companies, such as Morrison-Knudsen; defense contractors, such as General Dynamics; and computerized machine manufacturers, such as Cincinnati Milacron. These companies all produce customized products, which we call *jobs.* Companies producing customized products use **job costing** to record the cost of their products.

Many professional service organizations also use job costing. Examples include public accounting and consulting firms (such as Ernst & Young and Accenture) and law firms (such as

EXHIBIT 2.3	Production Methods and Accounting Systems	
Type of Production	**Accounting System**	**Type of Product**
Job (health-care services, custom homes, CPA firm)	Job Costing	Customized
Operations (computer terminals, automobiles, clothing)	Operation Costing	Mostly standardized
Continuous Flow Processing (oil refinery, soft drinks)	Process Costing	Standardized

Baker and McKenzie). These firms use job costing to keep track of costs for each client. Health-care organizations, such as Kaiser Permanente and the Mayo Clinic, record the costs of each patient's care using job costing. Look at Exhibit 2.3; which type of production and accounting system do you think NASA uses for the space shuttle program? (Answer: Job and job costing.)

Companies using **continuous flow processing** lie at the opposite end of the continuum from firms producing by job. Continuous flow processes mass-produce homogeneous products in a continuous flow. Companies manufacturing with continuous flow processes use **process costing** to account for product costs. Coca-Cola and PepsiCo use process costing to track costs of making soft drink syrup. Dow Chemical uses process costing to record the costs of chemical production. ExxonMobil uses process costing for its oil refining, and Merck uses process costing to record costs of pharmaceutical manufacturing.

Many organizations use job systems for some products and process systems for others. A home builder might use process costing for standardized homes with a particular floor plan. The same builder might use job costing when building a custom-designed house for a single customer. Honeywell, Inc., a high-tech company, uses process costing for most of its furnace thermostats and job costing for customized aerospace contracting products.

Many companies use a hybrid of job and process costing, called **operation costing. Operations** are a standardized method of making a product that is performed repeatedly in production. Some products share common production methods but differ in details. Consider jeans, such as those manufactured by Levi Strauss, which always have two legs and a closure such as a zipper or buttons. The amount and color of materials that make up the pair of jeans might differ depending on the style of jeans, but each pair of jeans has a common production process (i.e., cutting, sewing, trimming, washing). Consider desktop computers, such as those manufactured by Dell, which have different components but common methods of assembly. Consider a furniture manufacturer, such as Herman Miller, which makes different types of tables that require different materials but uses the same manufacturing process regardless of type. Each of these companies uses standardized methods for producing similar products even though the products differ in their specific materials. Operation costing resembles process costing for the production process. Thus accountants assign the same labor and overhead costs to each type of Herman Miller table, just as they would in process costing. Because each table requires different materials, the accountants assign specific materials to specific types of tables, just as they would in job costing.

Job and Process Costing Systems

This section compares job and process costing. We continue the Plantimum Builders example, using normal costing.

In job costing, firms collect costs for each "unit" produced. Often each department collects costs for evaluating the performance of departmental personnel. For instance, in April, Plantimum Builders started and completed three custom mobile home jobs (no beginning inventories). The data and costs follow:

	Direct Labor	Direct Materials	Direct Labor Hours ×	Predetermined Overhead Rate ($3/hr)	Total Cost of Job
Job. No. 1001	$ 8,000	$20,800	(400 × $3) =	$1,200	$30,000
Job. No. 1002	6,000	18,100	(300 × $3) =	900	25,000
Job. No. 1003	5,000	11,250	(250 × $3) =	750	17,000
Total	$19,000	$50,150		$2,850	$72,000

In process costing, firms accumulate costs in a department or production process during an accounting period (for example, one month), then spread those costs evenly over the units produced that month, computing an average unit cost. The formula follows:

$$\text{Unit Cost} = \frac{\text{Total Manufacturing Cost Incurred during the Period}}{\text{Total Units Produced during the Period}}$$

Assume Plantimum Builders had used process costing for the three jobs started and completed in April. The average cost per job would be computed as follows:

$$\frac{\underset{\$19,000}{\text{Direct Labor}} + \underset{\$50,150}{\text{Direct Materials}} + \underset{\$2,850}{\text{Applied Overhead}}}{3 \text{ jobs}} = \$24,000 \text{ per job}$$

Process costing does not require as much record keeping as job costing because it does not require keeping track of the cost of each job. However, process costing informs decision makers only about the average cost of the units, not the cost of *each particular* unit or job.

We have presented an overview of job and process costing. Next, we examine managerial issues in choosing between job and process costing.

Job versus Process Costing: Cost-Benefit Considerations

Why do firms prefer one accounting system to another? Cost-benefit analysis provides the answer. In general, the costs of record keeping under job costing systems exceed those under process costing. Consider the house builder. Under job costing, the house builder must accumulate costs for each house. If a truck delivers lumber to several houses, records of mere total cost of lumber issued will not suffice. The driver must keep records of the amount delivered to, and subsequently returned from, each house. If laborers work on several houses, they must keep track of the time spent on each house.

Process costing, however, requires recording only the total cost. For the house builder, process costing would report the average cost of all houses built. (In practice, house builders generally use job costing for custom-built houses and process costing for houses having a particular model type or floor plan.)

Under process costing, a firm does not report the direct cost incurred for a particular unit. If all units are homogeneous, this loss of information is probably minimal. Is it important for Kellogg's to know whether the cost of the 1,001st box of Raisin Bran differs from the 1,002nd box's cost? Not likely. The additional benefits from tracing costs to each box of Raisin Bran would not justify the additional record-keeping costs.

Although job costing provides more detailed information than process costing, it costs more to implement. Thus management and accountants must examine the costs and benefits of information and pick the method that best fits the organization's production operations.

Example   In this example, a custom house builder explains the benefits of job costing for companies that make heterogeneous products.

> We estimate the costs of each house for pricing purposes. Unless we know the actual costs of each house, we cannot evaluate our estimation methods. We use the information for performance evaluation and cost control, too. We assign a manager to each house who is responsible for seeing that actual costs don't exceed the estimate. If the actual costs come in under the estimate, the manager gets a bonus.
>
> We need a job system also to help us charge customers for the cost of customer changes. Usually, customers make changes as we build. If the changes have a small impact on costs, we absorb them. But if these changes add significant costs, we go to the customer with our computation of the cost of changes, and get an adjustment in the price of the house. Sometimes, we build on a cost-plus basis, which means customers pay us an amount equal to the cost of the job plus a profit. In this case we must know and document costs for each house so we can collect from the customer.

Management generally finds that the comparative costs and benefits of job and process costing indicate matching the cost system to the production methods as follows:

Nature of Production	Costing System Used
Heterogeneous Units, Each Unit Large	Job Costing
Homogeneous Units, Continuous Process, Many Small Units	Process Costing

Problem 2.3 for Self-Study

Classifying production as jobs or processes. Classify each of the following as the product of either a job or a continuous process:

- Work for a client on a lawsuit by lawyers in a law firm
- Diet cola
- Patient care in an emergency room for a college basketball player
- House painting by a company called Student Painters
- Paint

The solution to this self-study problem is at the end of this chapter on page 52.

Flow of Costs through Accounts

This section presents cost flows through accounts using a service company for our example. The flow of costs in service organizations resembles that in manufacturing. The service provided requires labor, overhead, and sometimes materials. In consulting, public accounting, and similar service organizations, the firm collects costs by job or client and uses an accounting method similar to that used in manufacturing job shops. The firm collects costs by job for performance evaluation, to provide information for cost control, and to compare actual with estimated costs for pricing of future jobs.

Example   For July, Corporate Training Group (CTG) has the following activity:

- Client A: 400 hours; Client B: 600 hours; Billing rate to clients: $200 per hour
- Labor costs (all consulting staff): $80 per hour
- Total consulting hours worked in July: 1,200 hours (CTG did not charge 200 hours to a client. The firm calls that time "Direct Labor—Unbillable.")
- Actual overhead costs for July: $22,000 (Overhead includes travel, secretarial salaries, telephone, copying, and postage.)
- CTG charges overhead to jobs based on labor hours worked using a predetermined rate of $20 per labor hour.
- Marketing and administrative costs: $12,000
- Training materials (books and handout materials): $10,000 materials in beginning Materials Inventory, $40,000 purchased; $15,000 used by Client A; $20,000 used by Client B; $15,000 remaining in Materials Inventory at the end of the month
- Corporate Training Group had no beginning Work-in-Process Inventory at the beginning of July.
- All transactions are on account.

The accountant billed both jobs to clients and transferred the costs from Work-in-Process to Cost of Services Billed. The entries to record these transactions are as follows:

(1)	Materials Inventory	40,000	
	Accounts Payable		40,000
	(To record purchase of training materials: $40,000)		
(2)	Work-in-Process: Client A	15,000	
	Work-in-Process: Client B	20,000	
	Materials Inventory		35,000
	(To record materials used by Client A: $15,000; and Client B: $20,000)		

(3)	Work-in-Process: Client A	32,000	
	Work-in-Process: Client B	48,000	
	Direct Labor—Unbillable	16,000	
	Accounts and Wages Payable		96,000
	(Client A: 400 hours @ $80 = $32,000; Client B: 600 hours @ $80 = $48,000; Unbillable: 200 hours @ $80 = $16,000)		
(4)	Work-in-Process: Client A	8,000	
	Work-in-Process: Client B	12,000	
	Overhead (applied)		20,000
	(Overhead applied to jobs at the rate of $20 per labor hour.)		
(5)	Overhead	22,000	
	Wages and Accounts Payable		22,000
	(Actual overhead: $22,000)		
(6)	Marketing and Administrative Costs	12,000	
	Wages and Accounts Payable		12,000
	(Actual cost: $12,000)		
(7a)	Accounts Receivable	200,000	
	Revenue: Client A		80,000
	Revenue: Client B		120,000
	(To record revenue at $200 per hour: 400 hours for Client A, 600 hours for Client B.)		
(7b)	Cost of Services Billed	135,000	
	Work-in-Process: Client A		55,000
	Work-in-Process: Client B		80,000
	(To record the cost of services billed to clients.)		

Note that 7a and 7b are two parts of the same entry.

Exhibit 2.4 shows the flow of costs through T-accounts. Exhibit 2.5 presents an income statement. The company treats the unbilled labor and unassigned overhead as expenses included with

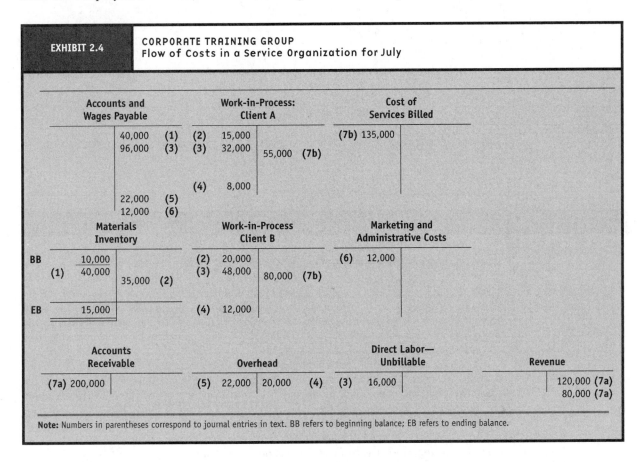

EXHIBIT 2.4

CORPORATE TRAINING GROUP
Flow of Costs in a Service Organization for July

Note: Numbers in parentheses correspond to journal entries in text. BB refers to beginning balance; EB refers to ending balance.

EXHIBIT 2.5	CORPORATE TRAINING GROUP Income Statement for the Month Ending July 31

Revenue from Services	$200,000
Less Cost of Services Billed	135,000
Gross Margin	65,000
Less:	
Direct Labor—Unbillable	16,000
Overhead (underapplied)	2,000[a]
Marketing and Administrative Costs	12,000
Operating Profit	$ 35,000

[a]$2,000 = $22,000 incurred − $20,000 applied to jobs.

marketing and administrative costs. We use the traditional income-statement format for demonstration purposes.

Problem 2.4 for Self-Study

Cost flows in a service organization. For the month of September, Touche Young & Company, an accounting firm, worked 200 hours for Client A and 700 hours for Client B. Touche Young bills clients at the rate of $80 per hour and pays the audit staff at the rate of $30 per hour. The audit staff worked 1,000 total hours in September, including 100 hours not billable to clients. Overhead costs were $10,000. (Examples of unbillable hours are hours spent in professional training and meetings unrelated to particular clients.) The firm assigned overhead as follows: Client A, $2,000; Client B, $7,000; and $1,000 unassigned. In addition, Touche Young & Company spent $5,000 in marketing and administrative costs. All transactions are on account. The firm has billed to the clients all work done in September.

a. Using T-accounts, show costs and revenue flows.
b. Prepare an income statement for the company for September.

The solution to this self-study problem is at the end of this chapter on page 52.

Ethical Issues in Job Costing

Many organizations have allegedly committed fraud in the way they assign costs to jobs. For example, the Defense Department has accused major defense contractors of overstating the costs of jobs. Fund-granting agencies, such as the National Science Foundation, have accused universities of overstating the costs of research projects. One or more of the following generally cause improprieties in job costing: misstating the stage of completion of jobs, charging costs to the wrong jobs or categories (for example, charging the cost of university yachts to research projects), or simply misrepresenting the costs of jobs.

To avoid the appearance of cost overruns on some jobs, job supervisors ask employees to wrongly charge costs to other jobs. If you work in consulting or auditing, you may encounter supervisors who ask you to allocate the time that you actually spent on jobs now in danger of exceeding their cost estimates to other jobs less likely to overrun cost estimates. At a minimum, this practice misleads managers who rely on accurate cost information for pricing, cost control, and other decisions. At worst, it also cheats people who may be paying for a job on a cost-plus-fee basis, where that job has cost less than the producer claims.

People who pay for jobs often insist on audits of financial records to avoid such deception. Government auditors generally work on the site of defense contractors, universities, and other organizations that have contracts with the government for large jobs.

Just-in-Time (JIT) Methods

Many companies (Toyota, Hewlett-Packard, and Yamaha, to name a few) use just-in-time methods for parts of their production process. **Just-in-time (JIT) methods** attempt to obtain materials just in time for production and to provide finished goods just in time for sale. This practice reduces, or potentially eliminates, inventories and the cost of carrying them. Just-in-time compels workers to immediately correct a process making defective units because they have no inventory where they can hide defective units. Eliminating inventories helps expose production problems. With no inventory to draw from for delivery to customers, just-in-time relies on high-quality materials and production.

Using a just-in-time system, production does not begin on an item until the firm receives an order. When the firm receives an order for a finished product, people in production order raw materials. As soon as production fills the order, production ends. In theory, a JIT system eliminates the need for inventories because no production takes place until the firm knows that it will sell the item. As a practical matter, companies using just-in-time inventory usually have a backlog of orders or stable demand for their products to assure continued production.

Because just-in-time production responds to an order receipt, JIT accounting can charge all costs directly to cost of goods sold. If inventories remain at the end of an accounting period, accountants remove the inventory amounts from the cost of goods sold account and charge them to inventory accounts.

Backflush Costing

What if a company's accountants record all manufacturing costs directly in Cost of Goods Sold, but at the end of the accounting period, the accountants learn that the company has some inventory? (Despite using just-in-time production, companies often find they have some inventory.) Companies that record costs directly in Cost of Goods Sold can use a method called *backflush costing* to transfer any costs back to the inventory accounts, if necessary.

Backflush costing is a method that works backward from the output to assign manufacturing costs to Work-in-Process inventories. Companies have probably used the term *backflush* because costs are "flushed back" through the production process to the points at which inventories remain. Exhibit 2.6 compares the traditional method of sequential costing with the backflush approach. Costs are initially recorded at the end of the production process, either in Finished Goods Inventory or in Cost of Goods Sold, on the grounds that the company has little or no Work-in-Process Inventory. If the company has inventories at the end of a period, the accountants can credit Cost of Goods Sold, as shown in Exhibit 2.6, and debit the inventory accounts for the amount of inventory. (Backflush costing looks more complicated than traditional sequential costing, but it is simpler in practice.) Look at Exhibit 2.6 for a Nissan plant that makes trucks; to what account would finished trucks that have not been sold be backflushed? (Answer: Finished Goods Inventory.)

Example   Biotech Corporation uses JIT. Direct materials cost $1.50 per unit, and other manufacturing costs (including labor) are $0.80 per unit. The company received an order for 10,000 units. Biotech incurred materials costs of $15,000 and other manufacturing costs of $8,000. The journal entries to record these events follow:

Cost of Goods Sold	15,000	
Accounts Payable		15,000
(To record materials.)		
Cost of Goods Sold	8,000	
Wages Payable and Manufacturing Overhead Applied		8,000
(To record the other manufacturing costs.)		

Accounting debits all of these costs directly to Cost of Goods Sold.

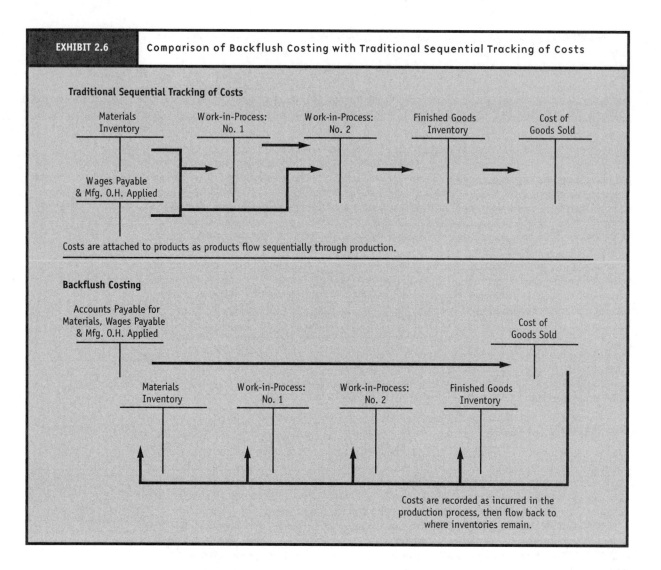

EXHIBIT 2.6   Comparison of Backflush Costing with Traditional Sequential Tracking of Costs

Traditional Sequential Tracking of Costs

Costs are attached to products as products flow sequentially through production.

Backflush Costing

Costs are recorded as incurred in the production process, then flow back to where inventories remain.

Assume 1,000 completed units remain in Finished Goods Inventory at the end of the period. Backflush costing removes the cost of 1,000 units from Cost of Goods Sold based on a unit cost of $2.30, which is $1.50 for materials and $0.80 for other manufacturing costs. The total cost removed and flushed back to ending inventory is $2,300 (= 1,000 units × $2.30 per unit). The journal entry to back out the inventory from Cost of Goods Sold follows:

Finished Goods Inventory	2,300	
Cost of Goods Sold		2,300
(To record inventory.)		

Exhibit 2.7 shows these transactions in T-accounts.

Traditional costing methods would charge the costs of these units to production, debiting the materials costs to a direct materials account. As production used the materials, traditional costing would transfer their costs to Work-in-Process Inventory and charge other manufacturing costs to Work-in-Process. As production completed goods, traditional costing transfers their costs into Finished Goods and finally into Cost of Goods Sold. Look at Exhibit 2.7; what would be the entry for recording inventory if the firm sold 9,500 units? (Answer: Credit Cost of Goods Sold $1,150 and debit Finished Goods Inventory $1,150.)

| EXHIBIT 2.7 | Backflush Cost Flows |

Accounts Payable

| | 15,000 |

Wages Payable and Mfg. O.H. Applied

| | 8,000 |

Cost of Goods Sold

| Materials | 15,000 | To Finished Goods | 2,300 |
| Other Manufacturing Costs | 8,000 | | |

Finished Goods Inventory

| Inventory | 2,300 | |

Spoilage and Quality of Production

Accountants typically include the cost of normal waste in the cost of work done this period. If Biotech Corporation incurs some normal wastage on a job, accountants would typically include that cost of materials in the cost of work done for the period. If the waste is not normal, accounting would remove it from the costs included in these computations and debit it to an expense account called "Abnormal Spoilage."

Companies concerned about quality production do not treat waste or spoiled goods as normal. Instead they remove waste and spoilage costs to avoid having waste costs buried in product costs. Some companies have been surprised to discover that, when they removed their waste and spoilage costs from other product costs, waste and spoilage costs were 20 to 30 percent of their total product costs.

Problem 2.5 for Self-Study

Traditional versus backflush cost flows. Influence "R" Us uses JIT production methods in making television commercials. For the month of January, the company incurred costs of $200,000 in making commercials. It assigned 20 percent of January's costs to one commercial for a clothing store that it has finished but not yet delivered or recorded in Cost of Goods Sold. Influence "R" Us has one Materials account for film, one Work-in-Process account, one Finished Goods account, and one Cost of Goods Sold account.

Show the flow of costs through T-accounts using (a) traditional costing and (b) backflush costing. Assume that the credit entries for these costs as recorded were $10,000 to Accounts Payable for film, $90,000 to Accounts Payable for overhead, and $100,000 to Wages Payable for labor. Also assume that actual overhead equaled applied overhead. The company had no beginning inventory on January 1.

The solution to this self-study problem is at the end of this chapter on page 53.

International Applications of JIT

Although Toyota gets credit as the first large company to install JIT, we suspect JIT has existed in some form for many decades, perhaps centuries, in various parts of the world. We now find JIT used in companies around the world. Countries like Japan with well-defined networks of suppliers and manufacturers are well suited to JIT. JIT is more difficult to implement in countries like the United States with dispersed suppliers and manufacturers. Efforts to increase international trade may increase the dispersion of suppliers, making JIT more difficult to implement.

Do Integrated Accounting Systems Satisfy Managerial Needs?

Firms frequently integrate product costing systems with other information systems, such as supply-chain management and customer information systems. These Enterprise Resource Planning Systems (ERPS) tend to centralize managerial accounting information systems, which reduces the flexibility of managers in divisions and subsidiaries to tailor managerial accounting for their own purposes. In some cases, we have seen managers (and managerial accountants) develop "shadow systems" that meet the specific needs of local managers.

Shadow systems usually indicate that the company-wide information system does not meet the needs of local managers. This problem often arises where most of the company uses a particular operating system, but a local business unit operates so differently that it needs a different system. Examples include public utilities that have expanded into other nonutility lines of businesses, oil companies that are organized as processes which have nonprocess subsidiaries, and conglomerates that have multiple types of business processes.

Summary

The following items correspond to the learning objectives presented at the beginning of the chapter.

1. **Understand the nature of manufacturing costs.** Three major categories of manufacturing costs are (1) direct materials that can be easily traced to a product, (2) direct labor of workers who transform materials into finished products and whose time can be easily traced to a product, and (3) manufacturing overhead, which represents all other manufacturing costs that do not fit into the first two categories.

2. **Explain the need for recording costs by department and assigning costs to products.** In recording costs by departments, the accounting system has served its function of providing data for departmental performance evaluation. The accounting system also assigns costs to products for managerial decision making, such as evaluating a product's profitability.

3. **Understand how the Work-in-Process account both describes the transformation of inputs into outputs in a company and accounts for the costs incurred in the process.** A key factor in a company's success is how well it controls the conversion costs (direct labor and overhead). Companies closely monitor those costs in the Work-in-Process Inventory account. The key equation in words is Beginning Balance plus Transfers In equals Transfers Out plus Ending Balance; in symbols, we write:

Key Equation

$$BB + TI = TO + EB$$

4. **Compare and contrast normal costing and actual costing.** Actual costing measures product costs using actual costs incurred. Normal costing uses actual direct material and direct labor costs, plus an amount representing "normal" manufacturing overhead. Under normal costing, a firm derives a rate for applying overhead to units produced before the production period, then uses this "predetermined rate" in applying overhead to each unit as the firm produces it.

Key Equation

$$\text{Predetermined Manufacturing Overhead Rate} = \frac{\text{Estimated Manufacturing Overhead}}{\text{Normal (or Estimated) Activity Level}}$$

5. **Know various production methods and the different accounting systems each requires.** Companies that produce customized products—or jobs—use job costing. Companies that

mass-produce homogeneous products—continuous flow processing—use process costing. Companies that produce batches of products using standardized methods—operations—use operation costing. Operation costing is a hybrid of job and process costing, where the materials differ by type of product but labor and overhead amounts are the same.

6. **Compare and contrast job costing and process costing systems.** In job costing, firms collect costs for each unit produced. In process costing, firms accumulate costs in a department or production process during an accounting period, then spread those costs evenly over the units produced during that period, to determine an average cost per unit. Job costing provides more detailed information than process costing, and the costs of record keeping under job costing systems exceed those under process costing.

Key Equation

$$\text{Unit Cost} = \frac{\text{Total Manufacturing Cost Incurred during the Period}}{\text{Total Units Produced during the Period}}$$

7. **Compare and contrast product costing in service organizations to that in manufacturing companies.** Service companies, like manufacturing companies, need accurate, relevant, and timely management accounting information. Service organizations often collect costs by departments for performance evaluation, and also by job or client. Service organizations differ in that they do not show inventories on the financial statements.

8. **Understand the concepts of customer costing and profitability analysis.** Companies often track revenues and costs by customer to determine the profitability of each customer. Management uses these data in making strategic decisions related to customers.

9. **Identify ethical issues in job costing.** Many organizations commit improprieties in the way they assign costs to jobs. To avoid the appearance of cost overruns on jobs, job supervisors sometimes ask employees to charge costs to the wrong jobs.

10. **Recognize components of just-in-time (JIT) production methods and understand how accountants adapt costing systems to them.** Management uses JIT methods to obtain materials just in time for production and to provide finished goods just in time for sale. JIT requires that workers immediately correct a process making defective units because there is no inventory where workers and supervisors can hide defective units. Accounting in a JIT environment charges all costs directly to Cost of Goods Sold, creating a significant savings in administrative time and costs, and charges them to Inventory accounts, when needed, using backflush costing.

11. **Know how to compute end-of-period inventory book value using equivalent units of production (Appendix 2.1).** The five steps to compute inventory book value are: (1) summarize the flow of physical units, (2) compute equivalent units, (3) summarize cost to be accounted for, (4) compute unit costs for the current period, and (5) compute the cost of goods completed and transferred out of Work-in-Process Inventory.

Key Terms and Concepts

Allocation base
Backflush costing
Continuous flow processing
Cost driver
Cost flow equation
Direct labor
Direct materials
Equivalent units (E.U.)*
Job

Job costing
Just-in-time (JIT) method
Manufacturing overhead
Normal costing
Operation costing
Operations
Predetermined overhead rate
Process costing

*Term appears in Appendix 2.1.

Appendix 2.1: Computing Costs of Equivalent Production

This appendix describes product costing methods when a firm has partially completed work on a product at the beginning or end of a period. For example, assume Davis Contractors, a house builder, is currently building several houses of a particular model. Davis had three partially built houses at the beginning of the second quarter of the year (April 1). Davis started four houses and completed five houses during the second quarter and had two partially built houses at the end of the quarter (June 30). The contractor knows that she has spent $795,000 on construction materials, labor, and overhead for these houses during the second quarter and that the cost of the beginning Work-in-Process Inventory for the three houses partially built on April 1 totals $42,000. The contractor wishes to know several other things, however, such as the cost of each house constructed in the second quarter, the cost of the ending Work-in-Process Inventory, and the cost of the houses completed.

The contractor has several potential uses for the information about the cost of each house. First, the contractor had set prices based on market conditions and the estimate that each house would cost $145,000 to build. If she estimated incorrectly, the contractor would consider changing the prices on the houses or possibly would stop building this type of house if costs were so high that the contractor would make insufficient profits. Second, the contractor holds construction job supervisors responsible for managing and scheduling workers, for minimizing waste, and for other activities that affect construction costs. Product costs can provide feedback about their performance. Third, Davis Contractors prepares the external financial statements for its creditors that require ending inventory valuation and the cost of finished houses sold.

Procedure for Applying Costs to Units Produced

This section describes the five steps required to compute product costs, the cost of ending Work-in-Process Inventory, and the cost of finished goods. Exhibit 2.8 presents the data required to do

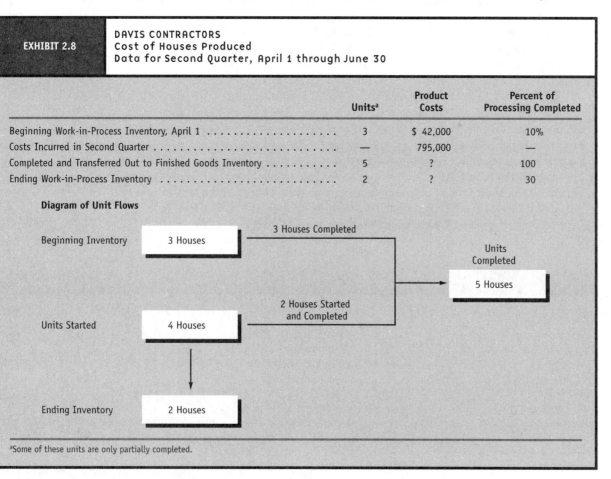

EXHIBIT 2.8	DAVIS CONTRACTORS Cost of Houses Produced Data for Second Quarter, April 1 through June 30

	Units[a]	Product Costs	Percent of Processing Completed
Beginning Work-in-Process Inventory, April 1	3	$ 42,000	10%
Costs Incurred in Second Quarter	—	795,000	—
Completed and Transferred Out to Finished Goods Inventory	5	?	100
Ending Work-in-Process Inventory	2	?	30

Diagram of Unit Flows

Beginning Inventory — 3 Houses — 3 Houses Completed

Units Completed — 5 Houses

2 Houses Started and Completed

Units Started — 4 Houses

Ending Inventory — 2 Houses

[a]Some of these units are only partially completed.

the analysis for the Davis Contractors example. Exhibit 2.8 shows that the contractor considered each of the three houses in the beginning Work-in-Process Inventory to be 10 percent complete, on average, and the two houses in the ending Work-in-Process Inventory each to be 30 percent complete on average. Assume the first-in, first-out (FIFO) cost flow assumption for inventory, for now. (Later, we discuss the effects of using the weighted-average method.) Exhibit 2.9 summarizes the five steps in the process and presents the analysis for Davis Contractors.

Step 1: Summarize the Flow of Physical Units. This appears in the top of the production cost report in Exhibit 2.9.

EXHIBIT 2.9	DAVIS CONTRACTORS Production Cost Report Using FIFO Second Quarter, April 1 through June 30		

	(Step 1) Physical Units	(Step 2) Compute Equivalent Units (E.U.)
Accounting for Units:		
Units to Account For:		
Beginning Work-in-Process (WIP) Inventory	3	
Units Started This Period	4	
Total Units to Account For	7	
Units Accounted For:		
Units Completed and Transferred Out:		
From Beginning Inventory	3	2.7[a] (90%)[b]
Started and Completed, Currently	2	2.0
Units in Ending WIP Inventory	2	0.6 (30%)[c]
Total Units Accounted For	7	5.3

	Total Costs	Units Costs
Accounting for Costs:		
(Step 3) Costs to Be Accounted For:		
Costs in Beginning WIP Inventory	$ 42,000	
Current Period Costs	795,000	
Total Costs to Be Accounted For	$837,000	
(Step 4) Cost per Equivalent Unit of Work Done This Period:		
$795,000/5.3 E.U.		$150,000 per E.U.
(Step 5) Costs Accounted For:		
Costs Assigned to Units		
Transferred Out:		
Costs from Beginning WIP Inventory	$ 42,000	
Current Costs Added to Complete		
Beginning WIP Inventory:		
2.7 E.U. × $150,000	= 405,000	
Current Costs of Units Started and Completed:		
2.0 E.U. × $150,000	= 300,000	
Total Costs Transferred Out	$747,000	$149,400 per Unit (= $747,000/5 Units Transferred Out)
Costs Assigned to Ending WIP Inventory:		
0.6 E.U. × $150,000	= 90,000	
Total Costs Accounted For	$837,000	

[a]Equivalent units required to complete beginning inventory. For example, 90 percent of 3 units must be added to the beginning inventory to complete it. Therefore, 2.7 (= 90% × 3) equivalent units are required to complete beginning inventory.
[b]Percent required to complete beginning inventory.
[c]Stage of completion of ending inventory.

Step 2: Compute Equivalent Units. Because the firm has some partially completed units at the beginning and end of the period, accounting must convert the work into equivalent (finished) units produced. **Equivalent units (E.U.)** represent the translation of partially completed work into equivalent whole units. For example, two units, each 50 percent complete, represent one equivalent unit. Three categories of work done require equivalent-unit computations to derive the equivalent work done in a period:

- For Davis Contractors, the three houses in beginning Work-in-Process (WIP) Inventory were 10 percent complete when the period started. Because Davis completed them during this period, Davis did 90 percent of the work on these houses during the second quarter. Therefore, Davis manufactured the equivalent of 2.7 units (= 3 houses $\times$ 90%) to complete the beginning inventory, as Exhibit 2.9 shows.
- Exhibit 2.8 shows that Davis started and completed two houses during the period, representing two equivalent units produced, as shown in Exhibit 2.9.
- The ending WIP Inventory represents the equivalent work done on units not completed and not yet transferred out during the period. Two houses that Davis had 30 percent complete at the end of the period fit into this category, representing 0.6 equivalent units (2 houses $\times$ 30%).

The equivalent units produced for the second quarter are 5.3 units (= 2.7 + 2.0 + 0.6), as Step 2 in Exhibit 2.9 shows.

We base equivalent unit computations on the basic cost flow equation. Here is an alternative way to find the equivalent units. If you know the equivalent work done in beginning and ending Work-in-Process inventories and the units transferred out, you can derive the equivalent units produced during the period as follows:

$$\begin{array}{l}\text{Equivalent Units} \\ \text{in the Beginning} \\ \text{Inventory}\end{array} + \begin{array}{l}\text{Equivalent Units} \\ \text{of Work Done} \\ \text{This Period}\end{array} = \begin{array}{l}\text{Equivalent Units} \\ \text{Transferred Out}\end{array} + \begin{array}{l}\text{Equivalent Units} \\ \text{in Ending} \\ \text{Inventory}\end{array}$$

In our example, to find the work done this period, use the following formula:

$$\begin{array}{l}\text{Equivalent Units} \\ \text{of Work Done} \\ \text{This Period}\end{array} = \begin{array}{l}\text{Equivalent Units} \\ \text{Transferred Out}\end{array} + \begin{array}{l}\text{Equivalent Units} \\ \text{in Ending} \\ \text{Inventory}\end{array} - \begin{array}{l}\text{Equivalent Units} \\ \text{in Beginning} \\ \text{Inventory}\end{array}$$

$$= 5.0 + 0.6 - (3.0 \times 10\%)$$

$$= 5.3 \text{ Equivalent Units of Work Done}$$

Step 3: Summarize Costs to Be Accounted For. This step records the costs in beginning Work-in-Process Inventory and the costs incurred during the period, as Step 3 of Exhibit 2.9 shows.

Step 4: Compute Unit Costs for the Current Period. Exhibit 2.9 shows that the cost per equivalent unit produced this period is $150,000. Note that this cost represents work done during this period only; it does not include costs in beginning inventory. Davis would use this unit cost to evaluate performance in controlling costs, and it would provide information to management about the cost of building houses that Davis can use to assess prices and the profitability of continuing to build this type of house. Look at Exhibit 2.9; what would be the total costs to be accounted for if the contractor considered the ending Work-in-Process Inventory to be only 20 percent complete? (Answer: still $837,000.)

Step 5: Compute the Cost of Goods Completed and Transferred Out of Work-in-Process and the Cost of Ending Work-in-Process Inventory. Exhibit 2.9 shows the cost of units transferred out, including the $42,000 from beginning inventory and the cost of the goods still in ending inventory, for which accounting assigns a cost of $150,000 per equivalent unit.

Exhibit 2.10 presents the flow of costs through T-accounts. Look at Exhibit 2.10 and assume the same beginning and ending inventory values; if current period costs were $805,000, what would be the value of Finished Goods Inventory? (Answer: $757,000.)

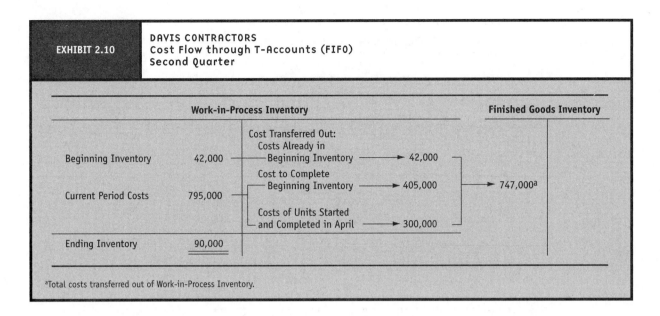

| EXHIBIT 2.10 | DAVIS CONTRACTORS
Cost Flow through T-Accounts (FIFO)
Second Quarter |

	Work-in-Process Inventory			Finished Goods Inventory
		Cost Transferred Out:		
Beginning Inventory	42,000	Costs Already in Beginning Inventory ⟶ 42,000		
Current Period Costs	795,000	Cost to Complete Beginning Inventory ⟶ 405,000	⟶ 747,000[a]	
		Costs of Units Started and Completed in April ⟶ 300,000		
Ending Inventory	90,000			

[a]Total costs transferred out of Work-in-Process Inventory.

Weighted-Average Method

The previous computations assumed FIFO, which means that accounting transferred out the cost of beginning inventory first, and that the costs assigned to ending inventory were the costs of goods produced during the current period. If Davis used the weighted-average method instead of FIFO, accounting would assign the cost of goods transferred out and the cost of goods in ending inventory a weighted-average cost that considers both the current period cost and the beginning inventory cost. The weighted-average cost is $149,464 per unit, which equals the total costs Davis must account for, $837,000, divided by the total equivalent units, 5.6. The 5.6 equivalent units equal 5.3 equivalent units for the period plus 0.3 in beginning inventory. The 5.6 equivalent units also equal the 5.0 units transferred out plus 0.6 equivalent units in ending inventory. This result must be true because

$$BB + TI = TO + EB,$$

so

$$0.3 + 5.3 = 5.0 + 0.6,$$

where TI is defined to be the equivalent units produced this period.

Solutions to Self-Study Problems

SUGGESTED SOLUTION TO PROBLEM 2.1 FOR SELF-STUDY

For each case, start with the formula

$$BB + TI = TO + EB.$$

$$A: TI = TO + EB - BB$$
$$= \$61,000 + \$32,000 - \$40,000$$
$$= \$53,000$$

$$B: BB = TO + EB - TI$$
$$= \$11,000 + \$16,000 - \$8,000$$
$$= \$19,000$$

$$C: TO = BB + TI - EB$$
$$= \$35,000 + \$8,000 - \$27,000$$
$$= \$16,000$$

SUGGESTED SOLUTION TO PROBLEM 2.2 FOR SELF-STUDY

Compute the predetermined overhead rates as follows.

	Variable Overhead	Fixed Overhead
Labor hours	$\dfrac{\$108,000}{12,000} = \$9$ per labor hr.	$\dfrac{\$120,000}{12,000} = \$10$ per labor hr.
Labor dollars	$\dfrac{\$108,000}{(\$20 \times 12,000)} = \$0.45$ per dollar	$\dfrac{\$120,000}{(\$20 \times 12,000)} = \$0.50$ per dollar
Output	$\dfrac{\$108,000}{120,000} = \$0.90$ per pizza	$\dfrac{\$120,000}{120,000} = \$1.00$ per pizza

SUGGESTED SOLUTION TO PROBLEM 2.3 FOR SELF-STUDY

> Lawsuit: job
> Diet cola: process
> Emergency room care: job
> House painting: job
> Paint: process

SUGGESTED SOLUTION TO PROBLEM 2.4 FOR SELF-STUDY

TOUCHE YOUNG & COMPANY
September

Accounts Receivable	Work-in-Process: Client A	Revenue
(5a) 72,000	(1) 6,000 | 8,000 (5b) (2) 2,000	72,000 (5a)

Wages and Accounts Payable	Work-in-Process: Client B	Cost of Services Billed
30,000 (1)	(1) 21,000 | 28,000 (5b) (2) 7,000	(5b) 36,000

	Direct Labor— Unbillable	
	(1) 3,000	
10,000 (3)		

	Overhead	Marketing and Administrative Costs
5,000 (4)	(3) 10,000 | 9,000 (2)	(4) 5,000

Entries: (1) Direct labor at $30 per hour. (2) Overhead applied. (3) Actual overhead incurred. (4) Marketing and administrative costs. (5) Services billed.

b.

TOUCHE YOUNG & COMPANY
Income Statement for the Month Ended September 30

Revenue from Services	$72,000
Less Cost of Services Billed	36,000
Gross Margin	$36,000
Less:	
Direct Labor—Unbillable	3,000
Overhead (underapplied)	1,000[a]
Marketing and Administrative Costs	5,000
Operating Profit	$27,000

[a]Actual overhead $10,000 − $9,000 assigned to jobs.

SUGGESTED SOLUTION TO PROBLEM 2.5 FOR SELF-STUDY

a. Traditional Costing

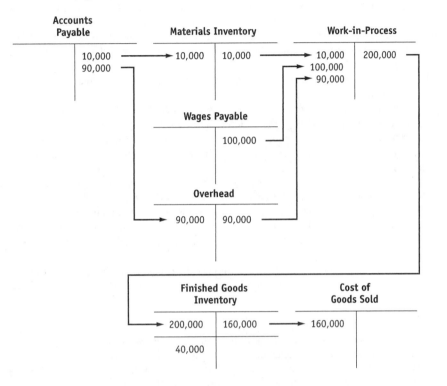

b. Backflush Costing

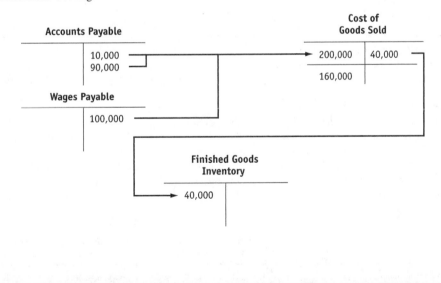

Questions, Exercises, Problems, and Cases

REVIEW QUESTIONS

1. Review the meaning of the concepts or terms given in Key Terms and Concepts.
2. Compare and contrast job costing and process costing systems.
3. Why don't most service organizations have inventories (other than supplies)?
4. What is a production operation?
5. Why is operation costing called a hybrid costing method?
6. What is the basic cost flow equation?

CRITICAL ANALYSIS AND DISCUSSION QUESTIONS

7. Describe the concept of customer profitability. Why is customer profitability important?
8. Management of a company that manufactures small appliances is trying to decide whether to install a job or process costing system. The manufacturing vice-president has stated that job costing gives the best control. The controller, however, has stated that job costing would require too much record keeping. What do you think of the manufacturing vice-president's suggestion and why?
9. What operating conditions of companies make just-in-time methods feasible?
10. How might JIT affect accounting methods?
11. Compare and contrast the problem of providing quality service in a service company to that of providing quality goods in a manufacturing company.
12. How does operation costing compare and contrast with job costing and process costing?
13. What types of savings can firms achieve with just-in-time methods compared with traditional production methods?
14. Explain the differences in accounting for the flow of costs using traditional accounting, where accountants charge costs first to inventory accounts, and using JIT.
15. Why must firms have reliable suppliers when using just-in-time methods?
16. Refer to the Managerial Application "Using the Basic Cost Flow Equation to Detect Fraud." How did the manager of the Gravins Division fraudulently increase profits? How was the fraud detected?
17. Name three companies not mentioned in the text that make products using processes.
18. Name three companies not mentioned in the text that produce jobs.

EXERCISES

Solutions to even-numbered exercises are at the end of the chapter after the cases.

19. **Cost flow model.** Marie Johnson is trying to compute unknown values in inventory accounts in three of her stores. Knowing of your expertise in cost flows, she asks for your help and provides you with the following information about each store:

	Store		
	Midwest	**Northeast**	**North**
Beginning inventory	$ 60,000	?	?
Transfers into inventory accounts	200,000	$200,000	$160,000
Transfers out of inventory accounts	220,000	180,000	150,000
Ending inventory	?	60,000	40,000

Tell Marie Johnson what the missing values (?) are for each of her stores.

20. **Cost flow model.** A fire has destroyed the inventory of the BBQ Company. Before paying for damages, the Comprehensive Insurance Company wants to know the amount of ending inventory that is missing. You have been hired to dig through the ashes and find as much information as you can. You find the following information about four of BBQ's big-selling inventory items:

	Product			
	Lighter Fluid	**Waterproof Matches**	**Burn Ointment**	**Fireplace Screens**
Beginning inventory	$ 40,000	$ 60,000	$ 60,000	?
Transfers into inventory accounts	180,000	340,000	120,000	$120,000
Transfers out of inventory accounts ...	80,000	380,000	140,000	120,000
Ending inventory	?	?	?	?

Compute the ending inventory, which is the amount destroyed by the fire, for any of the products that you can. You may not be able to compute ending inventory for all products. If you cannot compute the ending inventory, state what additional information you need.

21. **Cost flow model.** A flood has destroyed the inventory of the AquaMan Corporation. Before paying for damages, the JRC Insurance Company wants to know the amount of ending inventory that is missing. You have been hired to search through the water-sodden mess to

find as much information as you can. You find the following information about four of AquaMan's big-selling inventory items:

	Item			
	Rubber Rafts	Rubber Duckies	Galoshes	Diving Equipment
Beginning inventory	$ 60,000	$60,000	?	$160,000
Transfers into inventory accounts	480,000	90,000	$120,000	180,000
Transfers out of inventory accounts	540,000	75,000	150,000	240,000
Ending inventory	?	?	?	?

Compute the ending inventory, which is the amount destroyed by the flood, for any of the products that you can. You may not be able to compute ending inventory for all products. If you cannot compute the ending inventory, state what additional information you need.

22. **Cost flow model.** The law firm of Candice & Bergman has asked your help in computing damages in a lawsuit. The law firm's client claims an employee has stolen merchandise and is suspicious because this employee has just opened a discount electronics store. The law firm provides you with the following information from the accounting records:

	Product		
	Videocassette Recorders	Televisions	Compact Disc Players
Beginning inventory	$20,000	$20,000	$15,000
Transfers into inventory accounts	40,000	50,000	20,000
Transfers out of inventory accounts from sales	35,000	55,000	25,000
Ending inventory	?	?	?

You physically counted the ending inventory and found it to be as follows: videocassette recorders, $20,000; televisions, $5,000; and compact disc players, $10,000. Compute the ending inventory according to the accounting records and compare it to the physical count. What discrepancy, if any, between the physical count and the accounting records could be attributed to the theft?

23. **Cost flow model.** Franklin, LLP, an auditing firm, is reconstructing the records of a client called MultiChips, which is concerned that some of its inventory is missing. The accounting records provide the following information about MultiChips' inventories:

	Product		
	Computer Chips	Potato Chips	Poker Chips
Beginning inventory	$ 800,000	$160,000	$ 40,000
Transfers into inventory accounts	1,600,000	600,000	200,000
Transfers out of inventory accounts from sales	1,800,000	560,000	210,000
Ending inventory	?	?	?

You physically counted the ending inventory and found it to be as follows: computer chips, $600,000; potato chips, $140,000; and poker chips, $20,000. Compute the ending inventory according to the accounting records and compare it to the physical count. What discrepancy do you find between the physical count and the accounting records, if any?

24. **Just-in-time methods.** McNeal Products uses a just-in-time system. To produce 2,000 units for an order, it purchased and used materials costing $50,000, and incurred other manufacturing costs of $30,000, of which $10,000 was labor. All costs were on account.

After McNeal Products completed production of the 2,000 units and shipped 1,600 units, management needed the Finished Goods Inventory balance for the 400 units remaining in inventory for financial statement preparation. The firm incurred costs evenly across all products.

Show the flow of costs using journal entries and T-accounts using backflush costing.

25. **Just-in-time methods.** Sam's Circuits uses just-in-time production methods. To produce 1,200 units for an order, Sam's purchased and used materials costing $26,000 and incurred other manufacturing costs of $22,000, of which $8,000 was labor. All costs were on account.

    After Sam's completed production on the 1,200 units and shipped 1,100 units, management needed the Finished Goods Inventory balance for the 100 units remaining in inventory for financial statement preparation.

    Prepare journal entries and T-accounts for these transactions using backflush costing.

26. **Job costs in a service organization.** Loomis and Associates, a CPA firm, uses job costing. During January, the firm provided audit services for two clients and billed those clients for the services performed. Springsteen Productions was billed for 4,000 hours at $100 per hour, and RCI Records was billed for 2,000 hours at $100 per hour. Direct labor costs were $60 per hour. Of the 6,400 hours worked in January, 400 hours were not billable. The firm assigns overhead to jobs at the rate of $20 per billable hour. During January, the firm incurred actual overhead of $140,000. The firm incurred marketing and administrative costs of $20,000. All transactions were on account.

    a. Show how Loomis and Associates' accounting system would record these revenues and costs using journal entries.

    b. Prepare an income statement for January like the one in Exhibit 2.5.

27. **Job costs in a service organization.** Internet Designs, a Web site design and maintenance firm, uses job costing. During November, the firm provided Web site services for two clients and billed those clients for the services performed. Internet Designs billed Mountain View Company for $150,000 and Palatine Productions for $100,000. Direct labor costs were $80 per hour. Internet Designs worked 1,200 hours on the Mountain View account and 900 hours on the Palatine account. The firm worked an additional 100 hours that it did not charge to either account. The firm assigns overhead to jobs at the rate of $60 per billable hour. During November, the firm incurred actual overhead of $140,000. The firm incurred marketing and administrative costs of $60,000. All transactions were on account.

    a. Show how Internet Designs' accounting system would record these revenues and costs using journal entries.

    b. Prepare an income statement for November like the one in Exhibit 2.5.

28. **Job costs in a service organization.** Computer Systems, Inc., uses job costing. During June, the firm provided computer consulting services for three clients and billed those clients for the services performed. E-Gadgets was billed for 900 hours, E-Shop was billed for 300 hours, and E-Food was billed for 200 hours, all at $200 per hour. Direct labor costs were $100 per hour. Of the 1,600 hours worked in June, 200 hours were not billable. The firm assigns overhead to jobs at the rate of $60 per billable hour. During June, the firm incurred actual overhead of $100,000. The firm incurred marketing and administrative costs of $40,000. All transactions were on account.

    a. Show how these revenues and costs would appear in T-accounts.

    b. Prepare an income statement for June like the one in Exhibit 2.5.

29. **Job costs in a service organization.** Crafty Ideas, an advertising firm, uses job costing. During March, the firm designed ads for two clients and billed those clients for the services performed. Crafty Ideas billed Franklin Groceries for $75,000 and Truman Trust for $150,000. Direct labor costs were $25 per hour. Crafty Ideas worked 1,200 hours on the Franklin job and 2,000 hours on the Truman Trust job. The firm could not charge 300 hours to either job. The firm assigns overhead to jobs at the rate of $20 per billable hour. During March, the firm incurred actual overhead of $70,000. The firm incurred marketing and administrative costs of $20,000. All transactions were on account.

    a. Show the flow of these revenues and costs through T-accounts.

    b. Prepare an income statement for March like the one in Exhibit 2.5.

30. **Computing equivalent units (Appendix 2.1).** The Assembly Department had 60,000 units 60 percent complete in Work-in-Process Inventory at the beginning of April. During April, the department started and completed 160,000 units. The department started another 40,000 units and completed 30 percent as of the end of April. Compute the equivalent units of work performed during April using FIFO. Assume the department incurred production costs evenly throughout processing.

31. **Computing product costs with incomplete products (Appendix 2.1).** Refer to the data in Exercise **30.** Assume that the cost assigned to beginning inventory on April 1 was $70,000 and that the department incurred $382,000 of production costs during April. Prepare a production cost report like the one shown in Exhibit 2.9.

32. **Actual costs and normal costs.** American River Company uses a predetermined rate for applying overhead to production using normal costing. The rates for Year 1 follow: variable, 200 percent of direct labor dollars; fixed, 300 percent of direct labor dollars. Actual overhead costs incurred follow: variable, $20,000; fixed, $26,000. Actual direct materials costs were $5,000, and actual direct labor costs were $9,000. American River produced one job in Year 1.

    a. Calculate actual costs of the job.

    b. Calculate normal costs of the job using predetermined overhead rates.

33. **Applied overhead in a bank.** On January 1, a bank estimated its production capacity to be 800 million units and used that estimate to compute its predetermined overhead rate of $0.01 per check processed (one unit = one check processed). The units produced for the four quarters follow:

Quarter	Actual Units of Production (in millions)
1st	200 Checks
2nd	200 Checks
3rd	200 Checks
4th	100 Checks

    a. Compute the amount of total overhead applied under normal costing for each quarter.

    b. What was the estimated overhead for the year for the predicted capacity of 800 million units?

PROBLEMS

34. **Analyzing costs in a job company.** On February 1, Peterman Plumbing Company had two jobs in process with the following costs:

	Direct Materials	Direct Labor
Wilson	$3,000	$12,000
Baker	2,400	9,600

    In addition, overhead is applied to these jobs at the rate of 80 percent of direct labor costs.

    On February 1, Peterman had materials inventory totaling $6,000. During February, Peterman purchased $12,000 of materials and had none left in materials inventory at the end of the month. (However, Peterman had some materials in Work-in-Process Inventory at the end of the month.)

    During February, Peterman completed both the Wilson and Baker jobs and recorded them as Cost of Goods Sold. The Wilson job required no more materials in February, but it did require $3,600 of direct labor to complete. The Baker job required $6,000 of direct labor to complete.

    Peterman started a new job, Ottley, during February and put $4,800 of direct labor costs into this job. Unfortunately, Peterman lost the records of materials used on this job but knows all the materials available in February went into the Ottley job. The Ottley job is still in Work-in-Process Inventory at the end of the month.

    Peterman needs to know the total cost of the Wilson and Baker jobs, and the cost to date for the Ottley job, for billing purposes. Provide the cost of direct materials, direct labor, and overhead (at 80 percent of direct labor cost) for the three jobs.

35. **Job costing for the movies.** Movies and television shows are jobs. Some are successful, some are not. Studios must decide what to do with the cost of unsuccessful shows ("flops"). Some studios have been criticized for assigning the cost of flops to successful shows, which in turn reduces profits available under profit-sharing agreements with actors, actresses, directors, and others associated with the successful show.

    Studios point out that flops have to be paid for out of the profits from successful shows. For example, Orion Pictures was criticized for carrying the cost of flops in inventory instead of writing them off, thereby overstating both assets and profits.

    a. How does carrying "flops" in inventory overstate assets and profits?

b. When do you think the cost of a movie that turns out to be a flop should be written off (that is, expensed)?

36. **Comparing job costs to management's expectations.** Simon Construction Company uses a job costing system. It applies overhead to jobs at a rate of 60 percent of direct labor cost.

On August 1, the balance in the Work-in-Process Inventory account was $34,000. It had the following jobs in process on August 1:

	Job No.
478 (irrigation project)	$19,600
479 (parking lot construction)	9,400
480 (street repair)	5,000
Total	$34,000

Selected transactions for the month of August follow:

(1) Materials issued: Job 480, $682; Job 481, $4,200; Job 482, $2,600; indirect materials, $390; total, $7,872.

(2) Simon assigned labor costs as follows: Job 478, $331; Job 479, $2,651; Job 480, $7,800; Job 481, $5,891; Job 482, $1,720; indirect labor, $853; total, $19,246.

(3) It applies overhead for August to jobs using an overhead rate of 60 percent of direct labor costs. Actual overhead for the month was $11,623 including the indirect materials and indirect labor noted in **(1)** and **(2)** above.

(4) It completed Jobs 478 and 479 in August.

Simon Construction Company's management is concerned that costs are higher than anticipated. Managers had expected the cost of completed jobs to be as follows:

Job 478: $20,000, when complete

Job 479: $13,000, when complete

Job 480: $15,000, as of August 31

Job 481: $10,000, as of August 31

Job 482: $4,000, as of August 31

Compare the actual job costs to management's expected costs, and report your results.

37. **Analyzing costs in a job company.** On June 1, Williams Landscaping Company had two jobs in process with the following costs:

	Direct Materials	Direct Labor
Thomson	$1,000	$4,000
Reed Family	800	3,200

In addition, overhead is applied to these jobs at the rate of 100 percent of direct labor costs.

On June 1, Williams had materials inventory (for example, plants and shrubs) totaling $2,000. During June, Williams purchased $4,000 of materials and had none left in materials inventory at the end of the month. (However, Williams had some materials in Work-in-Process Inventory at the end of the month.)

During June, Williams completed both the Thomson and Reed Family jobs and recorded them as Cost of Goods Sold. The Thomson job required no more materials in June, but it did require $1,200 of direct labor to complete. The Reed Family job required $2,000 of direct labor to complete.

Williams started a new job, Sparks, during June and put $1,600 of direct labor costs into this job. Unfortunately, Williams lost the records of materials used on this job but knows all the materials available in June went into the Sparks job. The Sparks job is still in Work-in-Process Inventory at the end of the month.

Williams needs to know the total cost of the Thomson and Reed Family jobs and the cost to date for the Sparks job, for billing purposes. (Otherwise, all the little Williamses at home will go hungry in July.) Provide the cost of direct materials, direct labor, and overhead (at 100 percent of direct labor cost) for the three jobs.

38. **Comparing job costs to management's expectations.** Polebarn Construction Incorporated uses a job costing system. It applies overhead to jobs at a rate of 70 percent of direct labor cost.

    On November 1, the balance in the Work-in-Process Inventory account was $100,000. It had the following jobs in process on November 1:

Job No.	Total
15	$ 45,000
16	18,000
17	37,000
Total	$100,000

Selected transactions for the month of November follow:
   (1) Direct materials issued: Job 17, $23,000; Job 18, $15,500; Job 19, $29,000.
   (2) Polebarn assigned direct labor costs as follows: Job 15, $13,000; Job 16, $8,500; Job 17, $10,500; Job 18, $26,000; Job 19, $34,500.
   (3) It applies overhead for November to jobs using an overhead rate of 70 percent of direct labor costs. Actual overhead for the month was $70,352.
   (4) It completed Jobs 15 and 16 in November.

   Polebarn Construction Inc.'s management is concerned that costs are higher than anticipated. Managers had expected the cost of completed jobs to be as follows:

   Job 15: $70,000, when complete

   Job 16: $30,000, when complete

   Job 17: $65,000, as of November 30

   Job 18: $60,000, as of November 30

   Job 19: $83,000, as of November 30

   Compare the actual job costs to management's expected costs, and report your results.

39. **Compare just-in-time to a traditional accounting system.** Myers Manufacturing produces heat measurement meters. The company received an order for 8,000 meters. The company purchased and used $500,000 of materials for this order. The company incurred labor costs of $250,000 and other nonlabor manufacturing costs of $800,000.

    The accounting period ended before the company completed the order. The firm had 10 percent of the total costs incurred still in Work-in-Process Inventory and 20 percent of the total costs incurred still in Finished Goods Inventory.
    a. Use T-accounts to show the flow of costs using backflush costing.
    b. Use T-accounts to show the flow of costs using a traditional costing system.

40. **Compare just-in-time to a traditional accounting system.** Sanchez Manufacturing received an order for 10,000 units. The company purchased and used $100,000 of materials for this order. The company incurred labor costs of $45,000 and other nonlabor manufacturing costs of $75,000.

    The accounting period ended before the company completed the order. The firm had 5 percent of the total costs incurred still in Work-in-Process Inventory and 20 percent of the total costs incurred still in Finished Goods Inventory.
    a. Use T-accounts to show the flow of costs using backflush costing.
    b. Use T-accounts to show the flow of costs using a traditional costing system.

41. **Computing equivalent units and cost flows under process costing (Appendix 2.1).** Omar Production Company has a process cost accounting system. Omar incurred material, direct labor, and manufacturing overhead costs evenly during processing. On September 1, the firm had 20,000 units in process, 40 percent complete, with the following accumulated costs:

Material	$156,000
Direct Labor	80,000
Manufacturing Overhead	60,000

During September, Omar started 110,000 units in process and incurred the following costs:

Material	$1,244,000
Direct Labor	980,000
Manufacturing Overhead	735,000

During September, Omar completed 90,000 units. The units in ending inventory were, on average, 40 percent complete.

Prepare a production cost report such as the one in Exhibit 2.9 using FIFO.

42. **Equivalent units—solving for unknowns (Appendix 2.1).** For each of the following independent cases, calculate the information requested, using FIFO costing.

   a. Beginning inventory amounted to 2,000 units. The firm started and completed 4,500 units during this period. At the end of the period, the firm had 3,000 units in inventory that were 30 percent complete. Using FIFO costing, the equivalent production for the period was 5,600 units. What was the percentage of completion of the beginning inventory?

   b. The ending inventory included $8,700 for conversion costs. During the period, the firm required 4,200 equivalent units to complete the beginning inventory and started and completed 6,000 units. The ending inventory represented 2,000 equivalent units of work this period. What was the total conversion cost incurred during this period?

43. **Completing missing data.** After a dispute concerning wages, Blake Anderson destroyed all information systems files and tossed an incendiary device into the Alameda Company's record vault. Within moments, only a few readable, charred fragments remained from the company's factory ledger, as follows:

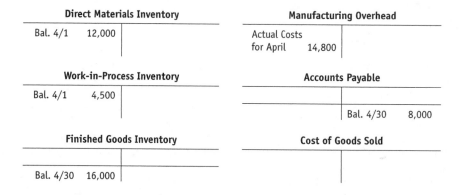

Sifting through the ashes and interviewing selected employees generated the following additional information:

(1) The controller remembers clearly that the firm based the predetermined overhead rate on an estimated 30,000 direct labor hours to be worked over the year and an estimated $180,000 in manufacturing overhead costs.

(2) The production superintendent's cost sheets showed only one job in process on April 30. The firm had added materials of $2,600 to the job and expended 150 direct labor hours at $12 per hour.

(3) The Accounts Payable are for direct materials purchases only, according to the accounts payable clerk. He clearly remembers that the balance in the account was $6,000 on April 1. An analysis of canceled checks (kept in the treasurer's office) shows that Alameda made payments of $40,000 to suppliers during the month.

(4) A charred piece of the payroll ledger shows that the firm recorded 2,600 direct labor hours for the month. The employment department has verified that pay rates were the same for all employees (this infuriated Blake, who thought that Alameda underpaid him).

(5) Records maintained in the finished goods warehouse indicate that the finished goods inventory totaled $11,000 on April 1.

(6) From another charred paper in the vault you discern that the cost of goods manufactured (that is, finished) for April was $89,000.

Compute the following amounts:

a. Work-in-Process Inventory, April 30
b. Direct materials purchased during April
c. Overhead applied to Work-in-Process
d. Cost of Goods Sold for April
e. Over- or underapplied overhead for April
f. Direct materials usage during April
g. Direct materials inventory, April 30

44. **Incomplete data—job costing.** Premier Printing, Inc., has not been profitable despite increases in sales. It has hired you to learn why. You turn to the accounting system for data and find it to be a mess. However, you piece together the following information for June:

Production

(1) Completed Job 11.
(2) Started and completed Job 12.
(3) Started Job 13.

Inventory Values

(1) Work-in-process inventory:

May 31: Job 11

Direct materials	$ 4,000
Labor (960 hours × $20)	19,200

June 30: Job 13

Direct materials	$ 3,200
Labor (1,040 hours × $20)	20,800

---

(2) Each job in work-in-process inventory was exactly 50 percent completed as to labor hours; however, all the direct materials necessary to do the entire job were charged to each job as soon as it was started.
(3) There were no direct materials inventories or finished goods inventories at either May 31 or June 30.

Overhead

(1) Actual manufacturing overhead was $40,000.
(2) The company had sold jobs 11 and 12. You find limited information about the cost of these two jobs from a spreadsheet. These two jobs make up the total cost of goods sold (before adjustment for over- or underapplied overhead) for the month of June:

Job 11

Materials	$ 4,000
Labor	?
Overhead	?
Total	$61,600

Job 12

Materials	?
Labor	?
Overhead	?
Total	?

---

(3) Overhead was applied to jobs using a predetermined rate per labor dollar that has been used since the company began operations.
(4) All direct materials were purchased for cash and charged directly to Work-in-Process Inventory when purchased. Direct materials purchased in June amounted to $9,200.
(5) Direct labor costs charged to jobs in June were $64,000. All labor costs were the same per hour for June for all laborers.

Write a report to management to show:

a. The cost elements (material, labor, and overhead) of cost of goods sold before adjustment for over- or underapplied overhead for each of the two jobs sold.

b. The value of each cost element (material, labor, and overhead) for each job in Work-in-Process Inventory at June 30.

c. Over- or underapplied overhead for June.

CASES

45. Evaluating cost systems used in financial services companies. John Frank, controller of Midwest Insurance Company, recently returned from a management education program where he talked to Peter Montgomery, his counterpart at Northern Insurance Company. Both companies had mortgage departments, but whereas Midwest made loans only to businesses, Northern made only home mortgage loans.

Peter Montgomery had described the use of standard costs at Northern as follows:

> We have collected data over several years that give us a pretty good idea how much each batch of loans costs to process. We receive loans in three main categories: (1) FHA and VA mortgages, (2) conventional home mortgages, and (3) development loans. Banks and other financial institutions make these loans initially and banks then package the loans and offer them to us as a package. The Mortgage Division establishes terms for ascertaining whether we accept the mortgage and for legal work on the loan. We assume that each loan in a category costs about the same. To calculate how much processing loans costs, we periodically have people in the Mortgage Division keep track of their time on each package of loans. Our overhead is about 130 percent of direct labor costs, so we assign overhead accordingly to each package of loans. We don't keep track of the actual costs of processing each package of loans. What we lose in knowing the actual cost of processing each package of loans, we make up by saving clerical costs that we would incur to keep track of the time spent on each package of loans.

A cost statement for a recent month appears in Exhibit 2.11.

Montgomery's comment about saving clerical costs struck a respondent chord with John Frank. Midwest's accounting costs had reached alarming levels, according to the company president, and Frank was looking for ways to reduce costs. Midwest kept track of the following costs for each loan: labor; telephone costs; travel; and outside services, such as appraisals, legal fees, and the cost of consultants. The costs of processing these loans often amounted to several thousand dollars. A sample of these loans and their processing costs appears in Exhibit 2.12.

When Frank told the Mortgage Division manager about the methods Northern used, the manager responded: "That sounds fine for them because each package of loans in a cate-

EXHIBIT 2.11	NORTHERN INSURANCE COMPANY Mortgage Division Loan Processing Costs Month of October		
Category of Loans	**Labor**	**Overhead**	**Number of Loan Packages Processed**
Standard Costs			
FHA and VA	$ 4,200	$ 5,460	14
Conventional	31,160	40,508	82
Development	20,440	26,572	73
Total	$55,800	$72,540	
Actual Costs	$58,172	$74,626	

				Outside Services		
EXHIBIT 2.12	**MIDWEST INSURANCE COMPANY** **Mortgage Division** **Loan Processing Costs** **Month of July**					
Loan No.	**Labor**	**Telephone**	**Travel**	**Appraisal**	**Legal**	**Other**
A48-10136	$ 1,184	$ 113	$ 415	$ 1,500	—	—
A48-11237	3,631	42	—	2,300	—	—
B42-19361	814	78	—	—	$1,500	$ 150
C39-21341	4,191	240	110	—	2,200	—
.	.	.	.	.	.	.
.	.	.	.	.	.	.
.	.	.	.	.	.	.
Total	$47,291	$4,843	$2,739	$11,800	$9,950	$1,470

gory has about the same processing costs. The processing costs of each loan in our company vary considerably. I believe it would be invalid to establish standards for our loans."

Frank thought the Mortgage Division manager's comments were reasonable, but he wanted to find some way to save clerical costs by not recording the costs of processing each loan. At the same time, he knew the firm would potentially benefit from having a standard against which to compare actual costs.

a. What would you advise Mr. Frank to do? Compare the advantages and disadvantages of the system each company uses.

b. Diagram the flow of costs for each company using the data available in Exhibits 2.11 and 2.12. Treat each loan or category of loans as a separate product in your diagram.

46. **Reconstructing missing data.** A severe tornado struck the only manufacturing plant of Oklahoma Hardware, Inc., just after midnight on December 1. All the work-in-process inventory was destroyed, but a few records were salvaged from the wreckage and from the company's headquarters. The insurance company has stated that it will pay the cost of the lost inventory if adequate documentation can be supplied. The insurable value of work-in-process inventory consists of direct materials, direct labor, and applied overhead.

The following information about the plant appears on the financial statements at the company's headquarters. This information pertains to the October before the tornado.

Materials inventory (includes direct and indirect materials), October 31	$ 49,000
Work-in-process inventory, October 31	86,200
Finished goods inventory, October 31	32,000
Cost of goods sold for the year through October 31	348,600
Accounts payable (materials suppliers) on October 31	21,600
Manufacturing overhead for the year to date through October 31 (actual)	184,900
Payroll payable on October 31	–0–
Withholding and other payroll liabilities on October 31	9,700
Overhead applied for the year to date through October 31	179,600

A count of the inventories on hand November 30 (just before the tornado) showed:

Materials inventory	$ 43,000
Work-in-process inventory	?
Finished goods inventory	37,500

The accounts payable clerk tells you that outstanding bills to materials suppliers totaled $50,100 as of the close of business on November 30 (just before the tornado hit) and that cash payments of $37,900 were made to them during the month of November.

The payroll clerk informs you that the payroll costs last month for the manufacturing section were $82,400, of which $14,700 was indirect labor.

At the end of November, the following balances were available from the main office:

Manufacturing overhead for the year to date through November 30 (actual)	$217,000
Cost of goods sold for the year to date through November 30	396,600

Among the fragments of paper that you found lying about, you learn that indirect materials requisitioned in November was $2,086. You also learn that the overhead during the month of November was overapplied by $1,200.

Compute the cost of the work-in-process inventory lost in the disaster.

47. **Job costing and ethics.** Andre Preneur supervises two consulting jobs in the consulting firm of Dewey, Cheatham, and Howe, which does studies on environmental cleanup. One of the consulting jobs is for the Canadian government, the other is for General Electric, Inc. After receiving the monthly financial reports on the two jobs, he immediately called his boss to report that costs were way over budget on the General Electric job.

"The job is only about three-fourths complete, but we've spent all the money that we had budgeted for the entire job," he said.

"You'd better watch these job costs more carefully in the future," his boss advised. "Meanwhile, charge the rest of the costs needed to complete the General Electric job to your Canadian government job. We're under budget on that job, plus we get reimbursed for costs on the government job."

a. What should Andre do?

b. Does it matter that Andre's consulting firm is reimbursed for costs on the Canadian government job? Explain.

48. **Comparison of just-in-time in the United States and Japan.** A comparison of U.S. and Japanese companies in the chemical industry showed more companies in Japan used just-in-time than in the United States. The Japanese companies had lower inventory levels and higher turnover rates. Why do you think Japanese companies were more likely to use just-in-time?

(**Source:** I. Meric, L. W. Ross, S. M. Weidman, and G. Meric, "A Comparison of the Financial Characteristics of U.S. and Japanese Chemical Firms," *Multinational Business Review,* vol. 5, no. 2, pp. 23–27.)

49. **Job cost information using equivalent units.** The Custer Manufacturing Corporation, which uses a job order cost system, produces various plastic parts for the aircraft industry. On October 9, Year 1, production was started on Job No. 487 for 100 front bubbles (windshields) for commercial helicopters.

Production of the bubbles begins in the Fabricating Department, where sheets of plastic (purchased as raw material) are melted down and poured into molds. The molds are then placed in a special temperature and humidity room to harden the plastic. The hardened plastic bubbles are then removed from the molds and hand-worked to remove imperfections.

After fabrication, the bubbles are transferred to the Testing Department, where each bubble must meet rigid specifications. Bubbles that fail the tests are scrapped, and there is no salvage value.

Bubbles passing the tests are transferred to the Assembly Department, where they are inserted into metal frames. The frames, purchased from vendors, require no work prior to installing the bubbles.

The assembled unit is then transferred to the Shipping Department for crating and shipment. Crating material is relatively expensive, and most of the work is done by hand.

The following information concerning Job No. 487 is available as of December 31, Year 1 (the information is correct as stated):

1. Direct materials charged to the job:

    a. One thousand square feet of plastic at $12.75 per square foot was charged to the Fabricating Department. This amount was to meet all plastic material requirements of the job assuming no spoilage.

b. Seventy-four metal frames at $408.52 each were charged to the Assembly Department.

c. Packing material for 40 units at $75 per unit was charged to the Shipping Department.

2. Direct labor charges through December 31 were as follows:

	Total
Fabricating Department	$1,424
Testing Department	444
Assembly Department	612
Shipping Department	256
Total	$2,736

3. There were no differences between actual and applied manufacturing overhead for the year ended December 31, Year 1. Manufacturing overhead is charged to the four production departments by various allocation methods, all of which you approve.

Manufacturing overhead charged to the Fabricating Department is allocated to jobs based on heat-room-hours; the other production departments allocate manufacturing overhead to jobs on the basis of direct labor-dollars charged to each job within the department. The following reflects the manufacturing overhead rates for the year ended December 31, Year 1.

	Rate per Unit
Fabricating Department	$.45 per heat-room-hour
Testing Department	.68 per direct labor dollar
Assembly Department	.38 per direct labor dollar
Shipping Department	.25 per direct labor dollar

4. Job No. 487 used 855 heat-room-hours during the year ended December 31.

5. Following is the physical inventory for Job No. 487 as of December 31:

Fabricating Department:
a. Fifty square feet of plastic sheet.
b. Four complete bubbles.
c. Eight hardened bubbles, one-fourth complete as to direct labor.

Testing Department:
a. Seven bubbles complete as to testing.
b. Fifteen bubbles that failed testing when two-fifths of testing was complete. No others failed.

Assembly Department:
a. Three complete bubbles and frames.
b. Thirteen frames with no direct labor.
c. Fifteen bubbles and frames, one-third complete as to direct labor.

Shipping Department:
a. Nine complete units; two-thirds complete as to packing material; one-third complete as to direct labor.
b. Ten complete units; 100 percent complete as to packing material; 50 percent complete as to direct labor.
c. One unit complete for shipping was dropped off the loading docks. There is no salvage.
d. Twenty-three units have been shipped prior to December 31.
e. There was no inventory of packing materials in the shipping department at December 31.

6. Following is a schedule of equivalent units in production by department for Job No. 487 as of December 31.

CUSTER MANUFACTURING CORPORATION
Schedule of Equivalent Units in
Production for Job No. 487
December 31

Fabricating Department
Bubbles (Units)

	Plastic (sq. ft.)	Materials	Labor	Overhead
Transferred in from direct materials	1,000	—	—	—
Production to date	(950)	95	89	95
Transferred out to other departments	—	(83)	(83)	(83)
Spoilage	—	—	—	—
Balance at December 31	50	12	6	12

Testing Department (Units)
Bubbles

	Transferred In	Labor	Overhead
Transferred in from other departments	83	—	—
Production to date	—	74	74
Transferred out to other departments	(61)	(61)	(61)
Spoilage	(15)	(6)	(6)
Balance at December 31	7	7	7

Assembly Department (Units)

	Transferred In	Frames	Labor	Overhead
Transferred in from direct materials	—	74	—	—
Transferred in from other departments	61	—	—	—
Production to date	—	—	51	51
Transferred out to other departments	(43)	(43)	(43)	(43)
Balance at December 31	18	31	8	8

Shipping Department (Units)

	Transferred In	Packing Material	Labor	Overhead
Transferred in from direct materials	—	40	—	—
Transferred in from other departments	43	—	—	—
Production to date	—	—	32	32
Shipped	(23)	(23)	(23)	(23)
Spoilage	(1)	(1)	(1)	(1)
Balance at December 31	19	16	8	8

a. What is the dollar amount of work-in-process inventory on December 31, Year 1, for Job No. 487 for each of the four departments: Fabricating, Testing, Assembly, and Shipping? The unused plastic in the Fabricating Department is part of that department's work-in-process inventory on December 31, Year 1.

b. What is the dollar amount of Cost of Goods Sold for the 23 units shipped for Job No. 487?

c. What is the cost of the units spoiled in Job No. 487?

SUGGESTED ADDITIONAL CASES

Anagene. Harvard Business School Case No. 102030. Case focuses on capacity utilization, including overhead rate computation and assigning capacity costs to products.

Colorscope, Inc. Harvard Business School Case No. 197040. Case focuses on cost control and process improvement.

20. Cost flow model.

Lighter Fluid:

$$BB + TI = TO + EB$$

$$\$40{,}000 + \$180{,}000 = \$80{,}000 + EB$$

$$EB = \$40{,}000 + \$180{,}000 - \$80{,}000$$

$$EB = \$140{,}000$$

Waterproof Matches:

$$\$60{,}000 + \$340{,}000 = \$380{,}000 + EB$$

$$EB = \$60{,}000 + \$340{,}000 - \$380{,}000$$

$$EB = \$20{,}000$$

Burn Ointment:

$$BB + TI = TO + EB$$

$$\$60{,}000 + \$120{,}000 = \$140{,}000 + EB$$

$$EB = \$60{,}000 + \$120{,}000 - \$140{,}000$$

$$EB = \$40{,}000$$

Fireplace Screens:

Cannot compute because we have two unknowns in the basic cost flow equation.

22. Cost flow model.

Use the cost flow equation,

$$BB + TI = TO + EB$$

to find what the ending inventory should be per the records.

Videocassette Recorders:

$$\$20{,}000 + \$40{,}000 = \$35{,}000 + EB$$

$$EB = \$20{,}000 + \$40{,}000 - \$35{,}000$$

$$EB = \$25{,}000$$

$5,000 (= $25,000 − $20,000 physical count) worth of videocassette recorders is missing.

Televisions:

$$\$20{,}000 + \$50{,}000 = \$55{,}000 + EB$$

$$EB = \$20{,}000 + \$50{,}000 - \$55{,}000$$

$$EB = \$15{,}000$$

$10,000 (= $15,000 − $5,000 physical count) worth of televisions is missing.

Compact Disc Players:

$$\$15{,}000 + \$20{,}000 = \$25{,}000 + EB$$

$$EB = \$15{,}000 + \$20{,}000 - \$25{,}000$$

$$EB = \$10{,}000$$

No discrepancy in compact disc players.

24. Just-in-time methods.

Journal Entries

(1) Cost of Goods Sold 80,000

      Accounts Payable—Materials 50,000

      Accounts Payable—Other Manufacturing Costs 20,000

      Wages Payable 10,000

      (To record costs of production.)

(2) Finished Goods Inventory .... 16,000[a]

      Cost of Goods Sold 16,000

      (To record inventory.)

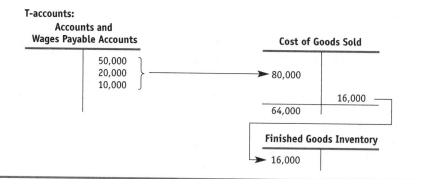

[a]$16,000 = 400 units at $40 per unit ($40 = $80,000/2,000 units).

26. Job costs in a service organization.

    a. Journal Entries:

(1) Work-in-Process—Springsteen Productions	240,000	
Work-in-Process—RCI Records	120,000	
Direct Labor—Unbillable	24,000	
Wages Payable		384,000
(2) Work-in-Process—Springsteen Productions	80,000	
Work-in-Process—RCI Records	40,000	
Overhead (Applied)		120,000
(3) Overhead	140,000	
Wages and Accounts Payable		140,000
(4) Marketing and Administrative Costs	20,000	
Wages and Accounts Payable		20,000
(5a) Accounts Receivable	600,000	
Revenue		600,000
(5b) Cost of Services Billed	480,000	
Work-in-Process—Springsteen Productions		320,000
Work-in-Process—RCI Records		160,000

    b.

LOOMIS AND ASSOCIATES
Income Statement
For the Month Ending January 31

Revenue from Services	$600,000
Less Cost of Services Billed	480,000
Gross Margin	$120,000
Less:	
Direct Labor—Unbillable	24,000
Overhead—Underapplied	20,000[a]
Marketing and Administrative	20,000
Operating Profit	$ 56,000

[a]$140,000 actual − $120,000 applied.

28. Job costs in a service organization.

a.

Wages and Accounts Payable			Work-in-Process: E-Gadgets			Cost of Services Billed	
	160,000	(1)	(1) 90,000			(5b) 224,000	
	100,000	(3)	(2) 54,000	144,000	(5b)		
	40,000	(4)					

Overhead			Work-in-Process: E-Shop			Marketing and Administrative Costs	
(3) 100,000	84,000	(2)	(1) 30,000			(4) 40,000	
			(2) 18,000	48,000	(5b)		

Accounts Receivable			Work-in-Process: E-Food			Revenues	
(5a) 280,000			(1) 20,000				280,000 (5a)
			(2) 12,000	32,000	(5b)		

Direct Labor— Unbillable	
(1) 20,000	

Entries:

(1) Labor costs at $100 per hour.
(2) Overhead at $60 per billable hour.
(3) Overhead actually incurred in June.
(4) Marketing and administrative costs.
(5) Services billed.

b.

COMPUTER SYSTEMS, INC.
Income Statement
For the Month Ending June 30

Revenue from Services	$280,000
Less Cost of Services Billed	224,000
Gross Margin	$ 56,000
Less:	
Direct Labor—Unbillable	20,000
Overhead—Underapplied	16,000[a]
Marketing and Administrative	40,000
Operating Profit (Loss)	$(20,000)

[a]$100,000 actual − $84,000 applied.

30. Computing equivalent units (Appendix 2.1).

To Complete Beginning Inventory: $[(1.0 - 0.60) \times (60{,}000 \text{ Units})]$	24,000 E.U.
Started and Completed	160,000 E.U.
In Ending Inventory: $.30 \times 40{,}000$ Units	12,000 E.U.
Total	196,000 E.U.

32. Actual costs and normal costs.

a. Actual Costs

Direct Materials	$ 5,000
Direct Labor	9,000
Variable Manufacturing Overhead	20,000
Fixed Manufacturing Overhead	26,000
Total Cost	$60,000

b. Normal Costs

Direct Materials	$ 5,000
Direct Labor	9,000
Variable Manufacturing Overhead	18,000[a]
Fixed Manufacturing Overhead	27,000[b]
Total Cost	$59,000

[a]$18,000 = 200\% \times \$9,000.
[b]$27,000 = 300\% \times \$9,000.

chapter 3

Activity-Based Management

Learning Objectives

1. Identify strategic and operational uses of activity-based management.

2. Differentiate between traditional cost allocation methods and activity-based costing.

3. Understand the concept of activity-based costing.

4. Identify the steps in activity-based costing.

5. Apply activity-based management and costing to marketing.

6. Use the cost hierarchy to organize cost information for decision making.

7. Distinguish between resources used and resources supplied, and measure unused resource capacity.

8. Explain the difficulties of implementing advanced cost-management systems.

Many companies, such as Hewlett-Packard, Procter & Gamble, Boeing, Caterpillar, and IBM, have implemented activity-based costing and management to improve the way they manage costs. These new methods have revealed startling new information about product profitability. A high-tech company in Oregon found, to the surprise of management, that one of its products, a printed circuit board, was generating negative margins of 46 percent.

This chapter deals with activity-based costing and management. **Activity-based costing (ABC)** and **activity-based management (ABM)** rest on this premise: *Products require activities; activities consume resources.* Activities involve action, such as purchasing raw materials. Purchasing raw materials requires resources—for example, a purchasing agent's time. Companies incur costs to acquire the time of purchasing managers. To understand a product's costs, one must identify the activities required to make the product, then identify the resources used to provide for those activities, and finally figure the cost of those resources. If managers want their products to be competitive, they must know both (1) the activities that go into making the goods or providing the services and (2) the cost of those activities.

ABCM has two parts: the costing part, known as activity-based costing (ABC), and the management part, known as activity-based management. ABC deals with learning about the cost of activities; ABM deals with how management uses that cost information. Effective management requires both ABC and ABM. Companies that collect activity-based cost information (i.e., ABC) but do not apply activity-based management go to a lot of work to obtain cost information for no purpose. Managers who do ABM without ABC make decisions without the appropriate information.

ABC analysis treats mostly indirect costs. Indirect costs include overhead costs incurred to manufacture a good or provide a service, indirect costs to market a product, and indirect costs incurred to manage the company. Unlike direct materials and direct labor that accountants can trace directly to a product, if accountants want to compute the full cost of products including both direct and indirect costs, then they must *allocate* indirect costs to products.

Activity-based costing is one way to allocate costs to products. Accountants also use simpler methods, which we and others call "traditional" cost allocation methods. We discuss those traditional methods later in this chapter.

Strategic Use of Activity-Based Management

Strategic activity-based costing and management work in two ways. First, managers use activity-based information to shift the mix of activities and products away from less profitable to more profitable applications. For example, activity-based costing might reveal that particular customers are more expensive to serve or particular products are more expensive to produce than a manager thought. Armed with this information, managers might take some or all of the following steps:

- Add surcharges for particular customers,
- "Fire" some customers,
- Seek to serve more profitable customers,
- Raise or lower product prices, and/or
- Drop products.

actions

Second, managers use activity-based information to help them become a low-cost producer or seller. Companies such as Wal-Mart in retailing, United Parcel in delivery services, and Southwest Airlines in the airline industry create a competitive advantage by managing activities to reduce costs and then to lower prices. Price cuts enable them to increase sales volume and market share.[1]

Reducing costs requires changes in activities. Top management can beg or command employees to reduce costs, but implementation requires changes in activities. To reduce a product's costs, managers will likely have to change the activities the product consumes. A manager who announces, "I want across-the-board cuts—everyone reduce costs by 20 percent," rarely gets the desired results. To make significant cost reductions, people must first identify the activities that a product uses. Then they must figure out how to rework those activities to improve production efficiency.

Activity Analysis

Activity analysis supports the second strategic use of activity-based costing and management noted previously; namely, to become a low-cost seller or producer. Activity analysis also supports tactical and intelligent cost cutting for managers who simply want their organizations to be competitive, sustainable enterprises.

Activity-based management starts with activity analysis. Activity analysis has four steps:

1. Chart, from start to finish, the activities used to complete the product or service.
2. Classify activities as value-added or non–value-added.
3. Eliminate non–value-added activities.
4. Continuously improve and reevaluate the efficiency of value-added activities or replace them with more efficient activities.

The value-added activities identified in step 2 make up the value chain. As shown in Exhibit 3.1, the **value chain** is a linked set of value-creating activities leading from raw material sources to the ultimate end use of the goods or services produced. Managers use the value chain to analyze the cost- and revenue-generating components of a company's activities. Managers continually analyze the value-chain activities to classify, eliminate, and improve the classifications. Exhibit 3.2 illustrates the continuous analysis.

Activity analysis provides a systematic way for organizations to evaluate the processes that they use to produce goods and services for their customers. Such an analysis can identify and eliminate activities that add costs but not value to the product. Non–value-added costs are costs of activities that the company can eliminate without reducing product quality, performance, or value. For example, storing bicycle frames until needed for production does not add to the finished bicycles' value. If management can find ways to eliminate storing bicycle frames, say, by

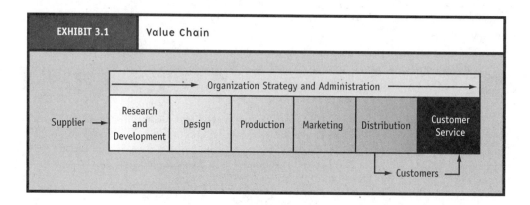

EXHIBIT 3.1	Value Chain

Organization Strategy and Administration

Supplier → | Research and Development | Design | Production | Marketing | Distribution | Customer Service

→ Customers →

---

[1]M. E. Porter, *Competitive Advantage* (New York: Free Press, 1985).

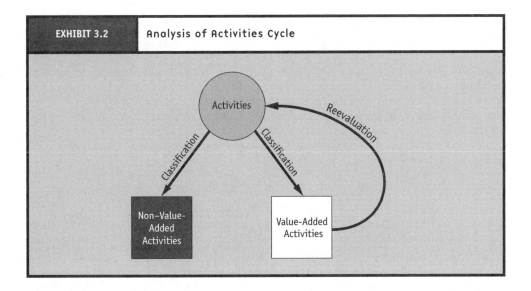

EXHIBIT 3.2 | Analysis of Activities Cycle

Activities

Reevaluation

Classification

Classification

Non–Value-Added Activities

Value-Added Activities

using just-in-time purchasing, the company could save money without reducing the quality of the finished product.

The following activities are candidates for elimination because they do not add value to the product.

1. *Storage.* Storage of materials, Work-in-Process, and finished goods inventories provide no value to the customer. Many companies have applied the just-in-time philosophy to purchasing and production to reduce or even eliminate storage.
2. *Moving items.* Moving parts, materials, and other items around the factory floor does not add value to the finished product. A steel mill in Michigan once had more than 100 miles of railroad tracks simply to move materials and partially finished products from one part of the factory to another. Eliminating a hundred miles or so of track reduced both labor and overhead costs and even eliminated some spoilage because train accidents sometimes damaged products.
3. *Waiting for work.* Idle time does not add value to products. Reducing the amount of time people wait to work on something reduces the cost of idle time.
4. *Production process components.* Managers should investigate the entire production process including purchasing, production, inspection, and shipping to identify activities that do not add value to the finished product.

You can see examples of non–value-added activities by observing activities in universities, health-care organizations, fast-food restaurants, construction sites, government agencies, and many other organizations.

Traditional Methods versus Activity-Based Costing

Writers have criticized traditional methods of cost allocation as being too simplistic and inaccurate. Consider the following scene. You and a friend go to dinner. After dinner, you and your friend will split the cost of the meal. Each of you is a cost object. (Please do not be offended by our calling you a "cost object." That's an accounting term of art.) You have tea (a $2.50 item on the menu) and a small salad (an $8.00 item on the menu) while your friend has an appetizer, expensive entree, and dessert. The bill for dinner totals $60 for the two of you. Traditional cost allocation methods assign the cost of the meal equally to the two cost objects—you and your friend. Your share of the meal's cost is $30, according to traditional methods of cost allocation. An activity analysis would reveal that your share of the meal costs is much less—perhaps about $14 after tax and tip.

Which Method to Use: A Cost-Benefit Decision

The traditional method is simple (e.g., just divide the total meal cost by two) but results in an inappropriate allocation. Activity analysis will provide a more appropriate result but costs more to do so. Somebody must figure out the cost of each item that each diner ordered and compute tax and tip. There is the trade-off that accountants and managers face: the less expensive, less accurate, traditional method versus the more expensive, more accurate, activity analysis. Managers must make a cost-benefit call whether the added benefits of activity-based information justify the additional costs of obtaining that information.

In our experience, and based on surveys of practice, managers make this cost-benefit decision in one of three ways.

1. *They reject activity analysis and stay with the simpler traditional method.* Managers tend to reject activity-based costing and management in small companies they can manage without sophisticated information systems. For example, construction companies are good candidates for activity-based analysis because they have lots of activities. Thoughtful managers and supervisors can manage the activities of small construction companies just by directly observing activities. Managers in organizations that do not care much about cost management also choose the simpler traditional approach because these managers would not use the activity-based information. Examples of these organizations include companies that are highly profitable because they lack competition or have a copyright on a product, some government organizations (although many do use activity-based costing, including the U.S. military), and some nonprofit organizations.

2. *They use activity-based costing because they want information that will help them be competitive.* These managers are usually in complex organizations that face a lot of competition.

3. *They use activity-based costing as a special analysis, but not as an ongoing information system.* For example, managers are concerned that certain customers are not profitable. They request analysts to do an activity-based cost analysis on their customers to ascertain whether to fire some customers or raise prices to particular customers. Having done the analysis and made the decisions, these managers no longer find activity-based information helpful.

Cost Pools: Plant versus Department versus Activity Center

Managers who use traditional methods have a choice between two methods depending on the cost pool they use. **Cost pools** are groups of costs. The three major types of cost pools are:

1. The "plant" (traditional),
2. The department (traditional), and
3. The activity center (activity-based costing).

We discuss the first two cost pools in this section; the third cost pool—activity center—is the basis for activity-based costing that we discuss later in this chapter.

The simplest allocation method, **plantwide allocation,** uses the entire plant as a cost pool. Although accountants call this method the *plantwide method,* in fact, the "plant" need not refer to a manufacturing facility but can mean a store, hospital, or multi-department segment of a company. A bank, for example, could apply overhead to different customer accounts, to different types of loans, and to other products using only one overhead rate for the entire bank.

Simple organizations having only a few departments and not much variety in activities in different departments might justify using the plantwide method.

When using the **department allocation method,** companies have a separate cost pool for each department. The company establishes a separate overhead allocation rate or set of rates for each department. Both plantwide and departmental methods are "traditional methods" in that they allocate overhead to products based on direct labor hours, or other direct input, which is generally not a causal cost driver.

Companies that use activity-based management philosophies, such as Hewlett-Packard, American Airlines, Procter & Gamble, Caterpillar, and DaimlerChrysler, use at least one cost pool for each activity center. Each company defines its own activity centers as parts of the company that perform some easily described activity.

For example, a motorcycle plant that one of the authors studied defined the paint quality inspection activity in the paint department as an activity center. This activity center handled all paint-related quality inspections to see that the manufacturing had properly applied the paint, with no paint runs, splatters, splotches, oversprays, and the like. The detailed activity-based costing system in this motorcycle plant separated the paint inspection costs from the paint spraying costs. In contrast, a cost system based on department cost pools combines all paint department costs into a single pool, instead of separating paint spraying from the inspection of paint spraying. In contrast, the plantwide allocation method would have a single cost pool for the entire motorcycle factory. The plantwide allocation method thus compiles no separate costs for the paint department, much less the quality inspection activity.

Should managers use plantwide, departmental, or activity-center cost pools? As noted previously—there is no single right answer. The choice requires managers to make cost-benefit decisions. Plantwide methods cost the least but provide the least accurate information. Maintaining cost pools by activity center costs the most but provides the most detailed information.

Activity-Based Costing

Activity-based costing (ABC) assigns costs first to activities, then to the products based on each product's use of activities.

Activity-Based Costing Methods

Activity-based costing requires accountants to follow four steps.

1. Identify the activities that consume resources, and assign costs to those activities. Purchasing materials would be an activity, for example.
2. Identify the cost driver(s) associated with each activity. A **cost driver** is a factor that causes, or "drives," an activity's costs. For the activity "purchasing materials," the cost driver could be "number of orders." (Each activity could have multiple cost drivers.)
3. Compute a cost rate per cost driver unit. The cost driver rate could be the cost per purchase order, for example.
4. Assign costs to products by multiplying the cost driver rate by the volume of cost drivers consumed by the product. For example, the cost per purchase order times the number of orders required for Product X for the month of December would measure the cost of the purchasing activity for Product X for December.

Step 1: Identify the Activities That Consume Resources

This is often the most interesting and challenging part of the exercise because it requires people to understand all the activities required to make the product. Managers attempt to identify those activities that have the greatest impact on costs.

A Deere and Company plant identified eight major activities required to produce one of its products. The company used one cost driver for each activity. Then it developed two cost rates for each cost driver, one for variable costs and one for fixed costs. For the materials handling activity, Deere used the number of loads or trips required to move parts around the plant as the cost driver. Most of the materials handling costs consisted of labor. The company had little fixed cost associated with materials handling.[2] To reduce materials handling costs, Deere and Company managers sought ways to reduce the number of trips required to move parts around the plant.

---

[2]See "John Deere Component Works," Harvard Business School, Case 187–107.

Researchers studying the cost of online education in a university used activity-based costing to measure the cost of teaching online. They identified six major instructor activities—planning the course, preparing the course for online delivery, delivering the course (including time spent dealing with student problems in getting access to the online course during the term), interacting with students (both in-person and online), evaluating student performance, and supervising teaching assistants. The researchers collected data about how much time instructors spent on each activity and then used that information to estimate the cost of similar online courses.[3]

Complexity as an Activity That Consumes Resources   One of the lessons of activity-based costing has been that costs depend not only on volume but also on complexity.[4] Imagine you produce 100,000 gallons per month of vanilla ice cream and your friend produces 100,000 gallons per month of 39 different flavors of ice cream. Further, assume you sell your ice cream only in one-liter containers, while your friend sells his in several sizes of containers. Your friend has more complicated systems for ordering, storage, packing in containers, and product testing (one department that has no trouble hiring help). Your friend has more machine setups, too. Presumably, you can set the machinery to one setting to obtain the desired product quality and taste; your friend has to reset the machines to produce each flavor. Although both of you produce the same total volume of ice cream, you can easily imagine that your friend's overhead costs would be considerably higher—the multiproduct plant must operate more hours per day to produce the same volume of output.

Low-volume products often require more machine setups for a given level of production output because the firm produces them in smaller batches. In the ice cream example, one batch of 1,000 gallons of the low-volume 39th flavor might require as much overhead cost for machine setups, quality inspections, and purchase orders as one batch of 100,000 gallons of the highest-volume flavor. Further, the low-volume product adds complexity to the operation by disrupting the production flow of the high-volume items. (You'll get a reminder of this fact the next time you stand in line at the store, bank, fast-food restaurant, or student-aid line when someone ahead of you has a special transaction.)

Step 2: Identify Cost Drivers

Exhibit 3.3 presents several examples of the kinds of cost drivers that companies use. Most cost drivers relate either to the volume of production or to the complexity of the production or marketing process. Look at Exhibit 3.3; which cost drivers on the list might a law firm use? (Answer: Labor hours, pages typed, miles driven, computer time spent, clients served, and number of different clients.)

How do managers decide which cost driver to use? The primary criterion for selecting a cost driver is *causal relation*. Choose a cost driver that *causes* the cost.

Other people recommend using the following two criteria for selecting cost drivers; however, we believe they are inferior to the causal criterion:

- *Benefits received.* Choose a cost driver to assign costs in proportion to benefits received. For example, if the Physics Department in a university benefits more from the university's supercomputer than does the History Department, the university should select a cost driver that recognizes the benefits to Physics. For example, the university might use the number of faculty and students in each department who use the computer to allocate the costs of the supercomputer if it wanted to allocate supercomputer costs proportional to the benefits.
- *Reasonableness.* Sometimes, managers cannot link costs to products based on causality or benefits received, so the managers assign costs on the basis of fairness or reasonableness. We noted above that Deere and Company selected eight cost drivers for certain products. It allocated the cost of a ninth activity, general and administrative overhead, to products

[3]See http://moby.ucdavis.edu/Mellon for information about these studies of the cost-effectiveness of online education. In comparing online and traditional lecture methods, the researchers found that, overall, costs were slightly higher and student performance was slightly better in the traditional lecture courses.

[4]R. D. Banker, G. Potter, and R. G. Schroeder, "An Empirical Analysis of Manufacturing Overhead Cost Drivers," *Journal of Accounting and Economics* 19, no. 1, 115–137; G. Foster and M. Gupta, "Manufacturing Overhead Cost Driver Analysis," *Journal of Accounting and Economics* 12, nos. 1–3, 309–337; and E. Noreen and N. Soderstrom, "Are Overhead Costs Strictly Proportional to Activity?" *Journal of Accounting and Economics* 17, no. 1, 255–278.

EXHIBIT 3.3	Examples of Cost Drivers

Machine Hours	Number of Surgeries
Computer Time	Purchase Orders
Labor Hours or Cost	Scrap/Rework Orders
Items Produced or Sold	Quality Inspections
Pounds of Materials Handled	Hours of Testing Time
Customers Served	Number of Parts in a Product
Pages Typed	Number of Different Customers
Flight Hours	Miles Driven
Machine Setups	

using the reasonableness approach; namely, it allocated these costs to products in the same percentages as it allocated the costs of the other eight activities to products.

Step 3: Compute a Cost Rate per Cost Driver Unit

In general, predetermined rates for allocating indirect costs to products result from a computation such as:

$$\text{Predetermined indirect cost rate} = \frac{\text{Estimated indirect cost}}{\text{Estimated volume of the allocation base}}$$

This formula applies to all indirect costs—whether manufacturing overhead, administrative costs, distribution costs, selling costs, or any other indirect cost.

Companies using activity-based costing compute the rate for each cost driver in each activity center. An **activity center** is a unit within an organization that performs a set of tasks. For example, accountants assign the costs of setting up machines to the activity center that sets up machines. In many companies, each activity center has only one cost driver, but an activity center can have more than one.

Example   If the cost driver is inspecting products for quality, then the company must estimate the inspection costs before the period starts in order to derive a cost rate per inspection. (Ideally, the company will keep track of the actual cost of inspections as it incurs them during the period so that it can compare actual and applied inspection costs.) The purpose of the cost driver is to allocate costs to products. The purpose of comparing estimates and actual amounts is to help managers ensure that the amount of costs incurred for inspections is under control.

Step 4: Assign Costs to Products

Workers and machines perform activities on each product they produce. The system then allocates costs to products by multiplying each cost driver's rate by the amount of cost driver activity used in making the product. The following illustrates this process.

Activity-Based Costing Illustrated

Assume the Ciudad Juarez factory makes two products—a mountain bike, a high-volume product; and a racing bike, a low-volume, specialized product.

The Ciudad Juarez factory allocates overhead to products in an amount equal to five times a product's direct labor costs, which are $30 and $60 per bike for the mountain and racing bikes, respectively. The direct materials costs are $100 and $200 per bike for the mountain and racing bikes. Adding overhead at the rate of 500 percent of direct labor costs gave the following product costs per unit.

	Mountain Bikes	Racing Bikes
Direct Materials	$100	$200
Direct Labor	30	60
Manufacturing Overhead	$150ᵃ	$300ᵃ
Total	$280	$560

ᵃAmount equals direct labor times 500 percent.

Assigning Costs Using Activity-Based Costing

Managers decide to experiment with activity-based costing at the Ciudad Juarez factory. First, they identify four activities as important cost drivers. These activities are (1) purchasing materials, (2) setting up machines to produce a different product, (3) inspecting products, and (4) running machines.

The managers estimated the amount of overhead and the volume-of-activity events for each activity. For example, they estimated the company would purchase 10,000 frames. These purchases would require annual overhead costs of $200,000 such as salaries of people who purchase, inspect, and store materials. For purchasing overhead, they assigned a cost of $20 (= $200,000/10,000 frames) to each frame that the factory purchased.

Machine operation requires energy and maintenance, which they estimated to cost $30 per machine hour. They estimated the rate for inspections to be $100 per hour in the inspection station and the machine setup rate to be $2,000 per setup. Exhibit 3.4 shows the predetermined annual rates computed for all four activities.

Picking the month of January for their study, the managers collected the following information about the actual number of cost driver units for each of the two products:

	Mountain Bikes	Racing Bikes
Purchasing materials	1,000 frames	200 frames
Machine setups	1,013 setups	30 setups
Inspections	1,200 hours	200 hours
Running machines	1,500 hours	500 hours

During January, the factory produced 1,000 mountain bikes and 200 racing bikes.

Exhibit 3.5 shows the overhead allocations for the two products derived by multiplying the actual number of cost driver units for each product times the predetermined rates computed previously.

EXHIBIT 3.4	Predetermined Annual Overhead Rates for Activity-Based Costing			
(1)	**(2)**	**(3)**	**(4)**	**(5)**
Activity	**Cost Driver**	**Estimated Overhead Cost for the Activity**	**Estimated Number of Cost Driver Units for Year 2**	**Rate (Column 3/Column 4)**
Purchasing materials	Number of frames purchased	$ 200,000	10,000 frames	$20 per frame
Machine setups	Number of machine setups	800,000	400 setups	$2,000 per setup
Inspections	Hours of inspections	400,000	4,000 hours	$100 per hour
Running machines	Machine hours	600,000	20,000 hours	$30 per hour
Total estimated overhead		$2,000,000		

EXHIBIT 3.5	Overhead Costs Assigned to Products Using Activity-Based Costing				
		Mountain Bikes		**Racing Bikes**	
Activity	Rate	Actual Cost Driver Units	Cost Allocated to Mountain Bikes	Actual Cost Driver Units	Cost Allocated to Racing Bikes
Purchasing materials	$20 per frame	1,000 frames	$ 20,000	200 frames	$ 4,000
Machine setups	$2,000 per setup	13 setups	26,000	30 setups	60,000
Inspections	$100 per inspection hour	200 hours	20,000	200 hours	20,000
Running machines	$30 per hour	1,500 hours	45,000	500 hours	15,000
Total cost allocated to each product			$111,000		$99,000
Total overhead				$210,000	

Unit Costs   Recall the factory produced 1,000 mountain bikes and 200 racing bikes in January. The direct materials cost $100 per unit for mountain bikes and $200 per unit for racing bikes. Direct labor costs were $30 per unit for mountain bikes and $60 per unit for racing bikes. Based on the overhead costs computed for the two product lines, which appear in Exhibit 3.5, overhead per unit was $111 (= $111,000/1,000 units) for mountain bikes and $495 (= $99,000/200 units) for racing bikes. After putting together the data shown in the top panel of Exhibit 3.6, the managers, to their surprise, find that the product costs derived from activity-based costing significantly differ from those derived with the traditional approach. Using the traditional approach, they had computed numbers shown in the bottom panel of Exhibit 3.6. They had assigned *considerably* more overhead to racing bikes and less to mountain bikes using activity-based costing. This result in our hypothetical example mirrors the actual situations we have seen: Typically activity-based costing assigns more costs to items produced in small runs than the traditional methods do.

EXHIBIT 3.6	Product Costs Using Activity-Based Costing

Activity-Based Costing

	Mountain Bikes	Racing Bikes
Direct Materials	$100	$200
Direct Labor	30	60
Overhead	111[a]	495[b]
Total Cost	$241	$755

Traditional Approach

	Mountain Bikes	Racing Bikes
Direct Materials	$100	$200
Direct Labor	30	60
Overhead	150	300
Total Cost	$280	$560

[a] $111 = overhead cost allocation to products using activity-based costing divided by number of units produced = $111,000/1,000 units.
[b] $495 = overhead cost allocation to products using activity-based costing divided by number of units produced = $99,000/200 units.

Analysis In analyzing the results, the Ciudad Juarez managers realize that ABC allocated more overhead to each racing bike than to each mountain bike because the factory performed more machine setups for the racing bikes. Also, the factory used as many total inspection hours for the lower-volume racing bike as for the mountain bike, meaning that the racing bike used more inspection hours per bike.

Activity-based costing revealed two facts. First, the mountain bikes cost less to make, and the racing bikes cost more, than the company had realized. Armed with this information, marketers decide to lower prices on the mountain bikes to make them more attractive in the market. Second, after taking a closer look at the production process for both bikes, management discovers that the Ciudad Juarez factory production methods are inefficient, so the company reworks the production process to reduce the number of setups, particularly on racing bikes.

Problem 3.1 for Self-Study

Compute Product Costs Using Activity-Based Costing. The following information is available for the month of December for the Ciudad Juarez factory:

Mountain bikes produced 600
Racing bikes produced 200

| | Cost Driver Units | |
Activities	Mountain Bikes	Racing Bikes
Purchasing materials	600 frames	200 frames
Machine setups	7 setups	24 setups
Inspections	100 hours	200 hours
Running machines	800 hours	600 hours

Compute the costs (1) in total and (2) per unit for both products using the activity-based costing rates. Use the actual cost driver units for December given in this self-study problem and the rates presented in the text. For mountain and racing bikes, respectively, assume the direct materials costs are $100 and $200 per unit and direct labor costs are $30 and $60 per unit. Round unit costs to the nearest dollar. Recall that overhead allocated to products equals the cost driver rate (for example, $20 per frame for materials handled according to the schedule of rates in Exhibit 3.4) times the cost driver units (for example, 600 frames for mountain bikes in December).

The solution to this self-study problem is at the end of the chapter on page 91.

Activity-Based Management and Costing in Marketing

Marketing activities also consume resources; territories, customer groupings, and other segments require activities to maintain themselves. Activity-based costing (ABC) costs the marketing activities needed to service each customer. The variability in marketing costs across customer types and distribution channels requires attention by the costing system. ABC also supports activity-based management by encouraging the elimination of low-volume customers, for whom the activities to process are the same as for large-volume customers. ABC also provides cost analysis to support the addition of a surcharge on small orders.

The principles and methods are the same as discussed earlier:

1. Identify activities, such as warehousing, credit and collection, transportation, personal selling, and advertising, focusing on the expensive ones.

2. Identify cost drivers. Some possible cost drivers are as follows:

Detailed Activity	ABC Drivers
Transportation—Loading and unloading, gasoline, repairs, and supervision	Deliveries or shipments, truck miles, units or value shipped
Advertising and sales promotion—Newspaper advertising, radio and television ads, and product demonstrations	Newspaper inches, cost per thousand consumers reached, sales transactions, or product units sold

3. Compute the cost rate for each cost driver. Compute unit costs for each activity by dividing the budgeted activity cost by the cost driver selected. For example, assume advertising for a month in the *Chicago Tribune* is $30,000, including the newspaper ad and the company advertising and graphics employees' salaries. The company has chosen column inches as the cost driver and runs a total of 300 inches per month. The cost per inch is $100.

4. Assign costs to each product by multiplying the rate for each cost driver by the number of cost driver units used for each product.

Managerial Application

Cost Management in Action: Why Hewlett-Packard Now Manages Suppliers Instead of Overhead

Supplier relations are becoming increasingly important as more and more companies outsource activities that were once done internally. Some of this increased reliance on suppliers is derived from the use of activity-based costing and management. Here we describe how Hewlett-Packard used activity-based costing to evaluate costly activities, then outsourced many of them.

A division of Hewlett-Packard was one of the early experimenters with activity-based costing. Because overhead costs were more than 50 percent of total product costs, managers wanted to identify the activities that drove overhead costs. Based on the costs of activities revealed by activity-based costing, management decided to outsource many of the activities that drove overhead costs. The result was that overhead costs decreased substantially, but the cost of goods purchased from suppliers increased to 70 percent of total product cost. The emphasis shifted from managing overhead costs to managing supplier relations.

Source: Interviews with Hewlett-Packard managers.

Cost Hierarchies

Some costs are fixed over the time horizon management uses in its decision making. Others vary with units produced. Still others vary, but not strictly with units produced. For example, the costs of machine setups generally vary with the number of batches a company runs. A new batch of products requires a machine setup whether the batch contains 1 unit or 1,000 units. The number of batches, not the number of units, generates the setup cost.

A hierarchy of costs like that in Exhibit 3.7 helps managers think about the major factors that drive costs.[5] The **cost hierarchy** categorizes costs according to whether they are capacity,

---

[5]R. Cooper and R. S. Kaplan, "Profit Priorities from Activity-Based Costing," *Harvard Business Review* (May–June 1991), 130–135.

EXHIBIT 3.7	Hierarchy of Product Costs

Activity Category	Examples
1. Capacity-Sustaining Activities	Plant Management
	Building Depreciation and Rent
	Heating and Lighting
2. Customer Activities	Market Research
	Customer Records
	Promotion
3. Product Activities	Product Specifications
	Product Testing
4. Batch Activities	Machine Setups
	Quality Inspections
5. Unit Activities	Energy to Run Machines
	Direct Materials

product, customer, batch, or unit costs. Variable costs, such as energy costs to run machines, appear at the bottom of the illustration as unit-level costs. Direct materials and piecework labor costs are also unit-level costs.

At the other extreme, at the top of the illustration, are capacity-related costs. These costs are essentially fixed by management's decisions to have a particular size of store, factory, hospital, or other facility. Although these costs are fixed with respect to volume, management can change them. Managers can make decisions that affect capacity costs; such decisions just require a longer time horizon to implement than do decisions to reduce unit-level costs.

The way the company manages its activities affects the two middle categories of costs. A company that makes products to order for a customer will have more product/customer-level costs than a company that provides limited choices. A company that schedules its work to make one product on Monday, a second product on Tuesday, and so on through Friday has batch-related costs lower than if it produced all five products on Monday, all five again on Tuesday, and so on through the week. In practice, managers can find many opportunities for reducing costs in these middle categories of product/customer-level and batch-related costs.

Management can use the cost hierarchy to ascertain which category of costs will change because of a management decision. If management makes decisions that affect units but not batches, products, customers, or capacity, management would analyze costs in category 5 (unit-level activities). For example, management of an airline choosing between peanuts and pretzels to serve passengers will probably focus only on unit costs, where they consider passengers to be "units" (not surprisingly).

If management makes decisions that affect capacity, the change in capacity will likely affect all activities in categories 1 through 5, and management should analyze costs in all five categories. For example, if airline management considers adding new aircraft to its fleet, it will consider all categories of activities. Assume the additional capacity will add flights and routes to the airline's schedule. Consequently, management will consider

1. Capacity costs, such as the costs of capital and depreciation of aircraft;
2. Customer costs, such as special promotions to attract customers to fly on the new aircraft;
3. Product costs (which are routes for airlines), such as developing schedules for new routes;
4. Batch costs (which are flights for airlines), such as fuel and baggage handling for new flights; and
5. Unit costs, such as credit card fees for additional customers attracted by the new flights and routes.

Problem 3.2 for Self-Study

Identify which of the following items generate capacity-sustaining costs, product-sustaining costs, customer-sustaining costs, batch costs, or unit costs.

1. Piecework labor
2. Long-term lease on a building
3. Energy to run machines
4. Engineering drawings for a product
5. Purchase order
6. Movement of materials for products in production
7. Change order to meet new customer specifications

The solution to this self-study problem is at the end of this chapter on page 91.

Distinguishing between Resources Used and Resources Supplied

In some situations, costs go up and down proportionately with the cost driver. For example, if the driver is units produced, then materials, energy, and piecework labor vary with the driver. Suppose workers receive $1.50 per crate to pick strawberries from a field. The cost driver would be "crates of strawberries" and the cost driver rate would be $1.50 per crate.

Now suppose the firm hires strawberry workers by the day and pays them $64 per day. Assume the cost driver is still "crates of strawberries." Management would compute the cost driver rate: estimated wages of strawberry workers for the day divided by the estimated number of crates of strawberries that workers can pick during the day. The grower estimates the workers will pick 32 crates per day, which gives a rate of $2 per crate (= $64 per-day wages/32 crates picked per day). In general, this cost driver rate could be higher, lower, or the same as the piecework rate. We assume the rate is $2 only to help you see the difference between the piecework rate and the cost driver rate when workers receive payments for time periods such as hours, days, or months.

The grower employs five workers. Each has the capacity to pick 32 crates per day, or a total of 160 crates per day for five workers. But assume that on Tuesday, the workers pick only 140 crates. That means there are 20 crates, or $40 (= $2 cost driver rate × 20 crates), of unused capacity on Tuesday. The grower has costs of $320, computed either of two ways:

$$\$320 = 5 \text{ workers} \times \$64 \text{ per day}$$

$$\$320 = \$2 \text{ per crate} \times 160\text{-crate capacity}$$

The grower supplies resources of $320 to the strawberry-picking activity. However, on Tuesday, the grower used only $280 (= $2 per crate × 140 crates actually picked) of strawberry-picking resources, leaving $40 of unused capacity (= $320 − $280). The grower knows the five workers could have picked more strawberries without increasing the resources supplied to the activity.

In general, activity-based costing estimates the cost of resources used. Activity-based costing measures **resources used** for an activity by the cost driver rate times the cost driver volume. In the strawberry example, resources used are $280.

The **resources supplied** to an activity are the expenditures or the amounts spent on the activity. In the strawberry example, resources supplied are the $320 paid to the strawberry pickers. Resources supplied are also called "resource capacity acquired" because the resources are acquired by the company for the activity. In the strawberry example, the grower acquires the capacity to pick strawberries for one day by paying the workers $320. Financial statements show resources supplied. The difference between resources supplied and resources used is **unused capacity.**[6]

---

[6]Failure to distinguish between resources used and resources supplied leads to suboptimal decisions. See E. Noreen, "Conditions under Which Activity-Based Costing Systems Provide Relevant Costs," *Journal of Management Accounting Research* 3, 159–168.

Knowing the difference between resources used and supplied helps managers to identify unused capacity. Finding unused capacity helps managers to reduce it or use it in creative ways. For example, the strawberry grower may look for ways to reduce the $40 (or 20 crates) of unused capacity. Suppose the grower finds that the people checking each case for quantity and quality have insufficient training. Consequently, the checkers slowed the picking process. The activity-based management information signaled the existence of unused capacity, which helped the grower and workers improve the production flow.

Managerial Application

Identifying Unused Capacity in the Recovery Room

In the current era of managed competition, health maintenance organizations (HMOs), and capitation, health-care organizations look for ways to reduce costs while improving the quality of care. Several health-care organizations recently experimented with a new anesthesia that would enable patients to leave the recovery room sooner. Managers hoped the new anesthesia would both reduce the costs of nurse staffing in the recovery room and increase customer satisfaction because patients would leave the surgery center earlier.

The managers faced the problem that resources used (patient time in the recovery room) did not equal resources supplied (expenditures to pay nurses to staff the recovery room). Researchers found that a particular new anesthesia reduced patient time in the recovery room by one-third. Although resources used in the recovery room were 33 percent less, would resources supplied also go down by 33 percent?

Researchers found the answer to be *no* in this case. They discovered that the resources supplied (that is, expenditures to pay nurses) went down by only 20 percent, despite the 33 percent decrease in patient time. Why? Primarily because the outpatient surgery center employed nurses in four-hour shifts. Once nurses went on duty, the managers could not save their wages, even if the patient census dropped in the recovery room.

In the end, managers realized that the new anesthesia would have three desirable effects:

1. Patients would go home sooner, which increased their satisfaction.
2. Costs would be lower; even a 20 percent reduction beats no reduction.
3. Both patient care and nurse morale would improve. Reducing resource usage by 33 percent and reducing resource supply by only 20 percent creates unused capacity. Nurses could use this "unused capacity" for many desirable purposes, including spending more time with each patient, devoting more time to patient follow-up, and doing unscheduled training.

Incidentally, turnover in other hospital departments provided ample jobs for nurses who would no longer be needed in the outpatient surgery-center recovery room.

Source: Based on M. W. Maher and M. L. Marais, "A Field Study on the Limitations of Activity-Based Costing When Resources Are Provided on a Joint and Indivisible Basis," *Journal of Accounting Research* 36, no. 1, 129–142.

Differences between resource supply and resource usage generally occur because managers have committed to supply a certain level of resources before using them. In the strawberry example, the grower committed to the $64-per-day wage before the actual picking of the strawberries. In the Managerial Application "Identifying Unused Capacity in the Recovery Room," the resources supplied are nurses hired for an entire shift of four hours before patients arrive. Unused capacity occurs in the health-care setting when nurses stand ready to provide patient care but no, or too few, patients require nursing services. Knowing the difference between resources used and resources supplied enables management to use nurses who are not engaged in patient care some other way. For example, during time not spent on patient care, nurses could make telephone calls or send e-mail messages to former patients to see whether they have complications from surgery or side effects from drugs administered during and after surgery.

In cases where the firm supplies resources as it uses them, the resource supply will generally equal the resource usage, resulting in no unused capacity. Good examples are materials costs and piecework labor. If the grower had paid the piecework labor rate of $1.50 per crate, the resources supplied would have been $1.50 per crate of strawberries picked and the resource used would also have been $1.50 per crate picked. There would have been no unused capacity. The next section expands on these ideas by suggesting a new reporting format that presents managers with important information about resources used, resources supplied, and unused capacity.

Activity-Based Reporting of Unused Resources

We now discuss an important way for managers to add value in companies. The previous sections have demonstrated two key concepts: the cost hierarchy and the difference between resources used and resources supplied. Conventional management reports do not distinguish these. Typical reports show costs as line items, as for Kaplan, Inc., in Exhibit 3.8. It is impossible for managers to distinguish resources used from resources supplied in such reports.

Here we present in Exhibit 3.9 a new format of report that compares resources used with resources supplied and classifies costs into cost hierarchies. This information will help managers to manage resources wisely. Note first that this format categorizes costs into the cost hierarchies discussed earlier in this chapter. Managers can look at the amount of costs in each hierarchy and figure out ways to manage those resources effectively. For example, managers see that batch-related activities receive $30,000 of resources supplied. Now they investigate how much of that $30,000 they can save by changing the production process—for example, by cutting the number of setups in half.

Perhaps of greater interest, the report shows managers the unused portion of the resources for each type of cost. Here's how it works. Take setup costs. Assume the cost driver is "hours of setup" and the cost driver rate is $100 per hour. Based on the information in the income statement, $20,000 was spent on setups. That represents 200 hours of setup capacity (= $20,000/$100 per setup hour). However, the company used only 140 hours (= $14,000 resources used/$100 cost driver rate) during the month. The report shows managers that $6,000 (or 60 hours) of unused setup resource is available.

All other things equal, managers could have used perhaps as much as 60 additional hours of setup in January without increasing expenditures. In reality, managers know that some unused resources are a good thing. Having some unstructured time for ad hoc training, for

EXHIBIT 3.8	**KAPLAN, INC.** **Traditional (Detailed) Income Statement** **January**	
Sales		$180,000
Costs		
Materials	$30,000	
Energy	10,000	
Short-term Labor	4,000	
Outside Contracts	6,000	
Setups	20,000	
Parts Management	7,000	
Purchasing	10,000	
Marketing	15,000	
Customer Service	4,000	
Engineering Changes	6,000	
Long-term Labor	7,000	
Depreciation (buildings)	20,000	
Administrative	13,000	
Total Costs		152,000
Operating Profits		$ 28,000

	Resources Used	Unused Capacity	Resources Supplied
EXHIBIT 3.9 KAPLAN, INC. Activity-Based Management Income Statement January			

	Resources Used	Unused Capacity	Resources Supplied	
Sales				$180,000
Costs				
Unit:				
Materials	$ 30,000	$ 0	$30,000	
Energy	10,000	0	10,000	
Short-term Labor	3,500	500	4,000	
Outside Contracts	6,000	0	6,000	
	$ 49,500	$ 500	$50,000	
Batch:				
Setups	$ 14,000	$ 6,000	$20,000	
Purchasing	9,000	1,000	10,000	
	$ 23,000	$ 7,000	$30,000	
Product- and Customer-Sustaining:				
Parts Management	$ 6,000	$ 1,000	$ 7,000	
Marketing	14,000	1,000	15,000	
Customer Service	2,000	2,000	4,000	
Engineering Changes	5,000	1,000	6,000	
	$ 27,000	$ 5,000	$32,000	
Capacity-Sustaining:				
Long-term Labor	$ 5,000	$ 2,000	$ 7,000	
Depreciation (buildings)	12,000	8,000	20,000	
Administrative	10,000	3,000	13,000	
	$ 27,000	$13,000	$40,000	
Total Costs	$126,500	$25,500		$152,000
Operating Profits				$ 28,000

Source: This statement is an extension of an idea presented in R. Cooper and R. Kaplan, "Activity-Based Systems: Measuring the Costs of Resource Usage," *Accounting Horizons* 6, no. 3, 1–13.

leisure, or for thinking about ways to improve work and the work environment can boost morale and productivity.

Note that some costs have more unused resources than others. The costs listed under unit-related costs at the top of the report show little or no unused resources. These costs vary proportionately with output and will often have little or no unused resources. Short-term labor, for example, is the cost of piecework labor or temporary help employed on an "as needed" basis. In a college, a part-time lecturer hired for only one class is an example of short-term labor. Many of us have worked as short-term laborers during the summer in resorts, on farms, fighting forest fires, in retail stores, or providing delivery services.

Capacity-related costs will have unused resources unless the company operates at full capacity. Long-term labor resources are the costs of employing people who are not laid off during temporary fluctuations in production. In colleges, permanent faculty and staff are examples of long-term labor.

Implementing Advanced Cost-Management Systems

Accountants cannot implement activity-based costing without becoming familiar with the operations of the company. Accountants become part of a team with management and people from production, engineering, marketing, and other parts of the company who all work to identify the activities that drive the company's costs. This often creates discomfort at first as accountants deal with unfamiliar areas, but in the long run their familiarity with the company's operating activities improves their productivity. Also, non-accounting personnel feel a greater sense of ownership of the numbers reported by the accounting system as accounting improves its credibility among non-accountants.

Implementing activity-based costing goes badly when influential people in the organization fail to buy into the process. People become accustomed to accounting methods in companies just as people in sports become accustomed to playing by one set of rules and oppose change to the unknown. In fact, specialists who advise companies about how to implement advanced cost-management systems believe that top-level employee resistance presents the single biggest obstacle to implementing activity-based management. For example, analysts at one company spent several months of their time and hundreds of hours of computer time to develop an activity-based costing system that revealed several hundred clearly unprofitable products that the company should eliminate. The key managers who made product elimination decisions agreed to eliminate only about 20 products. Why? The analysts had failed to talk to these key managers early in the process. When these managers saw the results, they raised numerous objections that the analysts had not anticipated. The moral is: If you are involved in trying to make a change, get all the people who are important to that change involved in the process early.

Cultural Differences in Implementing ABC

ABC simply works better in some cultures than in others. A researcher studying the attempt of Harris Semiconductor to implement ABC in Malaysia and the United States found that ABC's emphasis on cross-functional teams for implementation worked better in Malaysia than in U.S. plants. Further, he found that the U.S. plants' emphasis on short-term results created skepticism about ABC. Consequently, the U.S. plant managers did not use ABC to its fullest potential.[7] ABC is not a quick fix; it is a process that requires patience and participation to see results. Cultures that reward only short-term results are not fertile grounds for ABC.

Managerial Application

Impact of ABC on Shareholder Value

ABC might be an interesting exercise, but does it really pay off for shareholders? One study of ABC in U.K. companies attempted to answer this question by comparing the stock returns and various accounting ratios of companies adopting ABC with those of companies that did not. The researchers concluded that the ABC firms had superior financial performance because of better cost controls and asset utilization.

Source: T. Kennedy and J. Affleck-Graves, "The Impact of Activity-Based Costing Techniques on Firm Performance," *Journal of Management Accounting Research* 13, 19–45.

Summary

These items relate to the learning objectives stated at the beginning of the chapter.

1. **Identify strategic and operational uses of activity-based management.** Activity-based management can help a company develop strategy, long-range plans, and subsequent competitive cost advantage by focusing attention on activities.
2. **Differentiate between traditional cost allocation methods and activity-based costing.** The simplest allocation method, plantwide allocation, considers the entire plant to be one cost pool. The department allocation method uses a separate cost pool for each department. Activity-based costing uses a cost pool for each activity center.

---

[7]P. Brewer, "National Culture and ABC Systems," *Management Accounting Research* 9, no. 2, 241–260.

3. **Understand the concept of activity-based costing.** Activity-based costing first assigns costs to activities and then to the products based on each product's use of activities. Many believe that activity-based costing changes the way managers do their jobs. People manage activities, not costs. Activity-based costing thus focuses attention on the things that management can make more efficient or otherwise change. Traditional allocation systems can distort product costs. Although overhead costs are allocated on volume of production or sales, the demand for overhead activities is also driven by batch-related and product-sustaining activities.

4. **Identify the steps in activity-based costing.** Activity-based costing requires accountants to follow four steps: (1) identify the activities that consume resources and assign costs to those activities, (2) identify the cost drivers associated with each activity, (3) compute a cost rate per cost driver unit, and (4) assign cost to products by multiplying the cost driver rate by the volume of cost driver consumed by the product.

Key Equation

$$\text{Predetermined indirect cost rate} = \frac{\text{Estimated indirect cost}}{\text{Estimated volume of the allocation base}}$$

5. **Apply activity-based management and costing to marketing.** Activity-based costing identifies the marketing activities needed to service each customer or order more appropriately. The variability in marketing costs across customer types and distribution channels requires attention by the costing system. Activity-based costing also supports activity-based management by encouraging the elimination of accounts with high processing costs.

6. **Use the cost hierarchy to organize cost information for decision making.** Allocating all costs to units is misleading if some costs do not vary with the volume of units. To deal with this, management can set up a hierarchy of expenses—capacity-sustaining, product-sustaining, customer-sustaining, batch, and unit—and focus on the costs in the applicable category.

7. **Distinguish between resources used and resources supplied, and measure unused resource capacity.** Resources used for an activity are measured by the cost driver rate times the cost driver volume. Resources supplied to an activity are the expenditures for the activity. Differences between resource supply and resource usage (unused resource capacity) generally occur because managers have committed to supply a certain level of resources before using them. Activity-based management involves looking for ways to reduce unused capacity.

8. **Explain the difficulties of implementing advanced cost-management systems.** Accountants cannot implement activity-based costing without becoming familiar with the operations of the company. Accountants become part of a team with management and people from production, engineering, marketing, and other parts of the company who all work to identify the activities that drive the company's costs. One cause of difficulty in implementing activity-based costing is the failure to get influential people in the organization to buy into the process.

Key Terms and Concepts

Activity-based costing (ABC)	Department allocation method
Activity-based management (ABM)	Plantwide allocation method
Activity center	Resources supplied
Cost driver	Resources used
Cost hierarchy	Unused capacity
Cost pool	Value chain

SUGGESTED SOLUTION TO PROBLEM 3.1 FOR SELF-STUDY

		Mountain Bikes		Racing Bikes	
Activity	Rate	Actual Cost Driver Units	Costs Allocated to Mountain Bikes	Actual Cost Driver Units	Costs Allocated to Racing Bikes
Purchasing materials	$20 per frame	600 frames	$12,000	200 frames	$ 4,000
Machine setups	$2,000 per setup	7 setups	$14,000	24 setups	$48,000
Inspections	$100 per inspection hour	100 hours	$10,000	200 hours	$20,000
Running machines	$30 per hour	800 hours	$24,000	600 hours	$18,000
Total cost allocated to each product:			$60,000		$90,000

The costs of producing 600 mountain bikes and 200 racing bikes are as follows:

	Mountain Bikes	Racing Bikes
Direct Materials	$ 60,000 ($100 each)	$ 40,000 ($200 each)
Direct Labor	$ 18,000 ($30 each)	$ 12,000 ($60 each)
Overhead	$ 60,000 (see above)	$ 90,000 (see above)
Total	$138,000	$142,000

Unit Costs

	Mountain Bikes	Racing Bikes
Direct Materials	$100	$200
Direct Labor	30	60
Overhead	100[a]	450[b]
Total	$230	$710

[a]$100 = total allocation to products divided by number of units produced = $60,000/600 units.
[b]$450 = total allocation to products divided by number of units produced = $90,000/200 units.

SUGGESTED SOLUTION TO PROBLEM 3.2 FOR SELF-STUDY

Activity	Category
1. Piecework labor	Unit
2. Long-term lease on building	Capacity sustaining
3. Energy to run machines	Unit
4. Engineering drawings for a product	Product sustaining
5. Purchase order	Batch
6. Movement of materials for products in production	Batch
7. Change order to meet new customer specifications	Customer sustaining

Questions, Exercises, Problems, and Cases

REVIEW QUESTIONS

1. Review the meaning of the concepts and terms given in Key Terms and Concepts.
2. "Activity-based costing is great for manufacturing plants, but it doesn't really address the needs of the service sector." Do you agree? Explain.
3. If step 1 of ABC is to identify activities that consume resources, what is step 2?
4. What basis or cost driver does a company using a single plantwide rate typically select for the allocation of indirect costs?
5. What are the four basic steps required for activity-based costing?
6. Give the criterion for choosing cost drivers for allocating costs to products.
7. Why is the traditional approach to indirect cost allocation less expensive to implement than the activity-based costing approach?

CRITICAL ANALYSIS AND DISCUSSION QUESTIONS

8. What types of cultures most likely support implementing ABC? What types would not support ABC implementation?
9. What exactly is a cost driver? Give three examples.
10. Activity-based costing requires more record keeping and extensive teamwork among all departments. What are the potential benefits of a more detailed product cost system?
11. "One of the lessons learned from activity-based costing is that all costs are really a function of volume." True, false, or uncertain? Explain.
12. Allocating overhead based on the volume of output, such as direct labor hours or machine hours, seems fair and equitable. Why, then, do many people claim that high-volume products "subsidize" low-volume products?
13. Give examples of two non–value-added activities that may be found in each of the following organizations: (1) a university, (2) a restaurant, and (3) a bicycle repair shop.
14. "The total estimated overhead for the year will differ depending on whether you use department allocation or activity-based costing." Do you agree? Explain.
15. Many companies have experienced great technological change resulting in potential for erroneous product cost figures, assuming traditional labor-based cost drivers are used to allocate overhead to products. What is that technological change?
16. "Activity-based costing is for accountants and production managers. I plan to be a marketing specialist, so ABC won't help me." Do you agree with this statement? Explain.
17. Refer to the Managerial Application "Identifying Unused Capacity in the Recovery Room." If the new anesthesia reduces the number of minutes a patient stays in the recovery room after surgery, why wouldn't nursing costs necessarily be reduced proportional to the reduction in the number of minutes the patient stays in the recovery room?
18. Martha Clark, the vice-president of marketing, wonders how products can cost less under one cost system than under another: "Aren't costs cut-and-dried?" How would you respond?
19. According to a recent publication, "Activity-based costing is the wave of the future. Everyone should drop their existing cost systems and adopt ABC!" Do you agree? Explain.
20. What is the difference between a capacity-sustaining cost and a unit-level cost? How can managers use a hierarchy of overhead costs like the one presented in Exhibit 3.9?
21. Of the four categories of costs in the hierarchy, which one would you most expect to have unused resources? Why?
22. How are the unused resources measured?
23. How does activity-based management use the hierarchy of costs?
24. Would you expect companies that adopt ABC to add value to shareholders? How would you measure such added value?

EXERCISES

Solutions to even-numbered exercises are at the end of the chapter after the cases.

25. **Activity-based costing.** Michael Conway has just joined the Ciudad Juarez factory (text example) as the new production manager. He was pleased to see the company uses activity-

based costing. Conway believes he can reduce production costs if he reduces the number of machine setups. He has spent the past month working with purchasing and sales to better coordinate raw material arrivals and the anticipated demand for the company's products. In March, he plans to produce 1,000 mountain bikes and 200 racing bikes. Conway believes that with his efficient production scheduling he can reduce the number of setups for both mountain and racing bikes by about 50 percent.

a. Refer to Exhibit 3.5. Compute the amount of overhead allocated to each product line—mountain bikes and racing bikes—assuming annual setups are reduced by approximately 50 percent. Assume the number of machine setups in March is seven setups for mountain bikes and 15 setups for racing bikes. Assume the overhead costs of setting up machines decrease proportionately with the reduction in the number of setups; thus, the setup rate remains at $2,000 per setup. All other overhead costs will remain the same.

b. What information did activity-based costing provide that enabled Michael Conway to pursue reducing overhead costs? In general, what are the advantages of activity-based costing over the traditional volume-based allocation methods? What are the disadvantages?

26. **Activity-based costing.** The manager of Wildwater Adventurers uses activity-based costing to compute the costs of her raft trips. Each raft holds six paying customers and a guide. The company offers two types of raft trips—three-day float trips for beginners and three-day whitewater trips for seasoned rafters. The breakdown of the costs is as follows:

Activities (with cost drivers)	Float Trip Costs	Whitewater Trip Costs
Advertising (trips)	$215 per trip	$215 per trip
Permit to Use the River (trips)	30 per trip	50 per trip
Equipment Use (trips, people)	20 per trip + $5 per person (including guides)	40 per trip + $8 per person (including guides)
Insurance (trips)	75 per trip	127 per trip
Paying Guides (trips, guides)	300 per trip per guide	400 per trip per guide
Food (people)	60 per person (including guides)	60 per person (including guides)

a. Compute the cost of a four-raft, 28-person (including four guides) float trip.
b. Compute the cost of a four-raft, 28-person (including four guides) whitewater trip.
c. Recommend a minimum price per customer to the manager if she wants to cover her costs.

27. **ABC versus traditional costing.** DuraDisc Corporation produces two types of compact discs: standard and high-grade. The standard CDs are used primarily in computer drives and are designed for data storage rather than accurate sound reproduction. The company only recently began producing the higher-quality, high-grade model to enter the lucrative music-recording market. Since the new product was introduced, profits have seen only a modest increase. Management expected a significant profit increase related to rapidly growing sales of the high-grade discs. Management believes the accounting system may not be accurately allocating costs to products.

Management has asked you to investigate the cost allocation problem. You find that manufacturing overhead is currently assigned to products based on the direct labor costs in the products. Last year's manufacturing overhead was $880,000, based on production of 320,000 standard CDs and 120,000 high-grade CDs. Selling prices last year averaged $3.60 per standard disc and $5.80 per high-grade disc. Direct labor and direct materials costs for last year were as follows:

	Standard	High-Grade	Total
Direct Labor	$174,000	$ 66,000	$240,000
Direct Materials	125,000	114,000	239,000

Management believes the following three activities cause overhead costs. The cost drivers and related costs are as follows:

| | Costs Assigned | Activity Level | | |
		Standard	High-Grade	Total
Number of Production Runs	$400,000	30	10	40
Quality Tests Performed	360,000	12	18	30
Shipping Orders Processed	120,000	100	50	150
Total Overhead	$880,000			

a. How much of the overhead will be assigned to each product if the three cost drivers are used to allocate overhead? What would be the cost per unit produced for each product?

b. How much of the overhead would have been assigned to each product if direct labor cost had been used to allocate overhead? What would have been the total cost per unit produced for each product?

c. How might the results explain why profits did not increase as much as management expected?

28. **Activity-based costing in a nonmanufacturing environment.** Plantcare, Inc., is a garden care service. The company originally specialized in serving residential clients but has recently started contracting for work with larger commercial clients. Ms. Plantcare, the owner, is considering reducing residential services and increasing commercial lawn care.

Five field employees worked a total of 10,000 hours last year—6,500 on residential jobs and 3,500 on commercial jobs. Wages were $9 per hour for all work done. Direct materials used were minimal and are included in overhead. All overhead is allocated on the basis of labor hours worked, which is also the basis for customer charges. Because of greater competition for commercial accounts, Ms. Plantcare can charge $22 per hour for residential work but only $19 per hour for commercial work.

a. If overhead for the year was $62,000, what were the profits of commercial and residential service using labor hours as the allocation base?

b. Overhead consists of office supplies, garden supplies, and depreciation and maintenance on equipment. These costs can be traced to the following activities:

| Activity | Cost Driver | Cost | Activity Level | |
			Commercial	Residential
Office Supplies	Number of Clients Served	$ 8,000	15	45
Equipment Depreciation and Maintenance	Equipment Hours	18,000	3,500	2,500
Garden Supplies	Area Covered (computed as number of square yards of garden times number of times garden is serviced per year)	36,000	65,000	35,000
Total Overhead		$62,000		

Recalculate profits for commercial and residential services based on these activity bases.

c. What recommendations do you have for management?

29. **ABC versus traditional costing.** Nokian Corporation manufactures cellular phones and pagers. Overhead costs are currently allocated using direct labor hours, but the controller has recommended an activity-based costing system using the following data:

| Activity | Cost Driver | Cost | Activity Level | |
			Cellular Phones	Pagers
Production Setup	Number of Setups	$100,000	5	15
Material Handling and Requisition	Number of Parts	10,000	22	28
Packaging and Shipping	Number of Units Shipped	50,000	60,000	80,000
Total Overhead		$160,000		

a. Compute the amount of overhead allocated to each of the products under activity-based costing.

b. Compute the amount of overhead to be allocated to each product using labor hours as the allocation base. Assume 20,000 labor hours were used to assemble cellular phones and 80,000 labor hours were used to assemble pagers.

c. Should the company adopt an ABC system?

30. **ABC versus traditional costing.** Vicki Greenshade, CPA, provides consulting and tax preparation services to her clients. She charges a fee of $100 per hour for each service. Her revenues and expenses for the year are shown in the following income statement:

	Tax	Consulting	Total
Revenue	$80,000	$120,000	$200,000
Expenses:			
Filing, scheduling, and data entry	_____	_____	40,000
Supplies	_____	_____	36,000
Computer costs	_____	_____	20,000
Profit	_____	_____	$104,000

Vicki has kept records of the following data for cost allocation purposes:

		Activity Level	
Expenses	Cost Driver	Tax Preparation	Consulting
Filing, scheduling, and data entry	Number of Clients	72	48
Supplies	Number of Hours Billed	800	1,200
Computer costs	Computer Hours	1,000	600

a. Complete the income statement using Vicki's three cost drivers.

b. Recompute the income statements using hours billed as the only allocation base.

c. How might Vicki's decisions be altered if she were to use only hours billed to allocate expenses?

31. **When do ABC and traditional methods yield similar results?** Refer to Exercise **30.** In general, under what circumstances would the two allocation methods in parts **a.** and **b.** result in similar profit results?

32. **Resources used versus resources supplied.** Information about two activities for the Condor Corporation follows:

	Cost Driver Rate	Cost Driver Volume
Resources Used		
Energy	$ 6	500 machine hours
Marketing	25	200 sales calls
Resources Supplied		
Energy	$3,300	
Marketing	6,000	

Compute unused capacity for energy and marketing.

33. **Resources used versus resources supplied.** Information about resources for Publications, Inc., which produces brochures, follows:

	Cost Driver Rate	Cost Driver Volume
Resources Used		
Setups	$ 80	60 runs
Administrative	150	15 jobs
Resources Supplied		
Setups	$6,600	
Administrative	3,000	

Compute unused capacity for these items.

PROBLEMS

34. **Comparative income statements and management analysis.** Soft Bed Corporation manufactures two types of mattresses, Dreamer and Sleeper. Dreamer has a complex design that uses gel-filled compartments to provide support. Sleeper is simpler to manufacture and uses conventional padding. Last year, Soft Bed had the following revenues and costs:

	Dreamer	Sleeper	Total
Revenue	$600,000	$375,000	$975,000
Direct Materials	250,000	110,000	360,000
Direct Labor	100,000	50,000	150,000
Indirect Costs:			
Administration	_____	_____	50,000
Production Setup	_____	_____	75,000
Quality Control	_____	_____	90,000
Sales and Marketing	_____	_____	150,000
Operating Profit	_____	_____	$100,000

Soft Bed currently uses labor costs to allocate all overhead, but management is considering implementing an activity-based costing system. After interviewing the sales and production staff, management decides to allocate administrative costs on the basis of direct labor costs but to use the following bases to allocate the remaining overhead:

		Activity Level	
Activity	Cost Driver	Dreamer	Sleeper
Production Setup	Number of Production Runs	5	15
Quality Control	Number of Inspections	20	70
Sales and Marketing	Number of Advertisements	25	55

a. Complete the income statement using the activity bases above.
b. Write a brief report indicating how management could use activity-based costing to reduce costs.
c. Restate the income statement for Soft Bed using direct labor costs as the only overhead allocation base.
d. Write a report to management stating why product-line profits differ using activity-based costing compared with the traditional approach. Indicate whether activity-based costing provides more accurate information and why (if you believe it does provide more accurate information). Indicate in your report how the use of labor-based overhead allocation could result in Soft Bed management making suboptimal decisions.

35. **Comparative income statements and management analysis.** Athlete Feet, Inc., manufactures two types of shoes: X-Trainer and Court. Last year, Athlete Feet had the following costs and revenues:

ATHLETE FEET, INC.
Income Statement

	Court	X-Trainer	Total
Revenue	$720,000	$800,000	$1,520,000
Direct Materials	100,000	100,000	200,000
Direct Labor	360,000	240,000	600,000
Indirect Costs:			
Administration			100,000
Production Setup			160,000
Quality Control			150,000
Sales and Marketing			60,000
Operating Profit			$ 250,000

Athlete Feet, Inc., currently uses labor costs to allocate all overhead, but management is considering implementing an activity-based costing system. After interviewing the sales and production staff, management decides to allocate administrative costs on the basis of direct labor costs but to use the following cost drivers to allocate the remaining overhead:

		Activity Level	
Activity	**Cost Driver**	**Court**	**X-Trainer**
Production Setup	Number of Production Runs	350	450
Quality Control	Number of Inspections	600	400
Sales and Marketing	Number of Advertisements	120	80

a. Complete the income statement using the cost drivers above.
b. Write a report indicating how management might use activity-based costing to reduce costs.
c. Restate the income statement for Athlete Feet using direct labor costs as the only overhead allocation base.
d. Write a report to management stating why product-line profits differ using activity-based costing compared with the traditional approach. Indicate whether activity-based costing provides more accurate information and, if so, how. Indicate in your report how the use of labor-based overhead allocation could result in Athlete Feet management making suboptimal decisions.

36. Resources used versus resources supplied. Selected information about resources for Gary's Glassware is as follows:

	Cost Driver Rate	**Cost Driver Volume**
Resources Used		
Materials	$ 5	5,000
Energy	1	3,200
Setups	50	30
Purchasing	40	30
Customer Service	50	30
Long-term Labor	40	100
Administrative	50	200
Resources Supplied		
Materials	$25,000	
Energy	3,500	
Setups	1,750	
Purchasing	1,500	
Customer Service	1,600	
Long-term Labor	6,000	
Administrative	14,000	

a. Compute unused capacity for these items.
b. Write a short report stating why managers should know the difference between resources used and resources supplied. Give examples of how managers could use the information on resources used and resources supplied.

37. ABC and predetermined overhead rates. SunSpecs Corporation makes three types of sunglasses: Razors, Slims, and Eagles. SunSpecs presently applies overhead using a predetermined rate based on direct labor hours. A consultant recommended that SunSpecs switch to activity-based costing. Management decided to give ABC a try and identified the following activities, cost drivers, and estimated costs for Year 2 for each activity center.

Activity	Recommended Cost Driver	Estimated Costs	Estimated Cost Driver Units
Production Setup	Number of Production Runs	$ 60,000	200
Order Processing	Number of Orders	100,000	400
Materials Handling	Pounds of Materials Used	40,000	16,000
Equipment Depreciation and Maintenance	Machine Hours	120,000	20,000
Quality Management	Number of Inspections	100,000	800
Packing and Shipping	Number of Units Shipped	80,000	40,000
Total Estimated Overhead		$500,000	

The company estimated 10,000 labor hours would be worked in Year 2. Assume the following activities occurred in February of Year 2:

	Razors	Slims	Eagles
Number of Units Produced	2,000	1,000	800
Direct Materials Costs	$8,000	$5,000	$4,000
Direct Labor Hours	400	300	174
Number of Production Runs	2	4	12
Number of Orders	16	16	8
Pounds of Material Used	800	400	400
Machine Hours	800	400	400
Number of Inspections	20	20	20
Units Shipped	2,000	1,000	600

Direct labor costs are $20 per hour.

a. Compute an overhead allocation rate for each of the cost drivers recommended by the consultant and for direct labor.
b. Compute the production costs for each product for February using the cost drivers recommended by the consultant.
c. Management has seen your numbers and wants to know how you account for the discrepancy between the product costs using only direct labor hours as the allocation base and using activity-based costing. Write a brief response to management, including calculation of product costs using direct labor hours to allocate overhead.

38. **Choosing an ABC system.** BiWheeler, Inc., manufactures three bicycle models: a racing bike, a mountain bike, and a children's model. The racing model is made of a titanium-aluminum alloy and is called the Featherweight. The mountain bike is called the Peak and is made of aluminum. The steel-framed children's bike is called the Raider. Because of the different materials used, production processes differ significantly among models in terms of machine types and time requirements. However, once parts are produced, assembly time per unit required for each type of bike is similar. For this reason, BiWheeler had adopted the practice of allocating overhead on the basis of machine hours. Last year, the company produced 2,000 Featherweights, 4,000 Peaks, and 10,000 Raiders and had the following revenues and expenses:

BIWHEELER, INC.
Income Statement

	Featherweight	Peak	Raider	Total
Sales	$760,000	$1,120,000	$950,000	$2,830,000
Direct Costs				
Direct Materials	300,000	480,000	400,000	1,180,000
Direct Labor	28,800	48,000	108,000	184,800

	Featherweight	Peak	Raider	Total
Variable Overhead				
Machine Setup	_____	_____	_____	52,000
Order Processing	_____	_____	_____	128,000
Warehousing Costs	_____	_____	_____	186,000
Depreciation of Machines	_____	_____	_____	84,000
Shipping	_____	_____	_____	72,000
Contribution Margin	_____	_____	_____	$ 943,200
Fixed Overhead				
Plant Administration	_____	_____	_____	176,000
Other Fixed Overhead	_____	_____	_____	280,000
Operating Profit	_____	_____	_____	$ 487,200

The CFO of BiWheeler had heard about activity-based costing and hired a consultant to recommend cost allocation bases. The consultant recommended the following:

		Activity Level		
Activity	Cost Driver	Featherweight	Peak	Raider
Machine Setup	Number of Production Runs	16	28	36
Order Processing	Number of Sales Orders Received	400	600	600
Warehousing Costs	Number of Units Held in Inventory	200	200	400
Depreciation	Machine Hours	10,000	16,000	24,000
Shipping	Number of Units Shipped	1,000	4,000	10,000

The consultant found no basis for allocating the plant administration and other fixed overhead costs and recommended that these not be applied to products.

a. Using machine hours to allocate variable overhead, complete the income statement for BiWheeler. Do not attempt to allocate fixed overhead.

b. Complete the income statement using the cost drivers recommended by the consultant.

c. How might activity-based costing result in better decisions by BiWheeler management?

d. After hearing the consultant's recommendations, the CFO decided to adopt activity-based costing but expressed concern about not allocating some of the overhead (administration and other fixed overhead) to the products. In the CFO's view, "Products have to bear a fair share of all overhead or we won't be covering all our costs." How would you respond to this comment?

39. **Resources used versus resources supplied.** Selected information about resources for Jones Juice is as follows:

	Cost Driver Rate	Cost Driver Volume
Resources Used		
Materials	$ 5	2,500
Short-term Labor	25	250
Setups	80	30
Purchasing	60	75
Customer Service	30	17
Marketing	40	120
Administrative	30	125
Resources Supplied		
Materials	$12,500	
Short-term Labor	7,000	
Setups	2,500	
Purchasing	4,600	
Customer Service	650	
Marketing	5,500	
Administrative	3,800	

a. Compute unused capacity for these items.

b. Write a short report stating why managers should know the difference between resources used and resources supplied. Give examples of how managers could use information about resources used and resources supplied.

40. **Activity-based reporting.** Illuminate Corporation manufactures desk lamps and floor lamps. Information regarding resources for the month of March follows:

	Resources Used	Resources Supplied
Parts Management	$3,000	$3,500
Energy	5,000	5,000
Quality Inspections	4,500	5,000
Long-term Labor	2,500	3,500

	Resources Used	Resources Supplied
Short-term Labor	$ 2,000	$ 2,400
Setups	7,000	10,000
Materials	15,000	15,000
Depreciation	6,000	10,000
Marketing	7,000	7,500
Customer Service	1,000	2,000
Administrative	5,000	7,000

In addition, $2,500 was spent on 10 engineering changes with a cost driver rate of $250, and $3,000 was spent on four outside contracts with a cost driver rate of $750. There was no unused capacity for these two activities. Sales for March were $100,000. Management has requested that you:

a. Prepare a traditional income statement.

b. Prepare an activity-based income statement.

c. Write a short report explaining why the activity-based income statement provides better information to managers. Use information from Illuminate Corporation in examples.

41. **Benefits of activity-based costing** (adapted from the CMA exam). Many companies recognize that their cost systems are inadequate for today's global market. Managers in companies selling multiple products are making important product decisions based on distorted cost information. Most systems of the past were designed to focus on inventory valuation. If management should decide to implement an activity-based costing system, what benefits should they expect?

42. **Benefits of activity-based costing** (adapted from the CMA exam). Biotech, Inc. has just completed a major change in the method it uses to inspect its products. Previously 12 inspectors examined the product after each major process. The salaries of these inspectors were charged as direct labor to the operation or job. In an effort to improve efficiency, the Biotech production manager recently bought a computerized quality control system consisting of a microcomputer, 30 video cameras, peripheral hardware, and software. The cameras are placed at key points in the production process, taking pictures of the product and comparing these pictures with a known "good" image supplied by a quality control engineer. This new system allowed Biotech to replace the 12 quality control inspectors with just two quality control engineers.

The president of the company was confused. She was told that the production process was now more efficient, yet she notices a large increase in the factory overhead rate. The computation of the rate before and after automation is as follows:

	Before	After
Budgeted Overhead	$2,000,000	$2,500,000
Budgeted Direct Labor	1,200,000	1,000,000
Budgeted Overhead Rate	167%	250%

How might an activity-based costing system benefit Biotech, Inc. and clear up the president's confusion?

43. **Activity-based reporting.** The Halloway Corporation manufactures oxygen tanks for deep-sea divers. Information regarding resources for the month of March follows.

	Resources Used	Resources Supplied
Marketing	$28,000	$30,000
Depreciation	24,000	40,000
Outside Contracts	12,000	12,000
Materials	60,000	60,000
Setups	14,000	20,000
Energy	20,000	21,000
Parts Management	15,000	16,000
Engineering Changes	10,000	12,000
Short-term Labor	7,000	7,000
Long-term Labor	10,000	14,000
Administrative	20,000	26,000

In addition, $22,000 was spent on 800 quality inspections with a cost driver rate of $25, and $8,000 was spent on 200 customer-service cost driver units with a cost driver rate of $30. Sales for March were $350,000. Management has requested that you:

a. Prepare a traditional income statement.

b. Prepare an activity-based income statement.

c. Write a short report explaining why the activity-based income statement provides better information to managers. Use information for Halloway Corporation in examples.

CASES

44. **The Grape cola caper.**[8] Howard Rockness was worried. His company, Rockness Bottling, showed declining profits over the past several years despite an increase in revenues. With profits declining and revenues increasing, Rockness knew there must be a problem with costs.

Rockness sent an e-mail to his executive team under the subject heading, "How do we get Rockness Bottling back on track?" Meeting in Rockness's spacious office, the team began brainstorming solutions to the declining profits problems. Some members of the team wanted to add products. (These were marketing people.) Some wanted to fire the least efficient workers. (These were finance people.) Some wanted to empower the workers. (These people worked in the Human Resources Department.) And some people wanted to install a new computer system. (It should be obvious who these people were.)

Rockness listened patiently. When all participants had made their cases, Rockness said, "We made money when we were a smaller, simpler company. We have grown, added new product lines, and added new products to old product lines. Now we are going downhill. What's wrong with this picture?"

Rockness continued, "Here, look at this report. This is last month's report on the cola bottling line. What do you see here?" He handed copies of the report in Exhibit 3.10 to the people in his office.

Rockness asked, "Do you see any problems here? Should we drop any of these products? Should we reprice any of these products?" The room was silent for a moment, then everybody started talking at once. Nobody could see any problems based on the data in the report, but all made suggestions to Rockness ranging from "add another cola product" to "cut costs across the board" to "we need a new computer system so that managers can get this information more quickly." A not-so-patient Rockness stopped the discussion abruptly and adjourned the meeting.

He then turned to the quietest person in the room—his son, Rocky—and said, "I am suspicious of these cost data, Rocky. Here we are assigning indirect costs to these products

---

[8]This case was inspired by "The Classic Pen Company," Harvard Business School, Case 198–117.

EXHIBIT 3.10	Monthly Report on Cola Bottling Line				
	Diet	**Regular**	**Cherry**	**Grape**	**Total**
Sales	$75,000	$60,000	$13,950	$1,650	$150,600
Less:					
Materials	25,000	20,000	4,680	550	50,230
Direct labor	10,000	8,000	1,800	200	20,000
Fringe benefits on direct labor	4,000	3,200	720	80	8,000
Indirect costs @ 260% of direct labor	26,000	20,800	4,680	520	52,000
Gross margin	$10,000	$8,000	$2,070	$300	$20,370
Return on sales[a]	13.3%	13.3%	14.8%	18.2%	13.5%
Volume	50,000	40,000	9,000	1,000	100,000
Unit price	$1.50	$1.50	$1.55	$1.65	$1.506
Unit cost	1.30	1.30	1.32	1.35	1.302

[a]Return on sales before considering selling, general, and administrative expenses.

using a 260 percent rate. I really wonder whether that rate is accurate for all products. I want you to dig into the indirect cost data, figure out what drives those costs, and see whether you can give me more accurate cost numbers for these products."

"Will do, Dad."

Rocky first went to the accounting records to get a breakdown of indirect costs. Here is what he found:

Indirect labor	$20,000
Fringe benefits on indirect labor	8,000
Information technology	10,000
Machinery depreciation	8,000
Machinery maintenance	4,000
Energy	2,000
Total	$52,000

Then, he began a series of interviews with department heads to see how to assign these costs to cost pools. He found that one-half of indirect labor was for scheduling or for handling production runs, including purchasing, preparing the production run, releasing materials for the production run, and performing a first-time inspection of the run. Another 40 percent of indirect labor was used to set up machinery to produce a particular product. The time to set up the products varied, with the least time for cola and the most for Cherry and Grape. The remaining 10 percent of indirect labor was spent maintaining records for each of the four products, monitoring the supply of raw materials required for each product, and improving the production processes for each product.

Interviews with people in the Information Technology Department indicated that $10,000 was allocated to the cola bottling line. Eighty percent of this $10,000 information technology cost was for scheduling production runs. Twenty percent of the cost was for record keeping for each of the four products.

Fringe benefits were 40 percent of labor costs. The rest of the overhead was used to supply machine capacity of 10,000 hours of productive time.

Rocky then found the following cost driver volumes from interviews with production personnel.

- Setups: 560 person hours doing setups
- Production runs: 110 production runs
- Number of products: 4 products
- Machine-hour capacity: 10,000 hours

Diet cola used 200 setup hours, 40 production runs, and 5,000 machine-hours to produce 50,000 units. Regular cola used 60 setup hours, 30 production runs, and 4,000 machine-hours to produce 40,000 units. Cherry cola used 240 setup hours, 30 production runs, and 900 machine-hours to produce 9,000 units. Grape cola used 60 setup hours, 10 production runs, and 100 machine-hours to produce 1,000 units. Rocky learned that production people had difficulty getting the taste just right for the Cherry and Grape cola, so Cherry and Grape cola required more time per setup than either Diet or Regular cola did.

   a. Compute cost driver rates for each of the four cost drivers.

   b. Compute unit costs for each product: Diet, Regular, Cherry, and Grape colas.

   c. Prepare a report like the one in Exhibit 3.10 but with your revised indirect cost numbers for each product.

   d. Prepare a memorandum to (Howard) Rockness recommending what to do.

45. **The Grape cola caper: unused capacity.** Assume that all facts in Case **44** still hold except that the practical capacity of the machinery was 20,000 hours instead of 10,000 hours.

   a. Recompute the unit costs for each product: Diet, Regular, Cherry, and Grape colas.

   b. What is the cost of unused capacity? What do you recommend that Rockness Bottling do with this unused capacity?

   c. Now assume that Rockness considers producing a fifth product: Vanilla cola. Because Vanilla cola is in high demand in the Rockness Bottling's market, assume that it would use 10,000 hours of machine time to make 100,000 units. (Recall that the machine capacity in this case is 20,000 hours, while Diet, Regular, Cherry, and Grape consume only 10,000 hours.) Vanilla cola's per-unit costs would be identical to those of Diet cola except for the machine usage costs. What would be the cost of Vanilla cola? Calculate on a per-unit basis, then in total.

46. **Distortions caused by inappropriate overhead allocation base.**[9] Chocolate Bars, Inc. (CBI) manufactures creamy deluxe chocolate candy bars. The firm has developed three distinct products: Almond Dream, Krispy Krackle, and Creamy Crunch.

   CBI is profitable, but management is quite concerned about the profitability of each product and the product costing methods currently employed. In particular, management questions whether the overhead allocation base of direct labor-hours accurately reflects the costs incurred during the production process of each product.

   In reviewing cost reports with the marketing manager, cost accountant Steve Hoffman notices that Creamy Crunch appears exceptionally profitable while Almond Dream appears to be produced at a loss. This surprises both Steve and the manager, and after much discussion, they are convinced that the cost accounting system is at fault and that Almond Dream is performing very well at the current market price.

   Steve decides to hire Jean Sharpe, a management consultant, to study the firm's cost system over the next month and present her findings and recommendations to senior management. Her objective is to identify and demonstrate how the cost accounting system might be distorting the firm's product costs.

   Jean begins her study by gathering information and documenting the existing cost accounting system. It is rather simplistic, using a single overhead allocation base, direct labor-hours, to calculate and apply overhead rates to all products. The rate is calculated by summing variable and fixed overhead costs and then dividing the result by the number of direct labor-hours. The product cost is determined by multiplying the number of direct labor-hours required to manufacture the product by the overhead rate and adding this amount to the direct labor and direct material costs.

   CBI engages in two distinct production processes for each product. Process 1 is labor intensive, using a high proportion of direct materials and labor. Process 2 uses special packing equipment that wraps each individual candy bar and then packs it into a box of 24 bars. The boxes are then packaged into cases of six boxes. Special packing equipment is used on all three products and has a monthly capacity of 3,000 boxes, each containing 144 candy bars.

   To illustrate the source of the distortions to senior management, Jean collects the cost data for the three products, Almond Dream, Krispy Krackle, and Creamy Crunch (see Exhibit 3.11).

---

[9]Copyright Ed Deakin 1992. Used by permission.

EXHIBIT 3.11	CHOCOLATE BARS, INC. Cost Data		

	Almond Dream	Krispy Krackle	Creamy Crunch
Product Costs			
Labor-hours per unit	7	3	1
Total units produced	1,000	1,000	1,000
Material cost per unit	$ 8.00	$ 2.00	$9.00
Direct labor cost per unit	$42.00	$18.00	$6.00
Labor-hours per product	7,000	3,000	1,000
Total overhead = $69,500			
Total labor-hours = 11,000			
Direct labor costs per hour = $6.00			
Allocation rate per labor-hour = (a)			
Costs of Products			
Material cost per unit	$ 8.00	$ 2.00	$9.00
Direct labor cost per unit	42.00	18.00	6.00
Allocated overhead per unit (to be computed)	(b)	(c)	(d)
Product cost per unit	(e)	(f)	(g)

CBI recently adopted a general policy of discontinuing all products whose gross profit margin ([Gross margin/Selling price] × 100) percentages were less than 10 percent. By comparing the selling prices to the firm's costs and then calculating the gross margin percentages, Jean could determine which products, under the current cost system, should be dropped. The current selling prices of Almond Dream, Krispy Krackle, and Creamy Crunch are $85, $55, and $35 per case, respectively.

a. Complete Exhibit 3.11 under the current cost system and determine which product(s), if any, should be dropped.

b. What characteristic of the product that should be dropped makes it appear relatively unprofitable?

c. Calculate the gross profit margin percentage for the remaining products. Assume that CBI can sell all products it manufactures and that it will use the excess capacity from dropping a product to produce more of the most profitable product. If CBI maintains its current rule about dropping products, which additional products, if any, should CBI drop under the existing cost system? Overhead will remain $69,500 per month under all alternatives.

d. Recalculate the gross profit margin percentage for the remaining product(s) and ascertain whether any additional product(s) should be dropped.

e. Discuss the outcome and any recommendations you might make to management regarding the current cost system and decision policies.

47. **Multiple allocation bases.**[10] Refer to Case **46.** Jean Sharpe decides to gather additional data to identify the cause of overhead costs and figure out which products are most profitable.

Jean notices that $30,000 of the overhead originated from the equipment used. She decides to incorporate machine-hours into the overhead allocation base to see its effect on product profitability. Almond Dream requires two hours of machine time per unit, Krispy Krackle requires seven hours per unit, and Creamy Crunch requires six hours per unit. Additionally, Jean notices that the $15,000 per month spent to rent 10,000 square feet of factory space accounts for almost 22 percent of the overhead. Almond Dream is assigned 1,000 square feet, Krispy Krackle 4,000 square feet, and Creamy Crunch 5,000 square feet. Jean decides to incorporate this into the allocation base for the rental costs.

Because labor-hours are still an important cost driver for overhead, Jean decides that she should use labor-hours to allocate the remaining $24,500.

[10]Copyright Ed Deakin 1992. Used by permission.

CBI still plans to produce 1,000 cases each of Almond Dream, Krispy Krackle, and Creamy Crunch. Assume that CBI can sell all the products it manufactures and that it will use excess capacity, if it drops any products, to produce additional units of the most profitable product. Overhead will remain $69,500 per month under all alternatives.

a. Based on the additional data, determine the product cost and gross profit margin percentages of each product using the three allocation bases to determine the allocation assigned to each product.

b. Would management recommend dropping any of the products based on the criterion of dropping products with less than 10 percent gross profit margin?

c. Based on the recommendation you make in requirement **b.**, recalculate the allocations and profit margins to determine whether any of the remaining products should be dropped from the product line. If any additional products are dropped, substantiate the profitability of remaining products.

Recommended Cases for Chapter 3.

Activity-Based Management at Stream International. Harvard Business School Case No. 196134. This case presents various proposals based on an ABM analysis.

John Deere Component Works (A). Harvard Business School Case No. 187107. This is a classic case about the development of ABC at John Deere.

The Co-operative Bank. Harvard Business School Case No. 195196. This case applies ABC to a co-op financial institution that faces financial distress.

Indianapolis: Activity-based Costing of City Services (A). Harvard Business School Case No. 196115. This case is an application of ABC to a municipality.

Suggested Solutions to Even-Numbered Exercises

26. Activity-based costing.

a. and **b.** Cost per trip:

Activities	Float Trips (3-day)	Whitewater Trips (3-day)
Advertising	$ 215	$ 215
Permit to Use the River	30	50
Equipment Use	160 [= ($5 × 28) + $20]	264 [= ($8 × 28) + $40]
Insurance	75	127
Paying Guides	1,200 (= $300 × 4 guides)	1,600 (= $400 × 4 guides)
Food	1,680 (= $60 × 28)	1,680 (= $60 × 28)
Total	$3,360	$3,936

c. If the manager wants to cover her costs, she should charge $140 per customer for the three-day float trip ($3,360/24 paying customers) and $164 per customer for the three-day whitewater trip ($3,936/24 paying customers).

28. Activity-based costing in a nonmanufacturing environment.

a. *Using labor hours.*

	Commercial	Residential	Total
Revenue	$66,500[a]	$143,000[b]	$209,500
Direct Labor	31,500[c]	58,500[d]	90,000
Overhead	21,700[e]	40,300[f]	62,000
Profit	$13,300	$ 44,200	$ 57,500

[a]$66,500 = 3,500 hours × $19 per hour
[b]$143,000 = 6,500 hours × $22 per hour
[c]$31,500 = 3,500 hours × $9 per hour
[d]$58,500 = 6,500 hours × $9 per hour
[e]$21,700 = ($62,000/10,000 hours) × 3,500 hours
[f]$40,300 = ($62,000/10,000 hours) × 6,500 hours

b. *Using the three cost drivers.*

	Rate	Commercial	Residential	Total
Revenue[a]		$66,500	$143,000	$209,500
Direct Labor[a]		31,500	58,500	90,000
Overhead				
Office Supplies	$133.33[b]	2,000[e]	6,000	8,000
Equipment	3.00[c]	10,500[f]	7,500	18,000
Garden Supplies	0.36[d]	23,400[g]	12,600	36,000
Total Overhead		35,900	26,100	62,000
Profit		$ (900)	$ 58,400	$ 57,500

[a]From part **a.**
[b]$133.33 per client = $8,000/60 clients served
[c]$3.00 per hour = $18,000/6,000 equipment hours
[d]$0.36 per square yard = $36,000/100,000 square yards

[e]$2,000 = $133.33 × 15 commercial clients
[f]$10,500 = $3.00 × 3,500 equipment hours
[g]$23,400 = $0.36 × 65,000 square yards

c. Ms. Plantcare should reconsider reducing residential services in favor of the commercial business. From the results in part **b.**, commercial work is losing money, while the residential business is making a profit. The cost driver analysis shows that commercial work, which provides only about 30 percent of the revenues, incurs most of the equipment and garden supplies overhead costs. Allocating overhead costs based on direct labor, as in part **a.**, implies commercial business incurs about 35 percent of the total overhead whereas the cost driver analysis in part **b.** shows commercial business incurs more than one-half of the total overhead.

30. **ABC versus traditional costing.**

   a.

Account	Rate	Tax	Consulting	Total
Revenue		$80,000	$120,000	$200,000
Expenses				
Filing, scheduling, and data entry	$333.33[a]	24,000[d]	16,000	40,000
Supplies	18.00[b]	14,400[e]	21,600	36,000
Computer costs	12.50[c]	12,500[f]	7,500	20,000
Profit		$29,100	$ 74,900	$104,000

[a]$333.33 per client = $40,000/120 clients
[b]$18 per hour billed = $36,000/2,000 hours billed
[c]$12.50 per computer hour = $20,000/1,600 hours

[d]$24,000 = $333.33 per client × 72 clients
[e]$14,400 = $18 per hour × 800 hours
[f]$12,500 = $12.50 per computer hour × 1,000 hours

   b.

Account	Rate	Tax	Consulting	Total
Revenue		$80,000	$120,000	$200,000
Expenses	$48[a]	38,400[b]	57,600	96,000
Profit		$41,600	$ 62,400	$104,000

[a]2,000 hours billed = $200,000 revenue/$100 per hour. $48 per hour = ($40,000 + $36,000 + $20,000)/2,000 hours.
[b]$38,400 = $48 per labor-hour × 800 hours of labor

   c. The cost driver approach shows consulting generates 62 percent profit-to-revenue whereas tax generates only about 36 percent. Consulting appears to be more profitable. However, under labor-based costing in **b.** consulting work appears about equally profitable. Believing that to be the case, Vicki might erroneously concentrate more heavily in tax work.

32. Resources used versus resources supplied.

	Supplied − Used	= Unused
Energy	$3,300 − ($6 × 500)	= $300 (or $300/$6 = 50 hours)
Marketing	$6,000 − ($25 × 200)	= $1,000 (or $1,000/$25 = 40 sales calls)

Part Two

Managerial Decision Making

In the first chapter of this book, we described two major uses of managerial accounting information:

1. managerial decision making and
2. managerial planning, control, and performance evaluation.

This part of the book, Chapters 4 through 9, deals with *managerial decision making*. This use of accounting information addresses questions like the following:

- What costs will the University save if it cuts enrollment?
- What is the minimum price that a coffee shop should charge for a cup of espresso?
- Should a hospital build a new wing?
- Is it cheaper for Reebok to make shoes or to buy them from factories in Southeast Asia?

All these questions require decision-makers to look to the future. Managers attempt to estimate the future costs and benefits of alternatives. The data in the accounting records, of course, provide data about the past, but these data can help with information about the future.

chapter 4

Strategic Management of Costs, Quality, and Time

Learning Objectives

1. Distinguish between the traditional view of quality and the quality-based view.

2. Define quality according to the customer.

3. Compare the costs of quality control with the costs of failing to control quality.

4. Explain why firms make trade-offs in quality control costs and failure costs.

5. Describe the tools firms use to identify quality control problems.

6. Explain why just-in-time requires total quality management.

7. Explain why time is important in a competitive environment.

8. Explain how activity-based management can reduce customer response time.

9. Explain how traditional managerial accounting systems require modifications to support total quality management.

4

*T*his chapter includes topics that you might be surprised to find in a managerial accounting textbook, for example, quality control and response time to customers. In fact, managing costs, quality, and response time are closely related in organizations. To be competitive, managers must learn to improve the quality of their product while shortening delivery times while controlling costs. *Just* focusing on costs, as we did in Chapter 3, might lead managers to forgo quality improvement or fast delivery times. This chapter examines how managers can work to integrate effective cost control, high quality, and quick delivery.

Why Is Quality Important?

You might have decided never to deal with a company again because you experienced poor quality service or purchased defective merchandise. That company lost you as a customer. Managers know this can happen and want to provide quality products.

A recent survey asked chief financial officers to select the most important changes in their companies' strategies in recent years. The most frequently cited changes were to improve customer satisfaction and product quality. In today's competitive environment, improving quality has a high priority. To cite an extreme example, in one country that strives to be globally competitive, government officials executed several managers of a refrigerator plant for poor quality of products shipped.

Several prestigious, internationally renowned groups give awards to companies for quality. For example, in 1950 the Union of Japanese Scientists and Engineers established the Deming Prize, awarded annually to Japanese companies that focus on quality improvement. Congress created the Baldrige Quality Award in 1987 to recognize U.S. firms with outstanding records of quality improvement and quality management.

Many companies that focus on improving quality require their suppliers to comply with international standards for quality management called ISO 9000. These suppliers' ability to win contracts depends on their complying with ISO's standards. The ISO standards, which are developed by the International Organization for Standardization (http://www.iso9000.org) are guidelines for the design and development, production, final inspection and testing, installation, and servicing of products and processes. Guidelines also exist for assessing the quality of services. To register, a company must document its quality systems and go through a third-party audit of its manufacturing and customer service processes. The growing importance of ISO 9000 provides clear evidence of a global movement toward quality improvement.

Additional ISO standards called ISO 14000 focus on communicating the financial impact of environmental issues. These ISO 14000 standards promote the importance of accounting for environmental costs (such as hazardous waste disposal, waste treatment, and periodic environmental inspections), and communicating these costs to management and people outside the organization. Much like the ISO 9000 standards, the ISO 14000 standards call for external certification that firms must meet to comply with the demands of purchasing organizations. The new ISO standards force companies to take a hard look at the impact of their actions on the environment.

EXHIBIT 4.1	Traditional versus Quality-Based View

Traditional View	Quality-Based View
• *Quality increases costs.*	• *Quality decreases costs.*
The costs associated with producing quality products may be too high to be cost effective.	Reworking poor-quality parts and making warranty repairs cost more than avoiding these tasks in the first place.
• *Goods require inspection.*	• *Defect-free goods require no inspection.*
Product inspections ensure quality.	Establish quality before inspections.
• *Workers cause most defects.*	• *System causes most defects.*
Defects generally result from worker errors.	Defects generally result from production process deficiencies.
• *Require standards, quotas, goals.*	• *Eliminate standards, quotas, goals.*
Company must constantly strive to meet standards; once achieved, process improvements are no longer necessary.	The production process can always get better.
• *Buy from lowest-cost supplier.*	• *Buy on basis of lowest total cost, including costs of inspection, rework, and bad customer relations.*
Minimize cost of production materials.	Consider the consequences of purchasing poor-quality production materials (reworking, scrap, etc.)
• *Focus on short-run profits.*	• *Focus on long-run profits.*
Maximize short-run profits even if the result is poor quality.	High quality leads to loyal, repeat customers. This maximizes long-run profits.

Traditional versus Quality-Based View

The traditional view of quality assumes that improving quality always requires increasing costs. This view holds that firms can reduce total costs by producing lower-quality goods and tolerating some level of defective goods. The quality-based view holds that firms should always attempt to improve quality and that such attempts will succeed, without limit. The quality-based view also states that the firm should not wait for inspections of finished products to reveal defects and then rework defective goods. Instead, the firm must establish quality goals and procedures at the beginning of the process and aim for zero defects. Exhibit 4.1 compares the traditional view of managing quality with the newer quality-based view. The quality-based view holds that high quality pays for itself. Further, the quality-based view emphasizes constantly improving systems and processes.

Quality According to the Customer

Three success factors that firms focus on to meet customer requirements are service, quality, and cost. Some firms call these the *critical success factors*. Successful firms develop measures to assess performance based on their critical success factors.

Service

Service refers to all the product's features, both tangible and intangible. Tangible features include such qualities as performance and functionality. For example, a washing machine provides service by functioning to clean clothes. Intangible features include how salespeople treat customers. Service relates to the customer's expectations about the product's purchase and use. Organizations can develop a profile of the services that customers expect by asking them.

Quality

Quality refers to the organization's ability to deliver its service commitments. It means different things to different people. We define *quality* as keeping promises made to customers; quality exists when the product conforms to specifications. For example, a washing machine that provides service without breaking down shows quality.

EXHIBIT 4.2	Customer Satisfaction Measures

Factor	Examples of Performance Measures
Service	Number of customers
	Amount of purchases per customer
	Customer satisfaction surveys
Quality	Number of customer complaints per 1,000 orders filled
	Customer satisfaction surveys
Cost	Ratio of material in final product to material purchased
	Ratio of labor allowed for work done to total labor cost incurred
	Ratio of overhead allowed based on cost drivers used in production to total overhead cost incurred

Quality increases as customer satisfaction increases. If a customer expects a product life of three years and gets it, the quality is as high for that product as for another product the customer purchased expecting and getting a product life of five years.

Customers expect to get what they have paid for. High quality means rarely disappointing the customer. As organizations get better at keeping promises to customers, quality, by definition, increases.

A process that produces high-quality products usually has high efficiency ratings. When quality is poor, the firm must either rework products or destroy them, so the cost per unit of good output increases. As quality goes up, scrap and rework fall, reducing costs.

Cost

Lowering cost results from the organization's ability to use resources more efficiently to obtain its objectives. Achieving the same goals with fewer resources lowers costs and means that the organization is increasing efficiency.

Reducing costs is important because of the long-run relation between product cost and price. In the long run, the price of a product must exceed its costs or the organization will no longer make a profit on that product. All else equal, customers buy the product from the company with the lowest price, so maintaining a strong competitive advantage requires keeping costs low.

In choosing among all the products available to meet their needs, customers will buy the product that provides them with the preferred mix of quality, services, and price. If two products provide the same quality and services, the customer will choose the product with the lower price.

Customers value service, quality, and low costs; therefore, the organization must measure these attributes to manage the performance of its activities. Exhibit 4.2 presents some basic examples of performance measures. For example, companies routinely measure service and product quality with customer satisfaction surveys. Managers also look at the ratio of materials in the final product to materials purchased to measure cost performance. If the ratio is high, say, greater than 95 percent, that means the firm has wasted few materials, using materials in production efficiently. A ratio of 50 percent means that the firm wasted half of the materials purchased. This drives up the cost of the final product.

Quality Control

In responding to customers' expectations for quality, managers often ask: "How much will improved quality cost?" It turns out that improving quality is costly, but so is *failing* to improve quality.

The two costs of controlling and improving quality are prevention costs and appraisal costs:

1. Firms incur **prevention costs** to prevent defects in the products or services they produce. These include
   • Procurement inspection—Inspecting production materials upon delivery.
   • Processing control (inspection)—Inspecting the production process.
   • Design—Designing production processes to be less susceptible to quality problems.

- Quality training—Training employees to continually improve quality.
- Machine inspection—Ensuring machines operate properly within specifications.

2. Firms incur **appraisal costs** (also called **detection costs**) to detect individual units of products that do not conform to specifications. These include
   - End-process sampling—Inspecting a sample of finished goods to ensure quality.
   - Field testing—Testing products in use at the customer site.

Suppose you are the manager at Steve's Sushi, which makes sushi for delivery only. What costs of quality might Steve's incur? You may decide to inspect all ingredients before accepting delivery to ensure they meet specifications to help provide customers with the product they expect (prevention cost). You could also taste sample sushi for quality (appraisal cost).

Costs of Failing to Control and Improve Quality

Failing to control and improve quality also has costs: internal failure costs and external failure costs.

1. Firms incur **internal failure costs** when they detect nonconforming products and services *before* delivering them to customers. These include
   - Scrap—Materials wasted in the production process.
   - Rework—Correcting product defects in completed products.
   - Reinspection/retesting—Quality control testing after completing rework.
2. The firm incurs **external failure costs** when it detects nonconforming products and services *after* delivering them to customers. These include
   - Warranty repairs—Repairing defective products.
   - Product liability—Liability of a company resulting from product failure.
   - Marketing costs—Marketing necessary to improve company image tarnished from poor product quality.
   - Lost sales—Decrease in sales resulting from poor-quality products (i.e., customers will go to competitors).

As a manager at Steve's, you would probably throw away any prepared sushi that does not meet the strict quality standards established by Steve's (internal failure cost). You might worry about lost customers and lost future sales as a result of selling poor-quality sushi or failing to make delivery on time (external failure cost).

Trading Off Quality Control and Failure Costs

A quality-improvement program attempts to achieve zero defects while minimizing costs. Managers must make trade-offs among the four cost categories and must seek to reduce total costs of quality over time.

How would Steve's Sushi estimate the cost of quality? One employee examines ingredients as part of her daily duties. Assume the cost of ingredient inspections (a prevention cost) is $200 per week. The annual cost of quality for ingredient inspections totals $10,400. Assuming yearly sales of $1,000,000, this cost equates to 1.04 percent of sales.

Steve's must decide how much to spend on ingredient inspections and finished product inspections—more of one means less of the other. It may be cheaper to inspect the finished product rather than inspect all the ingredients delivered.

Managers often express costs of quality as a percent of sales. An example of a cost-of-quality report prepared for Steve's appears in Exhibit 4.3. Managers of Steve's Sushi would use the information to ascertain where they could reduce the overall cost of quality. For example, suppose "scrap" occurs because ingredients get too old. Improving inventory management could reduce scrap costs. "Customer complaints" is the cost of dealing with customers, including managerial time and reimbursement to irate customers. Perhaps the firm could reduce this cost by finding the source of customer complaints and dealing with the problem before it becomes a customer complaint.

Note in Exhibit 4.3 that external failure costs do not explicitly report the opportunity cost of lost business. Accounting-based cost-of-quality reports rarely do. Such reports often show the

EXHIBIT 4.3	STEVE'S SUSHI Cost of Quality Report Year Ended December 31		

Cost Categories		Costs of Quality	Percent of Sales (Sales = $1,000,000)
Prevention Costs			
Quality training	$ 5,800		
Materials (ingredients) inspection	10,400	$16,200	1.62%
Appraisal Costs			
End-of-process sampling		18,000	1.80
Internal Failure Costs			
Scrap		14,400	1.44
External Failure Costs			
Customer complaints		12,000	1.20
Total Costs of Quality		$60,600	6.06%

results of transactions but not the opportunity cost of lost business. To obtain qualitative measures of lost business, organizations often use customer satisfaction surveys and measures of repeat business.

Trends of Quality Costs

Companies that track quality costs and use the information to improve operations tend to see a long-run decline in total costs of quality. Exhibit 4.4 shows the general trend of quality costs as

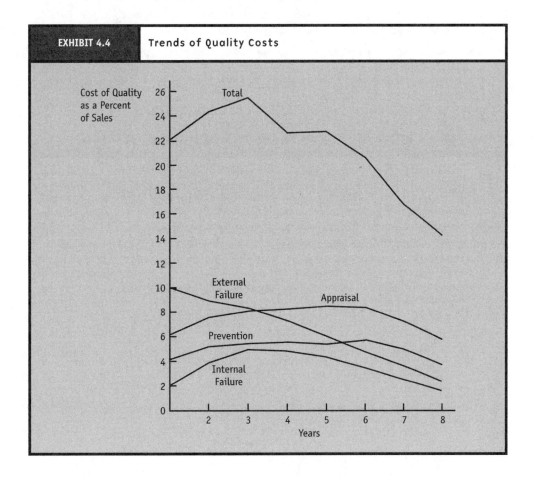

EXHIBIT 4.4	Trends of Quality Costs

firms improve processes within the business. Initially, management finds that external failure costs are relatively high; it takes action to detect (appraise) and prevent quality problems. As a result, appraisal and prevention costs rise in the first year or two. Management then will have reduced external failures, but internal failures rise in step with an increased effort to identify quality problems before they get to the customer. Exhibit 4.4 shows this movement in costs through Year 3 as appraisal, prevention, and internal failure costs rise while external failure costs decline. Accordingly, total costs of quality increase through Year 3.

Taking action to improve quality based on the cost-of-quality results should lead to improvements in the production process. Exhibit 4.4 shows the effect of these improvements in Years 4 through 8 as appraisal and prevention costs level off while internal and external failure costs decline. Ultimately, total costs of quality will decline as the firm optimizes the production process.

Problem 4.1 for Self-Study

Costs of quality. Carom Company makes skateboards. The following presents financial information for one year.

	Year 1
Sales	$500,000
Costs:	
Materials inspection	6,000
Scrap	8,000
Employee training	13,000
Returned goods	3,000
Finished goods inspection	15,000
Customer complaints	8,000

a. Classify the above items into prevention, appraisal, internal failure, or external failure costs.
b. Create a cost of quality report for Year 1 similar to Exhibit 4.3.

The solution to this self-study problem is at the end of the chapter on page 125.

Measuring the Cost of Quality in a Nonmanufacturing Setting

A high-tech company in the Midwest decided to measure the cost of internal failure in its order entry department, both to ascertain how much internal failure cost the company incurred and to identify where it should direct efforts to improve quality. The idea was to direct quality improvement efforts at high costs. Order entry starts immediately after the firm receives an order. Examples of internal failure include failure to obtain the customer's credit approval and payment terms for the order. The cost of internal failure, counting only the salary and fringe benefit costs for time spent correcting errors, exceeded 4 percent of the order entry department's annual budget, not including customer dissatisfaction from delayed fulfillment.

Collecting the cost information was not the goal but rather a first step in improving the order entry process. "The manager of the order entry department indicated that the changes would not have been pursued if cost information had not been presented."[1] However, the manager indicated that other information about the processes helped even more in making improvements. "Therefore, [cost of quality] information functioned as a catalyst to accelerate the improvement effort."[2]

---

[1]S. S. Kalagnanam and E. M. Matsumura, "Cost of Quality in an Order Entry Department," *Journal of Cost Management* (Fall 1995), 72.

[2]Ibid.

Does Quality Really Have a Cost?

As you may already understand, measuring increased customer satisfaction derived from additional spending on quality is difficult, as is measuring decreased customer satisfaction resulting from reduced quality costs. For example, if the firm reduces prevention costs, how do we measure lost sales resulting from this reduction? Conversely, how do we measure the increase in sales directly associated with an increase in prevention costs? Analysts cannot easily measure the specific change in sales under either scenario.

Companies throughout the world know about the "cost-of-quality" concept, but many believe that "quality is free." They believe that if they build quality into the product, the resulting benefits in customer satisfaction, reduced reworking and warranty costs, and other important factors will outweigh the costs of improving quality. Firms no longer focus on cost-benefit analyses in improving quality but on improving quality with the understanding that quality is free in the long run.

Those who subscribe to the quality-is-free concept believe that the only acceptable goal is zero defects. They attempt to improve the production process continuously by eliminating non–value-added activities and improving the process for all value-added activities. The result? Quality will improve, customers will be increasingly satisfied, and the cost of improving quality will pay for itself through increased sales and lower costs (leading to increased profit margins).

Although both approaches ("cost of quality" and "quality is free") strive for improved quality, the cost-of-quality approach assumes a cost-benefit trade-off when spending on quality improvement. The quality-is-free approach assumes the long-run benefits will always outweigh the costs of improving quality. One thing is certain: Quality is important to the success of any company.

Managerial Application

Firestone Blows It

"Good management—that is, management with real thought behind it—does not bother trying to make its way by trickery, for it knows that fundamental honesty is the keystone of the arch of business." Harvey Firestone, who founded Firestone Tire and Rubber Co. in 1900, spoke those words. "How unfortunate that Firestone is now associated with defective tires, SUV rollovers, denial of any problems and possible non-disclosure, even cover-up. . . . Because of poor-quality product and management's controversial handling of the crisis, the great company that Harvey Firestone dreamed of and built and its 100-year-old reputation is now tarnished."*

What happened at Firestone? Apparently, when management became aware of the tire tread separation, it was more concerned about the cost of fixing the problem, including recalls. In the end, because of poor product quality and bad management decisions, the company spent much more to clean up the mess than if the company had fixed the quality problem up front. Further, the company's reputation was tarnished and sales dropped. It has taken years for Firestone to rebuild the reputation for quality that it once had.

*M. Sheffert, "The High Cost of Low Ethics," *Financial Executive* 17, no. 6, 56.

Identifying Quality Problems

How does a company know whether it has a quality problem? Managers use several tools to identify quality problems. These tools—control charts, cause-and-effect analysis, and Pareto charts—provide signals about quality control.

A *signal* is information provided to a decision-maker. Tools used to identify quality control problems provide two types of signals. The first type, a **warning signal,** indicates something is wrong, in the same way that an increase in your body temperature signals a problem. The warning signal triggers an investigation to find the cause of the problem. The second type, a **diagnostic signal,** suggests the cause of the problem and perhaps a way to solve it.

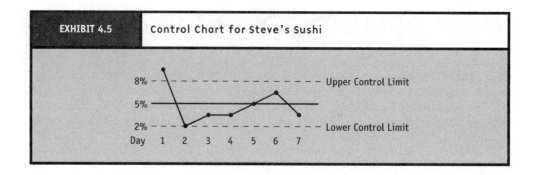

EXHIBIT 4.5   **Control Chart for Steve's Sushi**

Managers need both warning and diagnostic information about activities to identify problems that require attention. However, collecting most diagnostic information is expensive, so managers use warning signals to trigger this collection.

Control charts depict variation in a process and its behavior over time. They help managers distinguish between random or routine variations in quality and variations that they should investigate. They show the results of statistical process-control measures for a sample, batch, or some other unit. A specified level of variation may be acceptable, but deviation beyond some level is unacceptable.

Exhibit 4.5 shows an example of a control chart for the amount of scrap ingredients generated at Steve's Sushi each day. Management believes the scrap should range between 2 percent and 8 percent of total ingredients each day. If scrap is less than 2 percent, management worries that some poor-quality ingredients may be included in the sushi. If scrap exceeds 8 percent, management worries about wasting ingredients.

Pareto charts are graphs of skewed statistical distributions. Pareto charts get their name from Vilfredo Pareto, an Italian economist and sociologist who observed that approximately 20 percent of activities cause 80 percent of the problems. The Pareto distribution in statistics has this property.

Pareto charts are simple to construct, displaying the number of problems or defects as bars of varying lengths. Exhibit 4.6 shows an example of a Pareto chart for Steve's Sushi. Based on this Pareto chart, Steve's management can take actions to correct important problems. For example, management can train order-takers to triple check addresses, and it can develop a computer file of telephone numbers and addresses so that the address automatically appears when the customer places an order.

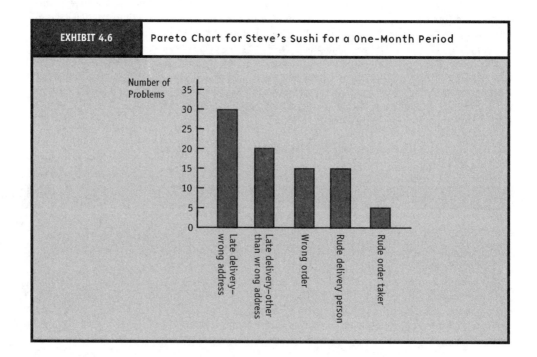

EXHIBIT 4.6   **Pareto Chart for Steve's Sushi for a One-Month Period**

Cause-and-effect analysis, which provides diagnostic signals, identifies potential causes of defects. To use this analysis, first define the effect (for example, wrong address for delivery) and then identify the causes of the problem. The potential causes fall into four categories: human factors, methods and design factors, machine-related factors, and materials/components factors. As management identifies the prevailing causes, it develops and implements corrective measures.

As companies increase their focus on quality in the face of intense global competition, quality control has become essential for any company wishing to compete effectively. Managers use control charts, Pareto charts, and cause-and-effect analysis to identify quality problems and find solutions.

Just-in-Time and Total Quality Management

The just-in-time philosophy closely relates to total quality management. The **just-in-time (JIT)** philosophy seeks to purchase or produce goods and services, or both, just when the company needs them. Companies that apply JIT find it not only reduces or even eliminates inventory carrying costs, it also requires high quality standards. The system must immediately correct processes or people making defective units because there is no place to send or hide defective units awaiting reworking or scrapping. Manufacturing managers find that JIT can prevent production problems from going undetected. But JIT also requires a smooth production flow without downtime to correct problems.

Think of JIT and quality requirements for a consulting job you have agreed to do. Suppose you schedule your time so that you have just enough time to complete a project before the job is due. If all goes as planned, you will finish inputting the report into your computer just in time.

Suppose your personal computer crashes in the midst of preparing the report. This presents a major problem for you because of the combination of your JIT philosophy and the defective hardware (or software) in your production process. JIT forces you to think through all the things that could go wrong and to correct them in advance of your project. If you use JIT for jobs, you need to be sure that your computer hardware and software are reliable (or that you have a backup) and that your means of delivering the product is reliable. In short, you need total quality management!

Companies using JIT find the following factors essential for success:

- **Total quality.** All employees must be committed to quality.
- **Smooth production flow.** Fluctuations in production lead to delays.
- **Purchasing quality materials.** Defective materials disrupt the production flow. Suppliers must be reliable, providing on-time deliveries of high-quality materials.
- **Well-trained, flexible workforce.** Workers must be well-trained and also be cross-trained to use various machines and work on various parts of the production process.
- **Short customer-response times.** Keeping the time to respond to customers short enables companies to respond quickly to customer needs.
- **Backlog of orders.** A company needs to have a backlog of orders to keep the production line moving with a JIT system. If there is no backlog, production will stop when the firm fills the last order.

Companies have found that JIT essentially requires total quality management. JIT eliminates buffers of inventory and time formerly used for solving problems with rework. With no buffers, processes must work right the first time. In practice, few companies have zero buffers, and processes do not always work perfectly the first time. Zero buffers and zero defects are, nevertheless, useful targets.

The Importance of Time in a Competitive Environment

Success in competitive markets increasingly demands shorter new-product development time and more rapid response to customers. Rapid response to customers can occur when work processes meet both quality and response goals. Response time improvement should be a major focus in quality improvement because it often drives simultaneous improvements in quality and productivity. Considering response time, quality, and customer satisfaction objectives together will provide benefits greater than the sum of the benefits from considering them separately.

Think of customer response time in two categories: (1) new-product development time and (2) operational measures of time.

New-Product Development Time

New-product development time refers to the period between a firm's first consideration of a product and its delivery to the customer. Firms that respond quickly to customer needs for new products may develop an advantage over competitors. For example, when Honda identified U.S. consumers' need for fuel-efficient cars, the firm's fast development capabilities gave it a competitive advantage for several years.

Not only does management want to shorten new-product development time, it wants to understand how quickly the company can recover its investment in a new product. **Break-even time (BET)** refers to time required before the firm recovers its investment in new-product development.

Analyzing break-even time requires identifying the differential cash flows related to the product—that is, the future cash inflows and outflows that result from introducing the new product. Overhead costs are irrelevant if adding a new product changes only the way the firm allocates overhead without changing the total cash outflow for overhead costs. Break-even time analysis should also include both positive and negative cash-flow effects that the new product may have on sales of existing products.

Break-even time works as follows:

1. Break-even time begins when management approves a project, rather than when cash outflows first occur.
2. Break-even time considers the time value of money by discounting all cash flows.[3]

Dallas Oil Company's research and development department presents a proposal for new product research that will require research, development, and design investments of $300 million (discounted cash flow). Sales will begin after three years and will generate an annual discounted net cash flow of $125 million starting in year four. Analysts compute the break-even time as follows:

$$\text{Break-even time} = \frac{\text{Investment}}{\text{Annual discounted cash flow}} + \frac{\text{Time period from approval of}}{\text{project until sales begin}}$$

$$= \frac{\$300 \text{ million}}{\$125 \text{ million}} + 3 \text{ years}$$

$$= 2.4 \text{ years} + 3 \text{ years}$$

$$= 5.4 \text{ years}$$

Although Hewlett-Packard and other successful companies use break-even time in assessing new-product development, this approach has several limitations:

1. Break-even time ignores all cash flows after the moment of break-even. Thus, managers using a decision criterion based on break-even time may reject projects with high profit potential in later years in favor of less-profitable projects with higher cash inflows in the early years. As a result, managers could pursue short-term projects with lower profits rather than long-term innovative projects that might contribute more to the long-run profitability of the company.
2. Break-even time does not consider strategic and nonfinancial reasons for product development. It focuses strictly on cash flows.
3. Break-even time varies greatly from one business to the next, depending on product life cycles and investment requirements. For example, an acceptable break-even time for the automobile industry may be five years, while the computer industry might demand a break-even time of two years or less.

---

[3]You do not need to know discounting techniques for this chapter. We discuss discounted cash flow techniques in Chapter 8.

Operational Measures of Time

Operational measures of time indicate the speed and reliability with which organizations supply products and services to customers. Companies generally use two operational measures of time: customer response time and on-time performance.

Customer response time (also called *delivery cycle time*) is the period that elapses from the moment a customer places an order for a product or requests service to the moment the firm delivers the product or service to the customer. That is, it is the time the firm takes to respond *to* the customer; it has nothing to do with any response *by* the customer. The quicker the response time, the more competitive the company. Several components of customer response time appear in Exhibit 4.7. Depending on the nature of the company, it may improve in any of the four areas—order receipt time, order waiting time, order manufacturing time, and order delivery time.

For example, Steve's order receipt time is minimal—an employee answers the phone and takes the order. The time elapsed between the order being taken at the phone and being passed to the preparation area varies—during rush times the order-taker cannot always transfer the order immediately as other calls are coming in. The firm could decrease this time by relocating the phone closer to the preparation area. It might decrease order preparation time by arranging the ingredients in a more efficient pattern. Order delivery time depends on distance to the customer, which Steve's cannot decrease, and efficient routing, which it can control.

On-time performance refers to situations in which the firm delivers the product or service at the time scheduled for delivery. For example, Steve's Sushi keeps records of the times at which it takes orders, promises delivery, and actually delivers the orders, and then measures performance as the ratio of on-time deliveries to total deliveries.

The Managerial Application "Reducing Delivery Time to Gain a Competitive Advantage" emphasizes the importance of reducing order delivery time for Ford Motor Company.

Managerial Application

Reducing Delivery Time to Gain a Competitive Advantage

Ford Motor Company (http://www.ford.com) recently began working with a United Parcel Service (http://www.ups.com) subsidiary to reduce the time it takes to ship vehicles from assembly plants to dealerships. Ford will take advantage of a high-tech information system developed by UPS that will allow car buyers to use a Web site to track a new vehicle through the delivery process. When implemented, the system is expected to reduce the time the average new vehicle is in transit, from 14 days to 8 days—nearly a 50 percent reduction in delivery time.

Frank Taylor, vice-president at Ford, says, "Speed is a competitive advantage. If you look at what happens in the total network today, it's lacking speed, and it's lacking precision, and the customer needs both. Speed and precision will drive cost down."

Source: Joseph Altman, Jr., "Ford, UPS Join Forces," *Associated Press,* February 3, 2000.

Using Activity-Based Management to Improve Customer Response Time

Exhibit 4.7 shows the chain of events from placement of a customer order to delivery. Reducing that time can increase output, increase customer satisfaction, and increase profits. For example, suppose a loan officer at a mortgage company can process 30 loan applications per month. If management can improve the process so that the loan officer can process 30 loan applications in one-half month, several good things happen. Customers are pleased that the bank processes their applications faster, and the cost per application goes down.

Activity-based management helps to reduce customer response time by identifying activities that consume the most resources, both in dollars and time. For example, mortgage loan applications can be delayed by the bank's need to verify credit, bank, employment, and other key information. Using computer networks substantially reduces such verification time.

Activity-based management also helps reduce customer response time by identifying non–value-added activities. For example, if you apply to graduate or law school, you will find

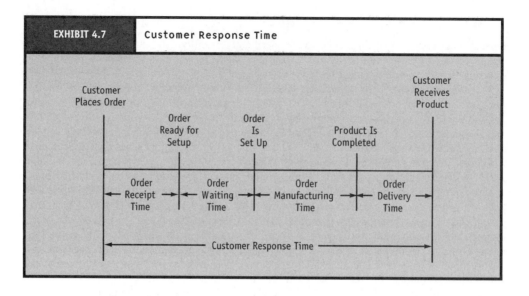

EXHIBIT 4.7   **Customer Response Time**

that many schools require transcripts from all the colleges you attended, even ones where you took only a few lower-division classes during the summer. Using activity-based management, admissions officers should consider whether obtaining these transcripts adds value to their universities. If not, why not eliminate this costly activity that slows down customer response time (i.e., the time it takes for the school to respond to the applicant)?

Many management accountants use customer response time to measure waste in the organization. Waiting, storing, moving, and inspecting add to customer response time and cost money. Eliminating the causes of long customer response times can reduce costs of non–value-added activities.

As we improve the efficiency of value-added activities and eliminate non–value-added activities, both customer response time and cost will fall. Of course, customers also value a quick response to their orders, which is another important benefit of short customer response time.

Using the Balanced Scorecard to Measure Performance

A **balanced scorecard** reports an integrated group of both financial and nonfinancial performance measures, which embody a company's vision and strategy. Management relays its strategies to employees in the form of performance measures they can use. One theme is: You manage what you measure. If employees see management measuring an item, they will likely focus on things that affect the item. For these performance measures to be effective, employees must have some control over actions affecting the measures.

Companies have used nonfinancial performance measures for decades. General Electric was well known for its use of nonfinancial performance measures in the 1950s and 1960s. The French approach, called *tableau de bord,* collects a variety of performance measures for "driving" the company much like the instrument panel of a car provides key indicators for driving the car. Like the *tableau de bord,* the balanced scorecard relies heavily on nonfinancial measures. Changes in these nonfinancial measures are likely lead indicators of changes in financial performance. For example, a decrease in delivery reliability will likely lead to lost customers and lower profits.

Exhibit 4.8 provides examples of measures that firms use for each of four typical sets of measures: financial, internal business process, learning and growth, and customer. The actual measures any company will use depend on the strategies it develops. Although financial measures tend to dominate most companies' performance assessments, proponents of the balanced scorecard believe that success in the other three areas will ultimately lead to improved financial performance and increased customer and employee satisfaction.

If a firm has developed its balanced scorecard effectively, the performance measures should bear a cause-and-effect relation to each other, ultimately leading to maximized profits and

---

EXHIBIT 4.8	Balanced Scorecard Performance Measure Examples

Financial
Return on investment
Economic value-added
Sales
Return on sales
Profit margin percentage

Internal Business Process
On-time deliveries as percentage of all deliveries
Customer response time
New-product development time
Defect-free units as percentage of completed units

Learning and Growth
Employee turnover
Hours of training per employee
Suggestions per employee

Customer
Number of customer complaints per week
Product returns as percentage of sales
Market share
Number of new customers

---

improved financial performance. If the firm improves one performance measure, improvement in other performance measures should follow. Focus on continual improvement requires that the firm take action to improve each performance measure, even on an incremental basis.

Traditional Managerial Accounting Systems Can Limit the Impact of Total Quality Management

A company that implements total quality management will likely find that its managerial accounting system reports little economic benefit from the initiative, even when it is successful. Managers often respond to the managerial accounting system instead of total quality management initiatives. For example, suppose total quality management requires expenditures on employee training that will improve quality but increase costs in the short run. Suppose further that the company records and reports cost increases but does not directly record quality improvements. Quality improvements result, for example, in less scrap in manufacturing and more repeat business from happier customers. The managerial system will likely report the lower scrap costs at the departmental level, but the profits from more sales likely never filter down to departmental level reports. If managers are evaluated solely "by the numbers," then they will choose not to increase cost to improve quality.

Effective implementation of total quality management requires five changes to traditional managerial accounting systems.[4]

1. The system should include information to help solve problems, like that coming from control charts and Pareto diagrams, not only financial information. Financial reports would indicate a decline in revenues, for example, but not indicate potential causes of the decline. Control charts could show an increase in customer complaints as a likely cause of the revenue decline. To carry this a step further, Pareto charts could list and rank the causes of increased customer complaints.

2. Line employees should collect the information and use it to get feedback and solve problems. Information should flow from the bottom up in the organization, not only from the top down. Traditional managerial accounting reports use data collected and aggregated by accountants, who present reports to managers, who then typically send some of the information down to the line employees. These reports may not mean much to line employees who are unfamiliar with accounting concepts.

---

[4]See C. Ittner and D. Larcker, "Total Quality Management and the Choice of Information and Reward Systems," *Journal of Accounting Research* 33 (Supplement), 1–34.

3. Information should be available quickly (e.g., daily) so that workers can get timely feedback. Frequent information accelerates identifying and correcting problems. Traditional managerial accounting systems often report weekly or monthly, which inhibits quick response to problems.

4. Information should be more detailed than that found in traditional managerial accounting systems. Instead of reporting only the cost of defects, for example, the information system should also report the types and causes of defects.

5. The firm should base rewards on quality and customer satisfaction measures of performance. This is the idea that "you get what you reward." If companies do not reward quality, they probably won't get it.

Summary

The following items correspond to the learning objectives presented at the beginning of the chapter.

1. **Distinguish between the traditional view of quality and the quality-based view.** Improving quality has become one of the most important strategic factors affecting companies today. Significant differences between the "traditional view" of quality and the emerging "quality-based view" relate to quality production, inspections, causes of defects, standards, purchasing, and customer focus. The primary difference is that the traditional view sees a trade-off between improved quality and lower costs, while the new view sees quality as free—it pays for itself.

2. **Define quality according to the customer.** The three critical success factors that relate to meeting customer requirements are service, quality, and cost. Service relates to the expectations the customer has about all the aspects, both tangible and intangible, of the product's purchase and use. Quality means giving the customer what the company promised; it is the degree to which the customer is satisfied. Cost is important because of the relation between product cost and price. In the long run, the price of a product must exceed its costs or the organization will no longer make a profit on that product.

3. **Compare the costs of quality control with the costs of failing to control quality.** The two costs of controlling quality are prevention costs (costs incurred to prevent defects in the products or services being produced) and appraisal costs (costs incurred to detect individual units of products that do not conform to specifications). The two costs of failing to control quality are internal failure costs (costs incurred when the firm discovers nonconforming products and services before delivery to customers) and external failure costs (costs incurred when the customers discover nonconforming products and services at delivery).

4. **Explain why firms make trade-offs in quality control costs and failure costs.** Trade-offs must be made in and among the four cost categories to reduce total costs of quality over time. The company works to achieve an allowable level of defective units.

5. **Describe the tools firms use to identify quality control problems.** Firms use control charts, cause-and-effect analyses, and Pareto charts to identify quality problems. Control charts show the results of statistical process-control measures for a sample, batch, or some other unit over time. The cause-and-effect analysis defines the effect and lists events that may be the causes of the problem. Pareto charts display the type and number of problems or defects in a product.

6. **Explain why just-in-time requires total quality management.** Companies using JIT find it requires high quality standards and smooth production flow with no downtime to correct problems.

7. **Explain why time is important in a competitive environment.** Success in competitive markets increasingly demands shorter new-product development time and more rapid response to customers. Response time improvements often drive simultaneous improvements in quality and productivity. Analysts focus on two aspects of time: (1) new-product development time, and (2) operational measures of time.

The shorter the new-product development time, the more likely the firm is to develop a competitive advantage. Operational measures of time indicate the speed and reliability with which organizations supply products and services to customers. The shorter the time to respond to customers, the more competitive the company.

8. **Explain how activity-based management can reduce customer response time.** Customer response time (the time a company spends responding to customer requests) can be reduced by identifying the activities that consume the most resources and making them more efficient, and by identifying non–value-added activities, which the company can eliminate.

9. **Explain how traditional managerial accounting systems require modifications to support total quality management.** First, systems should report information to aid in problem solving, not just financial information. Second, workers themselves should collect the information and use it to get feedback and solve problems. Third, the information should be available quickly so workers get timely feedback. Fourth, information should be more detailed than that found in traditional managerial accounting systems. Fifth, firms should base rewards on quality and customer satisfaction measures of performance.

Key Terms and Concepts

Appraisal costs (detection costs)	Just-in-time (JIT)
Balanced scorecard	New-product development time
Break-even time (BET)	On-time performance
Cause-and-effect analysis	Operational measures of time
Control charts	Pareto charts
Customer response time	Prevention costs
Diagnostic signal	Quality
External failure costs	Service
Internal failure costs	Warning signal

Solution to Self-Study Problem

SUGGESTED SOLUTION TO PROBLEM 4.1 FOR SELF-STUDY

a. and **b.**

CAROM COMPANY
Cost of Quality Report
For the Year Ended December 31

Cost Categories	Costs of Quality		Percent of Sales (Sales = $500,000)
Prevention Costs			
Materials inspection	$ 6,000		
Employee training	13,000	$19,000	3.8%
Appraisal Costs			
Finished goods inspection		15,000	3.0
Internal Failure Costs			
Scrap		8,000	1.6
External Failure Costs			
Returned goods	$ 3,000		
Customer complaints	8,000	11,000	2.2
Total Costs of Quality		$53,000	10.6%

REVIEW QUESTIONS

1. Review the meaning of the terms and concepts listed in Key Terms and Concepts.
2. What are the three factors that relate to meeting customer requirements?
3. How does the quality-based view differ from the traditional approach of managing quality by inspections?
4. The quality-based view focuses on higher *long-run* profits. Why?
5. What are the two costs of controlling quality?
6. What are the two costs of failing to control quality?

CRITICAL ANALYSIS AND DISCUSSION QUESTIONS

7. How does service relate to the expectations of the customer?
8. Can you think of any products in which one or several of the elements of service, quality, and cost are not important to the customer? Explain.
9. Review the Managerial Application "Reducing Delivery Time to Gain a Competitive Advantage." Why does Ford's management expect costs to decrease as a result of reducing delivery time?
10. For goods or services that you see produced, what are three examples of a warning signal and the related diagnostic signal you would use to identify quality problems?
11. How could control charts be used? Give two examples.
12. Why does just-in-time require total quality management?
13. Why is time important in a competitive environment?
14. Why would improvements in response time drive improvements in quality and productivity? Use a specific example.
15. Southwest Airlines has particularly emphasized the importance of on-time flight arrivals. Why?
16. Allegiance Insurance Company sends a questionnaire to policyholders who have filed a claim. The questionnaire asks these claimants whether they are satisfied with the way the claim has been handled. Why does Allegiance Insurance do this?
17. Course evaluations were introduced to college classrooms during the 1960s. Why do you think course evaluations were introduced?
18. Give two examples of cases in which you think managers would respond to the accounting system instead of to total quality management initiatives.

EXERCISES

Solutions to even-numbered exercises are at the end of the chapter after the problems.

19. **Quality according to the customer.** What are the three most important elements of service for each of the following products?
   a. Bridal gown
   b. Refrigerator
   c. English course at a university
   d. Cruise on a Princess ship
   e. Freshly squeezed orange juice
20. **Quality according to the customer.** What are the three most important elements of service for each of the following products?
   a. Cowboy boots
   b. Television
   c. Meal in a fine restaurant
   d. Student study guide for managerial accounting
   e. Dishwasher
21. **Quality according to the customer.** What are the three most important elements of service for each of the following products?
   a. Personal calculator
   b. MP3 player
   c. Money market account
   d. Taxicab ride through New York
   e. Sewing machine

22. **Costs of quality.** Cool Corporation manufactures freezers. The following table presents financial information for two years.

	Year 1	Year 2
Sales	$2,450,000	$2,200,000
Quality Costs:		
Quality training	16,500	18,800
Scrap	18,500	19,300
Production process design	198,000	130,000
Repair of returned goods	43,000	48,000
Rework (goods spoiled during production)	170,000	185,000
Preventive maintenance	135,000	95,000
Materials inspection	65,000	48,000
Finished product testing	94,000	124,000

   a. Classify the above costs into prevention, appraisal, internal failure, or external failure costs.
   b. Calculate the percentage of each prevention, appraisal, internal failure, and external failure cost to sales for Year 1 and Year 2.

23. **Costs of quality.** Scan It Company manufactures computer scanners. The following table presents financial information for two years.

	Year 1	Year 2
Sales	$2,000,000	$1,800,000
Quality Costs:		
Scrap	15,000	16,000
Repair of returned goods	35,000	40,000
Dealing with customer complaints	23,000	28,000
Rework (goods spoiled during production)	150,000	150,000
Materials inspection	55,000	40,000

   a. Classify the above items into prevention, appraisal, internal failure, or external failure costs.
   b. Calculate the percentage of each prevention, appraisal, internal failure, and external failure cost to sales for Year 1 and Year 2.

24. **Costs of quality.** Hien Corporation manufactures copy machines. The following table presents financial information for two years.

	Year 1	Year 2
Sales	$3,920,000	$3,520,000
Quality Costs:		
Scrap	28,800	30,100
Warranty repairs	70,000	75,000
Rework (goods spoiled during production)	272,000	195,000
Preventive maintenance	220,000	152,000
Materials inspection	105,000	75,000
Product testing	150,000	200,000

   a. Classify the above items into prevention, appraisal, internal failure, or external failure costs.
   b. Calculate the percentage of each prevention, appraisal, internal failure, and external failure cost to sales for Year 1 and Year 2.

25. **Reporting costs of quality.** Using the data in exercise **22,** prepare a cost of quality report for Year 1 and Year 2.

26. **Cost of quality report.** Using the data in exercise **23,** construct a cost of quality report for Year 1 and Year 2.

27. **Cost of quality report.** Using the data in exercise **24,** construct a cost of quality report for Year 1 and Year 2.

28. **Quality versus costs.** Assume Clearly Canadian has discovered a problem involving the mix of flavor to the seltzer water that costs the company $3,000 in waste and $2,500 in lost business per period. There are two alternative solutions. The first is to lease a new mix regulator at a cost of $4,000 per period. The new regulator would save Clearly Canadian $2,000 in waste and $2,000 in lost business. The second alternative is to hire an additional employee to manually monitor the existing regulator at a cost of $2,500 per period. This would save Clearly Canadian $1,500 in waste and $800 in lost business per period.

    Which alternative should Clearly Canadian choose?

29. **Quality versus costs.** Susan Scott has discovered a problem involving the mix of lye to the dry concrete mix that costs the company $20,000 in waste and $14,000 in lost business per period. There are two alternative solutions. The first is to lease a new mix regulator at a cost of $14,000 per period. The new regulator would save Susan $14,000 in waste and $8,000 in lost business. The second alternative is to hire an additional employee to manually monitor the existing regulator at a cost of $12,000 per period. This would save Susan $10,000 in waste and $8,000 in lost business per period.

    Which alternative should Susan choose?

30. **Quality versus costs.** Almaden Bicycles has discovered a problem involving the welding of bicycle frames that costs the company $3,000 in waste and $1,500 in lost business per period. There are two alternative solutions. The first is to lease a new automated welder at a cost of $3,500 per period. The new welder would save Almaden $1,500 in waste and $1,000 in lost business. The second alternative is to hire an additional employee to manually weld the frames at a cost of $3,000 per period. This would save Almaden $2,500 in waste and $1,000 in lost business per period.

    Which alternative should Almaden choose?

31. **Break-even time.** Domer Company's research and development department is presenting a proposal for new-product research. The new product will require research, development, and design investments of $500,000 (discounted cash flow). Sales will begin after two years and will generate an annual discounted net cash flow of $200,000 starting in year three.

    Calculate the break-even time for the new product.

PROBLEMS

32. **Quality improvement.** Custom Frames makes bicycle frames in two processes, tubing and welding. The tubing process has a capacity of 50,000 units per year; welding has a capacity of 75,000 units per year. Costs of quality information follow:

Design of product and process costs	$110,000
Inspection and testing costs	42,500
Scrap costs (all in the tubing dept.)	175,000

Demand is very strong. Custom Frames can sell whatever output it can produce at $50 per frame.

Custom Frames can start only 50,000 units into production in the tubing department because of capacity constraints on the tubing machines. Any defective units produced in the tubing department are scrapped. Of the 50,000 units started at the tubing operation, 5,000 units (10 percent) are scrapped. Scrap costs, based on total (fixed and variable) manufacturing costs incurred through the tubing operation, equal $35 per unit as follows:

Direct materials (variable)	$18
Direct manufacturing, setup, and materials handling labor (variable)	7
Depreciation, rent, and other overhead (fixed)	10
	$35

The good units from the tubing department are sent to the welding department. Variable manufacturing costs at the welding department are $3.50 per unit. There is no scrap in the welding department. Therefore, Custom Frame's total sales quantity equals the tubing department's output. Custom Frames incurs no other variable costs.

Custom Frame's designers have discovered that adding a different type of material to the existing direct materials would reduce scrap to zero, but it would increase the variable costs per unit in the tubing department by $2.00. Recall that only 50,000 units can be started each year.

a. What is the additional direct materials cost of implementing the new method?

b. What is the additional benefit to Custom Frames from using the new material and improving quality?

c. Should Custom Frames use the new materials?

d. What other nonfinancial and qualitative factors should Custom Frames consider in making the decision?

33. **Balanced scorecard.** A business executive says, "The financial perspective of the balanced scorecard indicates how the organization adds value to shareholders. I am involved with two organizations: a small business that is a partnership, so it has no shareholders, and a church that has no shareholders. While the balanced scorecard makes a lot of sense to me, the financial perspective is clearly irrelevant for these two organizations." How would you respond to this statement?

34. **Balanced scorecard.** John Donelan, the managing partner of the Dublin office of Donelan Consulting, saw the following diagram while visiting one of his clients, who owns a small manufacturing company.

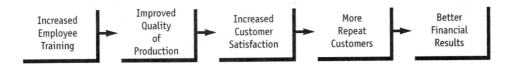

Mr. Donelan commented to his client that he could see how to link increased training to improved production quality and how that would result in better customer satisfaction with the products. "I wish I could apply this model to the consulting business, but I don't think it works in consulting. It works for you because you produce a tangible good. What we produce is advice, which is not very tangible."

Mr. Donelan's client responded, "You produce good advice, which helps us produce good products."

"Well, that's good," Mr. Donelan replied, "but it doesn't help me to apply your model to my business so that we can provide even better advice." (And be more profitable, he thought to himself.)

Using the balanced scorecard as a starting point, write a report to Mr. Donelan that explains how to implement the model shown in the diagram for Donelan Consulting. Be specific in stating how to measure the performance of each step in the sequence, from increased employee training to better financial results.

35. **Just-in-time and quality.** Individually or as a group, interview the manager of a retail (or wholesale) store such as a music store, an automobile parts store, or the parts department of an appliance dealership. Ask the manager how items are ordered to replace those sold. For example, do they order based on observing inventory levels, or do they place an order each time a customer buys an item? Do they appear to use just-in-time? If so, how important is total quality management to their just-in-time methods? Write a report to your instructor summarizing the results of your interview and analysis.

36. **Total quality management.** Individually or as a group, interview the manager of a fast-food restaurant. Ask the manager how quality of service is measured and used to evaluate the manager's performance. Write a report to your instructor summarizing the results of your interview.

37. **Quality control.** Eastsound operates daily round-trip flights between two cities using a fleet of three planes: the Viper, the Tiger, and the Eagle.

The budgeted quantity of fuel for each round trip is the average fuel usage, which over the past 12 months has been 150 gallons. Eastsound has set the upper control limit at 180 gallons and the lower control limit at 130 gallons. The operations manager received the following report for round-trip fuel usage for the period by the three planes.

Trip	Viper	Tiger	Eagle
1	156	155	146
2	141	141	156
3	146	144	167
4	152	161	156
5	156	138	183
6	161	170	177
7	167	149	189
8	186	159	171
9	173	152	176
10	179	140	185

a. Create quality control charts for round-trip fuel usage for each of the three planes for the period. What inferences can you draw from them?

b. Some managers propose that Eastsound present its quality control charts in monetary terms rather than in physical quantities (gallons). What are the advantages and disadvantages of using monetary fuel costs rather than gallons in the quality control charts?

38. **Break-even time.** Princeton Corporation's research and development department is presenting a proposal for new product research. The new product will require research, development, and design investments of $6 million (discounted cash flow). Sales will begin after four years and will generate an annual discounted net cash flow of $1.5 million starting in year three.

a. Calculate the break-even time for the new product.

b. What can Princeton Corporation do to reduce break-even time?

39. **Break-even time, working backward.** Tennessee Instruments is considering manufacturing the S-Card, a new type of sound card for personal computers. The new product development committee will not approve a new-product proposal if it has a break-even time of more than four years. If the project is approved, the investments to make the S-Card will begin on January 1, Year 1. The projected sales for the S-Card are $5 million each year for Years 1 through 4. The costs of manufacturing, distribution, marketing, and customer service are expected to be $3 million each year.

Assume that all cash flow numbers are discounted cash flows.

a. What is the maximum cash investment that the new product development committee will agree to fund for the S-Card project?

b. Why might Tennessee specify a policy not to fund new product proposals with an estimated breakeven of more than four years?

40. **Firestone blows it.** Using library and Web resources, research and write a report about how Firestone (now part of Bridgestone) has dealt with the quality problems that led to tire separation. Include anything you find about how Firestone/Bridgestone has changed its management decision-making process so that it can better deal with similar problems in the future.

41. **Johnson & Johnson's Tylenol recall.** Business ethicists give Johnson & Johnson high marks for the way it dealt with *potential* quality problems for Tylenol in the early 1980s. (These problems led to the difficult-to-remove caps on analgesic products.) Using library and Web resources, research and write a report about how Johnson & Johnson dealt with the problem. Indicate whether you think Johnson & Johnson would handle a similar problem in the same manner today.

42. **Customer response time.** The Clearsite Corporation, which manufactures custom motorcycle racing equipment and parts, engages in the following activities (not in sequence):

a. phone sales to retail motorcycle shops

b. processing mail-in orders

c. queuing orders to be shipped

d. sending each order to the appropriate production department at the end of each day

e. on-site salespeople calling in orders at the end of each day

f. shipping parts

g. quality inspection during production

   h. cataloging orders taken over the phone
   i. production department ordering special materials for ordered parts
   j. queuing orders in the production department
   k. setup of machinery to produce part according to specifications
   l. production of part
   m. on-site sales to retail motorcycle shops
   n. classifying orders according to process required for production
   o. quality inspection after production
   p. sending part to shipping department
   q. staffing on-site booths for taking orders at races
   r. holding parts until completion of other parts in order
   Categorize these activities according to the elements of customer response time shown in Exhibit 4.7. Write a short report to management detailing what you think could be done to reduce customer response time.

43. Quality problem. Based on your own experience, identify a quality problem (e.g., a bad meal in a restaurant). Indicate how the organization could deal with the problem. Include an assessment of the costs of preventing poor quality and the costs of failing to prevent poor quality in this case.

44. Arthur Andersen's quality problems. Using library and Web resources, research and write a report about the cause of Arthur Andersen & Co.'s apparent audit quality problems that included such well-known fiascos as Waste Management, Enron, and WorldCom.

RECOMMENDED ADDITIONAL CASES FOR CHAPTER 4.

  Romeo Engine Plant. Harvard Business School Case No. 197100. This case emphasizes team problem solving to achieve total quality management.

  Texas Instruments: Costs of Quality (A)(B). Harvard Business School Case No. 189021 (A case) and No. 189111 (B case). This is a classic case that has students analyze Texas Instruments' cost of quality program.

Suggested Solutions to Even-Numbered Exercises

20. Quality according to the customer. Answers will vary but may include:
   a. fit, design, and cost
   b. size, channel capacity, and cost
   c. taste, friendly waitpersons, and atmosphere
   d. accuracy, cost, and comprehensiveness
   e. cost, quietness, and energy efficiency

22. Costs of quality.
  a. and b.

	Year 1	%	Year 2	%
Sales	$2,450,000		$2,200,000	
Quality Costs:				
Prevention				
Preventive maintenance	135,000	5.5%	95,000	4.3%
Materials inspection	65,000	2.7	48,000	2.2
Quality training	16,500	0.7	18,800	0.9
Production process design	198,000	8.1	130,000	5.9
Appraisal				
Finished product testing	94,000	3.8	124,000	5.6
Internal Failure				
Scrap	18,500	0.8	19,300	0.9
Rework	170,000	6.9	185,000	8.4
External Failure				
Repair of returned goods	43,000	1.8	48,000	2.2

24. Costs of quality.
a. and b.

	Year 1	%	Year 2	%
Sales	$3,920,000		$3,520,000	
Quality Costs:				
Prevention				
Preventive maintenance	220,000	5.6%	152,000	4.3%
Materials inspection	105,000	2.7	75,000	2.1
Appraisal				
Product testing	150,000	3.8	200,000	5.7
Internal Failure				
Scrap	28,800	0.7	30,100	0.9
Rework	272,000	6.9	195,000	5.5
External Failure				
Warranty repairs	70,000	1.8	75,000	2.1

26. Cost of quality report.

SCAN IT COMPANY
Cost of Quality Report

	Year 1	%	Year 2	%
Sales	$2,000,000		$1,800,000	
Costs of Quality:				
Prevention				
Materials inspection	55,000		40,000	
Total prevention costs	$ 55,000	2.8%	$ 40,000	2.2%
Internal Failure				
Scrap	15,000		16,000	
Rework	150,000		150,000	
Total internal failure costs	$ 165,000	8.3	$ 166,000	9.2
External Failure				
Repair of returned goods	35,000		40,000	
Dealing with customer complaints	23,000		28,000	
Total external failure costs	$ 58,000	2.9	$ 68,000	3.8
Total Costs of Quality	$ 278,000	13.9%*	$ 274,000	15.2%

*Difference due to rounding.

28. Quality versus costs.

	Present	New Mix Regulator	Additional Employee
Costs:			
Waste	$3,000	$1,000	$1,500
Lost business	2,500	500	1,700
Lease		4,000	
Wages			2,500
Total	$5,500	$5,500	$5,700

Clearly Canadian is indifferent between leasing the new mix regulator or not because the costs would be the same. Clearly Canadian will not hire another employee because this would increase total quality costs. Of course, there might be non-financial factors not specified in this exercise that might affect the decision.

30. Quality versus costs.

	Present	New Welder	Additional Employee
Costs:			
Waste	$3,000	$1,500	$ 500
Lost business	1,500	500	500
Lease		3,500	
Wages			3,000
Total	$4,500	$5,500	$4,000

Almaden should hire an additional employee, because this is the alternative that incurs the least total quality costs. Of course, there might be non-financial factors not specified in this exercise that might affect the decision.

chapter 5

Cost Drivers and Cost Behavior

Learning Objectives

1. Distinguish between variable costs and fixed costs and between short run and long run, and define the relevant range.

2. Identify capacity costs, committed costs, and discretionary costs.

3. Describe the nature of the various cost behavior patterns.

4. Describe how managers use cost behavior patterns.

5. Explain how to use historical data to estimate costs.

6. Describe how analysts estimate cost behavior using regression, account analysis, and engineering methods.

7. Explain the costs, benefits, and weaknesses of the various cost estimation methods.

8. Identify the derivation of learning curves. (Appendix 5.1).

9. Interpret the results of regression analyses. (Appendix 5.2).

5

The first part of this chapter discusses methods of classifying costs into fixed and variable components. Some costs, such as rent, usually have only a fixed portion, whereas others, such as direct materials, usually have only a variable portion. Many costs, however, have both fixed and variable components. For example, delivery trucks incur both fixed costs per year (e.g., license fees) and variable costs per mile.

We express the total costs of an item as follows:

$$\begin{matrix} \text{Total} \\ \text{Cost} \\ \text{during} \\ \text{Period} \end{matrix} = \begin{matrix} \text{Fixed} \\ \text{Cost} \\ \text{during} \\ \text{Period} \end{matrix} + \left(\begin{matrix} \text{Variable} \\ \text{Cost per} \\ \text{Unit of} \\ \text{Activity} \end{matrix} \times \begin{matrix} \text{Units of} \\ \text{Activity} \\ \text{during} \\ \text{Period} \end{matrix} \right)$$

or, using briefer notation:

$$TC = F + VX,$$

where TC refers to the total cost for a time period, F refers to the total fixed cost for the time period, V refers to the variable cost per unit, and X refers to the number of units of activity for the time period. Nearly all managerial decisions deal with choices among different activity levels; hence, the manager must estimate which costs will vary with the activity and by how much.

Cost estimation works like this: Suppose management expects a temporary reduction in customers at a particular restaurant during the summer. Some costs will not decline. Other costs will. Management would estimate the relation between costs and meals served to ascertain how a decrease in meals served might affect total costs.

Because many costs do not fall neatly into fixed and variable categories, managers use statistical and other techniques for estimating **cost behavior.** These techniques help managers identify underlying cost behavior patterns.

The Nature of Fixed and Variable Costs

Short Run versus Long Run

Variable costs, also known as **engineered costs,** change in total as the level of activity changes. An engineered cost bears a definitive physical relationship to the activity measure. Direct materials cost is an engineered cost. It is impossible to manufacture more products without incurring greater materials costs.

Fixed costs do not change in total with changes in activity levels. During short time periods, say, one month, the firm operates with a relatively fixed sales force, managerial staff, and set of production facilities. Consequently, many of its costs are fixed. Over long time spans, no costs are fixed because staff size can be changed and facilities sold or expanded.

This fact provides the basis for the distinction drawn in economics between the long run and the short run and in accounting between fixed costs and variable costs. To the economist, the **short run** is a time

EXHIBIT 5.1	Long-Run versus Short-Run Nature of Costs

Why is there a gap between *D* and *E* in the diagram on the left? (Answer: To reflect the increase in fixed costs required to expand capacity from the 10,000-to-20,000-units range to the 20,000-to-30,000-units range.)

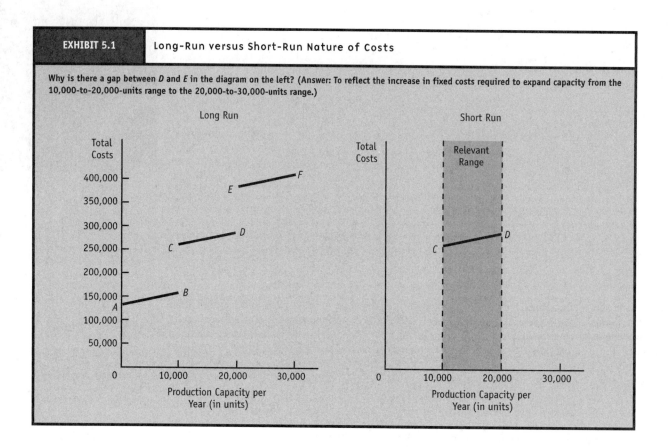

period long enough to allow management to change the level of production or other activity within the constraints of current total production capacity. Management can change total production capacity only in the **long run.**

To the manager, total costs that vary with activity levels in the short run are variable costs; costs that will not vary in the short run, no matter what the level of activity, are fixed costs. The accounting concepts of variable and fixed costs are, then, short-run concepts. They apply to a particular period of time and relate to a particular level of production capacity.

Consider, for example, the total costs (both variable and fixed) for the firm appearing in Exhibit 5.1. The graph on the left shows the total costs in the long run. If the production capacity of the firm is 10,000 units per year, total costs will vary as on line *AB*. If the firm acquires new production facilities to increase capacity to 20,000 units, total costs will be as on line *CD*. An increase in capacity to 30,000 units will increase the total costs as on line *EF*. These shifts in capacity represent long-run commitments. Of course, some overlap will occur; production of 10,000 units per year could be at the high-volume end of the *AB* line or at the low-volume end of the *CD* line.

In the short run, a firm has only one capacity level: namely, the capacity of the existing plant. The total costs in the short run appear at the right side of the graph in Exhibit 5.1 on the assumption that the capacity of the existing plant is 20,000 units per year. Note that line *CD* represents costs for the production level of approximately 10,000 units to 20,000 units only. Production levels outside this range require a different plant capacity, and the total cost line will shift up or down.

Relevant Range

Managers frequently use the notion of relevant range in estimating cost behavior. The **relevant range** is the range of activity over which the firm expects a set of cost behaviors to be consistent. For example, if the relevant range of activity shown in Exhibit 5.1 is between 10,000 and 20,000 units, the firm assumes that certain costs are fixed while others are variable within that range. The firm would not necessarily assume that costs fixed within the relevant range will stay fixed outside the relevant range. As Exhibit 5.1 shows, for example, costs step up from point *D* to point *E* when production increases from the right side of the 10,000-to-20,000 range to the left side of the 20,000-to-30,000 range.

Estimates of variable and fixed costs apply only if the contemplated level of activity lies within the relevant range. If the firm considers an alternative requiring a level of activity outside the relevant range, then the breakdown of costs into fixed and variable components requires a new computation.

Example   Exotic Eats, a profitable restaurant, features a menu of Far Eastern dishes. Because it is located in the financial district of a city, management keeps it open only from 11:00 AM until 2:00 PM, Monday through Friday, for lunch business. Although the restaurant can serve a maximum of 210 customers per day, it has been serving a daily average of 200 customers. The daily costs and revenues of operations follow:

Revenues		$1,000
Less Variable Costs	$400	
Less Fixed Costs	350	750
Operating Profits		$ 250

Based on this information, the restaurant's management considers doubling capacity. Cost behavior for doubling capacity is outside the relevant range. Initial calculations indicate that the number of customers would double. Management wants to know whether operating profits would double. A simple extrapolation indicates that the operating profits would *more* than double, as Exhibit 5.2 shows, because total revenues would double whereas total costs would not. Using Exhibit 5.2, what would profit be at 300 customers? (Answer: $550.)

This simple extrapolation assumes that the total revenues and total variable costs double to $2,000 and $800, respectively, whereas fixed costs remain constant at $350. When capacity changes, fixed costs are likely to increase as well.

The management of Exotic Eats realizes that with additional capacity and more customers, it must hire additional cooks; occupancy costs (e.g., space rental) would increase; and other fixed costs would increase. The projected new volume is outside the relevant range of volume over which the originally assumed cost behavior pattern would hold. Therefore, the original cost behavior pattern shown in Exhibit 5.2 would be invalid.

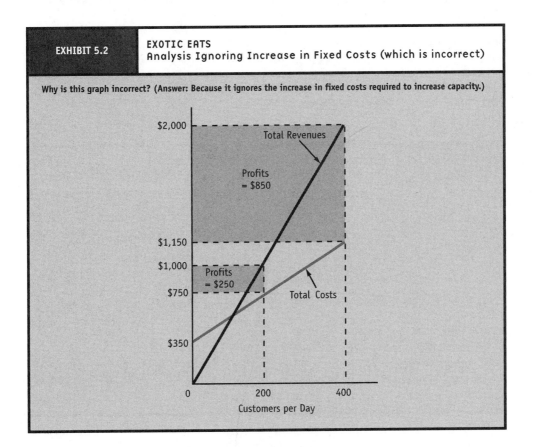

EXHIBIT 5.2

EXOTIC EATS
Analysis Ignoring Increase in Fixed Costs (which is incorrect)

Why is this graph incorrect? (Answer: Because it ignores the increase in fixed costs required to increase capacity.)

EXHIBIT 5.3	EXOTIC EATS Increase in Fixed Costs Accompanying Expansion

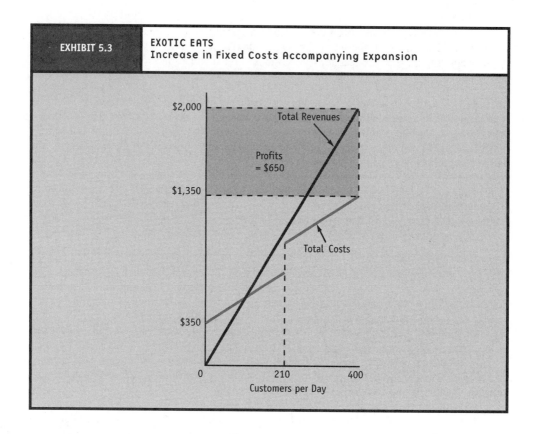

A revised, more realistic analysis of the cost behavior pattern estimates the unit variable cost of $2 per customer to be the same as before but estimates fixed costs to increase from $350 to $550 per day. Fixed costs would not double because some fixed costs would not increase (e.g., many of the administrative costs).

The revised cost behavior pattern appears in Exhibit 5.3. Look at Exhibit 5.3. What would profit be at 400 customers? (Answer: $650.) Exhibit 5.4 compares profits at the original activity level, 200 customers per day, with the projected increase to 400 per day. Management would use these cost estimates to decide whether to increase capacity. These decisions usually require discounted cash flow analysis in addition to the estimated change in cash flow discussed here. (Discounted cash flow analysis is discussed in Chapter 8.)

EXHIBIT 5.4	EXOTIC EATS Comparison of Profits at Original and Projected Activity Levels

	Status Quo: 200 Customers per Day	Alternative: 400 Customers per Day	
		Incorrect Assumption That Fixed Costs Are Constant	Correct Assumption That Fixed Costs Will Change
Revenues	$1,000	$2,000	$2,000
Less Variable Costs	400	800	800
Total Contribution Margin	$ 600	$1,200	$1,200
Less Fixed Costs	350	350	550
Operating Profits	$ 250	$ 850	$ 650

Types of Fixed Costs

In practice, where the short run stops and the long run starts is fuzzy. The managerial accountant divides fixed cost into subclassifications to explain the relation between particular types of fixed costs and current capacity.

Capacity Costs

Certain fixed costs, called **capacity costs,** provide a firm with the capacity to produce or sell or both. A firm incurs some capacity costs, known as **committed costs,** even if it temporarily shuts down operations. Committed costs result from an organization's ownership of facilities and its basic organizational structure. Examples include property taxes and some executive salaries. Other capacity costs cease if the firm's operations shut down but continue in fixed amounts if the firm carries out operations at any level. A firm can lay off a production worker if production ceases. Alternately, the wages of the security force is a committed cost because the security force must guard the plant no matter how little or how much activity goes on inside.

Discretionary Costs

Production or selling capacity requires fixed capacity costs. Companies also incur fixed **discretionary costs.** These costs are also called **programmed costs** or **managed costs.** Examples include research, development, and advertising to generate new business.

These costs are discretionary because the firm need not incur them in the short run to operate the business. They are, however, usually essential for achieving long-run goals. Imagine the long-run impact on Procter & Gamble of eliminating media advertising. Or consider the effects if Merck were to drop research and development. Although these companies would survive for a time, after a while they would lose their competitive edge and would most likely be less profitable companies.

Other Cost Behavior Patterns

We have made the following distinction between fixed and variable costs: Total fixed costs remain constant for a period of time (the short run) over a range of activity level (the relevant range); total variable costs change as the volume of activity changes within the relevant range.

Curved Variable Costs

The straightforward linear fixed and variable cost behavior patterns, shown in Exhibits 5.2 and 5.3, do not always arise in practice. For example, researchers of health-care institutions routinely find curvilinear cost behavior patterns.[1] Total variable cost behavior may be curvilinear, as Exhibit 5.5 shows with three different examples of variable cost behavior. **Curvilinear variable cost** functions indicate that the costs vary with the volume of activity, but not in constant proportion. For example, as volume increases, the unit prices of some inputs, such as materials and power, may decrease due to volume discounts, exhibiting decreasing marginal costs. The **marginal cost** is the cost of producing the next unit. Another example of curved cost behavior occurs when employees become more efficient with experience, as discussed in the following section.

Learning Curves

Systematic learning from experience frequently occurs, as when a firm initiates new products or processes or hires a group of new employees. As employees' experience increases, productivity improves and costs per unit decrease. Many high-tech companies, such as National Semiconductor, NVIDIA, and Sun Microsystems, experience learning effects on costs. NVIDIA expects learning to reduce its unit costs for producing graphics chips for the Microsoft Xbox. These

---

[1]See E. Noreen and N. Soderstrom, "The Accuracy of Proportional Cost Models: Evidence from Hospital Departments," *Review of Accounting Studies* 2, no. 1.

EXHIBIT 5.5	Examples of Curvilinear Total Variable Cost Behavior

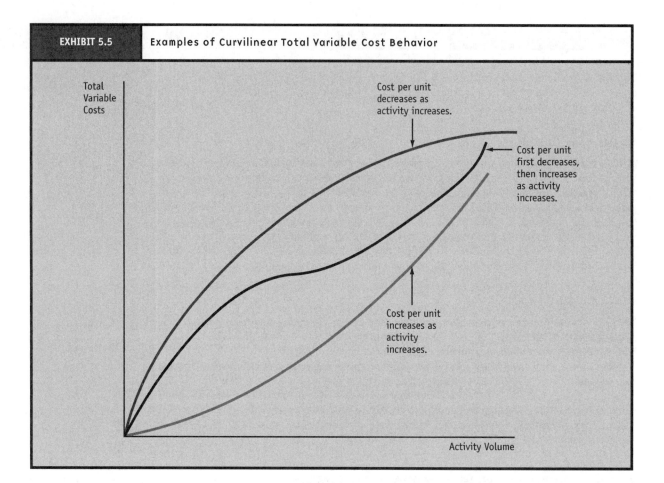

companies compete by learning quickly so that they can become low-cost producers and capture significant market share.

The effect of learning is often expressed as a **learning curve** (also known as an **experience curve**). The learning curve function shows how the amount of time required to perform a task goes down, per unit, as the number of units increases (see Exhibit 5.6).

Accountants model the nature of the learning phenomenon as a constant percentage reduction in the *average* direct labor input time required per unit as the *cumulative output* doubles. For example, assume a time reduction rate of 20 percent, that is, an 80 percent cumulative learning curve. Assume also that the first unit takes 125 hours. The *average* for two units should be 100 hours per unit (= 0.80 × 125 hours), a total of 200 hours for both units. Four units would take an average of 80 hours each (= 0.80 × 100 hours), or a total of 320 hours. Appendix 5.1 presents the mathematical formula for the learning curve.

The results in this example follow:

Quantity		Time in Hours	
Unit	Cumulative Units	Average per Unit	Cumulative
First	1	125	125
Second	2	100 (= 0.80 × 125)	200
Fourth	4	80 (= 0.80 × 100)	320
Eighth	8	64 (= 0.80 × 80)	512

Exhibit 5.6 shows the relation between volume and *average* labor hours in graph A. Note that four units require 80 hours per unit, on average. Eight units require only 64 hours per unit, on average. The relation between volume and *total* labor hours appears in graph B. The relation

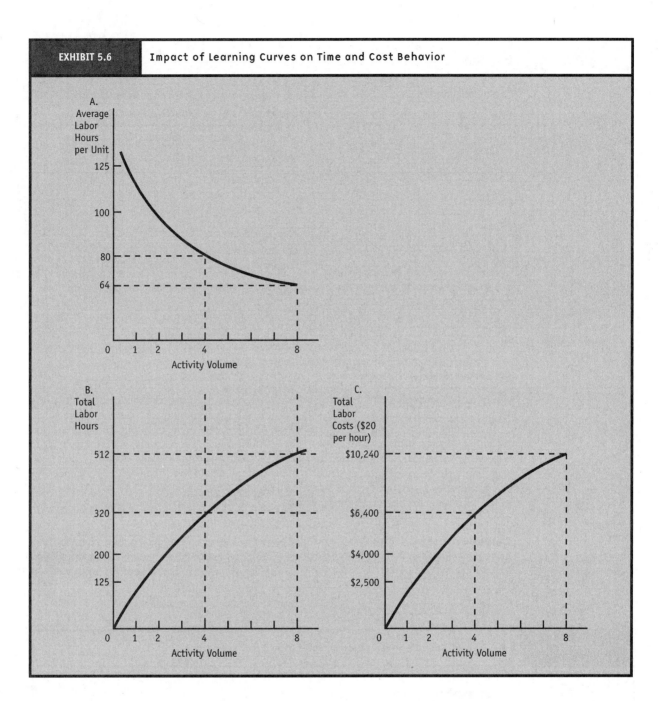

EXHIBIT 5.6   Impact of Learning Curves on Time and Cost Behavior

between volume and total labor costs appears in graph C. The labor cost is $20 per hour. Looking at Exhibit 5.6, what is the total labor cost of eight units? (Answer: $10,240.)

The possible consequences of learning for costs can affect decision making and performance evaluation. Suppose that you are trying to decide whether to make a new product that would be subject to the 80 percent cumulative learning curve. Using the data in Exhibit 5.6, if you assumed that the product would require labor costs of $2,500 (= $20 × 125 hours) per unit for the first eight units made, you would seriously overstate the costs for the eight units. If you used the $2,500 per unit as a standard for judging actual cost performance, you would set too loose a standard for all but the first unit.

To what costs do learning curves apply? The learning phenomenon results in savings of time; any labor-related costs could be affected. The learning phenomenon can also affect material costs, as in the semiconductor industry, if the cost of wasted materials decreases as experience increases.

Problem 5.1 for Self-Study

Computing cost decreases because of learning.   Bounce Electronics recently recorded the following costs, which are subject to a 75 percent cumulative learning effect.

Cumulative Number of Units Produced	Average Labor Cost per Unit	Total Labor Costs
1	$1,333.33	$1,333.33
2	1,000.00	2,000.00
4	?	?
8	?	?
16	?	?

Complete the chart by filling in the cost amounts for volumes 4, 8, and 16 units.

The solution to this self-study problem is at the end of the chapter on page 157.

Semivariable Costs

The term **semivariable costs** refers to costs that have both fixed and variable components, such as those represented by lines *CD, CE,* and *CF* in Exhibit 5.7, Graph A. Repair and maintenance costs or utility costs exemplify semivariable cost behavior, like line *CE.* Minimum repair service capability within a plant requires a fixed cost (*C*) for providing service and an extra charge for uses of the service above some fixed amount. If the charge per unit of, say, electricity decreases at certain stages as consumption increases, the cost curve would look like line *CF.* If the per-unit charge increases at certain stages as usage increases, the costs would look like line *CD.* The term *mixed costs* often denotes semivariable costs.

Example   Assume you purchase a cellular phone and service. You decide on a plan that provides you with up to 200 minutes of airtime for a flat rate of $39.99 a month. You will pay this rate for the service even if you use only 20 minutes of airtime. The charge for any calls you

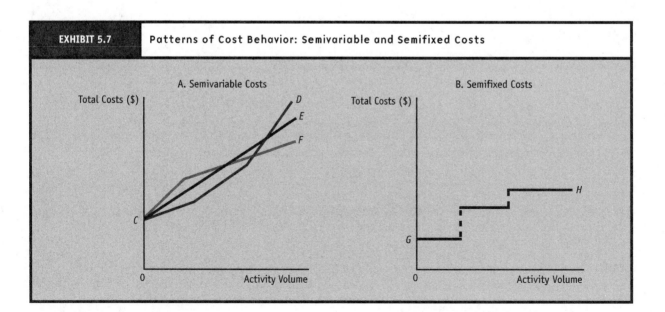

| EXHIBIT 5.7 | Patterns of Cost Behavior: Semivariable and Semifixed Costs |

make in excess of 200 minutes is $0.15 per minute. The semivariable cost pattern would be as follows:

Minutes of Airtime Used		Charge
0–200		$39.99
201	[$39.99 + 0.15(201 − 200)]	40.14
202	[$39.99 + 0.15(202 − 200)]	40.29
203	[$39.99 + 0.15(203 − 200)]	40.44

The cost would appear in a graph as follows:

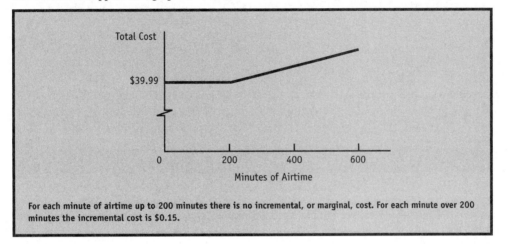

For each minute of airtime up to 200 minutes there is no incremental, or marginal, cost. For each minute over 200 minutes the incremental cost is $0.15.

Semifixed Costs

The term **semifixed costs** or **step costs,** refers to costs that increase in steps, such as those shown by the broken line *GH* in Exhibit 5.7, Graph B. Accountants sometimes describe semifixed costs as *step fixed costs*. If a quality-control inspector can examine 1,000 units per day, inspection costs will be semifixed, with a step up for every 1,000 units per day.

Example   Radio House hires one quality-control inspector for each 25,000 toy robots produced per month. The annual salary is $30,000 per inspector. Production has been 65,000 units, so the company has three inspectors. If a special order increases volume from 65,000 to 75,000 units, the firm need hire no additional inspectors. If the special order increases production to a level greater than 75,000 units (say, to 85,000 units), the firm must hire a fourth inspector.

The distinction between fixed and semifixed costs is subtle. A change in fixed costs (other than for inflation or other price changes) usually involves a change in long-term assets, whereas a change in semifixed costs often does not.

Simplifying Cost Analyses

Costs vary with the volume of activity in several ways. Some costs do not vary in the short run over a relevant range—they are *fixed*. Others vary with volume—that is, they are *variable*. Some costs, neither strictly fixed nor strictly variable, contain both components.

To simplify the analysis of cost behavior, decision makers usually assume that costs are either strictly fixed or linearly variable. They do this because the incremental cost of analyzing the more complex data often exceeds the incremental benefits of doing so. The assumed simple linear variable-fixed cost behavior usually sufficiently approximates the reality for decision-making purposes. Many cases require estimates and analysis of cost behavior with greater precision, however.

Problem 5.2 for Self-Study

Sketching cost graphs.   Draw graphs for the following cost behaviors.

a. Costs of direct materials used in producing a firm's products.

b. Wages of delivery truck drivers. The firm requires one driver, on average, for each $1 million of sales.

c. Leasing costs of a delivery truck, which are $250 per month and $0.18 per mile.

d. Fixed fee paid to an independent firm of CPAs for auditing and attesting to financial statements.

e. Compensation of sales staff with salary of $10,000 plus commission rates that increase as sales increase: 4 percent of the first $100,000 of annual sales, 6 percent of all sales from $100,000 to $200,000, and 8 percent for sales in excess of $200,000.

f. Cost of electricity, where the electric utility charges a flat rate of $50 for the first 5,000 units, $0.005 per unit for the next 45,000 units, and $0.004 per unit for all units in excess of the first 50,000 units.

The solution to this self-study problem is at the end of the chapter on pages 157–158.

Cost Estimation Methods

So far, we have assumed that analysts know the costs used for decision making. Now we discuss ways to obtain those costs. We call this **cost estimation** because, realistically, one never knows true costs. Wise analysts always look at cost numbers as *estimates* of the true costs, not the true costs.

Throughout the rest of this book, we use cost estimates in various types of decisions, planning exercises, and performance evaluation. For example, the estimated cost of setting up a Web site will help managers of Levi Strauss decide whether to add "clicks" to its distribution channels in Central Europe. The American Banking Association (ABA) estimates that in-person teller transactions cost approximately 100 times as much as online transactions. Where does the ABA get that information? It gets it from one or more of the cost estimation procedures that we discuss in this chapter.

We discuss the three methods of cost estimation that practitioners use: statistical regression analysis, account analysis, and engineering estimation. We start with a simple estimate of costs in which the only cost driver is the volume of output. Then we move to more complex applications involving several cost drivers. In practice, you may find analysts estimating costs for hundreds of cost drivers.

Estimating Costs Using Historical Data

When a firm has been carrying out activities for some time and expects future activities to be similar to those of the past, the firm can analyze the historical data to estimate the variable and fixed components of total cost and to estimate likely future costs. The procedure for analyzing historical cost data requires two steps:

1. Make an estimate of the past relation.
2. Update this estimate so that it is appropriate for the present or future period for which management wants the estimate. This step requires adjusting costs for inflation and for changes that have occurred in the relation between costs and activity. For example, if a firm expects the production process to be more capital-intensive in the future, the accountant should reduce variable costs and increase fixed costs.

Before developing cost estimates from historical data, analysts should take the following preliminary steps.

Preliminary Steps in Analyzing Historical Cost Data

Data analysts use the term *garbage in, garbage out* to indicate that the results of an analysis cannot be better than the input data. Before using cost estimates, the analyst should be confident that the estimates make sense and result from valid assumptions.

Keep in mind that we are trying to find fixed costs per period, F, and variable cost per unit, V, of some activity variable, X, in the relation

$$TC = F + VX.$$

Historical data comprise numerous observations. An observation is the total cost amount for a period and the level of activity carried out during that period. Thus we may have total labor costs by month (the **dependent variable**) and the number of units produced during each of the months (the **independent variable**). Exhibit 5.8 shows 12 observations, one for each month, for the suite of operating rooms at Chicago Hospital.

We should take the following steps in analyzing cost data:

1. **Review alternative cost drivers (independent variables).** A **cost driver** ideally measures the activity that *causes* costs. The cost drivers, if not the sole cause of costs, should directly influence costs. Operating room hours is an example of a cost driver in a hospital; machine hours is an example in a manufacturing firm; labor hours is an example in a service firm.
2. **Plot the data.** One simple procedure involves plotting each of the observations of total costs against cost-driver activity levels. Plotting the data may make it clear that either no relation or only a nonlinear relation exists between the chosen cost driver and actual costs.
3. **Examine the data and method of accumulation.** Do the time periods for the cost data and the activity correspond? Occasionally, accounting systems will record costs actually incurred late on a given day as occurring on the following day. Observations collected by the month may smooth over meaningful variations of the cost driver's activity level and cost that would appear if the accountant collected weekly data.

Be aware that a number of common recording procedures can make data appear to exhibit incorrect cost behavior patterns. Accounting systems often charge fixed overhead to production

EXHIBIT 5.8	CHICAGO HOSPITAL Operating Room Overhead Cost Data by Month		
Month		**Total Overhead**	**O.R. Hours**[a]
January		$ 558,000	590
February		433,000	460
March		408,000	440
April		283,000	290
May		245,500	230
June		308,000	320
July		358,000	390
August		445,500	480
September		533,000	560
October		658,000	700
November		558,000	590
December		693,000	740
Total		$5,481,000	5,790

[a]An operating room hour is one hour that one operating room is being used for surgery.

on a unit-by-unit basis. This "unitizing" of fixed costs makes fixed costs appear to be variable when they are not.

Sometimes an inverse relation seems to appear between activity and particular costs—when activity is high, costs are low; when activity is low, costs are high. An excellent example is maintenance. Firms sometimes purposefully do maintenance only when activity is slow. High maintenance levels often occur during plant shutdowns for automobile model changes, for example. The analyst would be naive to infer that low activity levels cause high maintenance costs.

These examples are a few of the data-recording methods that could lead the analyst astray. In general, we should investigate cost allocations, accruals, correcting and reversing entries, and relations between costs and activity levels to ensure that costs match activities in the appropriate time period for estimating costs.[2] Invalid relations between activity and costs will invalidate the analysis.

Statistical Regression Analysis

Having taken the preliminary steps to analyze the historical data, we now discuss the use of statistical analysis—specifically, a method called **regression analysis.** We discuss a simple estimation of variable and fixed overhead for the Chicago Hospital operating room suite. The Chicago Hospital operating room suite has 12 operating rooms used for a variety of surgeries ranging from simple vasectomies to major brain surgeries. This example discusses estimating overhead costs only—not costs of surgeons, nurses, or medical supplies—that can be directly traced to a particular surgery. (Each surgery is a "job" in cost language.) We assume that all data have been adjusted for the effects of inflation.

The task is to estimate the relation between total overhead costs and the activities that cause or at least are closely associated with those costs. For now, assume that, of the possible activity bases, the number of operating room hours during the month is the primary cause of overhead costs. Exhibit 5.8 shows total overhead costs and operating room hours each month for the past 12 months, adjusted for inflation. That is, the amounts presented are expressed in current dollars.

The cost equation to be estimated is:

$$
\begin{array}{c}
\text{Total Overhead} \\
\text{Costs per} \\
\text{Month}
\end{array}
=
\begin{array}{c}
\text{Fixed} \\
\text{Costs} \\
\text{per Month}
\end{array}
+
\left(
\begin{array}{c}
\text{Variable Overhead} \\
\text{Costs per} \\
\text{Operating} \\
\text{Room Hour}
\end{array}
\times
\begin{array}{c}
\text{Operating Room} \\
\text{Hours} \\
\text{Used during} \\
\text{Month}
\end{array}
\right)
$$

$$TC = F + VX.$$

Although the estimate is done by computer, it may be helpful to think about regression as fitting a line to the data points on a graph. Regression analysis "fits" this line to the data by the method of least squares. Least squares fits the data points to the line to minimize the sum of the squares of the vertical distances between the observation points and the regression line. The statistical regression locates the line that best fits the data points using the least-squares criterion. So think of regression analysis as giving you the best "fit" of the line to the data, although it might not be a perfect fit.

In our example, an observed actual value of total overhead cost is *TC*, and the line we fit by the least-squares regression will be of the form

$$\widehat{TC} = \hat{F} + \hat{V}X,$$

where the ^ on $\widehat{TC}$, $\hat{F}$, and $\hat{V}$ indicates that we have estimated the value of *TC*, *F*, and *V*.

The *V* in this cost equation is the cost driver rate. A **cost driver rate** is the rate at which the cost driver "drives" or causes costs. The cost driver rate in this example will be the rate at which the operating rooms incur costs for each hour of operating room usage.

Standard terminology designates the vertical distance between the actual and the fitted values, $TC - \widehat{TC}$, as the *residual*. The method of least squares fits a line to the data to minimize the sum of all the squared residuals, which makes the line the "best fit" to the data.

---

[2]For an extended discussion of these remarks, see W. E. Wecker and R. L. Weil, "Statistical Estimation of Incremental Costs from Accounting Data," Chapter 43 in R. L. Weil et al., eds., *Litigation Services Handbook*, 2nd edition (New York: John Wiley & Sons, 1995).

Virtually every computer system and spreadsheet software package for personal computers can execute regression analysis. Be aware, however, that one needs entire books to understand these methods fully.

Running the data for *TC* and *X* in Exhibit 5.8 through a least-squares regression computer program gives the following results:[3]

> Estimated Total
> Overhead   = $18,600 + ($908 × Operating Room Hours Used per Month)
> Costs per Month

We interpret the $18,600 and $908 amounts as follows. The first—the intercept—estimates the fixed overhead cost per month to be $18,600. The second—the coefficient on the independent variable, or cost driver, estimates the variable overhead cost per unit to be $908. In this example, the units are operating room hours used per month.

Using Regression to Estimate Cost Driver Rates

Using the least-squares regression equation,

$$TC = \$18,600 + (\$908 \times \text{Operating Room Hours per Month}),$$

assume a hospital administrator is attempting to estimate the overhead costs of the operating room suite for next month for budgeting purposes. To make that estimate, the administrator must estimate the volume of activity—operating room hours—for the month. Then she would insert the volume of activity into the cost equation that we just estimated using simple regression. If the administrator estimates the number of operating room hours to be 600 hours next month, then she estimates the operating suite's overhead costs to be $563,400 as follows:

$$TC = \$18,600 + (\$908 \times \text{Operating Room Hours per Month})$$

$$= \$18,600 + (\$908 \times 600 \text{ hours})$$

$$= \$563,400.$$

Warning   We should be wary of predicting total costs for operating room hours worked outside the range of observations. Any activity less than about 200 hours per month or more than about 800 hours per month is outside the range of observations. We should also be wary of our estimate of fixed costs because, at zero operating room hours per month, it is also outside the range of observations.

Multiple Regression

The preceding discussion dealt with only one independent variable. *Multiple regression* has more than one independent variable. We use Chicago Hospital data to illustrate multiple regression analysis with multiple cost drivers.

Assume that administrators at Chicago Hospital want to better understand the causes of costs. If they know the cost drivers, they can take actions to manage those costs better, thus reducing costs to HMOs which (should) reduce costs to members of the HMOs. After many interviews with the staff who work in the operating room suite, the administrators identified the following major cost drivers:

- Operating room hours (as used in the simple regression analysis, preceding).
- Operating room setup hours. These are the hours used to clean the operating room after a surgery and prepare it for the next surgery.
- Number of VIP patients. VIP stands for "Very Important Person," such as a City of Chicago councilperson, a member of the Chicago Bulls basketball team, or the owner of a very good restaurant. VIPs get special care, including extra staff on call during surgery and the highest-quality drugs.

---

[3]We obtained these results using the Regression option for Data Analysis in the Tools menu in Microsoft® Excel.

- Number of different operating rooms used. Each operating room has to be heated, lit, cleaned by maintenance personnel at the end of the day, and otherwise maintained. The more operating rooms used in a day, the more overhead costs. (That is, it would be less expensive to use one operating room for 10 surgeries scheduled sequentially than to use 10 operating rooms, one per surgery.)
- Number of special surgeries. Special surgeries include organ transplants, major cancer surgeries, and brain surgeries. Such major surgeries require greater overhead costs than more minor surgeries, all other things equal.

Exhibit 5.9 shows the cost driver volumes for the new cost drivers as well as the monthly costs and operating room hours that were presented in Exhibit 5.8.

The output for the multiple regression gives the following results:

$$TC = \$90,592 + (\$175 \times \text{Operating Room Hours}) +$$
$$(\$257 \times \text{Operating Room Setup Hours}) +$$
$$(\$3,839 \times \text{Number of VIP patients}) +$$
$$(\$2,043 \times \text{Number of Operating Rooms}) +$$
$$(\$6,050 \times \text{Number of Special Surgeries})$$

Now suppose the operating room administrator estimates the following level of activity for next month. What do you estimate the costs to be?

Estimated activity:

Operating room hours	600 hours
Operating room setup hours	280 hours
Number of VIP patients	6 patients
Average number of operating rooms used per day	8 rooms
Number of special surgeries	40 surgeries

EXHIBIT 5.9	CHICAGO HOSPITAL Multiple Cost Drivers

Cost Driver Volumes

	Total Overhead Costs Incurred During Month	Operating Room Hours Used During Month	Operating Room Setup Hours Used During Month	Number of VIP Patients During Month	Average Number of Operating Rooms Used per Day	Number of Special Surgeries During Month
January	$ 558,000	590	279	6	8	42
February	433,000	460	235	3	8	29
March	408,000	440	172	3	7	28
April	283,000	290	126	1	4	16
May	245,500	230	103	0	4	13
June	308,000	320	115	1	4	20
July	358,000	390	183	2	5	22
August	445,500	480	217	3	6	32
September	533,000	560	265	5	8	40
October	658,000	700	355	7	9	51
November	558,000	590	312	5	8	41
December	693,000	740	354	7	10	55
Total	$5,481,000	5,790	2,716	43	81	389

EXHIBIT 5.10	CHICAGO HOSPITAL Cost Estimation Using Multiple Regression Results		

Cost Driver	Cost Driver Rate (given in text)	Estimated Activity (given in text)	Estimated Cost[a]
Panel A: Cost estimation for next month			
Intercept			$ 90,592
Operating room hours	$ 175	600	105,000
Operating room setup hours	257	280	71,960
Number of VIP patients	3,839	6	23,034
Average number of operating rooms used per day	2,043	8	16,344
Number of special surgeries	6,050	40	242,000
Total estimated overhead for next month			$548,930
Panel B: Cost estimate for new customers			
Operating room hours	$ 175	100	$ 17,500
Operating room setup hours	257	40	10,280
Number of VIP patients	3,839	0	0
Average number of operating rooms used per day	2,043	1	2,043
Number of special surgeries	6,050	0	0
Total estimated overhead for new customer			$ 29,823

[a]Except for the intercept, which was estimated in the cost equation in the text, the estimated costs equal the cost driver rate times the estimated activity.

Given these estimates of activities, the administrator now estimates the overhead cost of the operating room suite for next month as shown in the last column of Panel A in the spreadsheet in Exhibit 5.10. Note that the estimated cost using multiple regression is different from the estimated cost obtained from simple regression. Without belaboring the point with discussion that is best left to statistics courses and textbooks, we simply note that models with different variables will give different results. It is likely that the multiple regression results are more accurate if (emphasize *if*) the cost drivers in the multiple regression model are appropriate. (Note that there is good reason for calling this process cost *estimation,* not cost truth.)

Financial Planning

The spreadsheet in Exhibit 5.10 becomes a financial planning model and basis for decision making. For example, suppose the hospital administrator is appalled at the overhead associated with VIP patients and decides to eliminate special treatment for all but benefactors who give large sums to the hospital. In so doing, she reduces the number of VIP patients in Exhibit 5.10 to 1 by simply replacing the 6 in the spreadsheet with 1. You can verify that the costs in the spreadsheet change to $3,839 for VIP patient overhead and to $529,735 for the total for next month.

Customer Profitability Analysis

Suppose the administrator is toying with the idea of becoming the surgery vendor for knee and hip replacements for other hospitals in the Chicago region. One health maintenance organization (HMO) has contacted Chicago Hospital about the possibility of doing its knee and hip replacements for a set monthly fee. The administrator for Chicago Hospital believes that three overhead cost drivers will be affected:

- Operating room hours will increase by 100 hours per month.
- Operating room setup hours will increase by 40 hours per month.
- The average number of operating rooms used will increase by 1 per day.

The administrator believes that no other overhead cost driver will be affected, nor will the intercept in the regression equation change. If so, the overhead cost increase is shown in Panel B of Exhibit 5.10 to be $29,823. The administrator can use this information to ascertain whether to take the HMO's offer.

In practice, analysts and managers use such estimates derived from cost estimation for thousands of applications, including cost management, standard setting, planning, all sorts of decision making, and many others. Keep in mind that such applications are only as good as the quality of the data and initial cost estimates.

Account Analysis

Now we turn to another method of estimating cost drivers. Using the **account analysis method**, analysts review each cost account and classify it according to its relation to a cost driver. Continuing the Chicago Hospital example, the administrator would classify each overhead cost for the operating room suite according to its cost driver. For example, the wages paid to staff who clean up operating rooms between surgeries would be assigned to the activity "operating room setup." Exhibit 5.11 shows the overhead costs assigned to the activities in the top row, "Costs." These amounts were summed over the same 12 months that were used in the previous regression analysis. We show only the totals for the 12-month period because the totals are the minimum data required to estimate the cost drivers. (We could have shown you the amounts for each month, but that would have taken 84 cells of space and not been interesting reading, to say the least.)

In practice, we recommend that analysts look at the detailed data—in this case, monthly data—to see whether there are outliers or other unusual patterns in the data. Analysts might find, for example, that the costs of VIP surgeries have increased dramatically over the 12-month period, suggesting that such costs will be higher in the future than predicted by the cost driver estimate.

After the analysts have assigned all costs to the appropriate activities, they should divide the sum of the costs for each activity by the sum of the cost driver volumes for the same activity. In Exhibit 5.11, the hospital administrator divides the costs by the sum of the cost driver volumes, in the second row. The cost driver volumes are the same as appeared in the last row of Exhibit 5.9.

The bottom row in Exhibit 5.11 shows the resulting cost driver rates. These rates correspond to the regression coefficients that are described in the text previously and that appear in Exhibit 5.10. The cost driver rates using account analysis are close to those estimated from multiple regression, but not exactly the same.

One item in Exhibit 5.11 that might seem puzzling is the category called "Fixed/Facility Costs." You can think of the cost driver in Exhibit 5.11 labeled "Fixed (Facility) Costs" ($93,763 per month) as corresponding to the "intercept" in Panel A of Exhibit 5.10.

Fixed (facility) costs are those that the organization incurs that are not related to a particular cost driver, but are required to keep the facility going. Building lease and depreciation, property taxes, and salaries of top administrators are classic examples of facility costs. We call them "fixed" because they do not vary with any of the cost drivers. In practice, they are not fixed in the long run—they can be changed with strategic decisions. For example, if Chicago Hospital gets out of the trauma center business, then it might subcontract its operating room business to another hospital. Doing so would eliminate some of its "fixed" costs. Note that the administrator calculated the "Fixed (Facility) Costs" estimate in Exhibit 5.11 as an amount per month. That is because the administrator wants to use the cost estimates to estimate monthly budgets.

EXHIBIT 5.11	CHICAGO HOSPITAL Account Analysis						
	Total Overhead	Operating Room Use	Operating Room Setup	VIP Patients	Number of Operating Rooms Used	Special Surgeries	Fixed (Facility) Costs
Costs	$5,481,000	$1,030,620	$719,740	$168,388	$169,614	$2,267,482	$1,125,156
Cost driver volumes . . .		5,790 hours	2,716 hours	43 patients	81 rooms	389 surgeries	12 months
Cost driver rates		$178 per hour	$265 per setup hour	$3,916 per patient	$2,094 per room	$5,829 per surgery	$93,763 per month

Problem 5.3 for Self-Study

Using cost estimates.   Assume that after reviewing the data used in the cost estimates for Chicago Hospital, you find some errors. After correcting those errors and re-estimating the cost drivers, you get the following results:

Intercept	$96,006
Operating room hours	$190 per hour
Setup hours	$232 per hour
VIP patients	$4,112 per patient
Operating rooms used	$1,456 per operating room used (average per month)
Special surgeries	$6,113 per special surgery

Refer to Exhibit 5.10. Using the new cost estimates above, revise the estimates of costs for next month shown in Panel A of Exhibit 5.10 and the cost estimate for the new customer shown in Panel B of Exhibit 5.10.

The solution to this self-study problem is at the end of the chapter on page 158.

Engineering Method of Estimating Costs

Yet a third method of cost estimation is the engineering method. The **engineering method of cost estimation** indicates what costs *should be*. The engineering method of cost estimation probably got its name because managers first used it in estimating cost using engineers' specifications of the inputs required to produce a unit of output. The engineering method is not confined to manufacturing. Banks, McDonald's, the U.S. Postal Service, hospitals, and other nonmanufacturing enterprises use time-and-motion studies and similar engineering methods to estimate what costs "should be" to perform a particular service.

Using the engineering method, analysts study the physical relation between the quantities of inputs and outputs. Analysts figure out the steps required to perform the task, the time needed to complete each step, the number and type of employees required, and the materials or other inputs needed. The accountant assigns costs to each of the inputs (wages, prices of material, insurance costs, etc.) to estimate the cost of outputs. Here are some examples of engineering study applications:

Company	Activity	Cost Driver
Wells Fargo Bank	Processing loans	Applications processed
U.S. Postal Service	Sorting mail	Pieces of mail sorted
The Gap store	Billing customers	Invoices processed
Internal Revenue Service	Processing tax returns	Returns processed
Prudential Insurance	Settling claims	Claims settled
American Airlines	Ticketing passengers	Passengers ticketed

Assume the administrator in the Chicago Hospital example uses the engineering method. To demonstrate, let's look at only the cost of operating room setup. The administrator would first identify the steps required to set up an operating room, the most efficient order for those steps, and the average amount of time that should be needed for each step. Next, she would figure the cost of each step.

For example, suppose it takes an average of 30 minutes to set up the equipment necessary for an operation, and the employee's time costs $30 per hour, including fringe benefits. The cost of this setup step is $15:

$$\frac{\text{Cost of}}{\text{one setup}} = \frac{\text{Time required to}}{\text{set up equipment}} \times \frac{\text{Cost of compensating}}{\text{employee for one hour}}$$

$$\$15 = 1/2 \text{ hour} \times \$30 \text{ per hour}$$

Analysts include other inputs, such as operating room cleanup, in the cost of operating room setup.

Assume the hospital wants to know what the costs of setting up operating rooms will be in the next month. The hospital expects to perform 250 operations next month. The analyst would estimate setup costs based on the $15 per operation setup, already measured, and the number of operations performed as follows:

$$\text{Total Setup Costs} = \text{Setup Cost per Operation} \times \text{Number of Operations}$$

$$\$3,750 = \$15 \times 250$$

The hospital can expect setup costs for the next month to be $3,750.

The engineering method is surprisingly costly to use. Analysis of time, motion, materials, operating characteristics of equipment, and the abilities of workers with varying skills requires experts. Expert engineers are expensive. Further, it is difficult to estimate indirect costs.

In short, the engineering method of estimating costs is most useful when input/output relations are well defined and fairly stable over time. For an aluminum manufacturer like ALCOA that has stable production methods over time, the engineering method results in good estimates of product costs, particularly for direct materials, direct labor, and certain overhead items like energy costs.

Data Problems

Whatever method is used to estimate costs, the results will only be as good as the data used. Collecting appropriate data is complicated by the following problems:

1. *Missing data.* Misplaced source documents or failure to record a transaction can result in missing data.
2. *Outliers.* Observations of extreme cost-activity relations may unduly affect cost estimates. For example, a hurricane affected operations in a Florida company in August, resulting in high overhead due to one-time costs that will not be incurred every month.
3. *Allocated and discretionary costs.* Fixed costs are often allocated on a volume basis and, as a result, may appear to be variable. Discretionary costs may also be budgeted so that they appear variable (e.g., advertising expense budgeted as a percentage of revenue).
4. *Inflation.* During periods of inflation, historical cost data do not accurately reflect future cost estimates.
5. *Mismatched time periods.* The time period for the dependent and independent variable may not match (e.g., running a machine in February but receiving and recording the energy bill in March).
6. *Trade-offs in choosing the time period.* Short, recent time periods may give a more accurate estimate of what will happen in the future. However, longer time periods may be more accurate for matching costs and activities. For example, using a machine this month may cause maintenance costs to be incurred next month. The activity and cost would not match on a monthly basis but would match on a yearly basis.

Managers should be aware of problems in the data. There is no substitute for experience when estimating how costs and activities are related.

Ethical Issues in Data Analysis

Managers who supervise the analysts doing the cost estimations sometimes pressure the analysts to "come up with the right answer." These managers might be motivated by desires to forecast low costs to get a pet project approved by even higher-level managers, or they might be motivated to forecast costs that are high so that it will be easy to beat those forecasts with lower costs, for example. Analysts can easily manipulate their analyses by, for example, deciding whether to include outliers, determining how to deal with missing data, or simply falsifying the data. But analysts who do this—and their managers—put themselves at great risk of penalty when they are caught.

Contrasting Approaches to Openness in Knowledge Sharing

Global Management

If you have ever made a mistake in a business setting, you know that different managers have different methods of dealing with errors. Some managers seek to cover up the problem, keeping it in-house and perhaps hoping that the error-maker will not even mention the error. Other managers want errors brought into the open. A study comparing U.S. and Chinese managers (in the People's Republic of China) examined whether Chinese or U.S. managers were more willing to reveal errors that they had made if the revelation would hurt them personally in their careers but would help their companies if revealed. The researchers found that Chinese managers were more likely to reveal their own errors, thereby putting the interests of the collective group—the company—ahead of their own private interests.[4] In general, different cultures foster different approaches to dealing with errors.

Managerial Application

United Airlines Uses Regression to Estimate Cost Behavior

In pricing and yield management, airlines continually seek to estimate the variable costs of additional passengers. In doing so, United Air Lines (UAL) analysts specified the regression model by regressing the change in total costs each period against the changes in revenue passenger miles and systemwide takeoffs. The analysts concluded that about 70 percent of UAL's costs varied with passenger traffic and takeoffs; that is, about 70 percent of UAL's costs were variable.

This result surprised other analysts, who thought that UAL's costs must be mostly fixed. These skeptics observed that UAL averages about 35 percent empty seats on its flights. They thought that when UAL carried a few extra passengers, these passengers would sit in the otherwise empty seats. Then, the only incremental costs would be about 25 percent of revenues for extra credit card fees, commissions, fuel, food, check-in agents, and baggage handling. The skeptics assumed UAL would not buy new airplanes and other major assets to handle the incremental passenger traffic.

The analysts at UAL who developed the regression estimates showed that the airline responded to an increase in demand for seats by expanding its total airline capacity, not only by putting the extra passengers in otherwise empty seats.

Source: Based on the authors' research.

Strengths and Weaknesses of Cost Estimation Methods

Each of the methods discussed has advantages and disadvantages. Probably the most informative estimate of cost behavior results from using several of the methods together, because each method has the potential to provide information not revealed by the others. Exhibit 5.12 summarizes the strengths and weaknesses of these methods. Look at Exhibit 5.12: When would you most likely expect to see the engineering method used? (Answer: In manufacturing settings.)

We have discussed a variety of cost estimation methods ranging from the simple account analysis approach to sophisticated techniques involving regression or learning curves. Which of these methods is best? In general, the more sophisticated methods will yield more accurate cost estimates than the simpler methods. However, even a sophisticated method yields only an imperfect estimate of an unknown cost behavior pattern.

[4]C. W. Chow, F. J. Deng, and J. L. Ho, "The Openness of Knowledge Sharing in Organizations: A Comparative Study of the United States and the People's Republic of China," *Journal of Management Accounting Research* 12.

EXHIBIT 5.12	Strengths and Weaknesses of Cost Estimation Methods	

Method	Strengths	Weaknesses
Engineering	• Based on studies of what future costs should be rather than what past costs have been.	• Not particularly useful when the physical relation between inputs and outputs is indirect. • Can be costly to use.
Account Analysis	• Provides a detailed expert analysis of the cost behavior in each account.	• Subjective.
Regression Method	• Uses all the observations of cost data. • The line is statistically fit to the observations. • Provides a measure of the goodness of fit of the line to the observations. • Relatively easy to use with computers and sophisticated calculators.	• The regression model requires that several relatively strict assumptions be satisfied for the results to be valid.

EXHIBIT 5.13	Sticky Costs

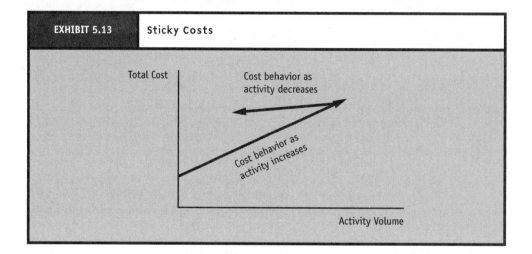

Analysts often simplify all cost estimation methods. The most common simplifications are the following.

1. Analysts often assume that cost behavior depends on only one cost driver. (Multiple regression is an exception.) In reality, however, costs are affected by a host of factors, including the weather, the mood of the employees, and the quality of the raw materials used.

2. Analysts often assume that cost behavior patterns are linear within the relevant range. We know that costs actually follow curvilinear, step, semivariable, and other patterns.

3. Analysts often assume that cost decreases are not "sticky." Exhibit 5.13 shows sticky cost behavior—when costs do not decrease with activity decreases as much as they increase with activity increases. For example, managers may be reluctant to fire workers when activity decreases, so labor costs do not decrease as much as activity decreases.[5]

You must consider on a case-by-case basis whether these assumptions are reasonable. You also must decide when it is important to use a more sophisticated, and more costly, estimation

---

[5]M. C. Anderson, R. D. Banker, and S. Janakiraman, "Are Selling, General and Administrative Costs 'Sticky'?," working paper, University of Texas at Dallas, 2001; shows that SGRA costs increase more when sales increase than they decrease when sales decrease by the same amount. The authors conclude that SGRA costs are "sticky."

method and when it is acceptable to use a simpler approach. Like the rest of managerial accounting, you must evaluate the costs and benefits of various cost estimation techniques.

Problem 5.4 for Self-Study

Plotting data and regression analysis output. Geoffrey Corporation, a manufacturer of stuffed animals, is interested in estimating its fixed and variable costs in the shipping department. Management has chosen the number of cartons packed as the cost driver and collected the following information for a year:

Total Overhead per Month	Total Cartons Packaged per Month
$20,500	500
22,300	650
22,300	625
23,000	700
21,000	550
21,400	570
24,500	725
21,000	525
21,500	600
23,200	675
21,400	560
22,500	640

A regression analysis shows the following:

$$TC = \$12,625 + (\$15.45 \times \text{Number of Cartons}).$$

a. Plot the data on a graph.
b. Draw the regression line.
c. What is the range of observations?

The solution to this self-study problem is at the end of the chapter on page 159.

Summary

The following items correspond to the learning objectives presented at the beginning of the chapter.

1. **Distinguish between variable costs and fixed costs and between short run and long run, and define the relevant range.** Total variable costs change as the level of activity changes. Total fixed costs do not change with changes in activity levels. The short run is a time period long enough to allow management to change the level of production or other activity within the constraints of current total production capacity. Management can change total production capacity only in the long run. The relevant range is the range of activity over which the firm expects a set of cost behaviors to be consistent.

2. **Identify capacity costs, committed costs, and discretionary costs.** Capacity costs are certain fixed costs that provide a firm with the capacity to produce or sell or both. Committed costs are costs that will continue regardless of production level. Discretionary costs need not be incurred in the short run to conduct business.

3. **Describe the nature of the various cost behavior patterns.** Curvilinear variable cost functions indicate that the costs vary with the volume of activity, but not in constant proportion. The learning curve function shows how the amount of time required to perform a task goes

down per unit as the number of units increases. Semivariable costs have both fixed and variable components. Semifixed costs increase in steps. A change in fixed costs usually involves a change in long-term assets, whereas a change in semifixed costs often does not.

4. **Describe how managers use cost behavior patterns.** Managers use cost behavior patterns to estimate how activities affect costs. This is particularly useful in forecasting costs.

5. **Explain how to use historical data to estimate costs.** In analyzing cost data, (1) review alternative cost drivers, (2) plot the data, and (3) examine the data and method of accumulation.

6. **Describe how analysts estimate cost behavior using regression, account analysis, and engineering methods.** Regression analysis is a statistical method that estimates the relation between cost drivers and costs. Using the account analysis method, analysts review each cost account and classify it according to cost driver. The engineering method of cost estimation studies the physical relation between the quantities of inputs and output. The accountant assigns costs to each of the inputs to estimate the cost of the outputs.

7. **Explain the costs, benefits, and weaknesses of the various cost estimation methods.** A simplifying assumption is that cost behavior patterns are linear within the relevant range. The cost analyst must consider on a case-by-case basis whether assumptions made are reasonable. The analyst must also decide when it is important to use a more sophisticated, and more costly, method and when it is acceptable to use a simpler approach.

8. **Identify the derivation of learning curves (Appendix 5.1).** The learning curve derivation in the appendix is known as the cumulative-average-time learning model.

Key Equation

$$Y = aX^b$$

$$\log Y = \log a + b(\log X)$$

9. **Interpret the results of regression analyses (Appendix 5.2).** In regression analysis the standard errors of the coefficients measure their variation and give an idea of the confidence we can have in the fixed and variable cost coefficients. The ratio between an estimated regression coefficient and its standard error is known as the *t*-statistic. If the absolute value is 2 or more, we can be relatively confident that the actual coefficient differs from zero. The R^2 attempts to measure how well the line fits the data; a value of 1.0 denotes a perfect fit. Some statistical problems that may affect interpretation of regression output include multicollinearity, autocorrelation, and heteroscedasticity.

Key Terms and Concepts

Account analysis method	Independent variable
Capacity costs	Learning curve (experience curve)
Committed costs	Long run
Cost behavior	Marginal cost
Cost driver	R^2*
Cost driver rate	Regression analysis
Cost estimation	Relevant range
Curvilinear variable cost	Semifixed costs (step costs)
Dependent variable	Semivariable costs
Discretionary costs (programmed costs, managed costs)	Short run
	Standard errors of the coefficients*
Engineering method of cost estimation	*t*-statistic*
Fixed costs	Variable costs (engineered costs)

*Term appears in Appendix 5.2.

Solutions to Self-Study Problems

SUGGESTED SOLUTION TO PROBLEM 5.1 FOR SELF-STUDY

Cumulative Number of Units Produced	Average Labor Cost per Unit	Total labor Costs
1	$1,333.33	$1,333.33
2	1,000 (= 75% × $1,333)	2,000
4	750 (= 75% × $1,000)	3,000
8	562.50 (= 75% × $750)	4,500
16	421.88 (= 75% × $562.50)	6,750

SUGGESTED SOLUTION TO PROBLEM 5.2 FOR SELF-STUDY

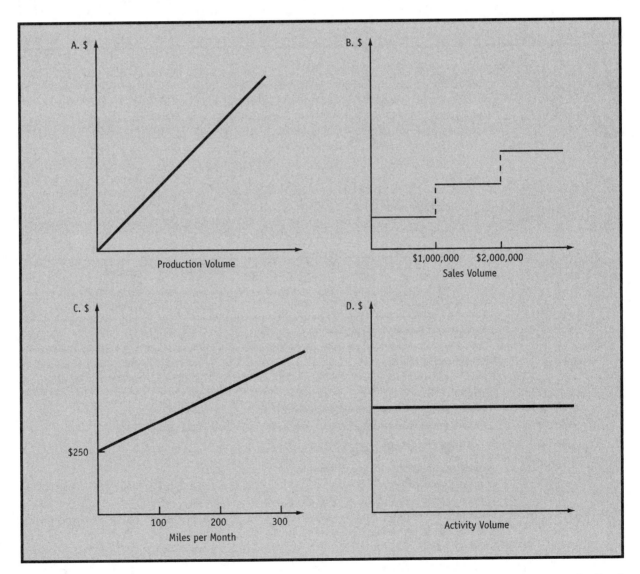

(continued)

SUGGESTED SOLUTION TO PROBLEM 5.2 FOR SELF-STUDY (continued)

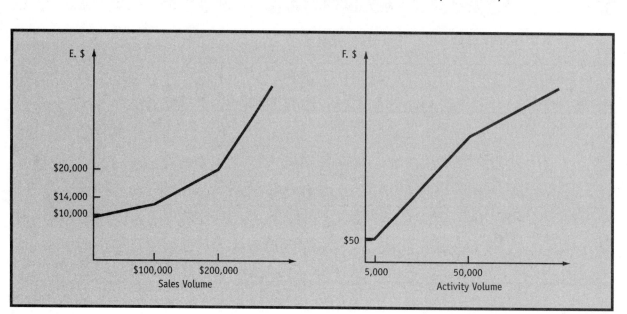

SUGGESTED SOLUTION TO PROBLEM 5.3 FOR SELF-STUDY

Cost Driver	Cost Driver Rate (given in text)	Estimated Activity (given in text)	Estimated Cost
Panel A: Cost estimation for next month			
Intercept			$ 96,006
Operating room hours	$ 190	600	114,000
Operating room setup hours	232	280	64,960
Number of VIP patients	4,112	6	24,672
Average number of operating rooms used per day	1,456	8	11,648
Number of special surgeries	6,113	40	244,520
Total estimated overhead for next month			$555,806
Panel B: Cost estimate for new customer			
Operating room hours	$ 190	100	$ 19,000
Operating room setup hours	232	40	9,280
Number of VIP patients	4,112	0	0
Average number of operating rooms used per day	1,456	1	1,456
Number of special surgeries	$6,113	0	0
Total estimated overhead for new customer			$ 29,736

SUGGESTED SOLUTION TO PROBLEM 5.4 FOR SELF-STUDY

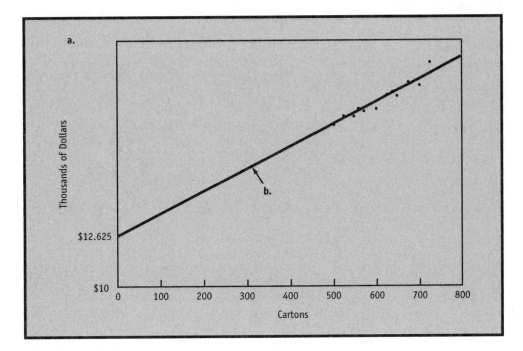

c. 500 to 725 cartons

Appendix 5.1: Deriving Learning Curves[6]

Mathematically, the learning curve effect can be expressed by the equation

$$Y = aX^b,$$

where

Y = average number of labor hours required per unit for X units

a = number of labor hours required for the first unit

X = cumulative number of units produced

b = index of learning, equal to the log of the learning rate divided by the log of 2.

For the 80 percent cumulative learning curve example in the text, $b = -0.322$, which we derive as follows.

If the first unit takes a hours, then the average for 2 units is $0.8a$ hours according to the model. Because $X = 2$, the equation gives $0.8a = a2^b$. Taking logs,

$$\log 0.8 + \log a = \log a + b(\log 2).$$

Simplifying,

$$b = \log 0.8/\log 2 = -0.322.$$

---

[6]The learning curve derivation in this appendix is known as the cumulative-average-time learning model.

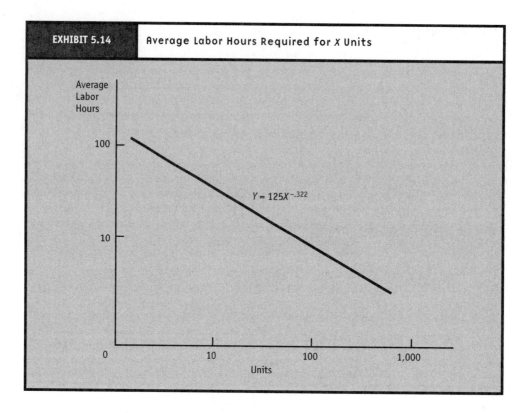

EXHIBIT 5.14	Average Labor Hours Required for *X* Units

Thus we can derive the average number of labor hours from the example in the text as follows:

X	Y	
1	125	
2	100	$Y = 125 \times (2^{-0.322}) = 100$
3	88	$Y = 125 \times (3^{-0.322}) = 88$
4	80	$Y = 125 \times (4^{-0.322}) = 80$
. . . .	.	
. . . .	.	
. . . .	.	
8	64	$Y = 125 \times (8^{-0.322}) = 64$

The function

$$Y = aX^b$$

is curvilinear, as shown in the text. The function is linear when expressed in logs, because

$$\log Y = \log a + b(\log X),$$

so the function is linear when plotted on log-log paper, as Exhibit 5.14 shows.

Operations management textbooks provide expanded discussions about learning curves.

Appendix 5.2: Interpreting Regression Analysis Output

This appendix expands the discussion in the text to help you understand and interpret regression output.

Standard Errors of the Coefficients and *t*-Statistics

The **standard errors of the coefficients** give an idea of the confidence we can have in the fixed and variable cost coefficients. The smaller the standard error relative to its coefficient, the more

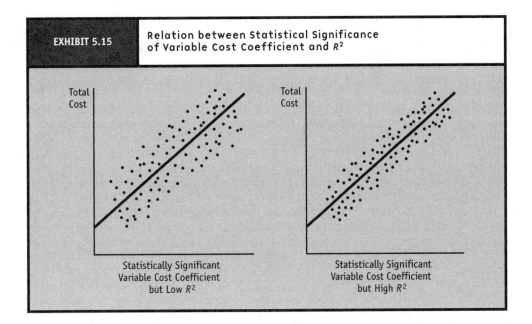

EXHIBIT 5.15 Relation between Statistical Significance of Variable Cost Coefficient and R^2

precise the estimate. (Such computational precision does not necessarily indicate that the estimating procedure is *theoretically* correct, however.)

The ratio between an estimated regression coefficient and its standard error is known as the *t*-value or ***t*-statistic.** If the absolute value of the *t*-statistic is approximately 2 or larger, we can be relatively confident that the actual coefficient differs from zero.[7]

If a variable cost coefficient has a small *t*-statistic, we may conclude that little, if any, relation exists between this particular activity (or independent variable) and changes in costs. If a fixed cost coefficient has a small *t*-statistic, we may conclude that these costs have little, if any, fixed cost component (which we would expect for operating room supplies or direct materials in manufacturing, for example).

R^2

The R^2 attempts to measure how well the line fits the data (that is, how closely the data points cluster about the fitted line). If all the data points were on the same straight line, the R^2 would be 1.00—a perfect fit. If the data points formed a circle or disk, the R^2 would be zero, indicating that no line passing through the center of the circle or disk fits the data better than any other. Technically, R^2 is a measure of the fraction of the total variance of the dependent variable about its mean that the fitted line explains. An R^2 of 1 means that the regression explains all of the variance; an R^2 of zero means that it explains none of the variance. R^2 is sometimes known as the "coefficient of determination."

Many users of statistical regression analysis believe that a low R^2 indicates a weak relation between total costs (dependent variable) and the activity base (independent variable). A low standard error (or high *t*-statistic) for the estimated variable cost coefficient signals whether or not the activity base performs well as an explanatory variable for total costs. With a large number of data observations, both low R^2 and significant regression coefficients can occur. Exhibit 5.15 illustrates this possibility.

Cautions When Using Regression

Computers easily perform statistical estimating techniques but often do not provide the necessary warnings. We conclude this section by providing several cautionary comments. A relation achieved in a regression analysis does not imply a causal relation; that is, a correlation between two variables does not imply that changes in one will cause changes in the other. An assertion of

---

[7]Statistics books provide *t*-tables that make the analysis of *t*-statistics more precise.

causality must be based on either *a priori* knowledge or some analysis other than a regression analysis.

Users of regression analysis should be wary of drawing too many inferences from the results unless they are familiar with such statistical estimation problems as *multicollinearity, autocorrelation,* and *heteroscedasticity* and how to deal with them. Statistics books deal with these statistical estimation problems.

Briefly, *multicollinearity* refers to the problem caused in multiple linear regression (more than one independent variable) when the independent variables are not independent of each other but are correlated. When severe multicollinearity occurs, the regression coefficients are unreliable. For example, direct labor hours worked during a month are likely to be highly correlated with direct labor costs during the month, even when wage rates change over time. If both direct labor hours and direct labor costs are used in a multiple linear regression, we would expect to have a problem of multicollinearity.

Autocorrelation problems arise when the data represent observations over time. Autocorrelation occurs when a linear regression is fit to data where a nonlinear relation exists between the dependent and independent variables. In such a case, the deviation of one observation from the fitted line can be predicted from the deviation of the prior observation(s). For example, if demand for a product is seasonal and production is also seasonal, a month of large total costs will more likely follow another month of large total costs than a month of small total costs. In such a case, we would have autocorrelation in the deviations of the data points from a fitted straight line.

Autocorrelation affects the estimates of standard errors of the regression estimates, and therefore it affects the *t*-statistics. If autocorrelation exists, the estimates of standard errors may be understated and the *t*-statistics may be overstated in the regression output.

Heteroscedasticity refers to the phenomenon that occurs when the average deviation of the dependent variable from the best-fitting linear relation is systematically larger in one part of the range of independent variable(s) than in others. For example, if the firm uses less-reliable equipment and employs less-skilled labor in months of large total production, variation in total costs during months of large total production is likely to be greater than in months of small total production. Heteroscedasticity affects the reliability of the estimates of standard errors of the regression coefficients (and therefore affects the reliability of the *t*-statistics).

Questions, Exercises, and Problems

REVIEW QUESTIONS

1. Review the meaning of the concepts or terms given in Key Terms and Concepts.
2. Which method of cost estimation does not rely primarily on historical cost data? What are the drawbacks of this method?
3. Name three methods of cost estimation.
4. The simplifying assumptions on which cost estimations are based include which of the following?
   a. Cost behavior depends on one activity variable (except multiple regression).
   b. Cost behavior patterns are not linear within the relevant range.
   c. Costs are only fixed.
   d. All of the above.
5. (See Appendix 5.2.) R^2
   a. measures how well the line fits the data.
   b. is a perfect fit when its value is 1.0.
   c. is the standard error of the coefficient.
   d. a. and b.
6. Multiple regression
   a. has one dependent variable.
   b. has more than one independent variable.
   c. has only one independent variable.
   d. a. and b.

CRITICAL ANALYSIS AND DISCUSSION QUESTIONS

7. "The concepts of short-run costs and long-run costs are relative—short run could mean a day, a month, a year, or even 10 years, depending on what you are looking at." Comment.

8. "My variable costs are $2 per unit. If I want to increase production from 100,000 units to 150,000 units, my total costs should go up by only $100,000." Comment.

9. What methods of cost estimation rely primarily on historical data? Discuss the problems an unwary user may encounter with the use of historical cost data.

10. What steps would you take to deal with a supervisor who asks you to falsify the results of your cost estimation?

11. In what cultures might analysts be more willing to reveal errors they made in estimating costs?

12. When estimating fixed and variable costs, it is possible to have an equation with a negative intercept. Does this mean that at zero production the company has negative fixed costs?

13. Refer to the Managerial Application "United Airlines Uses Regression to Estimate Cost Behavior." What independent variables did the analysts use in the regression? What did the analysts who developed the regression conclude? Based on your experience, do you agree with their conclusions?

14. (See Appendix 5.2.) How is regression used to identify what cost drivers might be used in activity-based costing?

15. (See Appendix 5.1.) Describe the phenomenon that gives rise to learning curves. To what type of costs do learning curves apply?

16. "Simplification of all costs into only fixed and variable costs distorts the actual cost behavior pattern of a firm. Yet businesses rely on this method of cost classification." Comment.

17. "The account analysis method uses subjective judgment. So we cannot really consider it a valid method of cost estimation." Comment.

18. Suggest ways that one can compensate for the effects of inflation when preparing cost estimates.

EXERCISES

Solutions to even-numbered exercises are at the end of the chapter.

19. **Graphs of cost relations.** Sketch cost graphs for the following situations:
    a. A 30 percent increase in fixed costs will enable Donelan Company to produce up to 75 percent more. Variable costs per unit will remain unchanged.
    b. Refer to part **a.** What if Donelan Company's variable costs per unit triple for the additional units it intends to produce?
    c. Richmond's variable marketing costs per unit decline as more units are sold.
    d. Anderson Paper pays a flat fixed charge per month for electricity plus an additional rate of $0.20 per unit for all consumption over the first 2,000 units.
    e. Indirect labor costs at KMD Bank consist only of supervisors' salaries. The bank needs one supervisor for every 20 clerks.
    f. National Plastics currently operates close to capacity. A short-run increase in production would result in increasing unit costs for every additional unit produced.

20. **Cost behavior in event of capacity change.** Slopeside Resort, a lodge located in a fast-growing ski resort, is planning to open its new wing this coming winter, increasing the number of beds by 40 percent. Although variable costs per guest-day will remain unchanged, total fixed costs will increase by 25 percent. Last year's costs follow:

Variable Costs	$50,000
Total Fixed Costs	30,000

   a. Sketch the cost function.
   b. Calculate the additional fixed operating costs that Slopeside Resort will incur next year.

21. **Cost behavior when costs are semivariable.** Data from the shipping department of Brawn Company for the past two months follows:

	Number of Packages Shipped	Shipping Department Costs
November	6,000	$12,000
December	9,000	15,000

    a. Sketch a line describing these costs as a function of the number of packages shipped.

    b. What is the apparent variable cost per package shipped?

    c. The line should indicate that these shipping costs are semivariable. What is the apparent fixed cost per month of running the shipping department during November and December?

22. **Identifying cost behavior.** Data from the shipping department of Wanda's Gourmet Foods for the past four months follow:

	Number of Packages Shipped	Shipping Department Costs
May	0	$1,500
June	2,000	3,500
July	2,500	4,500
August	1,500	3,000

    Are these costs fixed, semifixed, variable, or semivariable?

23. **Cost estimation using regression analysis.** Dali's Financial Services prepares tax returns for small businesses. Data on the company's total costs and output for the past six months appear in the table that follows. The results of regression analysis are also provided.

    a. Plot the data and the regression line on a graph. (See Problem 5.4 for Self-Study.)

    b. Estimate total monthly costs for a month when 330 tax returns are prepared, using the estimates from the regression output.

Month	Tax Returns Prepared	Total Costs
January	200	$160,000
February	280	192,000
March	300	198,000
April	260	180,000
May	260	186,000
June	240	170,000

Regression output: $TC = \$78,045 + (\$401 \times \text{Number of Tax Returns})$.

24. **Learning curve.** Phantom Co. makes technical products for mysterious customers. To make Product J24, the company recently recorded the following costs, which decline subject to an 85 percent cumulative learning curve.

Cumulative Number of Units Produced	Average Labor Costs per Unit
1	$5,000
2	4,250
4	?
8	?
16	?

    Complete the chart by filling in the cost amounts for volumes of 4, 8, and 16 units.

25. **Average cost calculations.** Abs Health Club has the following cost equation:

$$\text{Total Costs} = \$40,000 + \$80n,$$

where n = number of memberships.

    a. Calculate Abs's average fixed cost per membership when there are 1,000 memberships.

    b. What is the average variable cost per membership when there are 1,000 memberships?

    c. Calculate the average cost per membership when there are 1,000 memberships.

26. **Repair cost behavior.** The Shilling Company analyzed repair costs by month using linear regression analysis. The equation fit took the following form:

$$\text{Total Repair Costs} = \text{Fixed Costs} + \left(\text{Variable Repair Costs per Machine Hour Used during Month} \times \text{Machine Hours Actually Used during Month} \right)$$

$$TRC = a + bx.$$

The results were

$$TRC = \$20,000 - \$0.75x$$

Average monthly repair costs have been $18,800, and machine hours used have averaged 1,600 hours per month. Management worries about the ability of the analyst who carried out this work because of the *negative* coefficient for variable cost.

What is your evaluation of these results?

27. **Interpreting regression results.** The output of a regression of overhead costs on direct labor costs per month follows:

Regression Results

Equation:

Intercept $38,000

Slope 2.20

Statistical Data:

R^2 .... 0.85

Smalltime Consulting Services plans to operate at a level that would call for direct labor costs of $20,000 per month for the coming year.

a. Use the regression output to write the overhead cost equation.

b. Based on the cost equation, compute the estimated overhead cost per month for the coming year.

c. (See Appendix 5.2.) How well does this regression explain the relation between direct labor and overhead?

28. **Interpreting regression data.** A marketing manager of a company used a pocket calculator to estimate the relation between sales dollars for the past three years and monthly advertising expenditures (the independent variable). The regression results indicated the following equation:

$$\text{Sales Dollars} = \$97,000 - (1.45 \times \text{Advertising Dollars})$$

Do these results imply that advertising hurts sales? Why would there appear to be a negative relation between advertising expenditures and sales?

29. **Cost estimation using regression analysis.** Milky Chocolates has observed the following overhead costs for the past 12 months:

Month	Overhead Costs	Boxes of Output
January	$11,400	4,500
February	15,600	11,000
March	16,800	12,000
April	12,000	5,500
May	14,100	9,000
June	15,600	10,500
July	13,200	7,500
August	12,300	5,000
September	15,600	11,500
October	12,900	6,000
November	14,400	8,500
December	15,000	10,000

The results of the regression analysis are:

$$TC = \$8,781 + (\$0.63 \times \text{Number of Boxes})$$

a. Plot the data and the regression line (like Problem 5.4 for Self-Study).

b. Estimate total monthly costs for a month when 10,200 boxes of chocolate are produced.

PROBLEMS

30. **Multiple regression.** The managers of Peterson's Catering Company are analyzing the costs involved in providing catering services. Managers have selected the following cost drivers: units of meals produced, total deliveries, number of VIP services, number of new customers, and new products developed. Here are the cost data and levels of cost driver activity for the past 16 months.

Month	Total Overhead	Meals Produced	Deliveries	VIP Services	New Customers	New Products
1	$69,094	12,690	1,340	345	3	0
2	64,927	11,980	1,180	310	4	0
3	60,332	10,950	1,050	280	4	1
4	57,953	10,280	930	245	5	0
5	55,984	9,020	840	205	7	2
6	53,119	8,130	780	185	8	2
7	52,706	7,540	700	160	10	3
8	53,874	6,980	630	144	12	4
9	53,445	8,930	680	135	10	2
10	54,869	9,800	760	120	9	0
11	59,985	10,560	890	175	8	2
12	61,121	11,560	1,070	200	7	0
13	63,926	11,710	1,240	240	6	0
14	66,602	12,460	1,390	285	4	0
15	72,773	13,520	1,450	330	4	1
16	71,391	13,620	1,510	315	2	0
Totals	$972,101	169,730	16,440	3,674	103	17

Required:

a. Using multiple regression, find the cost driver rates for each of the cost drivers. (Note: You must use a computer program such as Microsoft® Excel to perform this step.)

b. Assuming the following level of cost driver volume for the next month, what is the estimated cost? (Don't forget to include the intercept of the regression in your estimate.)

12,000	Meals produced
1,100	Deliveries
300	VIP services
5	New customers
2	New products

c. Peterson's Catering Company is considering outsourcing deliveries. Compared to your answer in requirement **b.,** how much would be saved per month by outsourcing the delivery service (before considering the cost of outsourcing)?

31. **Account analysis.** Refer to problem **30.**

Required:

a. Indicate the information in addition to that provided in problem **30** required to perform account analysis.

b. Now assume that Peterson's Catering Company had the following breakdown of costs for the 16 months reported in problem **30:**

Total costs of meals produced	$334,368
Total costs for delivering	164,400
Total costs of VIP services	140,352
Total costs of developing new customers	154,904
Total costs of developing new products	18,700
Total facilities-level costs (total for all 16 months)	159,377
Total costs	$972,101

What are the cost driver rates for (1) meals produced, (2) deliveries, (3) VIP services, (4) new customers, and (5) new products developed using account analysis?

c. What are the estimated costs for a month assuming the following level of cost driver volumes? (Don't forget to include the facilities-level costs in your estimate.)

12,000	Meals produced
1,100	Deliveries
300	VIP services
5	New customers
2	New products

d. Peterson's Catering Company is considering outsourcing deliveries. Compared to your answer in requirement **c.,** how much would the company save by outsourcing the delivery service (before considering the cost of outsourcing)?

32. **Engineering method.** Refer to problems **30** and **31.** Peterson's Catering Company hired an engineering consulting firm to perform an engineering estimate of its business costs. The consulting firm came up with the following monthly cost estimates based on information for the current period:

Facilities costs	$9,500
Meal production-level costs	$1.90 per meal produced
Delivery costs	$11 per delivery
VIP services costs	$38 per service
New customer costs	$1,250 per new customer
New product costs	$1,000 per new product

Required:

a. Assuming the following level of cost driver volume for a month, what is the estimated cost using the engineering estimates? (Don't forget to include the facilities costs in your estimate.)

12,000	Meals produced
1,100	Deliveries
300	VIP services
5	New customers
2	New products

b. Peterson's Catering Company is considering outsourcing delivery. Compared to your answer in requirement **a.,** how much would the company save by outsourcing the delivery service (before considering the cost of outsourcing)?

33. **Multiple regression.** Analysts for American River Brewery have selected the following cost drivers: volume of beer produced (in hectoliters, i.e., 1 hL = 100 L), total amount of raw materials used (in kilograms), number of batches, volume of water used (in hL), number of cleaning procedures performed—cleanings in place (CIPs)—and number of new products. Here are the cost data and levels of cost driver activity for 18 months.

Month	Total Overhead	Beer Produced (hL)	Raw Material (kg)	Number of Batches	Water (hL)	CIPs	New Products
Jan.	$ 57,266.65	890	13,573	54	6,005	67	0
Feb.	61,020.23	980	15,013	58	6,588	72	1
Mar.	64,622.52	1,094	16,781	65	7,336	81	0
Apr.	68,630.16	1,212	18,551	73	8,002	88	0
May	70,652.68	1,262	19,370	75	8,435	93	0
June	79,927.29	1,494	23,182	89	9,940	110	2
July	82,867.34	1,557	24,202	95	10,420	106	3
Aug.	81,748.55	1,528	23,797	94	10,326	112	2
Sept.	68,819.71	1,215	18,537	72	8,284	87	0
Oct.	66,375.05	1,145	17,582	69	7,746	85	0
Nov.	63,767.19	1,072	16,369	64	7,168	76	0
Dec.	62,254.68	1,032	15,628	62	6,933	77	0
Jan.	56,837.54	872	13,158	50	5,902	61	1
Feb.	61,298.34	1,006	15,224	60	6,759	75	0
Mar.	63,179.60	1,041	15,763	62	6,990	81	1
Apr.	66,107.60	1,139	17,246	68	7,629	85	0
May	69,759.22	1,228	18,593	75	8,205	89	1
June	76,402.53	1,397	21,571	84	9,304	100	2
Totals	$1,221,536.88	21,164	324,140	1,269	141,972	1,545	13

Required:
a. Using multiple regression, find the cost driver rates for each of the cost drivers. (Note: You must use a computer program such as Microsoft® Excel to perform this step.)
b. Assuming the following level of cost driver volume for the next month, what is the estimated cost? (Don't forget to include the intercept of the regression in your estimate.)

1,650	hL of beer produced
25,500	kg of raw materials consumed
100	Batches
10,800	hL of water consumed
120	CIPs
1	New product

c. American River Brewery is considering a target for water consumption of 5.0 hL water per hL of beer produced. How much would American River Brewery have saved *in total* over the previous 18 months if it had reached this target in the previous 18 months?
34. Account analysis. Refer to problem **33**.
Required:
a. Indicate the information in addition to that provided in problem **33** required to perform account analysis.
b. Now assume that American River Brewery had the following breakdown of costs:

Total costs of beer produced	$ 292,429.28
Total costs of raw materials consumption	236,168.40
Total batch-level costs	69,173.19
Total costs of water consumption	141,935.36
Total costs of CIPs performed	29,392.65
Total costs of developing new products	6,204.64
Total facilities-level costs (total for all 18 months)	446,233.36
Total costs	$1,221,536.88

What are the cost driver rates using account analysis?

c. What are the estimated costs for a month assuming the following level of cost driver volumes? (Don't forget to include the facilities-level costs in your estimate.)

1,650	hL of beer produced
25,500	kg of raw materials consumed
100	Batches
10,800	hL of water consumed
120	CIPs
1	New product

35. **Engineering method.** Refer to problems **33** and **34.** American River Brewery hired an engineering consulting firm to perform an engineering estimate of beer production costs. The consulting firm came up with the following monthly cost estimates based on information for the current period:

Facilities costs	$26,008.00
Beer production-level costs	$13.5 per hL produced
Raw materials costs	$0.70 per kg consumed
Batch-level costs	$60 per batch
Water costs	$0.90 per hL consumed
CIP costs	$18.5 per CIP performed
New product costs	$500 per new product

Required:
Assuming the following level of cost driver volume for a month, what is the estimated cost using the engineering estimates? (Don't forget to include the facilities costs in your estimate.)

1,650	hL of beer produced
25,500	kg of raw materials consumed
100	Batches
10,800	hL of water consumed
120	CIPs
1	New product

36. **Interpreting regression results** (adapted from an example by G. Benston, *The Accounting Review* 41, pp. 657–672). The Philly Company manufactures widgets and digits. Philly assembles the widgets in batches, but makes digits one at a time. Philly believes that the cost of producing widgets is independent of the number of digits produced in a week. The firm gathered cost data for 156 weeks. The following notation is used:

C = Total manufacturing costs per week

N = Number of widgets produced during a week

B = Average number of widgets in a batch during the week

D = Number of digits produced during the week

A multiple linear regression fitted to the observations gave the following results:

$$C = \$265.80 + \$8.21N - \$7.83B + \$12.32D$$

a. According to the regression results, how much are weekly costs expected to increase if the number of widgets increases by 1?
b. What are the expected costs for the week if Philly produces 500 widgets in batches of 20 each and produces 300 digits during the week?
c. Interpret the negative coefficient $\$(7.83)$ estimated for the variable B.

37. **Regression analysis, multiple choice.** Lorenzo Company estimated the behavior pattern of maintenance costs. Data regarding maintenance hours and costs for the previous year and the results of the regression analysis follow:

Month	Hours of Activity	Maintenance Costs
January	240	$ 4,200
February	160	3,000
March	200	3,600
April	150	2,820
May	250	4,350
June	155	2,960
July	160	3,030
August	260	4,470
September	245	4,260
October	235	4,050
November	175	3,300
December	170	3,160
Sum for 12 months	2,400	$43,200
Average per month	200	$ 3,600

$$TC = F + VX$$
$$= \$684.65 + \$14.577X$$

a. In the equation $TC = F + VX$, the best description of the letter V is as the
  (1) independent variable.
  (2) dependent variable.
  (3) variable cost coefficient.
  (4) coefficient for the intercept.
b. The best description of TC in the preceding equation is as the
  (1) independent variable.
  (2) constant coefficient.
  (3) dependent variable.
  (4) variable coefficient.
c. The best description of the letter X in the preceding regression equation is as the
  (1) dependent variable.
  (2) coefficient for the intercept.
  (3) variable cost coefficient.
  (4) independent variable.
d. Based on the data derived from the regression analysis, 180 maintenance hours in a month means that the maintenance costs would be estimated at (rounded to the nearest dollar)
  (1) $3,309
  (2) $3,600
  (3) $3,461
  (4) $3,797
  (5) Some other amount

38. **Graphing costs and interpreting regression output** (adapted from CMA exam). Management of Tino's Tacos wants to estimate overhead costs accurately to plan the company's operations and assess its financial needs. A trade association publication reports that certain overhead costs tend to vary with tacos made. Management gathered monthly data on tacos and overhead costs for the past two years for five taco restaurants. No major changes in operations were made over this time period. The data follow:

Month No.	Number of Tacos	Overhead Costs
1	20,000	$42,000
2	25,000	49,500
3	22,000	44,750
4	23,000	45,000

(continued)

Month No.	Number of Tacos	Overhead Costs
5	20,000	40,750
6	19,000	37,750
7	14,000	35,250
8	10,000	32,250
9	12,000	34,500
10	17,000	37,500
11	16,000	35,750
12	19,000	39,000
13	21,000	43,000
14	24,000	46,500
15	23,000	46,500
16	22,000	43,500
17	20,000	40,000
18	18,000	38,250
19	12,000	33,750
20	13,000	35,500
21	15,000	36,750
22	17,000	36,250
23	15,000	35,500
24	18,000	37,500

An analyst entered these data into a computer regression program and obtained the following output:

Coefficients of the Equation:

Intercept $19,930

Independent Variable (slope) 1.0774

a. Prepare a graph showing the overhead costs plotted against tacos.

b. Use the results of the regression analysis to prepare the cost estimation equation and to prepare a cost estimate for 20,000 tacos for one month.

39. Interpreting regression results (adapted from CMA exam). Maya Company is making plans for the introduction of a new hair product that it will sell for $6 per unit. The following estimates have been made for manufacturing costs on 100,000 units to be produced the first year:

Direct materials $50,000

Direct labor .... $80,000 (the labor rate is $8 an hour × 10,000 hours)

Manufacturing overhead costs have not yet been estimated for the new product, but monthly data on total production and overhead costs for the past 24 months have been analyzed using regression. The following results were derived from the regression and will provide the basis for overhead cost estimates for the new product.

REGRESSION ANALYSIS RESULTS

Dependent variable—Factory overhead costs

Independent variable—Direct labor hours

Computed values:

Intercept $55,000

Coefficient of independent variable .... $ 3.20

Coefficient of correlation 0.953

R^2 .... 0.908

    a. The total overhead cost for an estimated activity level of 20,000 direct labor hours would be
        (1) $55,000
        (2) $64,000
        (3) $82,000
        (4) $119,000
        (5) Some other amount

    b. What is the expected contribution margin per *unit* to be earned during the first year on 100,000 units of the new product? (Assume all marketing and administrative costs are fixed.)
        (1) $4.38
        (2) $4.89
        (3) $3.83
        (4) $5.10
        (5) Some other amount

    c. How much is the variable manufacturing cost per *unit*, using the variable overhead estimated by the regression (and assuming direct materials and direct labor are variable costs)?
        (1) $1.30
        (2) $1.11
        (3) $1.62
        (4) $3.00
        (5) Some other amount

    d. What is the manufacturing cost equation implied by these results, where x refers to *units* produced?
        (1) $TC = \$80,000 + \$1.11x$
        (2) $TC = \$55,000 + \$1.62x$
        (3) $TC = \$185,000 + \$3.20x$
        (4) Some other equation

    e. (Answer if Appendix 5.2 was assigned reading.) What percentage of the variation in overhead costs is explained by the independent variable?
        (1) 90.8 percent
        (2) 42 percent
        (3) 48.8 percent
        (4) 95.3 percent
        (5) Some other amount

40. Interpreting multiple regression results (Appendix 5.2). To select the most appropriate activity base for allocating overhead, Chavez Manufacturing ran a multiple regression of several independent variables against its nonmaintenance overhead cost. The results were as follows for 24 observations:

Variable Name	Coefficient	Standard Error	t-Statistic
Direct labor hours	0.876	2.686	0.326
Units of output	10.218	5.378	1.900
Maintenance costs	$(12.786)	$1.113	(11.488)
Cost of utilities	$ 0.766	$0.079	9.696
Intercept	12.768	6.359	2.008

R^2 for the multiple regression = 0.90

    Discuss the appropriateness of each of these variables for use as an activity base. Which would you recommend selecting? Why?

41. Effect of learning on cost behavior. Nichols Incorporated manufactures bike parts for various bike manufacturers. One particular contract resulted in the following labor costs:

Cumulative Number of Units Produced, X	Average Labor Costs per Unit (in real dollars), Y
1	$1,333
2	1,000

(continued)

Cumulative Number of Units Produced, X	Average Labor Costs per Unit (in real dollars), Y
3	845
4	750
5	684
6	634
7	594
8	562

a. Sketch the relation between X and Y.

b. If there is a learning phenomenon, estimate the constant percentage reduction in labor costs, that is, the percent cumulative learning curve.

42. **Estimating health-care cost behavior.** The health-care industry has been faced with increasing pressure to control costs. Health-care costs have increased substantially more rapidly than general inflation rates. At the same time, health-care facilities face price competition for services because insurance companies and government-funded health programs are limiting opportunities for cost reimbursement.

To control costs, one must first relate the costs of providing services to the volume of activity. The first step is often to estimate a cost model, $TC = F + VX$, where X refers to the volume of activity. Examples of activity bases include patient days to estimate nursing staff costs or number of tests to estimate costs in a laboratory.

Although it may appear simple to estimate the relation $TC = F + VX$, analysts often find a lack of good data to make the estimates. For example, the cost of medical supplies shown in the accounting records is often the cost of *purchases,* not the cost of supplies *used.* Consequently, large purchases in one month followed by no purchases in the next month make these costs appear to behave in unrealistic ways.

Although recent pressures on health-care facilities to reduce costs have increased the incentives for administrators and doctors to improve record keeping, our research indicates the information needed to control costs is lacking in many health-care organizations. For example, hospitals often keep track of *charges* to patients but not the *costs* of the items being charged.

How would information that makes it possible to estimate the equation $TC = F + VX$ help health-care managers control costs?

43. **Learning curves, managerial decisions** (adapted from CMA exam). The Nippon Company purchases 80,000 pumps annually from Xing Brothers, Inc. The price has increased each year and reached $68 per unit last year. Because the purchase price has increased significantly, Nippon management has asked its analyst to estimate the cost to manufacture the pump in its own facilities. Nippon's products consist of stamping and castings. The company has little experience with products requiring assembly.

The engineering, manufacturing, and accounting departments have prepared a report for management that includes the following estimate for an assembly run of 10,000 units. The firm would hire additional production employees to manufacture the subassembly. It would not need extra equipment, space, or supervision.

The report estimates total costs for 10,000 units at $957,000, or $95.70 per unit. The current purchase price is $68 per unit, so the report recommends continued purchase of the product.

Components (outside purchases)	$120,000
Assembly labor[a]	300,000
Factory overhead[b]	450,000
General and administrative overhead[c]	87,000
Total Costs	$957,000
Fixed overhead	50 percent of direct labor dollars
Variable overhead	100 percent of direct labor dollars
Factory overhead rate	150 percent of direct labor dollars

[a]Assembly labor consists of hourly production workers.
[b]Factory overhead is applied to products on a direct labor dollar basis. Variable overhead costs vary closely with direct labor dollars.
[c]General and administrative overhead is applied at 10 percent of the total cost of material (or components), assembly labor, and factory overhead.

a. Was the analysis prepared by the engineering, manufacturing, and accounting departments of Nippon Company and the recommendation to continue purchasing the pumps that followed from the analysis correct? Explain your answer and include any supportive calculations you consider necessary.

b. Assume Nippon Company could experience labor cost improvements on the pump assembly consistent with an 80 percent learning curve. An assembly run of 10,000 units represents the initial lot or batch for measurement purposes. Should Nippon produce the 80,000 pumps in this situation? Explain your answer.

Suggested Solutions to Even-Numbered Exercises

20. Cost behavior in event of capacity change.

a.

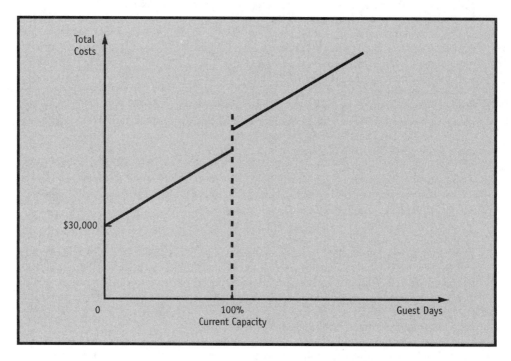

b. Additional fixed operating costs = 0.25($30,000)

= $7,500

22. Identifying cost behavior. Plotting the data, these costs appear to be semivariable. The fixed-cost component estimate is $1,500, and the variable cost component is $1 per package up to 2,000 packages [$1 = ($3,500 − $1,500)/2,000 packages]. With only four data points, you should view these estimates skeptically, however.

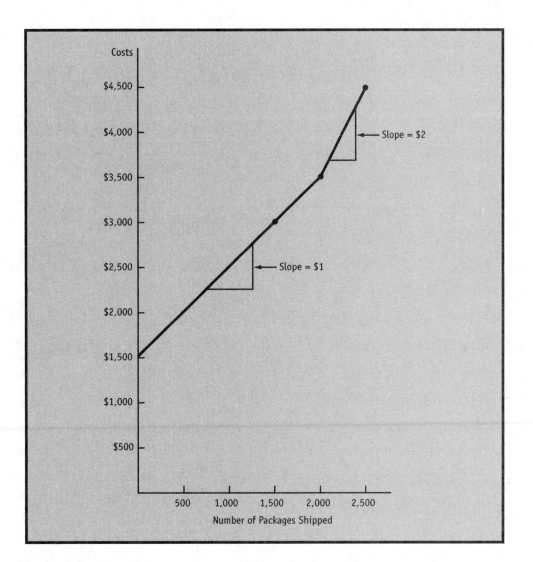

24. Learning curve.

Cumulative Number of Units Produced	Average Labor Costs per Unit
1	$5,000
2	4,250 ($5,000 × 85%)
4	3,612.50 ($4,250 × 85%)
8	3,070.63 ($3,612.50 × 85%)
16	2,610.04 ($3,070.63 × 85%)

26. Repair cost behavior. The most likely explanation for the inverse relation between production and repair costs is that the firm schedules repair work during slow, rather than busy, times. So repair costs increase when volume decreases.

28. Interpreting regression data. This problem frequently arises when applying analytical techniques to certain costs. Quite often the advertising expenditures result in sales being generated in the following month or later. In addition, many companies increase their advertising when sales are declining and cut back on advertising when manufacturing is at capacity. A better model might relate this month's sales to last month's advertising.

Similar problems exist for repair and maintenance costs because routine repairs and maintenance usually occur during slow periods.

chapter 6

Financial Modeling for Short-Term Decision-Making

Learning Objectives

1. Describe the use of financial modeling for profit-planning purposes.

2. Explain how to perform cost-volume-profit (CVP) analysis.

3. Describe the use of spreadsheets in financial modeling.

4. Identify the effects of cost structure and operating leverage on the sensitivity of profit to changes in volume.

5. Explain how to use sales dollars as the measure of volume.

6. Explain the effect of taxes on financial modeling.

7. Describe the use of financial modeling in a multiple-product setting.

8. Explain financial modeling with multiple cost drivers.

$\mathcal{F}$inancial modeling, a simple but appealing tool, can provide a sweeping overview of an organization's financial activities or can help managers make specific decisions.

Suppose that a student club wants to show movies on campus. The club can rent a particular movie for one weekend for $1,000. Rent for an auditorium, salaries to the ticket-takers and other personnel, and other fixed costs would total $800 for the weekend. The organization would sell tickets for $4 per person. In addition, it estimates that profits from the sale of soft drinks, popcorn, and candy are $1 per ticket holder. How many people would have to buy tickets for the club to break even and therefore justify renting the movie? (The answer is 360.)

The analysis relies on concepts of fixed and variable cost behavior that we first discussed in Chapter 1 and just covered in Chapter 5. This chapter presents the concept of financial modeling, more specifically a particular type of financial model, and demonstrates how managers can use it in a number of decision-making situations.

After reading this chapter, you should understand how to use financial modeling to project profits (or losses) and how to use the resulting information to make short-term decisions.

What Is Financial Modeling?

A model represents reality. You likely have seen models over the years, such as model airplanes, models of commercial buildings created by architects, or dolls and action figures. Another example is a simulator used to train airplane pilots. The simulator allows one to test skills under different conditions in an effort to study reactions of the pilot.

A **financial model,** which works in much the same fashion as a simulator, enables analysts to test the interaction of economic variables in a variety of settings. These models require that analysts develop a set of equations that represent a company's operating and financial relations. For example, these relations may include that of contribution margin to selling price, numbers of sales, inventory turnover ratios, and the relative proportion of various products sold (called product mix). They can include any financial relation that would help managers make decisions. The analyst then embeds the model in software, often a spreadsheet, allowing a user to compute the effect that changes to variables such as sales price or volume or costs might have on operating profits of the business. For example, a company may want to know the impact on cash flow, sales, and profitability of credit tightening proposed by one of its divisions. An analyst can construct an appropriate financial model and, in a matter of seconds, predict the outcome of various scenarios. (We explore this technique later in the chapter.)

Financial models offer several benefits to users. Once developed, analysts can use the model for business purposes without becoming overwhelmed by the related number crunching. Like the simulators just discussed, many models allow an organization to study the impact of a possible business action by reviewing the potential results before taking that action. The models help managers identify a bad project or decision ahead of time, before it negatively impacts the company involved.

Be warned about GIGO—garbage in, garbage out. Using financial models can present problems. Sound models do not automatically improve decision making. A model is only as good as the assumptions it uses. Faulty assumptions or bad data result in faulty output—sometimes worse than useless because it sends managers off in wrong directions.

The Cost-Volume-Profit Model

One basic financial model, the **cost-volume-profit (CVP) model,** summarizes the effects of volume changes on an organization's costs, revenue, and income. Users can extend such analysis to include the impact on profit of changes in selling prices, service fees, costs, income-tax rates, and the organization's mix of products or services. For example:

- What effect on profit can General Motors (http://www.generalmotors.com) expect if it builds a larger sport utility vehicle?
- How will NBC's (http://www.nbc.com) profit change if the ratings increase for its evening news program?
- How many online subscribers must America Online (http://www.aol.com) obtain to break even for the year?
- What happens if America Online reduces fees charged to its customers—will profits increase with an increase in subscribers?

Each of these questions concerns the effects on profits when some activity changes, and the CVP model can aid the analysis.

Although the word *profit* appears in its title, the cost-volume-profit model applies as well to not-for-profit enterprises. Managers in nonprofit organizations also routinely use CVP analysis to examine the effects of activity and other short-run changes on revenue and costs.

How the Model Works

We base much of our discussion in this chapter on illustrative data for Early Horizons Daycare, a daycare center providing service from 7 AM to 6 PM, weekdays only. Defining a unit of output as service provided for one child for a month, the accountant at Early Horizons developed the following cost and price estimates. (See Chapter 5 for information on how to make these estimates.)

Price per Child per Month	$ 600
Variable Cost per Child per Month	200
Fixed Costs per Month	5,000

Early Horizons Daycare has a capacity of 20 (units), after which it needs to hire more staff. The building has a capacity of 30; to service more than that the center must acquire additional space as well as more staff. The estimated variable costs include two snacks and lunch every day, various paper products and soap, a variable cost component of insurance, and supplies such as toys and crayons.

The fixed costs include rent, utilities, a fixed cost component of insurance, and minimum staffing requirements of three full-time "Big Friends," a part-time "Big Cook/Housekeeper," and some volunteers.

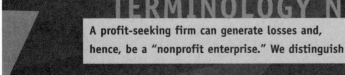

TERMINOLOGY NOTE

A profit-seeking firm can generate losses and, hence, be a "nonprofit enterprise." We distinguish the purpose of an organization by using the terms *profit-seeking* and *not-for-profit* enterprises.

Break-Even Point

Analysts can use the basic CVP model to find the **break-even point,** namely, the volume of activity that produces equal revenues and costs for the organization. The organization has no profit or loss at this sales level.

Suppose that Early Horizons has 12.5 children for one month (one child attends half-time and the rest are full-time). The following income statement shows that the operating profit for the month will be zero:

Sales Revenue (12.5 × $600)	$7,500
Less Variable Costs (12.5 × $200)	2,500
Contribution Margin	$5,000
Less Fixed Costs	5,000
Operating Profit	$ 0

Notice that the income statement (1) highlights the distinction between variable and fixed costs and (2) shows the total contribution margin, which is the amount contributed toward covering Early Horizon's fixed costs and generating income. Stated differently, each full-time child in daycare adds $400 to the firm's bottom-line profit. The $400 unit contribution margin is $600 selling price − $200 variable cost per child.

How could we compute Early Horizon's break-even point if we did not already know it is 12.5 children per month? An analyst can use either a contribution-margin approach or an equation approach.

Contribution-Margin Approach

Each full-time child pays $600, but $200 of this amount covers variable costs. Thus, $400 per child remains to cover the fixed costs of $5,000. We call this $400 amount the contribution margin per unit. The **contribution margin per unit** is the selling price per unit less variable costs per unit. When the firm has enrolled enough children so that these $400 contributions add up to $5,000, the organization will break even. We can therefore compute the 12.5 break-even volume as follows:

Break-Even Volume = Fixed Cost/Contribution Margin per Unit (per child per month)

For Early Horizons,

Break-Even Volume = $5,000/$400

= 12.5 children per month

Equation Approach

An alternative approach to finding the break-even point uses the equation:

Operating Profit = Sales Revenue − Costs

One expression of the income calculation is the following:

Sales Revenue − Variable Cost − Fixed Cost = Operating Profit

Expanding this yields:

(Selling Price per Unit × Sales Volume) − (Variable Cost per Unit × Sales Volume)

− Fixed Costs = Operating Profit

which equals

[(Selling Price per Unit − Variable Cost per Unit) × Sales Volume] − Fixed Costs = Operating Profit

The break-even point occurs where operating profit equals zero, so setting the expression above equal to zero and moving fixed costs to the other side of the equal sign, the equation becomes

[(Selling Price per Unit − Variable Cost per Unit) × Sales Volume] = Fixed Costs

Now solving for sales volume, we have

Sales Volume = Fixed Costs/(Selling Price per Unit − Variable Cost per Unit)

or

Sales Volume = Fixed Costs/Contribution Margin per Unit

For Early Horizons,

Break-Even Sales Volume = $5,000/($600 − $200)

= $5,000/$400

= 12.5 children per month

Note that both the equation and contribution-margin approaches get us to the same place—dividing fixed costs by the contribution margin per unit.

The CVP Model in Graphical Format

The contribution-margin and equation approaches both find the break-even point using the same data and concepts. Both methods reach the same conclusion, so personal preference dictates the approach to be used. Exhibit 6.1 graphs the relations.

The graph discloses more information than the break-even calculation and enables a manager to see the effects on profit of changes in volume. The graph shows sales volume on the horizontal axis and two diagonal lines: total revenues and total costs. The vertical distance between the lines on the graph is the profit or loss for a given sales volume (i.e., the difference between revenues and costs). If Early Horizons enrolls fewer than 12.5 children in a month, the organization will suffer a loss. The magnitude of the loss increases as enrollment declines. Conversely, the daycare center will have a profit if enrollment exceeds 12.5 children. Looking at Exhibit 6.1, what is the loss if Early Horizons Daycare serves no children? (Answer: $5,000, the fixed costs.)

Exhibit 6.2 is a profit-volume graph. The **profit-volume graph** shows one line that represents operating profits of the company for a given sales volume. It combines the two lines (revenues minus costs) shown in Exhibit 6.1.

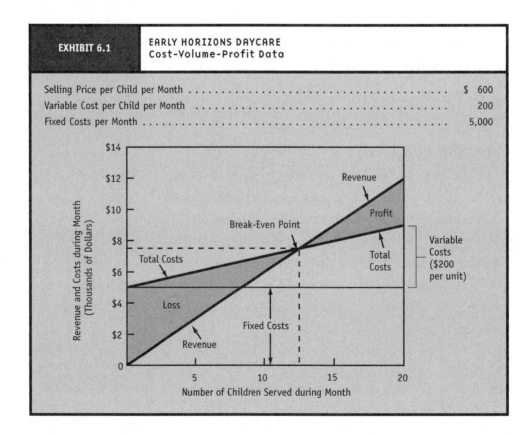

EXHIBIT 6.1	EARLY HORIZONS DAYCARE Cost-Volume-Profit Data

Selling Price per Child per Month	$ 600
Variable Cost per Child per Month	200
Fixed Costs per Month	5,000

EXHIBIT 6.2	EARLY HORIZONS DAYCARE Profit-Volume Graph

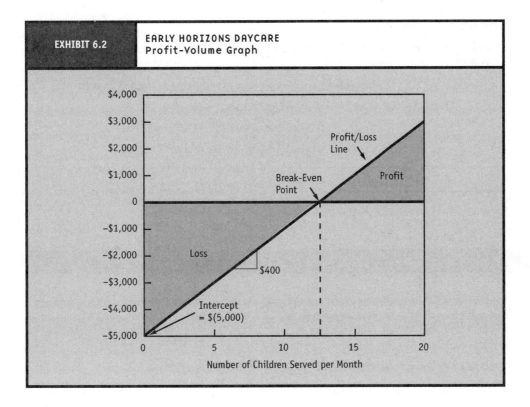

Target Profit

Finding the break-even point, where target profit is zero, is only one example of using the cost-volume-profit equation to find the unit sales necessary to achieve a specified profit. Suppose the owners of Early Horizons Daycare have 20 children enrolled for one month. The following income statement shows that the operating profit for the month would be $3,000.

Sales Revenue (20 × $600)	$12,000
Less Variable Costs (20 × $200)	4,000
Contribution Margin	$ 8,000
Less Fixed Costs	5,000
Operating Profit	$ 3,000

What if we did not know, and ask, "How many children lead to profits of $3,000?" Management will often ask this type of question. We call the answer to this question a "target profit." How could we compute Early Horizon's target profit of $3,000?

Contribution Margin Approach

The analyst can easily integrate target profit into the CVP model. In the previous break-even case, the daycare center had to enroll 12.5 children to break even. Now it must go one step further: Cover the fixed costs and earn $3,000 in operating profit. With each full-time child continuing to contribute $400, the calculation becomes:

Target Profit Volume = (Fixed Costs + Target Profit)/Contribution Margin

= ($5,000 + $3,000)/$400 per child

= $8,000/$400 per child

= 20 children

Equation Approach

Analysts can use the profit equation to find the target profit volume. Simply use the target profit of $3,000 in the following equation:

$$\text{Sales Revenue} - \text{Variable Cost} - \text{Fixed Cost} = \text{Operating Profit}$$

$$(\$600 \times \text{Sales Volume}) - (\$200 \times \text{Sales Volume}) - \$5{,}000 = \$3{,}000$$

$$(\$400 \times \text{Sales Volume}) - \$5{,}000 = \$3{,}000$$

$$\$400 \times \text{Sales Volume} = \$8{,}000$$

$$\text{Sales Volume} = \$8{,}000/\$400$$

$$\text{Sales Volume} = 20 \text{ children}$$

Early Horizons Daycare must enroll 20 children per month to reach the target profit of $3,000.

Applications of Financial Modeling

The cost-volume-profit model is one example of a financial model. Companies tailor their financial models to meet their particular needs. In this section we illustrate several uses of a financial model. Other analysts use other formats.

Sensitivity Analysis and Spreadsheets

The assumptions of the Early Horizons example were:

Price per Full-Time Child	$ 600
Variable Cost per Child	200
Monthly Fixed Cost	5,000
Target Operating Profit	3,000

A change in any of these variables requires new analysis. Most analysts use computer spreadsheets (e.g., Excel) for evaluating changes in the financial model variables (e.g., price per child, variable cost per child, and number of children enrolled). **Sensitivity analysis** shows how the financial model responds to changes in any or all of its variables. Typically, analysts focus on how changes will affect operating profit.

Exhibit 6.3 presents an example of how to set up a financial model in spreadsheet form and how to perform sensitivity analysis for Early Horizons Daycare. Assume Early Horizons Daycare expects to have 20 full-time children enrolled in the program each month. We call this the *base case*. The base case appears in column (1) and projects profit of $3,000. Management asked several questions. The answers appear in Exhibit 6.3 in the specified columns. Keep in mind each question is independent of the other—each relates to the base case only.

Column (2): What would happen to operating profit if the fixed costs declined by $500 per month (10 percent)?

Column (3): What would happen to operating profit if the variable costs increased $10 per child (5 percent)?

Column (4): What would happen to operating profit if the price per child increased $60 (10 percent) to $660 and volume decreased to 18 children?

The financial model in Exhibit 6.3 shows a sensitivity analysis—how operating profit changes as specified variables change. Column (2) shows that a 10 percent (= $500/$5,000) decrease in fixed costs results in a 16.67 percent (= $500/$3,000) increase in operating profit. Column (3) shows that a 5 percent (= $10/$200) increase in variable costs results in a 6.67 percent (= $200/$3,000) decrease in operating profit. Column (4) shows that a 10 percent (= $60/$600) increase in price and a 10 percent (= 2/20) decrease in volume results in a 9.33 percent (= $280/$3,000) increase in operating profit.

Using the financial model in Exhibit 6.3, management can begin to analyze how operating profit varies as model variables change. For example, operating profit is somewhat sensitive to

	EXHIBIT 6.3	EARLY HORIZONS DAYCARE Sensitivity Analysis			

	(1) Base Case	(2) Fixed Costs Decrease $500	(3) Variable Costs Increase $10	(4) Price Increases $60 Volume Decreases by 2 Children
Assumptions				
Price per child	$ 600	$ 600	$ 600	$ 660
Variable cost per child	$ 200	$ 200	$ 210	$ 200
Monthly fixed cost	$ 5,000	$ 4,500	$ 5,000	$ 5,000
Children enrolled	20	20	20	18
Financial Model Results **(Income Statement)**				
Sales revenue	$12,000	$12,000	$12,000	$11,880
Less variable cost	4,000	4,000	4,200	3,600
Total contribution margin	$ 8,000	$ 8,000	$ 7,800	$ 8,280
Less fixed cost	5,000	4,500	5,000	5,000
Operating profit	$ 3,000	$ 3,500	$ 2,800	$ 3,280

changes in fixed costs (16.67 percent change in profit for every 10 percent change in fixed cost) and less sensitive to changes in variable costs (6.67 percent change in profit for every 5 percent change in variable cost).

Not only does the model help managers analyze operating profit, but it can also help analyze target profits, target volumes, and other variables.

Problem 6.1 for Self-Study

Finding profits, break-even points, and quantities. The following information is for Sara's Ice Cream Company for April:

Sales (20,000 units)		$180,000
Fixed Manufacturing Costs	$22,000	
Fixed Marketing and Administrative Costs	14,000	
Total Fixed Costs		36,000
Total Variable Costs		120,000
Unit Price		9
Unit Variable Manufacturing Cost		5
Unit Variable Marketing Cost		1

Compute the following:

a. Operating profit when sales are $180,000 (as above)
b. Break-even quantity in units
c. Quantity of units that would produce an operating profit of $30,000

The solution to this self-study problem is at the end of this chapter on pages 197–198.

Step Costs (Semi-fixed Costs)

When the costs include step costs, which are fixed costs that increase in steps, we have to consider a different amount of fixed costs for each step. Let's examine how to deal with step costs for Early Horizons Daycare.

Assume the facility has been full with 20 children, and management is considering expanding. This would require hiring more "Big Friends" to increase capacity to 30 children, the maximum for the current space. Assume that each additional Big Friend would expand capacity by five children. Fixed costs would increase from $5,000 by $4,600, to $9,600, for the first step. The increased costs include hiring an additional Big Friend, increasing insurance, and hiring another part-time cook. The second step would require hiring a second Big Friend, which would increase fixed costs by an additional $2,800, to $12,400. Variable costs would remain at $200 per child per month and selling price at $600 per child per month. Management calculates the break-even point for each level of capacity as follows:

1. Status quo, 0–20 children:

$$\text{Break-Even Volume} = \text{Fixed Cost/Contribution Margin per Child}$$
$$= \$5,000/\$400$$
$$= 12.5 \text{ children}$$

2. First additional step, 21–25 children:

$$\text{Break-Even Volume} = \text{Fixed Cost/Contribution Margin per child}$$
$$= \$9,600/\$400$$
$$= 24 \text{ children}$$

3. Second additional step, 26–30 children:

$$= \$12,400/\$400$$
$$= 31 \text{ children}$$

Notice that with one additional step the break-even point is below capacity, so this is a viable alternative. However, with two additional steps the break-even point of 31 units exceeds full capacity of 30 units. Therefore, this alternative is not feasible.

From a profit-seeking perspective, adding the first step would not be wise. Although the facility would break even with 24 children, profits would be lower if the facility expanded from 20 to 25 children. This occurs because five additional children add $2,000 of contribution but require a step up in costs of $4,600.

Margin of Safety

The **margin of safety** is the excess of projected (or actual) sales units over the break-even unit sales level. The formula for margin of safety is

$$\text{Margin of Safety} = \text{Sales Units} - \text{Break-Even Sales Units}$$

In our example, assume the level of activity is 20 units. The break-even point is 12.5 units. Therefore, the margin of safety is 7.5 units. Sales volume can drop 37.5 percent (= 7.5/20) before the firm incurs a loss, other things held constant.

The margin of safety can also be measured in sales dollars. Use the same formula, except replace "units" with "dollars." Thus, given the preceding information, the margin of safety in sales dollars is

$$\text{Margin of Safety} = \text{Sales Dollars} - \text{Break-Even Sales Dollars}$$

In our example, sales dollars total $12,000 (= 20 × $600). The break-even point is 12.5 units, or $7,500 (= 12.5 × $600). Therefore, the margin of safety in sales dollars is $4,500. Sales dollars can drop $4,500 before the firm incurs a loss, other things held constant.

Problem 6.2 for Self-Study

Identifying CVP relations on a graph. The following graph contains cost-volume-profit and profit-volume graph elements. Identify the concept from the accompanying list that corresponds to the line segment or relation on the graph.

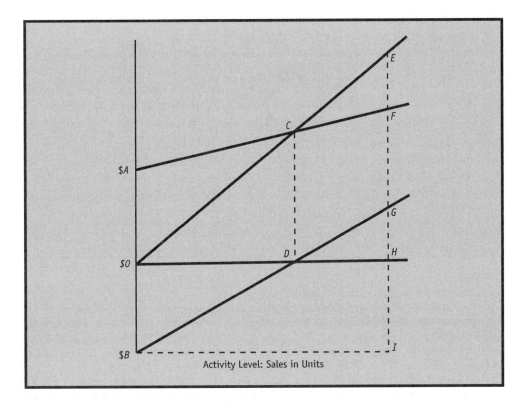

Line Segment or Relation	Concept
a. *0A*	**(1)** Variable Cost per Unit
b. *IG*	**(2)** Fixed Cost per Period
c. *0D*	**(3)** Revenue
d. *B0*	**(4)** Contribution Margin per Unit
e. *0H − 0D*	**(5)** Margin of Safety in Units
f. *B0/0D*	**(6)** Break-Even Sales in Units
g. *HF + HG*	**(7)** None of the above

Referring to the graph, answer each of the following as true or false (holding everything else constant).

h. If revenue is *CD*, the margin of safety is zero.
i. If revenue is *HE*, the margin of safety is *D0*.
j. Total fixed costs could never be larger than total variable costs.
k. If selling price increased, break-even sales in units would decrease.
l. If selling price increased, *HF* would increase.
m. *FE = HG*.

The solution to this self-study problem is at the end of this chapter on page 198.

Cost Structure and Operating Leverage

The **cost structure** of an organization refers to the proportion of fixed and variable costs to total costs. Cost structures differ widely among industries and among firms within an industry. Manufacturers using computer-integrated manufacturing systems have a large investment in plant and equipment, which results in a cost structure with high fixed costs. In contrast, for a builder of homes, a much higher proportion of costs is variable. The homebuilder has a cost structure with high variable costs relative to fixed costs.

EXHIBIT 6.4	Comparison of Cost Structures				
	Variable Company (1,000,000 units)		**Fixed Company (1,000,000 units)**		
	Amount	%	Amount	%	
Sales	$1,000,000	100	$1,000,000	100	
Less Variable Costs	750,000	75	250,000	25	
Contribution Margin	$ 250,000	25	$ 750,000	75	
Less Fixed Costs	50,000	5	550,000	55	
Operating Profit	$ 200,000	20	$ 200,000	20	
Break-Even Point	200,000 units		733,334 units		
Contribution Margin Ratio	0.25		0.75		

An organization's cost structure has a significant effect on the sensitivity of its profit to changes in volume. The extent to which an organization's cost structure is made up of fixed costs is called **operating leverage.** Operating leverage is high in firms with a high proportion of fixed costs, a small proportion of variable costs, and the resulting high contribution margin per unit. The higher the firm's fixed costs, the higher the break-even point. Once the break-even point is reached, profit increases significantly. Exhibit 6.4 presents an example of a Variable Company and a Fixed Company that demonstrates this point. The point is best demonstrated by comparing contribution margin ratios. The **contribution margin ratio** is the contribution amount per dollar of sales, or the contribution margin divided by sales.

Note that although these firms have the same sales revenue and operating profit, they have different cost structures. Variable Company's cost structure is dominated by variable costs with a lower contribution margin ratio of 0.25. So for every dollar of sales there is a contribution of 25 cents toward fixed costs and profit. Fixed Company's cost structure is dominated by fixed costs with a higher contribution margin of 0.75. So for every dollar of sales there is a contribution of 75 cents toward fixed costs and profit.

Suppose both companies experienced a 10 percent increase in sales. Variable Company's profits would increase by $25,000 (= 0.25 × $100,000), while Fixed Company's profits would increase by $75,000 (= 0.75 × $100,000). Looking at Exhibit 6.4, if variable costs for both companies were $500,000 and fixed costs were $200,000, would there be any difference in operating leverage? (Answer: No. Both companies would have the same operating leverage.)

Using Sales Dollars as a Measure of Volume

Firms that produce many types of products or that provide services find it convenient to measure volume in sales dollars instead of units. (Imagine defining a unit for a company like General Motors that makes cars, radios, batteries, and other products, or defining a unit for Accenture that provides management consulting services.) The formula to calculate the break-even point in sales dollars is

Break-Even Sales Dollars = Fixed Costs/Contribution Margin Ratio

With this measure, the cost-volume-profit equation remains the same as before, but we are now solving for total revenues (or total sales dollars). For Early Horizons Daycare the calculations for break-even points in both units and sales dollars are as follows:

Break-Even in Units

Break-Even Units = Fixed Costs/Contribution Margin per Unit (per child)

= $5,000/($600 − $200)

= 12.5 children per month

Break-Even in Sales Dollars

$$\text{Break-Even Sales Dollars} = \text{Fixed Costs/Contribution Margin Ratio}$$
$$= \$5{,}000/[(\$600 - \$200)/\$600]$$
$$= \$5{,}000/[\$400/\$600]$$
$$= \$5{,}000/0.667$$
$$= \$7{,}500$$

Thus the break-even volume expressed in sales dollars is \$7,500. The contribution margin ratio is the ratio of the unit contribution margin to unit price (= \$400/\$600).

With a slight modification, the break-even equation may also be used to determine target-profit level of sales. For instance, if managers of Early Horizons Daycare wanted profits of \$2,000, they would calculate the target volume as follows:

Target Profit in Units

$$\text{Target Profit in Units} = (\text{Fixed Costs} + \text{Target Profit})/\text{Contribution Margin per Unit}$$
$$= (\$5{,}000 + \$2{,}000)/(\$600 - \$200)$$
$$= \$7{,}000/\$400$$
$$= 17.5 \text{ children per month}$$

Target Profit in Sales Dollars

$$\text{Target Profit in Sales Dollars} = (\text{Fixed Costs} + \text{Target Profit})/\text{Contribution Margin Ratio}$$
$$= (\$5{,}000 + \$2{,}000)/[(\$600 - \$200)/\$600]$$
$$= \$7{,}000/[\$400/\$600]$$
$$= \$7{,}000/0.667$$
$$= \$10{,}500 \text{ per month}$$

Income Taxes

Profit-seeking enterprises must pay taxes on their profits, meaning that target profit figures are set high enough to cover the firm's tax obligation to the government. The relationship between an organization's before-tax profit and after-tax profit is expressed in the following formula:

$$\text{After-Tax Profit} = \text{Before-Tax Profit} - \text{Income Taxes}$$
$$= \text{Before-Tax Profit} - (\text{Before-Tax Profit} \times t)$$
$$= \text{Before-Tax Profit} \times (1 - t)$$

where t is the income-tax rate.

Starting from

$$\text{After-Tax Profit} = \text{Before-Tax Profit} \times (1 - t)$$

and dividing both sides by $(1 - t)$ gives:

$$\text{After-Tax Profit}/(1 - t) = \text{Before-Tax Profit}$$

Now we can find the desired before-tax profit that will generate the desired after-tax profit, given the company's tax rate.

Recall for Early Horizons Daycare, the before-tax amounts were: price per child is \$600, variable cost per child is \$200, and total fixed costs are \$5,000. Assume the tax rate is 40 percent for this example. Management wants to know how many children per month must be served for Early Horizons Daycare to generate an after-tax profit of $1,800 per month. Here are the calculations:

$$\text{After-Tax Profit}/(1 - t) = \text{Before-Tax Profit}$$

$$\$1,800/(1 - 0.4) = \text{Before-Tax Profit}$$

$$\$1,800/0.6 = \text{Before-Tax Profit}$$

$$\$3,000 = \text{Before-Tax Profit}$$

The before-tax profit can then be inserted into the formula for calculating a target profit (discussed earlier in this chapter) as follows:

$$\text{Target Profit in Units} = (\text{Fixed Costs} + \text{Target Profit})/\text{Contribution Margin per Unit (per child)}$$

$$= (\$5,000 + \$3,000)/(\$600 - \$200)$$

$$= \$8,000/\$400$$

$$= 20 \text{ children per month}$$

An income statement for the firm, set in a contribution margin format, reveals the same result.

Sales Revenue (20 × $600)	$12,000
Less Variable Costs (20 × $200)	4,000
Contribution Margin	8,000
Less Fixed Costs	5,000
Profit Before Taxes	3,000
Income Taxes ($3,000 × 40%)	1,200
Operating Profit	$ 1,800

Managerial Application

Calculating Break-Even Points for a Brewpub

Three entrepreneurs from California were looking for investors to finance their new brewpub. Brewpubs focus on two segments utilized by customers—food from the restaurant segment and freshly brewed beer from the beer production segment. In the process of raising capital from potential investors and banks, all parties involved (owners, investors, and banks) wanted to know what projected profits would be for the new business. After months of research, the investors created a financial model that provided this information. Projected profits were $300,000 for the first year (from sales of $1.95 million), with increases in each of the next four years.

One of the owners asked: "What if our projected revenues are too high? What will happen to profits if sales are lower than we expect? After all, we will have debt with the bank for well over one million dollars, and I don't want them coming after my personal assets if we don't have the money to pay them from the business!" Although the owners felt the financial model was reasonably accurate, they decided to find the break-even point and the resulting margin of safety.

Because a brewpub does not sell "units" of a specific product, the owners resorted to finding the break-even point in sales dollars. The owners knew the contribution margin ratio and all fixed costs from the financial model. With this information, they were able to calculate the break-even point and margin of safety. The worried owner was relieved to discover that sales could drop over 35 percent from initial projections before the brewpub incurred an operating loss.

Source: Reprinted by permission of Kurt Heisinger, Sierra College, March 2003.

Multiple Product Financial Modeling

Most companies produce and sell many products. Multiple products make using financial modeling more complex, as the following example shows.

Example   Sport Autos, a sports car dealership, sells two models, Sleek and Powerful. The relevant prices and costs of each appear in Exhibit 6.5. Average monthly fixed costs of the new car department are $100,000. Looking at Exhibit 6.5, what is the average contribution margin ratio of each product? (Answer: Sleek = 25 percent = $5,000/$20,000. Powerful = 33 percent = $10,000/$30,000.)

We expand the cost-volume-profit equation presented earlier to consider the contribution of each product:

Operating Profit = (Contribution Margin for Sleek Model × Sales Volume for Sleek Model)
       + (Contribution Margin for Powerful Model × Sales Volume for Powerful Model)
       − Fixed Costs

We expand the cost-volume-profit equation presented earlier to consider the contribution of each product:

Operating Profit = (Contribution Margin for Sleek Model × Sales Volume for Sleek Model)
       + (Contribution Margin for Powerful Model × Sales Volume for Powerful Model)
       − Fixed Costs

Based on the information for Sport Autos, the company's profit equation is

Operating Profit = ($20,000 − $15,000)(Sleek Model Sales Volume)
       + ($30,000 − $20,000)(Powerful Model Sales Volume) − $100,000

Operating Profit = ($5,000 × Sleek Model Sales Volume)
       + ($10,000 × Powerful Model Sales Volume) − $100,000

The chief executive of Sport Autos has been listening to a debate between two of the salespeople about the break-even point for the company. According to one, "We have to sell 20 cars a month to break even." But the other one claims that 10 cars a month would be sufficient. The chief executive wonders how these two salespeople could hold such different views. (It turns out that both are right.)

The break-even volume is the volume that provides a contribution that just covers all fixed costs. For Sport Autos, that is

($5,000 × Sleek Model Sales Volume) + ($10,000 × Powerful Model Sales Volume) = $100,000

The claim that 20 cars must be sold to break even is correct if the firm sells only the Sleek model ($5,000 × 20 = $100,000), whereas the claim that only 10 cars need to be sold is correct if the firm sells only the Powerful model ($10,000 × 10 = $100,000). In fact, Sport Autos has many possible product-mix combinations at which it would break even.

EXHIBIT 6.5	SPORT AUTOS Price and Cost Data				
		Sleek		**Powerful**	
Average Selling Price per Car			$20,000		$30,000
Less Average Variable Costs:					
Cost of Car	$11,000		$15,000		
Cost of Preparing Car for Sale	3,000		3,000		
Sales Commissions	1,000	15,000	2,000	20,000	
Average Contribution Margin per Car			$ 5,000		$10,000

EXHIBIT 6.6	SPORT AUTOS Combinations of Break-Even Quantities

Sleek Model		Powerful Model				
Quantity	Contribution	Quantity	Contribution	Total Contribution	Fixed Costs	Profit
20	$100,000	0	$ 0	$100,000	$100,000	$0
18	90,000	1	10,000	100,000	100,000	0
16	80,000	2	20,000	100,000	100,000	0
.	.	.	.	.	.	.
.	.	.	.	.	.	.
.	.	.	.	.	.	.
4	20,000	8	80,000	100,000	100,000	0
2	10,000	9	90,000	100,000	100,000	0
0	0	10	100,000	100,000	100,000	0

Exhibit 6.6 lists possible break-even points for Sport Autos. Looking at Exhibit 6.6, how many Sleek models must be sold to break even if four Powerful models are sold? (Answer: 12.)

This simple example demonstrates how complex multiple-product cost-volume-profit analysis can become. In a company with many products, billions of combinations of product volumes can provide a specific target profit. To deal with this problem, managers and accountants have several alternatives:

1. Assume that all products have the same contribution margin.
2. Assume a weighted-average contribution margin.
3. Treat each product line as a separate entity.
4. Use sales dollars as a measure of volume.

In addition to these simplifications, firms can conduct multiple-product analyses with a mathematical method known as linear programming, discussed in Chapter 7. We now look at each of these alternatives.

Assume the Same Contribution Margin

The analyst can often group products so that they have equal or nearly equal contribution margins. It does not matter whether the firm sells a unit of Product A or a unit of Product B if both have the same contribution margin. (This approach won't work for Sport Autos because Sleeks and Powerfuls have different contribution margins.)

Assume a Weighted-Average Contribution Margin

If we assume the product mix to be two Sleeks for every Powerful, the per-unit weighted average contribution margin is

	Sleeks	Powerfuls	Weighted-Average Contribution Margin
	$(2/3 \times \$5,000) + (1/3 \times \$10,000) =$		$6,667

The break-even point is:

Break-Even Units = Fixed Costs/Weighted-Average Contribution Margin per Unit

= $100,000/$6,667

= 15 cars

of which 2/3, or 10, are Sleeks and 1/3, or 5, are Powerfuls, according to the preceding product-mix assumption.

What is the effect of incorrect assumptions in this analysis about product mix? If the actual mix is richer than assumed (more Powerfuls, in our example), the firm requires fewer units than predicted to break even. The firm requires more units than predicted to break even if the mix is poorer than assumed. The data in Exhibit 6.6 demonstrate this point. If only Powerfuls are sold, for example, then only 10 cars must be sold to break even. However, 20 cars must be sold to break even if only Sleeks are sold.

Treat Each Product Line as a Separate Entity

This method requires allocating indirect costs to product lines. To illustrate, we must allocate part of Sport Autos's $100,000 monthly fixed costs that the two products share to Sleeks and Powerfuls. To do this, managers and accountants must find a reasonable method of allocating costs. Often the product lines share these costs, so any allocation method may be somewhat arbitrary.

Suppose that of the $100,000 common cost, Sport Autos allocates 40 percent to Sleeks and 60 percent to Powerfuls. We can then do break-even analysis and other cost-volume-profit analyses by product line as follows.

For Sleeks:

$$\text{Break-Even Units} = \text{Fixed Costs/Contribution Margin per Unit}$$
$$= \$40,000/(\$20,000 - \$15,000)$$
$$= 8 \text{ units.}$$

For Powerfuls:

$$\text{Break-Even Units} = \text{Fixed Costs/Contribution Margin per Unit}$$
$$= \$60,000/(\$30,000 - \$20,000)$$
$$= 6 \text{ units.}$$

Allocating indirect cost to product lines makes it possible for managers to analyze each product line's cost-volume-profit relations. Be wary, however, of any analysis that relies on arbitrary cost allocations. It would be a mistake to believe that Sleeks cause fixed costs of $40,000 and Powerfuls cause fixed costs of $60,000. The two product lines combined cause fixed costs of $100,000; the breakdown of those costs between product lines is arbitrary. Further, note that a change in the arbitrary allocation method changes the break-even volume.

For example, if we allocated the $100,000 as $20,000 to Sleeks and $80,000 to Powerfuls, break-even requires the sale of 4 Sleeks (= $20,000/$5,000 per unit) and 8 Powerfuls (= $80,000/$10,000 per unit).

Cost Allocation   In many situations, companies often resort to allocating costs on the basis of relative sales dollars or on the basis of quantities of the product lines. Other allocation bases used include relative number of employees per product line (particularly to allocate labor-related costs) or relative square feet of space used by each product line (particularly to allocate space-related costs).

Cost allocation pervades managerial reports. The accuracy of the basis used to allocate costs will have an impact on the accuracy of cost-volume-profit analysis. In an effort to be more accurate, many companies try to identify cost drivers—the activities that cause costs—to be used as the basis of allocation. Cost allocation is discussed in detail in Chapter 13.

Use Sales Dollars as a Measure of Volume

Earlier we referred to the sales-dollars approach to find break-even points when a company has multiple products or provides services. This approach can be used for Sport Autos as follows.

Assume Sport Autos has been selling 20 Sleeks and 10 Powerfuls per month. Sales have been $700,000, as shown in Exhibit 6.7. The contribution margin has been $200,000. Therefore, the weighted-average contribution margin ratio is as follows:

$$\text{Weighted-Average Contribution Margin Ratio} = \text{Total Contribution Margin/Total Sales}$$
$$= \$200,000/\$700,000$$
$$= 0.286$$

	Sleeks	Powerfuls	Total
EXHIBIT 6.7 — SPORT AUTOS Income Statement Month Ended April 30			
Sales	$400,000	$300,000	$700,000
Variable Costs	300,000	200,000	500,000
Contribution Margin	$100,000	$100,000	$200,000

We now calculate break-even in sales dollars assuming product mix is the same at break-even as at past sales levels.

Break-Even Sales Dollars = Fixed Costs/Weighted-Average Contribution Margin Ratio

= $100,000/0.286

= $350,000

Problem 6.3 for Self-Study

Finding break-even points in unit sales and sales dollars. Shades Company manufactures three inexpensive models of sunglasses with the following characteristics:

	Surfer	Skier	Runner
Price per Unit	$5	$6	$7
Variable Cost per Unit	$3	$2	$4
Expected Sales (units)	100,000	150,000	250,000

Total fixed costs for the company are $1,240,000.

Assume that the product mix at the break-even point would be the same as that for expected sales. Compute the break-even point in:

a. Units using the weighted-average method.
b. Sales dollars using the weighted-average method.

The solution to this self-study problem is at the end of this chapter on pages 198–199.

Using the Contribution Margin in Product Choice Decisions

The contribution margin plays an important role in making product choice decisions. Suppose Sport Autos wants to get into the business of selling relatively inexpensive sports cars and has the opportunity to sell one unit of either of the following cars (not both):

	Price
Sportster Coupe	$12,000
Sportster Convertible	15,000

Which would you sell? The Sportster Convertible? Is it more profitable? We cannot tell which product is more profitable until we consider their variable costs. Suppose that we find the following:

	Price	Variable Cost	Contribution Margin
Sportster Coupe	$12,000	$ 7,000	$5,000
Sportster Convertible	15,000	11,000	4,000

Although the Sportster Convertible's price is higher and it would provide more revenues, the Sportster Coupe's contribution to fixed costs and profits is higher. (This point raises an interesting incentive problem if sales personnel are paid a commission that is a percent of revenue. Sales personnel facing such a commission structure would have an incentive to sell the higher-priced but less profitable automobile.)

Simplifications and Assumptions

The financial model discussed in this chapter (often called the CVP model) simplifies costs, revenues, and volume to make the analysis easier. It is possible to describe the economic relations more completely than the model does, but to do so is costly. The careful user of financial models should be aware of the following common assumptions and be prepared to perform sensitivity analysis to see how the assumptions affect the model's results.

You can use the financial model most powerfully by analyzing how various alternatives affect operations. This analysis works because the model captures most of the important operating relationships of the firm in a single equation. We can analyze the effects of changes in any of the following variables on the remaining variables: selling price, number of units sold, variable cost, fixed cost, sales mix, and production mix.

Our illustrations in this chapter assumed a linear relation between revenues and volume and between cost and volume. You can, however, apply the model with nonlinear revenue and cost functions. Practice usually assumes cost and revenue curves to be linear over some **relevant range** of activity.

We also implicitly assumed that the analyst can predict the variables in the model with certainty and that selling price per unit, total fixed costs, and variable costs per unit will not change as the level of activity changes. This assumption implies that prices paid and charged are constant and that workers' productivity does not change during the period. Finally, to derive a unique break-even point for multiple products, we require that the production mix and sales mix not change as the level of activity changes.

Summary of Assumptions Required to Make the CVP Model Work

1. We can separate total costs into fixed and variable components.
2. Cost and revenue behavior is linear throughout the relevant range of activity. This assumption implies the following:
   a. Total fixed costs do not change throughout the relevant range of activity.
   b. Variable costs per unit remain constant throughout the relevant range of activity.
   c. Selling price per unit remains constant throughout the relevant range of activity.
3. Product mix remains constant throughout the relevant range of activity.

Assumptions of the cost-volume-profit model make it easy to use, but they also make it unrealistic. Before criticizing the model on this score, however, consider the costs and benefits of relaxing those assumptions to create more realism. Often the cost of more realism exceeds the benefits from improved decision-making.

Financial Modeling and ABC's Multiple-Cost Drivers

As indicated above, several assumptions must be made in using the CVP financial model described in this chapter. In addition, the use of a single cost driver is a significant limitation.

Picture the CVP model that we introduced for Early Horizons Daycare. The amount of revenue was based solely on the number of children enrolled. Variable costs, although not specifically mentioned, were driven by the number of children enrolled, and fixed costs were presumed to be fixed. The major factor, then, is children enrolled—a volume-related driver. Imagine in a more generic situation the number of items that could cause revenues and costs to change. Revenues are driven not only by volume but also by selling prices, number of competitive products, quality considerations, general economic conditions, target markets (e.g., upper- versus middle-income individuals), and promotional programs, among others. Similarly, costs for a university are influenced by the number of students, number of faculty, number of administrators, number and size of buildings, building operating condition (e.g., new, in need of repair, energy efficient), number of graduate teaching assistants, prominence and success of athletic programs, number of research grants, level of state support or private funding, number and types of programs offered (e.g., undergraduate versus doctoral), class size, commitment to technology, and other factors. Although these lists may appear to be fairly comprehensive, we have only touched the surface. Importantly, though, the lists show how multiple drivers affect financial performance.

The issue of multiple drivers should be familiar to you, as it was introduced in Chapter 3 with the discussion of activity-based costing (ABC). Just as ABC was shown to improve costing accuracy and related decision making, it also produces organizational benefits when coupled with the CVP model. An activity-based costing system can provide a much more complete picture of cost-volume-profit relationships, thus furnishing better information to managers.

Cost Hierarchy Review

Before we show the integration of CVP with the multiple-cost drivers of ABC, it is probably helpful if we quickly review the nature of unit-, batch-, product-, customer-, and facility-level activities and costs. Recall that:

- *Unit-level activities* are performed for each individual unit of product or service.
- *Batch-level activities* are performed to benefit multiple units of output equally and simultaneously (i.e., in batches). Related costs are traced easily to specific batches but not to individual output units.
- *Product-level activities* are needed to support a specific product or service, that is, an entire "product line." Such activities may include product design, product advertising, and maintaining product specifications.
- *Customer-level activities* are performed when meeting the needs of specific customers. Examples of related costs include those attributable to unique packaging, shipping, and distribution needs and to personnel who are assigned to handle specific customer accounts.
- *Facility-level activities* are required for an organization to have the capacity to produce goods and services. Such activities are at the highest level of the activity hierarchy and tend to support all organizational processes. Typical examples include the activities of top management and operating the physical plant.

These activity categories will change the nature of the CVP model. The basic model assumes that certain costs (the variable costs) vary with sales volume while others, the fixed costs, remain constant. With activity-based costing, costs vary because of drivers other than sales. The result is the following total cost expression:

$$\text{Total Cost} = (\text{Unit-Level Cost} \times \text{Number of Units}) + (\text{Batch-Level Cost} \times \text{Batch CDA})$$
$$+ (\text{Product-Level Cost} \times \text{Product CDA}) + (\text{Customer-Level Cost} \times \text{Customer CDA})$$
$$+ (\text{Facility-Level Cost} \times \text{Facility CDA})$$

where CDA = cost driver activity (e.g., number of batches, number of change orders, number of customers, number or size of facilities, and so on).

Observe that this calculation no longer focuses on the number of children enrolled as the sole cost driver. Instead, the impact of multiple cost drivers—the hallmark of an activity-based costing system—is introduced. As a result, some costs viewed as fixed under the traditional analysis are now considered variable with respect to the appropriate cost drivers under the ABC approach.

Using ABC in Financial Modeling

Using account analysis, multiple regression, and knowledge of cost behavior, the accountant for Early Horizons Daycare developed a set of cost drivers to use in a financial model. Here they are.

- **Unit-level.** The cost per child is estimated to be $20 per month, mostly to cover snacks and lunch.
- **Batch-level.** Each room used for a maximum of five children is considered a batch. The cost per month is estimated to be $700 per batch and includes items such as toys, crayons, and "Big Friends" (one Big Friend to each room).
- **Product-level.** Early Horizons often takes certain groups of children on field trips (e.g., to the local pumpkin patch). On average, one trip is taken each month. The product-level costs include bus rental and entrance costs. These costs are estimated to be $300 per field trip.
- **Customer-level.** Early Horizons offers daily transportation services to certain children. Rented vans and hired drivers are the customer-level costs involved and typically total $100 per child per month.
- **Facility-level.** These costs include building rent, utilities, salaried manager, accounting services, advertising, and insurance. Facility-level costs total $4,700 per month.

Armed with this information, Early Horizon's accountant developed the financial model shown in Exhibit 6.8.

Having gone to the trouble of developing the financial model shown in Exhibit 6.8, we can easily modify the numbers to consider alternative scenarios for financial planning and decision

EXHIBIT 6.8	Spreadsheet for EARLY HORIZONS Multiple Cost Drivers		
	(1) Base Case	(2) Increase Enrollment to 22	(3) Decrease Enrollment to 15
Assumptions			
Revenues			
Price per child	$ 600	$ 600	$ 600
Children enrolled	20	22	15
Costs			
Unit-Level	$ 20	$ 20	$ 20
Children enrolled	20	22	15
Batch-Level	$ 700	$ 700	$ 700
Number of rooms	4	5	3
Product-Level	$ 300	$ 300	$ 300
Number of field trips	1	1	1
Customer-Level	$ 100	$ 100	$ 100
Children transported	8	8	5
Facility-Level	$ 4,700	$ 4,700	$4,700
Number of facilities	1	1	1
Financial Model Results (Income Statement)			
Sales revenue	$12,000	$13,200	$9,000
Unit-level costs	400	440	300
Batch-level costs	2,800	3,500	2,100
Product-level costs	300	300	300
Customer-level costs	800	800	500
Facility-level costs	4,700	4,700	4,700
Operating profit	$ 3,000	$ 3,460	$1,100

making. For example, column (2) shows what is expected to happen to operating profit if enrollment increases from 20 to 22. Total revenues increase to $13,200. Total unit-level costs change because they are driven by the number of children enrolled. Total batch-level costs change because each room has a capacity of 5 children, and with 2 additional children, a new room must be used. Other costs remain the same, and operating profit increases by $460 to $3,460.

Column (3) shows what will happen with operating profit if enrollment decreases to 15 and children being transported decreases to 5. Total operating profit decreases by $1,900 (from the base case) to $1,100.

Summary

The following items relate to the learning objectives listed at the beginning of the chapter.

1. **Describe the use of financial modeling for profit-planning purposes.** Financial models help management to analyze financial relationships that are useful for decision making. Examples include the relation of contribution margin to sales, the relative proportion of various products sold (product mix), and the relation of changes in cost to operating profit.
2. **Explain how to perform cost-volume-profit (CVP) analysis.** The CVP model is one example of a financial model. It can be used to calculate required selling price, find new break-even points, find target profit points, conduct sensitivity analyses, compare alternatives, and calculate multiple break-even points. The margin of safety is the excess of projected sales units over the break-even unit sales level.

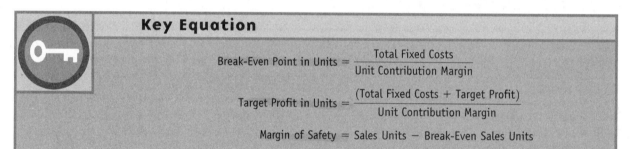

Key Equation

$$\text{Break-Even Point in Units} = \frac{\text{Total Fixed Costs}}{\text{Unit Contribution Margin}}$$

$$\text{Target Profit in Units} = \frac{(\text{Total Fixed Costs} + \text{Target Profit})}{\text{Unit Contribution Margin}}$$

$$\text{Margin of Safety} = \text{Sales Units} - \text{Break-Even Sales Units}$$

3. **Describe the use of spreadsheets in financial modeling.** Spreadsheets can be used to conduct "what-if" analyses. Once you have set up the basic formula, it is easy to determine the effect of changing price, costs, volume amounts, or any other variable deemed important to the analysis.
4. **Identify the effects of cost structure and operating leverage on the sensitivity of profit to changes in volume.** The cost structure of an organization is the proportion of fixed and variable costs to total costs. Operating leverage is high in firms with a high proportion of fixed costs, a small proportion of variable costs, and the resulting high contribution margin per unit. The higher the firm's leverage, the higher the degree of sensitivity of profits to volume changes.
5. **Explain how to use sales dollars as the measure of volume.** The cost-volume-profit equation remains the same as before, except the focus is on solving for *total revenue* required to break even or to reach a target profit rather than total units. Note that the contribution margin ratio is defined as the total contribution margin divided by total sales, or, alternatively, unit contribution margin divided by unit sales price.

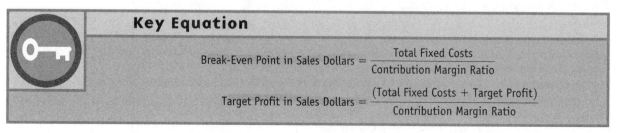

Key Equation

$$\text{Break-Even Point in Sales Dollars} = \frac{\text{Total Fixed Costs}}{\text{Contribution Margin Ratio}}$$

$$\text{Target Profit in Sales Dollars} = \frac{(\text{Total Fixed Costs} + \text{Target Profit})}{\text{Contribution Margin Ratio}}$$

6. **Explain the effect of taxes on financial modeling.** To solve for after-tax target profit points, simply input the after-tax target profit amount and tax rate into the following equation. Note that t is the tax rate. This will result in the before-tax target profit,

$$\text{After-Tax Profit}/(1 - t) = \text{Before-Tax Profit}.$$

The resulting before-tax profit is used in the following formulas to find the target profit in units or the target profit in sales dollars.

$$\text{Target Profit in Units} = \frac{(\text{Total Fixed Costs} + \text{Before-Tax Target Profit})}{\text{Unit Contribution Margin}}$$

$$\text{Target Profit in Sales Dollars} = \frac{(\text{Total Fixed Costs} + \text{Before-Tax Target Profit})}{\text{Contribution Margin Ratio}}$$

7. **Describe the use of financial modeling in a multiple-product setting.** Multiple products make using financial models more complex. To deal with this, managers can (1) assume that all products have the same contribution margin, (2) assume that a particular product mix does not change, (3) assume a weighted-average contribution margin, or (4) treat each product line as a separate entity.

Key Equation

Operating Profit = (Contribution Margin for Product 1

× Sales Volume for Product 1)

+ (Contribution Margin for Product 2

× Sales Volume for Product 2) − Fixed Costs

8. **Explain financial modeling with multiple cost drivers.** Developing a financial model with multiple cost drivers is a more refined way of assessing how changes to the model's variables will impact other variables. Costs are analyzed using the five cost hierarchy categories: unit-level, batch-level, product-level, customer-level, and facility-level.

Key Terms and Concepts

Break-even point	Margin of safety
Contribution margin per unit	Operating leverage
Contribution margin ratio	Profit-volume graph
Cost structure	Relevant range
Cost-volume-profit (CVP) model	Sensitivity analysis
Financial model	

Solutions to Self-Study Problems

SUGGESTED SOLUTION TO PROBLEM 6.1 FOR SELF-STUDY

a. Operating profit:

Sales Revenue (20,000 × $9)	$180,000
Less Variable Costs (20,000 × $6)	120,000
Contribution Margin	60,000
Less Fixed Costs	36,000
Operating Profit	$ 24,000

b. Break-even point:

$$\text{Break-Even Units} = \text{Fixed Costs/Contribution Margin per Unit}$$

$$= \$36,000/(\$9 - \$6)$$

$$= 12,000 \text{ units}$$

c. Target volume:

$$\text{Target Profit in Units} = (\text{Fixed Costs} + \text{Target Profit})/\text{Contribution Margin per Unit}$$

$$= (\$36,000 + \$30,000)/(\$9 - \$6)$$

$$= \$66,000/\$3$$

$$= 22,000 \text{ units}$$

SUGGESTED SOLUTION TO PROBLEM 6.2 FOR SELF-STUDY

a. $0A$ = (2) Fixed Cost per Period
b. IG = (7) None of the Above
c. $0D$ = (6) Break-Even Sales in Units
d. $B0$ = (2) Fixed Cost per Period; also, Operating Loss When Sales Are Zero
e. $0H - 0D$ = (5) Margin of Safety in Units
f. $B0/0D$ = (4) Contribution Margin per Unit
g. $HF + HG$ = (3) Revenue
h. True
i. False; if revenue is HE, the margin of safety is DH.
j. False
k. True
l. False
m. True

SUGGESTED SOLUTION TO PROBLEM 6.3 FOR SELF-STUDY

a. To find the break-even point in units, first compute the weighted-average contribution margin:

	Surfer	Skier	Runner
Product Mix	100,000 Units/ 500,000 Units = 0.20	150,000/ 500,000 = 0.30	250,000/ 500,000 = 0.50
Weighted-Average Contribution Margin	0.20($2)	+ 0.30($4)	+ 0.50($3) = $3.10

Or

$$[(100,000 \text{ Units})(\$2) + (150,000)(\$4) + (250,000)(\$3)]/500,000 = \$3.10$$

Then input the weighted-average contribution margin in the break-even formula:

$$\text{Break-Even Units} = \text{Fixed Costs/Weighted-Average Contribution Margin per Unit}$$

$$= \$1,240,000/\$3.10$$

$$= 400,000 \text{ units}$$

b. To find the break-even point in sales dollars, first compute the weighted-average contribution margin ratio:

Weighted-Average Contribution Margin Ratio = Total Contribution Margin/Total Sales

$$= [(\$2 \times 100,000) + (\$4 \times 150,000) + (\$3 \times 250,000)]/$$

$$[(\$5 \times 100,000) + (\$6 \times 150,000) + (\$7 \times 250,000)]$$

$$= (\$200,000 + \$600,000 + \$750,000)/(\$500,000 + \$900,000 + \$1,750,000)$$

$$= \$1,550,000/\$3,150,000$$

$$= 0.492 \text{ (rounded)}$$

Then input the weighted-average contribution margin ratio in the break-even formula:

Break-Even Sales Dollars = Fixed Costs/Weighted-Average Contribution Margin Ratio

= $1,240,000/0.492

= $2,520,000 (rounded)

Questions, Exercises, Problems, and Cases

REVIEW QUESTIONS

1. Review the meaning of the terms or concepts given in Key Terms and Concepts.
2. Define the profit equation.
3. Define the term *contribution margin*.
4. Name three common assumptions of a linear cost-volume-profit analysis.
5. What effect could the following changes, occurring independently, have on (1) the break-even point, (2) the unit contribution margin, and (3) the expected total profit?
   a. An increase in fixed costs.
   b. A decrease in wage rates applicable to direct, strictly variable labor.
   c. An increase in the selling price of the product.
   d. An increase in production and sales volume.
   e. An increase in building insurance rates.

CRITICAL ANALYSIS AND DISCUSSION QUESTIONS

6. How does the total contribution margin (unit contribution margin × total number of units sold) differ from the gross margin often seen on companies' financial statements?
7. Compare cost-volume-profit analysis with profit-volume analysis. How do they differ?
8. How do spreadsheets assist in financial modeling?
9. How does the profit equation change when the analyst uses the multiple-product financial model?
10. If companies that are operating below the break-even point cannot raise prices, what must they do to break even?
11. Fixed costs are often defined as "fixed over the short run." Does this mean that they are not fixed over the long run? Why or why not?
12. Why do accountants use a linear representation of cost and revenue behavior in cost-volume-profit analysis? Justify this use.
13. Assume the linear cost relation of the cost-volume-profit model for a single-product firm, and use the following answer key:
    (1) more than double
    (2) double
    (3) increase, but less than double
    (4) remain the same
    (5) decrease
    Complete each of the following statements, assuming that all other things (such as quantities) remain constant.
    a. If price doubles, revenue will _____.
    b. If price doubles, the total contribution margin (contribution margin per unit × number of units) will _____.
    c. If price doubles, profit will _____.
    d. If contribution margin per unit doubles, profit will _____.
    e. If fixed costs double, the total contribution margin will _____.
    f. If fixed costs double, profit will _____.
    g. If fixed costs double, the break-even point of units sold will _____.
    h. If total sales of units double, profit will _____.
    i. If total sales dollars double, the break-even point will _____.
    j. If the contribution margin per unit doubles, the break-even point will _____.
    k. If both variable costs per unit and selling price per unit double, profit will _____.
14. Is a company really breaking even if it produces and sells at the break-even point? What costs may not be covered?

15. Why does multiple product cost-volume-profit analysis often assume a constant product mix?

16. When would the sum of the break-even quantities for each of a company's products not be the break-even point for the company as a whole?

17. A sporting goods retailer is running a monthly special, with snow skis and snowboards being priced to yield a negative contribution margin. What would motivate a retailer to do this?

EXERCISES

Solutions to even-numbered exercises are at the end of the chapter.

18. **Break-even and target profits.** Analysis of the operations of Padillo Company shows the fixed costs to be $200,000 and the variable costs to be $8 per unit. Selling price is $16 per unit.

    a. Derive the break-even point expressed in units.
    b. How many units must the firm sell to earn a profit of $280,000?
    c. What would profits be if revenue from sales were $2,000,000?

19. **Cost-volume-profit; volume defined in sales dollars.** An excerpt from the income statement of the Donelan Company follows. Estimated fixed costs in Year 1 are $660,000.

DONELAN COMPANY
Income Statement
Year Ended December 31, Year 1

Sales		$3,000,000
Operating Expenses:		
Cost of Goods Sold	$1,425,000	
Selling Costs	450,000	
Administrative Costs	225,000	
Total Operating Costs		2,100,000
Profit		$ 900,000

    a. What percentage of sales revenue is variable cost?
    b. What is the break-even point in sales dollars for Donelan Company?
    c. Prepare a cost-volume-profit graph for Donelan Company.
    d. If sales revenue falls to $2,500,000, what will be the estimated amount of profit?
    e. What amount of sales dollars produces a profit of $1,000,000?

20. **Cost-volume-profit graph.** Identify each item on the accompanying graph:

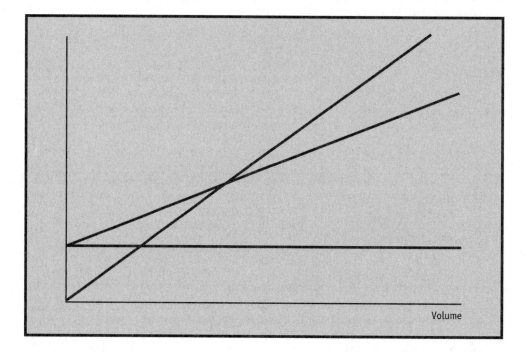

    a. the total cost line
    b. the total revenue line
    c. total variable costs
    d. variable cost per unit
    e. the total fixed costs
    f. the break-even point
    g. the profit area (or volume)
    h. the loss area (or volume)

21. **Profit-volume graph.** Identify the places on the following profit-volume graph of Bohemian Laboratories indicated by the letters.

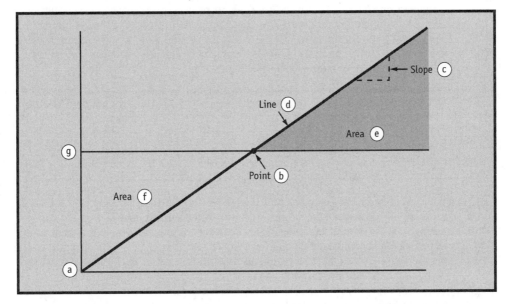

22. **Cost-volume-profit analysis.** PJ Company produces one type of sunglasses with the following costs and revenues for the year:

Total Revenues	$5,000,000
Total Fixed Costs	$1,000,000
Total Variable Costs	$3,000,000
Total Quantity Produced and Sold	1,000,000 Units

    a. What is the selling price per unit?
    b. What is the variable cost per unit?
    c. What is the contribution margin per unit?
    d. What is the break-even point in units?
    e. Assume an income-tax rate of 40 percent. What quantity of units is required for PJ Company to make an after-tax operating profit of $1,200,000 for the year?

23. **Break-even and target profits; volume defined in sales dollars.** The manager of Wong's Food Express estimates operating costs for the year will total $300,000 for fixed costs.
    a. Find the break-even point in sales dollars with a contribution margin ratio of 40 percent.
    b. Find the break-even point in sales dollars with a contribution margin ratio of 25 percent.
    c. Find the sales dollars required with a contribution margin ratio of 40 percent to generate a profit of $100,000.

24. **CVP—sensitivity analysis. spreadsheet recommended.** Quality Cabinet Construction is considering introducing a new cabinet-production seminar with the following price and cost characteristics:

Tuition	$200 per Student
Variable Costs (wood, supplies, etc.)	$120 per Student
Fixed Costs (advertising, instructor's salary, insurance, etc.)	$400,000 per Year

a. What enrollment enables Quality Cabinet Construction to break even?

b. How many students will enable Quality Cabinet Construction to make an operating profit of $200,000 for the year?

c. Assume that the projected enrollment for the year is 8,000 students for each of the following situations:

  (1) What will be the operating profit for 8,000 students?

  (2) What would be the operating profit if the tuition per student (that is, sales price) decreased by 10 percent? Increased by 20 percent?

  (3) What would be the operating profit if variable costs per student decreased by 10 percent? Increased by 20 percent?

  (4) Suppose that fixed costs for the year are 10 percent lower than projected, whereas variable costs per student are 10 percent higher than projected. What would be the operating profit for the year?

25. **Multiple-product profit analysis.** Cisco's Sumptuous Burritos produces two burritos, chicken and steak, with the following characteristics:

	Chicken	Steak
Selling Price per Unit	$4	$6
Variable Cost per Unit	$2	$3
Expected Sales (units)	100,000	150,000

The total fixed costs for the company are $100,000.

a. What is the anticipated level of profits for the expected sales volumes?

b. Assuming that the product mix would be 40 percent chicken and 60 percent steak at the break-even point, compute the break-even volume.

c. If the product sales mix were to change to four chicken burritos for each steak burrito, what would be the new break-even volume?

26. **Multiple-product profit analysis.** The Salinas Company produces and sells three products. Operating data for the three products follow.

	Selling Price per Unit	Variable Cost per Unit	Fixed Cost per Month
Product P	$3	$2	—
Product Q	5	3	—
Product R	8	5	—
Entire Company	—	—	$48,000

Define a unit as the sum of one unit of product R sold, two units of product Q sold, and three units of product P sold.

a. Draw a cost-volume-profit graph for the Salinas Company.

b. At what number of units does the Salinas Company break even?

c. Change the facts. Suppose a "unit" now consists of two units of product P for every two units of product Q and one unit of product R. At what number of units does Salinas Company break even?

27. **Solving for cost-based selling price.** Haun Company follows a cost-based approach to pricing. Prices are 150 percent of cost. The annual cost of producing one of its products follows:

Variable Manufacturing Costs	$15 per Unit
Fixed Manufacturing Costs	$50,000 per Year
Variable Selling and Administrative Costs	$2 per Unit
Fixed Selling and Administrative Costs	$75,000 per Year

a. Assume that Haun produces and sells 10,000 units. Calculate the selling price per unit.

b. Assume that Haun produces and sells 20,000 units. Calculate the selling price per unit.

PROBLEMS

28. Explaining sales and cost changes. You have acquired the following data for Years 1 and 2 for Sam's Splash Park.

	Year 1		Year 2		Dollar Increase
Revenue from Admissions	$750,000	100.0%	$840,000	100.0%	$90,000
Variable Costs of Operations	495,000	66.0	560,000	66.7	65,000
Contribution Margin	$255,000	34.0%	$280,000	33.3%	$25,000
Admission Price per Person	$10		$12		

Write a short report explaining the cause of the increase in total contribution margin between Year 1 and Year 2. Your report should consider the effect of each of the following: admission price change, change in volume, and change in operating costs per admission.

29. CVP analysis and financial modeling (adapted from CMA exam). Storage Devices Incorporated is a retailer for high-tech recording disks. The projected operating profit for the current year is $200,000 based on a sales volume of 200,000 units. The company has been selling the disks for $16 each; variable costs consist of the $10 purchase price and a $2 handling cost. The company's annual fixed costs are $600,000.

Management is planning for the coming year, when it expects that the unit purchase price of the disks will increase by 30 percent.

a. Calculate the company's break-even point for the current year in units.

b. What will be the company's operating profit for the current year if there is a 20 percent increase in projected unit sales volume?

c. What volume of dollar sales must be achieved in the coming year to maintain the current year's operating profit if the selling price remains at $16?

d. Would the use of a financial model be helpful to the firm in addressing issues such as those raised in requirements **b.** and **c.**? Explain.

30. CVP—missing data. Bonkoski Production has performed cost studies and projected the following annual costs based on 200,000 units of production and sales:

	Total Annual Costs (200,000 units)
Direct Material	$ 400,000
Direct Labor	360,000
Manufacturing Overhead	300,000
Selling, General, and Administrative	200,000
Total	$1,260,000

a. Compute Bonkoski's unit selling price that will yield a profit of $300,000, given sales of 200,000 units.

b. Assume management selects a selling price of $8 per unit. Compute Bonkoski's dollar sales that will yield a projected 20 percent profit on sales, assuming variable costs per unit are 60 percent of the selling price per unit and fixed costs are $420,000.

31. CVP analysis. A company is deciding which of two new thermostat systems to produce and sell. The Basic system has variable costs of $8.00 per unit, excluding sales commissions, and annual fixed costs of $520,000; the Deluxe system has variable costs of $6.40, excluding sales commissions, and fixed costs of $672,000. The company's selling price is $32 per unit for the Basic model and $38 for the Deluxe model. The company pays a 10 percent sales commission.

a. Which of the two systems will be more profitable for the firm if sales are expected to average 150,000 units per year?

b. How many units must the company sell to break even if it selects the Deluxe system?

c. Suppose the Basic system requires the purchase of additional equipment that is not reflected in the preceding figures. The equipment will cost $224,000 and will be depreciated over a 10-year life by the straight-line method. How many units must the company sell to earn $40,000 of income, after considering depreciation, if the Basic system is selected?

d. Ignoring the information presented in part **c.**, at what volume level will management be indifferent between the Basic system and the Deluxe system?

32. **CVP with taxes** (adapted from CMA exam). Illuminate Company, maker of quality flashlights, has experienced a steady growth in sales for the past five years. However, increased competition has led Mr. Schaberg, the CEO, to believe that to maintain the company's present growth requires an aggressive advertising campaign next year. To prepare the next year's advertising campaign, the company's accountant has prepared and presented to Mr. Schaberg the following data for the current year, Year 1:

Cost Schedule

Variable Costs:

Direct Labor	$10.00 per Flashlight
Direct Materials	4.50
Variable Overhead	2.00
Total Variable Costs	$16.50 per Flashlight

Fixed Costs:

Manufacturing	$ 40,000
Selling	30,000
Administrative	80,000
Total Fixed Costs	$150,000
Selling Price, per Flashlight	$ 40.00
Expected Sales, Year 1 (25,000 flashlights)	$1,000,000

Tax Rate: 35 Percent

Mr. Schaberg has set the sales target for Year 2 at a level of $1,120,000 (or 28,000 flashlights).

a. What is the projected after-tax operating profit for Year 1?

b. What is the after-tax break-even point in units for Year 1?

c. Mr. Schaberg believes that to attain the sales target (28,000 flashlights) requires an additional selling expense of $30,000 for advertising in Year 2, with all other costs remaining constant. What will be the after-tax operating profit for Year 2 if the firm spends the additional $30,000?

d. What will be the after-tax break-even point in sales dollars for Year 2 if the firm spends the additional $30,000 for advertising?

e. If the firm spends the additional $30,000 for advertising in Year 2, what is the sales level in dollars required to equal Year 1 after-tax operating profit?

f. At a sales level of 28,000 units, what is the maximum amount the firm can spend on advertising to earn an after-tax operating profit of $75,000?

33. **CVP—missing data; assumptions.** You are analyzing the financial performance of Sonoma Winery based on limited data from a *New York Times* article. The article says that despite an increase in sales revenue from $4,704,000 in Year 8 to $4,725,000 in Year 9, Sonoma recently reported a decline in net income of $129,500 from Year 8 to an amount equal to 2 percent of sales revenue in Year 9. The average total cost per unit increased from $2.200 in Year 8 to $2.205 in Year 9.

a. Compute the changes, if any, in average selling price and sales in units from Year 8 to Year 9.

b. Can you compute the total fixed costs and variable cost per unit during Year 9? If so, do so. If not, illustrate why with a graph and discuss any important assumptions of the cost-volume-profit model that this application violates.

34. **Alternatives to reduce break-even sales.** Shout Broadcasting operated at the break-even point of $2,250,000 during Year 1 while incurring fixed costs of $1,000,000. Management is considering two alternatives to reduce the break-even level. Alternative A trims fixed costs by $200,000 annually with no change in variable cost per unit; doing so, however, will reduce the quality of the product and result in a 10 percent decrease in selling price but no change in the number of units sold. Alternative B substitutes automated equipment for certain operations now performed manually. Alternative B will result in an annual increase of $300,000 in fixed costs but a 5 percent decrease in variable costs per barrel produced, with no change in product quality, selling price, or sales volume.

    a. What was the total contribution margin (contribution margin per unit times number of units sold) during Year 1?

    b. What is the break-even point in sales dollars under alternative A?

    c. What is the break-even point in sales dollars under alternative B?

    d. What should the company do?

35. **CVP analysis with semifixed (step) costs.** Logo Company has one product: printing logos on sweatshirts for businesses. The sales price of $20 remains constant per unit regardless of volume, as does the variable cost of $12 per unit. The company is considering operating at one of the following three monthly levels of operations:

	Volume Range (production and sales)	Total Fixed Costs	Increase in Fixed Costs from Previous Level
Level 1	0–10,000	$ 40,000	—
Level 2	10,001–25,000	80,000	$40,000
Level 3	25,001–40,000	100,000	20,000

    a. Calculate the break-even point(s) in units.

    b. If the company can sell everything it makes, should it operate at level 1, level 2, or level 3? Support your answer.

36. **CVP analysis with semifixed costs and changing unit variable costs.** The Arganon Company manufactures and sells crystal earrings. The sales price, $50 per unit, remains constant regardless of volume. Last year's sales were 15,000 units, and operating profits were $200,000. Fixed costs depend on production levels, as the following table shows. Variable costs per unit are 40 percent *higher* for level 2 (two shifts) than for level 1 (day shift only). The additional labor costs result primarily from higher wages required to employ workers for the night shift.

	Annual Production Range (in units)	Annual Total Fixed Costs
Level 1 (day shift)	0–20,000	$100,000
Level 2 (day and night shifts)	20,001–36,000	164,000

Arganon expects last year's cost structure and selling price not to change this year. Maximum plant capacity is 36,000. The company sells everything it produces.

    a. Compute the contribution margin per unit for last year for each of the two production levels.

    b. Compute the break-even points in units for last year for each of the two production levels.

    c. Compute the volume in units that will maximize operating profits. Defend your choice.

37. **CVP analysis with semifixed costs.** Melissa Mooring, director and owner of the Kids Education Center, has a master's degree in elementary education. In the seven years she has been running the Kids Education Center, her salary has ranged from nothing to $20,000 per year. "The second year," she says, "I made 62 cents an hour." (Her salary is what's left over after meeting all other expenses.)

    Could she run a more profitable center? She thinks perhaps she could if she increased the student–teacher ratio, which is currently five students to one teacher. (Government standards for a center such as this set a maximum of 10 students per teacher.) She refuses to increase the ratio to more than six-to-one. "If you increase the ratio to more than six-to-one, the children don't get enough attention. In addition, the demands on the teacher are far too great." She does not hire part-time teachers.

    Mooring rents the space for her center in the basement of a church for $900 per month, including utilities. She estimates that supplies, snacks, and other nonpersonnel costs are $80 per student per month. She charges $380 per month per student. Teachers receive $1,200 per month, including fringe benefits. She has no other operating costs. At present, she cares for 30 students and employs six teachers.

    a. What is the present operating profit per month of the Kids Education Center before Ms. Mooring's salary?

b. What is (are) the break-even point(s), before Ms. Mooring's salary, assuming a student–teacher ratio of 6:1?

c. What would be the break-even point(s), before Ms. Mooring's salary, if the student–teacher ratio increased to 10:1?

d. Ms. Mooring has an opportunity to increase the student body by six students. She must take all six or none. Should she accept the six students if she wants to maintain a maximum student–teacher ratio of 6:1?

e. (Continuation of part **d.**) Suppose that Ms. Mooring accepts the six children. Now she has the opportunity to accept one more, which requires hiring one more teacher. What would happen to profit, before her salary, if she accepts one more student?

38. **Break-even analysis for management education.** The dean of the Graduate School of Management at the University of California at Davis was considering whether to offer a particular seminar for executives. The tuition was $650 per person. Variable costs, which included meals, parking, and materials, were $80 per person. Certain costs of offering the seminar, including advertising the seminar, instructors' fees, room rent, and audiovisual equipment rent, would not be affected by the number of people attending (within a "relevant range"). Such costs, which could be thought of as step costs, amounted to $8,000 for the seminar.

    In addition to these costs, a number of staff, including the dean of the school, worked on the program. Although the salaries paid to these staff were not affected by offering the seminar, working on the seminar took these people away from other duties, thus creating an opportunity cost estimated at $7,000 for this seminar.

    Given this information, the school estimated the break-even point to be ($8,000 + $7,000)/($650 − $80) = 26.3 students. If the school wanted to at least break even on this program, it should offer the program only if it expected at least 27 students to attend.

    Write a report to the dean that evaluates the quality of this analysis. In particular, focus on concerns about the accuracy of the data and the limitations of cost-volume-profit analysis.

39. **Cost cutting to break even.** Cost-volume-profit analysis showed how much Auto, Inc. had to improve just to break even in Year 1. In that year, the break-even point was 2.2 million units, but the company was selling considerably fewer than 2 million units. Faced with a severe recession in the industry, Auto, Inc. had virtually no chance to increase sales enough to break even. Meanwhile, the company had received loan guarantees from the U.S. government, which evoked considerable criticism that the federal government was supporting a "failing" company.

    By Year 4, Auto, Inc. reduced its break-even point to 1.1 million units, and the company reported a profit for the first time in several years. The turnaround came despite continued low sales in the industry; it resulted primarily from severe cost cutting, which reduced fixed costs in constant dollars from $4.5 billion in Year 1 to $3.1 billion in Year 4. In addition, the company made improvements in its production methods, which enabled it to maintain its volume of output despite the reduction in fixed costs.

a. If Auto, Inc.'s break-even volume was 1.1 million units and its fixed costs were $3.1 billion, what was its average contribution margin per unit?

b. Why do you think management concentrated on reducing fixed costs to put Auto, Inc. above its break-even point?

c. As a shareholder of Auto, Inc., what concerns might you have about the company's massive cost cutting?

40. **CVP—partial data; special order.** Partial income statements of University Dining Hall Food Service for the first two quarters of Year 200X follow.

UNIVERSITY DINING HALL FOOD SERVICE
Partial Income Statements for First and Second Quarters of Year 200X

	First Quarter	Second Quarter
Sales at $3.60 per Meal (unit)	$ 36,000	$63,000
Total Costs	49,000	67,000
(Loss)	$(13,000)	$ (4,000)

Each dollar of variable cost per meal comprises 50 percent direct labor, 25 percent direct materials, and 25 percent variable overhead costs. University Dining Hall expects sales units, price per unit, variable cost per unit, and total fixed costs to remain at the same level during the third quarter as during the second quarter. University Dining Hall sold 17,500 meals in the second quarter.

a. What is the quarterly break-even point in meals (units)?

b. The dining hall has just received a special order from the university officials that requests 7,500 meals for visitors to campus at a price of $3.20 per meal (unit). If the dining hall accepts the order, it will not affect the regular market for 17,500 meals in the third quarter. The dining hall can produce the additional meals with existing capacity, but direct labor costs per meal will increase by 10 percent for *all* meals produced because of the need to hire and use new labor. Fixed costs will increase $3,000 per quarter if the dining hall accepts the new order. Should it accept the university officials' order?

c. Assume that the dining hall accepts the order in part **b.** What level of sales volume to student customers provides third-quarter profit of $6,800? (The third quarter would be just like the second quarter if the dining hall does not accept the university officials' order.)

41. **Financial modeling with multiple cost drivers.** Radio, Inc., manufactures portable radios. Last year the firm sold 25,000 radios at $25 each. Total costs amounted to $525,000, of which $150,000 were considered fixed. An activity-based costing study recently revealed that Radio's fixed costs include the following components:

Setup (40 setups at $400 per setup)	$ 16,000
Engineering (500 hours at $25 per hour)	12,500
Inspection (1,000 inspections at $30 per inspection)	30,000
General factory overhead	61,500
Total	$120,000
Fixed selling and administrative costs	30,000
Total	$150,000

Management is considering both the installation of new, highly automated manufacturing equipment and a move toward just-in-time inventory and production management. If the new equipment is installed, setups will be quicker and less expensive. Under the proposed JIT approach, there would be 300 setups per year at $50 per setup. Because a total quality program would accompany the move toward JIT, only 100 inspections are anticipated at a cost of $45 each.

After the installation of the new system, 800 hours of engineering would be required at $28 per hour. General factory overhead would increase to $166,100; however, the automated equipment would allow Radio, Inc., to cut its unit variable cost by 20 percent. Finally, the overall improvement in product quality would support a selling price of $26 per unit.

a. Upon seeing the analysis given in the problem, Radio's vice-president for manufacturing exclaimed to the controller, "I thought you told me this $150,000 cost was fixed. These don't look like fixed costs at all. What you're telling me now is that setup costs us $400 every time we start a production run. What gives?" As Radio's controller, write a short memo to the vice-president that clarifies the situation.

b. Compute Radio's new break-even point in units if the proposed automated equipment is installed.

c. Calculate how many units Radio, Inc., will have to sell to show a profit of $140,000, assuming the new technology is adopted.

d. If Radio, Inc., adopts the new manufacturing technology, will its break-even point be higher or lower? Will the number of sales units required to earn a profit of $140,000 be higher or lower? Are the results in this case consistent with what you would typically expect to find in a modern high-tech manufacturing facility? Explain.

CASES

42. **Financial modeling for a brewpub** (reprinted by permission of Kurt Heisinger, Sierra College, March 2003). Three entrepreneurs were looking to start a new brewpub near Sacramento, California, called Roseville Brewing Company (RBC). (See the Managerial Application "Calculating Break-Even Points for a Brewpub.") Brewpubs provide two products to

customers—food from the restaurant segment and freshly brewed beer from the beer production segment. Both segments are typically in the same building, which allows customers to see the beer-brewing process.

After months of research, the owners created a financial model that showed the following projections for the first year of operations:

Sales	
Beer sales	$ 781,200
Food sales	1,074,150
Other sales	97,650
Total sales	$1,953,000
Less cost of sales	525,358
Gross margin	1,427,642
Less marketing and administrative expenses	1,125,430
Operating profit	$ 302,212

In the process of pursuing capital through private investors and financial institutions, RBC was approached with several questions. The following represents a sample of the more common questions asked:

- What is the break-even point?
- What sales dollars will be required to make $200,000? To make $500,000?
- Is the product mix reasonable? (Beer tends to have a higher contribution margin ratio than food, and therefore product mix assumptions are critical to profit projections.)
- What happens to operating profit if the product mix shifts?
- How will changes in price affect operating profit?
- How much does a pint of beer cost to produce?

It became clear to the owners of RBC that the initial financial model was not adequate for answering these types of questions. After further research, RBC created another financial model that provided the following information for the first year of operations:

Sales		
Beer sales (40% of total sales)	$ 781,200	
Food sales (55% of total sales)	1,074,150	
Other sales (5% of total sales)	97,650	
Total sales		$1,953,000
Variable Costs		
Beer (15% of beer sales)	117,180	
Food (35% of food sales)	375,953	
Other (33% of other sales)	32,225	
Wages of employees (25% of sales)	488,250	
Supplies (1% of sales)	19,530	
Utilities (3% of sales)	58,590	
Other: credit card, misc. (2% of sales)	39,060	
Total variable costs		1,130,788
Contribution margin		$ 822,212
Fixed Costs		
Salaries: manager, chef, brewer	$ 140,000	
Equipment and building maintenance	30,000	
Advertising	20,000	

(continued)

Other: cleaning, menus, misc.	40,000	
Insurance and accounting	40,000	
Property taxes	24,000	
Depreciation	94,000	
Debt service (interest on debt)	132,000	
Total fixed costs		$ 520,000
Operating profit		$ 302,212

Answer the following questions using the information in the case.
   a. What were potential investors and financial institutions concerned with when asking the questions listed in the case?
   b. Why was the first financial model prepared by RBC inappropriate for answering most of the questions asked by investors and bankers? Be specific.
   c. If you were deciding whether to invest in RBC, how would you quickly check the reasonableness of RBC's projected operating profit?
   d. Why is the question "How much does a pint of beer cost to produce?" difficult to answer?
   e. Perform sensitivity analysis by answering the following questions.
      i. What is the break-even point in sales dollars for RBC?
      ii. What is the margin of safety for RBC?
      iii. Why can't RBC find the break-even point in units?
      iv. What sales dollars would be required to achieve an operating profit of $200,000? $500,000? What assumptions are made in this calculation?
   f. Assume total revenues remain the same, but the product mix changes so that each of the three revenue categories is weighted as follows: food 70%, beer 25%, other 5%. How will this shift in product mix affect projected profits?
   g. Although the financial model is important, what other strategic factors should RBC and its investors consider?

RECOMMENDED ADDITIONAL CASES FOR CHAPTER 6

San Francisco Giants. Harvard Business School Case no. 804092. This case examines how to improve profitability for a major league baseball team. It could also be assigned with Chapter 7.

Walker and Company: Profit Plan Decisions. Harvard Business School Case no. 197084. This case covers profit planning, as well as performance measurement and decision making. It could also be assigned with Chapter 9.

Suggested Solutions to Even-Numbered Exercises

18. Break-even and target profits.
   a. Break-Even Units = Fixed Costs/Unit Contribution Margin

$$= \$200,000/(\$16 - \$8)$$

$$= 25,000$$

   b. Target Profit Units = (Fixed Costs + Target Profit)/Unit Contribution Margin

$$= 60,000$$

   c. Contribution Margin Ratio $= \dfrac{(\text{Unit Selling Price} - \text{Unit Variable Cost})}{\text{Unit Selling Price}}$

$$= (\$16 - \$8)/\$16 = \$8/\$16 = 50\%$$

$$\text{Profit} = (0.5 \times \$2,000,000) - \$200,000$$

$$= \$800,000$$

20. Cost-volume-profit graph.

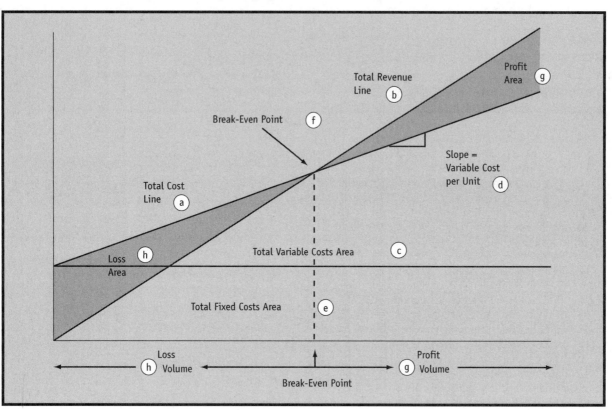

22. Cost-volume-profit analysis.

a. $5,000,000/1,000,000 Units = $5 per Unit.

b. $3,000,000/1,000,000 Units = $3 per Unit.

c. $5 − $3 = $2 per Unit.

d. Operating Profit = [(Sales Price per Unit − Variable Cost per Unit) × Unit Sales]

− Fixed Cost

0 = [($5 − $3) × Unit Sales] − $1,000,000

$$\text{Unit Sales} = \frac{\$1,000,000}{\$2} = 500,000 \text{ units}$$

e. After-Tax Profit/$(1 − t)$ = Before-Tax Profit

$1,200,000/$(1 − .4)$ = Before-Tax Profit

$2,000,000 = Before-Tax Profit

Then, go back to the equation shown in **d.** above and set operating profit to $2,000,000 as follows:

$2,000,000 = [($5 − $3) × Unit Sales] − $1,000,000

$$\text{Unit Sales} = \frac{\$3,000,000}{\$2} = 1,500,000 \text{ units}$$

24. Sensitivity analysis.

a. $$\text{Break-Even Point in Units} = \frac{\text{Fixed Costs}}{\text{Unit Contribution Margin}}$$

$$= \frac{\$400,000}{\$200 - \$120}$$

$$= \frac{\$400,000}{\$80} = 5,000 \text{ students}$$

b. Target Profit in Units $= \dfrac{\text{Fixed Costs} + \text{Target Profit}}{\text{Unit Contribution Margin}}$

$$= \frac{\$400,000 + \$20,000}{\$200 - \$120}$$

$$= \frac{\$600,000}{\$80} = 7,500 \text{ students}$$

c. (1) Profit $= (\$200 - \$120)8,000 - \$400,000$

$$= \underline{\$240,000}$$

(2) 10% price decrease. Now price = $180

Profit $= (\$180 - \$120)8,000 - \$400,000$

$$= \underline{\$80,000}$$

Profit decreases by $160,000 (67%).

20% price increase. Now price = $240

Profit $= (\$240 - \$120)8,000 - \$400,000$

$$= \underline{\$560,000}$$

Profit increases by $320,000 (133%).

(3) 10% variable cost decrease. Now variable cost = $108

Profit $= (\$200 - \$108)8,000 - \$400,000$

$$= \underline{\$336,000}$$

Profit increases by $96,000 (40%).

20% variable cost increase. Now variable cost = $144

Profit $= (\$200 - \$144)8,000 - \$400,000$

$$= \underline{\$48,000}$$

Profit decreases by $192,000 (80%).

(4) Profit $= (\$200 - \$132)8,000 - \$360,000$

$$= \underline{\$184,000}$$

Profit decreases by $56,000 (23%).

26. Multiple-product profit analysis.

a. A unit = production of three product Ps, two product Qs, and one product R.

Variable Cost per Unit $= (3 \times \$2) + (2 \times \$3) + (1 \times \$5) = \$17$.

Revenue per Unit $= (3 \times \$3) + (2 \times \$5) + (1 \times \$8) = \$27$.

b. $0 = \text{Total Revenue} - \text{Total Cost}$

$0 = \$27X - (\$17X + \$48,000)$

$\$10X = \$48,000$

$X = 4,800 \text{ Units}$.

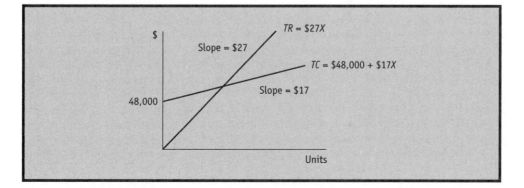

Not Required:

Total Revenue at Break-Even Level = 4,800 Units $\times$ \$27 = \$129,600.

c. A Unit = two product Ps, two product Qs, and one product R.

Variable Cost per Unit = (2 $\times$ \$2) + (2 $\times$ \$3) + (1 $\times$ \$5) = \$15.

Revenue per Unit = (2 $\times$ \$3) + (2 $\times$ \$5) + (1 $\times$ \$8) = \$24.

$$0 = \text{Total Revenue} - \text{Total Cost}$$
$$0 = \$24X - (\$15X + \$48,000)$$
$$\$9X = \$48,000$$
$$X = 5,333.3 \text{ Units.}$$

Not Required:

Total Revenue at Break-Even Level = 5,333.3 Units $\times$ \$24 = \$128,000.

chapter 7

Differential Cost Analysis for Operating Decisions

Learning Objectives

1. Explain the differential principle and know how to identify costs for differential analysis.

2. Explain the relation between costs and prices.

3. Explain how to base target costs on target prices.

4. Describe how to use differential analysis to measure customer profitability.

5. Explain why businesses apply differential analysis to product choice decisions.

6. Explain the theory of constraints.

7. Identify the factors underlying make-or-buy decisions.

8. Explain how to identify the costs of producing joint products and the relevant costs for decisions to sell or process further.

9. Explain the use of differential analysis to determine when to add or drop parts of operations.

10. Identify the factors of inventory management decisions.

11. Explain how linear programming optimizes the use of scarce resources (Appendix 7.1).

12. Identify the use of the economic order quantity model (Appendix 7.2).

*M*anagers use accounting information to make decisions, such as pricing, accepting special orders, and outsourcing. This chapter deals with several applications of one principle—**differential analysis,** the analysis of differences among particular alternative actions.[1] Owners typically judge management's performance on the basis of a firm's profitability. Thus managers want to know the differential effect of various alternative actions on profits. As you go through each application of differential analysis, we encourage you to keep the following questions in mind: What activities differ among the alternatives? How does that difference affect costs and profits?

Managers make decisions by choosing among alternatives. Each alternative represents a set of activities that will result in costs and profits. The differential analysis model, shown in Exhibit 7.1, extends the financial model discussed in Chapter 6.

The first column represents the alternative being considered. The second column presents the **status quo,** or the outcome expected if management makes no change. The third column shows the difference between the status quo and the alternative. If the difference is such that $profit_1 > profit_0$, the alternative is more profitable than the status quo. If $profit_0 > profit_1$, the status quo is more profitable. A *differential cost* is a cost that changes (differs) as a result of changing activities or levels of activities.

The following example illustrates differential analysis. To provide continuity, we use the facts from this example throughout the chapter. We use a manufacturing firm in this illustration because it is the most comprehensive and complex of any type of organization. The concepts apply as well to service, financial, merchandising, and other organizations.

EXHIBIT 7.1	Differential Analysis Model		
	Alternative	− Status Quo	= Difference
Revenue	$Revenues_1$	− $Revenues_0$	= *Change in Revenues*
Less Variable Costs	$Variable\ Costs_1$	− $Variable\ Costs_0$	= *Change in Variable Costs*
Total Contribution Margin (CM)	CM_1	− CM_0	= *Change in CM*
Less Fixed Costs	$Fixed\ Costs_1$	− $Fixed\ Costs_0$	= *Change in Fixed Costs*
Operating Profit	$Profit_1$	− $Profit_0$	= *Change in Profit*

[1]Differential analysis is also known as *incremental analysis* or, less accurately, *marginal analysis.* See Glossary for distinction.

Example   Assume the following status quo data for Ullman Educational Media, a company that produces tutorial videos for primary and preschool use.

Units Made and Sold	800 Units per Month
Maximum Production and Sales Capacity	1,200 Units per Month
Selling Price	$30

Activity Classification and Resulting Costs	Variable Cost (per unit)	Fixed Cost (per month)
Manufacturing	$17	$3,060
Marketing and Administrative	5	1,740
Total Costs	$22	$4,800

The management of Ullman Educational Media believes that it can increase volume from 800 units to 900 units per month by decreasing the selling price from $30 to $28 per unit. Would the price reduction be profitable? The differential analysis for this example indicates that the alternative would not increase profits. Exhibit 7.2 shows the alternative's profit is only $600, whereas the status quo generates $1,600 in profits.

Relevant Costs

Note in Exhibit 7.2 that this particular alternative does not affect all costs. Specifically, fixed costs from manufacturing, marketing, and administrative activities in this example do not change. Thus, only revenues and *total* variable costs are relevant to the analysis; fixed costs are not. We sometimes call differential analysis **relevant cost analysis** as it identifies only the costs (or revenues) relevant to the decision. A cost or revenue is *relevant* if an amount appears in the Difference column; all others are irrelevant. Thus, we could ignore fixed costs in this example. (This is not true in general. Fixed costs nearly always differ in long-run decisions involving changes in capacity, and they sometimes differ in short-run operating decisions, as we shall see later in this chapter.)

As you become familiar with differential analysis, you will find shortcuts by ignoring irrelevant costs (or revenues). For instance, you needed to work only with revenues and total variable costs in the previous example to get the correct answer.

Focus on Cash Flows

The emphasis on **cash flows** is fundamental for two reasons:

EXHIBIT 7.2	ULLMAN EDUCATIONAL MEDIA Differential Analysis of a Price Reduction		

	Alternative Price = $28 Units = 900	−	Status Quo Price = $30 Units = 800	=	Difference
Revenue	$25,200[a]	−	$24,000[c]	=	$1,200 higher
Less Unit-Level Costs (Variable)	19,800[b]	−	17,600[d]	=	2,200 higher
Total Contribution Margin	$ 5,400	−	$ 6,400	=	$1,000 lower
Less Facility-Level Costs (Fixed)	4,800	−	4,800	=	0
Operating Profit	$ 600	−	$ 1,600	=	$1,000 lower

[a]$25,200 = $28 × 900 Units.
[b]$19,800 = $22 × 900 Units.
[c]$24,000 = $30 × 800 Units.
[d]$17,600 = $22 × 800 Units.

1. Cash is the medium of exchange.

2. Cash is a common, objective measure of the benefits and costs of alternatives.

Consequently, differential analysis focuses mostly on differential cash flows caused by changes in activities. The previous example assumed both differential revenues and costs to be cash flows or near-cash flows (e.g., it assumed that revenues and costs on account are cash flows).

Uncertainty and Differential Analysis

Cost and revenue estimates for the status quo are usually more certain than estimates for alternatives. The status quo represents something known, whereas estimates for alternatives may be little more than educated guesses. When considering an alternative, the types of activities, the level of activities, and the cost of activities are all estimates subject to error. Analysts may easily omit some critical aspect of the alternative.

Most managers dislike risk and bear risk only if compensated. They prefer the known to the unknown, all other things being equal. Consequently, managers sometimes reject, because of risk, an alternative expected to be more profitable than the status quo. Managers often deal with risk and differential analysis by setting high standards for the alternative. For example, "The alternative must increase profits by 25 percent before we will accept it." Some organizations set incentives for managers to take risks in these situations.

Major Influences on Pricing

In making pricing decisions, companies weigh customers, competitors, and costs differently. Companies selling homogeneous products in highly competitive markets must accept the market price. Managers setting prices in markets with little competition, however, have some discretion. The pricing decision considers the value customers place on the product, the pricing strategies of competitors, and the costs of the product. Companies have become customer driven, focusing on delivering quality products at competitive prices. The three major influences on pricing decisions are customers, competitors, and costs:

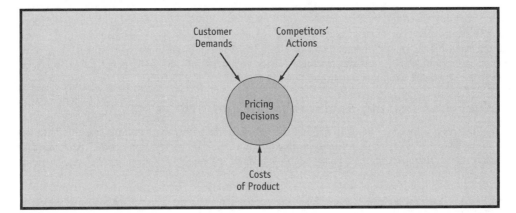

Customers

Managers examine pricing problems through the eyes of their customers. Increasing prices may cause the loss of a customer to a competitor, or it may cause a customer to substitute a less expensive product.

Competitors

Competitors' reactions also influence pricing decisions. A competitor's aggressive pricing may force a business to lower its prices to compete. On the other hand, a business without any competitors can set higher prices. If a business has knowledge of its competitors' technology, plant capacity, and operating policies, it is able to estimate the competitors' costs, which is valuable in its own pricing decisions.

Increasingly, managers consider their domestic and international competition in making pricing decisions. Firms with excess capacity because of low demand in domestic markets may price aggressively in their export markets. For instance, a software development company such as Microsoft, with high development costs and low variable costs, may seek out foreign markets. In a foreign market the company can exploit the high development costs already incurred while pricing lower than local competitors, who must incur high development costs before they can produce anything.

Costs

A product that is consistently priced below its cost can drain large amounts of resources from an organization. Financial modeling assists in measuring the profits that result from different combinations of price and output sold for a particular product.

Pricing is an area where newly evolving themes, such as customer satisfaction, continuous improvement, and the dual internal/external focus, come together. For instance, lower prices for quality products are conducive to customer satisfaction—an external focus. But when prices drop, costs must be reduced as well. The internal focus on continuous improvement is the key to cutting costs.

Short-Run versus Long-Run Pricing Decisions

The time horizon of the decision is critical in computing the relevant costs in a pricing decision. The two ends of the time-horizon spectrum are:

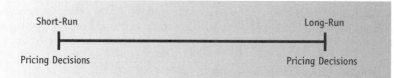

Short-run decisions include pricing for a one-time-only special order with no long-term implications. The time horizon is typically six months or less. Long-run decisions include pricing a main product in a major market. For example, a special order to Nike for shoes for an athletic team would be a short-run pricing decision, whereas introducing a new type of running shoe to the market would be a long-run pricing decision.

Short-Run Pricing Decisions: Special Orders

The differential approach helps in making special-order decisions. For example, assume Ullman Educational Media has an opportunity to make a one-time sale of 100 units at $25 per unit to a state prison system. Exhibit 7.3 presents an analysis of the effects of accepting the special order

EXHIBIT 7.3	ULLMAN EDUCATIONAL MEDIA Differential Analysis of a Special Order				
		Alternative	**− Status Quo**	**=**	**Difference**
Revenue		$26,500[a]	− $24,000	=	$2,500 higher
Less Unit-Level Costs (Variable)		19,800[b]	− 17,600	=	2,200 higher
Total Contribution Margin		$ 6,700	− $ 6,400	=	$ 300 higher
Less Facility-Level Costs (Fixed)		4,800	− 4,800	=	0
Operating Profit		$ 1,900	− $ 1,600	=	$ 300 higher

[a]$26,500 = $24,000 + ($25 × 100 Units).
[b]$19,800 = $17,600 + ($22 × 100 Units).

or not. Assume the regular market is 800 units sold at a price of $30 per unit. Exhibit 7.3 demonstrates that Ullman should accept the special order at $25 per unit because that price permits the firm to cover the differential costs of $22 per unit and provide a contribution of $3 per unit toward covering fixed costs and earning a profit.

Differential Approach to Pricing

The differential approach to pricing is useful for both short-run and long-run decisions. It presumes that the price must at least equal the **differential cost** of producing and selling the product. In the short run, this practice will result in a positive contribution to covering fixed costs and generating profit. In the long run, the practice will require covering all costs, *because both fixed and variable costs become differential costs in the long run.*

Consider the data for Ullman Educational Media in Exhibit 7.4. The minimum acceptable price in the short run is the differential cost of $22 per unit. In the long run, the minimum acceptable price is $28 per unit because the firm must cover both variable and fixed costs. A more desirable long-run price is the current price, $30, which provides a profit. The firm may set a price slightly higher than the variable cost for a special order as long as excess capacity exists and doing so will not affect the firm's regular market.

Suppose Ullman Educational Media wants to price aggressively. It can set a price slightly higher than the $22 minimum. Managers hope to underprice competitors and to capture a larger share of the market. If the firm is the only supplier of this product, it can charge a price higher than $28. If the firm sets the price too high, however, its high profits may entice competitors into the market.

Problem 7.1 for Self-Study

Applying differential analysis. Domer Technologies, Inc., produces a valve used in electric turbine systems. The costs of the valve at the company's normal volume of 5,000 units per month appear below. Unless otherwise specified, assume a selling price of $1,750 per unit.

Cost Data for Domer Technologies

Unit-Level Costs (5,000 units)	
Materials ($250 per unit)	$1,250,000
Labor ($175 per unit)	875,000
Overhead ($75 per unit)	375,000
Total Unit-Level Costs	$2,500,000
Customer-Level Costs (200 customers)	
Meetings with Customers ($5,000 per customer)	1,000,000
Facility-Level Costs	
Factory and Related Costs (fixed)	1,625,000
Total Costs	$5,125,000

EXHIBIT 7.4	ULLMAN EDUCATIONAL MEDIA Data for Pricing

Short-Run Differential Costs (variable costs)	$22 = Short-Run Minimum Price
Fixed Cost	6[a]
Long-Run Incremental Costs	$28 = Long-Run Minimum Price
Expected Profits	2
Target Selling Price	$30 = Long-Run Desired Price

[a]$6 = $4,800/800. This assumes a long-run volume of 800 units.

Market research estimates that a price increase to $1,900 per unit would decrease monthly sales volume to 4,500 units. The accounting department estimates total unit-level costs would decrease proportionately with volume. Total customers would decrease from 200 to 185 customers, and total facility-level costs would decrease from $1,625,000 to $1,617,500. Would you recommend that the firm take this action? What would be the impact on monthly revenues, costs, and profits?

The solution to this self-study problem is at the end of the chapter on page 237.

Long-Run Pricing Decisions

Many firms rely on full cost information reports when setting prices, as discussed in the Managerial Application "Pricing Practices in Various Countries." *Full cost* is the total cost of producing and selling a unit, which includes all the costs incurred by the activities that make up the value chain, as shown in Exhibit 7.5.

Typically, the accounting department provides cost reports to the marketing department, which then adds appropriate markups to the costs to set benchmark or target prices for all products normally sold by the firm.

Using the full costs for pricing decisions can be justified in three circumstances:

1. When a firm enters into a long-term contractual relationship to supply a product, most activity costs will depend on the production decisions under the long-term contract. Therefore, full costs are relevant for the long-term pricing decision.
2. Many contracts for the development and production of customized products and many contracts with governmental agencies specify prices as full costs plus a markup. Prices set in regulated industries such as electric utilities also are based on full costs.
3. Managers sometimes initially set prices based on full costs plus a profit and then make short-term adjustments to prices to reflect market conditions. Conversely, when demand for their products is high, they recognize the greater likelihood that the existing capacity of activity resources is inadequate to satisfy all the demand. Accordingly, they adjust the prices upward based on the higher incremental costs when capacity is fully utilized.

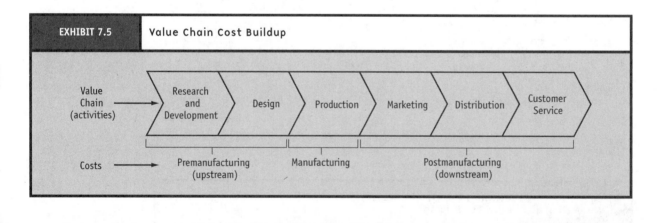

EXHIBIT 7.5   Value Chain Cost Buildup

Managerial Application

Pricing Practices in Various Countries

Surveys indicate the use of cost-based pricing appears to be more prevalent in the United States than in Ireland, Japan, and the United Kingdom. Although a majority of Japanese companies in assembly-type operations (e.g., electronics and automobiles) bases prices on costs, cost-based pricing is far less prevalent in Japanese process-type industries (e.g., chemicals, oil, and steel). When costs are used for pricing decisions, the pattern is consistent: Overwhelmingly, companies around the globe use full costs rather than variable costs. A later survey of U.S. industries supported these findings by showing that full-cost pricing dominated pricing practices (69.5 percent), while only 12.1 percent of the respondents used a variable-cost-based approach.

Ranking of Factors That Are Primarily Used to Price Products (1 is most important)

	United States	Japan	Ireland	United Kingdom
Market-based	2	1	1	1
Cost-based	1	2	2	2

Source: Eunsup Shim and Ephraim Sudit, "How Manufacturers Price Products," *Management Accounting,* February 1995 and authors' research.

Life-Cycle Product Costing and Pricing

The **product life cycle** covers the time from initial research and development to the time at which support to the customer is withdrawn. For motor vehicles, such as the Jeep Grand Cherokee, this time span may range from 10 to 20 years. For toys or fashion clothing products, the time span may be less than one year.

Managers estimate the revenues and costs for each product from its initial research and development to its final customer support. Life-cycle costing tracks costs attributable to each product from start to finish. The term *cradle-to-grave costing* conveys the sense of capturing all life-cycle costs associated with a product.

Life-cycle costs provide important information for pricing. For some products, particularly in electronics, the development period is relatively long. Many costs are incurred prior to manufacturing.

A product life-cycle budget highlights for managers the importance of setting prices that will cover costs in all the value-chain categories (shown in Exhibit 7.5). To be profitable, companies must generate revenue to cover costs in all six categories. Although we defer discussion of discounted cash flow analysis until Chapter 8, note that multiperiod costs and revenues should be discounted to their present value.

Using Target Prices to Set Target Costs

Simply stated, target costing is the concept of *price-based costing* (instead of *cost-based pricing*). A **target price** is the estimated price for a product or service that potential customers will be willing to pay. A target cost is the estimated long-run cost of a product or service that when sold enables the company to achieve targeted profit. **Target cost** is derived by subtracting the target profit from the target price.

For instance, a shoe manufacturer can sell a particular style for $33 a pair and wants profits of $6 per pair, thus leaving a $27 limit on costs per pair. Target costing is widely used. Mercedes and Toyota in the automobile industry, Panasonic and Sharp in the electronics industry, and Apple and Toshiba in the personal computer industry use target costing. Developing target prices and target costs requires the following four steps:

Step 1: Develop a product that satisfies the needs of potential customers.
Step 2: Choose a target price based on customers' perceived value for the product and the competitors' prices.
Step 3: Derive a target cost by subtracting the desired profit margin from the target price.
Step 4: Perform value engineering to achieve target costs.

Value engineering is a systematic evaluation of all aspects of research and development, design of products and processes, production, marketing, distribution, and customer service. Its objective is reducing costs while satisfying customer needs. Value engineering can result in improvements in product designs, changes in materials specifications, or modifications in process methods. Value engineering starts with an analysis of the value-chain activities.

Legal Issues Relating Costs to Prices

U.S. laws compel managers to consider costs when setting prices. For example, to comply with federal and many state laws, pricing must not be predatory. A business engages in **predatory pricing** when it deliberately prices below its costs in an effort to drive out competitors. Many legal jurisdictions define *costs* to be full costs. In other cases, courts have allowed companies to price as low as variable costs.

A related issue is "dumping." Under U.S. laws, **dumping** occurs when a foreign company sells a product in the United States at a price below the market value in the country of its creation, and this action materially injures (or threatens to materially injure) an industry in the United States. Dumping has occurred in the steel, semiconductor, and textile industries.

Customer Profitability and Differential Analysis

You know that companies choose products based on profitability. They also choose customers based on profitability. Differential costing is useful for deciding which customers a firm should keep and which it should stop servicing.

Assume Harrison and Associates, an advertising firm, performs ongoing services for three clients—Sonora Community Hospital, Beairds Department Store, and Servinties Resort. Exhibit 7.6 presents Harrison's typical revenues and costs by customer and is typical for the past few years.

Exhibit 7.6 shows a loss of $18,000 on services to Servinties. Should Harrison discontinue the Servinties account? The key question is: What are the differential revenues and costs for this client? You learn the following information:

- Dropping the Servinties account will save the cost of services incurred on the account.
- Dropping the Servinties account will have no effect on Harrison's total administrative salaries, rent, and other costs.
- Dropping the Servinties account will have no effect on the revenues or cost of services for the other accounts.

EXHIBIT 7.6	HARRISON AND ASSOCIATES Customer Profitability Analysis (in thousands)			
	Sonora Community Hospital	Beairds Department Store	Servinties Resort	Total
Revenue (fees charged)	$450	$270	$350	$1,070
Customer-Level Costs				
Cost of Services	$370	$220	$330	$ 920
Facility-Level Costs				
Administrative Salaries, Rent, and Other	44	26	38	108
Total Operating Costs	$414	$246	$368	$1,028
Operating Profit	$ 36	$ 24	$(18)	$ 42

	HARRISON AND ASSOCIATES Computations for Decision on Dropping the Servinties Account (in thousands)			
EXHIBIT 7.7				
		Drop Servinties (total minus Servinties)	Status Quo (total for company)	Difference
Revenue (fees charged)		$720	$1,070	$350 lower
Customer-Level Costs				
Cost of Services		$590	$920	$330 lower
Facility-Level Costs				
Administrative Salaries, Rent, and Other		108	108	0
Total Operating Costs		$698	$1,028	$330 lower
Operating Profit		$ 22	$ 42	$ 20 lower

Exhibit 7.7 presents the computations. Harrison's operating profits will be $20,000 higher if it keeps the Servinties account. The last column in Exhibit 7.7 shows that the cost savings from dropping the Servinties account, $330,000, is not enough to offset the loss of $350,000 in revenue. This is true because administrative salaries, rent, and other costs will not decrease if the Servinties account is dropped.

The conclusion would be different if, after dropping the Servinties account, Harrison could utilize the extra capacity to generate profits of more than $20,000 per year from another client. Before coming to a final decision, however, Harrison should seek ways to improve the profitability of the Servinties account. Harrison should also consider the effect the decision might have on its reputation for developing stable, long-run customer relations.

Using Activity-Based Costing to Analyze Customer Profitability

Customer costs often comprise the following four categories of activities:

1. Cost to acquire the customer
2. Cost to provide goods and services
3. Cost to maintain customers
4. Cost to retain customers

Managers use activity-based costing to understand the cost of activities in each of those four categories. For example, according to consultants from PricewaterhouseCoopers, analysts should develop costs of the following activities to compute customer costs:[2]

Customer Cost	Activities
Cost to acquire the customer	• Promote the product • Conduct campaign to win back lost customers • Run advertising campaigns
Cost to provide goods and services	• Process order • Deliver product • Process returns
Cost to maintain customers	• Bill customers • Process payments • Issue refunds
Cost to retain customers	• Follow-up calls

[2]J. A. Ness, M. J. Schroeck, R. A. Letendre, and W. J. Douglas, "The Role of ABM in Measuring Customer Value," *Strategic Finance* (April 2001), 44–49.

These consultants advise managers that focusing solely on revenues and ignoring costs leads to superior relations, but with the wrong customers. That is, managers have great relations with costly customers.

Problem 7.2 for Self-Study

Customer profitability. McKlintoff and Associates, an accounting firm, performs ongoing services for two clients, Jamoca Joe's and Levinon Industries. The following information about McKlintoff's revenue and costs (in thousands) by customer is typical of the past few years.

	Jamoca Joe's	Levinon Industries	Total
Revenue (fees charged)	$460	$700	$1,160
Customer-Level Costs			
Cost of Services	$425	$610	$1,035
Facility-Level Costs			
Salaries, Rent, and General Administration	40	60	100
Total Operating Costs	$465	$670	$1,135
Operating Profit	$ (5)	$ 30	$ 25

This shows a loss of $5,000 on services to Jamoca Joe's. Use differential analysis to determine whether McKlintoff should discontinue the Jamoca Joe's account. Assume only the revenues and cost of services for Jamoca Joe's will be affected if Jamoca Joe's is dropped.

The solution to this self-study problem is at the end of the chapter on page 238.

Product Choice Decisions

One of a manager's most important decisions is which goods to make or services to provide. Firms must choose among alternatives, just as students must choose how to allocate their limited study time between accounting and finance or their time between question 1 and question 2 on a final exam. Team salary caps limit the amount professional basketball teams can pay and, therefore, the number of top players each team can keep. In its Detroit Jeep plant, DaimlerChrysler must decide how many Limiteds to make, how many Classics, and how many of the other models. The Gap must decide how many items of each size to carry in its limited retail space.

We normally think of these product choice problems as short-run decisions. With enough time, students can study for *both* accounting and finance. In the short run, however, capacity limitations require choosing among options.

Example   The Cinadale Cookie Company has just purchased one machine that can make Plain Wafers, Chocolate-Covered Wafers, and Caramel-Filled Wafers, also covered in chocolate. The market for these products will absorb all that Cinadale can produce in any combination. Management wants to pick the most profitable product, or combination of products, to produce. The firm has only 400 hours of time available on the machine each month.

The time requirements for each of the three products, their selling prices, and their variable costs appear in Exhibit 7.8. For this example, assume that all marketing and administrative costs are fixed. Also assume that fixed manufacturing, marketing, and administrative costs are the same (that is, are not differential) whichever product or combination of products the firm produces. One unit is one case of cookies.

If the machine time were unlimited, the Cinadale Cookie Company should produce and sell all three products in the short run because all have a positive contribution margin. But with con-

EXHIBIT 7.8	Rationing Scarce Capacity			
		Plain	**Chocolate-Covered**	**Caramel-Filled**
Time Required on the Machine per Unit Produced		0.5 Hour	2.0 Hours	4.0 Hours
Selling Price per Unit		$5.00	$12.00	$16.00
Less Variable Costs to Produce One Unit		3.00	5.00	6.00
Contribution Margin per Unit		$2.00	$ 7.00	$10.00
Contribution Margin per Hour on the Machine (contribution margin per unit/time requirement in hours)		$4.00 per Hour[a]	$3.50 per Hour[b]	$2.50 per Hour[c]
Total Contribution from Using 400 Hours on the Machine		$1,600	$1,400	$1,000

[a]$4.00 per Hour = $2.00/0.5 Hour.
[b]$3.50 per Hour = $7.00/2.0 Hours.
[c]$2.50 per Hour = $10.00/4.0 Hours.

strained machine time, the most profitable product is *the one that contributes the most contribution margin per unit of time.* (Hint: If you face time constraints on an examination and must choose between question 1 and question 2, and if working on question 1 will earn you 1 point per minute and question 2 will earn you 2 points per minute, then work on question 2.)

The Plain Wafers have a per-unit contribution of $2.00. The Caramel-Filled Wafers have a per-unit contribution of $10.00. Yet the Plain Wafers are still the best product to produce given the capacity constraint on the machine. The Plain Wafers contribute $4.00 per hour of time on the machine, whereas the Caramel-Filled contribute only $2.50 per hour of time on the machine, as shown in Exhibit 7.8. Differential analysis indicates that the total contribution margin from using the machine to produce Plain Wafers is $1,600, whereas the contribution from producing Chocolate-Covered is $1,400, and that from producing Caramel-Filled is $1,000.

When there is only one scarce resource, the decision is easy: *Choose the product that gives the largest contribution per unit of the scarce resource used.* When each product uses different proportions of several scarce resources, the computational problem becomes more difficult. Appendix 7.1 describes linear programming, a mathematical tool for solving such multiply-constrained decision problems. Textbooks on operations research and quantitative methods describe these techniques in more detail.

Incorrect Use of Accounting Data

In general, decision makers should not rely on data that include cost allocations. You should particularly beware of cost information produced by the full-absorption method of product costing, which allocates fixed manufacturing costs to units produced by manufacturing companies. Full-absorption unit costs for short-run decision making will lead to incorrect decisions, as the following example demonstrates.

Example We have seen that production of Plain Wafers is optimal because the total monthly contribution is the highest of the three products. (Refer to Exhibit 7.8.) Suppose accountants have allocated fixed manufacturing costs in the amounts shown on line **(7)** of Exhibit 7.9. As line **(10)** of Exhibit 7.9 shows, full-absorption costing may lead to an incorrect assessment that Chocolate-Covered Wafers are most profitable and Plain Wafers are least profitable per machine hour.

This example shows how the use of accounting data intended for one purpose may not be useful for other purposes. External reporting requires full-absorption unit cost data. Most managerial decision models, on the other hand, require *variable* unit costs.

Unsophisticated users of accounting data often incorrectly assume that any calculated unit cost is a variable cost. You should not *assume* that the unit cost reported by an accounting system is a variable cost. Those unit costs often contain unitized fixed costs. When requesting data from the accounting department, be sure to specify what you need and how you will use it.

EXHIBIT 7.9	Rationing Scarce Capacity by Incorrectly Using Full-Absorption Unit Costs		

		Plain	Chocolate-Covered	Caramel-Filled
(1)	Time Required on the Machine per Unit Produced	0.5 Hour	2.0 Hours	4.0 Hours
(2)	Selling Price per Unit	$5.00	$12.00	$16.00
(3)	Direct Materials	$1.00	$ 2.00	$ 2.50
(4)	Direct Labor	1.50	2.00	2.50
(5)	Variable Manufacturing Overhead	0.50	1.00	1.00
(6)	Total Variable Costs per Unit	$3.00	$ 5.00	$ 6.00
(7)	Allocation of Fixed Costs at 100 Percent of Direct Labor	1.50	2.00	2.50
(8)	Full-Absorption Cost per Unit	$4.50	$ 7.00	$ 8.50
(9)	Gross Margin per Unit [line (2) minus line (8)]	$0.50	$ 5.00	$ 7.50
(10)	Gross Margin per Hour	$1.00 per Hour	$2.50 per Hour	$1.875 per Hour

Theory of Constraints and Throughput Contribution Analysis

As noted in the previous section, organizations often have constraints, or limits, on what can be accomplished. The **theory of constraints (TOC)** is a newly developing management method for dealing with constraints.

The theory of constraints focuses on increasing the excess of differential revenue over differential costs when the firm faces bottlenecks. A **bottleneck** is an operation in which the work to be performed equals or exceeds the available capacity. With multiple parts of a production process, each operation depends on the preceding operations. An operation cannot be started until the previous operation has completed its work.

Companies produce inventory because items must wait in line until the bottleneck is free. For example, assume Pete's Pizza suddenly has orders at 7 PM for pizza to be delivered to 20 locations. Pete's has one delivery car that can deliver to five locations per delivery. With more than five locations, the pizzas are cold when delivered. Pete's can deliver all the pizzas eventually, but Pete's guarantees delivery in 30 minutes or the customer gets half off the price. As a result of the delivery time constraint, a bottleneck develops in the delivery process, which results in large numbers of customers getting a discount on their pizzas.

The theory of constraints focuses on such bottlenecks. It encourages managers to find ways to increase profits by relaxing constraints and increasing throughput. At Pete's Pizza, this means finding ways to get pizzas delivered quickly without giving customers a discount.

The theory of constraints focuses on three factors:

1. **Throughput contribution.** Sales dollars minus short-run variable costs (e.g., materials, energy, and piecework labor).
2. **Investments.** The assets required for production and sales.
3. **Other operating costs.** All operating costs other than short-run variable costs. These costs are incurred to earn throughput contribution and include salaries and wages that are fixed costs, rent, utilities, and depreciation.

The objective of the theory of constraints is to maximize throughput contribution while minimizing investments and operating costs. The theory of constraints assumes a short time horizon. Five key steps in managing bottleneck resources are outlined below:

1. Recognize that the bottleneck resource determines throughput contribution of the product. For example, Pete's Pizza cannot deliver all the pizzas on time, which results in large discounts.

2. Search for and find the bottleneck resource by identifying resources with large quantities of inventory waiting to be worked on (e.g., lots of pizzas waiting over 30 minutes to be delivered).

3. Subordinate all nonbottleneck resources to the bottleneck resource. The needs of the bottleneck resource determine the production schedule of nonbottleneck resources. (A nonbottleneck process at Pete's is the preparation area, where the dough is made and appropriate toppings put on prior to cooking. The delivery rate should set the rate of preparation of pizzas for delivery.)

4. Increase bottleneck efficiency and capacity. The intent is to increase throughput contribution minus the differential costs of taking such actions (such as leasing another car and hiring another driver).

5. Repeat steps **1** through **4** for any new bottleneck.

Let's look at an example of how to manage constraints. Pete's Pizza has three operations—preparing, cooking, and delivering. During the dinner rush, delivery drivers can't keep up with the pizzamakers. This delivery bottleneck totals 60 hours per month. Pertinent information for those 60 hours per month follows:

	Preparation	Cooking	Delivery
Hourly Capacity	15 Units	12 Units	10 Units
Monthly Capacity during the Pertinent 60 Hours	900 Units	720 Units	600 Units
Monthly Production Possible during the Pertinent 60 Hours	600 Units	600 Units	600 Units

Each unit (that is, each pizza) has an average variable cost of $6 and a selling price of $15. Pete's output is constrained by the 600 units on-time delivery capacity. Several options exist that can relieve the bottleneck at the delivery operation. It is necessary to consider differential costs associated with each option:

1. **Eliminate the idle time on the bottleneck operation.** Assume Pete's can increase bottleneck output by hiring one employee to organize the preparation and cooking to ensure that pizzas are ready for delivery to five locations immediately upon arrival of the delivery car and to schedule pizza delivery so that the most efficient route is taken to deliver to the five locations. The additional cost for the employee time is $1,200 per month, and on-time delivery capacity is increased by 100 units per month. Thus, the throughput contribution increases by $900 [= 100 units × $9 (= $15 selling price − $6 variable costs)], which is less than the additional cost of $1,200. Pete's would not opt for this alternative.

2. **Shift parts that do not have to be made on the bottleneck machine to nonbottleneck machines or to outside facilities.** If Pete's can sell pizzas for pick-up instead of delivery, production would increase during the bottleneck hours to 720 units, which is the capacity of the cooking process. Assume the additional 120 units of pick-up pizzas will have a lower price of $12 and a lower variable cost of $5 per unit because delivery is not included. This option would increase throughput by $840 [= 120 × $7 (= $12 selling price − $5 variable costs)]. Assume Pete's would incur additional costs of $600 for the 60 pertinent hours per month for employees to sell pick-up pizzas. This alternative increases profits by $240 per month ($240 = $840 − $600). Pete's should implement this alternative.

3. **Increase the capacity of the bottleneck process.** Assume Pete's could hire another car and driver for the 60 bottleneck hours, increasing the delivery capacity to 720 units per month (which is the cooking constraint), costing an additional $900 for the 60 pertinent hours per month. This would increase throughput contribution by $1,080 [= 120 units × $9 (= $15 selling price − $6 variable costs)], which is $180 greater than the additional costs of $900. Although this alternative would increase profits, it would not increase profits by as much as alternative 2.

If Pete's management opted for alternative 2, it would then look for ways to increase the capacity of the new bottleneck, which is the cooking operation.

Theory of Constraints and Cost Assumptions

The theory of constraints assumes few costs are variable—generally only materials, purchased parts, piecework labor, and energy to run machines. Most direct labor and overhead costs are assumed to be fixed. This is consistent with the idea that the shorter the time period, the more costs are fixed, and the idea that the theory of constraints focuses on the short run. Generally, this assumption about cost behavior seems reasonable.

Theory of Constraints, Total Quality Management, and Just-in-Time

The theory of constraints identifies bottlenecks and possible disruptions that threaten throughput. When disruptions are hard to pinpoint or eliminate, quality control techniques from total quality management (TQM) may be utilized. Total quality management stabilizes and improves processes to decrease variation; it is well suited to removing disruptions in the process. One manager summarized the relations among recent management techniques well by saying, "Essentially, JIT (just-in-time) improves lead times and due-date performance, TQM (total quality management) improves people, and TOC (theory of constraints) provides focus for the entire improvement process."[3]

Make-or-Buy Decisions

A firm facing a **make-or-buy decision** must decide whether to meet its needs internally or to acquire goods or services from external sources (often called outsourcing). If Pillsbury grows its own farm products for its frozen foods, then it "makes." If it buys products from other farmers, then it "buys." Housing contractors who do their own site preparation and foundation work "make," whereas those who hire subcontractors "buy." Professional baseball teams that rely on the draft and their minor league system "make," whereas those that trade for established players "buy."

Whether to make or to buy depends on cost factors and on nonquantitative factors such as dependability of suppliers and the quality of purchased materials.

Managerial Application

Cost Management in Action: Why Hewlett-Packard Now Manages Suppliers Instead of Overhead

A division of Hewlett-Packard was one of the early experimenters with activity-based costing. Because overhead costs were more than 50 percent of total product costs, managers wanted to identify the activities that drove overhead costs. Based on the costs of activities revealed by activity-based costing, management decided to outsource many of the activities that drove overhead costs. The result was that overhead costs decreased substantially, but the cost of goods purchased from suppliers increased to 70 percent of total product cost. The emphasis shifted from managing overhead costs to managing supplier relations.

Source: Interviews with Hewlett-Packard managers.

---

[3]E. Noreen, D. Smith, and J. Mackey, *The Theory of Constraints and Its Implications for Management Accounting* (Great Barrington, Mass.: North River Press, 1995), p. 42.

		EXHIBIT 7.10	BEN & JERRY COOKIE COMPANY

EXHIBIT 7.10

BEN & JERRY COOKIE COMPANY
Differential Analysis of Make-or-Buy Decision

	Alternative: Buy	−	Status Quo: Make	=	Difference
Revenue	$24,000	−	$24,000	=	0
Less:					
Variable Costs to Produce and Sell	8,800ª	−	17,600	=	$8,800 lower
Variable Costs of Goods Bought	9,600ᵇ	−	—	=	9,600 higher
Total Contribution Margin	$ 5,600	−	$ 6,400	=	$ 800 lower
Less Fixed Costs	3,840	−	4,800	=	960 lower
Operating Profit	$ 1,760	−	$ 1,600	=	$ 160 higher

ª$8,800 = $11 × 800 Units.
ᵇ$9,600 = $12 × 800 Units.

Example   The Ben & Jerry Cookie Company has an opportunity to buy part of its product for $12 per unit. This purchase would affect prices, volume, and costs as follows:

	Alternative: Buy	Status Quo: Make
Unit Selling Price	$ 30	$ 30
Volume	800 per Month	800 per Month
Unit Variable Costs	$ 11	$ 22
Purchased Ingredients, per Unit	$ 12	$ 0
Total Fixed Costs	$3,840	$4,800

Exhibit 7.10 shows that the alternative to buy is more profitable. The $9,600 cost to buy is more than offset by the fixed and variable cost savings.

Problem 7.3 for Self-Study

Make-or-buy decision. Assume the Franklin Company, which manufactures wood stoves, has an opportunity to buy the handles for its stoves for $8 per unit. This purchase would affect prices, volume, and costs as follows:

	Buy	Make
Unit Selling Price	$ 340	$ 340
Volume (per month)	500	500
Unit Variable Costs	$ 88	$ 95
Purchased Parts (per unit)	$ 8	$ 0
Fixed Costs	$4,700	$5,500

Management wants you to decide whether the part should be made or bought.

The solution to this self-study problem is at the end of the chapter on page 238.

Joint Products: Sell or Process Further

Suppose you get multiple products from a single production process. For example, Georgia-Pacific gets various wood products from its lumber mills. Dairy producers such as Borden and Land O'Lakes get multiple products from raw milk.

Exhibit 7.11 presents the following information graphically. The firm initially introduces direct materials into processing. After incurring direct labor and manufacturing overhead costs, two identifiable products, Product A and Product B, emerge from the production process. The firm processes Product A further but sells Product B immediately. We call the point at which the identifiable products emerge the **splitoff point.** Costs incurred up to the splitoff point are the **joint costs.** We call costs incurred after the splitoff point **additional processing costs.**

Companies producing joint products must decide at each splitoff point whether to sell the individual products as they are or process further. Differential analysis is appropriate for these types of decisions.

Example   At Hanson Dairy the cows produce 10,000 gallons of raw milk per month. After milking, separating, and processing, which costs $11,000, the dairy has 7,000 gallons of whole milk and 3,000 gallons of cream. The milk could be sold at this point for $1.00 per gallon or processed further into 6,500 gallons of nonfat milk, with 500 gallons lost in the process. Further processing would cost $0.20 per gallon for the 6,500 gallons of output. The nonfat milk could then be sold for $1.25 per gallon. The cream could also be sold or processed further into sour cream, butter, and cheese.

The following is an analysis considering whether to process the milk further or sell now. The initial $11,000 is a joint cost and not differential for this decision. The differential costs are the additional processing costs of $0.20 per gallon.

	Alternative: Process Further	−	Status Quo: Sell	=	Difference
Revenue	$8,125	−	$7,000	=	$1,125 higher
Less Additional Processing Costs	1,300	−	0	=	1,300 higher
Contribution Margin before Costs Prior to Splitoff Are Considered	$6,825	−	$7,000	=	$ 175 lower

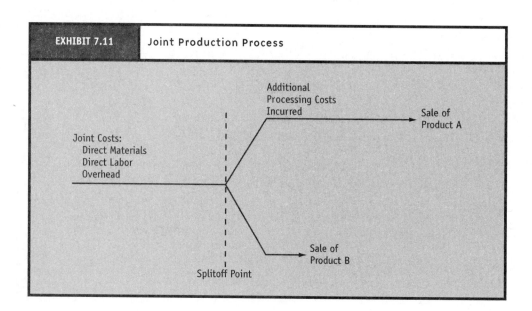

EXHIBIT 7.11	Joint Production Process

Of the joint products milk and cream, the milk should not be processed further. Costs to process the milk further would exceed expected revenues. The company could perform the same analysis for the cream.

Problem 7.4 for Self-Study

Sell or process further. The Demi Company processes logs into 200,000 board feet of lumber and 50,000 board feet of scrap lumber per year. The scrap lumber can be sold at splitoff for $5 per board foot or processed further into plywood to be sold for $6 per board foot. Further processing would incur variable costs of $0.50 per board foot. The equipment and space to process the scrap lumber would increase fixed costs by $25,000 per year.

Management wants you to decide whether the scrap lumber should be sold or processed further.

The solution to this self-study problem is at the end of the chapter on page 238.

Adding and Dropping Parts of Operations

Managers must decide when to add or drop products from the product line and when to open or abandon sales territories. For example, Microsoft decided to drop certain networking products. Sears decided to eliminate certain real estate and financial services operations. Tower Records closed many of its large retail stores.

These can be either long-run decisions involving a change in capacity or short-run decisions in which capacity does not change. This chapter deals with these short-run decisions.

The differential principle implies the following rule: *If the differential revenue from the sale of a product exceeds the differential costs required to provide the product for sale, then the product generates profits and the firm should continue its production.* This decision is correct even though the product may show a loss in financial statements because of overhead costs allocated to it. If the product's revenues more than covers its differential costs, and if no other alternative use of the production and sales facilities exists, the firm should retain the product in the short run.

Example Suppose that the Baltimore Company had three products and used common facilities to produce and sell all three. No single product affects sales of the others. The relevant data for these three products follow:

	Product			
	A	**B**	**C**	**Total**
Sales Volume per Month	800	1,000	600	—
Unit Sales Price	$ 30	$ 20	$ 40	—
Sales Revenue	$24,000	$20,000	$24,000	$68,000
Unit Variable Cost	$ 22	$ 14	$ 35	—
Fixed Cost per Month	—	—	—	$13,600

Management has asked the accounting department to allocate fixed costs to each product so that it can evaluate how well each product is doing. Total fixed costs were 20 percent of total dollar sales, so the accountant charged fixed costs to each product at 20 percent of the product's sales. For example, Product C received $4,800 (= 0.20 × $24,000 sales) of fixed costs.

The product-line income statements in the top panel of Exhibit 7.12 show an apparent loss of $1,800 for Product C. One of Baltimore's managers argued, "We should drop Product C. It is losing $1,800 per month." A second manager suggested performing a differential analysis to see the costs saved and revenues lost. The bottom panel of Exhibit 7.12, the differential analysis,

EXHIBIT 7.12	BALTIMORE COMPANY Differential Analysis of Dropping a Product

INCOME STATEMENT ANALYSIS

	Product			
	A	B	C	Total
Sales	$24,000	$20,000	$24,000	$68,000
Less Variable Costs	17,600	14,000	21,000	52,600
Total Contribution Margin	$ 6,400	$ 6,000	$ 3,000	$15,400
Less Fixed Costs Allocated to Each Product	4,800[a]	4,000[a]	4,800[a]	13,600
Operating Profit (Loss)	$ 1,600	$ 2,000	$ (1,800)	$ 1,800

DIFFERENTIAL ANALYSIS

	Alternative: Drop Product C	−	Status Quo	=	Difference
Sales	$44,000	−	$68,000	=	$24,000 lower
Less Variable Costs	31,600	−	52,600	=	21,000 lower
Total Contribution Margin	$12,400	−	$15,400	=	$ 3,000 lower
Less Fixed Costs	13,600	−	13,600	=	0
Operating Profit (Loss)	$ (1,200)	−	$ 1,800	=	$ 3,000 lower

[a]Fixed costs of $13,600 allocated in proportion to sales.

shows dropping Product C reduces the company's profits. The first manager incorrectly assumed that dropping the product would save fixed costs.

The firm should investigate more profitable uses of the facilities used to produce and sell Product C, because its contribution margin appears to be the weakest of the three products. Until such alternatives emerge, however, producing and selling Product C is profitable.

Problem 7.5 for Self-Study

Product decisions. Assume Baltimore Company did not drop Product C, but Product B's revenue and variable costs dropped to 50 percent of the levels shown in Exhibit 7.12. Should Baltimore drop Product B?

The solution to this self-study problem is at the end of the chapter on page 238.

Inventory Management Decisions

Inventory management affects profits in merchandising, manufacturing, and other organizations with inventories. Having the correct type and amount of inventory can prevent a production shutdown in manufacturing. In merchandising, having the correct type of merchandise inventory may mean making a sale. Inventories are costly to maintain, however. The costs include storage costs, insurance, losses from damage and theft, property taxes, and the opportunity cost of funds tied up in inventory. Key inventory management questions include the following:

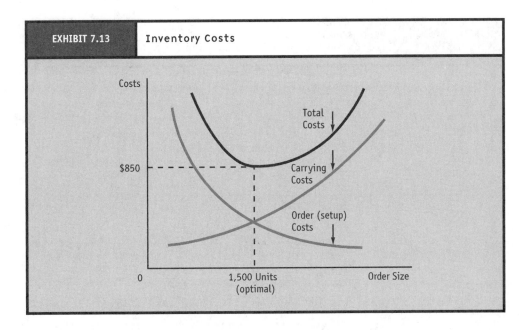

EXHIBIT 7.13   **Inventory Costs**

1. How many units of inventory should be on hand and available for use or sale?
2. How often should the firm order a particular item? What is the optimal size of the order?

Differential Costs for Inventory Management

Inventory management decisions involve two types of opposing costs. The firm incurs differential costs each time it places an order or makes a production run (e.g., the cost of processing each purchase order or the cost of preparing machinery for each production run). These are **setup** or **order costs.** The firm could minimize them by minimizing the number of orders or production runs.

By ordering or producing less frequently, however, each order or production run must be for a larger number of units. The firm will carry a larger average inventory. Larger inventories imply larger **carrying costs** for these inventories (e.g., the cost of maintaining warehouse facilities).

Management would like to find the optimal trade-off between these two types of opposing costs, carrying costs and order costs. Refer to Exhibit 7.13, based on the following example. (We refer to both order costs and setup costs as *order costs* for the rest of our discussion.) The problem is calculating the optimal number of orders or production runs each year and the optimal number of units to order or produce. The optimal number of units to order or produce is the **economic order quantity (EOQ).**

Example   Penn Merchandising sells 6,000 units of a product per year, spread evenly throughout the year. Each unit costs $2 to purchase. The differential cost of preparing and servicing an order is $100. The cost of carrying a unit in inventory is 30 percent of the unit's cost. Thus, if the firm places one order for the year, it will purchase 6,000 units and have, *on average,* 3,000 units (that is, $6,000) in inventory during the year. The carrying cost would be $1,800 (= $6,000 × 0.30) for the year. Exhibit 7.14 presents the inventory carrying costs, order costs, and total costs of the inventory. Note the trade-off between carrying costs and order costs: As one decreases, the other increases. The optimal number of orders per year is four, which has the lowest total costs (see column **(6)** in Exhibit 7.14).

A formal model (called the EOQ model) for deriving the optimal number of orders (or setups or production runs) and the optimal number of items in an order (or in a production run) appears in Appendix 7.2.

EXHIBIT 7.14	PENN MERCHANDISING Economic Order Quantity Calculation

Differential ordering costs per order are $100.
Annual requirement is 6,000 units.
Inventory carrying costs are 30 percent per year.
Purchase cost per unit is $2.00.

Orders (1)	Order Size[a] (2)	Average Number of Units in Inventory[b] (3)	Inventory Carrying Costs[c] (4)	Order Costs[d] (5)	Total Costs[e] (6)
1	6,000	3,000	$1,800	$ 100	$1,900
2	3,000	1,500	900	200	1,100
3	2,000	1,000	600	300	900
4	1,500	750	450	400	850[f]
5	1,200	600	360	500	860
6	1,000	500	300	600	900
12	500	250	150	1,200	1,350

[a]6,000 units/number of orders from column (1).
[b]Column (2)/2.
[c]Amount in column (3) × $2 cost per unit × 0.30.
[d]$100 × number of orders from column (1).
[e]Amount in column (4) + amount in column (5).
[f]Lowest total cost. Optimal number of orders is four per year.

Estimating the Costs of Maintaining Inventory

Managers, industrial engineers, analysts, and others who attempt to derive optimal solutions to inventory management problems typically use costs the accounting system provides. An important but difficult task for managerial accountants is estimating inventory order costs and carrying costs. Keep in mind that only *differential* costs matter. For example, suppose that the firm uses one purchasing agent whether customers place one order or 12 orders per year, and the number of orders made does not affect the agent's salary. Assume that the opportunity cost of the agent's time equals zero. Therefore, the agent's salary does not differ, and the analysis need not include it in differential order costs.

Order Costs   To estimate differential order costs, consider whether any salaries or wages differ due to the number of orders and whether there are opportunity costs of lost time. Production setups, in particular, usually result in lost time for production employees. Order costs should include differential costs of receiving and inspecting orders, costs of processing invoices from suppliers, and freight costs.

Carrying Costs   Differential carrying costs include insurance, inventory taxes, the opportunity costs of funds invested in inventory, and other costs that differ with the number of units held in inventory. If the firm pays additional wages or leases additional warehouse space because inventory quantity increases, these costs are differential carrying costs. Carrying costs should not include an allocated portion of warehouse depreciation or rent if these costs do not vary with the number of units in inventory. Such depreciation and rent are not differential carrying costs.

Innovations in Inventory Management and Flexible Manufacturing

Just-in-Time

Just-in-time (JIT) is a method of managing purchasing, production, and sales by which the firm attempts to produce each item only as needed for the next step in the production process or the firm attempts to time purchases so that items arrive just in time for production or sale. This practice can reduce inventory levels to virtually zero.

Just-in-time is a philosophy rather than a tool or set of tools. The objective is the elimination of all non–value-added activities and thus a reduction in cost and time. Like total quality management, JIT seeks continuous improvement involving all employees.

Just-in-time dovetails with total quality management in that it requires managers to lay out the production process so that there is a continuous flow once production starts. Because products are produced only as needed, managers must reduce setup costs to eliminate the need to produce in large batches.

Just-in-time requires reliable processing systems. Production must correct a process resulting in defective units immediately because the plan disallows accumulating defective units while they await reworking or scrapping. This is a major cost of carrying inventory, and its elimination is a major advantage of just-in-time. Economic order quantity models that omit this cost of carrying inventory overstate the optimal level of inventory. Manufacturing managers find that eliminating inventories can prevent production workers from hiding production problems.

All aspects of production, including developing the design, acquiring materials for production, producing the good or service, delivering the good or service to the customer, and providing service after the delivery, are encompassed by just-in-time, and all may be enhanced by total quality management. The performance measures used in a just-in-time system are inventory levels; failures, whether these are materials, people, or machine failures; moving; and storing. In a just-in-time system everyone works to keep these measures as close to zero as possible.

The use of just-in-time enables accountants to spend less time on inventory valuation for external reporting purposes and more time obtaining data for managerial decisions such as those discussed in this chapter.

Flexible Manufacturing

Another innovation that reduces both setup costs and inventory levels is flexible manufacturing. As this chapter discusses, reducing inventory levels means increasing the number of setups. Consider an automobile manufacturer that makes fenders for several models of cars. When it is time to change from left fenders to right fenders, or from fenders for cars to fenders for trucks, the production line stops while workers modify the machines to make the new fenders. Making only a few fenders of each type during a single production run requires many separate setups, so companies such as Ford Motor Company use flexible manufacturing methods to make these changeovers quickly, which reduces setup time and setup costs.

The use of flexible manufacturing practices to reduce setup costs enhances companies' abilities to use just-in-time. If setup costs are low, each production run can be small—perhaps only one unit. These innovations are likely to decrease the need for detailed record keeping for inventory valuation and to increase accountants' time spent on managerial activities.

Problem 7.6 for Self-Study

Inventory decisions. Compute the minimum total costs for JIT-not Incorporated, given the following facts:

Differential Costs per Order	$41
Total Units Purchased per Year	40,000 Units
Differential Carrying Costs per Unit of Inventory	$5.35 per Unit

Prepare a table like Exhibit 7.14, and find the minimum total costs of ordering and holding inventory. (Hint: Start with 50 annual orders.)

The solution to this self-study problem is at the end of the chapter on page 239.

The following items correspond to the learning objectives presented at the beginning of the chapter.

1. **Explain the differential principle and know how to identify costs for differential analysis.** Differential analysis is an extension of financial modeling. The relevant costs for differential analysis are the differential costs. The model focuses on cash flows because cash is the medium of exchange and because cash serves as a common, objective measure of the benefits and costs of alternatives.

2. **Explain the relation between costs and prices.** The three major influences on pricing decisions are customers, competitors, and costs. The differential approach to pricing presumes that the price must at least equal the differential cost of producing and selling the product. In the short run, this practice will result in a positive contribution to covering fixed costs and generating profit. In the long run, this practice will cover all costs because both fixed and variable costs are differential in the long run.

   Short-run decisions include pricing for a special order with no long-term implications. Typically the time horizon is six months or less. Long-run decisions include pricing a main product in a major market.

   Companies typically use full costs for pricing decisions in three circumstances: (1) when a firm enters into a long-term contractual relationship to supply a product; (2) for development and production of customized products and contracts with the government; and (3) when managers initially set prices to cover full costs plus a profit and then adjust to reflect market conditions.

3. **Explain how to base target costs on target prices.** Target pricing is based on customers' perceived value for the product and the prices competitors charge. Target costs equal target prices minus target profits.

4. **Describe how to use differential analysis to measure customer profitability.** Customer profitability is determined using differential analysis with the customer as the cost object. Customer costs generally fall under four categories: cost to acquire the customer, cost to provide goods and services, cost to maintain customers, and cost to retain customers.

5. **Explain why businesses apply differential analysis to product choice decisions.** Most firms can supply a number of goods and services, but manufacturing or distribution constraints limit what firms can produce. In the short run, capacity limitations require choices among alternatives.

6. **Explain the theory of constraints.** The theory of constraints focuses on revenue and cost management when dealing with bottlenecks. The objective is to increase throughput contribution (i.e., sales dollars minus direct materials costs), minimize investments, and manage production by letting the bottleneck set the pace for the rest of operations.

7. **Identify the factors underlying make-or-buy decisions.** Whether to make or buy depends on cost factors and on nonquantitative factors, such as dependability of suppliers and the quality of purchased materials.

8. **Explain how to identify the costs of producing joint products and the relevant costs for decisions to sell or process further.** The point at which the identifiable products emerge is the splitoff point. Costs incurred up to the splitoff point are the joint costs. Additional processing costs—costs incurred after the splitoff point—are the relevant costs for decisions to sell or process further.

9. **Explain the use of differential analysis to determine when to add or drop parts of operations.** In the short run, capacity does not change. If the differential revenue from the sale of a product exceeds the differential costs required to provide the product for sale, then the product generates profits, and the firm should continue its production.

10. **Identify the factors of inventory management decisions.** The optimal number of units to order or produce is the *economic order quantity,* which is the optimal trade-off between setup (or order) costs and carrying costs. In estimating order costs and carrying costs, only differential costs matter. Just-in-time inventory is a method of managing purchasing, production, and sales, by which (a) the firm attempts to produce each item only as needed for the next step in the production process, or (b) the firm attempts to time purchases so that items arrive just in time for sale or production. The use of total quality management and

flexible manufacturing practices to reduce setup costs enhances companies' abilities to use just-in-time inventory.
11. **Explain how linear programming optimizes the use of scarce resources (Appendix 7.1).** Linear programming (a) finds the product mix that will maximize profits given the constraints, (b) provides opportunity costs of constraints, and (c) allows for sensitivity analysis.
12. **Identify the use of the economic order quantity model (Appendix 7.2).** The economic order quantity model derives the optimal number of orders or production runs.

Key Terms and Concepts

Additional processing costs	Objective function*
Bottleneck	Other operating costs
Carrying costs	Predatory pricing
Cash flow	Product life cycle
Differential analysis	Relevant cost analysis
Differential cost	Setup or order costs
Dumping	Shadow price*
Economic order quantity (EOQ)	Splitoff point
Economic order quantity (EOQ) model**	Status quo
Investments	Target cost
Joint costs	Target price
Just-in-time (JIT)	Theory of constraints (TOC)
Linear programming*	Throughput contribution
Make-or-buy decision	Value engineering

*Term appears in Appendix 7.1.

**Term appears in Appendix 7.2.

Solutions to Self-Study Problems

SUGGESTED SOLUTION TO PROBLEM 7.1 FOR SELF-STUDY

	Alternative	− Status Quo =	Difference
Price	$1,900	$1,750	
Volume	4,500 units	5,000 units	
Revenue[a]	$8,550,000 −	$8,750,000 =	$200,000 lower
Unit-Level Costs[b]	2,250,000 −	2,500,000 =	250,000 lower
Customer-Level Costs[c]	925,000 −	1,000,000 =	75,000 lower
Facility-Level Costs[d]	1,617,500 −	1,625,000 =	7,500 lower
Operating Profit	$3,757,500 −	$3,625,000 =	$132,500 higher

[a]Number of units × sales price.
[b]Number of units × costs per unit. (Unit-level costs = $500.)
[c]Number of customers × costs per customer. (Customer-level costs = $5,000.)
[d]Number of facilities × costs per facility. (Company has one facility.)

Domer Technologies should raise its price to $1,900 per unit because profits are projected to increase to $3,757,500, an increase of $132,500.

SUGGESTED SOLUTION TO PROBLEM 7.2 FOR SELF-STUDY

	Alternative: Drop Jamoca Joe's	Status Quo: Total	Difference
Revenue (fees charged)	$700	$1,160	$460 lower
Customer-Level Costs			
Costs of Services	$610	$1,035	$425 lower
Facility-Level Costs			
Salaries, Rent, and General Administration (fixed)	100	100	0
Total Operating Costs	$710	$1,135	$425 lower
Operating Profit	$(10)	$ 25	$ 35 lower

McKlintoff should not drop Jamoca Joe's in the short run, as profits would drop by $35,000.

SUGGESTED SOLUTION TO PROBLEM 7.3 FOR SELF-STUDY

	Buy	—	Make	=	Difference
Revenue	$170,000	—	$170,000	=	$ 0
Less:					
Variable Costs to Produce and Sell	44,000	—	47,500	=	3,500 lower
Variable Costs of Goods Bought	4,000	—	0	=	4,000 higher
Total Contribution Margin	$122,000	—	$122,500	=	$ 500 lower
Less Fixed Costs	4,700	—	5,500	=	800 lower
Operating Profit	$117,300	—	$117,000	=	$ 300 higher

Operating profit for the Franklin Company increases by $300 if it purchases the handles rather than makes them.

SUGGESTED SOLUTION TO PROBLEM 7.4 FOR SELF-STUDY

	Process Further	—	Sell	=	Difference
Revenue	$300,000	—	$250,000	=	$50,000 higher
Less Additional Processing Variable Costs	25,000	—	0	=	25,000 higher
Total Contribution Margin before Considering Costs Prior to Splitoff Point	$275,000	—	$250,000	=	$25,000 higher
Less Additional Fixed Costs	25,000	—	0	=	25,000 higher
Operating Profit	$250,000	—	$250,000	=	$ 0

Operating profit for the Demi Company will be the same whether it processes the scrap lumber into plywood or sells scrap lumber at splitoff.

SUGGESTED SOLUTION TO PROBLEM 7.5 FOR SELF-STUDY

Baltimore should not drop Product B in the short run. It continues to have a positive contribution margin even if the revenue and variable costs drop by 50 percent.

SUGGESTED SOLUTION TO PROBLEM 7.6 FOR SELF-STUDY

Annual Orders	Order Size[a] in Units	Average Number of Units in Inventory	Inventory Carrying Costs[b]	Order Costs[c]	Total Costs
40	1,000	500.0	$2,675	$1,640	$4,315
.					
.					
.					
50	800	400.0	2,140	2,050	4,190
51	784	392.0	2,097	2,091	4,188
52	769	384.5	2,057	2,132	4,189
53	755	377.5	2,020	2,173	4,193
.					
.					
.					
60	667	333.5	1,784	2,460	4,244

[a]40,000 units/number of orders.
[b]Average units in inventory × $5.35.
[c]Number of orders × $41.

Minimum total costs are $4,188 at 51 orders per year.

Appendix 7.1: Linear Programming

Factors such as factory capacity, personnel time, floor space, and so forth constrain most managerial decisions. If the firm has enough time before implementing a decision, it can relax constraints by increasing capacity. In the short run, however, decision makers face a constrained amount of resources available to them. **Linear programming** solves problems of this type. We refer to linear programming as a *constrained optimization* technique because it solves for the optimal use of scarce (that is, constrained) resources.

Two simple examples demonstrate how linear programming works. We solve these using graphs and simple algebra. More complex problems require some systematic procedure like the *simplex method,* described in textbooks on operations research and quantitative methods. Most linear programming problem solutions result from computer implementation of the simplex method or variations of it.

Profit Maximization

Example   Moline Company produces two products, 1 and 2. The contribution margins per unit of the two products follow:

Product	Contribution Margin per Unit
1	$3
2	4

Fixed costs are the same regardless of the combination of Products 1 and 2 the firm produces; therefore, the firm wants to maximize the total contribution per period of these two products.

Both products have a positive contribution margin. If Moline Company faces no constraints, it should make (and sell) both products, eliminating our problem. When production of a unit of each product consumes the same quantity of a scarce resource, managers solve the problem by making and selling only the highest contribution item. For our example, if Product 1 and Product 2 each require one hour of machine time and the quantity of machine hours is finite, Moline will choose Product 2, all else being equal. Products usually do not consume equal amounts of scarce resources, however, so the problem is to find the optimal mix of products given the amount of a scarce resource each product consumes.

Moline Company uses two scarce resources to make the two products, labor time and machine time. Twenty-four hours of labor time and 20 hours of machine time are available each day. The amount of time required to make each product follows:

	Product	
	1	**2**
Labor Time	1 hour per unit	2 hours per unit
Machine Time	1 hour per unit	1 hour per unit

This problem formulation follows. (X_1 and X_2 refer to the quantity of Products 1 and 2 produced and sold.)

1. Maximize: $\$3X_1 + \$4X_2 =$ Total Contribution
2. Subject to: $X_1 + 2X_2 = 24$ Labor Hours
3. $X_1 + X_2 = 20$ Machine Hours

The first line, the **objective function,** states the objective of our problem as a linear equation. Here the objective is to maximize total contribution where each unit of Product 1 contributes $3 and each unit of Product 2 contributes $4. The lines that follow specify the parameters of the constraints. Line **(2)** is the labor time constraint, which states that each unit of Product 1 requires 1 labor hour and each unit of Product 2 requires 2 labor hours. Total labor hours cannot exceed 24 per period (that is, one day). Line **(3)** is the machine time constraint, which states that Product 1 and Product 2 each use 1 machine hour per unit, and total machine hours cannot exceed 20.

Exhibit 7.15 graphs the constraints. The shaded area shows feasible production; production does not use more scarce resources than are available. The lowercase letters show the corner

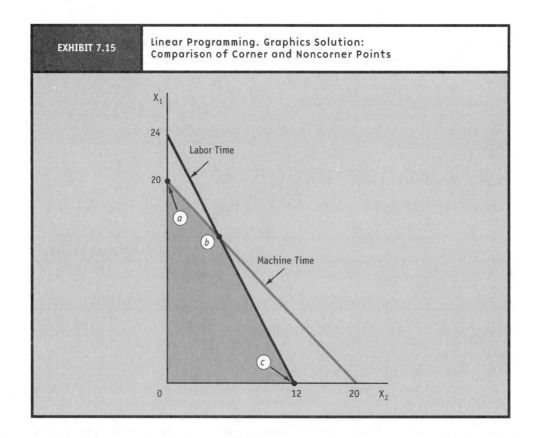

EXHIBIT 7.15	Linear Programming. Graphics Solution: Comparison of Corner and Noncorner Points

points. We find the optimal solution by deriving the total contribution margin at each point, using the following steps.

Step 1   Find the production level of Product 1 and Product 2 at each point. Points a and c are straightforward. At a, $X_1 = 20$ and $X_2 = 0$; at c, $X_2 = 12$ and $X_1 = 0$. Point b requires solving for two unknowns using the two constraint formulas:

Labor Time:	$X_1 + 2X_2 = 24$
Machine Time:	$X_1 + X_2 = 20$

Setting these two equations equal, we have

$$X_1 = 24 - 2X_2$$
$$X_1 = 20 - X_2,$$
$$24 - 2X_2 = 20 - X_2$$
$$4 = X_2.$$

If $X_2 = 4$, then

$$X_1 = 20 - X_2$$
$$= 20 - 4$$
$$= 16.$$

At point b, Moline produces 16 units of Product 1 and 4 units of Product 2.

Step 2   Find the total contribution margin at each point. (Recall that the unit contribution margins of Products 1 and 2 are $3 and $4.) Exhibit 7.16 shows the solution. It is optimal to produce at point b, where $X_1 = 16$ and $X_2 = 4$.

Why must the optimal solution be at a corner? If production moves away from the corner at point b in any feasible direction, total contribution will not increase and generally will be lower. Exhibit 7.17 shows a movement away from point b in four feasible directions.

Exhibit 7.18 compares contributions at those noncorner points with the contribution at corner point b. Although these examples show intuitively that the contribution margin declines away from the corner point, we can prove mathematically our assertion that the optimal solution always lies on a corner point.

Sensitivity Analysis

The contribution margins and costs in the objective functions are estimates, subject to error. Decision makers frequently need to know how much the estimates can change before the decision changes.

EXHIBIT 7.16	Optimal Product Mix				
		Production		**Contribution**	
Point		X_1	X_2	1	2	Total
a		20	0	$60	$ 0	$60
b		16	4	48	16	64
c		0	12	0	48	48

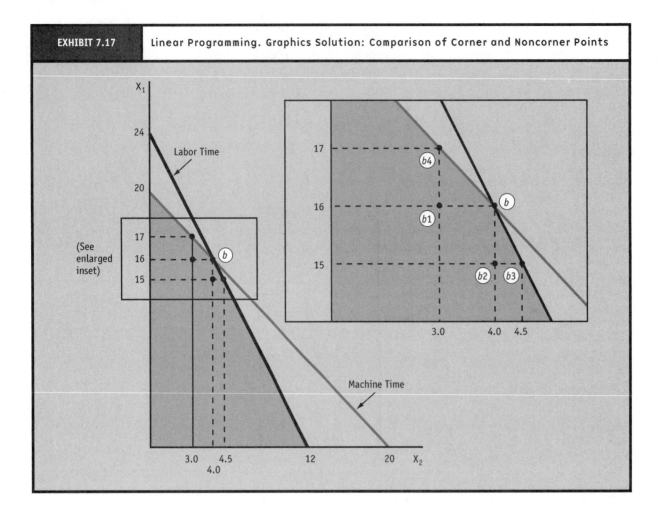

EXHIBIT 7.17	Linear Programming. Graphics Solution: Comparison of Corner and Noncorner Points

EXHIBIT 7.18	Comparison of Corner Point and Noncorner Points

	Production		Contribution		
Point	X_1	X_2	1	2	Total
b	16	4.0	$48	$16	$64
$b1$	16	3.0	48	12	60
$b2$	15	4.0	45	16	61
$b3^a$	15	4.5	45	18	63
$b4^b$	17	3.0	51	12	63

[a] Let $X_1 = 15$ and find X_2 as follows:

$$X_1 = 24 - 2X_2$$
$$15 = 24 - 2X_2$$
$$2X_2 = 9$$
$$X_2 = 4.5.$$

[b] Let $X_2 = 3$ and find X_1 as follows:

$$X_1 = 20 - X_2$$
$$= 20 - 3$$
$$= 17.$$

EXHIBIT 7.19	Optimal Product Mix: Revised Cost Estimates				
		Production		**Contribution**	
Point[a]		X_1	X_2	1	2	**Total**
a		20	0	$60	$ 0	$60
b		16	4	48	14[b]	62
c		0	12	0	42	42

[a]The graph in Exhibit 7.15 presents these points.
[b]Four units × $3.50 per unit.

To demonstrate our point, we use our earlier profit-maximization problem for Moline Company, which we formulated as follows:

Maximize: $$\$3X_1 + \$4X_2 = \text{Total Contribution}$$

Subject to: $$X_1 + 2X_2 = 24 \text{ Labor Hours}$$

$$X_1 + X_2 = 20 \text{ Machine Hours.}$$

Suppose that the variable cost estimate for Product 2 was $0.50 per unit too low, so Product 2's unit contribution margin should have been $3.50 instead of $4.00. What effect would this have? We have calculated the new contributions in Exhibit 7.19. If you compare this exhibit with Exhibit 7.16, you will see that the contribution for Product 2 changes; thus the total contribution changes. The optimal decision to produce 16 units of Product 1 and 4 units of Product 2 does not change, however. In spite of the change in costs and thus in contributions, the *decision* does not change. In this example, the unit contribution margin of Product 2 would have to drop to less than $3 per unit before the optimal decision would change, assuming that all other things remained constant.

Most linear programming computer programs can provide this type of sensitivity analysis. With it, managers and accountants can ascertain how much a cost or contribution margin can change before the optimal decision will change.

Opportunity Costs

Any constrained resource has an opportunity cost, which is the profit forgone by not having an additional unit of the resource. For example, suppose that Moline Company in our previous example could obtain one additional hour of machine time. With one more hour of machine time, the machine constraint would move out, as shown in Exhibit 7.20. We find the new production level at point *b* as follows:

$$X_1 = 24 - 2X_2$$

and

$$X_1 = 21 - X_2$$
$$24 - 2X_2 = 21 - X_2$$
$$X_2 = 3$$
$$X_1 = 18.$$

The new total contribution at point *b* would be $3(18) + $4(3) = $66, compared to $64 when machine time was constrained to 20 hours per day, as shown for point *b* in Exhibit 7.18. Thus the opportunity cost of not having an extra hour of machine time is $2 (= $66 − $64).

Linear programming computer programs regularly provide for opportunity costs, called **shadow prices.** Opportunity cost data indicate the benefits of acquiring more units of a scarce resource. For example, if Moline Company could rent one more machine hour for less than $2 per hour, the company would profit by doing so, all other things being equal.

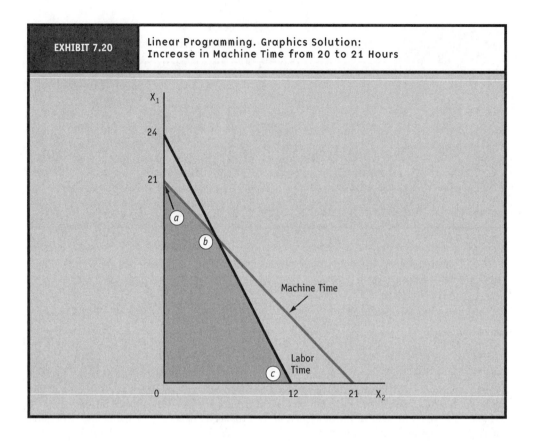

EXHIBIT 7.20 | Linear Programming. Graphics Solution: Increase in Machine Time from 20 to 21 Hours

Appendix 7.2: Economic Order Quantity Model

In our discussion of inventory management, we derived the optimal number of orders or production runs by trial and error. We also could derive the optimal number of orders or production runs per period from the following formula:

$$N = D/Q$$

where

$$Q = \sqrt{\frac{2K_0D}{K_c}}$$

N = the optimal number of orders or production runs for the period

Q = the economic order quantity, or the optimal number of items in an order or production run

D = the period demand in units

K_0 = the order or setup cost

K_c = the cost of carrying one unit in inventory for the period.

The formula $Q = \sqrt{2K_0D/K_c}$ results from using calculus to minimize total cost with respect to Q. The total cost (TC) formula is

$$\frac{\text{Total Cost}}{\text{per Period}} = \frac{\text{Carrying Costs}}{\text{per Period}} + \frac{\text{Order Costs}}{\text{per Period}}$$

$$TC = K_c\frac{Q}{2} + K_0\frac{D}{Q}.$$

Take the first derivative of TC with respect to Q, set it equal to zero, and solve for Q:

$$\frac{dTC}{dQ} = \frac{d}{dQ}\left(K_c \frac{Q}{2} + K_0 \frac{D}{Q} \right)$$

$$= \frac{K_c}{2} - \frac{K_0 D}{Q^2} = 0.$$

$$Q = \sqrt{\frac{2K_0 D}{K_c}}.$$

Example   The following facts for the Penn Merchandising example appeared in the text:

D = period demand = 6,000 units per year

K_0 = order costs = $100 per order

K_c = carrying cost = 30 percent of the cost of inventory of $0.60 per unit
     ($0.60 = 30 percent $\times$ $2.00 per unit).

Solving for Q (the optimal number of items in an order), we have

$$Q = \sqrt{\frac{2K_0 D}{K_c}}$$

$$= \sqrt{\frac{2 \times \$100 \times 6{,}000\ \text{Units}}{\$0.60}}$$

$$= \sqrt{2{,}000{,}000\ \text{Units}}$$

$$= 1{,}414\ \text{Units per Order}.$$

$$N = \frac{D}{Q}$$

$$= \frac{6{,}000\ \text{Units}}{1{,}414\ \text{Units}}$$

$$= 4.2\ \text{Orders per Year}.$$

From these equations, we derived the optimal order size, 1,414 units, and the optimal number of orders per year, 4.2. This result is approximately the same one we derived by trial and error earlier. Using the economic order quantity model is usually more efficient for finding the least costly size and number of orders (or productions).

This is known as the **economic order quantity (EOQ) model.** Textbooks on operations research and quantitative methods present many variations and applications of this model.

Questions, Exercises, Problems, and Cases

REVIEW QUESTIONS

1. Review the meanings of the concepts or terms given in Key Terms and Concepts.
2. When, if ever, are fixed costs differential?
3. How is the evaluation of short-term pricing decisions different from the evaluation of long-term decisions?
4. Should facility-sustaining costs be considered in making a short-term pricing decision?
5. When is the use of full cost information appropriate for pricing decisions?
6. Production of a special order will increase operating profit when the additional revenue from the special order is greater than
   a. the direct material costs in producing the order.
   b. the fixed costs incurred in producing the order.
   c. the indirect costs of producing the order.
   d. the differential costs of producing the order.

7. In considering a special order that will enable a company to make use of idle capacity, which of the following costs would probably not be differential?
   a. materials
   b. depreciation of buildings
   c. direct labor
   d. variable overhead

8. Inventory management problems usually involve two types of opposing costs. Describe these costs and sketch a graph showing how they change as order size changes. (Put order size on the horizontal axis.)

9. Describe the relevant costs for make-or-buy decisions.

10. True or false: The objective of the theory of constraints is to increase throughput contribution.

CRITICAL ANALYSIS AND DISCUSSION QUESTIONS

11. What additional costs must be taken into account when making a short-term pricing decision where surplus capacity is not available, and overtime, additional shifts, or other means must be used to expand capacity?

12. Describe two situations in which the use of full costs for pricing decisions is not appropriate.

13. Why is full cost information useful for long-term decisions?

14. "This whole subject of differential costing is easy—variable costs are the only costs that are relevant." Respond to this statement.

15. A manager in your organization just received a special order at a price that is "below cost." The manager points to the document and says, "These are the kinds of orders that will get you in trouble. Every sale must bear its share of the full costs of running the business. If we sell below our full cost, we'll be out of business in no time." What do you think of this remark?

16. If you are considering driving to a weekend resort for a quick break from school, what are the differential costs of operating your car for that drive?

17. If you are considering buying a second car, what are the differential costs of that decision? Are they the same as in Question **16**? Why or why not?

18. Assume that your company uses activity-based costing. You must set the price for a custom order and suggest that your boss use a cost-plus pricing approach. Your boss states, "We can't possibly use cost-plus pricing given the activity-based costing system we recently implemented!" Respond to your boss's comment. What recommendation would you make as to how to price a custom order?

19. "A proper evaluation of any project using differential analysis requires the consideration of all relevant costs—past, present, and future." Comment.

20. You are asked to provide margin figures for a product-choice decision. Do you give the gross margin per unit or contribution margin per unit? Why?

21. Interview the manager of a restaurant. Does the restaurant make or buy soups and desserts? Based on your interview, write a short report that explains why the restaurant makes or buys each of these items.

EXERCISES

Solutions to even-numbered exercises are at the end of the chapter.

22. **Product choice.** Renovation Enterprises renovated an old train station into warehouse space, office space, restaurants, and specialty shops. If used all for warehouse space, the estimated revenue and variable costs per year to Renovation would be $960,000 and $40,000, respectively. If used all for office space, the revenue and variable costs per year would be $982,800 and $70,000, respectively. If used all for restaurants and specialty shops, the revenue and variable costs would be $1,101,100 and $95,000, respectively. Fixed costs per year would be $600,000 regardless of the alternative chosen.

To which use should Renovation Enterprises put the old train station?

23. **Special order.** Anticipating unusually high sales for July, Radios, Inc., a producer of small two-way radios, plans to produce 20,000 radios, using all available capacity. Radios anticipates costs for the radios for July as follows:

Unit Manufacturing Costs		
Variable Direct Materials Cost	$1.20	
Variable Labor	2.50	
Variable Overhead	0.10	
Fixed Overhead	0.85	
Total Manufacturing Costs per Unit		$ 4.65
Unit Marketing Costs		
Variable	$0.90	
Fixed	2.20	
Total Marketing Costs per Unit		3.10
Total Unit Costs		$ 7.75
Selling Price per Unit		$15.00

On June 30, Radios received a contract offer from Communication Devices (a radio manufacturer) to supply 10,000 radios for delivery by July 31. In place of the standard sales price of $15 per radio, the Communication Devices offer would reimburse Radios' share of both variable and fixed manufacturing costs (that is, $4.65 per product) plus a fixed fee of $5,000. Variable marketing costs would be zero for this order. None of the fixed costs would be affected by this order. Radios would lose 10,000 units of sales to regular customers in July, but this order would not affect sales in any subsequent months.

Prepare a differential analysis comparing the status quo for July with the alternative case in which Radios accepts the special order. Write a brief report to Radios' management explaining why the company should or should not accept the special order.

24. **Finding the most profitable price-quantity combination.** The Giants Company is introducing a new product called Barry Dolls and must decide what price should be set. An estimated demand schedule for the product follows:

Price	Quantity Demanded (in units)
$10	40,000
12	36,000
14	28,000
16	24,000
18	18,000
20	15,000

Estimated costs follow:

Variable Manufacturing Costs	$4 per Unit
Fixed Manufacturing Costs	$40,000 per Year
Variable Selling and Administrative Costs	$2 per Unit
Fixed Selling and Administrative Costs	$10,000 per Year

a. Prepare a schedule showing the total revenue, total cost, and total profit or loss for each selling price.

b. Which price provides the most profits?

25. **Pricing decisions.** The marketing department of Coffee Express estimates the following monthly demand for espresso in these five price-volume relations at one of its outlets:

1	6,000 cups at $2.00 per cup
2	5,000 cups at $2.20 per cup
3	4,000 cups at $2.50 per cup
4	3,000 cups at $2.75 per cup
5	2,000 cups at $3.00 per cup

The fixed costs of $6,000 per month are the same for all these volumes. Variable costs are $0.75 per cup. Which of these prices should Coffee Express charge for its espresso?

26. **Identify differential costs.** Assume Nordican Boot Company is considering making a specially designed snow boot just for the Winter Olympics. Which of the following costs or activities would probably be differential in developing, marketing, producing, and selling the special snow boot?
   a. Product design work to design the boot.
   b. The company president's salary.
   c. Advertising the boot.
   d. The lease of the building in which the boot is made. The company would not use the building but would pay the lease whether it makes the boots or not.
   e. Catering costs incurred to provide food at the monthly board of directors meeting.
   f. Sales commissions paid to sales personnel who attempt to get sporting goods stores to carry the special boot.

27. **Special order.** Cisco's Sportswear makes jerseys for athletic teams. The Junior League group has offered to buy 80 jerseys for the teams in its league for $14 per jersey. The normal team price for such jerseys is $20. Cisco's purchases the plain jerseys for $12 per jersey and then sews a name and number to each jersey at a variable cost of $3 per jersey. Cisco's makes about 2,000 jerseys per year and has a capacity limit of 4,000 jerseys. The annual fixed cost of equipment used in the sewing process is $5,000, and other fixed costs allocated to jerseys are $2,000, bringing the total costs allocated to each jersey to $3.50.

   Compute the amount by which the operating profit of Cisco's would change if the special order were accepted. Should Cisco's accept the special order?

28. **Target costing and pricing.** Irish Products makes wheels for a variety of toys and sports equipment. Irish Products sells the wheels to manufacturers who assemble and sell the toys and equipment. The company's market research department has discovered a market for wheels for in-line skates, which Irish Products currently does not produce. The market research department has indicated that a set of four wheels for in-line skates would likely sell for $6.

   Assume the company desires an operating profit of 20 percent. What is the highest acceptable manufacturing cost for Irish Products to produce the sets of wheels?

29. **Target costing and pricing.** Donelan Products makes high-pressure lines for a variety of heavy road-improvement equipment. Donelan Products sells the lines to manufacturers who manufacture and sell the equipment. The company's market research department has discovered a market for high-pressure lines used in automated manufacturing equipment, which Donelan Products currently does not produce. The market research department has indicated that lines would likely sell for $50 per foot.

   Assume Donelan Products desires an operating profit of 40 percent of sales. What is the highest acceptable manufacturing cost per foot for which Donelan Products would produce the lines?

30. **Make or buy.** Ol' Salt Enterprises produces 1,000 sailboats per year. Although the company currently buys sails for the sailboats (one set of sails per boat), it is considering making sails in some space that it does not currently use. The company purchases each set of sails for $300. It could make the sails for variable costs of $250 per set, plus it would allocate $200,000 of fixed costs per year to the sail-making operation. However, this $200,000 is not a differential cost of making sails; it is part of the costs the company already incurs that it would allocate away from sailboat manufacture to sail making.

a. Prepare a differential analysis to show whether Ol' Salt Enterprises should make or buy the sails. What should you recommend to management? Explain why the $200,000 fixed costs allocated to sail making is or is not relevant to the decision.

b. If Ol' Salt buys the sails, then it would have unused factory space. Suppose Ol' Salt received an opportunity to rent out this unused factory space for $80,000 per year. Would that affect your recommendation in part **a.**?

31. **Throughput contribution.** Victoria Hair Salon styles hair in three operations—washing, cutting/setting, and drying—and charges $15 per styling. (Each styling is one "unit.") Victoria styles hair on a walk-in basis and does not take appointments; customers who face a wait walk across the street to another salon. Victoria's owners find it has a cutting/setting bottleneck on Saturdays due to a limited number of stylists. The bottleneck exists for a total of eight hours each Saturday. Pertinent information follows:

	Washing	Cutting/Setting	Drying
Hourly Capacity	30 Units	12 Units	15 Units
Saturday Capacity (8 hours)	240 Units	96 Units	120 Units
Actual Saturday Production	96 Units	96 Units	96 Units
Fixed Operating Costs per Saturday	$10	$75	$100

Each hair styling has variable costs of $5. Victoria's output is constrained by the 96 units of cutting/setting capacity. Two options exist that can relieve the bottleneck at the cutting/setting operation. Consider the differential costs associated with each of the following options to determine the impact on throughput.

Option a. Victoria can increase bottleneck output by hiring one nonstylist employee to prepare customers for the cutting/setting by washing and combing their hair. This would increase the cutting/setting capacity to 110 each Saturday. The cost for this additional employee is $64 per Saturday.

Option b. Victoria could hire another stylist for each Saturday, increasing the cutting/setting capacity to 108 each Saturday and costing an additional $120 per Saturday. (Note that the drying operation has a capacity of 120.)

Should Victoria's owner go ahead with either of the two options? Why or why not?

32. **Throughput contribution.** Stay Warm, Inc., produces extreme-weather parkas in three operations—cutting, assembling, and finishing. The parkas sell for $120 each. Stay Warm's managers find it has a cutting bottleneck due to limited layout space. Pertinent information per month follows:

	Cutting	Assembly	Finishing
Hourly Capacity	80 Units	100 Units	150 Units
Monthly Capacity (168 hours)	13,440 Units	16,800 Units	25,200 Units
Actual Monthly Production	13,440 Units	13,440 Units	13,440 Units
Fixed Operating Costs per Month	$11,200	$15,500	$12,000

Each parka has variable costs of $65. Stay Warm's output is constrained by the 13,440 units of cutting capacity. Only one option exists that can relieve the bottleneck at the cutting operation. Consider the differential costs associated with the following option to determine the impact on throughput.

Stay Warm can increase bottleneck output by renting additional space for the cutting operation, increasing the monthly cutting capacity to 15,000. The additional monthly cost of renting space and hiring additional cutters is $60,000.

Should Stay Warm go ahead with this option? Why or why not?

33. **Dropping a product line.** Tiger Products currently operates at 75 percent capacity. Worried about the company's performance, the general manager segmented the company's income statement product by product and obtained the following picture:

	Product		
	A	**B**	**C**
Sales	$20,000	$30,000	$38,000
Less Variable Costs	15,000	22,000	34,000
Total Contribution Margin	$ 5,000	$ 8,000	$ 4,000
Less Fixed Costs	3,000	5,000	7,000
Net Operating Profit (Loss)	$ 2,000	$ 3,000	$(3,000)

Should Tiger Products drop Product C, given that doing so would eliminate Product C's sales and variable costs and reduce the company's total fixed costs by only $5,000?

34. **Dropping a product line.** Timepiece Products, a clock manufacturer, operates at capacity. Constrained by machine time, the company decides to drop the most unprofitable of its three product lines. The accounting department came up with the following data from last year's operations:

	Manual	**Electric**	**Quartz**
Machine Time per Unit	0.4 Hour	2.5 Hours	5.0 Hours
Selling Price per Unit	$20	$30	$50
Less Variable Costs per Unit	10	14	28
Contribution Margin	$10	$16	$22

Which line should Timepiece Products drop? (Hint: Compute the contribution per machine hour because machine time is the constraint.)

35. **Product choice using linear programming** (Appendix 7.1). Gateway Products manufactures two products whose contribution margins follow:

Product	**Contribution Margin**
A	$10
B	13

Each month Gateway Products has only 12,000 hours of machine time and 14,400 hours of labor time available. The amount of time required to make Products A and B follows:

	Product A	**Product B**
Labor Time	4 Hours per Unit	2 Hours per Unit
Machine Time	2 Hours per Unit	3 Hours per Unit

The firm sells all units produced. Management wants to know the number of units of each product the company should make.

Set up the problem in the linear programming format and solve for the optimal production mix.

36. **Economic order quantity** (Appendix 7.2). The Sun Valley Foundry regularly uses 10,000 axles per year. It can purchase axles for $100 each. Ordering costs are $10 per order, and

the holding costs of items in inventory are 20 percent of cost per year. Prepare an analysis for management that answers the following question:

What are the economic order quantity and annual ordering costs?

37. **Economic order quantity** (Appendix 7.2). The purchasing agent responsible for ordering chairs estimates that Folsom Furniture sells 30,000 chairs evenly throughout each year, that each order costs $15 to place, and that holding each chair in inventory for a year costs $4 per chair.
    a. How many chairs should Folsom Furniture request in each order?
    b. How many times per year should Folsom Furniture order chairs?

38. **Product mix decisions** (Appendix 7.1; adapted from CPA exam). The Hanson Company manufactures two products, Zeta and Beta. Each product must pass through two processing operations. All materials enter production at the start of Process No. 1. Hanson has no work-in-process inventories. Hanson may produce either one product exclusively or various combinations of both products, subject to the following constraints:

	Process No. 1	Process No. 2	Contribution Margin per Unit
Hours Required to Produce One Unit of:			
Zeta	1	1	$4.25
Beta	2	3	5.25
Total Capacity per Day in Hours	1,000	1,275	

A shortage of technical labor has limited Beta production to 400 units per day. The firm has *no* constraints on the production of Zeta other than the hour constraints in the preceding schedule. Assume that all relations between capacity and production are linear.

What is the total contribution from the optimal product mix?

39. **Product mix decisions** (Appendix 7.1). Use the information for the Hanson Company in Exercise **38** and assume that the present Process No. 1 already costs the company $1.75 for each unit of Zeta. What is the maximum price that Hanson would be willing to pay for just enough additional time in Process No. 1 to produce one more unit of Zeta?

40. **Dropping a product line.** Hayley and Associates is a public accounting firm that offers three types of services—audit, tax, and consulting. The firm is concerned about the profitability of its consulting business and is considering dropping that line. If the consulting business is dropped, more tax work would be done. If consulting is dropped, all consulting revenues would be lost, all the variable costs associated with consulting would be saved, and 40 percent of the fixed costs associated with consulting would be saved. If consulting is dropped, tax revenues are expected to increase by 50 percent, the variable costs associated with tax would increase by 50 percent, and the fixed costs associated with tax would increase 20 percent. Revenues and costs associated with auditing would not be affected.

Segmented income statements for these product lines appear as follows:

Product

	Consulting	Tax	Auditing
Revenue	$300,000	$400,000	$500,000
Variable Costs	250,000	300,000	350,000
Contribution Margin	$ 50,000	$100,000	$150,000
Fixed Costs	50,000	60,000	80,000
Operating Profit	$ 0	$ 40,000	$ 70,000

Prepare a report to the management of Hayley and Associates advising whether to drop consulting and increase tax. Assume tax would not be increased if consulting were kept. Include a differential analysis.

41. **Differential costs: Special order.** Assume Road-Runner Shoes has a plant capacity that can produce 3,000 units per week (each unit is a pair of shoes). Its predicted operations for the week follow:

Sales (2,500 units at $30 each)	$75,000
Manufacturing Costs	
Variable	$15 per Unit
Fixed	$10,000
Marketing and Administrative Costs	
Variable (sales commissions)	$3 per Unit
Fixed	$1,500

Should Road-Runner accept a special order for 400 units at a selling price of $30 each? Assume these units are subject to half the usual sales commission rate per unit, and assume no effect on regular sales at regular prices. How will the decision affect the company's operating profit?

PROBLEMS

42. **Special order.** Easton Company has a capacity of 200,000 computer monitors per year. The company is currently producing and selling 160,000 monitors per year at a selling price of $400 per monitor. The cost of producing and selling one monitor at the 160,000-unit level of activity follows:

Variable Manufacturing Costs	$160
Fixed Manufacturing Costs	40
Variable Selling and Administrative Costs	80
Fixed Selling and Administrative Costs	20
Total Costs	$300

The company has received a special order for 10,000 monitors at a price of $250 per monitor. Because it need not pay a sales commission on the special order, the variable selling and administrative costs would be only $50 per monitor. The special order would have no effect on total fixed costs. The company has rejected the offer based on the following computations:

Selling Price per Monitor	$250
Variable Manufacturing Costs	160
Fixed Manufacturing Costs	40
Variable Selling and Administrative Costs	50
Fixed Selling and Administrative Costs	20
Net Loss per Monitor	$(20)

Management is reviewing its decision and wants your advice. Should Easton have accepted the special order? Show your computations.

43. **Solving for minimum price.** Assume that Dan & Barry's sells ice cream for $3 per quart. The cost of each quart follows:

Materials	$1.00
Labor	0.50
Variable Overhead	0.25
Fixed Overhead ($20,000 per month, 20,000 quarts per month)	1.00
Total Cost per Quart	$2.75

One of Dan & Barry's regular customers asked the company to fill a special order of 400 quarts at a selling price of $2.50 per quart for a special picnic. Dan & Barry's can fill the order using existing capacity without affecting total fixed costs for the month.

Dan & Barry's general manager was concerned about selling the ice cream below the cost of $2.75 per quart and has asked for your advice.

a. Prepare a schedule to show the impact of providing the special order of 400 quarts of ice cream on Dan & Barry's profits in addition to the regular production and sales of 20,000 quarts per month.

b. Based solely on the data given, what is the lowest price per quart at which the ice cream in the special order could be sold without reducing Dan & Barry's profits?

44. **Customer profitability analysis.** Squeaky Clean, a commercial laundry service, has two clients, Super 6 Motel and Seaside Inn. The following is information about Squeaky's revenues and costs (in thousands) by customer for the previous year:

	Super 6 Motel	Seaside Inn	Total
Revenues (fees charged)	$230	$350	$580
Operating Costs			
Cost of Services (variable)	$212	$305	$517
Salaries, Rent, and General Administration (fixed)	20	35	55
Total Operating Costs	$232	$340	$572
Operating Profits	$ (2)	$ 10	$ 8

The analysis apparently shows that Super 6 Motel is not profitable for Squeaky. Use differential analysis to decide whether Squeaky should discontinue the Super 6 Motel account.

45. **Customer profitability analysis.** Hillson & Brady (H&B), a janitorial service, has two clients, Greeley Hospital and Greeley Junior High School. The following is information about H&B's revenues and costs (in thousands) by customer for the previous year.

	Greeley Hospital	Greeley Junior High	Total
Revenues (fees charged)	$920	$1,400	$2,320
Operating Costs			
Cost of Services (variable)	$848	$1,220	$2,068
Salaries, Rent, and General Administration (fixed)	80	120	200
Total Operating Costs	$928	$1,340	$2,268
Operating Profits	$ (8)	$ 60	$ 52

This analysis apparently shows that Greeley Hospital is not profitable for H&B. Use differential analysis to determine whether H&B should discontinue the hospital account.

46. **Special order** (adapted from CMA exam). Nancy Boussard operates a small machine shop. She manufactures one standard product, which is available from many other similar businesses, in addition to custom-made products. Her accountant prepared the following annual income statement:

	Custom Sales	Standard Sales	Total
Sales revenue	$50,000	$25,000	$75,000
Materials	$10,000	$ 8,000	$18,000
Labor	20,000	9,000	29,000
Depreciation	6,300	3,600	9,900
Power	700	400	1,100

(continued)

	Custom Sales	Standard Sales	Total
Rent	6,000	1,000	7,000
Heat and Light	600	100	700
Other	400	900	1,300
Total Costs	$44,000	$23,000	$67,000
Operating Profit	$ 6,000	$ 2,000	$ 8,000

The depreciation charges are for machines (based on time) used in the respective product lines. The power charge is apportioned based on the estimate of power consumed. The rent is for the building space, which has been leased for 10 years at $7,000 per year. The rent, heat, and electricity are apportioned to the product lines based on the amount of floor space occupied. All other costs are current expenses identified with the product line causing them.

A valued custom-parts customer has asked Nancy to manufacture 10,000 special units. Nancy is working at capacity and would have to give up some other business to take this business. She can't renege on custom orders already agreed to, but she can reduce the output of her standard product by about one-half for one year while producing the custom part. The customer is willing to pay $6 for each unit. Materials will cost $2 per unit and the labor, $3.60 per unit. Nancy will have to spend $2,000 for a special device, which will be discarded when the job is done.

Should Nancy take the order? Explain your answer.

47. **Special order—multiple choice.** Meals.com, Inc., which produces and ships frozen meals, has the plant capacity to produce 10,000 units annually. Its predicted operations for the year follow:

Sales (8,000 units at $10 each)	$80,000
Manufacturing Costs	
Variable	$4 per Unit
Fixed	$10,000
Marketing and Administrative Costs	
Variable	$2 per Unit
Fixed	$8,000

Meals.com is considering a special order of 1,000 units from a prospective customer willing to pay $8 per unit. Assume this order will have no effect on regular sales at regular prices, on total fixed costs, or on variable costs per unit.

a. The effect of the special order on sales will be an increase of
  (1) $10,000.
  (2) $72,000.
  (3) $80,000.
  (4) $8,000.
  (5) Some other amount.
b. The effect of the special order on total variable costs will be an increase of
  (1) $8,000.
  (2) $6,000.
  (3) $5,000.
  (4) $4,000.
  (5) Some other amount.
c. The effect of the special order on total fixed costs will be an increase of
  (1) $0.
  (2) $2,250.
  (3) $8,000.
  (4) $1,250.
  (5) Some other amount.

d. The effect of the special order on fixed costs per unit will be
   (1) Zero.
   (2) An increase of $2.25.
   (3) A decrease of $2.25.
   (4) A decrease of some other amount.
   (5) An increase of some other amount.

e. How will the special order affect operating profit?
   (1) Increase it.
   (2) Decrease it.
   (3) Have no effect.

48. **Dropping a machine from service.** Granger Company has four machines of approximately equal capacity. Each was run at close to its full capacity during Year 4. Each machine is depreciated separately using an accelerated method. Data for each machine follow (00 refers to Year 0):

	No. 1	No. 2	No. 3	No. 4
Date Acquired	1/1/00	1/1/01	1/1/03	1/1/04
Cost	$ 2,500	$ 4,000	$ 5,000	$ 7,000
Operating Costs, Year 4:				
Labor	$15,000	$19,000	$18,000	$21,000
Materials	4,000	4,500	5,000	2,500
Maintenance	500	500	500	400
Depreciation (a fixed cost)	200	300	300	500
Total Operating Costs	$19,700	$24,300	$23,800	$24,400

Granger expects activity in Year 5 to be less than that in Year 4, so it will drop one machine from service. Management proposes that Granger drop No. 4 on the grounds that it has the highest operating costs. Do you agree or disagree with this proposal? Why?

49. **Make or buy.** Spectra, Inc., produces semiconductors of which part no. 200 is a subassembly. Spectra, Inc., currently produces part no. 200 in its own shop. The Alta Company offers to supply it at a cost of $200 per 500 units. An analysis of the costs Spectra incurs producing part no. 200 reveals the following information:

	Cost per 500 Units
Direct (Variable) Material	$ 80
Direct (Variable) Labor	90
Other Variable Costs	25
Fixed Costs[a]	50
Total	$245

[a]Fixed overhead comprises largely depreciation on general-purpose equipment and factory buildings.

Management of Spectra, Inc., needs your advice in answering the following questions:

a. Should Spectra, Inc., accept the offer from Alta if Spectra's plant is operating well below capacity?

b. Should the offer be accepted if Alta reduces the price to $180 per 500 units?

c. Suppose Spectra can find other profitable uses for the facilities it now uses in turning out part no. 200. How would that fact affect the price Spectra is willing to pay Alta?

50. **Cost estimate for bidding: consulting firm.** Art, Sam, and Kaye (ASK) operates a management consulting firm. It has just received an inquiry from a prospective client about its prices for educational seminars for the prospective client's supervisors. The prospective client wants bids for three alternative activity levels: (1) one seminar with 25 participants, (2) four seminars with 20 participants each (80 participants total), or (3) eight seminars with

144 participants in total. The consulting firm's accountants have provided the following differential cost estimates:

Startup Costs for the Entire Job	$ 600
Materials Costs per Participant (brochures, handouts, etc.)	100
Differential Direct Labor Costs:	
One Seminar	1,200
Four Seminars	5,000
Eight Seminars	8,800

In addition to the preceding differential costs, ASK allocates fixed costs to jobs on a direct-labor-cost basis, at a rate of 75 percent of direct labor costs (excluding setup costs). For example, if direct labor costs are $100, ASK would also charge the job $75 for fixed costs. ASK seeks to make a profit of 20 percent above cost for each job. For this purpose, profit is revenue minus all costs assigned to the job, including allocated fixed costs. ASK has enough excess capacity to handle this job with ease.

a. Assume ASK bases its bid on the average total cost, including fixed costs allocated to the job, plus the 20 percent markup on cost. What should ASK bid for each of the three levels of activity?

b. Compute the differential cost (including startup cost) and the contribution to profit for each of the three levels of activity.

c. Assume the prospective client gives three options. It is willing to accept either of ASK's bids for the one-seminar or four-seminar activity levels, but the prospective client will pay only 88 percent of the bid price for the eight-seminar package. ASK's president responds, "Taking the order for 12 percent below our bid would wipe out our profit! Let's take the four-seminar option; we make the most profit on it." Do you agree? What would be the contribution to profit for each of the three options?

51. **Differential cost analysis in a service organization** (contributed by Robert H. Colson). Columbo Connections, LLP, is a "head-hunting" firm that provides information about candidates for executive and cabinet-level positions. Major customers include corporations and the federal government.

The cost per billable hour of service at the company's normal volume of 5,000 billable hours per month follows. (A billable hour is one hour billed to a client.)

COLUMBO CONNECTIONS, LLP
Cost per Billable Hour of Service

Average Cost per Hour Billed to Client:		
Variable Labor—Consultants	$200	
Variable Overhead, Including Supplies and Clerical Support	40	
Fixed Overhead, Including Allowance for Unbilled Hours	160	
		$400
Marketing and Administrative Costs per Billable Hour (all fixed)		100
Total Hourly Cost		$500

Treat each question independently. Unless given otherwise, the regular fee per hour is $600.

a. How many hours must the firm bill per month to break even?

b. Market research estimates that a fee increase to $750 per hour would decrease monthly volume to 4,000 hours. The accounting department estimates that fixed costs would be $1,000,000 while variable costs per hour would remain unchanged. How would a fee increase affect profits?

c. Columbo Connections is operating at its normal volume. It has received a special request from a cabinet official to provide investigative services on a special-order basis. Because of the long-term nature of the contract (four months) and the magnitude (1,000 hours per month), the customer believes a fee reduction is in order. Columbo Connections has a capacity limitation of 6,000 hours per month. Fixed costs will not change if the firm accepts the special order. What is the lowest fee Columbo Connections would be willing to charge?

52. **Comprehensive differential costing problem.** Troy Manufacturing, Inc., produces exercise bicycles. The costs of manufacturing and marketing exercise bicycles at the company's normal volume of 3,000 units per month follow:

TROY MANUFACTURING
Costs per Unit

Unit Manufacturing Costs		
Variable Materials	$100	
Variable Labor	150	
Variable Overhead	50	
Fixed Overhead	200	
Total Unit Manufacturing Costs		$500
Unit Non-manufacturing Costs		
Variable	$100	
Fixed	100	
Total Unit Non-manufacturing Costs		200
Total Unit Costs		$700

Unless otherwise stated, assume that the situations described in the questions are not connected; treat each independently. Unless otherwise stated, assume a regular selling price of $1,000 per unit and a volume of 3,000 bicycles per month.

a. Market research estimates that volume could be increased to 3,500 units, which is well within production capacity limitations, if the price were cut from $1,000 to $900 per unit. Assuming that the cost behavior patterns implied by the data given above are correct, would you recommend taking this action? What would be the impact on monthly sales, costs, and income?

b. On March 1, the Veterans Administration offers Troy a contract to supply 500 units to Veterans Administration hospitals for a March 31 delivery. Because of an unusually large number of rush orders from its regular customers, Troy plans to produce 4,000 units during March, which will use all available capacity. If it accepts the government order, it would lose 500 units normally sold to regular customers to a competitor. The government contract would reimburse its "share of March manufacturing costs" plus pay a $50,000 fixed fee (profit). (No variable marketing costs would be incurred on the government's units.) What impact would accepting the government contract have on March income? (Part of your problem is to figure out the meaning of "share of March manufacturing costs.")

c. Troy has an opportunity to enter a new market. An attraction of the new market is that its demand is greatest when the domestic market's demand is quite low; thus, idle production facilities could be used without affecting normal business.

  An order for 1,000 units is being sought at a below-normal price to enter this market. For this order, shipping costs will total $75 per unit; total (marketing) costs to obtain the contract will be $4,000. No other variable marketing costs would be required on this order, and it would not affect domestic business. What is the minimum unit price that Troy should consider for this order of 1,000 units?

d. An inventory of 200 units of an obsolete model of the exercise bicycle remains in the stockroom. These must be sold through regular channels (thus incurring variable marketing costs) at reduced prices or the inventory will soon be valueless. What is the minimum acceptable selling price for these units?

e. Troy Manufacturing receives a proposal from an outside contractor who will make and ship 1,000 units per month directly to Troy Manufacturing's customers. The proposal would not affect Troy Manufacturing's fixed non-manufacturing costs, but its variable non-manufacturing costs would decline by 20 percent for these 1,000 units produced by the contractor. Troy Manufacturing's plant would operate at two-thirds of its normal level. Total fixed manufacturing costs would decline by 30 percent.

What in-house unit cost should the firm use to compare with the quotation received from the supplier? Should the firm accept the proposal for a price (that is, payment to the contractor) of $600 per unit?

f. Assume the same facts as in part **e.,** except that the firm will use idle facilities to produce 800 low-impact bicycles per month that would be sold to people with injuries or other physical impairments. It can sell these low-impact bicycles for $1,200 each, while the costs of production would be $700 per unit variable manufacturing cost. Variable non-manufacturing costs would be $100 per unit. Fixed non-manufacturing and manufacturing costs will not change whether the firm manufactures the original 3,000 regular bicycles or the mix of 2,000 regular bicycles plus 800 low-impact bicycles. What is the maximum purchase price per unit that Troy Manufacturing should be willing to pay the outside contractor? Should it accept the proposal for a price of $600 per unit?

53. **Product mix decision.** The Lorenzo Company has one machine on which it can produce either of two products, Y or Z. Sales demand for both products is such that the machine could operate at full capacity on either of the products, and Lorenzo can sell all output at current prices. Product Y requires one hour of machine time per unit of output and Product Z requires two hours of machine time per unit of output. Lorenzo charges depreciation of machines to products at the rate of $8 per hour.

The following information summarizes the per-unit cash inflows and costs of Products Y and Z.

	Per Unit	
	Product Y	**Product Z**
Selling Price	$30	$55
Materials	$ 4	$ 6
Labor	1	3
Machine Depreciation[a]	8	16
Allocated Portion of Fixed Factory Costs	6	10
Total Cost per Unit	$19	$35
Gross Margin per Unit	$11	$20

[a]This item under these circumstances could be referred to as "fixed costs."

Selling costs are the same whether Lorenzo produces Product Y or Z, or both; you may ignore them. Should Lorenzo Company plan to produce Product Y, Product Z, or some mixture of both? Why?

54. **Alternative concepts of cost** (adapted from CMA exam). Kathleen and Mary (KM) operate a small coffee shop. They produce regular coffee available from many other similar businesses, and also produce gourmet coffee for special orders. Their accountant prepared the following annual income statement:

	Gourmet	Regular	Total
Sales	$40,000	$20,000	$60,000
Coffee Beans	$6,000	$ 3,000	$ 9,000
Labor	10,000	4,000	14,000
Depreciation	3,000	1,500	4,500
Power	400	300	700
Rent	6,000	4,000	10,000
Heat and Light	500	150	650
Other	500	400	900
Total Costs	$26,400	$13,350	$39,750
Operating Profit	$13,600	$ 6,650	$20,250

The depreciation charges are for machines used in the respective products. The rent is for the building space, which Kathleen and Mary (KM) have leased for 10 years at $10,000 per year. The accountant apportions the rent and the heat and light to the product lines based on amount of floor space occupied. Material, labor, power, and other costs are variable costs that are directly related to the product causing them.

A valued customer has asked KM to supply 2,000 cups of gourmet coffee. KM is working at capacity and would have to give up some other business in order to take this business. They must produce special orders already agreed to, but could reduce the output of regular orders by about one-half for one year and use the freed machine time normally used for the regular orders to produce the special orders. The customer is willing to pay $3.50 per cup. The coffee beans will cost about $1.50 per cup, and the labor will be $1.00 per cup. KM will have to spend $1,000 for a special coffee machine that they will discard when the job is finished. The special order will also require additional power costing $250.

a. Calculate and present the differential cash cost of filling the special order, considering both the cost of the order and the costs saved by reducing work on standard products.

b. Should KM accept the order? Explain your answer.

CASES

55. Department closing. Prior to last year, Leastan Company had not kept departmental income statements. To achieve better management control, the company decided to install department-by-department accounts. At the end of last year, the new accounts showed that although the business as a whole was profitable, the Dry Goods Department had shown a substantial loss. The income statement for the Dry Goods Department, shown here, reports on operations for last year.

LEASTAN COMPANY
Dry Goods Department
Partial Income Statement

Sales	$250,000	
Cost of Goods Sold	187,500	
Gross Margin		$62,500
Costs:		
Payroll, Direct Labor, and Supervision	$ 16,500	
Commissions of Sales Staff[a]	15,000	
Rent[b]	13,000	
State Taxes[c]	1,500	
Insurance on Inventory	2,000	
Depreciation[d]	3,500	
Administration and General Office[e]	11,000	
Interest for Inventory Carrying Costs[f]	2,500	
Total Costs		65,000
Loss before Allocation of Income Taxes		$ (2,500)

Additional Computations:

[a]All sales staff are compensated on straight commission at a uniform 6 percent of all sales.
[b]Rent is charged to departments on a square-foot basis. The company rents an entire building, and the Dry Goods Department occupies 15 percent of the building.
[c]Assessed annually on the basis of average inventory on hand each month.
[d]8.5 percent of cost of departmental equipment.
[e]Allocated on basis of departmental sales as a fraction of total company sales.
[f]Based on average inventory quantity multiplied by the company's borrowing rate for three-month loans.

Analysis of these results has led management to suggest that it close the Dry Goods Department. Members of the management team agree that keeping the Dry Goods Department is not essential to maintaining good customer relations and supporting the rest of the company's business. In other words, eliminating the Dry Goods Department is not expected to affect the amount of business done by the other departments.

What action do you recommend to management of Leastan Company in the short run? Why?

56. **Sell or process further** (adapted from CMA exam). The management of Biggs Company is considering a proposal to install a third production department within its existing factory building. With the company's present production setup, 200,000 pounds per year of direct materials pass through Department I to produce 100,000 pounds each of Materials A and B. Material A then passes through Department II to yield 100,000 pounds of Product C. One hundred thousand pounds of Material B are presently being sold "as is" at a price of $20.25 per pound.

The costs for Biggs Company are as follows:

	Department I (Materials A and B)[a]	Department II (Product C)[a]	(Material B)[a]
Prior Department Costs	$ —	$33.25	$33.25
Direct Materials	20.00	—	—
Direct Labor	7.00	12.00	—
Variable Overhead	3.00	5.00	—
Fixed Overhead:			
Direct (Total = $675,000)	2.25	2.25	—
Allocated $(\frac{2}{3}, \frac{1}{3})$	1.00	1.00	—
	$33.25	$53.50	$33.25

[a]Cost per pound.

Common fixed overhead costs of $300,000 are allocated to the two producing departments on the basis of the space used by the departments: to Department I and to Department II.

The proposed Department III would process Material B into Product D. One pound of Material B yields one pound of Product D. Any quantity of Product D can be sold for $30 per pound. Costs under this proposal are as follows:

	Department I (Materials A and B)	Department II (Product C)	Department III (Product D)
Prior Department Costs	$ —	$33.00	$33.00
Direct Materials	20.00	—	—
Direct Labor	7.00	12.00	5.50
Variable Overhead	3.00	5.00	2.00
Fixed Overhead:			
Direct (Total = $850,000)	2.25	2.25	1.75
Allocated $(\frac{1}{2}, \frac{1}{4}, \frac{1}{4})$	0.75	0.75	0.75
	$33.00	$53.00	$43.00

If sales and production levels are expected to remain constant in the foreseeable future, if these cost estimates are expected to be true, and if there are no foreseeable alternative uses for the available factory space, should Biggs Company produce Product D? Show calculations to support your answer.

57. **Make-or-buy—Liquid Chemical Co.**[4] The Liquid Chemical Company manufactures and sells a range of high-grade products. Many of these products require careful packing. The company has a special patented lining made from a material known as GHL, and the firm operates a department to maintain its containers in good condition and to make new ones to replace those beyond repair.

Mr. Walsh, the general manager, has for some time suspected that the firm might save money and get equally good service by buying its containers from an outside source. After careful inquiries, he approached a firm specializing in container production, Packages, Inc.,

---

[4]Adapted from a case by Professor David Solomons. The case requires use of discounted cash flow analysis.

and asked for a quotation from it. At the same time, he asked Mr. Dyer, his chief accountant, to let him have an up-to-date statement of the costs of operating the container department.

Within a few days, the quotation from Packages, Inc., arrived. The firm proposed to supply all the new containers required—at that time, running at the rate of 3,000 per year—for $1,250,000 a year, the contract to run for a guaranteed term of five years and thereafter to be renewable from year to year. If the number of containers required increased, the contract price would increase proportionally. Also, independent of this contract, Packages, Inc., proposed to carry out purely maintenance work on containers, short of replacement, for a sum of $375,000 a year, on the same contract terms.

Mr. Walsh compared these figures with Mr. Dyer's cost figures, which covered a year's operations of the container department of the Liquid Chemical Company and appear in Exhibit 7.21.

Walsh concluded that he should immediately close the department and sign the contracts offered by Packages, Inc. He felt an obligation, however, to give the manager of the department, Mr. Duffy, an opportunity to question this conclusion before acting on it. Walsh told Duffy that Duffy's own position was not in jeopardy: Even if Walsh closed his department, another managerial position was becoming vacant to which Duffy could move without loss of pay or prospects. The manager Duffy would replace also earns $80,000 per year. Moreover, Walsh knew that he was paying $85,000 per year in rent for a warehouse a couple of miles away for other corporate purposes. If he closed Duffy's department, he'd have all the warehouse space he needed without renting.

Duffy gave Walsh a number of considerations to think about before closing the department. "For instance," he said, "what will you do with the machinery? It cost $1,200,000 four years ago, but you'd be lucky if you got $200,000 for it now, even though it's good for another five years. And then there's the stock of GHL (a special chemical) we bought a year ago. That cost us $1,000,000, and at the rate we're using it now, it'll last us another four years. We used up about one-fifth of it last year. Dyer's figure of $700,000 for materials includes $200,000 for GHL. But it'll be tricky stuff to handle if we don't use it up. We bought it for $5,000 a ton, and you couldn't buy it today for less than $6,000. But you'd get only $4,000 a ton if you sold it, after you'd covered all the handling expenses."

Walsh worried about the workers if he closed the department. "I don't think we can find room for any of them elsewhere in the firm. I believe Packages would take all but Hines and Walters. Hines and Walters have been with us since they left school 40 years ago. I'd feel bound to give them a supplemental pension on top of their regular pension benefits—$15,000 a year each for five years, say. Also, I'd figure a total severance pay of $20,000 for the other employees, paid in a lump sum at the time we sign the contract with Packages."

EXHIBIT 7.21	LIQUID CHEMICAL COMPANY Container Department	
Materials		$ 700,000
Labor		
Supervisor		50,000
Workers		450,000
Department Overheads		
Manager's Salary	$ 80,000	
Rent on Container Department	45,000	
Depreciation of Machinery	150,000	
Maintenance of Machinery	36,000	
Other Expenses	157,500	
		468,500
		$1,668,500
Proportion of General Administrative Overheads		225,000
Total Cost of Department for Year		$1,893,500

Duffy showed some relief at this. "But I still don't like Dyer's figures," he said. "What about this $225,000 for general administrative overheads? You surely don't expect to sack anyone in the general office if I'm closed, do you?" Walsh agreed.

"Well, I think we've thrashed this out pretty fully," said Walsh, "but I've been turning over in my mind the possibility of perhaps keeping on the maintenance work ourselves. What are your views on that, Duffy?"

"I don't know," said Duffy, "but it's worth looking into. We shouldn't need any machinery for that, and I could hand the supervision over to the current supervisor who earns $50,000 per year. You'd need only about one-fifth of the workers, but you could keep on the oldest and save the pension costs. You'd still have the $20,000 severance pay, I suppose. You wouldn't save any space, so I suppose the rent would be the same. I don't think the other expenses would be more than $65,000 a year."

"What about materials?" asked Walsh.

"We use 10 percent of the total on maintenance," Duffy replied.

"Well, I've told Packages, Inc., that I'd give them my decision within a week," said Walsh. "I'll let you know what I decide to do before I write to them."

Assume the company has a cost of capital of 10 percent per year and uses an income tax rate of 40 percent for decisions such as these. Liquid Chemical would pay taxes on any gain or loss on the sale of machinery or the GHL at 40 percent. (Depreciation for book and tax purposes is straight-line over eight years.) The tax basis of the machinery is $600,000.

Assume the company had a five-year time horizon for this project. Also assume that any GHL needed for Year 5 is purchased during Year 5.

a. What are the four alternatives available to Liquid Chemical?

b. What action should Walsh take? Support your conclusion with a net present value analysis of all the mutually exclusive alternatives. Be sure to consider factors not explicitly discussed in the case that you think should have a bearing on Walsh's decision.

c. What, if any, additional information do you think Walsh needs to make a sound decision? Why?

SUGGESTED ADDITIONAL CASES

Toyota Motor Corp.: Target Costing System. Harvard Business School Case No. 197031. This case examines the use of target costing at Toyota.

Sunk Costs: The Plan to Dump the Brent Spar (A)(B)(C)(D). Harvard Business School Case No. 903010 – 903013. This case discusses the conflict between environmentalists and Shell oil in disposing of the Brent Spar platform in the North Atlantic.

Sub-Micron Devices, Inc. Harvard Business School Case No. A170. This case considers differential costing issues as a supplier.

Suggested Solutions to Even-Numbered Exercises

22. **Product choice.**

- Alternative 1: Warehouse.
- Alternative 2: Office space.
- Alternative 3: Restaurant and specialty shops.

	Alternative		
	1	2	3
Revenue	$960,000	$982,800	$1,101,100
Less Variable Costs	40,000	70,000	95,000
Total Contribution Margin	$920,000	$912,800	$1,006,100
Less Fixed Costs	600,000	600,000	600,000
Operating Profit	$320,000	$312,800	$ 406,100

Renovation Enterprises should choose alternative 3.

24. Finding the most profitable price-quantity combination.

a.

Price (1)	Quantity Demanded (2)	Revenues (3)	Total Variable Manufacturing Costs[a] (4)	Total Variable Selling and Administrative Costs[b] (5)	Total Costs[c] (6)	Total Profits (7)
$10	40,000	$400,000	$160,000	$80,000	$290,000	$110,000
12	36,000	432,000	144,000	72,000	266,000	166,000
14	28,000	392,000	112,000	56,000	218,000	174,000
16	24,000	384,000	96,000	48,000	194,000	190,000
18	18,000	324,000	72,000	36,000	158,000	166,000
20	15,000	300,000	60,000	30,000	140,000	160,000

[a]Quantity demanded × $4.
[b]Quantity demanded × $2.
[c]Columns (4) + (5) + $50,000 (fixed costs).

b. Select a price of $16, because it results in the most profit.

26. Identify differential costs.

The following costs or activities would be differential:

a. Product design work.
c. Advertising the boot.
f. Sales commissions.

28. Target costing and pricing.

$$\text{Price} - (20\% \times \text{Price}) = \text{Highest Acceptable Cost}$$

$$\$6.00 - (20\% \times \$600) = \text{Highest Acceptable Cost}$$

$$\$4.80 = \text{Highest Acceptable Cost}$$

30. Make or buy.

a.

	Buy	−	Make	=	Difference
Variable Costs	$300,000	−	$250,000	=	$50,000

Ol' Salt should make the sails. The fixed costs are not differential.

b.

	Buy	−	Make	=	Difference
Variable Costs	$300,000	−	$250,000	=	$ 50,000
Revenue	(80,000)	−	0	=	(80,000)
Net Effect	$220,000	−	$250,000	=	$(30,000)

Ol' Salt should buy. (The rental opportunity makes buying the sails more attractive.)

32. Throughput contribution. The throughput contribution increases by $85,800 [= 1,560 units × ($120 selling price − $65 variable costs)], which exceeds the additional cost of $60,000 per month. Stay Warm should go ahead with this option because the differential throughput contribution exceeds the differential costs of relieving the bottleneck. (Then management should seek additional ways to further relieve the bottleneck.)

34. Dropping a product line.

	Manual	Electric	Quartz
Machine Time per Unit	0.4 Hour	2.5 Hours	5.0 Hours
Contribution Margin	$10.00	$16.00	$22.00
Contribution Margin per Machine Hour	$25.00[a]	$ 6.40[b]	$ 4.40[c]

[a]$25 = $10/0.4 hr.
[b]$6.40 = $16/2.5 hrs.
[c]$4.40 = $22/5 hrs.

Timepiece Products should drop the quartz line.

36. Economic order quantity.

$$D = 10{,}000 \text{ axles}$$

$$K_0 = \$10$$

$$K_c = 0.20 \times \$100 = \$20$$

$$Q = \sqrt{\frac{2 \times \$10 \times 10{,}000}{\$20}} = 100$$

$$N = \frac{D}{Q} = \frac{10{,}000}{100} = 100$$

Annual ordering costs = $1,000 (= 100 × $10).

38. Product mix decisions.

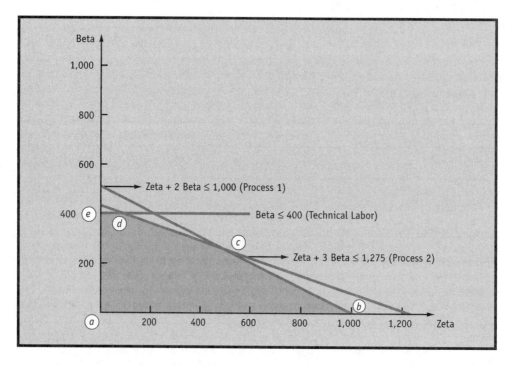

Problem Formulation:

Maximize Total Contribution Margin = 4.25 Zeta + 5.25 Beta.

Subject to:

Process 1 Constraint: Zeta + 2 Beta ≤ 1,000

Process 2 Constraint: Zeta + 3 Beta ≤ 1,275

Technical Labor Constraint: Beta ≤ 400.

Produce and Sell

Critical Points	Zeta	Beta	Total Contribution Margin[a]
a	0	0	0
b	1,000	0	$4,250.00*
c	450[b]	275[b]	$3,356.25
d	75[c]	400[c]	$2,418.75
e	0	400	$2,100.00

*Optimal solution.
[a]Total Contribution Margin = $4.25 Zeta + $5.25 Beta.
[b]Zeta + 2 Beta = 1,000 (Process 1 Constraint).
Zeta + 3 Beta = 1,275 (Process 2 Constraint).
Solving simultaneously:
(1,000 − 2 Beta) + 3 Beta = 1,275
Beta = 275.
Zeta + 2(275) = 1,000
Zeta = 450.
[c]Zeta + 3 Beta = 1,275
Beta = 400.
Solving simultaneously:
Zeta + 3(400) = 1,275
Zeta = 75.

40. Dropping a product line.

	Alternative	− Status Quo	= Difference
Revenue	$1,100,000[a]	− $1,200,000[d]	= $100,000 lower
Variable Costs	800,000[b]	− 900,000[e]	= 100,000 lower
Contribution Margin	$ 300,000	− $ 300,000	= $ 0
Fixed Costs	182,000[c]	− 1909,000[f]	= 8,000 lower
Operating Profit	$ 118,000	− $ 110,000	= $ 8,000 higher

[a]$1,100,000 = (1.5 × $400,000) + $500,000.
[b]$800,000 = (1.5 × $300,000) + $350,000.
[c]$182,000 = (1.2 × $60,000) + $80,000 + (0.6 × $50,000).
[d]$1,200,000 = $300,000 + $400,000 + $500,000.
[e]$900,000 = $250,000 + $300,000 + $350,000.
[f]$190,000 = $50,000 + $60,000 + $80,000.

Dropping consulting and increasing tax work would increase profits by $8,000.

chapter 8

Capital Expenditure Decisions

Learning Objectives

1. Explain the reasoning behind the separation of the investing and financing aspects of making long-term decisions.

2. Explain the role of capital expenditure decisions in the strategic planning process.

3. Describe the steps of the net present value method for making long-term decisions using discounted cash flows, and explain the effect of income taxes on cash flows.

4. Explain how spreadsheets help the analyst to conduct sensitivity analyses of capital budgeting.

5. Describe the internal rate of return method of assessing investment alternatives.

6. Explain why analysts will need more than cash flow analysis to justify or reject an investment.

7. Explain why the capital investment process requires audits.

8. Identify the behavioral issues involved in capital budgeting.

8

*E*arlier chapters applied the differential principle to several kinds of short-run operating decisions. In each case, the firm had fixed capacity. The manager must decide how best to use that fixed capacity in the short run. For example, how many units should we produce this month? Should a management consulting firm accept a one-time consulting assignment?

This chapter shifts attention to the long run. We focus on decisions to change operating capacity—for example, should Weyerhaeuser build a larger plant to manufacture paper? Should Citibank open a new branch? Should Nordstrom expand? Should Boston Consulting Group hire more staff consultants on long-term employment contracts? Should a job shop acquire new machinery to replace older, less efficient machinery? Should Track Auto acquire new technology that will perform services currently performed by workers? No decision affects the long-run success of a firm more than deciding which investment projects to undertake.

Short-run operating decisions and long-run capacity decisions both rely on a differential analysis of cash inflows and cash outflows. Long-run capacity decisions involve cash flows over several future periods, whereas typical operating decisions involve only short-run cash flows. When the cash flows extend over several future periods, the analyst must use some technique to make the cash flows comparable because the value of one dollar received now exceeds that of one dollar received in the future. Present value analysis, sometimes called discounted cash flow (DCF) analysis, provides the technique. The appendix at the end of this book further illustrates present value techniques. You should be familiar with its contents before you can understand much of this chapter.

Capital Budgeting: Investment and Financing Decisions

Capital budgeting involves deciding which long-term, or capital,[1] investments to undertake and how to finance them. These decisions involve **capital assets,** or long-term assets. A firm considering acquiring a new plant or new equipment must decide first whether to make the investment and then how to raise the funds required for the investment.

The principle of separating investment decisions from financing decisions results from the fact, or perhaps the assumption, that when a firm raises funds, the funds, once raised, support all the firm's assets, or the firm as a whole. Lenders and shareholders normally do not invest in specific assets but in the firm as a whole.

---

[1]No word in accounting has more ambiguity than the word *capital*. Sometimes, users mean the long-term assets of a firm. Other times, users—even the same users—mean the funds with which a firm acquires assets. Still other times, users—again, even the same users—mean the source of the funds used to acquire the assets, typically reported as long-term liabilities and owners' equity. In precise usage, *capital* means the assets themselves. The phrase *capital budgeting* means the process of choosing assets, but some users sloppily think of it as the process of allocating the funds among assets, as though there were a fixed amount of funds to be rationed among competing uses, as in normal budgeting. You will see that one of the assumptions of *capital budgeting* is that the firm can raise new funds at the same opportunity cost as the opportunity cost of the funds it already has on hand, and that the firm should treat the funds on hand as carefully and analytically as it treats new funds it might raise.

The capital budgeting decision involves estimating future cash flows, deciding on an appropriate interest rate for discounting those cash flows, and, finally, deciding on how to finance the project. This text focuses on estimating future cash flows and assumes the analyst already knows the appropriate discount rate. Corporate finance courses discuss how firms finance the projects—how firms raise cash. We also consider the sensitivity of capital investments to the estimates required to make those decisions.

Strategic Considerations

In its **strategic planning,** an organization decides on its major programs and the approximate resources to devote to them. The firm chooses its principal products or product lines and such nonproduction activities as major research and development projects. Strategic planning usually involves planning for several years into the future.

Wise capital investment decisions should fit the organization's strategic plans. When the president of Domino's Pizza decided to focus on delivery over in-store sales, that decision implied that Domino's Pizza should not pay to build stores in expensive locations with high levels of foot traffic. If the investment does not fit the organization's strategic plan, then the firm should probably reject that investment. If the investment appears sensible but does not fit the strategic plan, perhaps the firm should revise its strategic plan.

Strategic planning provides the context for capital expenditure decisions. General Motors' decision to invest in the Saturn automobile committed GM to the technology and concepts involved in making the Saturn for the foreseeable future. By deciding to expand outside its home base in Arkansas, Wal-Mart made the commitment to change from a small, regional company to a large, national company. Southwest Airlines' emphasis on leadership in cost management committed it to a market niche. The United States Postal Service decided to compete with Federal Express, DHL, and United Parcel Service, among others, in the market for mail and delivery services and changed itself from a bureaucratic to a market-oriented organization.

Managers generally understand the financial benefits from making long-term investments, but they might not think about the strategic implications. Some common examples of strategic benefits that long-term investments might provide are:

- Reducing the potential to make mistakes, thus improving the quality of the product (for instance, improving machine tolerances or reducing reliance on manual techniques).
- Making goods or delivering services that competitors can't (for instance, developing a patented process to make a product that competitors can't replicate).
- Reducing the cycle time to make the product (for instance, making a custom-designed product on the spot).
- Permanently reducing costs to provide such an advantage that competitors cannot afford to enter the market.

The Managerial Application "Environmental Investments" describes some strategic considerations for investing in environmental projects.

Conversely, some companies have unwittingly made strategic decisions by failing to make long-term investments. U.S. steel manufacturers fell far behind their Japanese counterparts after World War II when they failed to invest in new technology. Many bricks and mortar retailers who succeeded in the malls and in main street stores have not caught the e-business wave.

Managerial Application

Environmental Investments

Environmental accounting will present a major challenge for companies in this century. Consider, for example, the decision to install a pollution control device where the alternative, not installing the device, might lead to fines.

Although environmental projects provide many social benefits (not leading to quantifiable cash flows for the company), these investments also provide cash flow benefits by eliminating fines, legal costs, and cleanups. For example, oil companies probably saved billions of dollars by investing in safeguards in the Trans-Alaska Pipeline to prevent oil spills.

Discounted Cash Flow

Now we turn to the nuts and bolts of making capital expenditure decisions. Keep in mind two features of cash flows important for the analysis: the amount of cash flows and their timing.

As to the timing of cash flows, consider the following. If you have an opportunity to invest $1 today in return for $2 in the future, you will evaluate the attractiveness of the opportunity, in part, based on how long you have to wait for the $2. If you must wait only one week after making the initial investment, you will more likely accept the offer than if you have to wait 10 years to receive the $2. **Discounted cash flow (DCF) methods** aid in evaluating investments involving cash flows over time where there is a significant time difference between cash payment and receipt. Analysts use two discounted cash flow methods—the net present value (NPV) method and the internal rate of return (IRR) method.

The Discount Rate

The **discount rate** is the interest rate that analysts use in computing the present value of future cash flows. A firm considering a project whose risk equals the firm's average risk will use its cost of capital as the discount rate. If an investment has above-average risk, then the firm will use a discount rate larger than its cost of capital.

The appropriate discount rate has three separate elements:

1. A pure rate of interest reflecting the productive capability of capital assets. You can think of this rate as the rate a riskless borrower, such as the U.S. government, must pay to borrow for a period when the marketplace expects no inflation to occur over the term of the loan. (Economists debate the results of empirical research, but most would agree that the pure rate of interest generally lies between 0 and 5 percent.)
2. A risk factor reflecting the riskiness of the project. The greater a project's risk, the higher the discount rate. (An example would be investing a company's funds in a high-risk R&D project rather than in low-risk bonds. The federal government has the lowest probability of default, so government bonds usually have the lowest risk premiums.)
3. An increase reflecting inflation expected to occur over the life of the project. The higher the expected inflation, the higher should be the discount rate.

The **risk-free rate** includes the pure interest rate increased to reflect expected inflation. Many financial economists would say that, by definition, the U.S. government rate is the risk-free rate.

The **real interest rate** includes the pure interest rate and a premium for the risk of the investment, but no increase for expected inflation. The **nominal interest rate** includes all three factors—pure interest, risk premium, and expected inflation.

In our experience, analysts typically forecast project cash flows in nominal dollars—the actual dollar amounts they expect the project will generate in the future. Analysts generally expect that the larger the rate of inflation, the larger will be the nominal dollar receipts from the project. Analysts who forecast a project's cash flow in nominal dollars should use a nominal discount rate. The examples and analysis in this chapter all use cash flow forecasts in nominal dollars and nominal discount rates.

The Net Present Value Method

The net present value method involves the following steps:

1. Estimate the amounts of future cash inflows and future cash outflows in each period for each alternative under consideration.
2. Discount the future cash flows to the present using the project's discount rate. The **net present value of cash flows** of a project equals the present value of the cash inflows minus the present value of the cash outflows.
3. Accept or reject the proposed project, or select one from a set of mutually exclusive projects.

The Decision Rule   If the present value of the future cash inflows exceeds the present value of the future cash outflows for a proposal, the firm should accept the alternative. The firm should reject any alternative with negative net present value of future cash flows. If the firm must choose one from a set of mutually exclusive alternatives with the same life span, it should select the one with the largest net present value of cash flows.

This three-step procedure summarizes a process involving many estimates and projections. We begin the discussion of the process with the first step of identifying the cash flows.

In practice, analysts consider a variety of cash flows. The cash flows associated with an investment project divide into the **initial cash flows** (at the beginning of the project), the **periodic cash flows** (during the life of the project), and the **terminal cash flows** (at the end of the project). The following checklist presents these cash flows for your use in identifying cash flows. Don't forget that the analysis focuses on the time when cash flows in or out, not on the time when the firm records revenues and expenses for financial accounting purposes.

Initial Cash Flows   Cash flows occurring at the beginning of the project often include

1. Asset cost—outflow
2. Freight and installation costs—outflow
3. Cash proceeds from disposing of existing assets made redundant or unnecessary by the new project—inflow
4. Income tax effect of gain (loss) on disposal of existing assets—outflow (inflow)

Periodic Cash Flows   Cash flows occurring during the life of the project often include

1. Receipts from sales (cash, *not* revenues, which generally precede receipt of cash)—inflow
2. Opportunity costs of undertaking this particular project (lost other inflows)—outflow. (For example, the new equipment allows production of a new product that will decrease the sales of an existing product.)
3. Expenditures for fixed and variable production costs—outflow
4. Savings for fixed and variable production costs—inflow
5. Selling, general, and administrative expenditures—outflow
6. Savings in selling, general, and administrative expenditures—inflow
7. Income tax effects of flows **1** through **6**—opposite in sign to the cash flow that generates the tax consequences. The timing of the effect may be in a different period than the cash flow because the tax effect is based on financial accounting. (For instance, increased expenditures for production costs increase expenses, not necessarily during the same time period, which decrease taxes.)
8. Savings in taxes caused by deductibility of depreciation on tax return (sometimes called "depreciation tax shield")—inflow
9. Loss in tax savings from lost depreciation—outflow
10. Do *not* include noncash items, such as financial accounting depreciation expense (do include the tax effect, as stated in **8**) or allocated items of overhead not requiring differential cash expenditures.

Terminal Cash Flows   Cash flows occurring at the end of a project often include

1. Proceeds of salvage of equipment—inflow
2. Tax on gain (loss) on disposal—outflow (inflow)

A Basic Example of Discounted Cash Flow Analysis

The example in this section illustrates the steps of the net present value method. First we introduce the basics, and then we make the example more realistic.

JEP Realty Syndicators, Inc., contemplates the acquisition of computer hardware that will allow it to bring a new variety of real estate investment partnerships to the market. Exhibit 8.1 shows the cash inflows and cash outflows expected for the life of the investment.

		Year				
	0	1	2	3	4	5
New Asset Acquisition	($100,000)					
Old Asset Retirement	10,000					
Commissions and Fees		$120,000	$80,000	$60,000	$50,000	$40,000
Expenditures		(70,000)	(40,000)	(30,000)	(25,000)	(25,000)
Salvage Value						5,000
Net Cash Inflow (Outflow)	($ 90,000)	$ 50,000	$40,000	$30,000	$25,000	$20,000

EXHIBIT 8.1 — JEP REALTY SYNDICATORS, INC. Cash Flows Associated with New Real Estate Investment Products (basic)

When a firm acquires an asset for a specific project, the asset's cost will be a cash outflow at the start of the project. At the end of the project, the firm will scrap or sell the asset. The firm must include in the analysis the cash flow impact of the disposal and any tax implications thereof.

The equipment JEP may purchase will be obsolete for its intended purpose at the end of five years. However, it will have a scrap value of $5,000, which is equal to its book value at that time.

Often, when a firm undertakes a new investment, it already owns assets that it can sell or retire. The computer equipment JEP is considering acquiring would make its present system redundant. The market value of the present equipment, which is $10,000, is equal to the book value, so there will not be a tax effect due to gain or loss on equipment. Therefore, we include this disposal of the present equipment in the Year 0 column of Exhibit 8.1, as an initial cash flow.

Initial Cash Flows (Year 0):
1. Hardware and software purchase—$100,000 outflow.
2. Retirement of old equipment—$10,000 inflow.

Periodic Cash Flows (Years 1–5):
3. Receipt of commissions and underwriting fees—inflow. The decreasing pattern over the life of the investment is due to the expected entrance of competition into the market.
4. Expenditures for programmers, sales staff, and supplies—outflow.

Terminal Cash Flows (Year 5):
5. Salvage value—$5,000.

Expanded Example of Discounted Cash Flow Analysis

We now expand the example to include depreciation and taxes. Although each topic is discussed separately, Exhibit 8.2 presents the cash flow analysis for the expanded example including these factors.

Tax Effects

Depreciation Although depreciation is not a cash flow, it affects the tax cash flow because it is a deductible expense that affects taxable income and, therefore, the analysis must consider it. The equipment being purchased has a five-year life. JEP has estimated that the scrap value will

		Year				
	0	**1**	**2**	**3**	**4**	**5**
New Asset Acquisition	($100,000)					
Old Asset Retirement	10,000					
Commissions and Fees		$120,000	$80,000	$60,000	$50,000	$40,000
Expenditures		(70,000)	(40,000)	(30,000)	(25,000)	(25,000)
Salvage Value						5,000
Pretax Net Cash Inflow (Outflow)	($ 90,000)	$ 50,000	$40,000	$30,000	$25,000	$20,000
Depreciation		(19,000)	(19,000)	(19,000)	(19,000)	(19,000)
Taxable Income[a]		$ 31,000	$21,000	$11,000	$ 6,000	$ 1,000
Income Tax Payable[b]		(12,400)	(8,400)	(4,400)	(2,400)	(400)
Net Cash Inflow (Outflow)[c]	($ 90,000)	$ 37,600	$31,600	$25,600	$22,600	$19,600
Present Value Factor at 12 Percent[d]	× 1.00000	× 0.89286	× 0.79719	× 0.71178	× 0.63552	× 0.56743
Present Value of Cash Flows	($ 90,000)	$ 33,572	$25,191	$18,222	$14,363	$11,122
Net Present Value[e]	$ 12,469					

EXHIBIT 8.2 — JEP REALTY SYNDICATORS, INC. Cash Flows Associated with New Real Estate Investment Products* (expanded)

*Discount rate is 12 percent.
[a]Pretax Net Cash Flow − Depreciation except Year 0, which has no taxable income for this project.
[b]Taxable Income × .40.
[c]Pretax Net Cash Flow − Income Tax Payable.
[d]Taken from Table 2 of the Compound Interest and Annuity Tables at the end of the book.
[e]Sum of Present Values for Years 0–5.

be $5,000 and uses straight-line depreciation. The depreciation per year is equal to the purchase cost of $100,000 less the scrap value of $5,000, divided by the five-year life.

$$\text{Depreciation} = (\$100,000 - \$5,000)/5 \text{ years} = \$19,000$$

Income tax laws affect investment decisions through their effect on the type of depreciation method allowed. Tax laws change frequently and allow various approaches, so calculation of depreciation amounts will change as the tax rules change. We assume straight-line for this example. Analysts should check with their tax advisors at the time of the analysis. Although the method allowed may vary from time to time, the cash flow analysis is conducted in the same manner, adjusted for the amount of depreciation used and the time period in which the deductions fall. There is no taxable income or loss in Year 0. Although the cash flow is $(90,000), there is no tax effect because this is a cash flow, not a deduction for tax purposes.

JEP uses a discount rate of 12 percent for projects of this nature. The analysis shows that when all the factors are considered, the investment has a positive net present value and, therefore, JEP should undertake it.

Investment of Working Capital   Ordinarily, when a firm starts a new business, it expects to tie up cash in inventories and accounts receivable. Eventually it sells these inventories for cash and collects the accounts receivable. Cash flows out in the early periods and flows back in the later periods, usually much later. These factors require no special treatment because they are included in the analysis as cash flows at the time of occurrence. For example, the analyst should show cash outlay for materials in the period in which the firm makes cash payments and show cash received from sales when it collects cash. Of course, the firm will often collect cash from a sale in a period different from the period of sale.

The only time the analysis need recognize working capital occurs when the firm must let cash sit idle as a condition of undertaking the investment. For instance, assume that a company wanting to conduct business in a foreign country must, to satisfy its bank, deposit funds in a non–interest-bearing account that are to be held idle as collateral for a line of credit. The discounted cash flow analysis would show the cash deposit as a cash outflow in the period of deposit and a cash inflow in the period when the firm can retrieve the funds.

Problem 8.1 for Self-Study

Cash flow analysis. Kary Kinnard has an opportunity to open a franchised pizza outlet. He can lease the building, so he needs to invest only in equipment, which he estimates will cost $60,000. For tax purposes, assume he will depreciate the full amount for the equipment over six years using the straight-line method. For purposes of this analysis, assume the equipment will last six years, after which Kinnard will sell it for $6,000. He will pay taxes at 40 percent on the taxable gain from the disposal at the end of Year 6.

Kinnard estimates the following revenues, variable costs, and fixed costs from operations for the six-year period. He has included expected inflation in these estimates. Assume end-of-year cash flows.

	1	2	3	4	5	6
Revenues	$30,000	$36,000	$41,000	$45,000	$48,000	$50,000
Variable Costs	12,000	14,400	16,400	18,000	19,200	20,000
Fixed Costs (includes depreciation of $10,000 per year)	15,000	15,200	15,500	15,900	16,400	17,000

Use an after-tax cost of capital of 12 percent per year and an income tax rate of 40 percent for this analysis. The equipment will require a $60,000 cash outlay at the end of Year 0.

Prepare an analysis of all cash flows. Should Kinnard make the investment?

The solution to this self-study problem is at the end of the chapter on page 283.

Sensitivity of Net Present Value to Estimates

The calculation of the net present value of a proposed project requires three types of projections or estimates:

1. The amount of future cash flows
2. The timing of future cash flows
3. The discount rate

The amount predicted or estimated for each item will likely have some error. The net present value model exhibits different degrees of sensitivity to such errors.

Errors in predicting the amounts of future cash flows will likely have the largest impact of the three items. Given the sensitivity of the net present value to errors in the projections of cash flows, the manager will want accurate projections. Statistical techniques have been developed for dealing with the uncertainty inherent in predictions of cash flows.[2]

The degree of sensitivity of the net present value model to shifts in the pattern, but not in the total amount, of cash flows depends on the extent of the shifting. However, such shifts tend not to be as serious as errors in predicting the amount of cash flows.

The difficulty in estimating returns to alternative uses of capital causes uncertainty in the discount rate used to measure net present value. Financial economists have not yet developed

---

[2]Interested readers might consult the following book for additional discussion of capital budgeting under uncertainty: Harold Bierman, Jr., and Seymour Smidt, *The Capital Budgeting Decision,* 7th ed. (New York: Macmillan, 1988).

foolproof techniques for empirically verifying a firm's estimate of its cost of capital rate, but this rarely causes difficulty. In general, if a project appears marginally desirable for a given discount rate, it will ordinarily not be grossly undesirable for slightly higher rates. If a project is clearly worthwhile when analysts use a given discount rate, it is likely to be worthwhile even if they should have used a slightly higher discount rate.

Using Spreadsheets for Sensitivity Analysis

Personal computer spreadsheet programs, such as Microsoft Excel®, have become the preferred tools for analysts carrying out discounted cash flow (DCF) computations. These spreadsheet programs can help the user see the effect of changes in assumptions and estimates on the net present value. Thoughtful design of a computer spreadsheet enables the user to change assumptions (such as growth rates in sales, tax rates, or discount rates) with a few keystrokes. The net present value changes as the assumptions change, and the process takes only a few seconds.

For instance, Exhibit 8.3 presents a sensitivity analysis spreadsheet for the JEP Realty example. Panel A repeats the basic case on which we will perform a sensitivity analysis.

EXHIBIT 8.3	JEP REALTY SYNDICATORS, INC. Sensitivity Analysis

Panel A: Expanded Example from Exhibit 8.2

Discount Rate 12%

Year	0	1	2	3	4	5
New Asset Acquisition	($100,000)					
Old Asset Retirement	10,000					
Commissions and Fees		$120,000	$80,000	$60,000	$50,000	$40,000
Expenditures		(70,000)	(40,000)	(30,000)	(25,000)	(25,000)
Salvage Value						5,000
Pretax Net Cash Inflow (Outflow)	($ 90,000)	$ 50,000	$40,000	$30,000	$25,000	$20,000
Depreciation		(19,000)	(19,000)	(19,000)	(19,000)	(19,000)
Taxable Income		$ 31,000	$21,000	$11,000	$ 6,000	$ 1,000
Income Tax Payable		(12,400)	(8,400)	(4,400)	(2,400)	(400)
Net Cash Inflow (Outflow)	($ 90,000)	$ 37,600	$31,600	$25,600	$22,600	$19,600
Net Present Value	$ 12,469					

Panel B: Cell Formulas

	A	B	C
1	Discount Rate	12%	
2	Year	0	1
3	New Asset Acquisition	−100,000	
4	Old Asset Retirement	10,000	
5	Commissions and Fees		120,000
6	Expenditures		−70,000
7	Salvage Value		
8			
9	Pretax Net Cash Inflow (Outflow)	SUM(B3 . . . B7)	SUM(C3 . . . C7)
10	Depreciation		−19,000
11			
12	Taxable Income	0	SUM(C9 . . . C10)
13	Income Tax Payable	−(B12*.4)	−(C12*.4)
14			
15	Net Cash Inflow (Outflow)	+B9+B13	+C9+C13
16	Net Present Value	NPV(B1,C15 . . . G15)+B15	
17			*(continued)*

Panel B shows the cell formulas to set up the spreadsheet. The formula in cell B9 sums the cash inflows and outflows in cells B3 through B7, as cell C9 sums the cash inflows and outflows in cells C3 through C7. The formula in cell B13 calculates the income tax payable based on a 40 percent tax rate. The formula in cell B16 uses the discount rate entered in cell B1 to discount the

EXHIBIT 8.3	**JEP REALTY SYNDICATORS, INC.** Sensitivity Analysis (*continued*)					

Panel C: Change in Amounts of Cash Flows
Discount Rate 12%

Year	0	1	2	3	4	5
New Asset Acquisition	($100,000)					
Old Asset Retirement	10,000					
Commissions and Fees		$118,000	$79,000	$59,000	$49,000	$39,000
Expenditures		(70,000)	(40,000)	(30,000)	(25,000)	(25,000)
Salvage Value						5,000
Pretax Net Cash Inflow (Outflow)	($ 90,000)	$ 48,000	$39,000	$29,000	$24,000	$19,000
Depreciation		(19,000)	(19,000)	(19,000)	(19,000)	(19,000)
Taxable Income		$ 29,000	$20,000	$10,000	$ 5,000	$ —
Income Tax Payable		(11,600)	(8,000)	(4,000)	(2,000)	—
Net Cash Inflow (Outflow)	($ 90,000)	$ 36,400	$31,000	$25,000	$22,000	$19,000
Net Present Value	$ 9,770					

Panel D: Change in Timing of Cash Flows
Discount Rate 12%

Year	0	1	2	3	4	5
New Asset Acquisition	($100,000)					
Old Asset Retirement	10,000					
Commissions and Fees		$115,000	$75,000	$63,000	$55,000	$42,000
Expenditures		(70,000)	(40,000)	(30,000)	(25,000)	(25,000)
Salvage Value						5,000
Pretax Net Cash Inflow (Outflow)	($ 90,000)	$ 45,000	$35,000	$33,000	$30,000	$22,000
Depreciation		(19,000)	(19,000)	(19,000)	(19,000)	(19,000)
Taxable Income		$ 26,000	$16,000	$14,000	$11,000	$ 3,000
Income Tax Payable		(10,400)	(6,400)	(5,600)	(4,400)	(1,200)
Net Cash Inflow (Outflow)	($ 90,000)	$ 34,600	$28,600	$27,400	$25,600	$20,800
Net Present Value	$ 11,267					

Panel E: Change in Discount Rate
Discount Rate 13%

Year	0	1	2	3	4	5
New Asset Acquisition	($100,000)					
Old Asset Retirement	10,000					
Commissions and Fees		$120,000	$80,000	$60,000	$50,000	$40,000
Expenditures		(70,000)	(40,000)	(30,000)	(25,000)	(25,000)
Salvage Value						5,000
Pretax Net Cash Inflow (Outflow)	($ 90,000)	$ 50,000	$40,000	$30,000	$25,000	$20,000
Depreciation		(19,000)	(19,000)	(19,000)	(19,000)	(19,000)
Taxable Income		$ 31,000	$21,000	$11,000	$ 6,000	$ 1,000
Income Tax Payable		(12,400)	(8,400)	(4,400)	(2,400)	(400)
Net Cash Inflow (Outflow)	($ 90,000)	$ 37,600	$31,600	$25,600	$22,600	$19,600
Net Present Value	$ 10,263					

future cash flows of Years 1 through 5 to the present value of Year 0 and then adds the present value of the Year 0 cash flow.

Panel C shows the impact of changing the amount of cash flows. Forecasting cash flows accurately is critical in a cash flow analysis because the net present value is sensitive to the amount of cash flows, as shown in Panel C. Lowering the cash flows by a total of $6,000 over Years 1 through 5 lowers the net present value by $2,699. The net present value does not decline by the full $6,000, which is a nominal amount occurring in future years, not a discounted amount.

Panel D shows the impact of changing the timing of cash flows. Though the total net cash flow is the same in both cases, moving cash flows to later periods impacts the net present value of the project. The net present value drops by $1,202 simply because of moving the cash flows to later periods.

Panel E presents the impact of changing the discount rate. Assume a manager at JEP thinks a slightly higher discount rate would be appropriate. Raising the discount rate by 1 percent lowers the net present value to only $10,263, still a good investment.

Internal Rate of Return

The **internal rate of return (IRR),** sometimes called *the time-adjusted rate of return,* of a series of cash flows is the discount rate that equates the net present value of the series to zero. Stated another way, the IRR is the rate that discounts the future cash flows to a present value just equal to the initial investment. The IRR method is another discounted cash flow (DCF) method.

Spreadsheets have built-in functions for calculating the internal rate of return. Exhibit 8.4 presents the calculation using a spreadsheet for the JEP Realty basic example. The procedure is as follows: (1) insert cash flows, and (2) use IRR function. This formula uses data from the spreadsheet shown in Exhibit 8.3, Panel A. The internal rate of return for the example is 18 percent, or, at a discount rate of 18 percent, the net present value equals zero.

When using the internal rate of return to evaluate investment alternatives, analysts specify a **cutoff rate,** such as 12 percent for the JEP Realty Syndicators example. Generally, the analyst accepts a project if its internal rate of return exceeds the cutoff rate. The cutoff rate is sometimes called the *hurdle rate.*

EXHIBIT 8.4	JEP REALTY SYNDICATORS, INC. Internal Rate of Return					
A	B	C	D	E	F	G
1 New Asset Acquisition	($100,000)					
2 Old Asset Retirement	10,000					
3 Commissions and Fees		$120,000	$80,000	$60,000	$50,000	$40,000
4 Expenditures		(70,000)	(40,000)	(30,000)	(25,000)	(25,000)
5 Salvage Value						5,000
6 Pretax Net Cash Inflow (Outflow)	($ 90,000)	$ 50,000	$40,000	$30,000	$25,000	$20,000
7 Depreciation		(19,000)	(19,000)	(19,000)	(19,000)	(19,000)
8 Taxable Income		$ 31,000	$21,000	$11,000	$ 6,000	$ 1,000
9 Income Tax Payable		(12,400)	(8,400)	(4,400)	(2,400)	(400)
10 Net Cash Inflow (Outflow)	($ 90,000)	$ 37,600	$31,600	$25,600	$22,600	$19,600
11 Internal Rate of Return[a]	18%					

[a]Internal Rate of Return: IRR(B10 . . . G10)

Net Present Value and Internal Rate of Return: A Comparison

The decision to accept or reject an investment proposal can be made using either the internal rate of return method or the net present value method under most circumstances.[3] A comparison of the methods follows:

Net Present Value Method

1. Compute the investment's net present value, using the organization's adjusted cost of capital as the discount rate (hurdle rate).
2. Undertake the investment if its net present value is positive. Reject the investment if its net present value is negative.

Internal Rate of Return Method

1. Compute the investment's internal rate of return.
2. Undertake the investment if its internal rate of return is equal to or greater than the organization's adjusted cost of capital (hurdle rate). If not, reject the investment.

Problem 8.2 for Self-Study

Internal rate of return. Using the data from Problem 8.1 for Self-Study, create a spreadsheet analysis to estimate the internal rate of return.

The solution to this self-study problem is at the end of the chapter on page 283.

Justification of Investments in Advanced Production Systems

Movement toward computer-integrated manufacturing systems has changed manufacturing. Companies have found that these changes, along with revising management accounting systems, provide them a competitive edge in the marketplace.

Successes with technologically advanced systems have prompted other companies to consider making the same investments. However, many of these investments project a negative net present value. Managers often believe that such an investment is justified, but they are confused when the discounted cash flow analysis indicates rejection of the investment. The Managerial Application "Investing in Improved Technology" gives an example of a company that invested in a robot despite negative net present value results.

Managerial Application

Investing in Improved Technology

A small manufacturer in Medford, Massachusetts, considered buying a robot. The company controller calculated whether the $200,000 investment made financial sense. The controller found that net present value was negative. It wasn't even a close call.

The company bought the robot anyway, because the president wanted to inject new technology into the company's manufacturing operations. The investment has paid off. What standard procedures failed to see were intangibles such as improved quality, greater flexibility, and lower inventories that lead to long-term cash flows.

---

[3]More advanced managerial accounting and some finance texts discuss the conditions when the two methods need not give the same answer: mutually exclusive projects, projects with different lifetimes, or projects with intermixings of inflows and outflows (in contrast to the projects illustrated here where the initial cash flow is out and subsequent ones are in). When the two methods give different answers, the net present value method's answer is always the correct one.

Many apparently worthwhile investments in improved technology do not show a positive net present value when management uses traditional investment analysis. Technological innovations usually have a high investment outlay and a long time period before the project returns cash inflows. It is not unusual for an investment in automated equipment to take three or four years (or more) before it is fully operational. In companies with high discount rates, cash flows received or cash savings realized several years in the future have low present values. Further, as noted for the Medford, Massachusetts, company, technological improvements usually provide benefits that are not easily quantified. Analysts often omit such benefits from the cash flow projections.

Source: Authors' research.

Managers are often correct that the company would benefit from advanced manufacturing technology. Yet it is also difficult to find fault with the discounted cash flow model—it is economically and mathematically sound. The conflict lies in the difficulties of applying the discounted cash flow analysis to a computer-integrated manufacturing system investment decision. Some of these difficulties are as follows:

1. **Hurdle rate is too high.** Sometimes analysts use hurdle rates that are too high. The appropriate hurdle rate for any investment decision is the **cost of capital** adjusted for risk. In many cases, managers tend to overstate this risk. This is particularly a problem with investment in advanced technology because the acquisition cost of an advanced technology system can be large, and the benefits realized over a long period of time. With high hurdle rates, analysts severely discount these cash flows that occur far into the future.

2. **Bias toward incremental projects.** Companies generally require higher levels of management to authorize large investments; the larger the investment, the higher the authorization level. One result is an incentive for lower-level managers to request smaller, incremental projects to improve the manufacturing process rather than a large, comprehensive project. For example, if the investment limit for a plant manager is $50,000, the manager may institute a series of $45,000 improvements instead of requesting one investment in a million-dollar advanced technology manufacturing system. A series of small, incremental improvements may not have the same improving effect that could be gained with a full commitment to advanced manufacturing technology.

3. **Uncertainty about operating cash flows.** Analysts are often uncertain about the cash flows that will result with the implementation of an advanced technology. This uncertainty, which results from the complexity of the machinery and inexperience with such advanced technology, biases them against such investments.

4. **Exclusion of benefits that are difficult to quantify.** Advanced technology systems have extensive benefits that analysts cannot easily quantify. Some of these benefits are the following:
   - *Greater flexibility in the production process.* A flexible manufacturing process can produce batches of several distinct products in the same day. The machines can serve as backups for each other, which reduces machine downtime. Managers can more easily make engineering changes in order to adapt products to changing customer preferences.
   - *Shorter cycle times and reduced lead times.* You can imagine the difficulties in translating these into explicit statements of cash flow savings. The benefits are real but hard to model.
   - *Reduction of non–value-added costs.* These systems encourage employees to seek out activities that can be made more efficient or eliminated.

Because these benefits are difficult to quantify, analysts often exclude them from the discounted cash flow analysis. Excluding these benefits from a discounted cash flow analysis means valuing them at zero. It is better to make some estimate of these benefits, no matter how rough it is, than to exclude them. If making such an estimate is impracticable, then the investment criteria should compare these intangible benefits to the proposal's net present value. For example, if the net present value of a project is $(45,000), management might still decide that the nonquantifiable factors have present value greater than $45,000, which justifies the investment.

Problem 8.3 for Self-Study

Data analysis. This comprehensive problem illustrates the analysis of accounting data to derive cash flows for an investment decision and the choice among mutually exclusive alternatives. The last section of the answer to this problem presents a computer spreadsheet application.

Problem Data

Magee Company considers undertaking a new product line. If it does so, it must acquire new equipment with a purchase price of $140,000 at the beginning of Year 1. The equipment will last five years, and Magee expects to sell it at the end of the fifth year for its salvage value of $2,500 if there is no inflation. Magee forecasts equipment prices, including prices of used equipment of this sort, to rise at an annual rate of 12 percent, so the actual salvage expected to be realized at the end of the fifth year is $4,406 (= $2,500 $\times$ 1.12^5). Magee will pay taxes on any gain on disposal at 40 percent at the end of Year 6.

Magee Company owns old manufacturing equipment with both book and market value of $18,000 that it must retire, independent of whether it acquires the new machine.

Magee will depreciate any new equipment over five years for tax purposes using the following percentages: 20, 32, 19, 14.5, and 14.5.

Magee makes the following forecasts and projections:

1. Sales volume will be 15,000 units each year.
2. Sales price will be $7.00 per unit during Year 1 but will increase by 10 percent per year, to $7.70 in Year 2, $8.47 in Year 3, and so on.
3. Variable manufacturing costs are $3.00 per unit in Year 1, but will increase by 8 percent per year, to $3.24 in Year 2, and so on.
4. Selling costs are $5,000 per year plus $0.50 per unit in Year 1. Variable selling costs per unit will increase by 10 percent per year to $0.55 in Year 2, $0.61 in Year 3, and so on.
5. Income tax rates will remain at 40 percent of taxable income each year.
6. The after-tax cost of capital is 15 percent per year.

Magee makes the following assumptions about the timing of cash flows:

7. It will pay all variable manufacturing costs in cash at the beginning of each year.
8. It will pay all selling costs, fixed and variable, in cash at the end of each year.
9. It will collect cash from customers at the end of each year.
10. It will pay income taxes for each year's operations at the end of the year.

Magee makes the following assumptions about its operations and accounting:

11. Although it may deduct selling costs on the tax return in the year incurred, it may not deduct manufacturing costs until it sells the goods.
12. It will have sufficient other taxable income that losses on this project in any period will offset that income, saving $0.40 in income taxes for every $1.00 of operating loss.
13. It must produce enough each year to meet each year's sales, except that it must produce 20,000 units in Year 1 to provide a continuing supply of inventory of 5,000 units. It need produce only 10,000 units in Year 5, so that ending inventory will be zero.
14. It will use a LIFO cost flow assumption for inventories for income tax reporting.
15. It will charge all depreciation for a year to the cost of units it produces that year.

Construct a schedule of cash flows for acquiring the new asset.

Analyze the alternative and suggest a decision to management of Magee Company.

The solution to this self-study problem is at the end of the chapter on page 283–286.

Identifying Good Investments

How do organizations come up with good ideas for capital investments? Some ideas come naturally. If a computer is too obsolete to run today's software, it's time to consider a replacement. If business is booming, so that a company has space insufficient to produce all the goods and services the customers want to buy, it's time to consider adding space. (Note that we say time to *consider* the investment. One evaluates the financial implication of the investment and ascertains whether it makes sense in terms of the organization's strategy before making the investment.)

Organizations make three general types of long-term capital investments:

- Replacement and minor improvements
- Expansion
- Strategic moves

Replacements and minor improvements are simply that—replacement of existing assets as they wear out or become obsolete. Simple examples are the replacement of automobiles as they wear out or of computers as they become obsolete.

The ideas for replacement and minor improvements generally come from the people who use the assets. There is rarely a shortage of ideas for such changes. Companies' suggestion boxes are full of ideas for making replacement and minor improvement investments.

Expansion decisions come from desires for growth, either to meet the needs of an expanding market or to increase market share. Expansion decisions are not new ways of doing business; instead they expand existing businesses. Examples of expansion decisions are adding new stores by Wal-Mart, McDonald's, or Domino's Pizza. If American Airlines buys another airline to expand its routes, it is making an expansion decision.

Ideas for expansion decisions often come from marketing people or from top management who keep an eye on market opportunities. If the market for the organization's products is growing, then there is an almost obvious need for expansion. In some cases where the market is mature, management might expand to take market share away from competitors, as Wal-Mart has done in taking business from Kmart (now bankrupt) and small local retailers.

Strategic move investments reflect new initiatives for the company. Borders' decision to open an e-business channel was a strategic move. Amazon.com's decision to offer products in addition to books and CDs was a strategic move.

Ideas for strategic moves come from various sources. Some ideas come from visionary corporate leaders, such as Henry Ford, who decided to make a basic automobile affordable to working-class families, or Herb Kelleher, who decided that Southwest Airlines would be a no-frills, low-cost (and therefore low-ticket-price) airline at a time when the major airlines were competing on the basis of service instead of price.

Ideas also come from the marketplace. General Motors' motive to start Saturn came largely from competition from high-quality, low-priced imports. Japanese industrial leaders recognized after World War II that they could not compete on the same scale as U.S. steel, automobile, and other manufacturers, so they developed important market niches and focused on quality and efficiency.

Some companies have brainstorming groups that come up with ideas. One large forest products company used a strategic planning group, whose job was to come up with new strategic moves for the company. During the course of a year, the group would collect ideas and brainstorm until it had 400 ideas. Then the group would analyze each idea using nonfinancial criteria until approximately 40 ideas survived. Using discounted cash flow analysis, the group further winnowed the list to about four each year. Of these, management ultimately approved about one idea per year for implementation.

Audits and Capital Budgeting

The accuracy of a capital budgeting model relies heavily on the estimates used in the model, particularly the project's cash flows and life span. These estimates come from past experience, judgment, or the experience of others, such as competitors.

Comparing the estimates made in the capital budgeting process with the actual results, called *auditing* in this context, provides several advantages. Among these are the following:

1. Audits identify which estimates were wrong so that planners can incorporate that knowledge into future estimates to avoid making similar mistakes.
2. Management can use audits to identify and reward those planners who are good at making capital budgeting decisions, thus allowing decision makers to take into account the skill of the planner in making the capital investment decision.
3. Audits create an environment in which planners will not be tempted to inflate their estimates of the benefits associated with the project.

Audits bring an important discipline to a subjective judgmental process and provide insights for decision makers. Do not confuse these **internal audits** with the **external audits** done to satisfy SEC reporting rules.

Behavioral Issues

Planners who make capital budgeting estimates often bias their estimates, perhaps on purpose, perhaps unintentionally. Such factors as a desire to implement a project or meet performance evaluation measures often influence their objectivity in making estimates. Therefore, organizational policies, procedures, and performance measures should encourage and reward accurate estimations, and management should consider the planners' motivation and objectivity when evaluating capital investment projects.

Here is an example of how personal desire might influence a planner. A production manager who is anxious to have the latest equipment promotes its purchase by overestimating the benefits offered by the machine in terms of cost reduction, quality improvement, and cycle time reduction. A standard procedure of comparing projected results to those actually achieved and basing some feedback to the estimators based on the variation between projected and actual results will help to curb overoptimistic behavior. Controllers refer to such systematic procedures of projections and outcomes as *audits,* but they use procedures for these internal audits that differ from those used for external audits conducted under generally accepted auditing standards for external reporting.

Conflict often arises between the criteria used to evaluate individual projects and the criteria used to evaluate an organization's overall performance or the performance of a unit. An example of how performance measures influence a planner follows.

A manager of Desert Industries, a producer of microwave ovens, is considering acquiring machinery to produce another line of small kitchen appliances. The net present value of estimates of cash flows over the life of the equipment indicate that the firm should undertake the acquisition. The payoffs from the project, however, show large cash inflows in later years after negative cash flows (outflows) in the first two years. Desert Industries evaluates a manager's performance based on the annual operating profits, which the acquisition would reduce during the first two years. Thus, a conflict exists between the capital budgeting model, which looks to the far future by discounting it, and financial accounting performance measures, which ignore the future altogether. You can see that a firm with such evaluation procedures will sometimes reject a worthwhile investment because of its effect on short-run performance measures. Wise managers recognize these conflicts and reward employees for making the decision that best serves the company's long-run interests.

Summary

The following items correspond to the learning objectives presented at the beginning of the chapter.

1. **Explain the reasoning behind the separation of the investing and financing aspects of making long-term decisions.** Capital budgeting involves deciding which long-term, or capital, investments to undertake and how to finance them. A firm considering acquiring a new

plant or new equipment must first decide whether to make the investment and then decide how to raise the funds required for the investment.

2. **Explain the role of capital expenditure decisions in the strategic planning process.** Strategic planning provides the context for capital investments. For capital investments to make sense, they must implement a company's strategy.

3. **Describe the steps of the net present value method for making long-term decisions using discounted cash flows, and explain the effect of income taxes on cash flows.** Discounted cash flow (DCF) methods aid in evaluating investments involving cash flows over time where time elapses between cash payment and receipt. Estimate the amounts of future cash inflows and future cash outflows in each period for each alternative under consideration. Use for the discount rate—that is, the interest rate used in computing the present value of future cash flows—the firm's cost of capital. If the present value of the future cash inflows exceeds the present value of the future cash outflows for a proposal, accept the alternative.

   Although depreciation charges do not directly affect cash flow, they indirectly affect the after-tax cash flow because firms can deduct depreciation expenses on their tax returns, reducing cash outflow for taxes. Hence, the analyst should consider depreciation in any after-tax cash flow analysis. Income tax laws affect investment decisions through their effect on the type of depreciation method allowed.

4. **Explain how spreadsheets help the analyst to conduct sensitivity analyses of capital budgeting.** Analysts will likely err in predicting or estimating amounts, the timing of cash flows, or the discount rate. Errors in predicting the amounts of future cash flows will likely have the largest impact of the three items. In general, if a project appears marginally desirable for a given discount rate, it will ordinarily not be grossly undesirable for slightly higher rates. Spreadsheet programs help the user see the effect on the net present value of changes in assumptions and estimates.

5. **Describe the internal rate of return method of assessing investment alternatives.** The internal rate of return (IRR), sometimes called the *time-adjusted rate of return,* of a series of cash flows is the discount rate that equates the net present value of the series to zero. All spreadsheet programs of which we are aware have built-in functions to calculate the internal rate of return. When using the internal rate of return to evaluate investment alternatives, analysts specify a cutoff rate.

6. **Explain why analysts will need more than cash flow analysis to justify or reject an investment.** Justification of investments in advanced manufacturing systems is a difficult problem. Discounted cash flow analysis is the appropriate method for analyzing such an investment, but implementing the analysis presents a challenge. Managers should strive to make the best possible estimates of costs and benefits and ultimately make a judgment that recognizes the nonquantifiable benefits as well.

7. **Explain why the capital investment process requires audits.** Comparing the estimates made in the capital budgeting process with the actual results provides several advantages. Audits identify where estimates went wrong. Managers can use audits to identify good planners and then reward them. Systematic feedback to planners based on audits creates an environment in which planners will find less temptation to inflate their estimates of the benefits associated with their pet projects.

8. **Identify the behavioral issues involved in capital budgeting.** Planners respond to their environment. Factors such as desire to implement a project and performance evaluation measures will influence their objectivity in making estimates. Therefore, organizational policies, procedures, and performance measures should support accurate estimations and consider the effect these factors have on planners when evaluating capital investment projects.

Key Terms and Concepts

Capital assets	Cutoff rate
Capital budgeting	Discount rate
Cost of capital	Discounted cash flow (DCF) methods

Initial cash flows
Internal audit v. external audit
Internal rate of return (IRR)
Net present value of cash flows
Nominal interest rate

Periodic cash flows
Real interest rate
Risk-free rate
Strategic planning
Terminal cash flows

Solutions to Self-Study Problems

SUGGESTED SOLUTIONS TO PROBLEMS 8.1 AND 8.2 FOR SELF-STUDY

Year	0	1	2	3	4	5	6
Cash Inflows							
Revenues		$30,000	$36,000	$41,000	$45,000	$48,000	$50,000
Disposal of Machinery							6,000
Less Cash Outflows (Years 1–6)							
Purchase of Machinery	($60,000)						
Variable Costs		(12,000)	(14,400)	(16,400)	(18,000)	(19,200)	(20,000)
Fixed Costs[a]		(5,000)	(5,200)	(5,500)	(5,900)	(6,400)	(7,000)
Cash Flow before Taxes		$13,000	$16,400	$19,100	$21,100	$22,400	$29,000
Depreciation		(10,000)	(10,000)	(10,000)	(10,000)	(10,000)	(10,000)
Taxable Income[b]		$ 3,000	$ 6,400	$ 9,100	$11,100	$12,400	$19,000
Tax (40%)		(1,200)	(2,560)	(3,640)	(4,440)	(4,960)	(7,600)
Net Cash Flows[c]	(60,000)	$11,800	$13,840	$15,460	$16,660	$17,440	$21,400
Net Present Value (at 12%)	$ 3,899						
Internal Rate of Return		14%					

[a]Fixed costs less depreciation.
[b]Revenues less variable costs, fixed costs, and depreciation, plus disposal in Year 6.
[c]Cash flow before taxes less taxes.

Kinnard should undertake the project because it has a positive net present value and an internal rate of return exceeding the cutoff rate of 12 percent.

SUGGESTED SOLUTION TO PROBLEM 8.3 FOR SELF-STUDY

Acquiring the New Asset   Exhibit 8.5 derives the operating cash flows, including income tax effects. Exhibit 8.6, discussed later, combines operating and nonoperating cash flows. The calculations for the various lines of Exhibit 8.5 follow:

Line (1)   Magee sells 15,000 units each year and produces those amounts each year except in Year 1, when production is 20,000, or 5,000 units more than sales, and in Year 5, when production is 10,000, or 5,000 units fewer.

Line (2)   Variable cost per unit is $3.00 for Year 1 and $3.24 for Year 2 and increases at the rate of 8 percent per year thereafter to $3.50 in Year 3, $3.78 in Year 4, and $4.08 in Year 5.

Line (3)   Total variable costs result from multiplying line (1) by line (2). Magee pays this amount in cash at the beginning of the year, so transfers it to line (17) as a cash outflow at the beginning of each year.

Line (4)   Depreciation charge for the year results from multiplying the taxable depreciable basis, $140,000, by the percentages: 20, 32, 19, 14.5, and 14.5. Tax depreciation is relevant only because of its impact on tax-deductible cost of goods sold, which affects taxable income and income tax payments.

EXHIBIT 8.5	MAGEE COMPANY Analysis of Cash Flow Data by Year[a]					

	1	2	3	4	5	
Production and Selling Costs during Year						
(1)[a] Number of Units Produced	20,000	15,000	15,000	15,000	10,000	
(2) Variable Manufacturing Cost per Unit	$ 3.00	$ 3.24	$ 3.50	$ 3.78	$ 4.08	
(3) Total Variable Costs (at the beginning of year) = (1) × (2)	$ 60,000	$ 48,600	$ 52,500	$ 56,700	$ 40,800	
(4) Depreciation Charge for Year for Taxes	28,000	44,800	26,600	20,300	20,300	
(5) Total Manufacturing Costs for Taxes = (3) + (4)	$ 88,000	$ 93,400	$ 79,100	$ 77,000	$ 61,100	
(6) Manufacturing Cost per Unit for Taxes = (5)/(1)	$ 4.40	$ 6.23	$ 5.27	$ 5.13	$ 6.11	
(7) Variable Selling Cost per Unit	$ 0.50	$ 0.55	$ 0.61	$ 0.67	$ 0.73	
Revenues, End of Year						
(8) Number of Units Sold	15,000	15,000	15,000	15,000	15,000	
(9) Selling Price per Unit	$ 7.00	$ 7.70	$ 8.47	$ 9.32	$ 10.25	
(10) Total Revenues = (8) × (9)	$105,000	$115,500	$127,050	$139,800	$153,750	
Tax Return for Year						
(11) Revenues = (10)	$105,000	$115,500	$127,050	$139,800	$153,750	
(12) Less Manufacturing Costs of Sales	66,000	93,400	79,100	77,000	83,100	
(13) Less Selling Expenses	12,500	13,250	14,150	15,050	15,950	
(14) Taxable Income = (11) − (12) − (13)	$ 26,500	$ 8,850	$ 33,800	$ 47,750	$ 54,700	
(15) Income Taxes Payable = 0.40 × (14)	$ 10,600	$ 3,540	$ 13,520	$ 19,100	$ 21,880	
Cash Flow at:						
End of Year	0	1	2	3	4	5
Beginning of Year	1	2	3	4	5	6
(16) Revenues = (10)	—	$105,000	$115,500	$127,050	$139,800	$153,750
(17) Less Variable Costs = (3)	$ 60,000	48,600	52,500	56,700	40,800	—
(18) Less Selling Expenses = (13), Lagged . . .	—	12,500	13,250	14,150	15,050	15,950
(19) Less Income Taxes for Year = (15), Lagged	—	10,600	3,540	13,520	19,100	21,880
(20) Net Cash Inflow (Outflow) = (16) − (17) − (18) − (19)	$ (60,000)	$ 33,300	$ 46,210	$ 42,680	$ 64,850	$115,920
(21) Present Value at 15 Percent = $126,672	$ (60,000)	$ 28,957	$ 34,941	$ 28,063	$ 37,078	$ 57,633

[a]See text for discussion of line-by-line derivation.

Line (5)   Total manufacturing cost is the sum of the preceding two lines.

Line (6)   Manufacturing cost per unit is generally irrelevant for decision making in the absence of taxes. Because, however, inventory builds up in Year 1 for sale in Year 5, and because tax rules require full absorption costing, Magee must compute the full cost of the units put into inventory in Year 1. Any firm must compute such unit costs to derive tax effects whenever production volume differs from sales volume.

Line (7)   Variable selling costs of $0.50 per unit per year increase at the rate of 10 percent per year. The figure affects total selling costs later on line (13) and cash outflow for selling costs on line (18).

EXHIBIT 8.6	MAGEE COMPANY Analysis of All Cash Flows from Sale of Old Equipment and Purchase of New Equipment		
		Present Value at Beginning of Year 1	Undiscounted Cash Flows
Operating Cash Flows (Exhibit 8.5)		$126,672	$242,960
Cash Outlay for Equipment at Beginning of Year 1		(140,000)	(140,000)
Cash Proceeds from Selling Old Equipment		18,000	18,000
Salvage Proceeds from Selling Equipment at End of Year 5 ($4,406 × 0.49718)		2,191	4,406
Taxes at 40 Percent on Salvage Proceeds of $4,406 Paid at the End of Year 6 ($4,406 × 0.40 × 0.43233)		(762)	(1,762)
Total		$ 6,101	$123,604

Line (8)   Magee has forecast the number of units it will sell.

Line (9)   Selling price per unit increases at the rate of 10 percent per year. (The numbers here result from using this formula: Selling price at the end of Year $t = \$7.00 \times 1.10^{t-1}$. One might multiply each year's price by 1.10 to derive the next year's price. These two procedures do not differ significantly, but because of different rounding conventions, analysts may reach differing numbers by the fifth year.)

Line (10)   Total revenue results from multiplying the preceding two lines. The product appears on line **(11)** for tax purposes and on line **(16)** for cash flow calculations.

Line (11)   See discussion of line **(10)**.

Line (12)   Manufacturing cost comes from line **(5)** except for Years 1 and 5. In Year 1, manufacturing cost is the product of manufacturing cost per unit, line **(6)**, times number of units sold, line **(8)**: $\$4.40 \times 15,000 = \$66,000$. Magee uses a LIFO cost flow assumption. In Year 5, 10,000 units carry Year 5 manufacturing costs and 5,000 units carry Year 1 manufacturing costs: $\$61,100 + (\$4.40 \times 5,000) = \$83,100$.

Line (13)   Selling expenses are variable costs per unit on line **(7)** multiplied by the number of units sold from line **(8)** plus $5,000.

Line (14)   Taxable income is revenues, line **(11)**, minus expenses on lines **(12)** and **(13)**.

Line (15)   Income taxes are 40 percent of the amount on line **(14)**. Magee pays the amounts at the end of the year of sale.

Lines (16) through (20)   These lines show all cash flows. Be careful to align the timing of the cash flows. Note that the preceding lines show operations for a period. Magee assumes each cash flow occurs at a specific moment. Because the end of one year is also the beginning of the next, we find it convenient to label these moments with both their end-of-year and beginning-of-year designations to aid analysis. Note, for example, how the cash flows for variable manufacturing costs appear in one column, but the revenues from sale of the items produced appear in the next column.

Line (21)   The present values at the beginning of Year 1 result from multiplying the numbers on line **(20)** by the appropriate factor from the 15-percent column in Table 2 at the back of the book. The sum of the numbers on line **(21)** is $126,672.

Analysis of All Cash Flows   Exhibit 8.6 shows all the cash flows, operating and nonoperating, with present values at the beginning of Year 1. Magee pays taxes at the end of Year 6 on the salvage proceeds from the end of Year 5. Tax reporting often ignores salvage value in computing depreciation. The entire depreciable basis of $140,000 becomes deductible. Thus, the taxable gain on sale is equal to all the salvage proceeds, $4,406.

The net present value of this project is positive, $6,101. Magee should not undertake it, however, without considering the net present value of the alternative—selling the old equipment and not purchasing the new equipment.

If Magee sells the old and quits, the cash flow is $18,000. If Magee acquires the new equipment, the net present value of the estimated cash flows is about $6,000. Because the new equipment does not generate substantial amounts of positive cash flows in the last few years and because the result is worse than selling the old equipment outright, we prefer the outright sale, assuming that is a realistic business alternative. We would not conclude, however, that these data indicate a clear-cut decision either way. Whatever Magee Company does is not likely to be too costly, compared with the rejected alternative.

Questions, Exercises, Problems, and Cases

REVIEW QUESTIONS

1. Review the meaning of the concepts or terms given in Key Terms and Concepts.
2. The capital budgeting process comprises two distinct decisions. Describe these.
3. Assume a margin of error of plus or minus 10 percent in estimating any number required as an input for a capital budgeting decision. Under ordinary conditions, the net present value of a project is most sensitive to the estimate of which of the following?
   (1) Amounts of future cash flows
   (2) Timing of future cash flows
   (3) Cost of capital
4. Describe the factors that influence the market rate of interest a company must pay for borrowed funds.

CRITICAL ANALYSIS AND DISCUSSION QUESTIONS

5. "Under no conditions should the investment decision be made simultaneously with the financing decision." Comment.
6. "If an investment does not fit with an organization's strategic plan, it is probably not a good idea, even if the net present value is positive." Under what conditions would this be a true statement? When would it be false?
7. What advantages do audits provide?
8. How, if at all, should the amount of inflation incorporated in the cost of capital influence projected future cash flows for a project?
9. In *measuring* the cost of capital, management often measures the cost of the individual equities. A firm has no contractual obligation to pay anything to common shareholders. How can the capital they provide be said to have a cost other than zero?
10. At what level in the organization are approvals for strategic move investment decisions made? Are approvals for replacement decisions usually made at the same level of the organization as strategic move investment decisions? Why or why not?
11. Explain how you might analyze a capital budgeting decision where the cash flow data are nominal (including expected inflation of, say, 3 percent per year) but the quoted cost of capital of 10 percent per year is real (excluding anticipated inflation).
12. Sometimes capital investments with a positive net present value have a negative impact on earnings. For example, investing in certain types of research and development may result in a large expense at time of investment with the benefits coming a few years (or more) later. Suppose an executive tells you, "I will not approve any capital investment that decreases current earnings, no matter how high the net present value. If our earnings go down, our stockholders are hurt because stock prices will fall, and our managers will be hurt because their bonuses are tied to earnings." What is wrong with the executive's statement?
13. Describe the chain of influence, if any, between the rate of anticipated inflation in an economy and the opportunity cost of capital to a firm in that economy.
14. "But, Mr. Miller, you have said that the opportunity cost of capital is the rate of return on alternative investment projects available to the firm. So long as the firm has debt outstanding, one opportunity for idle funds will be to retire debt. Therefore, the cost of capital cannot be higher than the current cost of debt for any firm with debt outstanding." How should Mr. Miller reply?

15. Some people claim, "The internal rate of return is more difficult to compute than the net present value of a project. The internal rate of return method can never give a better answer than the net present value method." Why, then, do you suppose that so many people use the internal rate of return method?

EXERCISES

Solutions to even-numbered exercises appear at the end of the chapter after the cases.

16. **Computing net present value.** Compute the net present value of
    a. An investment of $15,000 that will yield $1,000 for 28 periods at 4 percent per period.
    b. An investment of $100,000 that will yield $250,000 eight years from now at 10 percent compounded semiannually.

17. **Computing net present value.** A firm has an after-tax cost of capital of 10 percent. Compute the net present value of each of the five projects listed in the following table.

| | After-Tax Cash Flow, End of Year | | | |
Project	0	1	2	3
A	$(10,000)	$4,000	$4,000	$4,000
B	(10,000)	6,000	4,000	2,000
C	(10,000)	2,000	4,000	6,000
D	(10,000)	3,000	5,000	4,000
E	(10,000)	4,000	4,000	3,000

18. **Computing net present value.** Hammersmith Homes is considering four possible housing development projects, each requiring an initial investment of $5,000,000. The cash inflows from each of the projects follow:

Year	Project A	Project B	Project C	Project D
1	$2,000,000	$4,000,000	0	$1,000,000
2	2,000,000	2,000,000	0	2,500,000
3	2,000,000	2,000,000	0	3,000,000
4	2,000,000	1,000,000	0	2,500,000
5	2,000,000	1,000,000	$10,000,000	1,000,000

   a. Compute the net present value of each of the projects. Hammersmith's cost of capital is 15 percent.
   b. Hammersmith can take on only one project; which should it choose? Explain why this project is superior to the others.

19. **Computing net present value.** Ralston Products is considering a project that requires an initial investment of $2,200,000 and that will generate the following cash inflows for the next five years:

Year	Cash Inflow at End of Year
1	$300,000
2	400,000
3	800,000
4	800,000
5	600,000

Calculate the net present value of this project if Ralston's cost of capital is
   a. 12 percent.
   b. 20 percent.

20. **Computing net present value.** Megatech, a computer software developer, is considering a software development project that requires an initial investment of $200,000 and subsequent investments of $150,000 and $100,000 at the end of the first and second years. Megatech expects this project to yield annual after-tax cash inflows for six more years: $90,000 at the end of each year for the third through eighth years. Megatech's after-tax cost of capital is 10 percent.

    Calculate the net present value of this project.

21. **Deriving cash flows and computing net present value.** The Southern Rail Lines (SRL) is considering replacing its power jack tamper, used to maintain track and roadbed, with a new automatic-raising power tamper. SRL spent $18,000 five years ago for the present power jack tamper and estimated it to have a total life of 12 years. If SRL keeps the old tamper, it must overhaul the old tamper two years from now at a cost of $5,000. SRL can sell the old tamper for $2,500 now; the tamper will be worthless seven years from now.

    A new automatic-raising tamper costs $23,000 delivered and has an estimated physical life of 12 years. SRL anticipates, however, that because of developments in maintenance machines, it should retire the new machine at the end of the seventh year for $5,000. Furthermore, the new machine will require an overhaul costing $10,000 at the end of the fourth year. The new equipment will reduce wages and fringe benefits by $4,000 per year.

    Track maintenance work is seasonal, so SRL normally uses the equipment only from May 1 through October 31 of each year. SRL transfers track maintenance employees to other work but pays them at the same rate for the rest of the year.

    The new machine will require $1,000 per year of maintenance, whereas the old machine requires $1,200 per year. Fuel consumption for the two machines is identical. SRL's cost of capital is 12 percent per year, and because of operating losses, SRL pays no income tax.

    Should SRL purchase the new machine?

22. **Observing the effects of using different discount rates.** Refer to the data and analysis developed for the Magee Company in Exhibits 8.5 and 8.6. Evaluate the alternatives using a cost of capital of 12 percent.

23. **Net present value and mutually exclusive projects.** Assume Raley Co. must choose between two mutually exclusive innovations for improving its computer system—one offered by AMD and the other by NEC. Raley's after-tax cost of capital is 12 percent.

    AMD's system costs $1 million and promises after-tax cash flows in personnel cost savings for four years: $400,000 at the end of Year 1 and Year 2, $300,000 at the end of Year 3, and $200,000 at the end of Year 4.

    NEC's system costs $1.5 million and promises after-tax cash flows for three years: $800,000 at the end of Year 1, $600,000 at the end of Year 2, and $500,000 at the end of Year 3.

    a. Compute the net present values of each of the alternatives.
    b. Compute the internal rate of return for each of the alternatives.
    c. Which alternative, if either, should Raley choose, and why?

24. **Net present value and mutually exclusive projects.** The Larson Company must choose between two mutually exclusive projects. The cost of capital is 12 percent. Given the following data, which project should Larson choose, and why?

After-Tax Cash Flows, End of Year

Project Label	0	1	2	3
M	$(500,000)	$175,000	$287,500	$400,000
N	(450,000)	477,000	195,000	60,000

25. **Computing internal rate of return.** What is the internal rate of return on the following projects, each of which requires a $20,000 cash outlay now and returns the cash flows indicated?
    a. $10,426.72 at the end of Years 1 and 2.
    b. $3,196.40 at the end of Years 1 through 10.
    c. $3,429.28 at the end of Years 1 through 13.
    d. $3,939.00 at the end of Years 1 through 15.
    e. $8,397.84 at the end of Years 3 through 7.

f. $3,618.80 at the end of Years 2 through 10.

g. $37,508.98 at the end of Year 5 only.

26. **Computing internal rate of return.** Compute the internal rate of return for each of the following projects, each of which requires an initial investment of $100,000 and provides the periodic cash flows indicated.

   a. $23,098 per period for five periods.

   b. $20,336 per period for six periods.

   c. $17,401 per period for eight periods.

   d. $16,144 per period for 12 periods.

   e. $17,102 per period for 15 periods.

27. **Working backward with net present value method.** A manager's favorite project requires an after-tax cash outflow on January 1 of $10,000 and promises to return $2,500 of after-tax cash inflows at the end of each of the next five years. The after-tax cost of capital is 10 percent per year.

   a. Use the net present value method to decide whether this favorite project is a good investment.

   b. How much would the projected cash inflow for the end of Year 5 have to increase for the project to be acceptable?

   c. How much would the projected cash inflow for the end of Year 5 have to increase for the project to have a net present value of $200?

28. **Computing internal rate of return.** Carlo Company is considering acquiring a machine that costs $40,000 and that promises to save $8,000 in cash outlays per year, after taxes, at the end of each of the next 12 years. Carlo expects the new machine to have no salvage value at the end of its useful life.

   a. Compute the internal rate of return for this project.

   b. Compute the internal rate of return, assuming that the cash savings were to last only six, instead of 12, years.

   c. Compute the internal rate of return, assuming that the cash savings were to last 20, rather than 12, years.

   d. Compute the internal rate of return, assuming that the cash savings would be $6,000 rather than $8,000 per year for 12 years.

PROBLEMS

29. **Deriving cash flows and computing net present value.** Coalinga Company is contemplating selling a new product. Coalinga can acquire the equipment necessary to distribute and sell the product for $100,000. The equipment has an estimated life of 10 years and has no salvage value. The following schedule shows the expected sales volume, selling price, and variable cost per unit of production:

Year	Sales Volume	Selling Price	Variable Cost of Production
1	10,000 Units	$5.00	$3.00
2	12,000	5.00	3.10
3	13,000	5.50	3.25
4	15,000	5.75	3.25
5	20,000	6.00	3.30
6	25,000	6.00	3.40
7	20,000	6.10	3.50
8	18,000	6.10	3.50
9	15,000	6.25	3.50
10	15,000	6.30	3.75

Production in each year must be sufficient to meet each year's sales. In addition, Coalinga will purchase 5,000 extra units in Year 1 to provide a continuing inventory of 5,000 units. Thus, production in Year 1 will be 15,000 units but in Year 10 will be only 10,000 units, so at the end of Year 10, ending inventory will be zero. Coalinga will use a LIFO (last in, first out) cost flow assumption. Coalinga's income tax rate is 40 percent, and its after-tax cost of capital is 9 percent per year. It receives cash at the end of the year when it makes sales and spends cash at the end of the year when it incurs costs. Coalinga estimates variable selling expenses at $1 per unit sold. Depreciation on the new distribution equipment is not a product cost but is an expense each period. For tax reporting, depreciation will follow these accelerated depreciation schedule percentages: 20 percent in the first year, 32 percent in the second, 19.2 percent in the third, 11.5 percent in the fourth, 11.5 percent in the fifth, 5.8 percent in the sixth, and zero thereafter. Coalinga Company generates sufficient cash flows from other operations so that it can use all depreciation deductions to reduce current taxes otherwise payable.

a. Prepare a schedule of cash flows for this project.

b. Compute the net present value of the project.

30. **Analyzing cash flows from alternatives.** Vatera Incorporated is considering replacing some machinery. The old machinery has book value and tax basis of $10,000. Its current market value is $5,000. Vatera does not have the alternative of simply selling the old machinery now. It must either use it for another year or replace it. Vatera has been depreciating the old equipment on a straight-line basis at the rate of $10,000 per year. If Vatera retains the machinery it will depreciate the remaining tax basis over one year and the financial book value over three years. The machinery will have no market value one year hence.

Vatera can acquire new machinery for $30,000, which will produce $10,000 of cash savings at the end of the first year. The new machinery will produce cash savings at the end of Year 2 that is 5 percent greater than at the end of Year 1, and at the end of Year 3 the savings will be 5 percent greater than at the end of Year 2. The new machinery will have a three-year life. Vatera will depreciate the equipment on a straight-line basis over three years for both tax and financial reporting purposes. It will sell the machinery for $2,000 at the end of Year 3 but will ignore salvage value in tax depreciation computations.

Vatera pays income taxes at the rate of 40 percent for both ordinary income and capital gains. The cost of capital for the new machinery, after taxes, is 12 percent per year. Vatera earns sufficient taxable income that it can deduct from its taxes payable at the beginning of Year 1 (= end of Year 0) the loss from disposition of the old machinery at the beginning of Year 1 (= end of Year 0).

Analyze the present value of the cash flows of the alternatives and make a recommendation to Vatera Incorporated.

31. **Analyzing cash flows from alternatives.** Oceanic Boatworks is considering purchasing a new machine for $1 million at the end of Year 0 to be put into operation at the beginning of Year 1. The new machine will save $250,000, before taxes, per year from the cash outflows generated by using the old machine. For tax purposes, Oceanic will depreciate the new machine in the following amounts: $100,000 in Year 1, $300,000 in Year 2, and $200,000 per year thereafter until fully depreciated or sold. The new machine will have no salvage value at the end of Year 5. Oceanic expects the new machine to have a market value of $400,000 at the end of three years.

If Oceanic acquires the new machine at the end of Year 0, it can sell the old one for $200,000 at that time. The old machine has a tax basis of $300,000 at the end of Year 0. If Oceanic keeps the old machine, the company will depreciate it for tax purposes in the amount of $100,000 per year for three years, when it will have no market value.

Oceanic pays taxes at the rate of 40 percent of taxable income and uses a cost of capital of 12 percent in evaluating this possible acquisition. Oceanic has sufficient otherwise-taxable income in Year 0 to save income taxes for each dollar of loss it may incur if it sells the old machine at the end of Year 0.

a. Compute the net present value of cash flows from each of the alternatives facing Oceanic Boatworks.

b. Make a recommendation to Oceanic Boatworks.

c. Assume that the cash flows described in the problem for Years 2 through 5 are real, not nominal, amounts, but the 12 percent cost of capital includes an allowance for inflation of 6 percent. Describe how this will affect your analysis. You need not perform new computations.

32. **Net present value graph and indifference cost of capital.** Specialized Consulting Service Company's after-tax net cash flows associated with two mutually exclusive projects, Alpha and Beta, are as follows:

	Cash Flow, End of Year		
Project	**0**	**1**	**2**
Alpha	$(100)	$125	—
Beta	(100)	50	$84

    a. Calculate the net present value for each project using discount rates of 0, 0.04, 0.08, 0.12, 0.15, 0.20, and 0.25.

    b. Prepare a graph as follows. Label the vertical axis "Net Present Value in Dollars" and the horizontal axis "Discount Rate in Percent per Year." Plot the net present value amounts calculated in part **a.** for project Alpha and project Beta.

    c. State the decision rule for choosing between projects Alpha and Beta as a function of the firm's cost of capital.

    d. What generalizations can you draw from this exercise?

33. **Deriving cash flows for asset disposition.** Custom Machining Company (CMC) purchased a made-to-order machine tool for grinding machine parts. The machine costs $160,000, and CMC installed it yesterday. Today, a vendor offers a machine tool that will do exactly the same work but costs only $80,000. Assume that the cost of capital is 12 percent, that both machines will last five years, that CMC will depreciate both machines on a straight-line basis for tax purposes with no salvage value, that the income tax rate is and will continue to be 40 percent, and that CMC earns sufficient income that it can offset any loss from disposing of or depreciating the "old" machine against other taxable income.

    How much, at a minimum, must the "old" machine fetch upon resale at this time to make purchasing the new machine worthwhile?

34. **Deriving cash flows for abandonment decision.** The Tiny Treasures Company must decide whether to continue selling a line of children's shoes manufactured on a machine that has no other purpose. The machine has a current book value of $12,000, and Tiny Treasures can sell it today for $8,000. Tiny Treasures depreciates the machine on a straight-line basis for tax purposes assuming no salvage value and could continue to use it four more years. If Tiny Treasures keeps the machine in use, it can sell it at the end of four years for $800, although this will not affect the depreciation charge for the next four years. The variable cost of producing a pair of shoes on the machine is less than the cash received from customers by $15,000 per year. To produce and sell the children's shoes requires cash outlays of $10,000 per year for administrative and overhead expenditures as well. Tiny Treasures Company pays taxes at a rate of 40 percent. The rate applies to any gain or loss on disposal of the machine as well as to other income. From its other activities, Tiny Treasures Company earns more income than any losses from the line of children's shoes or from disposal of the machine.

    a. Prepare a schedule showing all the cash and cost flows that Tiny Treasures Company needs to consider in order to decide whether to keep the machine.

    b. Should Tiny Treasures Company keep the machine if its cost of capital is 12 percent?

    c. Repeat part **b.** assuming a cost of capital of 20 percent.

35. **Managerial incentives of performance evaluation based on accounting data.** A firm with an opportunity cost of capital of 15 percent faces two mutually exclusive investment projects:

    (1) Acquire goods at the start of the year, ship them to Japan, and sell them at the end of the year. The internal rate of return on this project is 20 percent, and it has positive net present value.

    (2) Making certain expenditures today that will cause reported earnings for the year to decline. This will result, however, in large cash flows at the end of the second and third years. The internal rate of return on this project is 30 percent, and it has even larger net present value than the first project. Management observes that for the current year, the second project will result in smaller earnings reported to its shareholders than the first.

    How might management's observation influence its choice between the two investment projects?

CASES

36. **Present value of outsourcing decision.** See Case 57 (Liquid Chemical Co.) in Chapter 7.

37. **Merits of net present value.** A well-known university sponsors a continuing education program for engineers. One of its programs is called "Evaluating Project Alternatives by Discounted Cash Flow." The advertising copy for this program says, in part:

> **Why You Should Attend**   Traditionally, a large percentage of business decisions have been based solely on payback, which is the amount of time before the cash inflows from a project equal the cash outflows. Although the payback method has the advantage of computational simplicity, it is not a true measure of life-cycle cost effectiveness and can lead to erroneous accept-reject decisions.

Why Use Net Present Value
(1) Takes into account:
   Cash flows beyond the payback period.
   Timing of cash flows within the payback period.
(2) Does not discriminate against long-lived projects.
(3) Does not ignore the time value of money.
(4) Provides for:
   Return of and on debt and equity capital for a particular project.
   Income taxes, income tax write-offs.
   Inflation.
   Costs that escalate at a rate greater than the rate of inflation.
(5) Permits an accurate ranking of alternatives.
(6) Gives correct choice among independent alternatives.
(7) Maximizes return on investment.

Comment on the numbered points from the copy.

RECOMMENDED ADDITIONAL CASE FOR CHAPTER 8

Airbus A3XX: Developing the World's Largest Commercial Jet (A).   Harvard Business School Case No. 201028. This case considers the approval of a $13 billion investment for a new jumbo airplane.

Suggested Solutions to Even-Numbered Exercises

16. **Computing net present value.**
    a. Net Present Value = −$15,000 + ($1,000 × 16.66306)
                          = $1,663.
    b. Net Present Value = −$100,000 + ($250,000 × 0.45811)
                          = $14,528.

18. **Computing net present value.**
    a.

Year	Present Value Factor	Discounted Cash Flows Project A	Project B	Project C	Project D
0	1.00000	$(5,000,000)	$(5,000,000)	$(5,000,000)	$(5,000,000)
1	0.86957	1,739,140	3,478,280	0	869,570
2	0.75614	1,512,280	1,512,280	0	1,890,350
3	0.65752	1,315,040	1,315,040	0	1,972,560
4	0.57175	1,143,500	571,750	0	1,429,375
5	0.49718	994,360	497,180	4,971,800	497,180
		$ 1,704,320	$ 2,374,530	$ (28,200)	$ 1,659,035

b. Hammersmith should take Project B, which has the largest net present value. Even though all four projects have similar undiscounted total cash flow streams—that is, $10,000,000—Project B is superior because the bulk of the cash returns come in the earlier years.

20. Computing net present value.

Year (1)	Net Cash Flow (2)	10% Present Value Factor (3)	Present Value (4)[a]
0	$(200,000)	1.00000	$(200,000)
1	(150,000)	.90909	(136,364)
2	(100,000)	.82645	(82,645)
3	90,000	.75131	67,618
4	90,000	.68301	61,471
5	90,000	.62092	55,883
6	90,000	.56447	50,802
7	90,000	.51316	46,184
8	90,000	.46651	41,986
			$ (95,065)

[a](4) = (2) × (3).

22. Observing the effects of using different discount rates.

MAGEE COMPANY
Operating Cash Flows, End of Year
(cost of capital = 12 percent)

End of Year (1)	Cash Flow (2)	Present Value Factor at 12 Percent (3)	Present Value at 12 Percent = (2) × (3) (4)
0	$(60,000)	1.00000	$ (60,000)
1	33,300	0.89286	29,732
2	46,210	0.79719	36,838
3	42,680	0.71178	30,379
4	64,850	0.63552	41,213
5	115,920	0.56743	65,776
Total			$143,938

Present Value of All Cash Flows from Sale of Old Equipment and Purchase of New Equipment

Operating Cash Flow	$143,938
Net Cash Outlay for Equipment (= $140,000 − $18,000)	(122,000)
Salvage Proceeds End of Year 5: $4,406 × 0.56743	2,500
Taxes on Salvage End of Year 6: $4,406 × 0.40 × 0.50663	(893)
Net Present Value	$ 23,545

Present Value of Outright Sale

Sale Proceeds	$ 18,000

24. Net present value and mutually exclusive projects. Choose Project N. See the following table:

End of Year	Discount Factors at 12 Percent	Cash Flows in Thousands M	Cash Flows in Thousands N	Present Value of Cash Flows in Thousands M	Present Value of Cash Flows in Thousands N
0	1.00000	$(500)	$(450)	$(500.0)	$(450.0)
1	0.89286	175	477	156.3	425.9
2	0.79719	287.5	195	229.2	155.5
3	0.71178	400	60	284.7	42.7
				$ 170.2	$ 174.1

Net present value of cash flows discounted at 12 percent is larger for N.

26. **Computing internal rate of return.**

	Internal Rate of Return
a.	5 percent
b.	6 percent
c.	8 percent
d.	12 percent
e.	15 percent

28. **Computing internal rate of return.**
    Internal rate of return:
    a. 16.94%
    b. 5.47%
    c. 19.43%
    d. 10.45%

Part Three

Motivating Managers to Make Good Decisions

3

Managers often use accounting information to address planning and performance evaluation questions such as these:

- How many units of product do we expect to sell this year?
- What facilities, personnel, and other resources will be required to produce enough units to meet projected sales?
- What is our projected level of profits for the year?
- How do we measure the efficiency of production activities such as the use of materials or labor?
- How can we design performance measurement systems to encourage employees to act simultaneously in their own best interests and in the best interests of the organization?

Managerial accounting information helps managers deal with these issues. Managers use accounting to assign responsibility for actions, primarily through the use of budgets and standards. The accounting system provides information about actual performance that managers can compare with budgets and standards.

chapter 9

Profit Planning and Budgeting

9

$\mathcal{A}$ **budget** is a financial plan of the resources needed to carry out tasks and meet financial goals. A company's controller explained the use of budgeting in her organization as follows:

At our company, we view the budget as a blueprint for the company's activities, much like an architect makes a blueprint for the construction of a building. Like the architect's blueprint, our master budget helps us to plan and coordinate activities, to ascertain the means of achieving our goals, and to establish standards against which we measure our performance. All levels of management formally express what they each expect in the future for their business units. Simply stated, the budget expresses, in dollars, our plans for achieving company goals.[1]

This chapter shows how a **short-term operating budget** (management's quantitative action plan for the coming year) is established and how it fits into the overall plan for achieving organization goals. Before we investigate the details of developing a short-term operating budget, we discuss how strategic planning provides a context for the budget.

Strategic Planning

Companies generally start the strategic planning process by stating their **critical success factors,** which are the most important things for the company to do to be successful. For example, Southwest Airlines relies on several factors to maintain its competitive edge. It uses a point-to-point network of routes instead of the hub-and-spoke system used by most U.S. airlines, has efficient gate turnaround, and uses only one type of plane. These factors keep costs low and make Southwest a price leader.

Companies build on these critical success factors to expand operations. For example, McDonald's has developed expertise in the fast-food business over many years. McDonalds's management has realized that its expertise and worldwide reputation could be used to successfully expand throughout the world. The company continues to use its competitive advantages (e.g., name recognition, value, and consistency) to succeed in areas outside the United States.

The Organizational Plan

A **master budget** is part of an overall organization plan for the next year, made up of three components: (1) organizational goals, (2) the strategic long-range profit plan, and (3) the master budget (tactical short-range profit plan).

---

[1]**Source:** Interview with a company's controller.

Organizational Goals

Organizational goals are the broad objectives management establishes and company employees work to achieve. For example, consider the following quotation from internal documents of a company in the paper industry:

> Our organizational goal is to increase earnings steadily while maintaining our current share of industry sales and maintain profitability within the top one-third of our industry. We plan to achieve this goal while providing our customers with high-quality products and meeting our social responsibilities to our employees and the communities in which they live.[2]

Such broad goals indicate management's philosophy about the company. Many companies include such goals in published codes of conduct and annual reports to stockholders.

Strategic Long-Range Profit Plan

Although a statement of goals is necessary to guide an organization, it is important to detail the specific steps required to achieve them.[3] These steps are expressed in a **strategic long-range plan.** Because the long-range plans look into the intermediate and distant future, they are usually stated in rather broad terms. Strategic plans discuss the major capital investments required to maintain present facilities, increase capacity, diversify products and/or processes, and develop particular markets. For example, the previously mentioned paper company's strategies, as stated in its policy manual, included the following:

1. *Cost control.* Optimize contribution from existing product lines by holding product cost increases to less than the general rate of inflation. This will involve acquiring new machinery proposed in the capital budget as well as replacing our five least efficient plants over the next five years.
2. *Market share.* Maintain our market share by providing a level of service and quality comparable to our top competitors. This requires improving our quality control so that customer complaints and returned merchandise are reduced from a current level of 4 percent to 1 percent within two years.[4]

Each strategy statement was supported by projected activity levels (sales volumes, aggregate costs, and cash flow projections) for each of the next five years. At this stage, the plans were not stated in much detail, but they were well thought out. Hence, the plans provided a general framework for guiding management's operating decisions.

The Master Budget (Tactical Short-Range Profit Plan): Tying the Strategic Plan to the Operating Plan

Long-range plans are achieved in year-by-year steps. The guidance is more specific for the coming year than it is for more distant years. The plan for the coming year is called the master budget. The master budget is also known as the **static budget,** the budget plan, or the planning budget. The income statement portion of the master budget is often called the **profit plan.** The master budget indicates the sales levels, production and cost levels, income, and cash flows anticipated for the coming year. In addition, these budget data are used to construct a budgeted statement of financial position (balance sheet).

Budgeting is a dynamic process that ties together goals, plans, decision making, and employee performance evaluation. The master budget and its relationship to other plans, accounting reports, and management decision-making processes is diagrammed in Exhibit 9.1. The master budget derives from the long-range plan and considers conditions expected during the coming period. Such plans are subject to change as the events of the year unfold. Recently,

---

[2]Taken from the company's internal documents.

[3]J. March and H. Simon provide a classic discussion of organization goal setting. See *Organizations* (New York: John Wiley & Sons, 1958).

[4]Taken from the company's internal documents.

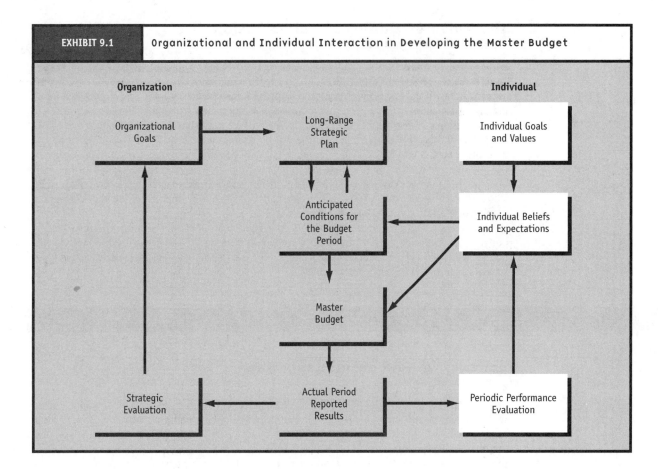

EXHIBIT 9.1 — Organizational and Individual Interaction in Developing the Master Budget

the long-range plan for a U.S. automobile manufacturer called for developing several new product lines, but unfavorable short-run economic conditions required their postponement.

Organizational and Individual Interaction in Developing the Master Budget

The conditions anticipated for the coming year are based in part on managers' near-term projections. Companies may gather this information from production managers, purchasing agents (materials prices), the accounting department, and employee relations (wage agreements), among others. As part of a **benchmarking** activity, some companies gather information through competitive intelligence, speaking to their competitors, customers, and suppliers. Benchmarking is the continuous process of measuring products, services, or activities against competitors' performances.

The Human Element in Budgeting

A number of factors, including their personal goals and values, affect managers' beliefs about the coming period. Although budgets are often viewed in purely quantitative, technical terms, the importance of this human factor cannot be overemphasized. The individual's relationship to the budget is diagrammed on the right side of Exhibit 9.1.

Budget preparation rests on human estimates of an unknown future. People's forecasts are likely to be greatly influenced by their experiences with various segments of the company. For example, district sales managers are in an excellent position to project customer orders over the next several months, but market researchers are usually better able to identify long-run market trends and make macro forecasts of sales. One challenge of budgeting is to identify who in the organization is best able to provide the most accurate information about particular topics.

The Value of Employee Participation in Developing Budgets

The use of input from lower- and middle-management employees is often called **participative budgeting** or *grassroots budgeting*. It has an obvious cost; it is time consuming. But it also has some benefits; it enhances employee motivation and acceptance of goals, and it provides information that enables employees to associate rewards and penalties with performance. Participative budgeting can also yield information that employees know but managers do not.

Some studies have shown that employees provide inaccurate data when asked to give budget estimates. They might request more money than they need because they expect their request to be cut. Employees who believe that the budget will be used as a standard for evaluating their performance may provide an estimate that will not be too hard to achieve. However, a recent study found that MBA students, acting as managers, behaved honestly. (See the Managerial Application "Honesty in Managerial Reporting.")

Managers usually view the technical steps required to construct a comprehensive tactical budget plan in the context of the effect that people have on the budget and the effect that the budget will have on them. Ideally, the budget will motivate people and facilitate their activities so that organizational goals can be achieved.

Managerial Application

Honesty in Managerial Reporting

Researchers conducted three experiments to learn whether managers would report honestly when they had strong incentives to be dishonest. The researchers wanted to see whether subjects (who were MBA students acting as managers) would sacrifice their wealth to make honest or, at least, partially honest reports. The subjects in the study had every reason to lie—the more they lied, the greater their payoff. Yet the experiments revealed considerable honesty. In two of the experiments, for example, subjects gave up 49 percent and 43 percent of their available payoff by reporting honestly or partially honestly.

Source: J. H. Evans III, R. L. Hannan, R. Krishnan, and D. V. Moser, "Honesty in Managerial Reporting," *The Accounting Review* 76, no. 4, 537–559.

Motivating Employees   When you assess the effect of budgets or any other part of a motivation system on people, ask the following two questions:

1. What types of behavior does the system motivate?
2. Is this the desired behavior?

Much of managerial accounting has developed to motivate people to behave in particular ways. Accounting reports allow superiors to make decisions about subordinates' future employment prospects. (For example, should employees be promoted?) In addition, employment contracts use accounting information, such as when an employee receives a bonus based on accounting performance measures.

Rewards for performing well depend on individual preferences and culture. Cultures that promote collectivism, including many Eastern countries, have less interest in rewarding or penalizing each individual; rewarding or penalizing the group or department is sufficient motivation.

Cultural Impact on the Budgeting Process

Researchers have found cultural differences in the way people accept top-down budgeting. Lower-level managers in Mexico, Singapore, and Hong Kong were more likely to accept top-down budgets than similar managers in Germany, the United Kingdom, the United States, New Zealand, Canada, and Australia. Lower-level managers in the latter countries wanted to actively participate in budgeting, not just accept top-down budgets. Researchers claimed that lower-level managers in the latter group of countries seemed less willing to accept the "fact" that top managers were more powerful than they.[5]

Goal Congruence **Goal congruence** occurs if members of an organization have incentives to perform in the common interest. Although complete goal congruence is rare, we observe team efforts in many cases. Examples include some military units and athletic teams. Many companies attempt to achieve this *esprit de corps* by, for example, carefully selecting employees whom management believes will be loyal. Observers of Japanese industry report that Japanese managers and owners have created team orientation with considerable goal congruence.

Complete goal congruence is, however, unlikely to occur naturally in most business settings. For example, employees may prefer to work less hard than the firm would like. Consequently, firms design performance evaluation and incentive systems to increase goal congruence by encouraging employees to behave more in the firm's interest.

The classroom setting is a good example. Examinations, written assignments—indeed, the entire grading process—are part of a performance evaluation and incentive system to encourage students to learn. Sometimes the system encourages the wrong type of behavior, because students may select easy courses to improve their grades instead of difficult courses in which they will learn more.

Problems of this type occur in all organizations where employees acting in their own best interests do not take actions that serve the best interests of the organization. Consider the case of a plant manager who believes that a promotion and bonus will follow from high plant-operating profits. Undertaking a needed maintenance program will cost money and reduce profits in the short run but benefit the company in the long run by improving product quality. The manager faces a classic trade-off between doing what *looks* good in the short run and doing what serves the best long-run interests of the company.

Tools for Planning and Performance Evaluation

Budgets provide estimates of expected performance. Comparing budgeted with actual results provides a basis for evaluating past performance and guiding future action. To be effective as *tools for performance evaluation*, budgets must be developed for individual responsibility centers.

Responsibility Centers

A **responsibility center** is a division or department in a firm responsible for managing a particular group of activities in the organization. The sportswear manager at Macy's is responsible for the activities of the sportswear department, for example. Accountants classify responsibility centers according to the activities for which the manager is responsible, as follows:

1. **Cost centers,** where management is responsible for costs. Manufacturing departments are examples because the managers are responsible for the costs of making products. There are two categories of cost centers, based on the types of costs incurred in the center.
   - **Engineered cost centers** have input-output relations sufficiently well established so that a particular set of inputs will provide a predictable and measurable set of outputs. Most production departments are engineered cost centers.
   - **Discretionary cost centers** are responsibility centers in which input-output relations are not well specified. Managers of such centers receive a cost budget that provides a ceiling on the center costs. Most administrative, research, and staff activities are discretionary cost centers.
2. **Revenue centers,** where management is responsible primarily for revenues. Marketing departments are revenue centers if the managers are responsible for revenues.
3. **Profit centers,** where management is responsible for both revenues and costs.
4. **Investment centers,** where management is responsible for revenues, costs, and assets. Most corporate divisions are profit centers or investment centers.

---

[5]S. J. Gray, S. B. Salter, and L. H. Radebaugh, *Global Accounting and Control: A Managerial Emphasis* (New York: Wiley, 2001).

Flexible Budgets

A **flexible budget** shows the expected relation between costs and volume. It has two components:

1. A fixed cost expected to be incurred regardless of the level of activity.
2. A variable cost per unit of activity. Variable costs change *in total* as the level of activity changes.

Example   Assume that studies of past cost behavior indicate the video booth at a Great America amusement park should incur total fixed costs of $100,000 per year and variable costs of $10 per video made. For planning purposes, management estimates that it will make 50,000 videos per year. The static cost budget for planning purposes is therefore $600,000 [= $100,000 + ($10 × 50,000)].

Suppose, however, that because of unexpected demand during the year, the booth made 70,000 videos. For performance evaluation purposes, management will not wish to compare the actual cost of producing 70,000 units with the expected cost of producing 50,000 units. The underlying levels of activity differ. To evaluate actual performance, accounting must express the budget in terms of what costs should have been to produce 70,000 units. The flexible budget is useful in this situation. It indicates the costs should have been $800,000 [= $100,000 + ($10 × 70,000)] during the year. This is the more appropriate budget for performance evaluation.

Establishing Budgets Using Cost Hierarchies

As we discuss how to develop a master budget, it is important to understand how the costs are affected by changes in related activities. To this end, it is helpful to categorize costs according to the hierarchy of costs covered in previous chapters. The cost hierarchy has five categories, as follows:

1. **Unit-level activities:** The work that converts resources into individual products and services is called unit-level activity. Examples include direct materials, direct labor, and energy to run the machines. (Note that direct labor is only a unit-level activity if management can easily adjust the level of labor relative to short-term production requirements.)
2. **Batch-level activities:** A batch refers to a number of units of service or product requiring the same setup of personnel or equipment. Examples include machine setups and quality inspections for specific batches of products.
3. **Product-level activities:** Product-level activities support a particular product or service line. Examples include design work, supervision, and advertising that are specific to each type of product or service.
4. **Customer-level activities:** Customer-level activities are performed to meet the needs of each customer. Examples include customer service and customer files.
5. **Facility-level activities:** Facility-level activities support the entire organization and are at the highest level of the hierarchy. Examples include top management, human resources, and research and development.

You will see in the discussion of the master budget that follows how we can use these categories of costs in the budgeting process.

The Process of Developing the Master Budget

Although each organization is unique in the way it puts together its budget, all budgeting processes share some common elements. After organizational goals, strategies, and long-range plans have been developed, work begins on the master budget, a detailed budget for the coming fiscal year with some less-detailed figures for subsequent years. (See the Managerial Application "Developing Master Budgets Throughout the World" for a discussion of the worldwide prevalence of master budgets.) Although budgeting is an ongoing process in most companies, the bulk of the work is usually done in the six months immediately preceding the beginning of the coming fiscal year. Final budget approvals by the chief executive and board of directors are made a month to six weeks before the beginning of the fiscal year.

To envision the master budgeting process, picture the financial statements most commonly prepared by companies: the income statement, the balance sheet, and the cash flow statement. Then imagine preparing these statements before the beginning of the fiscal period.

Managerial Application

Developing Master Budgets Throughout the World

Master budgets are used in companies throughout the world. More than 90 percent of all companies surveyed in Australia, the United Kingdom, and Japan utilize a master budget. Participants in the budgeting process vary from one country to the next. In Japan, 67 percent of the firms surveyed request division managers' participation compared with 78 percent in the United States. Budget goals and performance measures also vary from one country to the next. Return on investment is the most important measure used in the United States. Sales revenue is the most important measure used in Japan. However, both countries consider operating income to be the second most important performance measure. Although differences in priorities exist among countries, developing and using master budgets is common to most businesses throughout the world.

Source: T. Asada, J. Bailes, and M. Amano, "An Empirical Study of Japanese and American Budget Planning and Control Systems." Working paper, Tsu Kuba University and Oregon State University.

Where to Start? With Your Customers (Forecasting Sales)

Forecasting sales is perhaps the most difficult aspect of budgeting because it involves considerable subjectivity. To reduce subjectivity and gather as much information as possible, management often uses a number of methods to obtain forecasts from a number of different sources. We begin with a forecast of revenues for the budget period.

Sales Staff

Salespeople are in the unique position of being close to the customers, and they may possess the best information in the company about customers' immediate and near-term needs. As previously indicated, however, they may be tempted to bias their sales forecasts if such forecasts are used as the norm for performance evaluation.

For example, Sam is a district sales manager who expects his district's sales to be $1 million, although they could drop as low as $800,000 or run as high as $1.2 million. His bonus at the end of next year will be 1 percent of the excess of actual sales over the sales budget. So if the budget is $1 million and actual sales are also $1 million, he will receive no bonus.

If Sam provides a sales forecast that is too low, however, he will not be able to justify retaining his current number of employees. If his sales forecasts are consistently much below the actual sales results or below what management thinks his district should be doing, he will lose credibility. Thus, Sam decides on a conservative but reasonable sales forecast of $900,000, which, he believes, will give him a high probability of getting a bonus and a low risk of not meeting his other objectives.

Of course, if Sam's performance were compared using a different set of norms, he would have a different incentive. If, for instance, his bonus were a fixed percentage of sales, he would have incentive to maximize sales. Then he would be motivated to make an optimistic sales forecast to justify obtaining a larger sales staff. The high sales forecast also would be used to estimate the amount of production capacity needed, thus ensuring that adequate inventory would be available to satisfy customer needs. Of course, the managers and staff who receive forecasts usually recognize the subjectivity of the situation. As Sam's superior put it, "We've received sales forecasts from him for several years, and they're always a bit conservative. We don't ask him to revise his estimates. We simply take his conservatism into account when we put together the overall sales forecast."

Market Researchers

To provide a check on forecasts from local sales personnel, management often turns to market researchers. This group probably does not have incentives to provide a biased estimate of the budget. Furthermore, researchers have a different perspective on the market. They may know little about customers' immediate needs, but they can predict long-term trends in attitudes and the effects of social and economic changes on the company's sales, potential markets, and products.

The Delphi Technique

The **Delphi technique** is another method used to enhance forecasting and reduce bias in estimates. With this method, members of the forecasting group prepare individual forecasts and submit them anonymously. Each group member obtains a copy of all forecasts but is unaware of its source. The group then discusses the results. In this way, differences among individual forecasts can be addressed and reconciled without involving the personality or position of individual forecasters. After the differences are discussed, each group member prepares a new forecast and distributes it anonymously to the others. These forecasts are then discussed in the same manner as before. The process is repeated until the forecasts converge on a single best estimate of the coming year's sales level.

Trend Analysis

Trend analysis, which can range from a simple visual extrapolation of points on a graph to a highly sophisticated computerized time series analysis, also may be helpful in preparing sales forecasts.

Time series techniques use only past observations of the data series to be forecasted. No other data are included. This methodology is justified on the grounds that because all factors that affect the data series are reflected in the actual past observations, the past data are the best reflection of available information. This approach also is relatively economical because only a list of past sales figures is needed; no other data are gathered.

Forecasting techniques based on trend analysis often require long series of past data to derive a suitable solution. Generally, when these models are used in accounting applications, monthly data are required to obtain an adequate number of observations.

Econometric Models

Another forecasting approach is to enter past sales data into a regression model to obtain a statistical estimate of factors affecting sales (often called an **econometric model**). For example, the predicted sales for the coming period may be related to such factors as economic indicators, consumer-confidence indexes, back-order volume, and other internal and external factors that the company deems relevant.

Advocates of econometric models contend that they can include many relevant predictors and that manipulating the assumed values of the predictors makes it possible to examine a variety of hypothetical conditions and relate them to the sales forecast.

Sophisticated analytical models for forecasting are now widely available. Companies have software packages that allow economical use of these models. Nonetheless, it is important to remember that no model removes the uncertainty surrounding sales forecasts. Management often has found that the intuition of local sales personnel is a better predictor than sophisticated analysis and models. As in any management decision, cost-benefit tests should be used to determine which methods are most appropriate.

Victoria's Gourmet Coffee: A Comprehensive Illustration

To illustrate the budget preparation process, let's examine Victoria's Gourmet Coffee for a single period, assumed to be one month. Victoria's Gourmet Coffee produces gourmet coffee blends with spice flavors. We will continue this example in our discussion of performance evaluation in Chapter 10. An organization chart of Victoria's Gourmet Coffee appears in Exhibit 9.2. Each box in the organization chart is a responsibility center.

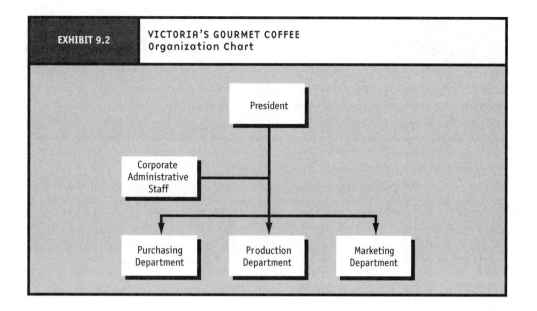

EXHIBIT 9.2 — VICTORIA'S GOURMET COFFEE Organization Chart

The development of Victoria's Gourmet Coffee's master budget for period 1 is illustrated throughout this section. The master budget contains the following components in exhibits, which are displayed and explained in the following pages.

Description	Exhibit
Sales Budget	9.3
Production Budget	9.4
Marketing Cost Budget	9.5
Administrative Cost Budget	9.6
Master Budget Profit Plan	9.7

The Sales Budget

Victoria's Gourmet Coffee produces one product, gourmet coffee blends. It expects to sell 70,000 units at $6 per unit (a unit is one can of coffee blend). Market researchers developed an initial sales forecast, estimating pessimistic, optimistic, and expected forecasts of total product sales in the market and Victoria's market share. The company defined optimistic as "probability of sales being this high or higher is 0.2"; they defined pessimistic as "probability of sales being this low or lower is 0.2." The marketing vice-president also had district sales managers prepare optimistic, pessimistic, and expected forecasts for their districts.

The chief marketing executive of the firm is responsible for preparing the sales budget. The marketing executive relies on inputs from market research groups as well as from salespeople or district managers in the field. The discussions among sales groups in budget preparation frequently identify problems in the firm's selling and advertising programs and broaden the participants' thinking about the firm's place in the market.

According to the marketing vice-president of Victoria's Gourmet Coffee, the market researchers and sales managers use two different databases:

The market research group uses consumer studies, economic forecasts, and past data about the company. The group provides a good macro-level forecast of economic conditions and consumer preferences for our products, but it explains little about the day-to-day efforts of our sales personnel.

This is where our sales managers' forecasts are most valuable. They know about potential customers, they know which of our present customers we are likely to lose, and they can forecast sales quite accurately for the first few months of the budget year. When I combine

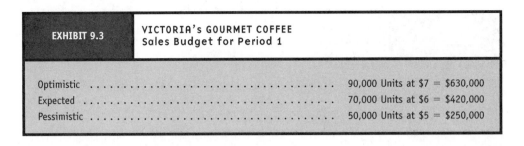

EXHIBIT 9.3	VICTORIA's GOURMET COFFEE Sales Budget for Period 1		
Optimistic	90,000 Units at $7	=	$630,000
Expected	70,000 Units at $6	=	$420,000
Pessimistic	50,000 Units at $5	=	$250,000

the forecasts of the market research group and the sales managers, I have a good idea of both the market conditions affecting the demand for our product and the immediate wishes of our customers.

The sales budget resulting from this approach is presented in Exhibit 9.3. To keep the example simple, we will use only the *expected* forecast in subsequent discussions.

The Production Budget

The sales budget, combined with estimates of beginning inventories and estimates of desired ending inventories, forms the basis of the production budget for Victoria's shown in the top panel of Exhibit 9.4.

EXHIBIT 9.4	VICTORIA'S GOURMET COFFEE Production Budget for Period 1	
UNITS TO BE PRODUCED		
Budgeted Sales, in Units (see sales budget)		70,000
Desired Ending Inventory (assumed)		8,000
Total Units Needed		78,000
Less Beginning Inventory (assumed)		(8,000)
Units to Be Produced		70,000
COSTS EXPECTED TO BE INCURRED		
Total Unit-Level Costs (for 70,000 units):		
Direct Materials (2 pounds per unit at $0.50 per pound)		$ 70,000
Direct Labor (.125 hour per unit at $20 per hour)		175,000
Manufacturing Overhead:		
Indirect Labor ($.10 per unit)		7,000
Supplies ($.04 per unit)		2,800
Power ($.03 per unit)		2,100
Total Unit-Level Costs		$256,900
Facility-Level Costs:		
Manufacturing Overhead:		
Power ($1,000 per period)		$ 1,000
Maintenance ($13,840 per period)		13,840
Rent ($6,000 per period)		6,000
Insurance ($1,000 per period)		1,000
Depreciation ($10,360 per period)		10,360
Total Facility-Level Costs		$ 32,200
Total Production Costs		$289,100

We compute the quantity of each product to be produced from the following equation:[6]

Units to Be Produced = Number of Units to Be Sold + Desired Units in Ending Inventory
— Units in Beginning Inventory

The costs to be incurred in producing the desired number of units for Victoria's Gourmet Coffee appear in the lower portion of Exhibit 9.4.

Direct Materials Direct materials are materials traceable to individual units produced. Direct materials costs are almost always variable. Management estimates that each finished unit at Victoria's will require 2 pounds of direct materials. The estimates of direct materials requirements result from engineering studies of material usage. The $0.50 cost per pound of the direct materials comes from projected prices. Hence, the budgeted, or standard, direct materials cost per finished unit is $0.50 × 2 pounds per finished unit = $1.00 per finished unit.[7]

Direct Labor Direct labor is work traceable directly to particular units of product. Engineering time-and-motion studies and studies of past labor time usage indicate that one unit requires 1/8 (or 0.125) hour of labor time. This estimate allows for normal, periodic rest periods, yet motivates employees to perform efficiently. The standard wage rate, including fringe benefits and payroll taxes (e.g., employer's share of social security and unemployment taxes), for production workers in Victoria's Gourmet Coffee's plant is $20.00 per hour. The direct labor cost per unit is $2.50 (= $20 per labor hour × 0.125 hour per unit of output).

Direct labor could be fixed (and therefore a product- or facility-level activity), as in high-tech companies having only a few workers, or variable (and therefore a unit-level activity). We assume direct labor is variable and a unit-level activity in this example.

Manufacturing Overhead Variable manufacturing overhead costs vary with units produced. Fixed manufacturing overhead costs give a firm the capacity to produce. As Exhibit 9.4 shows, indirect labor and supplies are variable overhead costs and considered to be unit-level activities. Power is a semivariable, or mixed, cost, having both variable and fixed components. The variable component of power is a unit-level activity (the cost varies in total with the unit level of output), and the fixed component is a facility-level activity (the cost is incurred regardless of the level of output). Maintenance, rent, insurance, and depreciation are fixed overhead costs and facility-level activities.

These estimates come from past experience. Managers should consider projected changes in costs and production methods to prepare estimates for the future. One can apply statistical regression methods to overhead to (1) separate fixed from variable overhead and (2) find the relationship between variable overhead and a measure of activity (e.g., direct labor hours or output).

Summary of Production Budget The budget in Exhibit 9.4 shows planned production department activity for the period of 70,000 units and costs of $289,100.

Exhibit 9.4 shows the expected fixed costs to be the sum of the estimates for:

Power (fixed cost portion)	$ 1,000
Maintenance	13,840
Rent	6,000
Insurance	1,000
Depreciation	10,360
Total	$32,200

---

[6]This equation comes from the basic accounting equation:

Beginning Balance + Transfers In = Transfers Out + Ending Balance

BB + TI = TO + EB

TI = TO + EB − BB

Units to Be Produced = Number of Units to Be Sold + Units in Ending Inventory
— Units in Beginning Inventory

[7]Managers and accountants use the terms *budgets* and *standards* interchangeably.

Exhibit 9.4 also shows the expected variable costs per unit to be the estimates for:

Direct Materials	$1.00
Direct Labor	2.50
Indirect Labor	0.10
Supplies	0.04
Power (variable cost portion)	0.03
Total	$3.67

If the level of production differs from the planned 70,000 units, we use the flexible budget to compute costs that the production department should have incurred for the actual units produced. The flexible budget for the production department is

Total Budgeted Manufacturing Costs for Production Department
= $32,200 + ($3.67 × Actual Units Produced)

Marketing Costs   The budget for marketing costs for Victoria's Gourmet Coffee's marketing department, based on expected sales of 70,000 units, appears in Exhibit 9.5. Travel costs are for customer-level activities related to sales personnel traveling to customer meetings. These costs are fixed in the short term. Salaries, advertising, and sales office costs are facility-level activities and are also considered to be fixed. Commissions are 2 percent of sales dollars, or $0.12 per unit at the budgeted price of $6 per unit ($0.12 = 0.02 × $6). Shipping costs are $0.02 per unit shipped. Hence, both are unit-level activities. Note that commissions and shipping costs are variable marketing costs because they vary with units *sold*. (Variable manufacturing costs vary with units *produced*.)

Summary of Marketing Budget   The budget in Exhibit 9.5 shows planned marketing department activity costs totaling $75,200.

Exhibit 9.5 shows the expected fixed costs to be the sum of the estimates for:

Salaries	$25,000
Advertising	30,000
Sales Office	8,400
Travel	2,000
Total	$65,400

Exhibit 9.5 also shows the expected variable costs per unit to be the estimates for:

Commissions	$0.12
Shipping	0.02
Total	$0.14

If the level of sales differs from the planned 70,000 units, we use the flexible budget to compute costs that the sales department should have incurred for the actual units sold. The flexible budget for the sales department is

Total Budgeted Marketing Costs = $65,400 + ($0.14 × Actual Units Sold).

Administrative Costs   Management estimates all the month's central corporate administrative costs in Exhibit 9.6 to be fixed. (In practice, some administrative costs might be fixed and others variable.) In addition, central corporate administrative costs are for facility-level activities.

Discretionary Fixed Costs   Many of the so-called fixed costs in the production, marketing, and administrative budgets are *discretionary costs*. Maintenance, donations, and advertising are examples. Although management budgets them as fixed costs, managers realize that these costs are not committed costs, like rent on a factory building, that are required to run the firm.

EXHIBIT 9.5	VICTORIA'S GOURMET COFFEE Marketing Cost Budget for Period 1		
Unit-Level Costs			
Commissions (2 percent of sales; see Exhibit 9.3, sales budget		$ 8,400[a]	
Shipping Costs ($.02 per unit shipped; see Exhibit 9.3, sales budget)		1,400	
Total Unit-Level Marketing Costs			$ 9,800
Customer-Level Costs			
Travel ($2,000 per period)		$ 2,000	
Total Customer-Level Costs			2,000
Facility-Level Costs			
Salaries ($25,000 per period)		$25,000	
Advertising ($30,000 per period)		30,000	
Sales Office ($8,400 per period)		8,400	
Total Facility-Level Costs			63,400
Total Marketing Cost Budget			$75,200

[a]Two percent × sales of $420,000 = $8,400.

When economic conditions make it doubtful that the firm will achieve its budgeted profit goals, management can cut discretionary costs. When managers state that they have reduced their fixed costs, or reduced their break-even points, they have often cut discretionary costs, not committed costs. For example, many companies recently made major cuts in expenses by laying off white-collar workers. Many executives believe those costs were discretionary because the firms continue to survive despite the cost cuts.

Discretionary costs are tempting cost-cutting targets because their reduction presents no serious short-term threats to production and marketing. The long-term consequences could be disastrous, however, if management cuts so-called discretionary functions like maintenance and advertising. Slashing the advertising budgets for companies like Nike, Miller Brewing Company, or Procter & Gamble could jeopardize those companies in the long run.

The Profit Plan (Budgeted Income Statement)   The *profit plan,* or *budgeted income statement,* appears in Exhibit 9.7 using a contribution margin format.

EXHIBIT 9.6	VICTORIA'S GOURMET COFFEE Administrative Cost Budget for Period 1	
Facility-Level Activities (all administrative costs are fixed)		
President's Salary		$10,000
Salaries of Other Staff Personnel		17,000
Supplies		2,000
Heat and Light		1,400
Rent		4,000
Donations and Contributions		1,000
General Corporate Taxes		8,000
Depreciation—Staff Office Equipment		1,400
Total Administrative Cost Budget		$44,800

EXHIBIT 9.7	VICTORIA'S GOURMET COFFEE Master Budget Profit Plan (income statement)

Sales (70,000 units at $6)	$420,000
Variable Manufacturing Cost of Goods Sold (70,000 units at $3.67)	(256,900)
Variable Marketing Costs (70,000 units at $.14)	(9,800)
Contribution Margin	$153,300
Fixed Manufacturing Costs	(32,200)
Fixed Marketing and Administrative Costs ($65,400 + $44,800)	(110,200)
Operating Profits	$ 10,900

After compiling the budget, management projects an operating profit of $10,900. (Recall that this figure is *before* taxes and miscellaneous income and expenses.) If top management is satisfied with this budgeted result and can find adequate cash to carry out the operations, it will approve the master budget. If management considers the budgeted results unsatisfactory, it will look for ways to improve budget profits using cost reductions or sales increases.

Using the Master Budget

The master budget includes a budgeted balance sheet, a cash flow budget, and other relevant budgets, as well as the profit plan developed in the preceding pages. Appendix 9.1 presents a comprehensive master budget including the profit plan, budgeted balance sheets, and the cash flow budget.

Preparing the master budget requires the participation of all managerial groups. As discussed in the Managerial Application "Using the Internet for Budgeting," many firms adopt electronic means to simplify the process. Once adopted, the budget becomes a major planning and control tool. Further, it becomes the authorization to produce and sell goods and services, to purchase materials, and to hire employees. In governmental units, the budget becomes the legal authorization for expenditures.

Managerial Application

Using the Internet for Budgeting

Many companies are attempting to streamline the budget process by using the World Wide Web. Employees of multinational companies are able to submit and retrieve budget-related information electronically. The controller of a multinational bank stated: "In the past, we have compiled our business plan using hundreds of spreadsheets, and our analysts have spent a disproportionate amount of time compiling and verifying data from multiple sources. Implementing a Web-based, enterprise-wide budgeting solution will help us develop business plans and allow our analysts to be proactive in monitoring quarterly results."

Source: Steve Hornyak, "Budgeting Made Easy," *Management Accounting* 80 (October 1998), 18–23.

Incentives for Accurate Forecasts

From our Victoria's Gourmet Coffee example, you can see the importance of the sales forecast to the entire budget process. If the sales forecast is too high and the company produces to meet the forecast, the company will have excess inventory. If the sales forecast is too low, the firm will likely lose sales opportunities because purchasing and production cannot meet demand. Rewarding managers only for accurate forecasting could create disincentives for better performance—managers would merely try to meet the forecast, not to beat it.

Companies use many methods of providing incentives for both accurate forecasting and good performance. These methods include comparing sales forecasts from year to year and obtaining forecasts from multiple sources. Appendix 9.2 discusses formal incentive models that simultaneously motivate accurate forecasts and good performance.

Comparison of the Flexible and Master Budgets

The following discussion compares the master budget with the flexible budget, as shown in Exhibit 9.8. This comparison ties the results of the planning process (i.e., the master budget) with flexible budgeting and forms the basis for analyzing differences between planned and actual results (discussed further in Chapter 10).

Flexible versus Master Budget Exhibit 9.8 compares the flexible budget with the master budget profit plan for Victoria's Gourmet Coffee. The master budget results in the profit shown in Exhibit 9.7.

To review, some of the important master budget amounts follow:

Sales Price per Unit	$6.00
Sales Volume per Period	70,000 Units
Variable Manufacturing Costs per Unit	$3.67
Variable Marketing Costs per Unit	$0.14
Fixed Manufacturing Costs per Period	$32,200
Fixed Marketing Costs per Period	$65,400
Fixed Administrative Costs per Period	$44,800

EXHIBIT 9.8	VICTORIA'S GOURMET COFFEE — Flexible Budget and Sales Volume Variance		
	Flexible Budget (based on actual sales volume of 80,000)	**Sales Volume Variance**	**Master Budget (based on a prediction of 70,000 units sold)**
Sales	$480,000[a]	$60,000 F	$420,000[d]
Less:			
Variable Manufacturing Costs	293,600[b]	36,700 U	256,900[e]
Variable Marketing Costs	11,200[c]	1,400 U	9,800[f]
Contribution Margin	$175,200	$21,900 F	$153,300
Less:			
Fixed Manufacturing Costs	32,200	—	32,200
Fixed Marketing Costs	65,400	—	65,400
Fixed Administrative Costs	44,800	—	44,800
Operating Profit	$ 32,800	$21,900 F	$ 10,900

[a]80,000 units sold at $6.00.
[b]80,000 units sold at $3.67.
[c]80,000 units sold at $0.14.
[d]70,000 units sold at $6.00.
[e]70,000 units sold at $3.67.
[f]70,000 units sold at $0.14.
  U denotes unfavorable variance
  F denotes favorable variance.

We base the flexible budget in this case on the actual sales and production volume.[8] Variable costs and revenues should change as volume changes. The flexible budget indicates expected budgeted revenues and costs at the actual activity level, which is sales volume in this case. You can think of the flexible budget as the cost equation:

$$TC = F + VX,$$

where TC = total budgeted costs, F = budgeted fixed costs, V = budgeted variable cost per unit, and X = actual volume.

Although management predicted sales volume to be 70,000 units, Victoria's produced and sold 80,000 units during the period. The sales volume variance is the difference in profits caused by the difference between the master budget sales volume and the actual sales volume. In this case, the difference of $21,900 between operating profits in the master budget and the flexible budget is a **sales volume variance.** It results from the 10,000-unit difference in sales volume from the sales plan of 70,000 units. We can also compute $21,900 by multiplying the 10,000-unit increase by the budgeted contribution margin per unit of $2.19 (= $6.00 − $3.67 − $0.14).

What Is the Meaning of *Favorable* and *Unfavorable*?   Note the use of F for "favorable" and U for "unfavorable" beside each of the variances in Exhibit 9.8. These terms describe the impact of the variance on the budgeted operating profits. A **favorable variance** means that the variance would *increase* operating profits, holding all other things constant. An **unfavorable variance** would *decrease* operating profits, holding all other things constant.

We do not use these terms in a normative sense. A favorable variance is not *necessarily* good, and an unfavorable variance is not *necessarily* bad. You should further note the variable cost variances—they are labeled unfavorable. Does this reflect unfavorable conditions in the company? Unlikely! These variable costs are *expected* to increase because the actual sales volume is higher than planned. In short, the labels *favorable* or *unfavorable* do not automatically indicate good or bad conditions. Rather, a favorable variance implies that actual profits are higher than budgeted, all other things (for example, other variances) being ignored; conversely, an unfavorable variance implies that actual profits are lower than budgeted, all other things being ignored. Ultimately, the accounting department will credit favorable variances and debit unfavorable variances to income statement accounts.

Information Use   The information presented in Exhibit 9.8 has a number of uses. First, it shows that the increase in operating profits between the master budget and flexible budget results from the increase in sales volume over the level planned. Sales variances are usually the responsibility of the marketing department, so this information may be useful feedback to personnel in that department, and managers may find it informative for evaluating performance. Second, the resulting flexible budget shows budgeted sales, costs, and operating profits after taking into account the volume increase but before considering differences in unit selling prices, differences in unit variable costs, and differences in fixed costs.

Problem 9.1 for Self-Study

Comparing the master budget to the flexible budget. Computer Supply, Inc., budgeted production and sales of 40,000 laptop computer cases for the month of April at a selling price of $11 each. The company actually sold 50,000 cases for $10 each. The company budgeted the following costs:

---

[8]The relevant activity variable is sales volume because this is a profit plan (that is, an income statement). If the objective were to compare the flexible production budget with the master production budget, the relevant activity variable would be production volume. Sales and production volumes are assumed to be equal throughout this example so that we can avoid allocating fixed manufacturing costs to inventories.

Standard Manufacturing Variable Costs per Unit	$4.00
Fixed Manufacturing Overhead Cost: Monthly Budget	$80,000
Marketing and Administrative Costs:	
Variable (per unit)	$1.00
Fixed (monthly budget)	$100,000

Prepare a report for management like the one in Exhibit 9.8 showing the master budget, flexible budget, and sales volume variance.

The solution to this self-study problem is at the end of the chapter on page 317.

Budgeting in Nonprofit Organizations

The master budget has added importance in nonprofit organizations because it is usually used as a basis for authorizing the expenditure of funds. In many governmental units, *the approved budget is a legal authorization for expenditure,* and the penalties for exceeding the authorized expenditures in the budget could be severe. This partially explains why a balanced budget takes on added importance in nonprofit organizations.

Ethical Issues in Budgeting

Not only do managers and employees provide information for the budget, their performance is evaluated by comparing the budget with actual results. This can often lead to serious ethical dilemmas. For example, as a manager, suppose you believe that, while it was possible to achieve a 10 percent increase in your department's sales, a 2 percent increase would be almost certain. If you tell upper management that a 10 percent increase is an appropriate budget, but you fall short of 10 percent, you will lose opportunities for merit pay increases and a promotion. Management may assume the reason you fell short of the 10 percent estimation was not because of market circumstances beyond your control, but because you did not perform well in making sales. On the other hand, if you report that only a 2 percent increase is possible, your performance is likely to exceed expectations, but the company will not provide for enough production capacity to fill the sales orders if the 10 percent increase comes through. What should you do? Should you prepare a budget that is in your best interest or one that presents your best estimate of reality (and is, therefore, in the best interest of the company)?

People in companies face these dilemmas all the time. We hope companies provide incentives for people to report truthfully, which means the company must reward both honest estimates and good performance. But the reality is that many companies put considerable pressure on employees to achieve continually more difficult targets. Fraudulent financial reporting often occurs because managers cannot meet increasingly difficult budgets.

Establishing an Operating Budget in the Real World

This chapter provides the basic framework for establishing an operating budget. The following example demonstrates how an actual company develops its budget.

Developing a Budget: The River Beverages Case[9]

Overview   River Beverages is a food and soft drink company with worldwide operations. The company is organized into five regional divisions with each vice-president reporting directly to

[9]Prepared by Thomas B. Rumzie under the direction of Michael W. Maher. Copyright © 2004 Michael W. Maher.

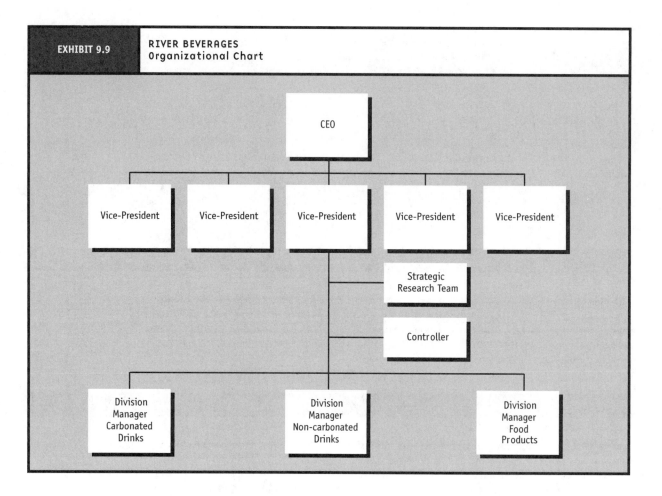

EXHIBIT 9.9

RIVER BEVERAGES
Organizational Chart

the CEO, Cindy Wilkins. Each vice-president has a strategic research team, a controller, and three divisions—Carbonated Drinks, Non-carbonated Drinks, and Food Products (see Exhibit 9.9). Management feels that the structure works well for River because different regions have different tastes and the divisions' products complement one another.

Industry   The beverage industry in the United States has become mature as it has grown in stride with population growth. Most of the industry growth has come from the nonalcoholic beverage market, which is growing by about 1.1 percent annually. In the nonalcoholic arena, soft drinks are the largest segment. Bottled water is the next largest segment, followed by juices. The smallest but fastest-growing segment is ready-to-drink tea, which is growing by over 90 percent in volume but accounts for only about 3 percent of the beverages consumed.

Sales Budgets   Susan Johnson, plant manager at River Beverage's Non-carbonated Drink plant in St. Louis (see Exhibit 9.10), recently completed the annual budgeting process. According to Johnson, division managers have decision-making authority in their business units except for capital financing activities. Budgets are used to keep the division managers focused on corporate goals.

In the beginning of December, division managers submit a report to the vice-president for the region summarizing capital, sales, and income forecasts for the upcoming fiscal year, which begins July 1. Although the initial report is not prepared in much detail, it is prepared with care because it is used in the strategic planning process.

Next, the strategic research team begins a formal assessment of each market segment in its region. The team develops sales forecasts for each division and compiles them into a company forecast. The team considers economic conditions and current market share in each region. Management believes the strategic research team is effective because it is able to integrate division products. In addition, the team ensures continuity of assumptions and achievable sales goals for the company as a whole. The work done by the strategic research team is shared with top man-

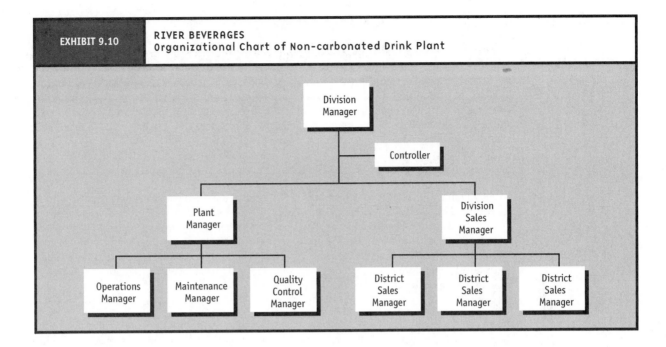

EXHIBIT 9.10   **RIVER BEVERAGES**
Organizational Chart of Non-carbonated Drink Plant

agement and division managers. Division managers typically do not share the information from the strategic research team with the district sales managers because the division managers want the district sales managers to derive their own estimates independent of such input.

In early February, the district sales managers estimate sales for the upcoming budget year. The district sales managers are ultimately responsible for the forecasts they prepare. The district sales forecasts are then compiled, coordinated by the division sales manager, and returned to the division manager. The division manager reviews the forecasts but does not make any revisions without first consulting the division and district sales managers. Next, the district sales forecasts are reviewed by the strategic research team and the division controller. Finally, top management reviews each division's competitive position, including plans to increase market share, capital spending, and quality improvement plans.

Plant Budgets   After the sales budget is approved by top management, it is broken down to a sales budget for each plant. The budget is broken down further by price, volume, and product type. Plant managers budget variable costs, contribution margins, fixed costs, and pretax income using information from the sales budget given to the plant.

Plant managers derive budgeted pretax income by subtracting standard variable costs and budgeted fixed costs from the sales forecast. If actual sales fall below forecasts, the plant manager is still responsible for budgeted pretax income.

The operations and maintenance managers work together to develop cost standards and cost reduction targets for all departments. Budgeted cost reductions from productivity improvements, unfavorable variances, and fixed costs are developed for each department, operation, and cost center in the plant.

Before plant managers submit their budgets, a member of the strategic research team and the division controller visit the plant. These visits are conducted to keep management in touch with what is happening at the plant level and to help management understand how plant managers determined their budgets. The visits also allow management to provide budget preparation guidance if necessary.

By April 1, plant managers submit their final budgets, and the controller consolidates them for the vice-president. The vice-president reviews the budgets to ensure they are in line with corporate objectives. After the vice-presidents and CEO have made all changes, the budgets are submitted to the board of directors for approval. The board votes on the final budget in early June.

Sales and Manufacturing Relations   "We are expected to meet our approved budget," remarked Kevin Greely, a division controller at River. Greely continued, "A couple years ago one of our major restaurant customers switched to another brand. Even though we lost sales of more than one million cases of our product annually, we were not allowed to make revisions to our budget."

Budgets are rarely adjusted after approval. However, if there is a decline in sales early in the year, plant managers may file an appeal to revise the budgeted profit for the year. If sales decline late in the year, management does not revise the budgeted amounts. Rather, plant managers are asked to cut costs wherever possible and delay any unnecessary expenditures until the following year. It is important to remember that River sets budgets so that it is able to see where to make cuts or where it can find any operating inefficiencies. Plant managers are not forced to meet their goals, but they are encouraged to cut costs below budget.

The sales department is primarily responsible for product price, sales mix, and delivery timing, while plant managers are responsible for plant operations. Kevin Greely remarked,

As you might imagine, problems occur between plant and regional sales managers from time to time. For example, rush orders may cause production costs to be higher than normal for some production runs. Another problem may occur when a sales manager runs a promotional campaign that causes margins to shrink. In both instances, a plant manager's profit budget will be affected negatively while a sales manager's forecasted sales budget will be affected positively. Such situations are often passed up to the division level for resolution; however, it is important to remember that the customer is always the primary concern.

Incentives   River Beverage management has devised what it thinks is an effective system to motivate plant managers. First, plant managers are promoted only when they have displayed outstanding performance in their current position. Next, River has monetary incentives in place that reward plant managers for reaching profit goals. Finally, charts are produced each month that display budgeted items versus actual results. Although not required to do so, most plant managers publicize the charts and use them as a motivational tool. The charts allow department supervisors and staff to compare activities in their department to similar activities in other plants around the world.

CEO's Message   Cindy Wilkins, CEO of River Beverages, looks to the future and comments,

Planning is an important aspect of budget preparation for every level of our organization. I would like to decrease the time spent on preparing the budget, but I feel that it keeps people thinking about the future. The negative aspect of the budgeting process is that sometimes it overcontrols our managers. We need to stay nimble enough to react to customer demands, while staying structured enough to achieve corporate objectives. For the most part, our budget process keeps our managers aware of sales goals and alerts them when sales or expenses are off track.

Summary

The following items correspond to the learning objectives presented at the beginning of the chapter.

1. **Explain the use of a budget as a tool for planning and performance evaluation.** A budget is an estimate of financial statements prepared before the actual transactions occur. Budgets are generally developed for a particular expected level of activity. Budgets also provide estimates of expected performance and serve as standards for evaluating performance.
2. **Explain how a budget can affect employee motivation.** Budgets motivate people to perform because they are standards or targets for people to achieve.
3. **Compare the four types of responsibility centers.** Managers are responsible for (1) costs in cost centers, (2) revenues in revenue centers, (3) both costs and revenues in profit centers, and (4) revenues, costs, and assets in an investment center.
4. **Describe the master budget.** The master budget is a complete blueprint of the planned operations of a firm for a period. It begins with the sales budget, then adds the production budget, and finishes with the budgeted income statement.
5. **Explain the difference between a flexible budget and master budget.** The master budget is based on *estimated* sales and production volume and is prepared before the budget period begins. The flexible budget is based on *actual* sales and production volume and is prepared after the budget period ends. The difference in operating profits from the flexible budget to

the master budget is called a *sales volume variance* and results from the difference between budgeted sales volume and actual sales volume.

6. **Describe ethical dilemmas in budgeting.** Managers and employees often encounter ethical dilemmas in the budgeting process because they are involved in the creation of the budget, and their performances are subsequently evaluated by comparing the budget with actual results.

7. **List the components of a comprehensive master budget (Appendix 9.1).** A comprehensive master budget includes individual schedules for a materials purchases budget, a capital budget, a cash outlays budget, a receivables and collections budget, and a cash budget, all of which support the budgeted income and retained earnings statement. Finally the budgeted balance sheet is developed.

8. **Describe an incentive model for accurate reporting (Appendix 9.2).** An incentive plan has three components: (1) It relates rewards positively to forecasted sales, (2) it provides incentives for the sales manager to increase sales beyond the forecast, and (3) it penalizes the sales manager when sales fall lower than forecasted.

Key Terms and Concepts

Batch-level activities	Master budget
Benchmarking	Organizational goals
Budget	Participative budgeting
Cost center	Product-level activities
Critical success factors	Profit center
Customer-level activities	Profit plan
Delphi technique	Responsibility center
Discretionary cost centers	Revenue center
Econometric model	Sales volume variance
Engineered cost centers	Short-term operating budget
Facility-level activities	Static budget
Favorable variance	Strategic long-range plan
Flexible budget	Trend analysis
Goal congruence	Unfavorable variance
Investment center	Unit-level activities

Solution to Self-Study Problem

SUGGESTED SOLUTION TO PROBLEM 9.1 FOR SELF-STUDY

COMPUTER SUPPLY, INC.
Flexible Budget and Sales Volume Variance
April

	Flexible Budget (based on 50,000 units)	Sales Volume Variance	Master Budget (based on 40,000 units)
Sales Revenue	$550,000[a]	$110,000 F	$440,000
Less:			
Variable Manufacturing Costs	200,000	40,000 U	160,000
Variable Marketing and Administrative Costs	50,000	10,000 U	40,000
Contribution Margin	$300,000	$ 60,000 F	$240,000
Less:			
Fixed Manufacturing Costs	80,000	—	80,000
Fixed Marketing and Administrative Costs	100,000	—	100,000
Operating Profits	$120,000	$ 60,000 F	$ 60,000

[a] $550,000 = 50,000 × $11. Note the only change is volume, not sales price.

This appendix presents the comprehensive master budget for Victoria's Gourmet Coffee. First, we summarize the profit plan developed in the chapter. Second, we tie the profit plan into the other budgets, such as the cash budget and the capital budget. Finally, we present the budgeted balance sheet. The master budget ties together the financial activities of the firm for the budget period. Hence, it can aid both planning and coordination. For example, planning for cash needs during a period requires knowing cash inflows and outflows from operating activities and also knowing cash requirements resulting from the capital budget.

Exhibit 9.11 summarizes the information from the chapter about projected sales and production volumes, revenues, and costs. Exhibit 9.12 presents the master budget profit plan from the chapter.

Materials Purchases Budget

The purchasing department is responsible for purchasing materials for Victoria's Gourmet Coffee. Exhibit 9.13 presents the materials purchases budget. The production budget is the basis for the materials purchases budget. For simplicity in presentation, we assume that payments to suppliers equal purchases each period.

Capital Budget

The capital budget, Exhibit 9.14, shows Victoria's Gourmet Coffee's plan for acquisition of depreciable, long-term assets during the next period. Management plans to purchase major items of equipment, financing part of the cost by issuing notes payable to equipment suppliers. The capital budget deducts the expected proceeds of the note issuance from the cost of the acquisitions to estimate current cash outlays for equipment. An accepted alternative treatment would have viewed the note issuance as a cash inflow, with the entire cost of the equipment included in cash outflows.

Cash Outlays Budget

Exhibit 9.15 presents a schedule of the planned cash outlays for the budget period. Each period, Victoria's Gourmet Coffee pays the income taxes accrued in the previous period. Income taxes payable at the start of the budget period appear as $6,200 on the beginning balance sheet (first column of Exhibit 9.19). The firm expects to declare and pay dividends of $5,000 in the budget period.

Receivables and Collections Budget

Victoria collects most of each period's sales in the period of sales, but there is a lag in some collections. The budget for cash collections from customers appears in Exhibit 9.16. Collecting for sales of a given period normally occurs as follows: 85 percent in the period of sale and 15 percent in the next period. We could introduce sales discounts and estimates of uncollectable accounts into the illustration, but we omit them for simplicity. The estimated accounts receivable at the start of the budget period of $71,400 appears on the balance sheet (first column of Exhibit 9.19). The amount represents 15 percent of the previous period's sales of $476,000: $71,400 = 0.15 × $476,000. In the budget period, the firm expects to collect 85 percent of sales, leaving $63,000 in Accounts Receivable at the end of the budget period ($63,000 = 15 percent of budget period sales of $420,000).

EXHIBIT 9.11	VICTORIA'S GOURMET COFFEE Summary of Sales, Production, and Cost Budgets for Period 1

SALES BUDGET[a]

70,000 Units at $6	$420,000

PRODUCTION BUDGET[b]

Units to Be Produced

Budgeted Sales in Units (see sales budget)	70,000 Units
Desired Ending Inventory (assumed)	8,000
Total Units Needed	78,000 Units
Beginning Inventory (assumed)	(8,000)
Units to Be Produced	70,000 Units

Cost Expected to Be Incurred

Direct Materials (2 pounds per unit at $.50 per pound)		$ 70,000
Direct Labor (.125 hour per unit at $20 per hour)		175,000
Manufacturing Overhead:		
Indirect Labor ($.10 per unit)	$ 7,000	
Supplies ($.04 per unit)	2,800	
Power ($1,000 per period plus $.03 per unit)	3,100	
Maintenance ($13,840 per period)	13,840	
Rent ($6,000 per period)	6,000	
Insurance ($1,000 per period)	1,000	
Depreciation ($10,360 per period)	10,360	44,100
Total Production Costs		$289,100

MARKETING COST BUDGET[c]

Variable Costs

Commissions (2 percent of sales)	$ 8,400	
Shipping Costs ($.02 per unit shipped)	1,400	
Total Variable Marketing Costs		$ 9,800

Fixed Costs

Salaries ($25,000 per period)	$25,000	
Advertising ($30,000 per period)	30,000	
Sales Office ($8,400 per period)	8,400	
Travel ($2,000 per period)	2,000	
Total Fixed Marketing Costs		65,400
Total Marketing Cost Budget		$ 75,200

ADMINISTRATIVE COST BUDGET[d]

President's Salary	$ 10,000
Salaries of Other Staff Personnel	17,000
Supplies	2,000
Heat and Light	1,400
Rent	4,000
Donations and Contributions	1,000
General Corporate Taxes	8,000
Depreciation—Staff Office Equipment	1,400
Total Administrative Cost Budget	$ 44,800

[a]**Source:** Exhibit 9.3.   [c]**Source:** Exhibit 9.5.
[b]**Source:** Exhibit 9.4.   [d]**Source:** Exhibit 9.6.

EXHIBIT 9.12	VICTORIA'S GOURMET COFFEE Master Budget Profit Plan for Period 1

Sales (70,000 units at $6)	$420,000
Less:	
Variable Manufacturing Cost of Goods Sold (70,000 units at $3.67)	(256,900)
Variable Marketing Costs (70,000 units at $0.14)	(9,800)
Contribution Margin	$153,300
Less:	
Fixed Manufacturing Costs	(32,200)
Fixed Marketing and Administrative Costs ($65,400 + $44,800)	(110,200)
Operating Profits	$ 10,900

Source: Exhibit 9.7.

EXHIBIT 9.13	VICTORIA'S GOURMET COFFEE Materials Purchases Budget

Quantities to Be Purchased (in pounds):	
Units to Be Produced (see Exhibit 9.11)	70,000 Units
Purchases Required at 2 Pounds per Unit	140,000 Pounds
There are no materials inventories.	

EXHIBIT 9.14	VICTORIA'S GOURMET COFFEE Capital Budget for Period 1

	Period 1
Acquisition of New Factory Machinery	$12,000
Miscellaneous Capital Additions	2,000
Total Capital Budget	$14,000
Borrowings for New Machinery—Long-Term Notes Payable	(6,000)
Current Cash Outlay	$ 8,000

Cash Budget

Cash flow is important. No budget is more important for financial planning than the cash budget, illustrated in Exhibit 9.17. This budget helps management plan to avoid unnecessary idle cash balances or unneeded, expensive borrowing. Almost all firms prepare a cash budget. The budgeted amounts for cash outflows and collections from customers come from Exhibits 9.15 and 9.16, respectively. Management estimates the other income, interest, and miscellaneous revenues to be $2,000 for the period.

EXHIBIT 9.15	VICTORIA'S GOURMET COFFEE Cash Outflows Budget for Period 1	
		Period 1
Materials (Exhibit 9.11)		$ 70,000
Labor (Exhibit 9.11)		175,000
Manufacturing Overhead (Exhibit 9.11)[a]		33,740
Marketing Costs (Exhibit 9.11)		75,200
Administrative Costs (Exhibit 9.11)[b]		43,400
Capital Expenditures (Exhibit 9.14)		8,000
Payments on Short-Term Notes[c]		13,000
Interest[c]		3,000
Income Taxes[d]		6,200
Dividends[c]		5,000
Total Cash Outflows		$432,540

[a]Manufacturing Overhead Costs − Depreciation = $44,100 − $10,360 = $33,740.
[b]Administrative Costs − Depreciation = $44,800 − $1,400 = $43,400.
[c]Assumed for illustration.
[d]The firm pays income taxes on earnings of previous period in current period. We assume the amount in this case.

EXHIBIT 9.16	VICTORIA'S GOURMET COFFEE Receivables and Collections Budget for Period 1	
		Period 1
Accounts Receivable, Start of Period:		
From the Period Immediately Preceding the Budget Period (15 percent of $476,000)		$ 71,400
Budget Period Sales		420,000
Total Receivables		$ 491,400
Less Collections:		
Current Period (85 percent of $420,000)		$(357,000)
Previous Period (15 percent of $476,000)		(71,400)
Total Collections		$(428,400)
Accounts Receivable, End of Period		$ 63,000

Budgeted (Pro Forma) Income and Retained Earnings Statement

The budgeted income and retained earnings statement and the budgeted balance sheet pull together all the preceding budget information. Exhibit 9.18 illustrates the budgeted income and retained earnings statement. At this stage in the budgeting process, management's attention switches from decision making, planning, and control to external reporting to shareholders. In other words, management becomes interested in how the income statement and balance sheet

EXHIBIT 9.17	VICTORIA'S GOURMET COFFEE Cash Budget for Period 1	

	Period 1
Cash Receipts:	
Collections from Customers (Exhibit 9.16)	$428,400
Other Income[a]	2,000
Total Receipts	$430,400
Cash Outflows (Exhibit 9.15)	(432,540)
Increase (Decrease) in Cash during Period	$ (2,140)
Cash Balance at Start of Period[a]	79,800
Cash Balance at End of Period	$ 77,660

[a]Assumed for illustration.

EXHIBIT 9.18	VICTORIA'S GOURMET COFFEE Budgeted (pro forma) Income and Retained Earnings Statement for Period 1	

	Period 1
Sales (70,000 units at $6)	$420,000
Less Cost of Goods Sold (Exhibit 9.11)	(289,100)
Gross Margin	$130,900
Less Marketing Expenses (Exhibit 9.11)	(75,200)
Less Administrative Expenses (Exhibit 9.11)	(44,800)
Operating Profits (Exhibit 9.12)	$ 10,900
Other Income (Exhibit 9.17)	2,000
	$ 12,900
Less Interest Expense (Exhibit 9.15)	(3,000)
Pretax Income	$ 9,900
Less Income Taxes[a]	(3,861)
Net Income	$ 6,039
Less Dividends (Exhibit 9.15)	(5,000)
Increase in Retained Earnings	$ 1,039
Retained Earnings at Start of Period (Exhibit 9.19)	56,500
Retained Earnings at End of Period (Exhibit 9.19)	$ 57,539

[a]Income taxes average approximately 39 percent of pretax income. The amount $3,861 is shown as the end-of-period income taxes payable in Exhibit 9.19.

will reflect the results of its decisions. Accordingly, accountants prepare the budgeted income statement and balance sheet in accordance with generally accepted accounting principles. The statement in Exhibit 9.18 is an income statement rather than a profit plan, and we present it using full absorption costing as required for external reporting.

Compilation of all the data for the period indicates a budgeted income of $6,039. If top management finds this budgeted result satisfactory and has available cash adequate to carry out the operations as indicated by Exhibit 9.17, it will approve the master budget. If management does not consider the budgeted results satisfactory, it will consider ways to improve the budgeted results through cost reductions or altered sales plans.

Budgeted Balance Sheet

The final exhibit of this series, Exhibit 9.19, shows the budgeted balance sheets at the start and end of the period. (Accountants prepare the budget before the beginning of the budget period; hence, they must estimate the beginning balance sheet. For example, accountants would prepare a budget for the calendar year during the preceding September through November.)

Here, as in the budgeted income statement, management will have to decide whether the overall budgeted results will be acceptable. Will cash balances be satisfactory? Do the receivables meet management's objectives? Will the final capital structure and debt-equity ratio conform to management's expectations? If the budgeted balance sheet and income statement are satisfactory, they will become the initial benchmarks against which management will check actual performance in the ensuing period.

Summary of the Master Budget

The master budget summarizes management's plans for the period covered. Preparing the master budget requires the participation of all managerial groups, from local plant and sales managers

EXHIBIT 9.19	VICTORIA'S GOURMET COFFEE Budgeted Balance Sheet for Period 1		
		Start of Period 1	End of Period 1
ASSETS			
Current Assets			
Cash (Exhibit 9.17)		$ 79,800	$ 77,660
Accounts Receivable (Exhibit 9.16)		71,400	63,000
Finished Goods Inventory		33,040[a]	33,040[a]
Total Current Assets		$184,240	$173,700
Plant Assets			
Equipment		460,000[a]	474,000[a]
Less Accumulated Depreciation		(162,000)[a]	(173,760)[a]
Total Assets		$482,240	$473,940
EQUITIES			
Current Liabilities			
Accounts Payable		$ 96,540[a]	$ 96,450[a]
Short-Term Notes and Other Payables		41,000[a]	28,000[a]
Income Taxes Payable (Exhibits 9.15 and 9.18)		6,200	3,861
Total Current Liabilities		$143,740	$128,401
Long-Term Liabilities			
Long-Term Equipment Notes		82,000[a]	88,000[a]
Total Liabilities		$225,740	$216,401
Shareholders' Equity			
Capital Stock ($20 par value)		$200,000[a]	$200,000[a]
Retained Earnings (Exhibit 9.18)		56,500[a]	57,539[a]
Total Shareholders' Equity		$256,500	$257,539
Total Equities		$482,240	$473,940

[a]Assumed for purposes of illustration.

to the top executives of the firm and the board of directors. Once management adopts the budget, it becomes the major planning and control instrument.

Master budgets are almost always static budgets; that is, they consider the likely results of the operations at the one level of operations specified in the budget. Computerizing the process makes it less costly to develop multiple master budgets that take into account various uncertainties facing the firm, such as market conditions, material prices, labor difficulties, and government regulations.

Appendix 9.2: Incentive Model for Accurate Reporting

How does management provide employees with incentives both for accurate reporting and for high performance?

Example   Assume that the Harris Raviv Company solicits sales forecasts from each of its district sales managers. These forecasts become budgets that management compares with actual sales to evaluate performance.

The firm's general manager of marketing wants to provide each district sales manager with a salary and a bonus. Previously, sales managers earned a bonus by beating the budget. The sales managers, however, began to "low-ball" the forecasts. Management knew this was happening, but it did not know how high the forecasts *should* have been because it did not have the information the managers had. The general manager of marketing explained:

> Managers could always counter our arguments with data that we could not audit. Their low estimates wreaked havoc with our production schedules, purchasing, and hiring decisions.
>
> Next we tried to give them incentives for accurate forecasts. We rewarded them if the actual sales were close to the forecasts, and penalized if actual and forecast deviated a lot. With this system, the managers forecast sales at a level that was sufficiently low to be achievable, then they "managed" their sales such that actual was almost right at the forecast. The consequences were that they had disincentives to beat the budget. Also, our internal auditors found numerous cases where managers had delayed sales orders until the following year and even turned down some orders because they did not want the current year's sales to overshoot the forecast.

The incentive plan to deal with this problem has three components:

1. Rewards are positively related to forecasted sales to give managers incentives to forecast high rather than low. If b_1 is a bonus coefficient that is a percentage of forecasted sales, and forecasted sales are $\hat{Y}$, then this component of the bonus is

$$b_1\hat{Y}$$

2. The plan provides incentives for the sales manager to increase sales beyond the forecast. If b_2 is the bonus coefficient for the excess of Y over $\hat{Y}$, forecast sales, then this component of the bonus is

$$b_2(Y - \hat{Y}), \quad \text{for } Y \geq \hat{Y}.$$

3. When actual sales, Y, are less than the forecast, $\hat{Y}$, the plan penalizes the sales manager. If b_3 is the bonus coefficient for the shortfall, $Y - \hat{Y}$, then this component of the bonus is

$$-b_3(\hat{Y} - Y), \quad \text{for } \hat{Y} > Y.$$

If B is the dollar bonus paid to the manager, the overall bonus plan is

$$B = \begin{cases} b_1\hat{Y} + b_2(Y - \hat{Y}), & \text{for } Y \geq \hat{Y} \text{ (actual sales meet or exceed the forecast);} \\ b_1\hat{Y} - b_3(\hat{Y} - Y), & \text{for } \hat{Y} > Y \text{ (the forecast exceeds actual sales).} \end{cases}$$

EXHIBIT 9.20	HARRIS RAVIV COMPANY Incentives for Accurate Forecasting Bonus Paid to District Sales Managers (thousands omitted from sales and bonus amounts)

Let $b_1 = 5$ percent, $b_2 = 3$ percent, and $b_3 = 7$ percent

$$B = \begin{cases} .05\,\hat{Y} + .03(Y - \hat{Y}), & \text{for } Y \geq \hat{Y} \\ .05\,\hat{Y} - .07(\hat{Y} - Y), & \text{for } \hat{Y} \times Y. \end{cases}$$

Forecasted Sales, $\hat{Y}$

		$1,000	$1,100	$1,200
Actual	$1,000	50[a]	48[d]	46[g]
Sales,	$1,200	53[b]	55[e]	53[h]
Y	$1,200	56[c]	58[f]	60[i]

[a]$50 = .05($1,000).
[b]$53 = .05($1,000) + .03($1,100 − $1,000).
[c]$56 = .05($1,000) + .03($1,200 − $1,000).
[d]$48 = .05($1,100) − .07($1,100 − $1,000).
[e]$55 = .05($1,100).

[f]$58 = .05($1,100) + .03($1,200 − $1,100).
[g]$46 = .05($1,200) − .07($1,200 − $1,000).
[h]$53 = .05($1,200) − .07($1,200 − $1,100).
[i]$60 = .05($1,200).

The coefficients are set such that

$$b_3 > b_1 > b_2 > 0,$$

and a rule of thumb is that b_3 should be at least 30 percent greater than b_1, and b_1 should be at least 20 percent greater than b_2. Management intends for this incentive plan to reward both accurate forecasts and outstanding performance.

Harris Raviv Company established an incentive system using the methods described here. Exhibit 9.20 shows the bonus that would result from various combinations of forecasted sales and actual sales. For example, if the forecast is $1,100,000 and the actual sales are $1,000,000, the district sales manager receives a bonus of $48,000; if both the forecast and actual sales are $1,100,000, the sales manager receives a bonus of $55,000; and so forth.

Implications

What are the implications of this incentive system? If you read down a column in Exhibit 9.20, you will see that after making the forecast, the manager receives a larger reward for more sales even if an increase in sales makes the forecast inaccurate. Reading across the rows reveals that the manager receives the highest bonus when the forecast equals actual sales; hence, the manager has an incentive to make accurate forecasts.

This system provides incentives for accurate forecasting and sales output simultaneously. Although our example has dealt with sales forecasts, the method described applies to virtually any type of forecasting (for example, production levels, costs, and productivity). Note that top management can adjust the bonus coefficients, b_1, b_2, and b_3, to suit the needs of the particular situation.

In summary, analysts have developed incentive methods that provide rewards for both accurate forecasts and good performance. Rewards are positively related to forecasted sales to give incentives to forecast high rather than low. Employees receive additional rewards for beating the forecast and penalties for results worse than forecast.

Questions, Exercises, Problems, and Cases

REVIEW QUESTIONS

1. Review the meaning of the concepts or terms listed in Key Terms and Concepts.
2. What is the difference between a cost center and a profit center?
3. What is the difference between a profit center and an investment center?
4. Why is it difficult to assess the effectiveness of discretionary cost centers?

CRITICAL ANALYSIS AND DISCUSSION QUESTIONS

5. Who, among university administrators, is most likely to be responsible for each of the following?
   a. Quantity of supplies used in executive education classes that the business school conducts
   b. Electricity for equipment the university's printing operations use
   c. Charge for classroom maintenance the business school uses
   d. Finance professors' salaries
6. Provide an example of how general economic trends would affect sales forecasting in the airline industry.
7. A superior criticized a sales manager for selling high-revenue, low-profit items instead of lower-revenue but higher-profit items. The sales manager responded, "My income is based on commissions that are a percent of revenues. Why should I care about profits? I care about revenues!" Comment.
8. "The flexible budget is a poor benchmark. You should develop a budget and stay with it." Comment.
9. Why is the sales forecast so important in developing the master budget?
10. When would the master budget profit equal the flexible budget profit?
11. Managers in some companies claim that they do not use flexible budgeting, yet they compute a sales volume variance. How is that different from flexible budgeting?
12. For governmental agencies, a budget places a legal limit on expenditures. As employees are asked for input into the budgeting process, what types of biases are likely to be encountered? Explain why these biases exist.
13. Describe the process you would go through to develop a budget for your college expenses.
14. A company rewards its production department employees for meeting budgeted cost levels by giving out bonuses. If the department's costs exceed the budget, employees do not get a bonus. What problems might arise with such a plan?
15. Refer to the Managerial Application on page 303 about budgeting throughout the world. Why do companies all around the globe use master budgets? Why is it important to find out who within a company participates in the budget process?
16. Several articles and books in the business press have heralded 3M for its product innovation and entrepreneurship. At the same time, good financial planning and tight cost controls are important to 3M. 3M accomplishes its objectives by using financial targets to set goals and measure performance. In particular, the company seeks to derive 25 percent of total sales each year from new products.

    Many groups are involved in budgeting for new products. People from marketing estimate market demand. Research and development, manufacturing, and finance people budget costs and revenues. If new equipment is involved, manufacturing, engineering, and finance work out the cost of that equipment and how fast it will run. Why are people from so many different functions involved in the budgeting process?
17. Refer to the Managerial Application on page 310 about budgeting on the Internet. Explain how using the World Wide Web might make the budgeting process more efficient for a multinational company.

EXERCISES

Solutions to even-numbered exercises are at the end of the chapter.

18. **Solving for materials requirements.** Jamison Company expects to sell 42,000 units of finished goods over the next three-month period. The company currently has 22,000 units of finished goods on hand and wishes to have an inventory of 24,000 units at the end of the three-month period. To produce one unit of finished goods requires four units of raw materials. The company currently has 100,000 units of raw materials on hand and wishes to have an inventory of 110,000 units of raw materials on hand at the end of the three-month period. The company does not have, nor does it wish to have, work-in-process inventory.

    How many units of raw materials must the Jamison Company purchase during the three-month period?

19. **Solving for budgeted manufacturing costs.** Williams Company expects to sell 400,000 cases of paper towels during the current year. Budgeted costs per case are $24 for direct materials, $18 for direct labor, and $6 (all variable) for manufacturing overhead. Williams began the period with 80,000 cases of finished goods on hand and wants to end the period with 20,000 cases of finished goods on hand.

    Compute the budgeted manufacturing costs of the Williams Company for the current period. Assume no beginning or ending inventory of work-in-process.

20. **Solving for cash collections** (Appendix 9.1). Lyndhurst Corporation normally collects cash from credit customers as follows: 50 percent in the month of sale, 30 percent in the first month after sale, 18 percent in the second month after sale, and 2 percent never collected. Lyndhurst Corporation expects its sales, all on credit, to be as follows:

January	$1,000,000
February	1,200,000
March	800,000
April	1,000,000

    a. Calculate the amount of cash Lyndhurst Corporation expects to receive from customers during March.
    b. Calculate the amount of cash Lyndhurst Corporation expects to receive from customers during April.

21. **Solving for cash payments** (Appendix 9.1). Sierra Corporation purchases raw materials on account from various suppliers. It normally pays for 70 percent of these in the month purchased, 20 percent in the first month after purchase, and the remaining 10 percent in the second month after purchase. Raw materials purchases during the last five months of the year follow:

August	$ 700,000
September	900,000
October	1,250,000
November	1,750,000
December	950,000

    Compute the budgeted amount of cash payments to suppliers for the months of October, November, and December.

22. **Sales volume variance analysis.** Myers Company prepared a budget last period that called for sales of 14,000 units at a price of $12 each. Variable costs per unit were budgeted to be $5. Fixed costs were budgeted to be $21,000 for the period. During the period, actual sales totaled 14,200 units.

    Prepare a variance report to show the difference between the master budget and the flexible budget.

	Flexible Budget (14,200 Units)	Sales Volume Variance	Master Budget (14,000 Units)
Sales Revenue	170,400ᵃ	$2,400 F	168,000ᵇ
Less Variable Costs	71,000ᶜ	$1,000 U	70,000ᵈ
Contribution Margin	99,400	$1,400 F	98,000
Less Fixed Costs	21,000	—	21,000
Operating Profit	78,400	$1,400 F	77,000

ᵃ$170,400 = 14,200 Units × $12.
ᵇ$168,000 = 14,000 Units × $12.
ᶜ$71,000 = 14,200 Units × $5.
ᵈ$70,000 = 14,000 Units × $5.

23. **Sales volume variance analysis.** Reid Company prepared a budget last period that called for sales of 60,000 units at a price of $75 each. Variable costs per unit were budgeted to be $10. Fixed costs were budgeted to be $2,000,000 for the period. During the period, actual sales totaled 58,000 units.

    Prepare a variance report to show the difference between the master budget and the flexible budget.

24. **Graphic comparison of budgeted and actual costs.**

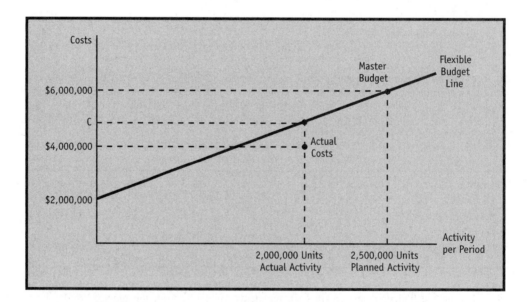

    a. Given the data shown in the graph, what is the budgeted variable cost per unit?
    b. What is the flexible budget cost for an activity level of 2,000,000 units (C on the graph)?
    c. If the actual activity had been 4,000,000 units, what would have been the flexible budget cost amount?

25. **Preparing flexible budgets** (adapted from CPA exam). Exhibit 9.21 provides information (totals) concerning the operations of the Maxum Company for the current period. The firm has no inventories. Prepare a flexible budget for the company.

EXHIBIT 9.21	MAXUM COMPANY		
		Actual	**Master Budget**
Sales Volume		170 Units	200 Units
Sales Revenue		$18,400	$20,000
Manufacturing Cost of Goods Sold:			
Variable		6,880	7,800
Fixed		485	500
Cost of Goods Sold		$ 7,365	$ 8,300
Gross Profit		$11,035	$11,700
Operating Costs:			
Marketing Costs:			
Variable		$ 2,060	$ 2,200
Fixed		1,040	1,000
Administrative Costs, All Fixed		995	1,000
Total Operating Costs		$ 4,095	$ 4,200
Operating Profits		$ 6,940	$ 7,500

26. **Sales volume variance analysis.** Using the data from Exhibit 9.21 and the flexible budget from exercise **25,** prepare a variance report to show the difference between the master budget and the flexible budget.

27. **Interpreting the flexible budget line.** The graph shows a flexible budget line with some missing data. Fill in the missing amounts for **(a)** and **(b)**.

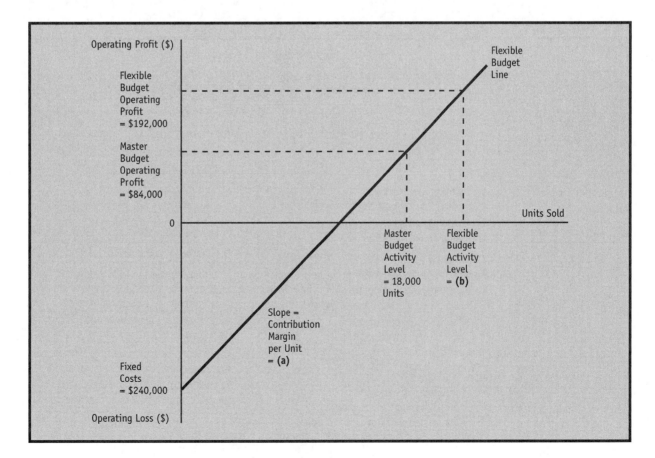

28. **Interpreting the flexible budget line.** Label **(a)** and **(b)** on the graph and give the number of units sold for each.

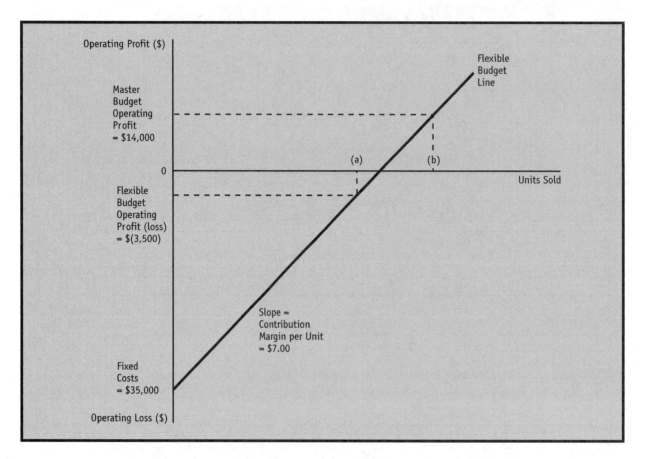

29. **Incentives for accurate forecasting** (Appendix 9.2). Compute the bonus, B, paid to a company's franchise managers using the following formulas:

$$B = b_1\hat{Y} + b_2(Y - \hat{Y}), \quad \text{for } Y \geq \hat{Y}$$

$$B = b_1\hat{Y} - b_3(\hat{Y} - Y), \quad \text{for } \hat{Y} > Y$$

where

$b_1 = 4\%$
$b_2 = 2\%$
$b_3 = 6\%$
$\hat{Y} =$ forecasted sales revenue
$Y =$ actual sales revenue.

Let Y and $\hat{Y}$ each have values of $2,500, $3,000, and $3,500.

30. **Incentives for accurate forecasting** (Appendix 9.2). Compute the monthly bonus, B, paid to an automobile dealership using the following formulas:

$$B = b_1\hat{Y} + b_2(Y - \hat{Y}), \quad \text{for } Y \geq \hat{Y}$$

$$B = b_1\hat{Y} - b_3(\hat{Y} - Y), \quad \text{for } \hat{Y} > Y$$

where

$b_1 = \$100$ per car
$b_2 = \$70$ per car
$b_3 = \$150$ per car
$\hat{Y} =$ forecasted sales of cars (in units)
$Y =$ actual number of cars sold.

31. Flexible budgeting-manufacturing costs. As a result of studying past cost behavior and adjusting for expected price increases in the future, Baker Company estimates that its manufacturing costs will be as follows:

Direct Materials	$8.00 per Unit
Direct Labor	$6.00 per Unit
Manufacturing Overhead:	
Variable	$3.00 per Unit
Fixed	$100,000 per Period

Baker adopts these estimates for planning and control purposes.

a. Baker expects to produce 20,000 units during the next period. Prepare a schedule of the expected manufacturing costs.

b. Suppose that Baker produces only 16,000 units during the next period. Prepare a flexible budget of manufacturing costs for the 16,000-unit level of activity.

c. Suppose that Baker produces 25,000 units during the next period. Prepare a flexible budget of manufacturing costs for the 25,000-unit level of activity.

32. Marketing cost budget. Refer to the marketing cost budget of Victoria's Gourmet Coffee shown in Exhibit 9.5. Prepare a flexible marketing cost budget for the period, assuming the following levels of sales and shipments and a selling price of $6 per unit.

	Case 1	Case 2	Case 3
Units	60,000	75,000	64,000

33. Administrative cost budget. Refer to the administrative budget of Victoria's Gourmet Coffee in Exhibit 9.6. Prepare a flexible administrative cost budget for the period, assuming that production and sales were 80,000 units. Is the term *flexible budget* a misnomer in this case? Explain.

34. Sales volume variance analysis. Budgeted sales and variable costs for Brook Electronics for the year were as follows:

	Total Sales	Total Variable Costs
Product X (5,000 units)	$ 50,000	$ 20,000
Product Y (200 units)	10,000	8,000
Product Z (50,000 units)	125,000	75,000
Total Budgeted	$185,000	$103,000

Actual sales for the period were as follows:

Product X (5,300 units)	$ 55,650
Product Y (240 units)	11,520
Product Z (48,000 units)	96,000
Total Actual Sales	$163,170

Prepare a variance report to show the difference between the master budget and the flexible budget for each of the three products.

35. Estimating flexible selling expense budget and computing sales volume variance. Blakow Products estimates that it will incur the following selling expenses next period:

Salaries (fixed)	$ 20,000
Commissions (0.05 of sales revenue)	17,875
Travel (0.03 of sales revenue)	10,725
Advertising (fixed)	50,000
Sales Office Costs ($4,000 plus $0.05 per unit sold)	7,250
Shipping Costs ($0.10 per unit sold)	6,500
Total Selling Expenses	$112,350

    a. Derive the cost equation for selling expenses. (Hint: $y = a + bx + cy$.)

    b. Assume that Blakow sells 50,000 units during the period. Budgeted sales totaled 65,000 units at a budgeted sales price of $5.50 per unit. Prepare a variance report to show the difference between the master budget and the flexible budget.

PROBLEMS

36. Master budget profit plan. The following information is available for Year 1 for Simba Products:

Revenues (100,000 units)		$725,000
Manufacturing Costs:		
Materials	$ 42,000	
Variable Costs	35,600	
Fixed Costs (excluding depreciation)	81,900	
Depreciation (fixed)	249,750	409,250
Marketing and Administrative Costs:		
Marketing (variable)	$105,600	
Marketing Depreciation	37,400	
Administrative (fixed) (excluding depreciation)	127,300	
Administrative Depreciation	18,700	289,000
Total Costs		698,250
Operating Profits		$ 26,750

All depreciation costs are fixed and are expected to remain the same for Year 2. Sales volume is expected to increase by 18 percent, but prices are expected to fall by 5 percent. Materials costs are expected to decrease by 8 percent. Variable manufacturing costs are expected to decrease by 2 percent per unit. Fixed manufacturing costs, other than depreciation, are expected to increase by 5 percent.

    Variable marketing costs change with volume. Administrative costs are expected to increase by 10 percent.

    Prepare a master budget profit plan for Year 2. Use a format similar to the one shown in Exhibit 9.7.

37. Prepare budgeted financial statements. Products Express has the following data from Year 1 operations, which are to be used for developing Year 2 budget estimates:

Revenues (100,000 units)		$746,000
Manufacturing Costs:		
Materials	$133,000	
Variable Costs	180,900	
Fixed Costs (excluding depreciation)	72,000	
Depreciation (fixed)	89,000	474,900
Marketing and Administrative Costs:		
Marketing (variable)	$95,000	
Marketing Depreciation	22,600	
Administrative (fixed) (excluding depreciation)	90,110	
Administrative Depreciation	8,400	216,110
Total Costs		691,010
Operating Profits		$54,990

All depreciation costs are fixed. Sales volume and prices are expected to increase by 12 percent and 6 percent, respectively. On a per-unit basis, expectations are that materials costs will increase by 10 percent and variable manufacturing costs will decrease by 4 percent. Fixed manufacturing costs are expected to decrease by 7 percent.

Variable marketing costs will change with volume. Administrative cash costs are expected to increase by 8 percent.

Prepare a master budget profit plan for Year 2. Use a format similar to the one shown in Exhibit 9.7.

38. **Production budget.** Floral Products, Inc., manufactures floral containers. The controller is preparing a budget for the coming year and asks for your assistance. The following costs and other data apply to container production:

Direct Materials per Container:

    1 pound Z-A Styrene at $.40 per Pound

    2 pounds Vasa Finish at $.80 per Pound

Direct Labor per Container:

    1/4-hour at $8.60 per Hour

Overhead per Container:

Indirect Labor	$.12
Indirect Materials	.03
Power	.07
Equipment Costs	.36
Building Occupancy	.19
Total Overhead per Unit	$.77

You learn that equipment costs and building occupancy are fixed and are based on a normal production of 20,000 units per year. Other overhead costs are variable. Plant capacity is sufficient to produce 25,000 units per year.

Labor costs per hour are not expected to change during the year. However, the Vasa Finish supplier has informed Floral that it will impose a 10 percent price increase at the start of the coming budget period. No other costs are expected to change.

During the coming budget period, Floral expects to sell 18,000 units. Finished goods inventory is targeted to increase from 4,000 units to 7,000 units to prepare for an expected sales increase the year after next. Production will occur evenly throughout the year. Inventory levels for Vasa Finish and Z-A Styrene are expected to remain unchanged throughout the year. There is no work-in-process inventory.

Prepare a production budget and estimate the materials, labor, and overhead costs for the coming year.

39. **Marketing expense budget.** Stallworth Corporation has just received its marketing expense report for January, which follows.

Item	Amount
Sales Commissions	$135,000
Sales Staff Salaries	32,000
Telephone and Mailing	16,200
Building Lease Payment	20,000
Heat, Light, and Water	4,100
Packaging and Delivery	27,400
Depreciation	12,500
Marketing Consultants	19,700

You have been asked to develop budgeted costs for the coming year. Because this month is typical, you decide to prepare an estimated budget for a typical month in the coming year, and you uncover the following additional data:

- Sales volume is expected to increase by 5 percent.
- Sales prices are expected to increase by 10 percent.
- Commissions are based on a percentage of sales revenue.
- Sales staff salaries will increase 4 percent next year regardless of sales volume.

- Telephone and mailing expenses are scheduled to increase by 8 percent even with no change in sales volume. However, these costs are variable with the number of units sold, as are packaging and delivery costs.
- Building rent is based on a five-year lease that expires in three years.
- Heat, light, and water are scheduled to increase by 12 percent regardless of sales volume.
- Packaging and delivery vary with the number of units sold.
- Depreciation includes furniture and fixtures used by the sales staff. The company has just acquired an additional $1,900 in furniture that will be received at the start of next year and will be depreciated over a 10-year life using the straight-line method.
- Marketing consultant expenses were for a special advertising campaign that runs from time to time. During the coming year, the costs are expected to average $35,000 per month.

Prepare a budget for marketing expenses for a typical month in the coming year.

40. **Budgeted purchases and cash flows** (adapted from CPA exam). Phillips Corporation seeks your assistance in developing cash and other budget information for May, June, and July. At April 30, the company had cash of $5,500, accounts receivable of $437,000, inventories of $309,400, and accounts payable of $133,055. The budget is to be based on the following assumptions:

Sales
- Each month's sales are billed on the last day of the month.
- Customers are allowed a 3 percent discount if payment is made within 10 days after the billing date. Receivables are recorded in the accounts at their gross amounts (not net of discounts).
- The billings are collected as follows: 60 percent within the discount period, 25 percent by the end of the month, and 9 percent by the end of the second month. Six percent are uncollectable.

Purchases
- Of all purchases of merchandise and selling, general, and administrative expenses, 54 percent is paid in the month purchased and the remainder in the following month.
- The number of units in each month's ending inventory equals 130 percent of the next month's units of sales.
- The cost of each unit of inventory is $20.
- Selling, general, and administrative expenses, of which $2,000 is depreciation, equal 15 percent of the current month's sales.

Actual and projected sales follow:

	Dollars	Units
March	$354,000	11,800
April	363,000	12,100
May	357,000	11,900
June	342,000	11,400
July	360,000	12,000
August	366,000	12,200

Choose the best answer for each of the following.

a. Budgeted purchases in dollars for May are
   (1) $357,000.
   (2) $238,000.
   (3) $225,000.
   (4) $244,800.
   (5) None of the above.

b. Budgeted purchases in dollars for June are
   (1) $292,000.
   (2) $243,600.
   (3) $242,000.

(4) $228,000.

(5) None of the above.

c. Budgeted cash collections during May are

(1) $355,656.

(2) $355,116.

(3) $340,410.

(4) $333,876.

(5) None of the above.

d. Budgeted cash disbursements during June are

(1) $285,379.

(2) $287,379.

(3) $292,900.

(4) $294,900.

(5) None of the above.

e. The budgeted number of units of inventory to be purchased during July is

(1) 15,860.

(2) 15,600.

(3) 12,260.

(4) 12,000.

(5) None of the above.

41. **Comprehensive budget plan** (adapted from CPA exam). Fancy Mugs Corporation, a manu-facturer of coffee cups, decided in October Year 1 that it needed cash to continue opera-tions. It began negotiating for a one-month bank loan of $100,000 starting November 1 Year 1. The bank would charge interest at the rate of 1 percent per month and require the com-pany to repay interest and principal on November 30 Year 1. In considering the loan, the bank requested a projected income statement and cash budget for November.

The following information is available:

- The company budgeted sales at 120,000 units per month in October Year 1, December Year 1, and January Year 2, and at 90,000 units in November Year 1. The selling price is $2 per unit.
- The inventory of finished goods on October 1 was 24,000 units. The number of units of finished goods inventory at the end of each month equals 20 percent of unit sales antici-pated for the following month. There is no work in process.
- The inventory of raw materials on October 1 was 22,800 pounds. At the end of each month, the raw materials inventory equals no less than 40 percent of production require-ments for the following month. The company purchases materials as needed in mini-mum quantities of 25,000 pounds per shipment.
- Selling expenses are 10 percent of gross sales. Administrative expenses, which include depreciation of $500 per month on office furniture and fixtures, total $33,000 per month.
- The manufacturing budget for coffee cups, based on normal production of 100,000 units per month, follows:

Materials (1/2 pound per cup, 50,000 pounds, $2.00 per pound)	$ 50,000
Labor	40,000
Variable Overhead	20,000
Fixed Overhead (includes depreciation of $4,000)	10,000
Total	$120,000

a. Prepare schedules computing inventory budgets by months for

(1) Production in units for October, November, and December.

(2) Raw material purchases in pounds for October and November.

b. Prepare a projected income statement for November.

42. **Ethical issues** (adapted from CMA exam). KJ Company manufactures furniture and car-riages for infants. The accounting staff is currently preparing next year's budget. Kyle Lans-ing is new to the firm and is interested in learning how this process occurs. He has lunch with the sales manager and the production manager to discuss further the planning process. Over the course of lunch, Kyle discovers that the sales manager lowers sales projections 5 to 10 percent before submitting her figures, while the production manager increases cost

estimates by 10 percent before submitting his figures. When Kyle asks about why this is done, the response is simply that everyone around here does it.

a. What do the sales and production managers hope to accomplish by their methods?

b. How might this backfire and work against them?

c. Are the actions of the sales and production managers unethical?

CASES

43. Solving for unknowns; cost-volume-profit and budget analysis (adapted from a problem by D. O. Green). A partial income statement of IBN Corporation for Year 0 follows. The company uses just-in-time inventory, so production each year equals sales. Each dollar of finished product produced in Year 0 contained $.50 of direct materials, $0.33333 of direct labor, and $0.16667 of overhead costs. During Year 0, fixed overhead costs were $40,000. No changes in production methods or credit policies are anticipated for Year 1.

IBN CORPORATION
Partial Income Statement for Year 0

Sales (100,000 units at $10)		$1,000,000
Cost of Goods Sold		600,000
Gross Margin		$ 400,000
Selling Costs	$150,000	
Administrative Costs	100,000	250,000
Operating Profits		$ 150,000

Management has estimated the following changes for Year 1:

- 30 percent increase in number of units sold
- 20 percent increase in unit cost of materials
- 15 percent increase in direct labor cost per unit
- 10 percent increase in variable overhead cost per unit
- 5 percent increase in fixed overhead costs
- 8 percent increase in selling costs because of increased volume
- 6 percent increase in administrative costs arising solely because of increased wages

There are no other changes.

a. What must the unit sales price be in Year 1 for IBN Corporation to earn a $200,000 operating profit?

b. What will be the Year 1 operating profit if selling prices are increased as before, but unit sales increase by 10 percent rather than 30 percent? (Selling costs would go up by only one-third of the amount projected previously.)

c. If selling price in Year 1 remains at $10 per unit, how many units must be sold in Year 1 for the operating profit to be $200,000?

44. Budgeting case: River Beverages

Review the River Beverages case starting on page 313.

Required

a. Discuss the budgeting process at River Beverages. Begin with the division manager's initial reports, and end with the board of directors' approval. Discuss the activities in each process and the reasoning for the activity.

b. Should the plants be set up as profit centers or cost centers?

RECOMMENDED ADDITIONAL CASES

Amgen, Inc.: Planning the Unplannable. Harvard Business School Case No. 492052. This case explores difficulties in forecasting in a dynamic biotech company.

Walker and Company: Profit Plan Decisions. Harvard Business School Case No. 197084. This case requires the student to make decisions, develop a profit plan, calculate free cash flow, and develop performance measures.

Hanson Ski Products. Harvard Business School Case No. 187038. This case involves profit planning.

18. Solving for materials requirements.

$$\begin{array}{c} \text{Finished Units} \\ \text{to Be Produced} \end{array} = \begin{array}{c} \text{42,000 Units} \\ \text{to Be Sold} \end{array} + \begin{array}{c} \text{24,000 Units in} \\ \text{Ending Inventory} \end{array} - \begin{array}{c} \text{22,000 Units in} \\ \text{Beginning Inventory} \end{array}$$

$$\begin{array}{c} \text{Units to Be} \\ \text{Produced} \end{array} = 44,000$$

$$\begin{array}{c} \text{Units of Raw} \\ \text{Materials to} \\ \text{Be Produced} \end{array} = \begin{array}{c} \text{4 Units of} \\ \text{Raw Materials} \\ \text{per Finished Unit} \end{array} \times \text{44,000 Finished Units} = 176,000$$

$$\begin{array}{c} \text{Units of Raw Materials} \\ \text{to Be Purchased} \end{array} = \begin{array}{c} \text{176,000 Units} \\ \text{to Be Used} \end{array} + \begin{array}{c} \text{110,000 Units Desired} \\ \text{Ending Inventory} \end{array} - \begin{array}{c} \text{100,000 Units} \\ \text{in Beginning Inventory} \end{array}$$

$$= 186,000.$$

20. Solving for cash collections (Appendix 9.1).

a. Budgeted cash collections in March:

From January Sales (0.18 × $1,000,000)	$180,000
From February Sales (0.30 × $1,200,000)	360,000
From March Sales (0.50 × $800,000)	400,000
Total Budgeted Collections in March	$940,000

b. Budgeted cash collections in April:

From February Sales (0.18 × $1,200,000)	$216,000
From March Sales (0.30 × $800,000)	240,000
From April Sales (0.50 × $1,000,000)	500,000
Total Budgeted Collections in April	$956,000

22. Sales volume variance analysis.

	Flexible Budget (14,200 Units)	Sales Volume Variance	Master Budget (14,000 Units)
Sales Revenue	$170,400[a]	$2,400 F	$168,000[b]
Less Variable Costs	71,000[c]	$1,000 U	70,000[d]
Contribution Margin	$99,400	$1,400 F	$98,000
Less Fixed Costs	21,000	—	21,000
Operating Profit	$ 78,400	$1,400 F	$ 77,000

[a]$170,400 = 14,200 Units × $12.
[b]$168,000 = 14,000 Units × $12.
[c]$71,000 = 14,200 Units × $5.
[d]$70,000 = 14,000 Units × $5.

24. Graphic comparison of budgeted and actual costs.

a. $1.60 per Unit

$$V = (TC - F) \div X$$

$$= (\$6,000,000 - \$2,000,000) \div 2,500,000$$

$$= \$1.60.$$

b. $5,200,000

$$TC = F + VX$$
$$= \$2,000,000 + (\$1.60 \times 2,000,000)$$
$$= \$5,200,000.$$

c. $8,400,000

$$TC = F + VX$$
$$= \$2,000,000 + (\$1.60 \times 4,000,000)$$
$$= \$8,400,000.$$

26. Sales volume variance analysis.

	Flexible Budget (170 Units)	Sales Volume Variance	Master Budget (200 Units)
Sales Revenue	$17,000	$3,000 U	$20,000
Variable Costs:			
Manufacturing	6,630	1,170 F	7,800
Marketing	1,870	330 F	2,200
Contribution Margin	$ 8,500	$1,500 U	$10,000
Fixed Costs:			
Manufacturing	500	—	500
Marketing	1,000	—	1,000
Administrative	1,000	—	1,000
Operating Profit	$ 6,000	$1,500 U	$ 7,500

28. Interpreting the flexible budget line.

a. Flexible Budget Activity Level (actual units sold):

$$\text{Profit} = (P - V)X - F$$
$$\$(3,500) = \$7X - \$35,000$$
$$\$7X = \$(3,500) + \$35,000$$
$$X = \frac{\$(3,500) + \$35,000}{\$7}$$
$$X = 4,500 \text{ Units.}$$

b. Master Budget Activity Level:

$$\$14,000 = \$7X - \$35,000$$
$$\$7X = \$14,000 + \$35,000$$
$$X = \frac{\$14,000 + \$35,000}{\$7}$$
$$X = 7,000 \text{ Units.}$$

30. Incentives for accurate forecasting (Appendix 9.2).

$$B = \begin{cases} \$100\,\hat{Y} + \$70(Y - \hat{Y}), & \text{for } Y \geq \hat{Y}; \\ \$100\,\hat{Y} - \$150(\hat{Y} - Y), & \text{for } \hat{Y} > Y. \end{cases}$$

Forecasted Sales, $\hat{Y}$

		20	21	22	23	24
	20	$2,000[a]	$1,950[f]	$1,900[i]	$1,850	$1,800
Actual	**21**	2,070[b]	2,100[g]	2,050[j]	2,000	1,950
Sales,	**22**	2,140[c]	2,170[h]	2,200	2,150	2,100
Y	**23**	2,210[d]	2,240	2,270	2,300	2,250
	24	2,280[e]	2,310	2,340	2,370	2,400

[a]$2,000 = \$100(20)$
[b]$2,070 = \$2,000 + \$70(21 - 20)$
[c]$2,140 = \$2,000 + \$70(22 - 20)$
[d]$2,210 = \$2,000 + \$70(23 - 20)$
[e]$2,280 = \$2,000 + \$70(24 - 20)$
[f]$1,950 = \$100(21) - \$150(21 - 20)$
[g]$2,100 = \$100(21)$
[h]$2,170 = \$2,100 + \$70(22 - 21)$, etc.
[i]$1,900 = \$100(22) - \$150(22 - 20)$
[j]$2,050 = \$2,200 - \$150(22 - 21)$, etc.

32. Marketing cost budget.

Fixed Costs:

Salaries	$25,000
Advertising	30,000
Sales Office Costs	8,400
Travel	2,000
Total	$65,400

Variable Costs:

Shipping Costs = $0.02 per Unit Sold and Shipped.

Commissions = 2 Percent of Sales, or 0.02 × Units Sold × Selling Price per Unit.

Variable Costs = ($0.02 × Units Shipped) + ($0.02 × $6 Selling Price × Units Sold).

Marketing Cost Flexible Budget:

$65,400 + ($0.02 × Units Shipped) + ($0.12 × Units Sold).

Case 1:

$65,400 + ($0.02 × 60,000) + ($0.12 × 60,000)

= $65,400 + $1,200 + $7,200

= $73,800.

Case 2:

$65,400 + ($0.02 × 75,000) + ($0.12 × 75,000)

= $65,400 + $1,500 + $9,000

= $75,900.

Case 3:

$65,400 + ($0.02 × 64,000) + ($0.12 × 64,000)

= $65,400 + $1,280 + $7,680

= $74,360.

34. Sales volume variance analysis.

Product X: Total sales volume variance is $1,800 favorable, as shown below.

	Flexible Budget (5,300 Units)	Sales Volume Variance	Master Budget (5,000 Units)
Sales	$53,000	$3,000 F	$50,000
Variable Costs	21,200	1,200 U	20,000
Contribution Margin	$31,800	$1,800 F	$30,000

Product Y: Total sales volume variance is $400 favorable, as shown below.

	Flexible Budget (240 Units)	Sales Volume Variance	Master Budget (200 Units)
Sales	$12,000	$2,000 F	$10,000
Variable Costs	9,600	1,600 U	8,000
Contribution Margin	$ 2,400	$ 400 F	$ 2,000

Product Z: Total sales volume variance is $2,000 unfavorable, as shown below.

	Flexible Budget (48,000 Units)	Sales Volume Variance	Master Budget (50,000 Units)
Sales	$120,000	$5,000 U	$125,000
Variable Costs	72,000	3,000 F	75,000
Contribution Margin	$ 48,000	$2,000 U	$ 50,000

chapter 10

Profit and Cost Center Performance Evaluation

Learning Objectives

1. Explain the reasons for conducting variance analyses.

2. Describe how to use the budget for performance evaluation.

3. Identify the different types of variances between actual results and the flexible budget.

4. Assign responsibility for variances.

5. Describe the role of variance analysis in service organizations.

6. Explain the difference between price and efficiency variances.

7. Identify the relation between actual, budgeted, and applied fixed manufacturing costs.

8. Explain why an effective performance measurement system requires employee involvement.

9. Explain how to compute the mix variance (Appendix 10.1).

10

Chapter 9 presented profit planning and budgeting, which includes preparing a master budget based on budgeted sales volume and a flexible budget based on actual sales volume. This chapter presents variance analysis. Variance analysis provides detailed comparisons of the profits achieved with those budgeted. As you encounter variance analysis in practice, remember that each organization calculates variances in a unique way, based on the nature of the organization and the needs of its decision makers. Nevertheless, all organizations follow the basic structure presented in this chapter.

Variance Analysis

This chapter continues the Victoria's Gourmet Coffee example discussed in Chapter 9. Recall that we showed the master budget, the flexible budget, and the resulting sales volume variance in Exhibit 9.8. Here we present the actual financial performance of Victoria's Gourmet Coffee for period 1.

Actual Results

Period 1 *actual* results for Victoria's Gourmet Coffee follow:

Sales Price per Unit	$6.10
Sales Volume for the Period	80,000 Units
Variable Manufacturing Costs per Unit	$3.82
Variable Marketing Costs per Unit	$0.16
Fixed Manufacturing Costs for the Period	$34,000
Fixed Marketing Costs for the Period	$64,400
Fixed Administrative Costs for the Period	$44,600

Exhibit 10.1, which is a profit variance report, compares the above actual results with the master and flexible budget. For your convenience in following the discussion, we carry Columns (5), (6), and (7) in Exhibit 10.1 forward from Exhibit 9.8 in Chapter 9. We calculate Column (1) in Exhibit 10.1 from the facts presented in the preceding display of data. Now, we compute variances from the budget based on the actual results presented above and the budgeted amounts presented in Chapter 9. These variances appear in Columns (2), (3), and (4) of Exhibit 10.1.

Overview of the Profit Variance

Exhibit 10.1 shows that the source of the total variance from the profit plan is $15,700 favorable. The **profit variance analysis** shows the causes of the total profit variance (that is, the $15,700 difference between the profit budgeted in the master budget and the profit earned for the period). Column (2) in Exhibit 10.1 summarizes purchasing and production variances. Columns (3) and (4) show marketing and administrative variances.

EXHIBIT 10.1

VICTORIA'S GOURMET COFFEE
Profit Variance Analysis: A Comparison of Actual Results with the Profit Plan

	Actual (based on actual sales volume of 80,000 units) (1)	Purchasing and Production Variances (2)	Marketing and Administrative Cost Variances (3)	Sales Price Variance (4)	Flexible Budget (based on actual sales volume of 80,000 units)[f] (5)	Sales Volume Variance[f] (6)	Master Budget (based on a plan of 70,000 units sold)[f] (7)
Sales	$488,000[a]	—	—	$8,000 F	$480,000	$60,000 F	$420,000
Less:							
Variable Manufacturing Costs	305,600[b]	$12,000 U	—	—	293,600	36,700 U	256,900
Variable Marketing Costs	12,800[c]	—	$1,440 U[d]	160 U[e]	11,200	1,400 U	9,800
Contribution Margin	$169,600	$12,000 U	$1,440 U	$7,840 F	$175,200	$21,900 F	$153,300
Less:							
Fixed Manufacturing Costs	34,000	1,800 U	—	—	32,200	—	32,200
Fixed Marketing Costs	64,400	—	1,000 F	—	65,400	—	65,400
Fixed Administrative Costs	44,600	—	200 F	—	44,800	—	44,800
Operating Profits	$ 26,600	$13,800 U	$ 240 U	$7,840 F	$ 32,800	$21,900 F	$ 10,900

Total Profit Variance from Flexible Budget = $6,200 U

Total Profit Variance from Master Budget = $15,700 F

[a] 80,000 units sold at $6.10 per unit.
[b] 80,000 units sold at $3.82 per unit.
[c] 80,000 units sold at $/16 per unit.

[d] $1,440 U = ($12,800 − $11,200) − $160.
[e] $160 U = 0.02 × $8,000 F Sales Price Variance.
[f] Amounts are from Exhibit 9.8.

U denotes unfavorable variance.
F denotes favorable variance.

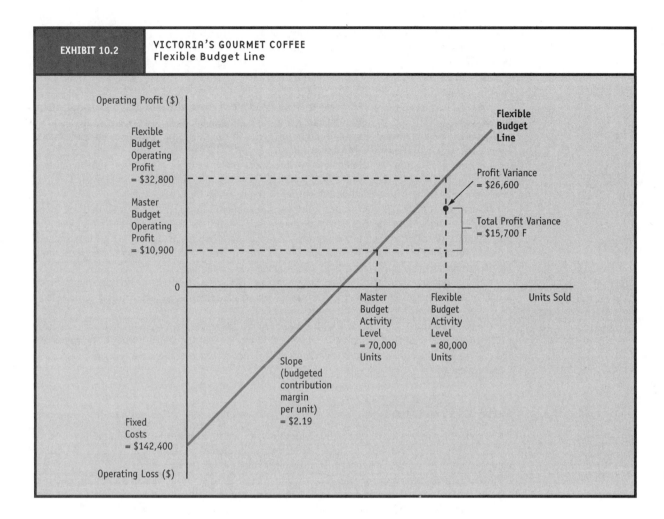

EXHIBIT 10.2	VICTORIA'S GOURMET COFFEE
	Flexible Budget Line

Flexible Budget Line   Exhibit 10.2 summarizes these results graphically. Note that the flexible budget line shows expected profits for various activity levels for a given level of fixed costs. Any change in fixed costs would *shift* the flexible budget line up or down.

Responsibility for Marketing and Administrative Variances

This section describes variance calculations for each major group responsible for variances in organizations: marketing, administration, purchasing, and production. We calculate each responsibility center's variances, *holding all other things constant.* Hence, we separate marketing variances from production, production variances from purchasing, and so forth. After accountants compute variances, managers investigate the causes of these variances and take corrective action if needed.

Marketing

Top management usually assigns responsibility for sales volume, sales price, and marketing cost variances to marketing managers.

The $21,900 favorable sales volume variance measures the favorable impact on profits of higher-than-expected sales volume, as the exhibit shows. However, the sales volume variance may be a function of factors outside the marketing department's influence, such as unexpected or unpredictable changes in the market. The sales volume variance is a contribution margin variance,

The company incurred the following actual costs in April:

Actual Manufacturing Costs:	
Variable Costs per Unit	$4.88
Fixed Overhead	$83,000
Actual Marketing and Administrative Costs:	
Variable (50,000 units at $1.04)	$52,000
Fixed	$96,000

Prepare a profit variance report for management like the one in Exhibit 10.1. (Note that this self-study problem is a continuation of Problem 9.1 for Self-Study in Chapter 9.)

The solution to this self-study problem is at the end of the chapter on page 366.

Cost Variance Analysis

Although the focus of this chapter is on a manufacturing company, the same concepts can be applied to nonmanufacturing organizations. Service organizations can use labor and overhead variances to assess efficiency and control costs. Financial institutions can use labor variances to assess transaction and check-processing efficiency. Fast-food restaurants use labor variances to assess efficiency in preparing and serving food.

Production Cost Variance Analysis

This section describes variance calculations for the major groups responsible for purchasing and production variances in organizations. We calculate each responsibility center's variances, *holding all other things constant.* After accountants compute variances, managers investigate the causes of these variances and take corrective action if needed.

Exhibit 10.3 presents the data for direct materials, direct labor, and manufacturing overhead, and gives the following variances for each: direct materials ($5,050 unfavorable), direct labor ($7,050 unfavorable), variable manufacturing overhead ($100 favorable), and fixed manufacturing overhead ($1,800 unfavorable). Managers want to identify the *cause* of production problems. This information helps managers to do that.

We prepare the flexible budget for each variable manufacturing cost by multiplying the *standard quantity of input allowed to produce the actual output* (called the standard quantity) by the standard price. If each unit of output produced has a standard of 1/8 hour of direct labor time, and if 80,000 units of output are *actually produced,* then the standard quantity of direct labor allowed is 10,000 hours (= 1/8 hour × 80,000 units).

The standard quantity (10,000 hours) times the standard wage rate per hour ($20) results in the flexible budget for direct labor of $200,000. The difference between the flexible budget and actual results is the variance (favorable if the actual costs are lower than the flexible budget, and unfavorable if the actual costs are higher than the flexible budget). See Exhibit 10.3 for the direct materials, direct labor, and variable manufacturing overhead variance calculations for Victoria's Gourmet Coffee.

EXHIBIT 10.3	VICTORIA'S GOURMET COFFEE Manufacturing Variances Flexible Budget		

	Actual	Flexible Budget (standard allowed based on actual production output of 80,000 units)	Variance
Variable Costs:			
Direct Materials	162,000 Pounds at $0.525 = $85,050	160,000 Pounds at $0.50 = $80,000	$ 5,050 U
Direct Labor	10,955 Hours at $18.90 = $207,050 (rounded to nearest dollar)	10,000 Hours (= 80,000 units × 1/8 hour) at $20 = $200,000	7,050 U
Variable Manufacturing Overhead	$ 13,500	80,000 Units at $0.17 = $ 13,600	100 F
Total Variable Manufacturing Costs	$305,600	$293,600	$12,000 U

	Actual	Budget	Variance
Fixed Costs:			
Fixed Manufacturing Overhead	$ 34,000	$ 32,200	$ 1,800 U

Reasons for Materials, Labor, and Variable Manufacturing Overhead Variances

Variance reports include explanations for the variances. These explanations help managers to ascertain whether they should investigate variances and take corrective action, whether they should reward people responsible for variances, or whether they should take other managerial action.

Variances can occur for many reasons:

1. **A variance is simply the difference between a predetermined norm or standard and the actual results.** Some difference should be expected simply because one measure is expected and the other is actual. For example, if you and several of your friends were each to flip a coin ten times, not all of you would come up with five heads, even though five heads (= 50 percent of ten coin flips) might be the expected value. In short, some variances will occur even when standards are unbiased expected values.

2. **The standards themselves may be biased.** Sometimes managers set standards intentionally loose or tight. Sometimes they are unintentionally biased, such as when the firm accidentally omits expected labor wage increases or an allowance for waste on direct material usage. The Managerial Application "An Antidote to Biased Standards: How Workers Develop Their Own Standards at NUMMI" demonstrates how a particular plant's management dealt with biased standards.

3. **Systematic reasons,** as discussed in the rest of this chapter.

An Antidote to Biased Standards: How Workers Develop Their Own Standards at NUMMI

The Toyota-General Motors joint venture in Fremont, California, known as New United Motor Manufacturing, Inc. (NUMMI; http://www.nummi.com), has succeeded in allowing employees to set their own work standards. The NUMMI plant was once a General Motors plant notorious for poor quality, low productivity, and morale problems. But workers who were ashamed of their products now leave notes on cars saying, "I helped build this one." The NUMMI plant has won numerous J. D. Powers and Associates plant quality awards.

At the old GM Fremont plant, industrial engineers who had little, if any, work experience in making cars would shut themselves in a room and ponder how to set standards. The industrial engineers ignored the workers, who in turn ignored the standards.

At NUMMI, workers themselves have set the standards. Worker team members have timed one another, looking for the most efficient and safest way to do the work. The workers are more informed about how to do the work right than industrial engineers. They are more motivated to meet the standards they set, instead of those set by industrial engineers working in an ivory tower.

Involving the workers has had benefits in addition to improved motivation and standards. These include improved safety, higher quality, easier job rotation because of easier tasks, and more flexibility because workers are both assembly-line workers and industrial engineers. For example, if orders for the product change, NUMMI can change the speed of the assembly line to respond. At the old GM Fremont plant, the assembly line ran at one speed, and responses to changes in orders came either from inventory or from adding or dropping entire shifts.

Source: Authors' research at the NUMMI Web site and literature review.

Separating Variances into Price and Efficiency Components

To this point, we have described the variable manufacturing cost variances (materials, direct labor, and variable overhead) as the difference between actual costs and the flexible budget. However, many managers wish to see variable manufacturing cost variances split into *price* and *efficiency* components. The price component is the difference between the budgeted (or standard) price and the actual price paid for each unit of input. The efficiency variance measures the efficiency with which the firm uses inputs to produce outputs.

A **price variance** measures the difference between the price set as the norm—that is, the standard or budgeted price—and the actual price.

An **efficiency variance** measures the difference between the actual quantity of inputs used and those allowed at standard to make a unit of output. Victoria's Gourmet Coffee allows 2 pounds of direct material for each unit produced. If it used 162,000 pounds to produce 80,000 units, an unfavorable efficiency variance of 2,000 pounds in quantity, or $1,000 (= 2,000 pounds × $0.50 standard price per pound), would result.

Problem 10.2 for Self-Study

Price and efficiency variances. Define price and efficiency variances. How might the manager of a coffeehouse use materials price and efficiency variances?

The solution to this self-study problem is at the end of the chapter on page 367.

Variable Cost Variance Model

A general model for variance calculations appears in Exhibit 10.4. We have divided direct materials and direct labor variances into price and efficiency components. The terms *price* and *efficiency* variances are general categories. Although terminology varies from company to company, the following specific variance titles are frequently used:

Input	Price Variance Category	Efficiency Variance Category
Direct Materials	Price (or Purchase Price) Variance	Usage or Quantity Variance
Direct Labor	Rate Variance	Efficiency Variance
Variable Overhead	Spending Variance	Efficiency Variance

We shall avoid unnecessary labeling by simply referring to these variances as either *price* or *efficiency* variances. Looking at Exhibit 10.4, what would the price variance be if the actual price was \$5.50, the standard price was \$5.10, and the actual quantity was 50,000? (Answer: \$20,000 = (\$5.50 – \$5.10) × 50,000.)

We apply the cost variance model to the calculation of direct materials and direct labor variances for Victoria's Gourmet Coffee in Exhibit 10.5.

Interpret the computations in Column (3) of Exhibit 10.5 carefully. Note that the term *SQ* refers to the *standard quantity of input allowed to produce the actual output*. SQ is not the *expected* production volume. If each unit of output produced has a standard of 1/8 hour of direct labor time, and if 80,000 units of output are *actually produced*, then SQ = 10,000 hours (= 1/8 hour × 80,000 units). Note that Column (3) is the flexible *production* budget.

Column (3) shows the *standard cost allowed to produce the actual output*, whereas Column (1) shows the *actual costs incurred to produce the actual output*. The differences between Columns (1) and (3) are the variable manufacturing cost variances, which you can further separate into price and efficiency variances.

This overview of manufacturing variances provides the essential calculations for management use of variances. Most companies carry out this analysis in much greater detail, reporting variances for each type of material, for each category of labor, and for major cost components of variable overhead (for example, power to run machines, indirect materials and supplies, and indirect labor).

Reasons for Materials Price and Efficiency Variances

Materials price variances, which measure the difference between the actual and standard price of materials, occur for numerous reasons. They may result from failure to take purchase discounts, from using a better (or worse) grade of raw material than expected so that the price paid was higher (or lower) than expected, or from changes in the market supply or demand for the raw material that affected prices.

A number of factors cause **materials efficiency variances.** When management, industrial engineers, and others set standards for the amount of direct materials that a unit of output should

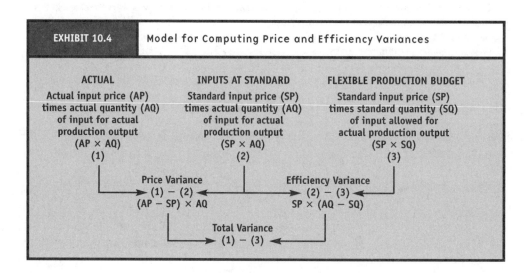

EXHIBIT 10.4	Model for Computing Price and Efficiency Variances

ACTUAL	INPUTS AT STANDARD	FLEXIBLE PRODUCTION BUDGET
Actual input price (AP) times actual quantity (AQ) of input for actual production output (AP × AQ) (1)	Standard input price (SP) times actual quantity (AQ) of input for actual production output (SP × AQ) (2)	Standard input price (SP) times standard quantity (SQ) of input allowed for actual production output (SP × SQ) (3)

Price Variance
(1) − (2)
(AP − SP) × AQ

Efficiency Variance
(2) − (3)
SP × (AQ − SQ)

Total Variance
(1) − (3)

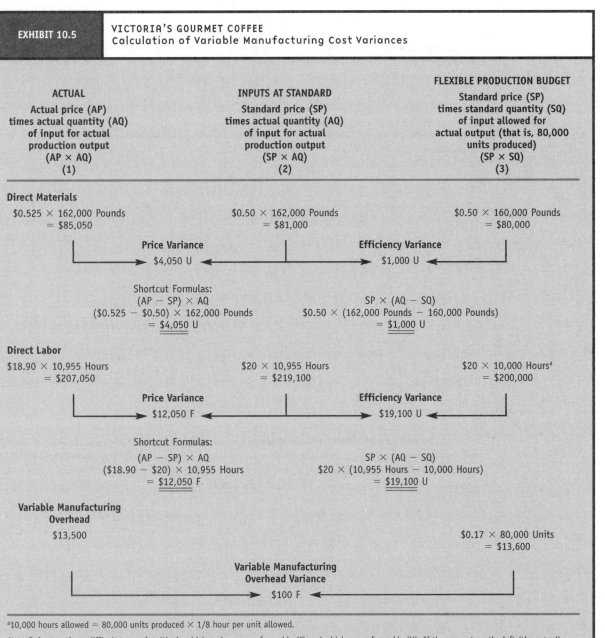

EXHIBIT 10.5

VICTORIA'S GOURMET COFFEE
Calculation of Variable Manufacturing Cost Variances

ACTUAL	INPUTS AT STANDARD	FLEXIBLE PRODUCTION BUDGET
Actual price (AP) times actual quantity (AQ) of input for actual production output (AP × AQ) (1)	Standard price (SP) times actual quantity (AQ) of input for actual production output (SP × AQ) (2)	Standard price (SP) times standard quantity (SQ) of input allowed for actual output (that is, 80,000 units produced) (SP × SQ) (3)

Direct Materials

$0.525 × 162,000 Pounds = $85,050	$0.50 × 162,000 Pounds = $81,000	$0.50 × 160,000 Pounds = $80,000

Price Variance
→ $4,050 U ◄

Efficiency Variance
→ $1,000 U ◄

Shortcut Formulas:
(AP − SP) × AQ
($0.525 − $0.50) × 162,000 Pounds
= $4,050 U

SP × (AQ − SQ)
$0.50 × (162,000 Pounds − 160,000 Pounds)
= $1,000 U

Direct Labor

$18.90 × 10,955 Hours = $207,050	$20 × 10,955 Hours = $219,100	$20 × 10,000 Hours[a] = $200,000

Price Variance
→ $12,050 F ◄

Efficiency Variance
→ $19,100 U ◄

Shortcut Formulas:
(AP − SP) × AQ
($18.90 − $20) × 10,955 Hours
= $12,050 F

SP × (AQ − SQ)
$20 × (10,955 Hours − 10,000 Hours)
= $19,100 U

Variable Manufacturing Overhead

$13,500

$0.17 × 80,000 Units
= $13,600

Variable Manufacturing Overhead Variance
→ $100 F ◄

[a]10,000 hours allowed = 80,000 units produced × 1/8 hour per unit allowed.

Note: It is sometimes difficult to see intuitively which variances are favorable (F) and which are unfavorable (U). If the amount on the left (the actual) exceeds the amount on the right (the budget or standard), the variance is *unfavorable* because higher costs than budgeted mean lower profits than budgeted. The reverse is true for favorable cost variances: The amounts on the left (actuals) are lower than those on the right. We set up all the cost variance calculations in this book consistently, with actual costs on the left, standard or budget on the right.

use, they usually allow for material defects, inexperienced workers who ruin materials, improperly used materials, and so forth. If the firm uses materials more efficiently than these standards, favorable efficiency variances result; usage worse than these standards results in unfavorable variances.

Sometimes purchasing, not production, causes a materials efficiency variance. In an effort to reduce prices (and create a favorable price variance), the purchasing department may have bought inferior materials, or it may have ordered the wrong materials.

Reasons for Labor Price and Efficiency Variances   Direct labor price (or wage) variances can occur because managers do not correctly anticipate changes in wage rates. Wage

rates established by a union contract may differ from the forecasted amount, for example. Also, a wage rate change may occur, but the firm will not have adjusted standards to reflect it.

The **direct labor efficiency variance** measures labor productivity. Managers watch this variance because they can usually control it. Many of the things that create variances affect all competitors about the same. Labor wage rates going up dramatically because of a union contract settlement usually affects all companies in an industry, so little competitive advantage or disadvantage results. Labor efficiency is unique to a firm, however, and can lead to competitive advantages or disadvantages.

Labor efficiency variances have many causes. The workers themselves may be poorly motivated or poorly trained and so less productive, whereas highly motivated and well-trained workers can generate favorable efficiency variances. Other causes include poor materials, faulty equipment, poor supervision, and scheduling problems.

Note that the labor price variance in the Victoria's Gourmet Coffee example was favorable, whereas the labor efficiency variance was unfavorable. A manager would probably ask first: "Did we use workers who were paid less and not as efficient as expected?" Although firms go to great lengths to break down variances into small components that they can easily understand and trace to particular responsibility centers, managers should not overlook the fact that variances are usually interrelated.

Variable Overhead Price and Efficiency Variances

Separating variable overhead variances into price and efficiency components helps managers in their efforts to control overhead costs. For example, energy costs in many firms are both sufficiently large and controllable to warrant special attention.

The manager can use the same method to compute price and efficiency variances for variable overhead as for other variable manufacturing costs. The computation requires a measure of overhead input activity, however, not yet presented in the Victoria's Gourmet Coffee example. Suppose the variable overhead at Victoria's Gourmet Coffee consisted of machines' operating costs, such as power and maintenance. The longer the machines run, the more variable overhead cost is incurred. A **variable overhead price variance** results when the cost per machine hour is either more or less than the standard cost allowed per machine hour. A **variable overhead efficiency variance** results if the machine hours required to make the actual production output exceed the standard machine hours allowed to make that output. For example, suppose the firm makes a large batch of units that consumed several hundred machine hours. Subsequently, the firm found these units to be defective and destroyed them; thus the accounting system did not count them as part of the actual production output. (Managers implicitly assume only good units are counted as part of the actual production output.)

Assume the standard for machine usage was 40 units per machine hour at a standard cost allowed of $6.80 per hour. (This is equivalent to $0.17 per unit of output, because $6.80/40 = $0.17.) Also assume the actual production output of 80,000 units required 2,100 machine hours, so the efficiency variance was $680 U, as Exhibit 10.6 shows. The actual costs for variable overhead totaled only $13,500, so the price variance was $780 F.

The manager should interpret variable overhead price and efficiency variances with care. The accountant sometimes selects the input activity base (machine hours in our example) without regard to the cause of variable overhead costs. For example, if a company uses direct labor hours to apply variable overhead, an unfavorable efficiency variance results when the company inefficiently uses direct labor hours. That variance means nothing if none of the variable overhead costs is associated with direct labor costs. This particular problem occurs in capital-intensive companies in which variable overhead mostly relates to machine usage.

In general, managers are wise to establish a detailed breakdown of variable overhead into cost categories that relate logically to the input activity base, as is done with activity-based costing. For example, the following variable overhead costs could be applied on the following input activity bases:

Cost	Activity Base
Indirect Labor	Direct Labor Hours
Power to Run Machines	Machine Hours
Materials Inventory Carrying Costs	Materials Inventory

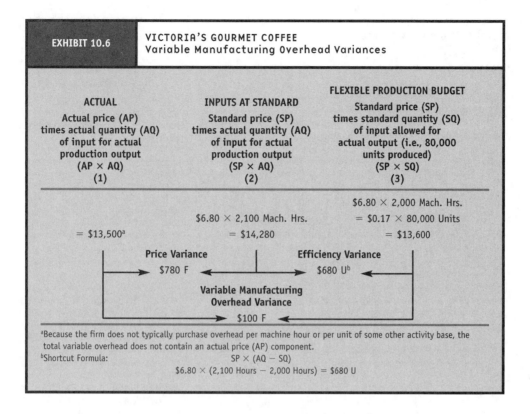

Overview of Price and Efficiency Variances

Exhibit 10.7 presents an overview of variances. The top panel reproduces Columns (1) through (5) of the profit variance analysis discussed earlier in the chapter, and the bottom panel illustrates the breakdown of the variable manufacturing costs into direct materials, direct labor, and variable manufacturing overhead. However, the bottom panel provides further detail by breaking down the direct materials, direct labor, and variable overhead variances into more detailed price and efficiency variances. We are now able to identify how much of the overall variances are caused by factors related to price, and how much are caused by factors related to efficiency.

Problem 10.3 for Self-Study

Computing variable cost variances. (This problem continues the previous problems for self-study.) During the past month, the following events took place at Computer Supply, Inc.:

1. Produced and sold 50,000 laptop computer cases at a sales price of $10 each. (Budgeted sales were 40,000 units at $11.)
2. Standard variable costs per unit (that is, per case) were as follows:

Direct Materials: 2 Pounds at $1 per Pound	$2.00
Direct Labor: 0.10 Hour at $15 per Hour	1.50
Variable Manufacturing Overhead: 0.10 Labor Hour at $5 per Hour	0.50
Total	$4.00 per Case

(continued on page 355)

EXHIBIT 10.7	VICTORIA'S GOURMET COFFEE Overview of Variance Analysis

Profit Variance Analysis

	Actual (based on actual sales volume of 80,000 units) (1)	Purchasing and Production Variances (2)	Marketing and Administrative Cost Variances (3)	Sales Price Variance (4)	Flexible Budget (based on actual sales volume of 80,000 units) (5)
Sales	$488,000	—	—	$8,000 F	$480,000
Less:					
Variable Manufacturing Costs	305,600	$12,000 U	—	—	293,600
Variable Marketing Costs	12,800	—	$1,440 U	160 U	11,200
Contribution Margin	$169,600	$12,000 U	$1,440 U	$7,840 F	$175,200
Less:					
Fixed Manufacturing Costs	34,000	1,800 U	—	—	32,200
Fixed Marketing Costs	64,400	—	1,000 F	—	65,400
Fixed Administrative Costs	44,600	—	200 F	—	44,800
Operating Profits	$ 26,600	$13,800 U	$ 240 U	$7,840 F	$ 32,800

Total Profit Variance from
Flexible Budget = $6,200 U

Cost Variance Analysis

ACTUAL Actual price (AP) times actual quantity (AQ) of input for actual production output (AP × AQ) (1)	INPUTS AT STANDARD Standard price (SP) times actual quantity (AQ) of input for actual production output (SP × AQ) (2)	FLEXIBLE PRODUCTION BUDGET Standard price (SP) times standard quantity (SQ) of input allowed for actual output (that is, 80,000 units produced) (SP × SQ) (3)

Direct Materials

$0.525 × 162,000 Pounds = $85,050	$0.50 × 162,000 Pounds = $81,000	$0.50 × 160,000 Pounds = $80,000

Price Variance
$4,050 U ◄

Efficiency Variance
$1,000 U ◄

Direct Labor

$18.90 × 10,955 Hours = $207,050	$20 × 10,955 Hours = $219,100	$20 × 10,000 Hours = $200,000

Price Variance
$12,050 F ◄

Efficiency Variance
$19,100 U ◄

Variable Manufacturing Overhead

$13,500	$6.80 × 2,100 Mach. Hours = $14,280	$6.80 × 2,000 Mach. Hours = $13,600

Price Variance
$780 F ◄

Efficiency Variance
$680 U ◄

Totals $305,600	$8,780 F	$20,780 U	$293,600
Total Variances		$12,000 U ◄	

3. Actual production costs were as follows:

Direct Materials Purchased and Used: 110,000 Pounds at $1.20	$132,000
Direct Labor: 6,000 Hours at $14	84,000
Variable Overhead	28,000

Compute variable manufacturing cost variances in as much detail as possible.

The solution to this self-study problem is at the end of the chapter on page 367.

Variable Overhead in Service Organizations

Variable overhead is often significant for service industry firms, governmental agencies, and nonprofit groups. These types of organizations set standards and perform variance analyses for planning and performance evaluation purposes. For example, a county building department might have a standard for the number of days required to process an application for a building permit. Financial institutions might have a standard for the number of days required to process a loan application. United Parcel Service (UPS) has standards for several delivery tasks. One example is a standard of 3 feet per second established as the pace at which drivers should walk to a customer's door. Companies use these standards to establish the flexible budget, which is ultimately compared with actual results in performing variance analysis.

Example   American Parcel Delivery is a parcel service that competes with the U.S. Postal Service and United Parcel Service. Each driver is responsible for picking up and delivering parcels in a particular geographic area. One major cost is fuel for the pick-up and delivery vans. The firm uses a fuel efficiency variance to evaluate the performance of drivers. The firm calculates a standard amount of fuel consumption per parcel, whether delivered or picked up, for each territory. These allowances take the population density of the territory into account—allowing more fuel per parcel for sparsely populated territories, less for densely populated territories. Drivers control this variance primarily by scheduling trips to avoid unnecessary driving.

For a particular territory, the standard was 0.08 gallon of fuel per parcel. The driver assigned to this territory handled 1,100 parcels during March; hence, the budget allows 88 gallons (= 1,100 parcels × 0.08 gallon per parcel). The driver actually used 93 gallons in March. We show the variance calculations below. Note the similarity of these calculations to those presented for direct labor costs in Exhibits 10.5 through 10.7. American Parcel attributes part of this variance to the lower cost per gallon for fuel (not the responsibility of the driver) and part to the additional usage of fuel (the responsibility of the driver).

AMERICAN PARCEL DELIVERY
Example, Variable Overhead Variance—Fuel Costs

Facts

Actual:

Output	1,100 Parcels Picked Up or Delivered
Fuel Required	93 Gallons
Cost per Gallon	$1.58 per Gallon

Standard:

Fuel Allowed	0.08 Gallon per Parcel Picked Up or Delivered
Cost per Gallon	$1.60 per Gallon

Actual	Variance	Flexible Budget
		$1.60 per Gallon × (0.08 Gallon × 1,100 Parcels)
$1.58 per Gallon × 93 Gallons		= $1.60 × 88 Gallons
= $146.94	$6.14 U	= $140.80

Fixed Manufacturing Cost Variances

Fixed costs are often treated as period costs in comparing budgeted and actual costs. This practice is appropriate for controlling fixed cost expenditures for managerial purposes. Manufacturing companies, however, use *full absorption costing* to value inventory. Full absorption costing unitizes fixed manufacturing costs and adds these unit fixed costs to unit variable manufacturing costs to compute the cost of a unit of inventory produced.

Companies frequently use a predetermined overhead rate to apply fixed overhead to units produced. For example, assume the following facts for Victoria's Gourmet Coffee:

Estimated (budgeted) Fixed Manufacturing Costs	$32,200
Estimated Production Volume	70,000 Units
Actual Production Volume	80,000 Units
Actual Fixed Manufacturing Costs	$34,000

If Victoria's Gourmet Coffee used full-absorption, standard costing, it would apply its fixed manufacturing costs to units as follows:

$$\text{Applied Fixed Manufacturing Cost per Unit} = \frac{\text{Estimated Fixed Manufacturing Cost per Period}}{\text{Estimated Production Volume per Period}}$$

$$= \frac{\$32,200}{70,000} \text{ Units Planned}$$

$$= \$0.46 \text{ per Unit}$$

Note that we use production, not sales, volumes to unitize fixed manufacturing costs. If you were to unitize fixed marketing costs, you would divide the estimated cost by estimated sales volume.

During the period, the firm produced 80,000 units, so 80,000 units times $0.46 per unit equals $36,800 applied to Work-in-Process Inventory. The amount "applied" is the amount of fixed manufacturing overhead debited to Work-in-Process Inventory. The firm could apply fixed manufacturing costs using an input basis such as machine hours. Assume the standard is 40 units per machine hour, or 1/40 hour per unit. Then you would compute the rate per hour as follows:

$$\text{Fixed Manufacturing Cost Rate per Hour} = \frac{\$32,000}{70,000 \text{ Units} \times 1/40}$$

$$= \frac{\$32,200}{1,750 \text{ Hours}}$$

$$= \$18.40 \text{ per Hour}$$

The amount applied would still be $36,800 (= $18.40 per Hour × 1/40 Hour per Unit × 80,000 Units = $18.40 per Hour × 2,000 Hours).

Production Volume Variance

The **production volume variance** is the difference between the budgeted and applied fixed costs. For Victoria's Gourmet Coffee, the production volume variance is:

$$\text{Production Volume Variance} = \frac{\text{Budgeted Fixed}}{\text{Manufacturing Costs}} - \frac{\text{Applied Fixed}}{\text{Manufacturing Costs}}$$

$$\$4,600 \text{ F} = \$32,200 - \$36,800$$

This variance is favorable, as indicated by the F.

If management had accurately estimated the production volume to be 80,000 units, the estimated unit cost would have been

$$\frac{\$32,200}{80,000 \text{ Units}} = \$0.4025 \text{ per Unit.}$$

Applied fixed manufacturing overhead would have been $32,200 (= $0.4025 per unit × 80,000 units actually produced), which equals the budget amount. Thus, if management correctly estimated the production volume, no production volume variance would occur.

The production volume variance applies only to fixed costs, and it emerges if companies allocate a fixed period cost to products on a predetermined basis. The production volume vari-

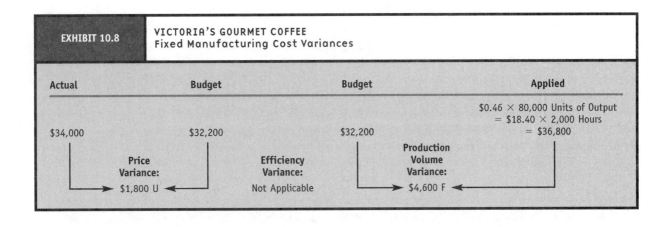

Actual		Budget		Budget		Applied

EXHIBIT 10.8 — **VICTORIA'S GOURMET COFFEE** / Fixed Manufacturing Cost Variances

$0.46 × 80,000 Units of Output
= $18.40 × 2,000 Hours
= $36,800

$34,000 $32,200 $32,200

Price Variance: $1,800 U

Efficiency Variance: Not Applicable

Production Volume Variance: $4,600 F

ance appears to have little or no benefit for managerial purposes. Some accountants argue that this variance signals a difference between expected and actual production levels, but so does a simple production report comparing actual and planned production volumes.

The production volume variance comes from the use of predetermined fixed-cost rates in full-absorption costing, unlike other cost variances that accountants compute to help managers. Manufacturing firms use predetermined rates and full-absorption costing for external reporting, so you will probably encounter production volume variances sometime during your career. Do not assume the production volume variance is useful simply because companies compute it, however.

Price (Spending) Variance   Recall from the chapter that the **price variance** (sometimes called the **spending variance**) **for fixed manufacturing costs** is the difference between the actual costs and the budgeted costs. Compute the fixed manufacturing price variance for Victoria's Gourmet Coffee as follows:

$$\text{Price Variance} = \frac{\text{Actual Fixed}}{\text{Manufacturing Costs}} - \frac{\text{Budgeted Fixed}}{\text{Manufacturing Costs}}$$

$1,800 U = $34,000 − $32,200.

Although we use manufacturing costs for this example, you can compute the price variance this way for any fixed cost.

The fixed manufacturing cost variance used for management and control of fixed manufacturing costs is the price variance, whereas the fixed-manufacturing-cost production volume variance occurs only when we compute inventory values using full-absorption costing and predetermined overhead rates.

Relation of Actual, Budgeted, and Applied Fixed Manufacturing Costs   We summarize the fixed manufacturing cost variances and the relation among actual, budget, and applied fixed manufacturing costs in Exhibit 10.8. Note the price variance is unfavorable because the actual exceeds the budget, but the production volume variance is favorable because the budget is less than the applied. Note that the master and flexible budgets for fixed costs do not differ here because we assume fixed costs do not vary with volume. If fixed costs differed in the flexible budget from the master budget, we would use the flexible budget fixed costs to compute these variances because we use the flexible budget for performance evaluation and control purposes.

Problem 10.4 for Self-Study

Fixed cost variances. During the past month, the following events took place at Computer Supply, Inc.

1. The company produced 50,000 computer cases. Actual fixed manufacturing cost was $83,000.

2. Budgeted fixed manufacturing cost was $80,000. Budgeted direct labor hours worked were 4,000 hours for budgeted production of 40,000 cases. Full-absorption costing, if used, applies fixed manufacturing costs to units produced on the basis of direct labor hours. Five thousand standard labor hours were allowed to make 50,000 computer cases.

Compute the fixed manufacturing price and production volume variances.

The solution to this self-study problem is at the end of the chapter on page 367.

Activity-Based Standard Costing

Activity-based costing is commonly used with standard costing. Hewlett-Packard, a pioneer in the development of activity-based costing, uses it to develop standard overhead costs. Using activity-based costing, a company has multiple cost drivers.

For example, assume Mesozoic Company uses activity-based costing to set standard variable costs for producing wooden crates to ship fruits and vegetables. Assume the company has the following three activity centers: indirect materials, energy costs, and quality testing. (Companies typically have more than three activity centers, but we want to keep the example simple.) Management selects the following cost drivers for these activity centers:

Activity Center	Cost Driver
1. Indirect Materials	Board feet of direct materials used
2. Energy	Machine hours
3. Quality Testing	Minutes of test time

Variance Analysis for Activity-Based Costing

We use the same approach to variance analysis for activity-based costing as for traditional costing. The price variance is the difference between standard prices and actual prices for the actual quantity of input used for each cost driver. The efficiency variance measures the difference between the actual amount of input, or cost driver units used, and the standard allowed to make the output. We multiply this difference in quantities by the standard price per cost driver unit to get the dollar value of the variance.

To make this idea concrete, assume the following data for Mesozoic Company for the three activities for the month of June:

	Standard Price per Unit	Standard Quantity of Input Allowed to Produce 10,000 Units of Output	Actual Cost	Actual Quantity of Input Used
1. Indirect Materials	$0.05 per board foot	100,000 board feet	$5,180	110,000 feet
2. Energy	$0.02 per minute of machine time	250,000 minutes of machine time	$5,300	240,000 minutes
3. Quality Testing	$0.50 per test minute	30,000 minutes of test time	$16,000	34,000 test minutes

Exhibit 10.9 shows the results of the variance analysis. In effect, we have taken the principle underlying variance computations shown throughout this chapter and applied it to a situation having three activity centers. If a company had 40 activity centers, the computations would look like Exhibit 10.9, but with 40 computations of variances instead of only three.

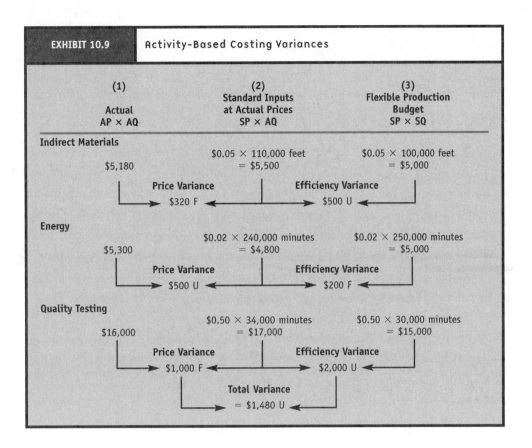

EXHIBIT 10.9   Activity-Based Costing Variances

	(1) Actual AP × AQ	(2) Standard Inputs at Actual Prices SP × AQ	(3) Flexible Production Budget SP × SQ
Indirect Materials	$5,180	$0.05 × 110,000 feet = $5,500	$0.05 × 100,000 feet = $5,000
	Price Variance $320 F	Efficiency Variance $500 U	
Energy	$5,300	$0.02 × 240,000 minutes = $4,800	$0.02 × 250,000 minutes = $5,000
	Price Variance $500 U	Efficiency Variance $200 F	
Quality Testing	$16,000	$0.50 × 34,000 minutes = $17,000	$0.50 × 30,000 minutes = $15,000
	Price Variance $1,000 F	Efficiency Variance $2,000 U	
	Total Variance = $1,480 U		

Even with only three activity drivers, we think you can see the potential for managers to get much more information from activity-based costing than from the traditional approach. For example, producing 10,000 units in June required 34,000 minutes of quality-test time instead of the 30,000 minutes allowed by the standard. Does this "inefficiency" reflect poorer-quality materials than expected? Does it represent extra concern about putting out a quality product? Is the standard three minutes per crate too low? In short, activity-based costing raises numerous specific questions that managers can address to improve quality and productivity.

Variance Analysis in High-Technology Companies

The variance analysis model used in this chapter generally applies to all types of organizations; however, high-technology firms apply the model somewhat differently. Most changes toward high technology involve substituting computerized equipment for direct labor. Examples include automatic teller machines in banks, robots in manufacturing plants, and word processors in various organizations. The result is less direct labor and more overhead.

The substitution of computerized equipment implies that the firm should treat labor more appropriately as a fixed cost than as a variable cost.[1] In high-technology manufacturing companies, employees monitor and maintain machines rather than produce output. For these companies, labor variances may no longer be meaningful because direct labor is a capacity cost, not a cost expected to vary with output. Variable overhead may associate more with machine usage than labor hours. Some high-technology manufacturing organizations have found that the two largest variable costs involve materials and power to operate machines. In these companies, the emphasis of variance analysis is placed on direct materials and variable manufacturing overhead.

---

[1]In practice, many low-technology companies also treat direct labor as a fixed cost.

Quality Control and Variance Investigation

Managers may receive reports that contain hundreds or even thousands of variances. Managerial time is a scarce resource—following up and investigating variances is costly. When confronted with variance reports, managers ask: Which variances should we investigate?

Managers can deal with the decision of whether to investigate a variance as they do other decisions—on a cost-benefit basis. Hence they should investigate variances if they expect the benefits from investigation to exceed the costs of investigation. These benefits may include improvements from taking corrective action, such as repairing defective machinery, training workers who were performing their tasks incorrectly, or changing a standard purchase order so that the firm can purchase cheaper materials. Further, managers generally believe that periodically investigating or auditing employees improves performances. Because measuring the benefits and costs of investigation is often difficult, decisions about the value of investigating variances rely considerably on managerial judgments.

The major cost of **variance investigation** is the opportunity cost of employees' time. Investigators spend time, as do those being investigated. Although measuring costs and benefits of variance investigation is difficult, in many cases the benefits are clearly too low or costs are clearly too high to make investigation worthwhile. In other cases, variances are so large that management obviously must do something about them.

Managers use a variety of methods to help them ascertain which variances to investigate, including rules that have worked well in the past (for example, any variance greater than 10 percent of standard cost, any variance that has been unfavorable for three months in a row, and so on). Although we emphasize that managerial experience and good judgment are the most important ingredients for variance investigation decisions, accountants have developed some decision aids to assist managers.

Tolerance Limits

Quality control techniques have long relied on the use of *tolerance limits*. Quality is allowed to fluctuate within predetermined tolerance limits. Applying this concept to variances requires establishing predetermined limits within which variances may fluctuate. These limits may differ for various cost items. For example, managers usually allow greater tolerance for direct materials prices than for labor efficiency, because they have less control over the former due to market fluctuations. Some managers set tighter tolerance limits for unfavorable variances than for favorable variances.

Example   The manager of a kitchen that makes meals for a college cafeteria wants to set tolerance limits on labor time variances so that variances fall outside the limits less than 5 percent of the time. Based on past experience, expected labor time is 58 minutes to prepare the lunch each day. Labor time to fix lunch is between 73.7 and 42.3 minutes 95 percent of the time.

Exhibit 10.10 presents a control chart of actual observations reported to the kitchen manager for five days. A time series of observations allows the manager to see trends and look for cumulative effects of variances. The manager gets this report at 9:00 A.M. each day for the five previous working days. The kitchen manager received the report shown in Exhibit 10.10 at 9:00 A.M. Friday. The manager would have investigated the labor time variance for Monday, presumably on Tuesday, because it fell outside the tolerance limits. In addition, the manager would probably investigate this labor variance after receiving the report on Friday because of the trend indicating a shift away from standard.

Decision Models

Although control charts provide data about variances, they do not incorporate the costs and benefits of variance investigation. Given the costs, C, and the benefits, B, from investigation, and the probability, p, that the benefits can be obtained, the decision rule is to investigate when expected benefits exceed expected costs:

$$pB > C$$

The following example shows how to apply this cost-benefit analysis.

Example   Electromagnet, Inc., uses a stamping machine to make a product in 10,000-unit batches. An employee adjusts this machine at the beginning of a batch. During the production

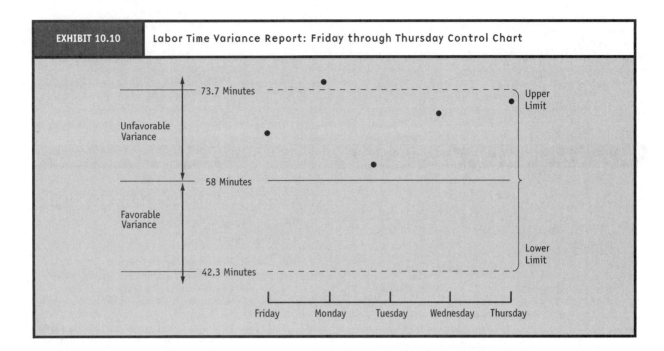

| EXHIBIT 10.10 | Labor Time Variance Report: Friday through Thursday Control Chart |

run, another employee calculates and reports the materials variances. If the machine is out of adjustment, it will use considerably more materials than needed. Hence, adjusting the machine during a production run could save materials costs.

Midway through a particular production batch, the stamping department manager receives a report indicating a large negative materials variance. Based on past experience, the manager estimates a 70 percent chance of the machine's running out of adjustment when the system reports a large negative materials variance.

The manager faces the decision of whether to investigate. Shutting down the machine would result in idle worker time, loss of materials, and lost managerial time. After computing the opportunity cost of lost time and the cost of lost materials, the department manager estimates the cost of variance investigation, C, to be $1,000. If the machine needs adjustment, making the adjustment will cost $1,200, but the firm will save $3,200 in materials cost.

Expected benefits equal the materials cost savings, $3,200, minus the cost of machine adjustments, $1,200 in this case. The computations follow:

$$pB > C$$
$$0.70(\$3,200 - \$1,200) > \$1,000$$
$$0.70(\$2,000) > \$1,000$$
$$\$1,400 > \$1,000.$$

The expected benefits ($1,400) exceed the estimated costs ($1,000), so the manager decides to investigate. This simple example shows how to model the variance investigation decision by applying statistical decision theory tools.[2] Statistical analysis can provide decision aids to managers. Ultimately, these decision aids are only *aids;* they do not replace managerial judgment and good sense.

Problem 10.5 for Self-Study

Variance investigation. Pep Seco, the manager of a soft-drink bottling plant, watches the variance reports like a hawk because Pep knows the consequences of the machinery being out of adjustment. Pep just received a variance report indicating a possible problem. Based on years of experience, Pep figures the probability that the machinery is out of adjustment is 0.40 in light of the variance report. Investigation to learn whether the machinery is out of adjustment would cost

---

[2]We have assumed that decision makers are risk-neutral in this example.

$10,000 (mostly Pep's time, which has a high opportunity cost). If the machinery is out of adjustment, it would cost $20,000 to fix, but correcting the problem would save the company $50,000 (not counting the cost of the adjustment). Should Pep investigate? Why or why not?

The solution to this self-study problem is at the end of the chapter on page 367.

Employee Participation

Many organizations involve workers in creating ideas for improving performance. In some Japanese companies that we have studied, every worker is expected to submit an idea for improvement at least once a week. Competent managers know that workers have good ideas for improving the operations of a company. After all, the workers are much closer than the managers to an organization's production and sales activities.

Worker involvement has three benefits:

1. Many managers believe that when workers take on real decision-making authority, their commitment to the organization and its goals increases.
2. When decision-making responsibility lies with workers closer to the customer, the company becomes more responsive to customers.
3. Giving decision-making responsibility to workers uses their skills and knowledge and provides them with motivation to further develop their skills and knowledge in an effort to improve the organization's performance.

Effective worker involvement decentralizes decision-making authority and empowers workers.

How do companies evaluate their own performance in getting workers involved and committed? Exhibit 10.11 shows performance measures that organizations can use to assess how well they are doing in terms of worker involvement and commitment. Increasing the percentages on these performance measures demonstrates increasing worker involvement and commitment to the organization.

Effective worker involvement presents three challenges for management.

1. Management must create a system that conveys the organization's goals and critical success factors to all members. Information, training sessions, and the performance indicators themselves will determine the extent to which employees understand what behavior is desired of them.
2. The measures the organization uses to judge individual performance will determine the success of the system in promoting goal congruence. Management must analyze the performance measures chosen by each organizational unit to ensure that they (a) promote the desired behavior, (b) are comprehensive, (c) support the achievement of organizational goals, and (d) reflect the unit's role in the organization.
3. Management must apply the performance measures consistently and accurately. The measures used to evaluate performance should reflect each unit's understanding of its contribution to the organization.

EXHIBIT 10.11	Performance Measures of Worker Involvement and Commitment

1. Worker Development: Measured by percentage of workers in mentor programs
2. Worker Empowerment: Measured by percentage of workers authorized to issue credit
3. Worker Recognition: Measured by percentage of workers recognized by awards
4. Worker Recruitment: Measured by percentage of employment offers accepted
5. Worker Promotion: Measured by percentage of positions filled from within the company
6. Worker Succession Planning: Measured by percentage of eligible positions filled through succession planning

Summary

The following items correspond to the learning objectives presented at the beginning of the chapter.

1. **Explain the reasons for conducting variance analyses.** Variance analysis investigates and analyzes the variance to find causes, to ascertain whether the firm needs to take corrective steps, and to reward or penalize employees, when appropriate.

2. **Describe how to use the budget for performance evaluation.** Accountants compare actual results achieved with budgets to derive variances for performance evaluation. Comparison of actual results with the flexible and master budgets ties the results of the planning process to flexible budgeting and forms the basis for analyzing differences between planned and actual results.

3. **Identify the different types of variances between actual results and the flexible budget.** Variances include purchasing and production variances, marketing and administrative cost variances, sales price variance, and sales volume variance.

4. **Assign responsibility for variances.** Variances for each responsibility center are separated from those for other centers and calculated holding all other things constant. Sales volume, sales price, and marketing cost variances are the responsibility of marketing. Administrative variances are often the hardest to manage because they are not engineered; management usually budgets administrative costs with discretion. Although discretionary budgets can provide a ceiling for expenditure, they do not provide a norm like a flexible manufacturing cost budget. Purchasing departments are responsible for materials variances related to price as they purchase the materials to make products and provide services. The production department is responsible for the fixed manufacturing cost variance and the remaining variable manufacturing cost variances not assigned to purchasing. These include materials variances, labor variances, and variable overhead variances.

5. **Describe the role of variance analysis in service organizations.** Service organizations use profit variance analysis but define output based on services provided, such as billable hours in consulting firms or patient-days in hospitals.

6. **Explain the difference between price and efficiency variances.** The price variance is the difference between the budgeted (or standard) price and the actual price paid for each unit of input. The efficiency variance measures the efficiency with which the firm uses inputs to produce outputs.

7. **Identify the relation between actual, budgeted, and applied fixed manufacturing costs.** Companies frequently use a predetermined overhead rate to apply fixed overhead to units produced. The price variance is the difference between the actual fixed overhead and the budgeted fixed overhead. The production volume variance is the difference between the budgeted fixed overhead and the applied fixed overhead.

8. **Explain why an effective performance measurement system requires employee involvement.** Worker involvement is important for three reasons: (1) It increases commitment to the organization and its goals, (2) it leads to more responsive and informed decision making, and (3) it uses worker skills and knowledge.

9. **Explain how to compute the mix variance (Appendix 10.1).** When companies use multiple inputs to produce output, the efficiency variance can be divided into mix and yield components to demonstrate how much of the variance was caused by a deviation in input mix from the standard and how much was caused by the over- or underuse of inputs, holding the mix constant.

Key Terms and Concepts

Direct labor efficiency variance	Mix variance*
Direct labor price (or wage) variance	Price variance
Efficiency variance	Price variance (or spending variance) for fixed
Materials efficiency variance	manufacturing costs
Materials price variance	Production volume variance

---

*Terms appear in Appendix 10.1.

Profit variance analysis   Variance investigation
Variable overhead efficiency variance   Yield variance*
Variable overhead price variance

Appendix 10.1: Mix and Yield Variances

Most organizations use multiple inputs to produce their output. Massachusetts General Hospital uses a combination of registered nurses, licensed practical nurses, and nurse's aides to provide nursing care to patients. Bethlehem Steel Company uses a combination of iron ore and other raw materials to make its product. A **mix variance** shows the impact on profits of using something other than the budgeted mix of inputs.

Example Engineering Associates, a consulting firm, has bid on a particular job assuming 1,000 hours of partner time at a cost of $100 per hour and 2,000 hours of staff time at $40 per hour. If it gets the job, these hour and cost assumptions become the flexible budget. During the job, scheduling problems arise—the partner spends 2,000 hours because the staff member spends only 1,000 hours. If the cost is actually $100 and $40 for partner and staff time, respectively, no labor price variance occurs. Further, the 3,000 hours required is exactly what was expected. Nevertheless, the job is $60,000 over the flexible budget, as shown in the following calculation:

$$\text{Actual Cost} = (2{,}000 \text{ Hours} \times \$100) + (1{,}000 \text{ Hours} \times \$40)$$

$$= \$200{,}000 + \$40{,}000$$

$$= \$240{,}000.$$

$$\text{Budgeted Cost} = (1{,}000 \text{ Hours} \times \$100) + (2{,}000 \text{ Hours} \times \$40)$$

$$= \$100{,}000 + \$80{,}000$$

$$= \$180{,}000.$$

$$\text{Actual Cost} - \text{Budgeted Cost} = \$240{,}000 - \$180{,}000$$

$$= \$60{,}000.$$

The $60,000 unfavorable efficiency variance results from a mix variance: the substitution of 1,000 hours (= 2,000 hours actual − 1,000 hours budgeted) of partner time at $100 for 1,000 hours of staff time at $40. The mix variance is the difference in labor costs per hour of $60 (= $100 − $40) times the 1,000 hours substituted.

The general model for a mix variance is as follows:

Standard Price of the Inputs × **Actual Proportions** of the Actual Total Quantity × Actual Total Quantity of Inputs	−	Standard Price of the Inputs × **Standard Proportions** of the Actual Total Quantity × Actual Total Quantity of Inputs

Exhibit 10.12 shows the model for computing a mix variance. Columns (2) and (3) in the bottom part of Exhibit 10.12 show the mix variance that we computed above.

This example demonstrates the general concept of a mix variance. You should note two factors always present in a mix variance. First, we assumed that partner time was *substitutable* for staff time. Second, the prices must be different. If the cost per hour were the same for both partner and staff, the substitution of hours would not affect the total cost of the job.

Note that Exhibit 10.12 would have called the mix variance an efficiency variance if we had not calculated a separate mix variance. We call the portion of the efficiency variance that is not a mix variance a **yield variance.** The yield variance measures the input-output relation holding the standard mix of inputs constant.

In this example, we deliberately make the yield variance equal to zero to show that the entire variance results from the mix. Problem 10.6 for Self-Study presents a case in which there is a yield variance. Managers use mix variances not only to measure performance when inputs are substitutes, as in the preceding example, but also to measure marketing performance with respect

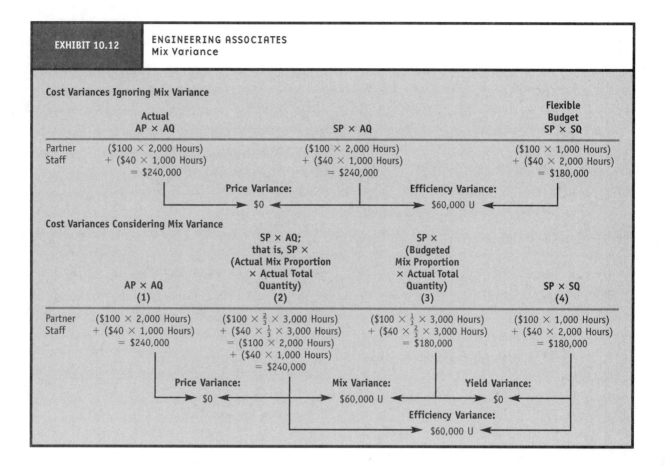

EXHIBIT 10.12	ENGINEERING ASSOCIATES Mix Variance

Cost Variances Ignoring Mix Variance

	Actual AP × AQ	SP × AQ	Flexible Budget SP × SQ
Partner Staff	($100 × 2,000 Hours) + ($40 × 1,000 Hours) = $240,000	($100 × 2,000 Hours) + ($40 × 1,000 Hours) = $240,000	($100 × 1,000 Hours) + ($40 × 2,000 Hours) = $180,000

Price Variance: $0 ← Efficiency Variance: $60,000 U

Cost Variances Considering Mix Variance

	AP × AQ (1)	SP × AQ; that is, SP × (Actual Mix Proportion × Actual Total Quantity) (2)	SP × (Budgeted Mix Proportion × Actual Total Quantity) (3)	SP × SQ (4)
Partner Staff	($100 × 2,000 Hours) + ($40 × 1,000 Hours) = $240,000	($100 × $\frac{2}{3}$ × 3,000 Hours) + ($40 × $\frac{1}{3}$ × 3,000 Hours) = ($100 × 2,000 Hours) + ($40 × 1,000 Hours) = $240,000	($100 × $\frac{1}{3}$ × 3,000 Hours) + ($40 × $\frac{2}{3}$ × 3,000 Hours) = $180,000	($100 × 1,000 Hours) + ($40 × 2,000 Hours) = $180,000

Price Variance: $0 ← Mix Variance: $60,000 U ← Yield Variance: $0

Efficiency Variance: $60,000 U

to sales mix. Companies with multiple products assume a particular sales mix in constructing their sales budget. If the actual mix of products sold differs from the budgeted mix, and if the products are substitutes, managers often compute a mix variance to measure the impact of the change in mix from the budget.

Problem 10.6 for Self-Study

Mix variance. Alexis Company makes a product, AL, from two materials, ST and EE. The standard prices and quantities follow:

	ST	EE
Price per Pound	$ 2	$3
Pounds per Unit of AL	10	5

In May, Alexis Company produced 7,000 units of AL, with the following actual prices and quantities of materials used:

	ST	EE
Price per Pound	$1.90	$2.80
Pounds Used	72,000	38,000

Compute materials price, mix, yield, and efficiency variances.

The solution to this self-study problem is at the end of the chapter on page 368.

Solutions to Self-Study Problems

SUGGESTED SOLUTION TO PROBLEM 10.1 FOR SELF-STUDY

COMPUTER SUPPLY, INC.
Profit Variance Analysis
April

	Actual (based on 50,000 units)	Purchasing and Production Variances	Marketing and Administrative Variances	Sales Price Variances	Flexible Budget (based on 50,000 units)	Sales Volume Variance	Master Budget (based on 40,000 units)
Sales Revenue	$500,000	—	—	$50,000 U	$550,000	$110,000 F	$440,000
Less:							
Variable Manufacturing Costs	244,000	$44,000 U	—	—	200,000	40,000 U	160,000
Variable Marketing and Administrative Costs	52,000	—	$2,000 U	—	50,000	10,000 U	40,000
Contribution Margin	$204,000	$44,000 U	$2,000 U	$50,000 U	$300,000	$60,000 F	$240,000
Less:							
Fixed Manufacturing Costs	83,000	3,000 U	—	—	80,000	—	80,000
Fixed Marketing and Administrative Costs	96,000	—	4,000 F	—	100,000	—	100,000
Operating Profits	$ 25,000	$47,000 U	$2,000 F	$50,000 U	$120,000	$ 60,000 F	$ 60,000

Total Profit Variance from Flexible Budget = $95,000 U

Total Profit Variance from Master Budget = $35,000 U

SUGGESTED SOLUTION TO PROBLEM 10.2 FOR SELF-STUDY

Definitions. The price variance measures the difference between the actual and standard price per unit, times the actual number of units. This variance measures how well the company is controlling the cost of items purchased. The efficiency variance measures the difference between the actual quantity of inputs and the standard quantity allowed to make the actual output, times the standard price per unit.

Uses. The manager of a coffee shop should monitor the price variance carefully. One can never tell when a revolution or natural disaster might break out in a coffee-producing country that would lead to an increase in the price of coffee beans. Coffeehouses are in a competitive business with low margins, in general, so failure to pass on the materials (that is, coffee beans) price increase to customers could take the company right out of business. Efficiency variances should measure waste in using coffee beans.

SUGGESTED SOLUTION TO PROBLEM 10.3 FOR SELF-STUDY

All based on 50,000 units produced

	Actual (AP × AQ)	Price Variance	Actual Inputs at Standard (SP × AQ)	Efficiency Variance	Flexible Production Budget (SP × SQ)
Direct Materials	$1.20 × 110,000 Pounds = $132,000	$22,000 U	$1 × 110,000 Pieces = $110,000	$10,000 U	$1 × 100,000[a] Pounds = $100,000
Direct Labor	$14 × 6,000 Hours = $84,000	$ 6,000 F	$15 × 6,000 Hours = $90,000	$15,000 U	$15 × 5,000 Hours[b] = $75,000
Variable Overhead	$28,000	$ 2,000 F	$5 × 6,000 Hours = $30,000	$ 5,000 U	$5 × 5,000 Hours[b] = $25,000

[a]Standard direct materials pounds allowed in production per unit times actual units produced (2 pounds × 50,000 units).
[b].10 hour × 50,000 units produced.

SUGGESTED SOLUTION TO PROBLEM 10.4 FOR SELF-STUDY

	Actual	Price Variance	Budget	Efficiency Variance	Budget	Production Volume Variance	Applied
Fixed Overhead	$83,000	$3,000 U	$80,000	Not Applicable	$80,000	$20,000 F	$100,000[a]

[a]Fixed overhead rate = $80,000/4,000 = $20 per standard labor hour; 5,000 standard labor hours allowed × $20 = $100,000.

SUGGESTED SOLUTION TO PROBLEM 10.5 FOR SELF-STUDY

Pep should figure out whether $pB > C$. In this case, $p = 0.40$, $B = \$50,000 - \$20,000 = \$30,000$, and $C = \$10,000$. We find that $.40 × \$30,000 > \$10,000$, so Pep should investigate.

SUGGESTED SOLUTION TO PROBLEM 10.6 FOR SELF-STUDY

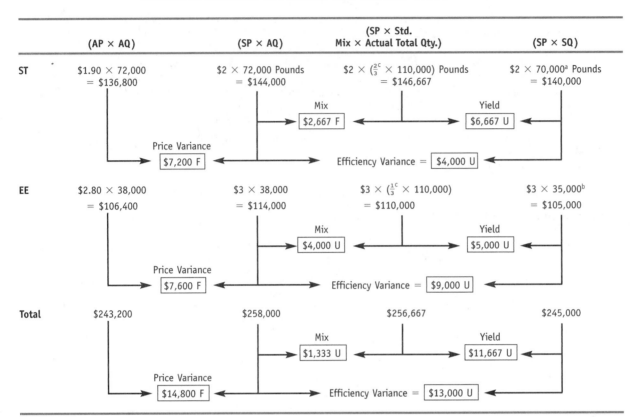

	(AP × AQ)	(SP × AQ)	(SP × Std. Mix × Actual Total Qty.)	(SP × SQ)
ST	$1.90 × 72,000 = $136,800	$2 × 72,000 Pounds = $144,000	$2 × ($\frac{2^c}{3}$ × 110,000) Pounds = $146,667	$2 × 70,000[a] Pounds = $140,000
			Mix $2,667 F ← → Yield $6,667 U ←	
		Price Variance $7,200 F ← →	Efficiency Variance = $4,000 U ←	
EE	$2.80 × 38,000 = $106,400	$3 × 38,000 = $114,000	$3 × ($\frac{1^c}{3}$ × 110,000) = $110,000	$3 × 35,000[b] = $105,000
			Mix $4,000 U ← → Yield $5,000 U ←	
		Price Variance $7,600 F ← →	Efficiency Variance = $9,000 U ←	
Total	$243,200	$258,000	$256,667	$245,000
			Mix $1,333 U ← → Yield $11,667 U ←	
		Price Variance $14,800 F ← →	Efficiency Variance = $13,000 U ←	

[a]70,000 Pounds = 7,000 Units × 10 Pounds per Unit.
[b]35,000 Pounds = 7,000 Units × 5 Pounds per Unit.
[c]Mix percentage ratio of ST pounds to total and EE pounds to total. For ST, 10/(10 + 5) = 2/3. For EE, 5/(10 + 5) = 1/3. 110,000 total = 72,000 ST plus 38,000 EE.

Questions, Exercises, Problems, and Cases

REVIEW QUESTIONS

1. Review the meaning of the concepts or terms given in Key Terms and Concepts.
2. An important point in variance analysis is that
   a. every variance must be investigated.
   b. a responsibility center's variances are calculated holding all other things constant.
   c. often variances cannot be separated.
   d. all of the above.
3. Which function is normally responsible for sales volume variances?
   a. marketing
   b. administration
   c. production
   d. top management
4. How would management evaluate performance without a budget?
5. Could some responsibility centers differ as to the type of budget items for which they are accountable? That is, might some responsibility centers be responsible only for costs, some only for revenues, and some for both? Give examples.
6. Refer to Exhibit 10.10 on page 361. How does "percentage of positions filled from within the company" measure worker involvement and commitment?
7. What is the difference between a standard and a budget?
8. Which function is normally responsible for sales price variances?
   a. marketing
   b. administration

    c. production
    d. top management
  9. Describe the basic decision that management must make when considering whether to investigate a variance.
10. "Manage by exception" is a term often used by management. How can the analysis of variances assist in this process?
11. Why should management want to divide variable production cost variances into price and efficiency variances?
12. Why are the variances for fixed costs different from the variances for variable costs?
13. For control purposes, why is an efficiency variance not calculated for fixed manufacturing overhead?
14. The price variance is calculated with which of the following?
    a. $AQ \times (AP - SP)$
    b. $SQ \times (AP - SP)$
    c. $AP \times (AQ - SQ)$
    d. $SP \times (AQ - SQ)$
15. A firm incurred fixed manufacturing overhead costs of $500,000 for the year. Fixed overhead applied to units produced during the year totaled $600,000. What are some of the reasons for this difference?

CRITICAL ANALYSIS AND DISCUSSION QUESTIONS

16. Refer to the Managerial Application "An Antidote to Biased Standards: How Workers Develop Their Own Standards at NUMMI" on page 349. What were the benefits of worker involvement in setting the standards at NUMMI?
17. How would a coffee shop use labor and materials variance information?
18. Why is a materials efficiency variance typically not calculated for the purchasing activity?
19. Why might the total variable manufacturing overhead variance not be divided into price and efficiency components?
20. How would you compute price and efficiency variances for taxicab drivers where the major variable costs are drivers' wages and automobile costs?
21. How could a CPA firm use mix variances to evaluate performance? (Appendix 10.1)

EXERCISES

Solutions to even-numbered exercises are at the end of the chapter after the cases.

22. Profit variance analysis. Sierra Company prepared a budget last period that called for sales of 14,000 units at a price of $12 each. Variable costs per unit were budgeted to be $5. Fixed costs were budgeted to be $21,000 for the period. During the period, production was exactly equal to actual sales of 14,200 units. The selling price was $12.15 per unit. Variable costs were $5.90 per unit. Fixed costs were $20,000.
    Prepare a profit variance report to show the difference between the master budget and the actual profits.
23. Analyzing contribution margin changes. The Diaz Company, which sells hard hats for construction, provided the following data for Years 1 and 2:

	Year 1	Year 2
Sales Volume	14,000 Hats	10,000 Hats
Sales Revenue	$1,750,000	$1,500,000
Variable Costs	(1,470,000)	(1,050,000)
Contribution Margin	$ 280,000	$ 450,000

    What impact did the changes in sales volume and in sales price have on the contribution margin? (Hint: Compare the actual, flexible budget, and master budget portion of the profit variance analysis. Use Year 1 as the "Master Budget.")
24. Profit variance analysis. Mason prepared a budget last period that called for sales of 200 units at a price of $100 each. Variable manufacturing costs were budgeted to be $39 per

unit, and variable marketing costs were budgeted to be $11 per unit. Total fixed manufacturing, marketing, and administrative costs were budgeted to be $500, $1,000, and $1,000, respectively.

During the period, actual sales totaled 170 units (units produced equaled units sold), and actual sales revenue totaled $18,400. Actual variable manufacturing and marketing costs totaled $6,880 and $2,060, respectively. Actual fixed manufacturing, marketing, and administrative costs totaled $485, $1,040, and $995, respectively.

Prepare a profit variance report to show the difference between the master budget and the actual profits.

25. **Estimating flexible selling expense budget and computing variances.** Kirkwood Products estimates the following selling expenses next period:

Salaries (fixed)	$ 20,000
Commissions (0.05% of sales revenue)	17,875
Travel (0.03% of sales revenue)	10,725
Advertising (fixed)	50,000
Sales Office Costs ($4,000 plus $0.05 per unit sold)	7,250
Shipping Costs ($0.10 per unit sold)	6,500
Total Selling Expenses	$112,350

   a. Derive the cost equation ($y = a + bx$) for selling expenses. (Hint: $y = a + bx + cy.$)
   b. Assume that Kirkwood sells 50,000 units during the period at an average price of $6 per unit. The company had budgeted sales for the period to be: volume, 65,000 units; price, $5.50. Calculate the sales price and volume variance.
   c. The actual selling expenses incurred during the period were $80,000 fixed and $30,000 variable. Prepare a profit variance analysis for sales revenue and selling expenses.

26. **Materials and labor variances.** Thong Company's budget contains these standards for materials and direct labor for a unit:

Material—2 Pounds at $.50 per Pound	$1.00
Direct Labor—1 Hour at $9.00	9.00

   Although the firm budgeted 100,000 units of output for September, it produced only 97,810. It purchased and used 200,000 pounds of materials for $105,500. Direct labor costs were $905,000 for 99,200 hours.
   a. Compute the materials variance.
   b. Compute the labor variance.

27. **Evaluate cause of variances.** Refer to the information in the previous exercise for Thong Company. Based on the information for Thong Company, write a short report explaining the cause of the variances that you computed.

28. **Materials and labor variances.** The Olhm Walnut Company presents the following data for October:

	Standards per Batch	Actual
Materials	1 Pound at $2.50 per Pound	49,000 Pounds
Labor	1.5 Hours at $3.00 per Hour	70,000 Hours
Batches Produced		48,000 Batches

   During the month, the firm purchased 49,000 pounds of materials for $127,500. Wages earned were $214,000. Compute the labor and material variances.

29. **Evaluate cause of variances.** Refer to the information in the previous exercise for Olhm Walnut Company. Based on the information for Olhm Walnut Company, write a short report explaining the cause of the variances that you computed.

30. **Solving for materials quantities and costs.** Nate's Pool Services uses from one to three chemicals to clean swimming pools. Variance data for the month follow (F indicates favorable variance; U indicates unfavorable variance):

	Chemical A	Chemical B	Chemical C
Materials Price Variance	$ 42,000 F	$ 25,000 F	$ 21,000 U
Materials Efficiency Variance	40,000 U	30,000 U	48,000 U
Net Materials Variance	$ 2,000 F	$ 5,000 U	$ 69,000 U
Pools Cleaned Requiring This Chemical	100,000	110,000	125,000

The budget allowed two pounds of each kind of chemical for each pool cleaning requiring that kind of chemical. For chemical A, the average price paid was $0.20 per pound less than standard; for chemical B, $0.10 less; for chemical C, $0.07 greater. The firm purchased and used all chemicals during the month.

For each of the three types of chemicals, calculate the following:
a. Number of pounds of material purchased.
b. Standard price per pound of material.

31. **Non-manufacturing variances.** Maxum's Sales uses standard costs and variances for controlling costs. As a result of studying past cost data, it has established standards as follows: variable costs, $6 per sales call; 9 sales calls per unit sold. Actual data for May, June, and July follow:

	Sales Calls	Units Sold	Actual Costs
May	290,000	30,000	$1,880,000
June	310,000	40,000	1,840,000
July	260,000	20,000	1,580,000

Compute the variable cost price and efficiency variances for each month.

32. **Labor and variable overhead variances** (adapted from CPA exam). The following data relate to the current month's activities of Animated Video Productions:

Actual Total Direct Labor	$43,400
Actual Hours Worked	14,000
Standard Hours Allowed for Actual Output (flexible budget)	15,000
Actual Total Variable Overhead	$22,900
Standard Variable Overhead Rate per Direct Labor Hour	$ 1.50
Standard Direct Labor Wages per Hour	$ 3.00

Compute the labor and variable overhead variances.

33. **Overhead variances.** Skyward Company, which uses standard costing, shows the following overhead information for the current period:

Actual Overhead Incurred	$13,600, of Which $3,500 Is Fixed
Budgeted Fixed Overhead	$3,300
Variable Overhead Rate per Machine Hour	$ 3
Standard Hours Allowed for Actual Production	3,500
Actual Machine Hours Used	3,200

Calculate the variable and fixed overhead variances in the same format as Exhibit 10.2.

34. **Finding purchase price.** Information on Wong Company's direct materials cost is as follows:

Standard Price per Materials Unit	$3.60
Actual Quantity Used	1,600
Materials Price Variance	$240 F

What was the actual purchase price per unit, rounded to the nearest cent?

35. **Solving for labor hours.** Lucas Consulting reports the following direct labor information for clerical staff in its tax department:

Month: April	
Standard Rate	$15 per Hour
Actual Rate Paid	$17 per Hour
Standard Hours Allowed for Actual Production	1,600 Hours
Labor Efficiency Variance	$860 U

What are the actual hours worked, rounded to the nearest hour?

36. **Overhead variances.** Casio Corporation estimated its overhead costs for Year 0 to be as follows: fixed, $300,000; variable, $2.50 per unit. Casio expected to produce 60,000 units during the year.
    a. Compute the rate to be used to apply overhead costs to products (assume units will be used as the allocation base).
    b. During Year 0, Casio incurred overhead costs of $400,000 and produced 65,000 units. Compute overhead costs applied to units produced.
    c. Refer to part **b.** Compute the amount of underapplied or overapplied overhead for the year.

37. **Overhead variances.** Solaris Company uses a predetermined rate for applying overhead costs to production. The rates for Year 0 follow: variable, $2 per unit; fixed, $1 per unit. Actual overhead costs incurred follow: variable, $95,000; fixed, $45,000. Solaris expected to produce 45,000 units during the year but produced only 40,000 units.
    a. What was the amount of budgeted fixed overhead costs for the year?
    b. What was the total underapplied or overapplied overhead for the year?
    c. Compute all possible fixed overhead variances.

38. **Variance investigation.** Tech Company's production manager is considering whether to investigate a computer-integrated manufacturing process. The investigation costs $7,000. If the manager finds that the process is out of control, correcting it costs $20,000. If the process is out of control and is corrected, the company saves $45,000 until the next scheduled investigation. The probability of the process being in control is 0.65, and the probability of the process being out of control is .35, given recent variance reports.
    Should management investigate the process? Why or why not?

39. **Variances from activity-based costs.** Assume Texas Instruments uses activity-based costing for variable overhead costs. For June, it has three cost drivers with the following standard and actual amounts for 10,000 units of output.

Activity Center	Cost Driver	Standard Rate per Cost Driver Unit	Standard Input for 10,000 Units of Output	Actual Costs	Actual Number of Inputs Used
Quality testing	Test minutes	$0.50	40,000 test minutes	$20,000	38,000 test minutes
Energy	Machine hours	$1.00	40,000 machine hours	$40,000	42,000 machine hours
Indirect labor	Direct labor hours	$1.00	60,000 labor hours	$56,800	56,000 labor hours

Prepare an analysis of the variances like that in Exhibit 10.10.

40. **Variance investigation.** The accounting system has reported a large unfavorable variance for Durango Company's production process. Conducting an investigation costs $7,000. If the process is actually out of control, the benefit of correction will be $40,000. The probability is .30 that the large negative variance indicates the process is out of control.
    Should management investigate the process?

PROBLEMS

41. **Profit variance analysis in a service organization.** Baker and Klatt (BK) is a law firm that gets a large portion of its revenue from corporate clients. Last year, BK's billable hours for

corporate clients were up 20 percent from expected levels, but, as the following data show, profits from corporate clients were lower than anticipated.

	Actual Results	Master Budget
Billable Hours[a]	30,000 Hours	25,000 Hours
Revenue	$3,300,000	$3,000,000
Production Costs:		
Professional Salaries (all variable)	1,850,000	1,500,000
Other Variable Costs (e.g., supplies, certain computer services)	470,000	400,000
General Administrative (all fixed)	680,000	700,000
Corporate Client Profit	$ 300,000	$ 400,000

[a]These are hours billed to clients. Hours worked exceed this amount because of nonbillable time (e.g., slack periods, time in training sessions) and because BK does not charge all time worked for clients.

Prepare a profit variance analysis for Baker and Klatt.

42. **Finding missing data.** Find the values of the missing items **(a)** through **(q)**.

	Actual Results, 750 Units	Purchasing and Production Variances	Marketing and Administrative Variances	Sales Price Variance	Flexible Budget (a)	Sales Volume Variance	Master Budget, 800 Units
Sales Revenue	$1,890			(b)	$2,025	(c)	(d)
Variable Manufacturing Costs	(f)	$60 F			(e)	$38 F	(g)
Variable Marketing and Administrative Costs	(h)	—	(j)	—	(i)	(k)	$216
Contribution Margin	$1,180	(l)	(m)	(n)	(o)	(p)	(q)

43. **Comprehensive problem.** Best Brewing, which produces coffee makers, has the following master budget income statement for the month of July:

	Master Budget (based on 16,000 units)
Sales Revenue (16,000 units at $20)	$320,000
Less:	
Variable Manufacturing Costs	$176,000[a]
Variable Marketing and Administrative Costs	$ 16,000[b]
Contribution Margin	$128,000
Less:	
Fixed Manufacturing Costs	$ 40,000
Fixed Marketing and Administrative Costs	$ 70,000
Operating Profit	$ 18,000

[a]16,000 budgeted units at $11 per unit.
[b]16,000 budgeted units at $1 per unit.

The company uses the following estimates to prepare the master budget:

Sales Price	$20 per Unit
Sales and Production Volume	16,000 Units
Variable Manufacturing Costs	$11 per Unit
Variable Marketing and Administrative Costs	$1 per Unit
Fixed Manufacturing Costs	$40,000
Fixed Marketing and Administrative Costs	$70,000

Assume that the actual results for July were as follows:

	Actual
Sales Price	$19 per Unit
Sales and Production Volume	20,000 Units
Variable Manufacturing Costs	$230,880
Variable Marketing and Administrative Costs	$22,000
Fixed Manufacturing Costs	$42,000
Fixed Marketing and Administrative Costs	$68,000

Compare the master budget, flexible budget, and actual results for the month of July.

44. Finding missing data. Find the values of the missing items **(a)** through **(u)**.

	Achieved Based on Actual Sales Volume	Cost and Sales Price Variances	Flexible Budget Based on Actual Sales Volume	Sales Volume Variance	Master Budget Based on Budgeted Sales Volume
Units	(b)		(a)	2,000 F	10,000
Sales Revenue	(i)	$18,000 F	(h)	(j)	$150,000
Less:					
Variable Manufacturing Costs	(n)	9,000 U	$96,000	(k)	80,000
Variable Marketing and Administrative Costs	$21,600	(o)	24,000	$4,000 U	(c)
Contribution Margin	(p)	(r)	$60,000	(l)	$ 50,000
Less:					
Fixed Manufacturing Costs	(q)	2,000 F	(d)		(e)
Fixed Marketing and Administrative Costs	$18,000	(t)	15,000		(f)
Operating Profits	(s)	(u)	$20,000	(m)	(g)

45. **Assigning responsibility.** Melrose Furniture Company is organized into two divisions, Assembling and Finishing. The Assembling Division combines raw materials into a semifinished product. The product then goes to the Finishing Division for painting, polishing, and packing.

   During May, the Assembling Division had significantly higher raw materials costs than expected because poor-quality raw materials required extensive rework. As a result of the rework, Assembly transferred fewer units than expected to the Finishing Division. The Finishing Division incurred higher labor costs per unit of finished product because workers had substantial idle time. The president of the company is upset about these events.

   a. Who should the firm hold responsible for the raw materials variance in the Assembling Division? Explain.

   b. Who should the firm hold responsible for the labor (idle time) variance in the Finishing Division? Explain.

46. **Controls over planning function.** Keating Federal Bank set up an independent planning department at corporate headquarters. This department is responsible for most aspects of budgeting (revenue and expense forecasting, profit planning, capital investment). Planning department personnel are responsible to the vice-president for administration. The resulting budgets are incorporated into the control system that the controller's department designed and administered.

   Outline an effective control system for the planning department's activities (that is, how the firm should evaluate the performance of the planning department).

47. **Computing variances for marketing costs.** Hoyt's Telemarketing, Inc., uses telephone solicitation to sell products. The company has set standards that call for $450 of sales per hour of telephone time. Telephone solicitors receive a commission of 10 percent of dollar sales. The firm expects other variable costs, including costs of sales in the operation, to be 45 percent of sales revenue. It budgets fixed costs at $411,500 per month. The firm computes the number of sales hours per month based on the number of days in a month minus

an allowance for idle time, scheduling, and other inefficiencies. This month the firm expected 180 hours of telephone calling time for each of 40 callers.

During the month, the firm earned $2,700,000 of revenues. Marketing and administrative cost data for the period follow:

	Actual	Master Budget
Cost of Sales	$810,000	$972,000
Telephone Time Charges	32,200	32,400
Delivery Services	161,100	194,400
Uncollectable Accounts	121,500	145,800
Other Variable Costs	112,700	113,400
Fixed Costs	409,000	411,500

Using sales dollars as a basis for analysis, compute the variances between actual, flexible budget, and master budget for all costs including cost of sales. (Hint: Consider sales volume as an output measure.)

48. **Analysis of cost reports** (adapted from CMA exam). Judy is the production manager of Test Images, a division of the larger corporation, Image View, Inc. Judy has complained several times to the corporate office that their cost reports used to evaluate her plant are misleading. She states, "I know how to get good quality product out. Over a number of years, I've even cut raw materials used to do it. The cost reports don't show any of this; they're always negative, no matter what I do. There's no way you can win with accounting or the people at headquarters who use these reports."

A copy of the latest report follows.

TEST IMAGES Cost Report
Month of November (in thousands)

	Master Budget	Actual Cost	Excess Cost
Raw Material	$ 500	$ 550	$ 50
Direct Labor	700	650	(50)
Overhead	150	180	30
Total	$1,350	$1,380	$ 30

Identify and explain changes to the report that would make the cost information more meaningful to the production managers.

49. **Change of policy to improve productivity** (adapted from CMA exam). Quincy Quilt Company has been experiencing declining profit margins and has been looking for ways to increase operating income. It cannot raise selling prices for fear of losing business to its competitors. It must either cut costs or improve productivity.

Quincy uses a standard cost system to evaluate the performance of the assembly department. All negative variances at the end of the month are investigated. The assembly department rarely completes the operations in less time than the standard allows (which would result in a positive variance). Most months the variance is zero or slightly negative. Reasoning that the application of lower standard costs to the products manufactured will result in improved profit margins, the production manager had recommended that all standard times for assembly operations be drastically reduced. The production manager has informed the assembly personnel that she expects them to meet these new standards.

Will the lowering of the standard costs (by reducing the time of the assembly operations) result in improved profit margins and increased productivity?

50. **Ethics and standard costs** (adapted from CMA exam). Western Farms is a producer of items made from local farm products that are distributed to supermarkets. Over the years, price competition has become increasingly important, so Doug Gilbert, the company's controller, is planning to implement a standard cost system for Western Farms. He asked his cost accountant, Joe Adams, to gather cost information on the production of strawberry jam (Western Farms' most popular product). Joe reported that strawberries cost $0.80 per quart, the price he intends to pay to his good friend who has been operating a strawberry farm in

the red for the past couple of years. Due to an oversupply in the market, the prices for strawberries have dropped to $0.50 per quart. Joe is sure that the $0.80 price will be enough to pull his friend's strawberry farm out of the red and into the black.

Is Joe Adams's behavior regarding the cost information he provided to Doug Gilbert unethical? Explain your answer.

51. **Hospital supply variances.** Assume Ashland Community Hospital had the following supplies costs for two products used in its operating room. Standard costs for one surgery: Item X, 5 pieces at $50 each; Item Y, 10 pieces at $75 each. During August the following data apply to the hospital:

Surgeries Performed	1,500
Supplies Purchased and Used:	
Item X	11,000 Pieces at $40
Item Y	20,000 Pieces at $76

Compute materials price and efficiency variances.

52. **Labor variances.** Assume Near and Far Burgers has two categories of direct labor: unskilled, which costs $6 per hour, and skilled, which costs $10 per hour. Management established standards per "equivalent meal," which it has defined as a typical meal consisting of a sandwich, a drink, and a side order. Managers set standards as follows: skilled labor, 6 minutes per equivalent meal; unskilled labor, 15 minutes per equivalent meal. During July, Near and Far Burgers sold 10,000 equivalent meals and incurred the following labor costs:

Skilled Labor: 900 Hours	$ 9,600
Unskilled Labor: 2,300 Hours	14,000

Compute labor price and efficiency variances.

53. **Hospital supply variances** (Appendix 10.1). Refer to Problem **51.** Compute mix and yield variances for the surgical supplies.

54. **Labor variances** (Appendix 10.1). Refer to Problem **52.** Compute mix and yield variances for the labor costs.

55. **Comprehensive cost variance.** Here are budget and standard cost data for July for Tino's Lasagna:

Budgeted sales	2,500 lasagnas at $10 per lasagna
Budgeted production	2,500 lasagnas
(Tino's uses just-in-time production methods.)	
Budgeted marketing and administrative costs	$2,500 per month (all fixed)
Standard costs to make one lasagna:	
Pasta	1/2 pound at $1 per pound
Labor	1/4 hour per lasagna at $10 per hour
Production overhead	$5,000 per month (fixed) plus $0.50 per lasagna for extra ingredients, veggie, olive, and beef

For July, the results were as follows:

3,000 lasagnas made and sold; revenue was $28,000.

1,525 pounds of pasta used at $1.05 per pound.

800 labor hours used at $10 per hour.

Production overhead costs were $5,500 fixed and $1,750 variable.

Marketing and administrative costs were $3,250.

a. Compute as many variances as possible.

b. Write a brief report to the management of Tino's that gives your evaluation of performance and suggests ways management might improve the company's performance.

56. **Performance evaluation in a service industry.** Southern Seaside Insurance Company estimates that its overhead costs for policy administration should be $100 for each new policy obtained and $5 per year for each $1,500 face amount of insurance outstanding. The company set a budget of 5,000 new policies for the coming period. In addition, the company estimated that the total face amount of insurance outstanding for the period would equal $12,000,000.

   During the period, actual costs related to new policies amounted to $495,000. A total of 4,800 new policies were obtained.

   The cost of maintaining existing policies was $55,000. Had the firm incurred these costs at the same prices as were in effect when it prepared the budget, the costs would have amounted to $60,000. However, $14,000,000 in policies were outstanding during the period. Prepare a schedule to indicate the differences between a master production budget and actual costs for this operation.

57. **Solving for materials and labor.** Sparky Company makes fireplace screens. Under the flexible budget, when the firm uses 75,000 direct labor hours, budgeted variable overhead is $75,000, whereas budgeted direct labor costs are $450,000. All data apply to the month of February.

   The following are some of the variances for February (F denotes favorable; U denotes unfavorable):

Variable Overhead Price Variance	$12,000 U
Variable Overhead Efficiency Variance	$20,000 U
Materials Price Variance	$30,000 F
Materials Efficiency Variance	$20,000 U

   During February, the firm incurred $400,000 of direct labor costs. According to the standards, each fireplace screen uses one pound of materials at a standard price of $4.00 per pound. The firm produced 100,000 units in February. The materials price variance was $.30 per pound, whereas the average wage rate exceeded the standard average rate by $.50 per hour.

   Compute the following for February, assuming there are beginning inventories but no ending inventories of materials:
   a. pounds of materials purchased
   b. pounds of material usage over standard
   c. standard hourly wage rate
   d. standard direct labor hours for the total February production

58. **Controlling labor costs.** Loomis Convalescent Home has a contract with its full-time nurses that guarantees a minimum of $2,000 per month to each nurse with at least 12 years of service. One hundred employees currently qualify for coverage. All nurses receive $20 per hour.

   The direct labor budget for Year 1 anticipates an annual usage of 400,000 hours at $20 per hour, or a total of $8,000,000. Management believes that, of this amount, $200,000 (100 nurses × $2,000) per month (or $2,400,000 for the year) was fixed. Thus the budgeted labor costs for any given month resulted from the formula

   Budgeted Labor Costs = $200,000 + ($14.00 × Direct Labor Hours Worked).

   Data on performance for the first three months of Year 1 follow:

	January	February	March
Nursing Hours Worked	22,000	32,000	42,000
Nursing Costs Budgeted	$508,000	$648,000	$788,000
Nursing Costs Incurred	440,000	640,000	840,000
Variance	68,000 F	8,000 F	52,000 U

   The results, which show favorable variances when hours worked were low and unfavorable variances when hours worked were high, perplex a hospital administrator. This administrator had believed the control over nursing costs was consistently good.

a. Why did the variances arise? Explain and illustrate, using amounts and diagrams as necessary.

b. Does this budget provide a basis for controlling nursing costs? Explain, indicating changes that management may make to improve control over nursing costs and to facilitate performance evaluation of nurses.

59. **Computing non-manufacturing cost variances.** Nicholson Insurance Company estimates that its overhead costs for policy administration should amount to $80 for each new policy obtained and $2 per year for each $1,000 face amount of insurance outstanding. The company set a budget of selling 6,000 new policies during the coming period. In addition, the company estimated that the total face amount of insurance outstanding for the period would equal $12,000,000.

During the period, actual costs related to new policies amounted to $430,000. The firm sold a total of 6,200 new policies.

The cost of maintaining existing policies was $27,000. Had the firm incurred these costs at the same prices as were in effect when it prepared the budget, the costs would have been $26,000. However, some costs changed. Policies worth $13,000,000 were outstanding during the period.

Prepare a schedule to show the variances between the flexible budget and actual costs for this operation.

60. **Behavioral impact of implementing standard cost system** (adapted from CMA exam). Windsor Healthcare, Inc., a manufacturer of custom-designed home health-care equipment, has been in business for 15 years. Last year, in an effort to better control the costs of their products, the controller implemented a standard cost system. Reports are issued monthly for tracking performance, and any negative variances are further investigated.

The production manager complained that the standards are unrealistic, stifle motivation by concentrating only on negative variances, and are out of date too quickly. He noted that his recent switch to titanium for the wheelchairs has resulted in higher material costs but decreased labor time. The net result was no increase in the total cost of producing the wheelchair. The monthly reports continue to show a negative material variance and a positive labor variance, despite the fact that there are indications that the workers are slowing down.

a. Describe several ways that a standard cost system strengthens management cost control.

b. Describe at least two reasons why a standard cost system may negatively impact the motivation of production employees.

61. **Comprehensive problem: Tondamakers, Inc.** Tondamakers produced and sold 1,000 Tonda riding lawnmowers in Year 1, its first year of operation. Actual costs of production are as follows:

Actual Results for the Year:	
Direct Materials: 11,000 Pounds at $19	$209,000
Direct Labor: 2,050 Hours at $31	$ 63,550
Manufacturing Overhead ($205,000 fixed)	$245,000
Actual Marketing and Administrative Costs ($320,000 fixed)	$380,000
Total Revenue: 1,000 Units at $940	$940,000
Actual Machine Hours Worked	550 Hours
Standard Variable Costs per Unit:	
Materials: 10 Pounds at $20	$ 200
Labor: 2 Hours at $30	$ 60
Variable Overhead: .5 Machine Hours at $80	$ 40
Budget Information:	
Budgeted Fixed Manufacturing Costs	$200,000
Master Budget Sales Volume	900 Units
Budgeted Marketing and Administrative Costs	$350,000 + $50 per Unit Sold
Budgeted Sales Price	$1,000 per Unit

Prepare profit and cost variance analyses such as those in Exhibit 10.8.

CASES

62. **Cost data for multiple purposes: Safety Auto Accessories.** Safety Auto Accessories manufactures an automobile safety seat for children that it sells through several retail chains. Safety Auto makes sales exclusively within its five-state region in the Midwest. The cost of manufacturing and marketing children's automobile safety seats at the company's forecasted volume of 15,000 units per month follows:

Variable Materials	$300,000
Variable Labor	150,000
Variable Overhead	30,000
Fixed Overhead	180,200
Total Manufacturing Costs	$660,200
Variable Non-manufacturing Costs	$ 75,000
Fixed Non-manufacturing Costs	105,000
Total Non-manufacturing Costs	$180,000
Total Costs	$840,200

Unless otherwise stated, you should assume a regular selling price of $70 per unit. Ignore income taxes and other costs the problem does not mention.

Early in July, the senior management of Safety Auto Accessories met to evaluate the firm on performance for the first half of the year. The following exchange ensued.

Bob Wilson (president): "Our performance for the first half of this year leaves much to be desired. Despite higher unit sales than forecast, our actual profits are lower than what we expected."

Sam Brown (sales manager): "I suspect production needs to shape up" (he said smugly). "We in sales have pursued an aggressive marketing strategy and the three-quarters of a million sales revenue higher than forecast is proof enough of our improved performance."

Linda Lampman (production manager): "Wait a minute, now! We managed to bring down unit costs from $44.00 to $43.00 with no help from sales, I must add! What's the use of production plans when sales can change them anytime it likes? In February, Sam wanted a rush order for 4,000. In March, it was 8,000 units. Then in April he said to hold off on production; then in June he wanted 6,000. You know what I think. . . ."

Wilson: "Hold on, now! I refuse to let this degenerate into a witch hunt. We have to examine this problem with more objectivity." (He turned to his assistant, who had been quietly taking notes.) "Do you have any ideas, Smith?"

Suppose you are Smith. Write a report to the president analyzing the company's performance. Include a comparison of the actual results to the flexible budget and to the master budget. You know that planned production and sales for each month of the year is 15,000 units per month. You also know that 108,000 units were produced and sold in the first six months of this year, and the income statement for the first six months was as follows:

Sales Revenue		$7,020,000
Manufacturing Costs:		
Variable Materials	$2,160,000	
Variable Labor	1,134,000	
Variable Overhead	324,000	
Fixed Overhead	1,026,000	4,644,000
Gross Margin		$2,376,000
Marketing Costs:		
Variable Marketing	$ 648,000	
Fixed Marketing	650,000	1,298,000
Operating Profit		$1,078,000

63. **Incentive plans at McDonald's.** McDonald's Corporation is one of the world's largest and most successful food service companies. As in all service companies, the way the service employees perform their jobs affects the success of the company.

   The performance of managers of McDonald's company-owned restaurants is critical to the quality and efficiency of service provided by McDonald's. Over the past two decades, McDonald's has tried several incentive compensation plans for its company-owned restaurant managers. We describe five of those plans here.

   - *Plan 1:* Manager's bonus is a function of the restaurant's sales volume increase over the previous year.
   - *Plan 2:* Manager's bonus is based on subjective evaluations by the manager's superiors. Bonuses are not tied explicitly to any quantitative performance measure.
   - *Plan 3:* Manager's bonus comprises the following components:
      (1) A bonus of 10 percent of salary is paid if the manager meets the budgeted costs. This budget is based on sales volume and the standard allowed per unit.
      (2) Management visits each restaurant each month and evaluates its performance with regard to quality, cleanliness, and service. Founder Ray Kroc identified these three key success factors for the company. Managers in restaurants receiving an A get a bonus of 10 percent of salary, managers of restaurants receiving a B get a bonus of 5 percent of salary, and managers of restaurants receiving a C receive no bonus for this component of the plan.
      (3) An additional bonus up to 10 percent of salary is earned based on increases in sales volume over the previous year. (The manager can still receive the bonus if volume does not increase because of circumstances beyond the manager's control.)
   - *Plan 4:* Superiors evaluate the manager as to the following six performance indicators: quality, service, cleanliness, training ability, volume, and profit. Each indicator is scored 0, 1, or 2. A manager receiving a score of 12 points receives a bonus of 40 percent of salary, a score of 11 points provides a bonus of 35 percent of salary, and so forth.
   - *Plan 5:* The manager receives a bonus of 10 percent of the sales volume increase over the previous year plus 20 percent of the restaurant's profit.

   Evaluate each of these incentive plans. Are there better alternatives? Be sure to consider the important things a manager and a restaurant should do to contribute to McDonald's overall company success.

64. **Performance Evaluation: River Beverages.** The River Beverages case at the end of Chapter 9 (see pp. 313–316) focuses on establishing an operating budget. Review the information before reading the next section, which is a continuation of the case.

   Performance Measurement Corporate headquarters generates the variance reports for each business unit. River Beverages has a sophisticated information system that automatically generates reports based on input that is downloaded daily from each plant. The reports can also be generated manually by managers in the organization. Most managers generate variance reports several times during the month, allowing them to solve problems before things get out of control.

   Corporate reviews the variance reports, looking closely at over-budget variance problems. Plant managers are questioned only about costs that exceed the budget. According to management, this ensures that the plant managers are staying on top of problem areas and keeping the plant operating as efficiently as possible. One week after the variance reports are generated, plant managers are required to submit a response outlining the causes of any variances and how they plan to prevent the problems in the future. If a plant manager has repeated problems, corporate may send a specialist to the plant to work with the plant manager to solve the problems.

   1. Do you think the variance analysis process at River Beverages is effective?
   2. What suggestions would you make to provide for a more efficient and effective variance analysis process at River Beverages?

65. **Trust versus incentives.** Product-specific sales incentives (PSIs), or "spiffs," have created conflicts in relations between salespeople and customers for more than 50 years. PSIs are incentives, from money to merchandise, offered by manufacturers to salespeople to encourage them to promote certain products above those of competitors. This practice can motivate salespeople to recommend products that might be inferior or more expensive, compared to other products. Customers often look to salespeople for expert advice when buying items that are complex or unfamiliar to them. PSIs energize sales, yet jeopardize trust and integrity in the marketplace. If a customer relies on a salesperson's advice when the sales-

person is motivated by a PSI, that advice becomes suspect. Consumer organizations state that spiffs are like bribes.

Retailers can compensate their employees less when compensation from PSIs is allowed. Manufacturers must inform the retailer that a PSI is being paid to the salespeople, and it must be paid to all salespeople in the store that sell the specific product model, but consumers do not legally need to be notified. Researchers Chonko and Hunt[3] found that for salespeople the predominant ethical problems with PSIs were bribery and misleading the customer. Women and subordinates were more likely to have ethical dilemmas than men and senior management. Some managers believe that use of PSIs contributes to distrust among consumers, salespeople, and corporate America.

Should retailers allow PSIs for their salespeople?

Suggested Solutions to Even-Numbered Exercises

22. Profit variance analysis.

	Actual (14,200 units)	Cost Variances	Sales Price Variance	Flexible Budget (14,200 units)	Sales Volume Variance	Master Budget (14,000 units)
Sales Revenue	$172,530[a]		$2,130 F	$170,400[c]	$2,400 F	$168,000[d]
Less Variable Costs	83,780[b]	$12,780 U		71,000	$1,000 U	70,000
Contribution Margin	$ 88,750	$12,780 U	$2,130 F	$ 99,400	$1,400 F	$ 98,000
Less Fixed Costs	20,000	1,000 F	—	21,000	—	21,000
Operating Profit	$68,750	$11,780 U	$2,130 F	$ 78,400	$1,400 F	$ 77,000

[a]$172,530 = 14,200 Units × $12.15
[b]$83,780 = 14,200 Units × $5.90
[c]$170,400 = 14,200 Units × $12
[d]$168,000 = 14,000 Units × $12

24. Profit variance analysis.

	Actual (170 units)	Manufacturing Variances	Marketing and Administrative Variances	Sales Price Variance	Flexible Budget (170 units)	Sales Volume Variance	Master Budget (200 units)
Sales Revenue	$18,400			$1,400 F	$17,000	$3,000 U	$20,000
Variable Costs:							
Manufacturing	6,880	$250 U			6,630	1,170 F	7,800
Marketing	2,060		$190 U		1,870	330 F	2,200
Contribution Margin	$ 9,460	$250 U	$190 U	$1,400 F	$ 8,500	$1,500 U	$10,000
Fixed Costs:							
Manufacturing	485	15 F			500	—	500
Marketing	1,040		40 U		1,000	—	1,000
Administrative	995		5 F		1,000	—	1,000
Operating Profit	$ 6,940	$235 U	$225 U	$1,400 F	$ 6,000	$1,500 U	$ 7,500

---

[3]T. J. Radin, "The Myth of the Salesperson: Intended and Unintended Consequences of Product-Specific Sales Incentives," *Journal of Business Ethics* 36, 79–92; and Chonko and Hunt, "Ethics in Marketing Management: An Empirical Examination," *Journal of Business Research* 13, 339–359.

26. Materials and labor variances.

	Actual Costs	Flexible Budget	Variance
Materials	$105,500	$0.50 × (97,810 units × 2 pounds) = $ 97,810	$ 7,690 U
Labor	$905,000	$9.00 × (97,810 units × 1 hr.) = $880,290	$24,710 U

28. Materials and labor variances.

	Actual Costs	Flexible Budget	Variance
Materials	$127,500	$2.50 × (48,000 batches × 1 lb.) = $120,000	$7,500 U
Labor	$214,000	$3.00 × (48,000 batches × 1.5 hrs.) = $216,000	$2,000 F

30. Solving for materials quantities and costs.
Chemical A

a. Price variance is $0.20 F per pound.
Total price variance is $42,000 F.

$$\text{Pounds Purchased and Used} = \frac{\$42,000}{\$.20} = 210,000.$$

b. Standard pounds allowed for 100,000 units (pools cleaned) = 200,000.

210,000 lbs. − 200,000 lbs. = 10,000 lbs. used over standard.

Efficiency variance = $40,000 U.

$$\text{So,}\ \frac{\$40,000}{10,000\ \text{lbs.}} = \$4.00 = \text{the standard unit price.}$$

Chemical B

a. $\text{Pounds Purchased and Used} = \dfrac{\$25,000}{\$0.10} = 250,000.$

b. $\text{Standard Unit Price} = \dfrac{\$30,000}{250,000\ \text{lbs.} - 220,000\ \text{lbs.}} = \$1.00.$

Chemical C

a. $\text{Pounds Purchased and Used} = \dfrac{\$21,000}{\$0.07} = 300,000.$

b. $\text{Standard Unit Price} = \dfrac{\$48,000}{300,000\ \text{lbs.} - 250,000\ \text{lbs.}} = \$0.96.$

32. Labor and variable overhead variances.

	Actual Costs	Flexible Budget	Variance
Direct Labor	$43,400	$3.00 × 15,000 hrs. = $45,000	$1,600 F
Variable Overhead	$22,900	$1.50 × 15,000 hrs. = $22,500	$ 400 U

34. Finding purchase price.

Actual Costs (AP × AQ)	Price Variance	Input at Standard Prices (SP × AQ)
AP × 1,600		$3.60 × 1,600 = $5,760

$240 F

$$1,600 \times AP = \$5,760 - \$240$$

$$AP = \frac{\$5,520}{1,600}$$

$$AP = \$3.45$$

36. Overhead variances.

a. $\dfrac{\$300,000}{60,000 \text{ Units}} = \$5.00$ per Unit

$5.00 + $2.50 = $7.50 per Unit.

b.   Fixed Overhead Applied = $5.00 per Unit × 65,000 Units

= $325,000.

Variable Overhead Applied = $2.50 per Unit × 65,000 Units

= $162,500.

Total Applied Overhead = $325,000 + $162,500

= $487,500

or $7.50 × 65,000 units = $487,500.

c. $487,500 Applied − $400,000 Actual = $87,500 Overapplied.

38. Variance investigation.

Investigate if $pB > C$:

Where: p = Probability process is out of control;

B = Dollar amount of savings from correcting the problem; and

C = Cost of investigation.

$$0.35 \times (\$45,000 - \$20,000) = \$8,750 > \$7,000.$$

Yes, this process should be investigated because the value of the expected savings exceeds the cost of investigation.

40. Variance investigation.

Investigate if $pB > C$:

Where: p = Probability process is out of control;

B = Dollar amount of savings from correcting the problem; and

C = Cost of investigation.

$$0.30 \times \$40,000 = \$12,000$$

$$\$12,000 > \$7,000 \text{ cost.}$$

This process should be investigated because the expected value of the savings is greater than the cost of investigation.

chapter 11

Investment Center Performance Evaluation

Learning Objectives

1. Identify the benefits and disadvantages of decentralization.

2. Identify the issues that must be addressed when using return on investment as a divisional performance measure.

3. Identify examples of differential analysis to make-or-buy decisions with different transfer prices.

4. Discuss transfer pricing issues and methods.

5. Discuss multinational transfer prices.

6. Identify types of costs to be considered in measuring divisional operating costs.

7. Identify issues in measuring the investment base for calculating return on investment.

8. Explain the contribution approach alternative to return on investment for division performance measurement.

9. Describe the purpose of the return on investment calculation, and identify its shortcomings.

10. Explain how to calculate economic value added, and identify its use.

ompanies such as Coca-Cola, McDonald's, and IBM have multiple divisions. Central corporate
management sets broad corporate policies, establishes long-range plans, raises funds, and conducts
other coordinating activities. But corporate management must oversee hundreds of corporate affiliates and divisions. How do companies like these measure and control the performance of their divisions in
such widely diverse and geographically dispersed operating environments?

Such firms rely heavily on their accounting systems to measure performance and to help control and
coordinate their activities. This chapter discusses concepts and methods of measuring performance and
controlling activities in multidivisional companies. These concepts and methods are used extensively in
both manufacturing and non-manufacturing organizations.

Divisional Organization and Performance

The term *division* means different things in different companies. Some companies use the term when
referring to segments organized according to product groupings, whereas other companies use it when
referring to geographic areas served. We use the term **division** to refer to a segment that conducts both
production and marketing activities.

A division may be either a **profit center,** responsible for both revenues and operating costs, or an
investment center, responsible for assets in addition to revenues and operating costs. Many companies
treat the division almost as an autonomous company. Headquarters provides funds for its divisions, much
as shareholders and bondholders provide funds for the company.

A partial organization chart for a high-tech company appears in Exhibit 11.1. This chart shows how
the company's divisions fit into the entire organization. The organization chart in Exhibit 11.1 presents
only a part of this complex organization. Corporate executives hold managers of divisions responsible for
revenues, costs, and assets invested in the divisions and groups. Managers hold most operating units
below the division level responsible for either revenues or costs alone. Performance measures often are
calculated based on profit, revenues minus costs, and return on investment, which are affected by management policies regarding transfer pricing, measurement of costs, and measurement of investment base.

The Nature of Divisionalized Organizations

Top managers delegate or **decentralize** authority and responsibility. The major advantages of decentralization follow:

1. Decentralization enables local personnel to respond quickly to a changing environment.
2. Decentralization frees top management from detailed operating decisions.
3. Decentralization divides large, complex problems into manageable pieces.
4. Decentralization helps train managers and provides a basis for evaluating their decision-making
   performance.
5. Decentralization motivates: Ambitious managers will be frustrated if they implement only the decisions of others. Delegation allows managers to make their own decisions.

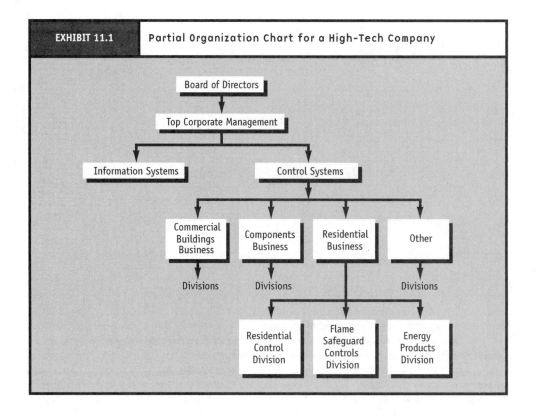

EXHIBIT 11.1   **Partial Organization Chart for a High-Tech Company**

Decentralization has disadvantages, however. Local managers may not act to achieve the overall goals of the organization. For example, a division manager may decide to purchase materials from an outside supplier even though another division of the firm could produce the materials at a lower incremental cost using currently idle facilities. Top management must be alert to situations where the benefits of decentralized authority and the possible conflicts between the goals of a division and those of the organization as a whole require trade-offs. Thus, divisional planning and control systems attempt to create **behavioral congruence** (or **goal congruence**) to encourage division managers to act in ways consistent with organizational goals.[1]

Consider the following interdivisional conflict. Assume a division purchased materials externally rather than from a division inside the company with idle capacity. By purchasing from an outside source, the company earned lower combined profits from the two divisions than if it had purchased the materials from the division inside the company. Should the performance measure for each division reflect the results of its actual transactions? Or should the cost of idle capacity in one division be charged against the profits of the other division? These questions are not easy to answer. The accounting system needs to inform top management of situations in which individual divisions are hurting overall company performance.

Separating a Manager's Performance Evaluation from Divisional Performance Evaluation

In measuring performance, top management should generally distinguish between an organizational division and the division manager. Managers often perform well despite the division's poor performance because of factors outside the manager's control.

For example, a natural disaster that affected the cost of materials would be outside the manager's control. Assume further that during the same period the manager improved efficiency in the use of the materials, cutting waste by 5 percent. However, if this improvement is not enough to compensate for the higher price of the materials, it will still negatively affect the performance

---

[1]For an expanded discussion of these points, see J. A. Brickley, C. W. Smith, Jr., and J. L. Zimmerman, *Managerial Economics and Organizational Architecture,* 3rd ed. (Burr Ridge, Ill.: 2004); R. Simons, *Performance Measurement and Control Systems for Implementing Strategy: Text and Cases* (Upper Saddle River, N.J.: 2000); and R. N. Anthony and V. Govindarajan, *Management Control Systems,* 11th ed. (Burr Ridge, Ill.: 2004).

measurement of the division, and hence the manager. Many measures used to evaluate divisions can be adjusted to account for the controllability of the revenues, costs, and investments by the manager.

Return on Investment as the Performance Measure

Because management expects each division to contribute to the company's profits, managers commonly use divisional operating profit to measure performance. Divisional operating profit by itself, however, does not provide a basis for measuring a division's performance in generating a return on the funds invested in the division. For example, the fact that Division A reported an operating profit of $50,000 does not necessarily mean that it was more successful than Division B, which had an operating profit of $40,000. The difference between these profit levels could be entirely attributable to a difference in the size of the divisions. Management must therefore use some means to relate the division profit measure to the amount of funds invested in the division. Management commonly achieves a comparable statistic by measuring the **division return on investment,** or **ROI,** calculated as follows:

$$\text{Division Return on Investment (ROI)} = \frac{\text{Division Operating Profit}}{\text{Division Investment}}$$

$$= \frac{\text{Division Revenue} - \text{Division Operating Costs}}{\text{Division Investment}}$$

In the preceding example, if management invested $500,000 and $250,000 in Division A and Division B, respectively, the ROIs would be 10 percent (= $50,000/$500,000) and 16 percent (= $40,000/$250,000). Thus Division B earned a higher profit given its investment base than Division A, even though Division A generated a larger absolute amount of profit.

The manager must answer several important questions before applying ROI as a control measure:

1. *How does the firm measure revenues,* particularly when it transfers part of a division's output to another division rather than selling it externally?
2. *Which costs does the firm deduct in measuring divisional operating costs*—only those that the division can control, or also a portion of allocated central corporate administration and staff costs?
3. *How does the firm measure investment:* total assets or net assets; at historical cost or some measure of current cost?

We consider these questions in the following sections.

Transfer Pricing: Measuring Divisional Revenue and Costs for Transactions inside the Organization

When goods or services are transferred from one unit of an organization to another, the transaction is recorded in the accounting records. The value assigned to the transaction is called the *transfer price.* Assessing this value allows for considerable discretion because this exchange takes place inside the organization. Transfer prices are widely used for decision making, product costing, and performance evaluation; hence, it is important to consider alternative transfer pricing methods and their advantages and disadvantages.

Applying Differential Analysis to Transfer Pricing

Assume E-Z Computing, which manufactures and sells various computer products, has two decentralized divisions, Production and Marketing. Marketing has always purchased a particular mouse from Production at $50 per unit. Production is considering raising the price to $60 per unit.

Assume the Production Division's costs related to mouse production are as follows:

Variable costs per unit: $50
Monthly fixed costs: $10,000

Marketing handles the promotion and distribution of the mouse it purchases from Production and sells each mouse for $100. Marketing incurs monthly fixed costs of $5,000. Marketing sells 1,500 units per month.

Each of the following situations is a type of make-or-buy decision, where either Production makes the mouse for Marketing or Marketing buys the mouse from outside suppliers.

Case 1: Transfer Pricing When Production Division Is *Below Capacity*. (Assume a transfer of $50 per unit.)

Case 2: Transfer Pricing When Production Division Is *At Capacity*. (Assume a transfer of $60 per unit.)

Case 1: Transfer Pricing When Production Division Is Below Capacity

First consider each division's profits and the company's profits if Marketing purchases the mouse from Production for $50 per unit. As Panel A of Exhibit 11.2 shows, the Production Division has a loss of $10,000, the Marketing Division makes a profit of $70,000, and the company makes a profit of $60,000.

Now assume that Marketing buys units from an outside supplier for $60 per unit. The facilities Production uses to manufacture these units would remain idle. As shown in Exhibit 11.2, Panel B, the result of purchasing units from an outside supplier reduces companywide operating profits by $15,000 compared to the Panel A results. The differential cost for the company to make the units is $50 per unit, whereas the differential cost to buy is $60 per unit. The cost savings for making over buying is $15,000 [= ($60 − $50) × 1,500 units].

Case 2: Transfer Pricing When Production Division Is At Capacity

Using the same data as above for E-Z Computing, we make one change in our assumptions; namely,

EXHIBIT 11.2	**Case 1: Production Division Below Capacity**		
Panel A: Set transfer price of $50 per unit; Marketing buys internally from Production		**Production**	**Marketing**
Sales:			
$50 × 1,500 (sales to Marketing)		$75,000	
$100 × 1,500 (sales to outsiders)			$150,000
Variable Costs:			
$50 × 1,500 (Production's costs)		75,000	
$50 × 1,500 (transfer from Production)			75,000
Fixed Costs		10,000	5,000
Operating Profits		($10,000)	$ 70,000
Total Company Operating Profits	$60,000		
Panel B: Marketing buys externally for $60 per unit		**Production**	**Marketing**
Sales:			
$100 × 1,500			$150,000
Variable Costs: $60 × 1,500			90,000
Fixed Costs		$10,000	5,000
Operating Profits		($10,000)	$ 55,000
Total Company Operating Profits	$45,000		

EXHIBIT 11.3	Case 2: Production Division At Capacity

Panel A: Set transfer price of $60 per unit	Production	Marketing
Sales:		
$60 × 1,500 (sales to Marketing)	$90,000	
$100 × 1,500		$150,000
Variable Costs:		
$50 × 1,500	75,000	
$60 × 1,500 (transfer from Production)		90,000
Fixed Costs	10,000	5,000
Operating Profits	$ 5,000	$ 55,000
Total Company Operating Profits	$60,000	

Panel B: Marketing buys externally for $60 per unit	Production	Marketing
Sales:		
$60 × 1,500 (sales to outsiders)	$90,000	
$100 × 1,500		$150,000
Variable Costs:		
$50 × 1,500	75,000	
$60 × 1,500 (purchase from outsiders)		90,000
Fixed Costs	$10,000	5,000
Operating Profits	$ 5,000	$ 55,000
Total Company Operating Profits	$60,000	

assume Production does not have idle capacity if Marketing buys from an outside supplier. Instead, if Marketing buys from an outside supplier, Production can sell all the units that it can produce to outside customers at $60 per unit (i.e., Production operates at capacity whether it sells internally or externally). Which option yields the highest total company operating profit for E-Z Computing: Marketing buys from Production or buys from outside supplier?

As shown in Exhibit 11.3, the company's profits are the same whether Marketing buys from Production or from outside. All parties are indifferent to purchasing inside or outside the organization. Production's profits are $5,000 either way, Marketing's profits are $55,000 either way, and E-Z's profits are $60,000 either way. If Production can sell to outsiders for a price greater than $60 per unit, then E-Z Computing will benefit from Production's selling to outsiders and having Marketing buy from other outsiders.

Alternative Ways to Set Transfer Prices

Management's problem is to set transfer prices so that the buyer and seller have goal congruence with respect to the organization's goals. Although there is no easy solution to the transfer pricing problem, there are three general alternative ways to set transfer prices:

1. Top management intervenes to set the transfer price for each transaction between divisions.
2. Top management establishes transfer price policies that divisions follow.
3. Division managers negotiate transfer prices among themselves.

Each of these approaches has advantages and disadvantages. We discuss these alternatives in the next sections.

Top Management Intervention

The disadvantage of top management intervention is that top management may become swamped with pricing disputes, and division managers will lose the flexibility and other advantages of autonomous decision making. Thus, direct intervention may give the right transfer price for a particular transaction, but it reduces the benefits from decentralization.

As long as transactions between divisions are infrequent, the benefits of direct intervention may outweigh the costs. However, if transfer transactions are common, direct intervention can be costly by requiring substantial top-management involvement in decisions that should be made at the divisional level.

Centrally Established Transfer Price Policies

A transfer pricing policy should allow divisional autonomy yet encourage managers to pursue corporate goals consistent with their own personal goals. Additionally, the use of transfer prices to set the selling division's revenue and the buying division's cost should be compatible with the company's performance evaluation system.

The Economic Transfer Pricing Rule
The **economic transfer pricing rule** for making transfers to maximize a company's profits is to *transfer at the differential outlay cost to the selling division (typically variable costs), plus the opportunity cost to the company of making the internal transfers ($0 if the seller has idle capacity or selling price minus variable costs if the seller is operating at capacity).*

To demonstrate the economic transfer pricing rule, consider the E-Z Computing example. The seller, the Production Division, could sell in outside markets to Computer Warehouse, a discount store, for $60 per mouse and has a variable cost of $50 per mouse, which we shall assume is its differential cost.

Now recall Case 1 discussed earlier in this chapter. The Production Division is operating below capacity and has no opportunity cost of the internal transfer because no outside sale is forgone. In this case the transfer price should be $50 per mouse. If the Production Division received a price of $50 for the product, then it would be indifferent between producing and selling it and *not* producing and selling it. The buyer, the Marketing Division, pays $50, which is Production's differential cost of producing the mouse. It is in E-Z's interest for the Marketing Division to pay the Production Division's cost of producing the mouse and not more.

Charging a transfer price above the differential cost plus opportunity cost when the selling division is under capacity can lead to incorrect decisions. For example, assume the Production Division insists on a transfer price of $58 per mouse. An outside company offers to sell the mouse to the Marketing Department at a price of $57. The Marketing Division will be inclined to buy from the outside company because the $57 price is less than what it would pay to the Production Division: $58 (the transfer price). Had the transfer price been set correctly at the $50 differential cost, the Marketing Division would have made the correct decision to buy from Production.

Now recall Case 2. The Production Division is operating at capacity and would have to give up one unit of outside sales for every unit transferred internally. In Case 2, the opportunity cost of transferring the product to a division inside the company is the forgone contribution of selling the unit in an outside market. Consequently, the optimal transfer price would be $60 for the at-capacity case. Exhibit 11.4 summarizes these cases.

If the selling division (the Production Division in our example) is operating at capacity, then it is indifferent between selling in the outside market for $60 or transferring internally at $60. Consequently, as a rule of thumb, the economic transfer pricing rule can be implemented as follows:

1. If the selling division is operating below capacity, it should transfer at the differential cost of production (usually the variable cost).
2. If the selling division is operating at capacity, it should transfer at market price.

In both the below-capacity and at-capacity cases, the selling division is no worse off if it makes the internal transfer.

The selling division does not earn a contribution on the transaction in the below-capacity case, however. Further, it earns only the same contribution for the internal transfer as it would for a sale to the outside market in the at-capacity case. Thus, the general rule stated above is

EXHIBIT 11.4	**Application of the Economic Transfer Pricing Rule**			

	Differential Outlay Cost	+	Opportunity Cost of Transferring Internally	=	Transfer Price
If the seller (that is, Production Division) has idle capacity	$50	+	0	=	$50
If the seller has no idle capacity	$50	+	$10	=	$60
($10 opportunity cost = $60 selling price − $50 variable cost)					

optimal for the company but does not benefit the selling division for an internal transfer. (We assume that the selling division will transfer internally if it is indifferent between an internal transfer and an external sale.)

Transfer Prices Based on Market Price

Externally based **market price-based transfer pricing** is generally considered the best basis when there is a competitive market for the product and market prices are readily available. It is considered a good estimation of differential cost plus opportunity cost, as opportunity cost is based on what can be earned from selling to external markets. An advantage of using market prices in a competitive market is that both the buying and selling divisions can buy and sell as many units as they want at the market price. Managers of both buying and selling divisions are indifferent between trading with each other or with outsiders. From the company's perspective, this is fine as long as the selling division (the Production Division in our example) is operating at capacity.

Transfer Prices Based on Costs

Full-Absorption Costs
Although the rule "transfer at differential outlay cost to the selling division plus the opportunity cost to the company of making the internal transfer" assumes the company has a measure of differential or variable cost, this is not always the case. Consequently, full-absorption costs are sometimes used in manufacturing firms.

Activity-Based Costing
Many companies are implementing activity-based costing to improve the accuracy of costs in cost-based transfer pricing. Deere and Co., maker of John Deere equipment, developed activity-based costing in part to improve the accuracy of cost numbers used for transfer pricing.

Cost-Plus Transfers
We also find companies using **cost-plus transfer pricing** based on either variable costs or full-absorption costs. These methods generally apply a normal markup to costs as a surrogate for market prices when intermediate market prices are not available.

Standard Costs or Actual Costs
Basing transfer prices on actual costs causes the buying division to suffer the costs of inefficiencies in the selling division. The problem of isolating the variances that have been transferred to subsequent buyer divisions becomes extremely complex. To promote responsibility in the selling division, standard costs, not actual costs, are usually used as a basis for transfer pricing in cost-based systems.

For example, suppose E-Z Computers transferred based on variable costs. The standard variable cost of producing the mouse is $50, but the actual cost of producing it turns out to be $52 because of inefficiencies in the Production Division. Should Production pass this inefficiency on to the buying division? The answer is usually no, to give the Production Division incentives to be efficient. In these cases, companies will use standard costs for the transfer price. If standards are out of date or otherwise do not reflect reasonable estimates of costs, then the actual cost may be a better measure to use in the transfer price.

Other Motivational Aspects of Transfer Pricing Policies

When the transfer pricing rule does not give the supplier a profit on the transaction, motivational problems can arise. For example, if transfers are made at differential cost, the transfer policy fails to motivate the supplier to transfer internally because the supplier earns no contribution toward profits on the transferred goods. This situation can be remedied in several ways.

A supplier whose transfers are almost all internal is usually organized as a cost center. The center manager is normally held responsible for costs, not for revenues. Hence, the transfer price does not affect the manager's performance measures. In companies where such a supplier is a profit center, the artificial nature of the transfer price should be taken into consideration when evaluating the results of that center's operations.

A company could set up a supplying center that does business with both internal and external customers as a profit center for external business when the manager has price-setting power and as a cost center for internal transfers when the manager does not have price-setting power. The company could measure performance on external business as if the center were a profit center and evaluate internal business as if the center were a cost center.

Dual Transfer Prices   A company may install a **dual transfer pricing** system to provide the selling division with a profit but charge the buying division with costs only. That is, accounting could charge the buyer the cost of the unit, however cost might be determined, and credit the selling division with cost plus some profit allowance. The difference could be accounted for by a special centralized account. This system would preserve cost data for subsequent buyer divisions, and it would encourage internal transfers by providing a profit on such transfers for the selling divisions.

Other Incentives for Internal Transfers   We have seen a few companies use dual transfer prices to encourage internal transfers. However, there are other ways to encourage internal transfers. Many companies recognize internal transfers and, using balanced scorecard principles, incorporate them explicitly in their reward systems. Other companies base part of a supplying manager's bonus on the purchasing center's profits. These approaches create incentives for managers to transfer internally in organizational settings.

Division Managers Negotiate Transfer Prices

An alternative to a centrally administered transfer pricing policy is to permit managers to negotiate the price for internally transferred goods and services. Under this system, the managers involved act much as if they headed independent companies. The major advantage to **negotiated transfer pricing** is that it preserves the autonomy of the division managers. In the E-Z Computers case, the two managers have room to negotiate the price between $50 and $60. The two managers might choose to "split the difference" or develop some other negotiating strategy. The two primary disadvantages are that a great deal of management effort may be consumed in the negotiating process, and the final price and its implications for performance measurement may depend more on the manager's ability to negotiate than on what's best for the company.

Problem 11.1 for Self-Study

Transfer pricing.   The Nykee Shoe Company has two divisions, Production and Marketing. Production manufactures Nykee shoes, which it sells to both the Marketing Division and to other retailers (the latter under a different brand name). Marketing operates several small shoe stores in shopping centers. Marketing sells both Nykee and other brands. Relevant facts for Production are as follows:

Production is operating far below its capacity.

Sales price to outsiders	$28.50 per pair
Variable cost to produce	$18.00 per pair
Fixed costs	$100,000 per month

The following data pertain to the sale of Nykee shoes by Marketing:
   Marketing is operating far below its capacity.

Sales price	.$40 per pair
Variable marketing costs	.$1 per pair

The company's variable manufacturing and marketing costs are differential to this decision, while fixed manufacturing and marketing costs are not.

a.   What is the minimum price that can be charged by the Marketing Division for the shoes and still cover the company's differential manufacturing and marketing costs?

b.   What is the appropriate transfer price for this decision?

c.   If the transfer price is set at $28.50, what effect will this have on the minimum price set by the Marketing manager?

d.   How would your answer to **b.** change if the Production Division was operating at full capacity?

The solution to this self-study problem is at the end of the chapter on page 403.

Global Transfer Pricing Practices

Surveys of corporate practices indicate that nearly half of companies that use transfer prices base transfer prices on costs. About one-third of companies use a market price-based system, and the rest rely on negotiations between division managers. Generally, we find that when companies use negotiated prices, the prices negotiated fall between the market price at the upper limit and some measure of cost at the lower limit. Managers who do business in various countries will find cultural differences in negotiating behavior (e.g., Australians tend to be more conciliatory than U.S. managers).[2]

Is there an optimal transfer pricing policy that dominates all others? The answer is no. An established policy will, most likely, be imperfect in the sense that it will not always work to induce the economically optimal outcome. However, as with other decisions, management must weigh the cost of any system against its benefits. Improving a transfer pricing policy beyond some point (say, to obtain better measures of variable costs and market prices) will result in the costs of the system exceeding the benefits. Thus, management tends to settle for a system that seems to work reasonably well rather than devise a textbook-perfect system.

Multinational and Multistate Transfer Pricing

In international transactions, transfer prices may affect tax liabilities, royalties, and other payments because of different laws in different countries (or states). Because tax rates differ by country, companies have incentives to set transfer prices that will increase revenues (and profits) in low-tax countries and increase costs (thereby reducing profits) in high-tax countries.

These same issues apply to interstate transactions. Companies have incentives to transfer profits from high-tax states like Massachusetts and California to low-tax states like New Hampshire and Nevada.

Tax avoidance by foreign companies using inflated transfer prices has spawned a major political issue in the United States. Foreign companies who sell goods to their U.S. subsidiaries at inflated transfer prices artificially reduce the profit of the U.S. subsidiaries. According to some political observers, the United States could collect as much as $9 billion to $13 billion per year in additional taxes if transfer pricing were calculated according to U.S. tax laws. (Many foreign companies dispute this claim.)

---

[2]See C. W. Chan, "Transfer Pricing Negotiation Outcomes and the Impact of Negotiator Mixed-Motives and Culture: Empirical Evidence from the U.S. and Australia," *Management Accounting Research* 9, 139–161.

To understand the effects of transfer pricing on taxes, consider the case of the Kashmere Jacket Corp. The Kashmere Jacket Corp.'s facility in the Republic of Tax (ROT) imports materials from the company's facility in the nation Great Incentives (GI). The tax rate in ROT is 60 percent, while the tax rate in GI is 10 percent.

During the current year, Kashmere incurred production costs of $2 million in GI. Costs incurred in ROT, aside from the materials imported from Kashmere's facilities in GI, amounted to $6 million. Sales revenues in ROT were $24 million. The government tax regulators argue that Kashmere should record a transfer price of $3 million for the materials imported from its facility in GI because that is the price that companies would pay on the open market in "arms-length" transactions. Kashmere Jacket Corp., however, tries (without success) to claim the appropriate transfer price is $10 million. What would Kashmere Jacket Corp.'s total tax liability in both jurisdictions be if it used the $3 million transfer price? What would the liability be if it used the $10 million transfer price?

Assuming the $3 million transfer price, the tax liabilities are computed as follows:

	Country GI	Country ROT
Revenues	$3,000,000	$24,000,000
Third-Party Costs	2,000,000	6,000,000
Transferred Goods Costs		3,000,000
Taxable Income	1,000,000	15,000,000
Tax Rate	× 10%	× 60%
Tax Liability	$ 100,000	$ 9,000,000
Total Tax Liability	$9,100,000	

Assuming the $10 million transfer price, the liabilities are computed as follows:

	Country GI	Country ROT
Revenues	$10,000,000	$24,000,000
Third-Party Costs	2,000,000	6,000,000
Transferred Goods Costs		10,000,000
Taxable Income	8,000,000	8,000,000
Tax Rate	× 10%	× 60%
Tax Liability	$ 800,000	$ 4,800,000
Total Tax Liability	$5,600,000	

Kashmere Jacket Corp. can save $3,500,000 in taxes simply by changing its transfer price.

Managerial Application

Just-in-Time Production in Japan and the Internal Revenue Service in the United States

A Japanese motorcycle manufacturer that used just-in-time production methods for its manufacturing facility in Japan sold its motorcycles to its U.S. subsidiary using full cost as the transfer price. During a recent period, demand in the United States for motorcycles dropped. At one point the U.S. subsidiary found itself with more than a year's supply of motorcycles on hand. Meanwhile, the Japanese manufacturing plant was reluctant to reduce production below its efficient operating level, and, because it followed the just-in-time philosophy, it did not stockpile finished goods inventory in Japan.

As inventories grew at the U.S. subsidiary, so did expenses to store and sell the mounting inventory of products. The U.S. subsidiary showed declining profits and eventually incurred losses. The U.S. Internal Revenue Service claimed the Japanese manufacturer should have lowered its transfer price, stopped shipping motorcycles to the U.S. subsidiary, or both. According to the IRS, the Japanese manufacturer should bear some of the costs of the U.S. subsidiary's high inventory levels. The Japanese manufacturer disagreed. The case was settled out of court.

Source: Based on the authors' research.

International (and state) taxing authorities look closely at transfer prices when examining the tax returns of companies engaged in related-party transactions that cross national (and state) borders. Companies must frequently have adequate support for the use of the transfer price that they have chosen for such a situation, as discussed in the Managerial Application "Just-in-Time Production in Japan and the Internal Revenue Service in the United States."

Problem 11.2 for Self-Study

Multinational transfer pricing. Refer to the information for Kashmere Jacket Corp. in the text. Assume the tax rate for both countries (GI and ROT) is 40 percent. What would the tax liability be for Kashmere Jacket Corp. if it set the transfer price at $3 million? At $10 million?

The solution to this self-study problem is at the end of the chapter on page 404.

Measuring Division Operating Costs

In measuring divisional operating costs, management must decide how to treat the following costs: (1) controllable direct operating costs; (2) noncontrollable direct operating costs; (3) controllable indirect operating costs; and (4) noncontrollable indirect operating costs. *Direct* versus *indirect* refers to whether the cost associates directly with the division; *controllable* versus *noncontrollable* refers to whether the division manager can affect the cost. Exhibit 11.5 shows examples of each. In each case it must be decided whether or not to include costs as costs to the division in calculating division operating profit for performance evaluation of the division and of the division manager.

Direct Costs

Management virtually always deducts a division's direct operating costs from divisional revenues in measuring divisional operating profits. From top management's perspective, any cost necessary for that division to operate is a direct cost, even if the division manager cannot control the cost. If top management believes that division managers should not be held responsible for things outside their control, it can separate the measure of costs assigned to a *division* from the costs assigned to a division *manager.* The latter measure could exclude direct costs of the division that the division manager cannot control (for example, the division manager's salary).

EXHIBIT 11.5	Examples of Direct (Indirect) and Controllable (Noncontrollable) Costs	
Direct		**Indirect**
Controllable		
Labor used in the division's production		Costs of providing centralized services, such as data processing and employee training
Noncontrollable		
Salary of the division manager (controlled by top management)		Company president's salary

Indirect Controllable Operating Costs

Divisions can at least partially control indirect controllable costs. Firms usually centralize particular services because of economies of scale. In some companies, costs would exceed benefits if each division had its own legal staff, research department, data-processing department, and so forth.

For example, many companies have centralized employee-training departments. Should management charge divisions for sending their people to these centralized departments? As you may expect, the experiences in most companies follow fundamental laws of economics: The use of centralized services and the price charged for those services are inversely related. When companies charge a high price for employee training, people's attendance from the divisions drops, and vice versa.

Top management can use this experience to decide on the desired usage and set the price accordingly. Some companies treat centralized service departments as profit or investment centers; if so, the transfer pricing issues discussed earlier are relevant.

Indirect Noncontrollable Operating Costs

Indirect noncontrollable operating costs may be necessary costs to the company (for example, the salaries and staff support of corporate top management). The most frequent arguments against allocating these costs down to divisions are based on the divisions' inability to control the amount of costs incurred.

One argument advanced for allocation is that, unless the company allocates these costs to the divisions, the divisions will underprice their products and cause the company as a whole to operate at a loss. In other words, the revenues the divisions generate would be insufficient to cover both the direct operating costs of the divisions and the indirect operating costs incurred at central headquarters.

A top manager of a retail company told us that the company allocated central headquarters' costs to the stores to keep them aware of these costs. "We want our store managers to recognize that it's not enough for stores to make a profit for the company to be profitable." The corporate manager went on to say that part of a store manager's bonus was based on the store's profit after central headquarters' costs had been allocated to stores. "This makes them very aware of central headquarters' costs, and it makes us [top management] sensitive to their criticisms about [central headquarters'] administrative costs."

Measuring the Investment in Divisions

Most companies use some measure of funds employed or invested in each division when calculating return on investment (ROI). In this section we discuss (1) which assets firms include in the investment base and (2) which valuation basis firms use.

Assets Included in the Investment Base

Management obviously should include assets physically located in a division and used only in the division's operations in the investment base. More difficult problems arise with assets shared among divisions and assets that centralized services departments acquire (for example, buildings and equipment used in personnel training). Management often allocates the cost of a shared manufacturing plant between divisions. We explain the ROI calculation in detail on pages 397 to 401.

Valuation of Assets in the Investment Base

Once the firm chooses the assets in the investment base, it must assign them a monetary value. Most firms use acquisition cost as the valuation basis. Management can obtain the necessary amounts directly from the company's accounts.

Using book values of assets, particularly fixed assets, in the ROI denominator can have undesirable results. The manager of a division with old, low-cost, and almost fully depreciated assets may be reluctant to replace the assets with newer, more efficient, but more costly assets. Replacing old assets with new, more costly ones decreases the numerator—operating profits—of the

ROI calculation because of increased depreciation charges. It also increases the denominator—cost of total assets—of the ROI calculation. Each of these effects reduces calculated ROI.

If using book values in the investment base affects divisional investment behavior this way, management may deal with the problem in two possible ways. One, it may state all assets at gross book value rather than at net book value. This approach states assets at full acquisition cost regardless of age. Another approach is to state assets at their current replacement cost or net realizable value.

In general, the older the assets, the higher the ROI under net book value compared to gross book value. If replacement cost increases over time, ROI is higher under historical cost compared to current replacement cost.

Contribution Approach to Division Reporting

In previous sections, we discussed some of the factors you should consider in calculating ROI. In this section, we discuss several additional considerations in using and interpreting ROI as a basis for evaluating divisional performance.

We suggest that a firm should decide how it is going to calculate ROI and then use it consistently. Exhibit 11.6 presents a divisional performance report in a format that facilitates a variety

| EXHIBIT 11.6 | The Contribution Approach to Division Reporting (all dollar amounts in thousands) |

			Company Breakdown into Two Divisions	
	Company as a Whole	Division A	Division B
Revenues	$6,500	$2,500	$4,000
Variable Manufacturing Cost of Goods Sold	2,300	800	1,500
Manufacturing Contribution Margin	$4,200	$1,700	$2,500
Variable Selling and Administrative Costs	600	200	400
Contribution Margin	$3,600	$1,500	$2,100
Fixed Costs Directly Attributable to the Division	2,400	475	1,925
Division Contribution to Unallocated Costs and Profit	$1,200	$1,025	$ 175
Unallocated Costs	800[a]		
Operating Profit	$ 400		

		Further Breakdown of Division A into Two Product Lines	
	Division A	Product 1	Product 2
Revenues	$2,500	$1,300	$1,200
Variable Manufacturing Cost of Goods Sold	800	500	300
Manufacturing Contribution Margin	$1,700	$ 800	$ 900
Variable Selling and Administrative Costs	200	100	100
Contribution Margin	$1,500	$ 700	$ 800
Fixed Costs Directly Attributable to the Division	475	275	200
Division Contribution to Unallocated Costs and Profit	$1,025	$ 425	$ 600
Unallocated Costs	425[b]		
Operating Profit	$ 600		

[a]These costs are not direct costs of the division and could be allocated only by an arbitrary allocation method.
[b]These costs are not direct costs of the product line and could be allocated only by an arbitrary allocation method.

of uses. For example, management could use the report to evaluate the division and its manager's performance without regard to costs allocated to divisions or to product lines. Further, the report provides data about the division's performance after the firm allocates all central administrative costs. Some corporate managers like to see a bottom line that takes into account all costs, even indirect costs that accounting has allocated to divisions.

Components of Return on Investment

The rate of return on investment has two components: profit margin percentage and investment (or asset) turnover ratio.

$$\text{Return on Investment} = \text{Profit Margin Percentage} \times \text{Investment Turnover Ratio}$$

$$\frac{\text{Profit Margin}}{\text{Divisional Investment}} = \frac{\text{Profit Margin}}{\text{Divisional Revenues}} \times \frac{\text{Divisional Revenues}}{\text{Divisional Investment}}$$

To illustrate the usefulness of dividing ROI into its components, assume the following information about Division A:

Year	Sales	Profit	Investment
1	$1,000,000	$100,000	$ 500,000
2	2,000,000	160,000	1,000,000
3	4,000,000	400,000	2,500,000

The following table shows the ROI for each of the three years and the associated profit margin percentages and investment turnover ratios.

Year	ROI	=	Profit Margin Percentage	×	Investment Turnover Ratio
1	20%	=	10%	×	2.0
2	16%	=	8%	×	2.0
3	16%	=	10%	×	1.6

The **profit margin percentage** indicates the portion of each dollar of revenue that is profit. Management often uses it as a measure for assessing efficiency in producing and selling goods and services. The profit margin percentage for Division A in this example decreased from 10 percent to 8 percent between Year 1 and Year 2.

The **investment turnover ratio** is the ratio of divisional sales to the investment in divisional assets. It indicates potentially useful information on how effectively management used the funds invested in the division. Returning to the preceding example, Division A could not increase its ROI between Year 2 and Year 3, despite an increase in its profit margin percentage, because its investment turnover ratio decreased. The division could not generate $2 of revenue for each dollar invested in Year 3, as it had done in previous years.

Studying profit margin percentages and investment turnover ratios for a given division over several periods will provide more useful information than comparing these ratios for all divisions in a particular period. Some divisions, due to the nature of their activities, require more invested funds than others; some have higher profit margins than others.

Setting Minimum Desired ROI

If the ROI is to measure divisional performance effectively, management must set a standard or desired rate each period. Management usually specifies a minimum desired ROI for each division, given its particular operating characteristics. Some divisions face greater risk than others; hence, management may have higher expectations for them. Some divisions have a low investment base (for example, professional services, consulting); thus, ROI is sometimes quite high. In short, management should recognize the particular characteristics of a division in setting minimum ROI for a division.

Critics of ROI argue that managers may turn down investment opportunities that are above the minimum acceptable rate but below the ROI currently being earned. For example, suppose that the division currently earns

$$ROI = \frac{\$1,000,000}{\$4,000,000} = 25\%.$$

Suppose the manager has an opportunity to make an additional investment. This investment would return $400,000 per year for five years for a $2 million investment. At the end of five years, the $2 million investment would be returned. Assume that there is no inflation. The ROI each year is

$$ROI = \frac{\$400,000}{\$2,000,000} = 20\%.$$

The company desires an ROI of at least 15 percent. This investment clearly qualifies, but it would lower the investment center ROI from 25 percent to 23.3 percent:

$$ROI = \frac{(\$1,000,000 + \$400,000)}{(\$4,000,000 + \$2,000,000)} = 23.3\%.$$

A comparison of the old (25 percent) and new (23.3 percent) ROIs would imply performance has worsened; consequently, a manager might decide not to make such an investment.

An alternative to ROI, and a contemporary measure of divisional performance, is **economic value added (EVA®)**[3]. Economic value added is the amount of earnings generated above the cost of funds invested to generate those earnings. Common practice refers to this cost of funds invested as the *cost of capital.* Although students and managers tend to confuse the concept with its methods of measurement, we shall refer to the *cost of capital* because of its common usage. The EVA resembles another measure, developed by General Motors in the 1920s and later refined by General Electric in the 1950s, called *residual income.* The concept of residual income remained largely unused in incentive compensation plans until some consultants recently repackaged it under the name "economic value added." Economic value added is defined as follows:

$$EVA® = NOPAT - (WACC \times Investment)$$

where
$$NOPAT = \text{Net Operating Profit After Tax,}$$
$$WACC = \text{Weighted-Average Cost of Capital, and}$$
$$Investment = \text{Total Assets} - \text{Noninterest-Bearing Current Liabilities.}$$

This formula applies to a division but also holds true for an entire company. Just use "company-wide measures" for "divisional measures of NOPAT, WACC, or investment" in the formula. The following discussion clarifies the components of the economic value added equation.

NOPAT (Net Operating Profit After Tax)

NOPAT measures the after-tax operating profits of a division or company. In principle, NOPAT is based on the same concept as operating income on an income statement or the operating profit numbers in the ROI formula. In practice, analysts generally use after-tax numbers, not before-tax numbers, to reflect tax expense.

NOPAT starts with the operating income or operating profit number from an income statement. You can find "operating income" on any published financial statement. To measure the after-tax operating profit in the ROI calculation, simply deduct income taxes as an expense.

The division's total assets (often called total investment, similar to ROI) and noninterest-bearing debt are relatively straightforward and come from the division's balance sheet.

---

[3]EVA® is a registered trademark of Stern Stewart & Co., New York, N.Y.

The weighted-average cost of capital is a bit more complicated. We measure it as the average of the after-tax cost of all long-term borrowing and the cost of equity. The **weighted-average cost of capital (WACC)** is calculated as follows:

$$WACC = \frac{\left(\begin{array}{c}\text{After-Tax}\\\text{Cost of Debt}\end{array} \times \begin{array}{c}\text{Market Value}\\\text{of Debt}\end{array}\right) + \left(\begin{array}{c}\text{Cost of}\\\text{Equity}\end{array} \times \begin{array}{c}\text{Market Value}\\\text{Equity}\end{array}\right)}{\text{Market Value of Debt } + \text{ Market Value of Equity}}$$

The weighted-average cost of funds is typically measured by the treasury or finance department within the company. Finance texts and courses discuss development of the appropriate cost of capital for companies and divisions. In our observations of economic value added in practice, organizations frequently use the information published in Ibbotson Associates' *Cost of Capital Quarterly* as a starting point for their cost of capital computations.[4] Modifying the published cost of capital data to apply it to a particular division's investment base can be something of an art as analysts grapple with how their division differs from industry averages. In practice, analysts generally compute a weighted-average cost of capital that takes into account both the debt and equity sources of capital.

Using data from the example discussed at the beginning of this section, we will calculate the economic value added amount both before the proposed investment and after the proposed investment.

Assume the company's minimum desired ROI of 15 percent is its weighted-average cost of capital (the finance department performed the weighted-average cost of capital calculation using the formula above). Furthermore, assume the division has no noninterest-bearing current liabilities (for the sake of simplicity) and the division's tax rate is 20 percent. With this information, we can calculate the economic value added amount. Remember that the division manager was initially evaluated using ROI, and as a result rejected an investment that met the company's overall minimum ROI criteria.

Before the investment, the economic value added amount is $200,000 as calculated in the following equation.

$$EVA = NOPAT - (WACC \times Investment)$$

$$EVA = [\$1,000,000 \times (1 - 0.20)] - [0.15 \times (\$4,000,000 - \$0)]$$

$$= \$800,000 - \$600,000$$

$$= \$200,000.$$

The economic value added amount from the additional investment is $20,000 as calculated in the following equation:

$$EVA = [\$400,000 \times (1 - 0.20)] - [0.15 \times (\$2,000,000 - \$0)]$$

$$= \$320,000 - \$300,000$$

$$= \$20,000.$$

Hence, *after the additional investment,* the economic value added amount for the division increases to $220,000 (= $200,000 + $20,000). The additional investment increases the economic value added amount, appropriately improving the measure of performance, whereas the use of ROI worsened the measure of performance. Using economic value added as a performance measure encourages managers to take on all projects that will increase the division's overall economic value added amount.

Managers generally recognize the goal congruence problem with ROI, and they may take it into account when a new investment lowers the ROI. This may explain why in practice economic value added does not dominate ROI as a performance measure. Further, ROI is expressed as a percentage that managers can intuitively compare with related percentages—such as the cost of capital, the prime interest rate, and the Treasury Bill rate. Most companies use ROI, but many use a combination of economic value added and ROI.

Using EVA in incentive plans gives managers incentives to eliminate assets that earn less than the cost of capital and invest in those that earn more. Top management in many companies, including Coca-Cola, Quaker Oats, Eli Lilly, Herman Miller, Ryder Systems, and Monsanto, have been enthusiastic about EVA. Even the U.S. Postal Service has adopted EVA to encourage

---

[4]See http://valuation.ibbotson.com/.

its managers to reduce losses. The jury is still out on whether EVA is a sustainable incentive device.[5] As discussed in the Managerial Application "Does Economic Value Added Beat Earnings?" researchers question whether EVA is more highly correlated with stock returns than are more traditional accounting measures such as net income or return on investment. EVA in some form is unlikely to be a passing fad, however, because it is based on the fundamental concept of economic profit, which is the profit generated after considering all costs, including the opportunity cost of capital. The notion that companies earning an economic profit will add wealth to their owners is well grounded in economic theory and in practice.

Like residual income before it, EVA attempts to operationalize the concept of economic profit. Whether EVA or a variation of EVA, designers of incentive compensation plans continue providing incentives for managers to earn an economic profit for as long as humans are economically oriented beings.

Managerial Application

Does Economic Value Added Beat Earnings?

Research indicates that division managers are more likely to make decisions in the best interest of shareholders if their performance is evaluated using residual income than if it is not. Thus, residual income/EVA may be an effective incentive tool from the perspective of shareholders. However, it is not clear whether EVA dominates net income as a preferred measure of company performance in the stock market. In fact, some research indicates that stock returns are more closely correlated with net income than with EVA.

Sources: J. S. Wallace, "Adopting Residual Income-Based Compensation Plans: Do You Get What You Pay For?" *Journal of Accounting and Economics* 24, no. 3, 275–300; and G. C. Biddle, R. M. Bowen, and J. S. Wallace, "Does EVA Beat Earnings? Evidence on Associations with Stock Returns and Firm Values," *Journal of Accounting and Economics* 24, no. 3, 301–336.

Modifying the Accounting Numbers

Many consultants and analysts modify the numbers presented in external financial statements that comply with GAAP. Keep in mind that the data used in external reports must comply with GAAP, but those in incentive compensation plans need not. Designers of incentive plans should examine desired manager and employee behavior to ascertain how to modify the accounting numbers to provide incentives for that behavior.

One of the consulting firms that implements economic value added has 164 possible adjustments to the accounting numbers. In our experience, most companies use only a few adjustments to the GAAP accounting numbers, and some use none. The main adjustments that companies seem to make, if any, are these:

- Capitalize expenditures on research and development and then amortize the capitalized expenditures over their useful life.
- Capitalize expenditures on customer development, advertising, and promotion if these expenditures will benefit future years and then amortize the capitalized expenditures over their useful life.
- Capitalize expenditures on employee training that will benefit future years and then amortize the capitalized expenditures over their useful life.
- Make price-level adjustments so that assets, revenues, and expenses are stated in current-year currency values.
- Use market values of assets at the beginning and end of fiscal periods to reflect the actual decline in the economic value of assets.

---

[5]For alternative points of view on this subject, see P. A. Dierks and A. Patel, "What Is EVA and How Can It Help Your Company?" *Management Accounting* 79, no. 9, 52–58.

- Restate inventories to reflect replacement cost.
- Do not amortize goodwill.

We advise you not to consider this list as either a recommended guideline or a complete list of adjustments. Each organization has a unique situation and requires a unique set of adjustments.

Problem 11.3 for Self-Study

Return on investment and economic value added. The Venus Division of Hyperspace Company has assets of $2.4 billion, current liabilities of $400 million, operating profits of $600 million before taxes, and a weighted-average cost of capital of 20 percent. The company's tax rate is 30 percent.

Compute return on investment before taxes and economic value added.

The solution to this self-study problem is at the end of the chapter on page 404.

Summary

The following items correspond to the learning objectives presented at the beginning of the chapter.

1. **Identify the benefits and disadvantages of decentralization.** Decentralization enables local personnel to respond quickly to a changing environment, frees top management from detailed operating decisions, divides complex problems into manageable pieces, helps train managers and provide a basis for evaluating performance, and motivates managers. The disadvantage is that it may promote non–goal-congruent behavior.

2. **Identify the issues that must be addressed when using return on investment as a divisional performance measure.** Several questions must be addressed before applying return on investment as a control measure: How does the firm measure revenues? Which costs does the firm deduct in measuring divisional operating costs? How does the firm measure investment?

3. **Identify examples of differential analysis to make-or-buy decisions with different transfer prices.** See Exhibits 11.2 through 11.4 for examples applying differential analysis to make-or-buy decisions involving transfer prices.

4. **Discuss transfer pricing issues and methods.** Two general rules exist when establishing a transfer price: (1) If the selling division is operating at capacity, the transfer price should be the market price; and (2) if the selling division has idle capacity, and the idle facilities cannot be used for other purposes, the transfer price should be at least the variable costs incurred to produce the goods.

5. **Discuss multinational transfer prices.** Because tax rates are different in different countries, companies have incentives to set transfer prices that will increase revenues (and profits) in low-tax countries and increase costs (thereby reducing profits) in high-tax countries.

6. **Identify types of costs to be considered in measuring divisional operating costs.** In measuring divisional operating costs, management must decide how to treat the following costs: (1) controllable direct operating costs; (2) noncontrollable direct operating costs; (3) controllable indirect operating costs; and (4) noncontrollable indirect operating costs. *Direct* versus *indirect* refers to whether the cost associates directly with the division; *controllable* versus *noncontrollable* refers to whether the division manager can affect the cost.

7. **Identify issues in measuring the investment base for calculating return on investment.** Two issues arise when measuring the investment base: (1) how to allocate the cost of shared assets; and (2) what value to use for the assets.

8. **Explain the contribution approach alternative to return on investment for division performance measurement.** The contribution approach allows management to evaluate the division and its managers' performance without regard to costs arbitrarily allocated to divisions or to product lines. The report also provides data about the division's performance after the firm allocates all central administrative costs.

9. **Describe the purpose of the return on investment calculation, and identify its shortcomings.** The rate of return on investment has two components: profit margin and investment turnover. A shortcoming of return on investment is that it may not lead managers to accept good investment opportunities if the ROI of the investment is lower than the present ROI of the division.

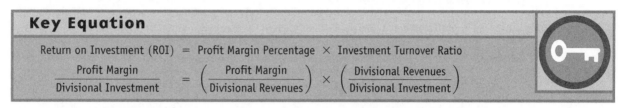

Key Equation

Return on Investment (ROI) = Profit Margin Percentage × Investment Turnover Ratio

$$\frac{\text{Profit Margin}}{\text{Divisional Investment}} = \left(\frac{\text{Profit Margin}}{\text{Divisional Revenues}} \right) \times \left(\frac{\text{Divisional Revenues}}{\text{Divisional Investment}} \right)$$

10. **Explain how to calculate economic value added, and identify its use.** The calculation of economic value added alleviates the shortcoming of the return on investment measurement.

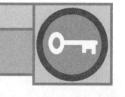

Key Equation

EVA = Net Operating Profit After Tax − [Weighted-Average Cost of Capital × (Total Assets − Noninterest-Bearing Debt)]

Key Terms and Concepts

Behavioral (goal) congruence
Cost-plus transfer pricing
Decentralize
Division
Division return on investment (ROI)
Dual transfer pricing
Economic transfer pricing rule
Economic value added (EVA®)

Investment center
Investment turnover ratio
Market price-based transfer pricing
Negotiated transfer pricing
Profit center
Profit margin percentage
Weighted-average cost of capital (WACC)

Solutions to Self-Study Problems

SUGGESTED SOLUTION TO PROBLEM 11.1 FOR SELF-STUDY

a. From a company's perspective, the minimum price would be the variable cost of producing and marketing the goods, $19. If the company were centralized, we would expect this information to be conveyed to the manager of Marketing, who would be instructed not to set a price below $19.

b. The transfer price that correctly informs the Marketing manager about the differential costs of manufacturing is $18.

c. If the Production manager set the price at $28.50, the Marketing manager would set the minimum price at $29.50 (= $28.50 + $1.00). In fact, prices of $28, $25, or anything greater than $19 would have generated a positive contribution margin from the production and sale of shoes.

d. If the Production Division had been operating at capacity, there would have been an implicit opportunity cost of internal transfers. The implicit opportunity cost to the company is the lost contribution margin ($28.50 − $19 = $9.50) from not selling in the wholesale market.
The transfer price should have been:

Differential cost   Implicit opportunity cost to company
of production   +   if goods are transferred internally

= $19.00 + $9.50

= $28.50

Marketing would have appropriately treated the $28.50 as part of its differential cost of buying and selling the shoes.

SUGGESTED SOLUTION TO PROBLEM 11.2 FOR SELF-STUDY

For the $3 million transfer, the total tax is (40% × $1,000,000) + (40% × $15,000,000) = $6,400,000. For $10 million, the total tax is (40% × $8,000,000) + (40% × $8,000,000) = $6,400,000. With equal tax rates, there is no advantage to inflating the transfer price.

SUGGESTED SOLUTION TO PROBLEM 11.3 FOR SELF-STUDY

$$ROI = \frac{\$0.6 \text{ Billion}}{\$2.4 \text{ Billion}} = 25\%$$

$$EVA = [\$0.6 \text{ Billion} \times (1.00 - 0.30)] - [0.2 \times (\$2.4 \text{ Billion} - \$0.4 \text{ Billion})]$$

$$= \$0.42 \text{ Billion} - \$0.40 \text{ Billion}$$

$$= \$0.02 \text{ Billion (that is, EVA of \$20 million).}$$

Questions, Exercises, Problems, and Cases

REVIEW QUESTIONS

1. Review the meaning of the concepts or terms given in Key Terms and Concepts.
2. Why may transfer prices exist even in highly centralized organizations?
3. Why do some consider market-based transfer prices optimal under many circumstances?
4. What are the limitations to market price-based transfer prices?
5. What are the advantages of a centrally administered transfer price (that is, direct intervention)? What are the disadvantages of such a transfer price?
6. Why do companies often use prices other than market prices for interdivisional transfers?
7. What are the disadvantages of a negotiated transfer price system?

CRITICAL ANALYSIS AND DISCUSSION QUESTIONS

8. "An action that is optimal for a division may not be optimal for the company as a whole." Explain.
9. Why are transfer prices necessary?
10. In what sense is the word *price* in the term *transfer price* a misnomer?
11. Refer to this chapter's Managerial Application "Just-in-Time Production in Japan and the Internal Revenue Service in the United States." Why did the Internal Revenue Service dispute the transfer prices? Did the IRS want the prices set higher or lower? Why?
12. What factors should companies consider when setting transfer prices for products sold from a division in one country to a division in another country?
13. Division A has no external markets. It produces a product that Division B uses. Division B cannot purchase this product from any other source. What transfer pricing system would you recommend for the interdivisional sale of the product? Why?
14. Describe the economic basis for transfer pricing systems.
15. "It may be desirable to use a different ROI measure for evaluating the performance of a division and the performance of the division's manager." Explain.
16. "The return on investment measure may be biased in favor of divisions with older plant and equipment." Explain.
17. What are the advantages of using the ROI measure rather than the value of division profits as a performance evaluation technique?
18. Under what conditions would the use of ROI measures inhibit goal-congruent decision making by a division manager?
19. What are the advantages of using economic value added (EVA®) instead of ROI?
20. Describe why the "general transfer pricing rule" will lead to the decision that benefits the company as a whole in the case where the selling division is under capacity.

EXERCISES

Solutions to even-numbered exercises are at the end of the chapter after the cases.

21. **Transfer pricing.** Spring Waters, Inc., produces bottled drinks. The New York Division acquires the water, adds carbonation, and sells it in bulk quantities to the New Jersey Division of Spring Waters and to outside buyers. The New Jersey Division buys carbonated water in bulk, adds flavoring, bottles it, and sells it.

    Last year, the New York Division produced 1,500,000 gallons, of which it sold 1,300,000 gallons to the New Jersey Division and the remaining 200,000 gallons to outsiders for $0.40 per gallon. The New Jersey Division processed the 1,300,000 gallons, which it sold for $1,500,000. New York's variable costs were $440,000 and its fixed costs were $120,000. The New Jersey Division incurred an additional variable cost of $320,000 and $200,000 of fixed costs. Both divisions operated below capacity.

    a. Prepare division income statements assuming the transfer price is at the external market price of $0.40 per gallon.

    b. Repeat part **a.** assuming a negotiated transfer price of $0.30 per gallon is used.

    c. Respond to the statement: "The choice of a particular transfer price is immaterial to the company as a whole."

22. **Return on investment computations.** The following information relates to the operating performance of three divisions of Walmat Retail Corporation for last year.

	Miami Division	Kansas City Division	Seattle Division
Divisional Profit Margin before Allocating Central Corporate Expenses to Divisions	$ 500,000	$ 500,000	$ 500,000
Divisional Investment	$ 4,000,000	$ 5,000,000	$ 6,000,000
Divisional Sales	$24,000,000	$20,000,000	$16,000,000
Divisional Employees	22,500	12,000	10,500

    Walmat evaluates divisional performance using rate of return on investment (ROI) after allocating a portion of the central corporate expenses to each division. Central corporate expenses for last year were $450,000.

    a. Compute the ROI of each division before allocation of central corporate expenses.

    b. Compute the ROI of each division assuming central corporate expenses are allocated based on divisional investments (that is, allocate 4/15 to the Miami Division, 5/15 to the Kansas City Division, and 6/15 to the Seattle Division).

    c. Repeat part **b.**, allocating central corporate expenses based on divisional sales.

    d. Repeat part **b.**, assuming that management allocates central corporate expenses based on the number of employees.

23. **ROI computations with a capital charge.** The following information relates to the operating performance of three divisions of Thrills Unlimited theme parks for last year.

	Western Division	Central Division	Eastern Division
Operating Profit	$ 500,000	$3,000,000	$ 4,500,000
Investment	5,000,000	9,000,000	18,000,000

    a. Compute the rate of return on investment (ROI) of each division for last year.

    b. Assume that the firm levies a charge on each division for the use of funds. The charge is 10 percent on investment, and the accounting system deducts it in measuring divisional net income. Recalculate ROI using divisional net income after deduction of the use-of-funds charge in the numerator.

    c. Which of these two measures do you think gives the better indication of operating performance? Explain your reasoning.

24. **ROI computations with replacement costs.** The following information relates to the operating performance of two divisions of McClatchen Corporation, a newspaper publisher, for last year.

	Toronto Division	Phoenix Division
Operating Profit	$ 800,000	$1,200,000
Total Assets (based on acquisition cost)	4,000,000	7,500,000
Total Assets (based on current replacement costs)	6,000,000	8,000,000

    a. Compute the return on investment (ROI) of each division, using total assets stated at acquisition cost as the investment base.
    b. Compute the ROI of each division, using total assets based on current replacement cost as the investment base.
    c. Which of the two measures do you think gives the better indication of operating performance? Explain your reasoning.

25. **ROI computations comparing net and gross book value.** The following information relates to the operating performance of two divisions of World Electronics, Inc., for last year.

	National Division	International Division
Operating Profit	$ 4,000,000	$ 5,000,000
Total Assets (at gross acquisition cost)	20,000,000	50,000,000
Total Assets (net of accumulated depreciation)	15,000,000	15,000,000

    a. Compute the return on investment (ROI) of each division, using total assets at gross book value as the investment base.
    b. Compute the ROI of each division, using total assets net of accumulated depreciation (net book value) as the investment base.
    c. Which of the two measures do you think gives the better indication of operating performance? Explain your reasoning.

26. **Comparing profit margin and ROI as performance measures.** College Coffee Shops operates coffeehouses on college campuses in three districts. The operating performance for each district follows.

	District		
	New Orleans	Chicago	Denver
Sales	$1,900,000	$8,500,000	$10,000,000
Operating Profit	200,000	500,000	1,000,000
Investment	2,000,000	6,250,000	8,000,000

    a. Using the operating profit margin percentage as the criterion, which is the most profitable district?
    b. Using the rate of return on investment as the criterion, which is the most profitable district?
    c. Which of the two measures better indicates operating performance? Explain your reasoning.

27. **Profit margin and investment turnover ratio computations.** The Striped Chocolate Division of the International Confection Company had a rate of return on investment (ROI) of 12 percent (= $1,200,000/$10,000,000) during 2002, based on sales of $20,000,000. In an effort to improve its performance during 2003, the company instituted several cost-saving programs, including the substitution of automatic equipment for work previously done by workers and the purchase of raw materials in large quantities to obtain quantity discounts. Despite these cost-saving programs, the company's ROI for 2003 was 10 percent (= $1,100,000/$11,000,000), based on sales of $20,000,000.
    a. Break down the ROI for 2002 and 2003 into profit margin and investment turnover ratios.
    b. Explain the reason for the decrease in ROI between the two years using the results from part **a.**

28. **ROI and economic value added computations.** A bank considers acquiring new computer equipment. The computer will cost $160,000 and result in a cash savings of $70,000 per year (excluding depreciation) for each of the five years of the asset's life. It will have no salvage value after five years. Assume straight-line depreciation (depreciation expensed

evenly over the life of the asset). The company's tax rate is 15 percent, and there are no current liabilities associated with this investment.

    a. What is the ROI for each year of the asset's life if the division uses beginning-of-year net book value asset balances for the computation?

    b. What is the economic value added each year if the weighted-average cost of capital is 25 percent?

29. **Transfer pricing** (adapted from CPA exam). Cassie's Computer Parts has two decentralized divisions, Hardware and Pre-Fab. Pre-Fab has always purchased certain units from Hardware at $230 per unit. Because Hardware plans to raise the price to $260 per unit, Pre-Fab desires to purchase these units from outside suppliers for $230 per unit. Hardware's costs follow: variable costs per unit, $200; annual fixed costs, $30,000. Annual production of these units for Pre-Fab is 1,500 units.

    If Pre-Fab buys from an outside supplier, the facilities Hardware uses to manufacture these units would remain idle. What would be the result if Cassie's Computer Parts' management enforces a transfer price of $260 per unit between Hardware and Pre-Fab?

30. **Transfer pricing.** The consulting group in an accounting firm offers its products to outside clients at a price of $200 per hour. Last month, the consultants billed 10,000 hours to outside clients, incurred variable costs of $70 per hour billed to outside clients, and incurred $500,000 in fixed costs.

    The firm's auditing group can acquire consulting services from outsiders or from the firm's own consultants. If it acquires the services from outsiders, it must pay $180 per hour. It would pay $200 for consulting services from the internal group.

    a. What are the costs and benefits of the alternatives available to these two groups, the consultants and the auditors, and to the accounting firm as a whole, with respect to consulting services? Assume the consulting group operates at capacity.

    b. How would your answer change if the accounting firm's consulting group had sufficient idle capacity to handle all the auditors' needs?

31. **ROI and economic value added using the Internet.** Select one of the following companies (or any company of your choosing) and use the Internet to explore the company's most recent annual report.

American Airlines (http://www.americanair.com)

Intel (http://www.intel.com)

IBM (http://www.ibm.com)

Wal-Mart (http://www.walmart.com)

    a. Calculate the company's overall return on investment (ROI). Also, calculate the company's overall economic value added amount. (Assume a weighted-average cost of capital of 10%. Calculate the tax rate from the company's income statement by taking the tax expense divided by income before taxes.) List and explain any assumptions you make.

    b. Does the company include a calculation of ROI in its online annual report? If it does, do your calculations agree with those of the company? If not, what would be some possible explanations?

32. **ROI and economic value added.** The Bella Vista Woodwork Company uses return on investment and economic value added as performance evaluation measures for its division managers. The company's minimum ROI is 14 percent, and its weighted-average cost of capital is 10 percent. Assume a tax rate of 20 percent. Financial data for the company's three divisions follow. (All foreign currencies have been converted to U.S. dollars.)

	U.S. Division	Asia Division	Europe Division
Sales	$300,000	$375,000	$450,000
Operating Income	25,500	28,000	29,500
Assets	150,000	125,000	175,000
Current Liabilities	10,000	5,000	15,000

    a. Compute the return on investment for each division.

    b. Compute the economic value added amount for each division.

    c. Which division's manager is performing the best using ROI? Which division's manager is performing the best using economic value added? Explain your results.

PROBLEMS

33. **Transfer pricing.** Keller Company produces computers and computer components. The company is organized into several divisions that operate essentially as autonomous companies. The firm permits division managers to make investment and production-level decisions. The division managers can also decide whether to sell to other divisions or to outside customers.

Networks Division produces a critical component for computers manufactured by Computers Division. It has been selling this component to Computers for $2,000 per unit. Networks recently purchased new equipment for producing the component. To offset its higher depreciation charges, Networks increased its price to $2,200 per unit. The manager of Networks has asked the president to instruct Computers to purchase the component for the $2,200 price rather than to permit Computers to purchase externally for $2,000 per unit. The following information is obtained from the company's records: Computers' annual purchases of the component, 400 units; Networks' variable costs per unit, $1,400; Networks' fixed costs per unit, $400.

   a. Assume that the firm has no alternative uses for Networks' idle capacity. Will the company as a whole benefit if Computers purchases the component externally for $2,000? Explain.
   b. Assume that the firm can use the idle capacity of Networks for other purposes, resulting in cash operating savings of $150,000. Will the company as a whole benefit if Computers purchases the component externally for $2,000? Explain.
   c. Assume the same facts as in part **b.** except that the outside market price drops to $1,800 per unit. Will the company as a whole benefit if Computers purchases the component externally for $1,800? Explain.
   d. As president, how would you respond to the manager of Networks? Discuss each scenario described in parts **a., b.,** and **c.**

34. **Biases in ROI computations.** Gabriel Sports Products uses rate of return on investment (ROI) as a basis for determining the annual bonus of divisional managers. The firm allocates central corporate expenses to the divisions based on total sales. The calculation of ROI for 2000 for two of its divisions follows:

	Tennis Products Division	Golf Products Division
Division Contribution to Central Corporate Expenses and Operating Profit	$100,000	$ 500,000
Share of Central Corporate Expenses	(10,000)	(25,000)
Divisional Operating Profit	$ 90,000	$ 475,000
Divisional Investment (assets)	$600,000	$4,750,000
ROI	15 Percent	10 Percent

Indicate several factors that, if present, would bias the ROI measure as Gabriel Sports has calculated it and lead to possible inequities in determining the annual bonus.

35. **Issues in designing ROI measures.** The Safety Alarm Corporation manufactures and sells a patented electronic device for detecting burglaries. The firm uses return on investment as a measure for the control of operations for each of its 16 U.S. divisions.

Recently the firm has organized a new division in Brazil. Safety Alarm contributed the necessary funds for the construction of manufacturing and sales facilities in Brazil, whereas it obtained debt financing locally for working capital requirements. The new division will remit annually the following amounts to the U.S. central corporate office: (1) a royalty of $10 for each burglary device sold in Brazil, (2) a fee of $40 per hour plus traveling expenses for central corporate engineering services used by the division, and (3) a dividend equal to 10 percent of the funds Safety Alarm committed. The division will retain for its own use the remaining funds that operations generate. The division will receive the right to produce and market in Brazil any future electronic devices the central corporate research and development staff develops.

List some of the questions that the firm must address in designing an ROI measure for this division.

36. **Evaluating profit impact of alternative transfer decisions** (adapted from CMA exam). Alfonso Company manufactures a line of men's colognes and after-shave lotions. The firm manufactures the products through a series of mixing operations with the addition of certain aromatic and coloring ingredients; the firm packages the finished product in a company-produced glass bottle and packs it in cases containing six bottles.

Management of Alfonso believes the bottle design heavily influences the sale of its product. Management has developed a unique bottle of which it is quite proud.

Cologne production and bottle manufacturing have evolved over the years in an almost independent manner; in fact, a rivalry has developed between management personnel as to which division is more important to Alfonso. This attitude is probably intensified because the bottle manufacturing plant was purchased intact 10 years ago, and no real interchange of management personnel or ideas (except at the top corporate level) has taken place.

Since the acquisition, the cologne manufacturing plant has absorbed all bottle production. Management considers each area a separate profit center and evaluates each area as a separate profit center. As the new corporate controller, you are responsible for the definition of a proper transfer value to use in crediting the bottle production profit center and in debiting the packaging profit center.

At your request, the bottle division general manager has asked certain other bottle manufacturers to quote a price for the quantity and sizes the cologne division demands. These competitive prices follow:

Volume	Total Price	Price per Case
2,000,000 Cases	$ 4,000,000	$2.00
4,000,000 Cases	7,000,000	$1.75
6,000,000 Cases	10,000,000	$1.67 (rounded)

A cost analysis of the internal bottle plant indicates that it can produce bottles at these costs:

Volume	Total Cost	Cost per Case
2,000,000 Cases	$3,200,000	$1.60
4,000,000 Cases	5,200,000	1.30
6,000,000 Cases	7,200,000	1.20

These costs include fixed costs of $1,200,000 and variable costs of $1 per case.

These figures resulted in discussion about the proper value to use in the transfer of bottles to the cologne division. Corporate executives are interested because a significant portion of a division manager's income is an incentive bonus based on profit center results.

The cologne production division incurred the following costs in addition to the bottle costs:

Volume	Total Cost	Cost per Case
2,000,000 Cases	$16,400,000	$8.20
4,000,000 Cases	32,400,000	8.10
6,000,000 Cases	48,400,000	8.07

After considerable analysis, the marketing research department furnishes you with the following price-demand relation for the finished product:

Sales Volume	Total Sales Revenue	Sales Price per Case
2,000,000 Cases	$25,000,000	$12.50
4,000,000 Cases	45,600,000	11.40
6,000,000 Cases	63,900,000	10.65

a. The Alfonso Company has used market-based transfer prices in the past. Using the current market prices and costs, and assuming a volume of 6,000,000 cases, calculate the income for
 (1) the bottle division.
 (2) the cologne division.
 (3) the corporation.
b. Is this production and sales level the most profitable volume for
 (1) the bottle division?
 (2) the cologne division?
 (3) the corporation?
 Explain your answer.

CASES

37. **Impact of division performance measures on management incentives.** The Owens Group manages several fitness centers in Europe and Asia. The home office staff of The Owens Group evaluates managers of the Owens divisions by keeping track of the rate of return each division earns on the average level of assets invested at the division. The home office staff considers 20 percent, which is The Owens Group's after-tax cost of capital, to be the minimum acceptable annual rate of return on average investment. When a division's rate of return drops below 20 percent, division management can expect an unpleasant investigation by the home office and perhaps some firings. When the rate of return exceeds 20 percent and grows through time, the home office staff is invariably pleased and rewards division management. When the rate of return exceeds 20 percent but declines over time, the home office staff sends out unpleasant memoranda and cuts the profit-sharing bonuses of the division managers.

In Division A, average assets employed during the year amount to $60,000. Division A has been earning 40 percent per year on its average investment for several years. Management of Division A is proud of its extraordinary record—earning a steady 40 percent per year.

In Division B, average assets employed during the year also amount to $60,000. Division B has been earning 25 percent per year on its average investment. In the preceding three years, the rate of return on investment was 20 percent, 22 percent, and 23 percent, respectively. Management of Division B is proud of its record of steadily boosting earnings.

New investment opportunities have arisen at both Division A and Division B. In both cases, the new investment opportunity will require a cash outlay today of $30,000 and will provide a rate of return on investment of 30 percent for each of the next eight years. The average amount of assets invested in the project will be $30,000 for each of the next eight years. Both new investment opportunities have positive net present value when the discount rate is 20 percent per year (the after-tax cost of capital of The Owens Group).

When word of the new opportunities reached the home office staff, the prospects of the two new investments pleased the staff, because both investments would yield a better-than-average return for The Owens Group.

Management of Division A computed its rate of return on investment both with and without the new investment project and decided not to undertake the project. Management of Division B computed its rate of return on investment both with and without the new investment project and decided to undertake it.

When word of the two divisions' actions reached the home office staff, it was perplexed. Why did Division A's management turn down such a good opportunity? What in the behavior of the home office staff induced Division A's management to reject the new project? Is management of Division B doing a better job than management of Division A? What may the home office do to give Division A an incentive to act in a way more consistent with the well-being of The Owens Group?

38. **Capital investment analysis and decentralized performance measurement—a comprehensive case.**[6] The following exchange occurred just after Diversified Electronics rejected a capital investment proposal.

---

[6]This case requires knowledge of discounted cash flow methods.

Ralph Browning (Product Development): I just don't understand why you have rejected my proposal. This new investment is going to be a sure money maker for the Residential Products division. No matter how we price this new product, we can expect to make $230,000 on it before tax.

Sue Gold (Finance): I am sorry that you are upset with our decision, but this product proposal just does not meet our short-term ROI target of 15 percent after tax.

Browning: I'm not so sure about the ROI target, but it goes a long way toward meeting our earnings-per-share growth target of 20 cents per share after tax.

Phil Carlson (Executive Vice-President): Ralph, you are right, of course, about the importance of earnings per share. However, we view our three divisions as investment centers. Proposals like yours must meet our ROI targets. It is not enough that you show an earnings-per-share increase.

Gold: We believe that a company like Diversified Electronics should have a return on investment of 12 percent after tax, especially given the interest rates we have had to pay recently. This is why we have targeted 12 percent as the appropriate minimum ROI for each division to earn next year.

Carlson: If it were not for the high interest rates and poor current economic outlook, Ralph, we would not be taking such a conservative position in evaluating new projects. This past year has been particularly rough for our industry. Our two major competitors had ROIs of 10.8 percent and 12.3 percent. Though our ROI of about 9 percent after tax was reasonable (see Exhibit 11.9), performance varied from division to division. Professional Services did very well with 15 percent ROI, while the Residential Products division managed just 10 percent. The performance of the Aerospace Products division was especially dismal, with an ROI of only 6 percent. We expect divisions in the future to carry their share of the load.

Chris McGregor (Aerospace Products): My division would be showing much higher ROI if we had a lot of old equipment like Residential Products or relied heavily on human labor like Professional Services.

Carlson: I don't really see the point you are trying to make, Chris.

Diversified Electronics, a growing company in the electronics industry, had grown to its present size of more than $140 million in sales. (See Exhibits 11.7, 11.8, and 11.9 for financial data.) Diversified Electronics has three divisions, Residential Products, Aerospace

EXHIBIT 11.7	DIVERSIFIED ELECTRONICS Income Statement for Year 1 and Year 2 (all dollar amounts in thousands, except earnings-per-share figures)		
		Year Ended December 31	
		Year 1	**Year 2**
Sales		$141,462	$148,220
Cost of Goods Sold		108,118	113,115
Gross Margin		$ 33,344	$ 35,105
Selling and General		13,014	13,692
Profit before Taxes and Interest		$ 20,330	$ 21,413
Interest Expense		1,190	1,952
Profit before Taxes		$ 19,140	$ 19,461
Income Tax Expense		7, 886	7,454
Net Income		$ 11,254	$ 12,007
Earnings per Share		$5.63	$6.00

EXHIBIT 11.8	DIVERSIFIED ELECTRONICS Balance Sheets for Year 1 and Year 2 (all dollar amounts in thousands)		

		December 31	
		Year 1	Year 2
Assets			
Cash and Temporary Investments		$ 1,404	$ 1,469
Accounts Receivable		13,688	15,607
Inventories		42,162	45,467
Total Current Assets		$ 57,254	$ 62,543
Plant and Equipment:			
Original Cost		107,326	115,736
Accumulated Depreciation		42,691	45,979
Net		$ 64,635	$ 69,757
Investments and Other Assets		3,143	3,119
Total Assets		$125,032	$135,419
Liabilities and Owners' Equity			
Accounts Payable		$ 10,720	$ 12,286
Taxes Payable		1,210	1,045
Current Portion of Long-Term Debt		—	1,634
Total Current Liabilities		$ 11,930	$ 14,965
Deferred Income Taxes		559	985
Long-Term Debt		12,622	15,448
Total Liabilities		$ 25,111	$ 31,398
Common Stock		47,368	47,368
Retained Earnings		52,553	56,653
Total Owners' Equity		$ 99,921	$104,021
Total Liabilities and Owners' Equity		$125,032	$135,419

EXHIBIT 11.9	DIVERSIFIED ELECTRONICS Ratio Analysis		

		Year 1	Year 2
$\text{ROI} = \dfrac{\text{Net Income}}{\text{Total Assets}}$		$\dfrac{\$11,254}{\$125,032} = 9.0\%$	$\dfrac{\$12,007}{\$135,419} = 8.9\%$

Products, and Professional Services, each of which accounts for about one-third of Diversified Electronics' sales. Residential Products, the oldest division, produces furnace thermostats and similar products. The Aerospace Products division is a large job shop that builds electronic devices to customer specifications. A typical job or batch takes several months to complete. About half of Aerospace Products' sales are to the U.S. Defense Department. The newest of the three divisions, Professional Services, provides consulting engineering services. This division has grown tremendously since Diversified Electronics acquired it seven years ago.

EXHIBIT 11.10	DIVERSIFIED ELECTRONICS Financial Data for New Product Proposal

1. Projected Asset Investment:

   Land Purchase . . . . $ 200,000

   Plant and Equipment[a]   800,000

       Total $1,000,000

2. Cost Data, before Taxes (first year):

   Variable Cost per Unit $3.00

   Differential Fixed Costs[b] $170,000

3. Price/Market Estimate (first year):

   Unit Price $7.00

   Sales . . . .   100,000 Units

4. Taxes: The company assumes a 40 percent tax rate for investment analyses. Depreciation of plant and equipment according to tax law is as follows: Year 1, 20 percent; Year 2, 32 percent; Year 3, 19 percent; Year 4, 14.5 percent; Year 5, 14.5 percent. Taxes are paid for taxable income in Year 1 at the end of Year 1, taxes for Year 2 at the end of Year 2, etc.

5. Inflation is assumed to be 10 percent per year and applies to revenues and costs except depreciation for years 2 through 8 (i.e., Year 2 amounts will reflect a 10 percent increase over the Year 1 amounts shown in the data above).

6. The project has an eight-year life. Land will be sold for $400,000 at the end of Year 8. Assume the gain on the sale of land is taxable at the 40% rate.

---

[a]Annual capacity of 120,000 units.

[b]Includes straight-line depreciation on new plant and equipment, depreciated for eight years with no net salvage value at the end of eight years.

Each division operates independently of the others, and corporate management treats each as a separate entity. Division managers make many of the operating decisions. Corporate management coordinates the activities of the various divisions, which includes review of all investment proposals over $400,000.

Diversified Electronics measures return on investment as the division's net income divided by total assets. Each division's expenses include the allocated portion of corporate administrative expenses.

Since each of Diversified Electronics' divisions is located in a separate facility, management can easily attribute most assets, including receivables, to specific divisions. Management allocates the corporate office assets, including the centrally controlled cash account, to the divisions on the basis of divisional revenues.

Exhibit 11.10 shows the details of Ralph Browning's rejected product proposal.

a. Why did corporate headquarters reject Ralph Browning's product proposal? Was their decision the right one? If top management used the discounted cash flow (DCF) method instead, what would the results be? The company uses a 15 percent after-tax cost of capital (i.e., discount rate) in evaluating projects such as these.

b. Evaluate the manner in which Diversified Electronics has implemented the investment center concept. What pitfalls did they apparently not anticipate? What, if anything, should be done with regard to the investment center approach and the use of ROI as a measure of performance?

c. What conflicting incentives for managers can occur between the use of a yearly ROI performance measure and DCF for capital budgeting?

39. **Honeywell, Inc.: Relative performance evaluation.**[7] A major issue in divisional performance evaluation is the process companies use to separate performance results that division managers can control from those that outside environmental factors cause. For instance, firms could hold division managers accountable for achieving a fixed target, independent of the performance of other divisions operating in similar product markets, or evaluate their

---

[7]Based on the authors' research.

performance relative to the performance of other divisions. The latter approach, known as relative performance evaluation, is analogous to "grading on the curve."

The Aviation and Space Controls group of divisions at Honeywell, Inc., experimented with relative performance evaluation. Honeywell is a technology-oriented company, particularly in the Aviation and Space Controls Business. They have historically emphasized growth, customer satisfaction, and new product development. As the Aviation and Space Controls Business has become more cost competitive, with less cost-plus contracting, in recent years top management has become more interested in providing incentives to reduce costs. Honeywell has also increased its emphasis on financial measures of performance. The firm changed incentive contracts for top management and division managers to emphasize return on investment. Aviation and Space Controls, in particular, experimented with a "peer company analysis" to create self-reassessment of the status quo.

The strategic planning group that performed the peer group analysis first identified the business segments of 22 competitors in the aerospace and defense industry. Of these 22 competitors, nine are prime contractors (e.g., Boeing and Lockheed), who are in aerospace and defense, but do not face the same market environment. Of the remaining 13 competitors, public data were not available for two competitors, leaving 11 competitors that Aviation and Space Controls' managers believed faced the same market environment as they did.

Honeywell used these results initially to identify highly ranked competitors and to examine their characteristics to see what Aviation and Space Controls could do to improve its financial performance. Over time, the firm will incorporate these comparisons with peer companies into the evaluation of division managers' performance.

a. What are the advantages to Honeywell of using relative performance evaluation?

b. As a division manager, would you rather have your performance evaluated using relative performance evaluation ("grading on the curve") or without regard to your competitors?

40. Transfer Pricing: Custom Freight Systems (A).[8] "We can't drop our prices below $210 per hundred pounds," exclaimed Greg Berman, manager of Forwarders, a division of Custom Freight Systems. "Our margins are already razor thin. Our costs just won't allow us to go any lower. Corporate rewards our division based on our profitability and I won't lower my prices below $210."

Customer Freight Systems is organized into three divisions: Air Cargo provides air cargo services; Logistics Services operates distribution centers and provides truck cargo services; and Forwarders provides international freight forwarding services. Freight forwarders typically buy space on planes from international air cargo companies. This is analogous to a charter company that books seats on passenger planes and resells them to passengers. In many cases freight forwarders will hire trucking companies to transport the cargo from the plane to the domestic destination.

Management believes that the three divisions integrate well and are able to provide customers with one-stop transportation services. For example, a Forwarders branch in Singapore would receive cargo from a shipper, prepare the necessary documentation, and then ship the cargo on Air Cargo to the San Francisco Forwarders station. The San Francisco Forwarders station would ensure the cargo passes through customs and ship it to the final destination with Logistics Services (see Exhibit 11.11).

Management evaluates each division separately and rewards division managers based on return on investment (ROI). Responsibility and decision-making authority are decentralized. Each division has a sales and marketing organization. Division salespeople report to the Vice-President of Sales for Custom Freight Systems as well as a division sales manager. Custom Freight Systems feels that it has been successful motivating division managers by paying bonuses for high division profits.

Recently, the Logistics division was completing a bid for a customer. The customer had freight to import from an overseas supplier and wanted Logistics to submit a bid for a distribution package that included air freight from the supplier, receiving the freight and providing customs clearance services at the airport, warehousing, and distributing to customers.

Because this was a contract for international shipping, Logistics needed to contact different freight forwarders for shipping quotes. Logistics requested quotes from the Forwarders division and United Systems, a competing freight forwarder. Divisions of Custom Freight Systems are free to use the most appropriate and cost-effective suppliers.

[8]Prepared by Thomas B. Rumzie under the direction of Michael W. Maher. Copyright 2002, Michael W. Maher.

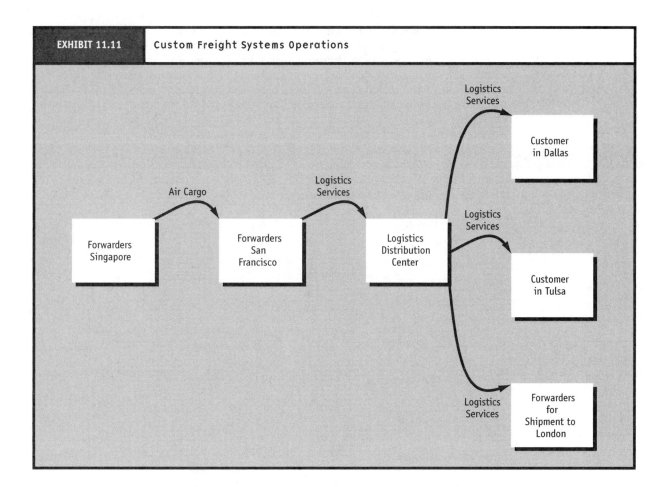

EXHIBIT 11.11   Custom Freight Systems Operations

Forwarders Singapore → *Air Cargo* → Forwarders San Francisco → *Logistics Services* → Logistics Distribution Center → *Logistics Services* → Customer in Dallas; *Logistics Services* → Customer in Tulsa; *Logistics Services* → Forwarders for Shipment to London

Logistics received bids of $210 per hundred pounds from Forwarders and $185 per hundred from United Systems. Forwarders specified in its bid that it will use Air Cargo, a division of Custom Freight Systems. Forwarder's variable costs were $175 per hundred, which included the cost of subcontracting air transportation. Air Cargo, which was experiencing a period of excess capacity, quoted Forwarders the market rate of $155. Typically, Air's variable costs are 60 percent of the market rate.

The price difference between the two different bids alarmed Susan Burns, a contract manager at Logistics. Burns knows this is a competitive business and is concerned because the total difference between the high and low bids was a lot of money for the contract estimated at 4,160,000 pounds during the first year. Burns contacted Greg Berman, the manager of Forwarders, and discussed the quote. "Don't you think full markup is unwarranted due to the fact that you and the airlines have so much excess capacity?" Burns complained.

Burns soon realized that Berman was not going to drop the price quote. "You know how small margins are in this business. Why should I cut my margins even smaller just to make you look good?" Berman asked.

Burns went to Bennie Espinosa, vice-president of Custom Freight Systems and chairperson for the corporate strategy committee. "That does sound strange," said Espinosa. "I need to examine the overall cost structure and talk to Berman. I'll get back to you by noon Monday."

a. Which bid should the Logistics division accept: the internal bid from the Forwarders division or the external bid from United Systems?

b. What should the transfer price be on this transaction?

c. What should Bennie Espinosa do?

d. Do the reward systems for the division managers support the best interests of the Forwarders division and the best interests of Custom Freight Systems? Give examples that support your conclusion.

41. **Transfer Pricing: Custom Freight Systems (B).** Assume all the information is the same as in Custom Freight Systems **(A),** but instead of receiving one outside bid, Logistics receives two. The new bid is from World Services for $195 per hundred pounds. World offered to use Air Cargo for air cargo. Air Cargo will charge World $155 per hundred pounds. The bids from Forwarders and United Systems remain the same as in part **A,** $210 and $185, respectively.
    Which bid should Logistics Services take? Why?

Suggested Solutions to Even-Numbered Exercises

22. **Return on investment computations.**

    a. Miami Division: $\dfrac{\$500,000}{\$4,000,000} = 12.5\%$

    Kansas City Division: $\dfrac{\$500,000}{\$5,000,000} = 10\%$

    Seattle Division: $\dfrac{\$500,000}{\$6,000,000} = 8.33\%$

    b. Miami Division: $\dfrac{\$500,000 - (\$4,000,000 \div \$15,000,000)(\$450,000)}{\$4,000,000} = 9.5\%$

    Kansas City Division: $\dfrac{\$500,000 - (\$5,000,000 \div \$15,000,000)(\$450,000)}{\$5,000,000} = 7.0\%$

    Seattle Division: $\dfrac{\$500,000 - (\$6,000,000 \div \$15,000,000)(\$450,000)}{\$6,000,000} = 5.33\%$

    c. Miami Division: $\dfrac{\$500,000 - (\$24,000,000 \div \$60,000,000)(\$450,000)}{\$4,000,000} = 8.0\%$

    Kansas City Division: $\dfrac{\$500,000 - (\$20,000,000 \div \$60,000,000)(\$450,000)}{\$5,000,000} = 7.0\%$

    Seattle Division: $\dfrac{\$500,000 - (\$16,000,000 \div \$60,000,000)(\$450,000)}{\$6,000,000} = 6.33\%$

    d. Miami Division: $\dfrac{\$500,000 - (\$22,500 \div \$45,000)(\$450,000)}{\$4,000,000} = 6.88\%$

    Kansas City Division: $\dfrac{\$500,000 - (\$12,000 \div \$45,000)(\$450,000)}{\$5,000,000} = 7.6\%$

    Seattle Division: $\dfrac{\$500,000 - (\$10,500 \div \$45,000)(\$450,000)}{\$6,000,000} = 6.58\%$

24. **ROI computations with replacement costs.**

    a. Toronto Division: $\dfrac{\$800,000}{\$4,000,000} = 20\%$ Phoenix Division: $\dfrac{\$1,200,000}{\$7,500,000} = 16\%$

    b. Toronto Division: $\dfrac{\$800,000}{\$6,000,000} = 13.33\%$ Phoenix Division: $\dfrac{\$1,200,000}{\$8,000,000} = 15\%$

    c. Analysts make two principal arguments for using acquisition cost in the denominator as in **a.** First, it is easily obtained from the firm's records and does not require estimates of current replacement costs. Second, it is consistent with the measurement of net income in the numerator (that is, depreciation expense is based on acquisition cost and unrealized holding gains are excluded). There are also two principal arguments for using current replacement cost in the denominator as in **b.** First, it eliminates the effects of price changes and permits the division which uses the depreciable assets most efficiently to show a better ROI. Second, as discussed in the chapter, it may lead division managers to make better equipment replacement decisions. If acquisition cost is used as the valuation basis in calculating ROI, divisions with older, more fully depreciated assets may be reluctant to replace them and thereby introduce higher, current amounts in the denominator. If current replacement cost is used in the denominator, the asset base will be the same regardless of whether or not the assets are replaced. Thus, the replacement decision can be made properly (that is, based on net present value) independent of any effects on ROI.

26. **Comparing profit margin and ROI as performance measures.**

The return on investment (ROI), profit margin percentage, and asset turnover ratio of the three divisions are as follows:

	Return on Investment	=	Profit Margin Percentage	×	Asset Turnover Ratio
New Orleans District:	$\dfrac{\$200,000}{\$2,000,000}$	=	$\dfrac{\$200,000}{\$1,900,000}$	×	$\dfrac{\$1,900,000}{\$2,000,000}$
	10%	=	10.53%	×	.95
Chicago District:	$\dfrac{\$500,000}{\$6,250,000}$	=	$\dfrac{\$500,000}{\$8,500,000}$	×	$\dfrac{\$8,500,000}{\$6,250,000}$
	8%	=	5.88%	×	1.36
Denver District:	$\dfrac{\$1,000,000}{\$8,000,000}$	=	$\dfrac{\$1,000,000}{\$10,000,000}$	×	$\dfrac{\$10,000,000}{\$8,000,000}$
	12.5%	=	10%	×	1.25

a. Using the profit margin percentage, the ranking of the districts is New Orleans, Denver, and then Chicago.

b. Using ROI, the ranking of districts is Denver, New Orleans, and then Chicago.

c. The ROI is a better measure of overall performance because it relates to the investment, or capital, required to generate those profits. New Orleans had the largest profit margin percentage. However, it required more capital to generate a dollar of sales than did Denver. Thus, its overall profitability is less. Note that Chicago had the largest asset turnover ratio. However, it generated the smallest amount of operating profit per dollar of sales, resulting in the lowest ROI of the three districts.

28. **ROI and EVA computations.**

$$\text{Annual Income} = \$70,000 - \frac{\$160,000}{5 \text{ years}} = \$38,000$$

Year	Investment Base	a. ROI $\$38,000 \div$ Base	b. EVA [$\$38,000 \times (1 - .15)$] $- [(\text{Base} - \$0) \times .25]$
1	$160,000	23.8%	($ 7,700)
2	128,000[a]	29.7	300
3	96,000	39.6	8,300
4	64,000	59.4	16,300
5	32,000	118.8	24,300

[a]Base decreases by annual depreciation of $32,000.

30. **Transfer pricing.**

a.

	Auditors (Buyers)	Consultants (Sellers)	Total Accounting Firm
Buy Services Internally	Pay $200	Receive $200	Pays $ 0
		Pay 70	Pays 70
			Pays $70
Buy Services Externally	Pay $180	Receive $200	Receives $20
		Pay 70	Pays 70
			Pays $50

Hence, it is advantageous to buy consulting services externally. Note that this result depends on whether the consulting group operates at capacity. (See **b.**)

b.

	Auditors (Buyers)	Consultants (Sellers)		Total Accounting Firm	
Buy Services Internally	Pay $200	Receive	$200	Pays	$ 0
		Pay	70	Pays	70
				Pays	$ 70
Buy Services Externally	Pay $180	Receive	$ 0	Pays	$180
		Pay	0	Pays	0
				Pays	$180

Hence, it is better to buy consulting services internally.

32. ROI and economic value added.

a. Return on investment.

$$\text{U.S. ROI} = \frac{\$25,500}{\$150,000} = 0.17$$

$$\text{Asia ROI} = \frac{\$28,000}{\$125,000} = 0.224$$

$$\text{Europe ROI} = \frac{\$29,500}{\$175,000} = 0.169$$

b. Economic value added.

	U.S.	Asia	Europe
Net Operating Income after Taxes (20%)	$20,400	$22,400	$ 23,600
Cost of Capital Employed			
($150,000 − $10,000) × 0.10	(14,000)		
($125,000 − $5,000) × 0.10		(12,000)	
($175,000 − $15,000) × 0.10			(16,000)
Economic Value Added	$ 6,400	$10,400	$ 7,600

c. The manager of the Asia Division is doing the best job based on ROI because it has the highest return. The Asia Division manager is also doing best with EVA of $10,400. Although Europe has the next highest EVA, it is earned with substantially more assets ($175,000 versus $150,000) and more capital employed ($160,000 versus $140,000) than the United States. Coupled with the fact that the United States has a slightly higher ROI, the United States probably earns the overall second place as to divisional performance.

chapter 12

Incentive Issues

Learning Objectives

1. Describe key characteristics of divisional incentive compensation plans.

2. Explain how incentive plans can affect the development phase of the product life cycle.

3. Compare and contrast expectancy and agency approaches to motivation.

4. Describe the balanced scorecard as a way to tie performance measures to organizational goals.

5. Explain the importance of performance measures for the four balanced scorecard perspectives.

6. Explain what constitutes fraudulent financial reporting.

7. Define the two most common types of fraud and demonstrate their impact on financial statements.

8. Identify the incentives for committing financial fraud.

9. Explain how environmental conditions influence fraudulent conduct.

10. Identify controls that can be instituted to prevent financial fraud.

This chapter discusses issues in the design and use of management performance evaluation and incentive plans. Ideally, these plans motivate managers to act in the organization's best interests. As self-interested utility maximizers, managers may prefer to act in ways that are in their own best interests but not in those of the organization. Good performance evaluation and incentive plans induce "win-win" results such that managers are motivated to behave in ways that are mutually beneficial to their organizations and to themselves.

Divisional Incentive Compensation Plans

Alfred Sloan, one of the first advocates of incentive compensation plans for management, instituted the General Motors bonus plan in 1918 to align interests between managers and the stockholders of the firm. General Motors had decentralized operating decisions, and, before instituting the bonus plan, the managers had little incentive to think of the overall welfare of the organization. Instead, they tended to focus on their own performance measurements, sometimes at the expense of the corporation's welfare. Once the bonus plan was installed, the executives were more attentive to how their individual efforts affected the welfare of the entire organization.

Today, nearly all managers of decentralized profit centers in large corporations are eligible for bonuses and other nonsalary incentives that often make up 25 to 50 percent of their salaries. The form of bonus plans varies across corporations. Payments can be made in cash, in the stock of the company, in stock options, in performance shares, in stock appreciation rights, and in participating units. The bonus can be made contingent on corporate results or on divisional profits. It may be based on annual performance or on performance over several years. It may be paid out immediately, deferred, or spread over several years.

Management can evaluate a company's performance using both accounting numbers and returns to stockholders, the latter reflecting a market assessment of how well the company is doing. Divisions normally do not have their own shares trading in capital markets, and the impact of one division's performance on the total company's share value may be small. Consequently, stock market assessments of performance are less useful at the divisional level than at the company level.

Our study of divisional incentive compensation plans revealed that most of these plans have the following characteristics:

1. Cash bonuses and profit sharing plans reward managers for short-term performance.
2. Deferred compensation, such as stock and stock options, is available to managers several years after they earn the compensation.[1] Deferring receipt of proceeds from stock gives managers incentives to take actions that increase long-run share value.
3. Firms give special awards for particular actions or extraordinary performance. For example, Johnson & Johnson (http://www.jnj.com/home.htm) presents a special stock award to employees responsible

---

[1]Stock options give an individual the right to purchase a specified number of shares of the company's stock at a specified price within a specified time period.

for developing new products. Top management and the board of directors believe new-product development is critical to the future success of the company.

When designing incentive systems, management must ascertain two things: (1) the behavior the system motivates and (2) the behavior management desires. Although incentive plans universally attempt to motivate good performance, each organization has its own particular set of problems that affect incentive system design.

For example, when Pillsbury (http://www.pillsbury.com) acquired Burger King, Pillsbury's executives had little experience in managing fast-food restaurants. The company wanted to provide incentives for Burger King's senior managers to remain with the company. Consequently, the incentive system provided for lucrative deferred compensation that the hamburger chain's managers would forgo if they quit. Each company's top management and board of directors must match its incentive system to its particular set of circumstances in deciding what type of behavior is desired.

Some critics point out that rewarding managers for performance reflected in annual accounting numbers gives managers incentives to take actions that make the numbers look good but not actions that benefit organizations in the long run. A classic example would be a division's failure to develop new production methods and new products that may substantially increase expenses in the short run but provide more value for shareholders in the long run. Using accounting numbers in performance measurement may also give managers incentives to make accounting choices and otherwise manipulate accounting data to put their performance in the most favorable light, as discussed later in this chapter in the section on fraudulent financial reporting. The Managerial Application "Conflicts in an Incentive Compensation Plan" demonstrates a conflict of interest for division controllers due to the incentive plan.

Managerial Application

Conflicts in an Incentive Compensation Plan

A large, multidivision manufacturer of industrial and consumer electrical products is organized into divisional profit centers. The firm rewards each division manager, at least in part, on the basis of the accounting profits and rate of return on assets that the division earned. Each division has its own controller, who reports directly to the central corporate controller. This direct reporting line, bypassing the division president, gives division controllers a feeling of independence from the division presidents, who would otherwise be their bosses. Central corporate management wants independent scorekeepers providing unbiased reports about ongoing operations.

In spite of this organizational design, the division controllers' compensation results in part from the same formula as that of the division presidents—a function of accounting profits and the rate of return on assets. Thus, division controllers have a financial stake in the reported profits of their divisions, giving them an incentive, at the margin, to boost reported profits.

The division controllers are aware of the potential conflict between their charge from central corporate management and their compensation packages. They feel conflict. At periodic meetings of controllers, they express their dissatisfaction to top management but so far have not been able to persuade top management to change the compensation plan.

Source: This example comes from a study by the authors. At management's request, we do not reveal the company's name.

Incentives and the Product Life Cycle

One of the major problems with short-run incentive plans is that managers are penalized in the current period for developing products that might produce long-run benefits. One reason is that, for external financial reporting, generally accepted accounting principles require that firms write off such costs as expenses when incurred.

A product's life cycle generally has four stages:

1. *Design and development:* Low sales volume; high research, design, and development costs.
2. *Growth:* Sales increase.

3. *Maturity:* Profits decline due to high competition.
4. *Decline:* Market for product contracts.

Product design people establish 80 to 90 percent of what the product's costs will be by the way they design the product. Manufacturing can influence only a small percentage of a product's costs once a product has been designed. The development stage of the life cycle is where the design and production techniques can be honed to greatest efficiency. Investment at this stage can improve efficiency and lower costs throughout the life cycle of the product.

When these costs are written off in the current period, managers are penalized for developing products that could produce long-term profits. Managers who invest little in new-product development may thus appear to have more efficient performance in the short run. But in the long run the company will suffer. Therefore, an incentive plan should create incentives for managers to incur design and development costs now that are good investments for the future. One successful method of accomplishing this objective is to defer writing off new-product design and development costs until the product has reached the growth and maturity stages.

Views of Behavior

We discuss two views of human behavior that address the key parts of incentive compensation plans. These are not necessarily opposing views, but they provide alternative perspectives on motivational issues.

Expectancy Theory View

Expectancy theory maintains that people act in ways to obtain the rewards that they desire and prevent the penalties that they wish to avoid. To motivate people, incentive plans must

1. Provide rewards that are desirable, and
2. Provide a high probability that behaving as the organization desires will lead to those rewards. This part is the "expectancy" that desired behavior will lead to desired rewards.

Exhibit 12.1 reflects the basic elements of the expectancy view. Appropriate performance measures and rewards increase employees' belief in the probability that good service will be rewarded.

Agency Theory View

Agency theory deals with relations between principals (e.g., supervisors) and agents (e.g., workers) where the principals assign responsibility to the agents and the agents work on behalf of the principals. Classic principal-agent relations include the following:

Principal	Agent
Shareholders	Board of Directors
Board of Directors	Top Management
Top Management	Division Managers
Division Managers	Department Managers

Note that most people in an organization serve in both a principal role and an agent role.

Agency theory differs from expectancy theory in that it focuses on the relations between principals and agents, whereas expectancy theory focuses on what motivates the individuals (that is, agents) without explicitly considering who is the principal, or boss. Expectancy theory focuses on what motivates people, whereas agency theory focuses on the cost to the principal caused by agents pursuing their own interests instead of the principal's interests. This concept is known as **agency cost,** which includes both the costs incurred by principals to control agents' actions and the cost to the principals if agents pursue their own interests that are not in the interests of the principals. The former includes rewards, penalties, monitoring devices, and audits to

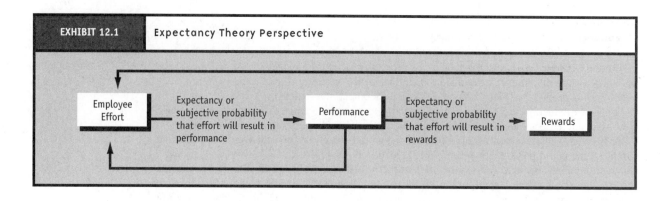

EXHIBIT 12.1   Expectancy Theory Perspective

motivate agents to behave as desired by principals. The latter includes so-called divergent behavior, which is behavior that is not aligned with principals' interests. Agents who spend time playing solitaire on their computers instead of preparing a report for the boss incur agency costs from the boss's point of view.

Agency theory assumes that employees will not necessarily behave as their employers desire. At the extreme, employees may have incentives to steal from the company.

According to the agency view, the objective of a good incentive compensation system is to minimize agency costs. One could spend so much money on monitoring devices that no employee could ever do anything out of line with organizational objectives. However, such actions are unlikely to be sensible given the high costs of the monitoring devices compared with the costs of divergent behavior (that is, agent's behavior that diverges from the wishes of the principal). In reality, organizations seek to minimize total agency costs, as shown in Exhibit 12.2, which balances the costs of controls and incentives against the costs of divergent behavior.

How Do Extrinsic and Intrinsic Rewards Affect Incentive Systems?

Extrinsic rewards are rewards that come from outside the individual, such as rewards from a teacher, a parent, an organization, or a spouse. Extrinsic rewards include grades, money, praise, and prizes. **Intrinsic rewards** come from the individual, such as the satisfaction from studying hard, providing help to someone in need, or doing a good job. Getting a bonus is an extrinsic reward. Getting satisfaction from one's own performance is an intrinsic reward.

Wise managers provide opportunities for intrinsic rewards from desired behavior.

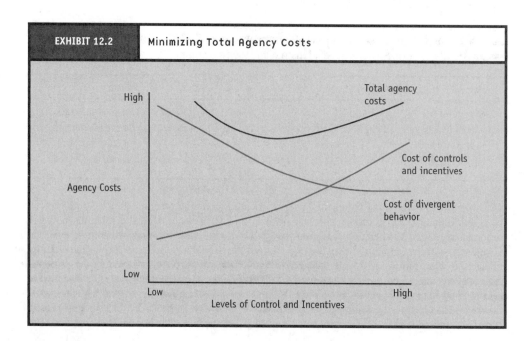

EXHIBIT 12.2   Minimizing Total Agency Costs

The **balanced scorecard** is a model of lead and lag indicators of performance that includes both financial and nonfinancial performance measures. For example, consider how the balanced scorecard can help Davis First National Bank, a community bank with several branches, improve performance. If the bank speeds up the loan processing function, it will increase customer satisfaction. Satisfied customers provide word-of-mouth advertising that will lead to a larger customer base, which means more revenue and better financial performance. Exhibit 12.3 shows the links among performance measures for a bank: from increased employee training to faster loan approvals to higher customer satisfaction to better financial results.

Carrying the balanced scorecard concept to its logical conclusion, one should be able to show each person in the organization how her or his job contributes to the ultimate goal of the organization. All employees, from receptionists to accountants to salespeople, should be able to see how their work leads to the financial success of the organization. The balanced scorecard represents a fundamental change in management style for companies that previously focused only on achieving financial objectives.

Four Basic Balanced Scorecard Perspectives

Although organizations differ in the way they implement the balanced scorecard, most appear to use four categories, or perspectives, of performance measures, as Exhibit 12.4 shows. The financial

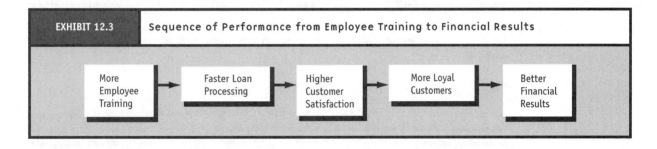

EXHIBIT 12.3   Sequence of Performance from Employee Training to Financial Results

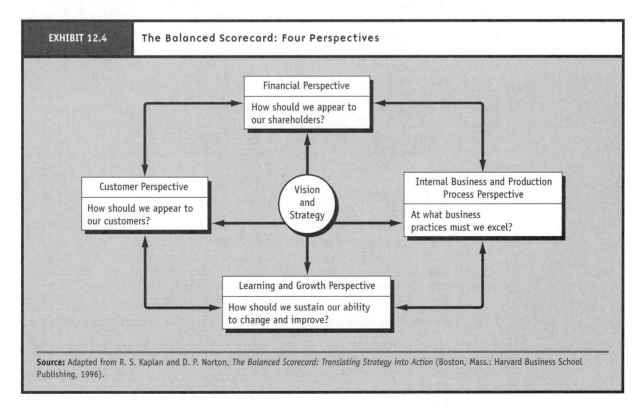

EXHIBIT 12.4   The Balanced Scorecard: Four Perspectives

Source: Adapted from R. S. Kaplan and D. P. Norton, *The Balanced Scorecard: Translating Strategy into Action* (Boston, Mass.: Harvard Business School Publishing, 1996).

perspective indicates whether the company's strategy and operations add value to shareholders. For organizations that do not have shareholders, the *financial perspective* indicates how well the strategy and operations contribute to improving the financial health of the organization. The *customer perspective* indicates how the company's strategy and operations add value to customers. The *internal business and production process perspective* indicates how well the internal business processes are working, first to add value to customers and then to shareholders. Finally, the *learning and growth perspective* indicates how well the infrastructure for innovation and long-term growth is working. In many ways, this is the most exciting perspective because it is the source of the future value of the organization.

At Davis First National Bank, top management discovered a large gap between the capabilities of many people working in the bank and the capabilities required for significantly improved performance. Although management knew the short-term costs would be high, it nevertheless developed an extensive training program to educate employees about the business practices of their customers. As a result, employees were able to devise creative ways to anticipate businesses' short-term loan needs based on regional economic forecasts from a local university. For example, when the president of a specialty sawmill called in a panic to say that he needed funds to employ workers overtime because of an unexpected increase in business, he was told that the bank was transferring funds into his business account as he spoke. To be sure, he was a loyal customer after that.

Building the Incentive Plan around the Balanced Scorecard

We next examine how to build an incentive plan around the four perspectives of the balanced scorecard.

The Learning and Growth Perspective

For incentive purposes, the learning and growth perspective focuses on the capabilities of people. Managers would be responsible for developing employee capabilities. Key measures for evaluating managers' performance would be employee satisfaction, employee retention, and employee productivity.

Employee Satisfaction   Employee satisfaction recognizes that employee morale is important for improving productivity, quality, customer satisfaction, and responsiveness to situations. Managers can measure employee satisfaction by sending surveys, interviewing employees, or observing employees at work.

Employee Retention   Firms committed to retaining employees recognize that employees develop organization-specific intellectual capital and are a valuable nonfinancial asset to the company. Further, finding and hiring good talent to replace people who leave is costly. Firms measure employee retention as the inverse of employee turnover—the percentage of people who leave each year.

Employee Productivity   Employee productivity recognizes the importance of output per employee. Output might be physical, such as miles driven, pages produced, or lawns mowed, or financial, such as revenue per employee or profits per employee. A simple measure of productivity for loan officers at a bank is the number of loans processed per loan officer per month.

A good incentive system rewards managers who promote high employee satisfaction, low employee turnover, and high employee productivity. An environment that supports employees provides greater opportunities for improving internal business processes, as discussed next.

The Internal Business and Production Process Perspective

A cause-and-effect relationship exists between the learning and growth perspective and the internal business and production process perspective. Employees who do the work are the best source of new ideas for better business processes. For example, an autoworker demonstrated that increasing the height of an automobile assembly line made it easier for workers to screw on the lug nuts for wheels. Raising the height of the assembly line improved productivity and reduced back injuries. At Davis First National Bank, employees developed permanent loan application files on the bank's Web site for repeat customers. With a few keystrokes, customers could update their files and usually complete their loan applications within 10 minutes. These innovations in production were possible because the workers were experienced (i.e., had not left the company) and were sufficiently happy with their jobs that they wanted to improve business processes.

Supplier Relations   Supplier relations are critical for success, particularly in retail and manufacturing assembly. Companies depend on suppliers to receive goods and services on time, at a low price, and at high quality. Entire companies can virtually cease production if they have a problem with a supplier. Good supplier relations are key to corporate success because more and more companies outsource important parts of the supply chain.

To provide incentives for good supplier relations, companies develop supplier rating systems that indicate which suppliers are certified for delivery of their products without inspection. The International Organization for Standardization (ISO) certifications are a starting point but are usually not sufficient for top-level suppliers. (For further information, see http://www.isonet .com or search the Internet for "iso9000.") If not certified, suppliers' products must be inspected upon receipt, which increases the cost of goods to the company.

Company managers should have incentives to get suppliers certified, working with them to reduce their costs and increase quality. Thus, an important part of any incentive plan is evaluation of supplier performance.

Davis First National Bank outsourced statement preparation for bank accounts and billing for loan payments. Any errors made by the companies performing those services reflected badly on the bank, just as if the employees of the bank performed the services themselves. Therefore, the bank appointed a manager to be in charge of each outsourced service. Although the work was done outside the bank, each service was like a responsibility center for the manager in charge. For example, Suzanne Reid was in charge of loan payments. Instead of having internal employees, she was responsible for the performance of the outside companies that processed loan payments. Errors by the outside supplier reflected badly on her own performance evaluation. She had incentives to get the best supplier and to manage it well.

Process Improvement Incentives   Customers value receiving goods and services reliably and on time. Suppliers can satisfy customers if they hold large amounts of inventory to ensure that goods are on hand. But holding lots of inventory leads to high inventory carrying and storage costs, inventory obsolescence, and a host of other problems that we have documented in earlier chapters. To avoid excessive inventory buildup, one possible alternative is for the supplier to work on reducing throughput time. Throughput time is the total time from when the order is received by the company until the customer receives the product. Shortening throughput time can be useful if the customer wants the goods or services as soon as possible.

Davis First National Bank had a problem with the throughput time for processing loans. Employees received no extrinsic rewards for turning around loans quickly, so loans sometimes took months to complete. To remedy this situation, management first classified loans as either "fasttrack" or "deadline." Fasttrack loans, usually for customers who had immediate needs for funds, were to be processed as quickly as possible. These loans cost more to process because they involved use of overnight delivery services and overtime pay. Davis First National also charged a higher loan-processing fee for these loans than for the deadline loans.

Deadline loans were to be processed so that they were completed by a particular date, usually four weeks from the application date. Customers with deadline loans did not have immediate needs but wanted loan applications completed within a reasonable time frame. For these loans, the bank emphasized cost minimization along with reliable and timely service, so the customers were charged a lower loan-processing fee compared with the fasttrack loans.

The bank found that it was more efficient to separate the loan processing staff into two groups, one for each type of loan. That way, employees could focus attention on their particular type of loan.

An assistant manager was placed in charge of fasttrack loans. He and his staff were responsible for minimizing throughput, doing quality work, and keeping costs to a reasonable level (but not for minimizing costs). Another assistant manager was placed in charge of deadline loans. He and his staff were responsible for minimizing costs, maximizing loan quality, and meeting loan completion deadlines.

The Customer Perspective

The customer perspective focuses on how the organization should look to its customers for success. Designing an incentive compensation system around customers' expectations requires, first, that the company define its customers and, second, that it know their expectations. Southwest Airlines, for instance, focuses on nonbusiness travelers who want low price and are not bothered by the inconvenience of having to line up to obtain their seats. Knowing those customers would be willing to drive or take the train as an alternative to flying, Southwest Airlines knows it must charge a sufficiently low price to make air travel competitive with auto or train travel. Its methods may not appeal to business travelers who do not want to wait in line at the airport to get a good seat and who are willing to pay more for the convenience of an assigned seat. However, business travelers are not Southwest's primary customers.

Federal Express developed successfully by knowing its customers and their expectations. It knew that its customers wanted the function of overnight delivery with defect-free quality. It also found that its particular customers were willing to pay a premium for that function and quality compared with what they could expect from such competitors as the U.S. Postal Service.

Knowing your customers and their expectations is not enough. An organization must also provide incentives to managers and employees to meet customers' expectations. Federal Express's incentive compensation plan encourages employees to go out of their way to be sure its packages are delivered reliably and on time.

Companies use the following performance measures, among others, when considering the customer perspective:

- Customer satisfaction
- Customer retention
- Market share
- Customer profitability

Customer Satisfaction   Customer satisfaction measures indicate whether the company is meeting customers' expectations or even delighting them. You have probably completed customer satisfaction forms for restaurants, hotels, or automobile repair shops.

Customer Retention   Customer retention or loyalty measures indicate how well a company is doing in keeping its customers. A rule of thumb says that it costs five times as much to get a new customer as to keep an existing one. While we might quibble with the number five, the point is well taken. Once you have a customer, it is much easier to keep that customer than to convince a new one to do business with you.

Market Share   Market share measures a company's proportion of the total business in a particular market. Companies typically measure market share in terms of dollar sales, unit volume, or number of customers.

Customer Profitability   Customer profitability refers to how much profit your customers make for you. Having satisfied and loyal customers and a large market share is well and good, but these accomplishments are not sufficient for profitability. One way to have happy, loyal customers is for an organization to provide a quality product well below cost. But that action would mean the company would not stay in business for long.

As noted in the Managerial Application "Does Customer Satisfaction Pay Off?" researchers have found evidence that better customer satisfaction leads to increased customer profitability. The researchers discovered, however, that increasing customer satisfaction appears to pay off only up to a point. One could think of this result as the difference between happy and ecstatic customers—euphoria is nice for the customers but does little for the economic value of the company.

Customer Perspective in Nonprofit Organizations   The customer perspective rises to the top of the various perspectives in nonprofit organizations because managers of nonprofits care more about servicing their students, patients, and clients than about generating profits. Nevertheless, financial goals are important in nonprofit organizations because they must be financially sound to sustain themselves, but nonprofit mission statements emphasize servicing their customers above all else.

Does Customer Satisfaction Pay Off?

Many companies use customer satisfaction measures in their incentive compensation plans. These measures are supposed to be lead indicators of financial performance at a future date. Are they? Studies by two Wharton School researchers, Christopher Ittner and David Larcker, found the answer, mostly, to be "yes." Using data from a telecommunications company, they first found a positive relation between customer satisfaction and customer retention. That is, satisfied customers were more likely to purchase services again than were dissatisfied customers. These results diminished at higher levels of satisfaction, however. That is, after some point of customer satisfaction, increasing it even more does not improve customer retention.

Second, using data from a bank, the researchers found a relation between customer satisfaction and profitability, with the effect of customer satisfaction coming mostly through increased revenues in the form of new customers. That is, branches with more satisfied customers saw more customer growth. This translated into more revenue for those branches. Third, the authors looked at the relation between customer satisfaction with companies as measured by the American Customer Satisfaction Index* and the stock market performance of those companies, and at other evidence that customer satisfaction measures of companies were economically relevant to the stock market. Taken as a whole, the results indicate a positive link between customer satisfaction and companies' financial performance.

*The American Customer Satisfaction Index is described in detail in National Quality Research Center, *American Customer Satisfaction Index—Methodology Report* (Milwaukee, Wisc.: American Society for Quality Control, December 1995).

Source: C. D. Ittner and D. F. Larcker, "Are Non-Financial Measures Leading Indicators of Financial Performance? An Analysis of Customer Satisfaction," *Journal of Accounting Research* 36 (Supplement).

The Financial Perspective

The balanced scorecard uses financial performance measures, such as net income and return on investment, because they are universally used in for-profit organizations. Financial performance measures provide a common language for analyzing and comparing companies. People who provide funds to companies, such as financial institutions and shareholders, rely heavily on financial performance measures in deciding whether to lend or invest funds. Properly designed financial measures can provide an aggregate view of an organization's success.

Financial measures by themselves are insufficient for providing incentives for success. Financial measures tell a story about the past, but not about the future.

In the end, financial measures are important but are not sufficient to guide performance in creating value. Nor are the nonfinancial measures, by themselves, sufficient for providing the bottom-line score. The balanced scorecard, as the name implies, looks for a balance of multiple performance measures—both financial and nonfinancial—to guide organizational performance toward success.

Implementing the Balanced Scorecard

We have presented four perspectives for the balanced scorecard and discussed numerous performance measures. There is nothing sacrosanct about having *four* perspectives—companies have been known to use more or fewer. Managers should use the performance measures that provide the right incentives. They should be mindful that there is a cost of data collection for each performance measure and that having too many performance measures can be confusing to employees, particularly if some seem contradictory. Thus, there is a trade-off between the costs and benefits of additional performance measures.

For example, as discussed in the Managerial Application "Successfully Implementing the Balanced Scorecard: The FMC Experience," FMC initially selected dozens of performance measures to implement the balanced scorecard. After much discussion and clustering of measures, management settled on 16 performance measures, four for each of the four perspectives. And of these, the company targeted four performance measures as critical success indicators.

The method of weighting various performance measures presents a problem for designers of balanced scorecards. Assigning a particular weight to each performance measure (e.g,, customer satisfaction will count 15 percent of the total performance score) does not allow for flexibility in assessing performance and for recognizing unforeseen problems arising during the performance period. For example, assume the designers assigned a weight of 15 percent to customer satisfaction, but a particular division did superb work in improving customer satisfaction. Top management might want to reward such performance more than implied by the 15 percent weighting. Research has shown that the use of flexibility, such as assigning weights to performance measures after the performance period and incorporating subjective performance evaluations, resulted in complaints about favoritism. Management at the research site put together a team to review the company's balanced scorecard. This team recommended creating an incentive pay plan with two components: (1) a formula-based component using quantitative measures of division revenues, customer satisfaction indicators, and the like, and (2) a discretionary component based on qualitative factors such as leadership and teamwork.[2]

Typically, implementing the balanced scorecard takes months or even years. Further, it is an iterative process because targets, performance measures, and even strategies change over time. People who are comfortable with only a single objective performance measure that never changes, such as return on investment, will probably find the balanced scorecard frustrating. On the other hand, using the balanced scorecard can provide a more realistic view about the complexities and trade-offs that organizations face.

Managerial Application

Successfully Implementing the Balanced Scorecard: The FMC Experience

FMC Corporation, a highly diversified company based in Chicago, Illinois, did a comprehensive strategic review to ascertain how best to increase shareholder value. Over the next several years, it developed and implemented the balanced scorecard to give the company a greater external focus.

The process of developing the balanced scorecard started with top management developing strategic objectives for the company. The balanced scorecard implementation team, with the help of numerous middle managers, developed performance measures and targets for the Lithium Division, which was the site of the pilot implementation. In total, the team developed four performance measures for each of the four balanced scorecard perspectives, or 16 performance measures in total. Of those 16, management thought four were particularly important for the company:

- On-time delivery
- Cost control
- Developing sources of raw materials
- Developing new products

The measures, which included both objective, "hard" measures and subjective, "soft" measures, were communicated to the employees in terms of what performance on these measures meant to the employees' jobs. For example, managers explained how meeting on-time delivery targets improved customer relations, increased repeat business, improved job security, and increased prospects for pay increases and promotions. This communication step was critical for assuring the performance measures were not just a management and staff idea but would be implemented by the people doing the work.

In setting targets for the measures, the balanced scorecard team looked at how FMC's best competitors were doing and what customers would demand in the future. For example, if 10 per-

---

[2]C. D. Ittner, D. F. Larcker, and M. W. Meyer, "Subjectivity and the Weighting of Performance Measures: Evidence from a Balanced Scorecard," *The Accounting Review* 78, no. 3, 725–758.

cent of FMC's deliveries were late, while only 5 percent of the best competitor's deliveries were late, and future customers would expect 99 percent on-time delivery, then FMC should substantially improve its on-time deliveries to be competitive.

The implementation at FMC appears to have gone well. Implementation has spread from the pilot study at the Lithium Division to other parts of the company.

Source: R. S. Kaplan and D. P. Norton, *The Balanced Scorecard,* video, Harvard Business School Management Productions, Boston, Mass., 1993.

Problem 12.1 for Self-Study

Divisional incentive systems.

a. What two key questions must management answer in designing incentive systems?
b. What incentives are given to managers when accountants write off design and development costs as overhead in the period when these costs are incurred?

The solution to this self-study problem is at the end of the chapter on page 442.

Motivational Issues in Designing Incentive Systems for Division Managers and Their Subordinates

We now turn to several specific choices that designers of incentive compensation plans must make. All these choices speak to the issue, "What behavior should the incentive compensation plan motivate?" The answer to that question is, "It depends on the situation faced by each company." There are no universal right or wrong answers, but there are likely right or wrong answers in a particular situation. Our aim is to provide you with an overview of the choices, not to suggest which are the correct choices for all situations. (Personal and corporate income tax regulations also affect the design of incentive compensation plans. Those issues are beyond the scope of this book.)

Basing Rewards on Current or Future Performance?

Rewards for performance can be based on current performance or future performance. If the basis is current, the compensation awards are usually in the form of cash or stock that can be cashed immediately or soon after the award. For example, a manager might be rewarded if the stock price increases 50 percent by the end of the year 2007. Or a manager might be rewarded if earnings increase by an average of 10 percent per year over the next three years.

An advantage of compensating based on future performance is that it provides "golden handcuffs" for managers because they have incentives to stay with the company, and it also focuses attention on the long run. Many commentators argue that managers, particularly in the United States, are too short-term oriented. They take actions that look good now, in the short run, but that are detrimental in the long run. A good example is the failure of many U.S. companies to invest in new technology. That decision kept earnings high in the short run but was detrimental in the long run.

A disadvantage of deferred compensation is that managers may view it as coming too far in the future to be motivational. Recall from expectancy theory that the reward must be attractive to be motivating. Giving a manager a reward in stock to be paid in, say, the year 2020 is less attractive than a payment at the end of the current year.

Our research indicates that most companies use a combination of current and deferred awards for top managers but pay mostly current awards for lower managers and their subordinates. When making deferred awards to divisional managers and below, companies usually defer the award for only three to five years. Three to five years appears to be a reasonable compromise that motivates the manager to think about the future but is not so distant as to lose incentive effects.

Basing Rewards on Division Performance or Companywide Performance?

Should a manager's rewards depend on the performance of the manager's responsibility center or the company as a whole? For example, should the bank manager of a branch of Davis First National Bank be evaluated based on the performance of the manager's branch bank alone or on the performance of the bank as a whole? Compensation based on the manager's responsibility center alone focuses managers' attentions on their own responsibility centers. However, that may be to the detriment of other responsibility centers and to the performance of the company as a whole.

Basing compensation on the performance of the company as a whole gives managers incentives to consider the impact of their actions on the whole company. In large companies, however, managers may not see much of a relation between their actions and the performance of the company. For example, Hewlett-Packard has numerous divisions. One particular division's performance has very little impact on that of the company as a whole. Thus, large companies like Hewlett-Packard base most of a division manager's compensation on the performance of the manager's own division.

Most companies reward division managers for both division and companywide performance. Companies that are decentralized and have many divisions doing diverse activities tend to weight the performance evaluation more on each division's performance and less on companywide performance. So ITT, a decentralized and diverse company, bases nearly all division managers' compensation on the performance of the divisions. Caterpillar, which, although large, is highly integrated and much more centralized than ITT, ties more of its division managers' compensation to companywide performance.

Using Fixed Formulas or Subjectivity in Providing Rewards?

Some companies base rewards on a fixed formula. For example, one company that we studied set up the incentive plan so that a manager would receive a bonus of 10 percent of the manager's base salary for each percentage point by which annual earnings growth exceeded 5 percent. A manager knew, for example, that if her division's earnings growth was 9 percent for a particular year (that is, four percentage points above the 5 percent threshold percent) and her base salary was $100,000 per year, then her bonus would be $40,000 (= 4 percentage points times 10 percent per point times $100,000). This bonus was paid in addition to the manager's base salary.

Other companies use more subjectivity in providing compensation above the base salary. The advantage of the subjective approach is that it considers factors not explicitly captured in the formula approach. For example, suppose a manager's return on investment dips because the manager is incurring research, employee training, and advertising expenses that should have a payoff in the future. It is difficult to capture such things in an explicit formula.

The advantage of the formula-based plan is that the managers know precisely what is expected of them and what reward they will get if they achieve expectations. The subjective approach is subject to favoritism, political maneuvering, and even a "good old boy network" approach to incentive compensation. Incentive compensation can become more a function of how well managers are liked by their superiors than a function of performance.

In our experience, managers who do not fully trust their superiors tend to prefer the formula-based approach. We find the subjective approach widely used in compensating top managers. Formula-based compensation is more widely used at lower levels. Although we see subjective performance evaluations at low levels in organizations, it is not as prevalent there as at higher levels. Recent research supports these observations.[3]

---

[3]An article by M. Gibbs, K. A. Merchant, W. A. Van der Stede, and M. E. Vargus, "Determinants and Effects of Subjectivity in Incentives," *The Accounting Review* 79, no. 2 (2004), 409–436, indicates that companies use subjective bonuses when performance is difficult to quantify. This article also finds that the impact of subjective bonuses on productivity and satisfaction are greater the longer the employee's tenure.

Performance Evaluation Based on Accounting Results or on Stock Performance?

Tying managers' performance to the company's stock performance has the obvious benefit of aligning managers' incentives with those of shareholders. However, division managers in large companies may see little link between their actions and the performance of the company's stock. Further, a company's stock can fluctuate widely based on factors over which the manager has no control.

Tying a manager's compensation to stock performance loads a lot of risk on managers. Further, this type of risk is not easy for managers to diversify, if they can at all, because the performance is based on just one stock—that of the company.

Despite these problems with stock-based performance, companies generally provide at least some incentive for managers to worry about stock performance. Stock options, which provide rewards for upside performance but no out-of-pocket penalty for downside performance, are one way to shield managers from some risk yet give them an orientation to how well the company's stock is doing.

One of the benefits of economic value added is that it both orients managers to focus on creating value for shareholders and relies on nonstock performance measures. In the final analysis, companies generally base most of divisional managers' compensation on accounting-based performance (including economic value added) and performance on nonfinancial measures such as those included in the balanced scorecard.

Absolute Performance Evaluation or Relative Performance Evaluation?

Undoubtedly, you have taken classes that use relative performance evaluation and classes that use absolute performance evaluation. In ones that use relative performance evaluation, the instructor "grades on the curve"; that is, your grade depends on how you perform relative to everyone else. In classes that use absolute performance evaluation, the instructor grades on an absolute scale, so your grade is not affected by how others do.

Companies that use relative performance evaluation compare divisional performance with that of other divisions in the same industry. Thus, the manager of a division that earned a return on investment of 20 percent might not be evaluated as positively as one whose division earned 10 percent, if in the first case the industry average return on investment was 30 percent, and in the second, 6 percent. Just as grading on the curve shields students from the risk of an extremely difficult or unfair test, relative performance evaluation shields a manager from the risk of managing a division in a poorly performing industry.

The disadvantage of relative performance evaluation is that it does not provide incentives for managers to move out of low-performing into high-performing industries. In the example just given, it is probably not in the company's best interest for a division to be in an industry that had an average return on investment of 6 percent. Most companies would want that manager to seek new, more profitable opportunities.

Cash Awards, Stock Awards, or Prizes?

Cash awards have the advantage of being liquid and highly attractive. Stock awards, on the other hand, are usually not redeemable into cash until sometime in the future. In some companies, there is an unwritten rule that managers not sell company stock until they leave the company or retire. Stock awards better align the interests of managers with those of shareholders than cash awards do. Stock options, which give an individual the right to purchase a certain number of shares at a specified price within a certain time period, provide incentives for managers to increase stock value. At the same time, stock options protect managers from losses because, if the stock declines in value before the option is exercised, the managers simply do not exercise the option to purchase the stock.

Some companies give prizes instead of either cash or stock. One small company that we studied awarded managers points for performing well. The managers could trade in the points for automotive accessories or sporting goods such as golf clubs or hunting rifles. Managers who received these awards told us this was a highly motivating reward. One of them told us, "A cash bonus would be eaten up paying the bills and soon forgotten. Every time I use my new fishing rod I remember the work I put in to earn it." Applying expectancy theory, the prizes were more attractive and, therefore, more motivating than cash awards.

Nonprofit organizations range from small, often informal organizations, such as sports clubs, student organizations, and parent support groups for sports and music, to large, well-established organizations such as the United Way, the Lutheran Church, most universities, the Department of Defense, and the Environmental Protection Agency. We can apply the concepts in this chapter to nonprofit organizations with some modification of the concepts. Naturally, a nonprofit organization has something other than earning a profit as its goal. Thus, managers should have incentives to perform well on nonfinancial dimensions.

Financial performance in nonprofit organizations has more to do with proper accountability for the use of funds than for achieving profit targets. Even so, nonprofit organizations generally attempt to break even in terms of attracting enough funds to cover expenses. They do not try to maximize profits, however.

Because they are not seeking to earn profits, nonprofit organizations are not managed by the numbers, as are many for-profit companies. Whereas a for-profit company can evaluate a division manager's performance by how well the manager's division performs in the market, market-based comparisons are usually not available or relevant for nonprofit organizations. Consider a country's military organization. How would one evaluate the performance of military commanders based on the performance of their units in the market? Instead, many nonprofits are managed as bureaucracies. In bureaucracies, the key performance measures involve adherence to rules set down by top authorities.

Other nonprofit organizations rule more by culture or shared values. For example, the parents in a particular soccer support organization share the values of providing support for their children's soccer activities. The culture binds them and provides a powerful force for performing to achieve common goals.

In voluntary and charitable organizations such as United Way, incentive compensation plans rely heavily on intrinsic rewards. People generally earn a lower salary than they would in the private sector. Further, nonprofits do not offer opportunities for large financial payoffs for excellent performance. However, voluntary and charitable organizations attract people for whom the intrinsic reward from doing good work compensates for the lost financial compensation available in the private sector. Government agencies may also attract people who get intrinsic rewards from the work and/or people who like the security and benefit packages that are often available in government organizations.

Increasing Use of Management Methods Developed in the Private Sector

Despite differences between for-profit and nonprofit organizations, nonprofit organizations increasingly use management methods developed in the private sector. The balanced scorecard seems particularly appropriate to nonprofit organizations. Surprisingly, even economic value added is attracting attention among nonprofits.

For example, the U.S. Postal Service is under a mandate to break even financially and to manage itself more like a for-profit enterprise. The U.S. Postal Service controls billions of dollars of assets in buildings, vehicles, and sorting equipment, so management adopted economic value added, discussed in Chapter 11, to help control its capital costs. Management applied a cost of capital to the assets for each responsibility center using the borrowing rate mandated by Congress—one-eighth of a percent over the three-month Treasury Bill rate.

With stiff competition from the private sector, such as United Parcel Service and Federal Express, the U.S. Postal Service must also concentrate on customer service; something that economic value added does not directly address. While economic value added provides an orientation toward effective management of resources, it does not directly motivate customer satisfaction, which is essential for the U.S. Postal Service to compete effectively with its private sector competitors. To become an effective competitor that manages its assets well, the U.S. Postal Service would seem well advised to adopt a balanced scorecard with economic value added as one of the financial measures.

This section of the chapter deals with ethical issues in financial reporting. We focus on motives and opportunities for committing fraud by managers and employees in companies. We have added this discussion for a simple reason: An increasing number of former students have come to us stressing the importance of discussing real ethical dilemmas people face on the job. This discussion should take place in a variety of classes, they say, and not be limited to classes on ethics. We agree.

Many managers and other employees are often placed under enormous pressure to meet high short-term financial-performance standards such as profits and return on investment. Consequently, managers and other employees may be tempted to "cook the books" by carrying obsolete inventory on the books, overstating revenues, or understating costs, or by other methods.

All of you are likely to encounter some form of pressure to fudge the numbers. Some of you will design systems to detect and deter fraudulent or other unethical behavior, or you will work in the growing field of forensic accounting, in which you might assist attorneys as expert witnesses or as consultants. All of you will benefit from an understanding of the conditions conducive to fraudulent financial reporting.

The purpose of this discussion is to help you understand conditions conducive to fraudulent financial reporting. Before continuing, we want to emphasize that, in our view, the vast majority of people in business organizations behave ethically. Even people who behave ethically, though, or people they know, sometimes find themselves in situations that create pressure to behave unethically.

Fraudulent financial reporting is intentional conduct resulting in materially misleading financial statements. In recent years, managers at high-flying companies, such as Enron, WorldCom, and Adelphia, and stalwarts, such as Xerox, have committed, or at least been formally charged with committing, financial fraud. One of the largest and most venerable accounting firms, Arthur Andersen & Co., was involved with many fraudulent clients and quickly died. Common examples of fraudulent financial reporting occur when companies recognize revenue before making the sale and when companies do not write down obsolete inventory.

Stealing is not the same as financial fraud, but falsifying financial reports to cover up a theft would likely be financial fraud. Unintentional errors in preparing financial statements do not constitute fraudulent financial reporting.

For financial reporting to be fraudulent,

1. it must result from intentional or reckless conduct, and
2. the resulting misstatements must be material to the financial statements.

To be material, the misstatement must be large enough to affect the judgment of a responsible person relying on the information. Simply stated, to be material, the misstatement must be important.

For a law enforcement agency such as the Securities and Exchange Commission (SEC) to prove fraud requires proving either intent to commit fraud or reckless conduct, both difficult tasks. Consequently, when the SEC brings charges against people for violating the antifraud provisions of the securities laws, it often settles the cases out of court by having the accused sign "consent" documents. The signer of a consent decree says, in effect, "Maybe I did or maybe I didn't commit fraud, but I promise not to do it again." The cases we discuss in the following sections involve alleged fraud because the SEC has generally not proven financial fraud.

Who Commits Fraud?

Employees at all levels in the organization, from top management to low-level employees, might participate in fraudulent financial reporting. Enforcement agencies sometimes find the company's external auditors responsible for their clients' fraudulent financial reporting.

We focus on the use of accounting information by managers inside organizations. Department and division managers may commit fraud when reporting to their superiors. For example, managers at certain PepsiCo bottling plants misled their superiors at corporate headquarters in Purchase, New York, by failing to write off obsolete or unusable bottle inventories.

Fraudulent reporting inside a company misleads top management and the board of directors as well as stockholders and other outsiders who rely on the company's financial information. Also, top managers sometimes commit fraud by misleading outsiders. Most cases reported by the media involve top management.

In many cases, management or the board of directors solves the problem involving potential fraud before financial reporting occurs and the firm files fraudulent financial statements with the Securities and Exchange Commission (SEC). Often, people start out bending the rules a little, only to find that, over time, bending the rules escalates into broken laws.

Types of Fraud

People have tried many types of fraud, including omitting liabilities from financial statements, overstating assets on the balance sheet, and preparing false appraisals or other documents to support loans. Subsequent investigation showed that many of the savings and loan companies that failed in the 1980s had relied on fraudulent loan documentation. Our research indicates the two most common types of fraud involve improper revenue recognition and overstating inventory.

Improper Revenue Recognition

Eventually, total revenue will equal total cash (or other assets) received from customers. Improper revenue recognition occurs when the firm reports the profit-increasing effects of revenue in the wrong accounting period—typically, but not always, too early. Improper revenue recognition results if a firm backdates sales to report revenue on December 30, Year 1, when the firm should have reported the sales as having occurred in January of Year 2. Such a misrepresentation shows both the revenue and the cost of goods sold in Year 1 instead of Year 2.

For example, according to allegations by the SEC, MiniScribe, a Denver-based computer disk drive manufacturer, backdated invoices for sales made on the first day of the year to the last day of the previous year. The company also had shipped bricks to distributors and booked them as sales of disk drives. The early recognition of revenue and booking of nonexistent revenues increased profits reported to shareholders. In other cases, companies have shipped products to company-owned warehouses but claimed the shipments were sales.

To compensate for the effects of previous fraud, perpetrators must continue to commit fraud. Note that early revenue recognition, resulting from backdating invoices or prematurely recording a sale, has only a temporary effect on reported revenues and profits. Pulling a sale out of Period 2 to report it in Period 1 improves sales and profits for Period 1 but reduces sales to be reported in Period 2. Now Period 2 does not look as good as it should, so the perpetrator moves sales from Period 3 back to Period 2 to cover for the sales previously moved from Period 2 to Period 1. The perpetrator must continue this practice to avoid reporting a revenue shortfall. The Managerial Application "Software Company's Stock Tanks after Premature Revenue Recognition Disclosed" describes how a software company got caught reporting premature revenue recognition.

Managerial Application

Software Company's Stock Tanks after Premature Revenue Recognition Disclosed

Within three weeks, MicroStrategy's stock dropped from a high of $333 per share to $86.75 per share. MicroStrategy was a software company headed by Michael J. Saylor, who proposed to contribute $100 million to the development of a free online university. The company "aggressively promoted itself and became a Wall Street darling, easily shrugging off criticism that its accounting was too liberal, enabling it to recognize revenue months if not years before it should have been reported."

Although the company's auditors, PricewaterhouseCoopers, had certified the year-end financial statements, the auditors questioned how the company could justify reporting revenue so quickly for contracts just signed. The auditors forced the company to defer reporting about one quarter of the $205.4 million in revenue it had reported for the previous year.

Source: Floyd Norris, "MicroStrategy Shares Plunge on Restatement," *New York Times,* March 21, 2000, p. C1.

Example The following example shows how one can get deeper and deeper into trouble with premature revenue recognition.

Financial Fraud: The Early Revenue Recognition Problem

Year 1: December 28

Buyer: "We really want your product, but we can't process the paperwork until January 3, Year 2."

Salesperson thinks: "No problem. We'll date everything December 28, Year 1, so I'll get credit for the sale in Year 1."

Year 2: December 28

Salesperson thinks: "I haven't heard from the buyer yet. I know they normally purchase an order about now. I'll just ship their normal order and date everything December 28, Year 2."

Year 3: December 28

Salesperson thinks: "I'm under a lot of pressure to make my sales budget. I know someone will want this stuff. I'll ship it to some customers and record the sale on December 28, Year 3. If the customers return the merchandise, I'll just say it's a mistake."

The salesperson starts in Year 1 with a minor indiscretion. By Year 3, the salesperson has committed a major fraud.

Overstating Inventory

Overstated ending inventory leads to overstated earnings. Recall the inventory equation:

Cost of Goods Sold = Beginning Inventory + Purchases − Ending Inventory

The higher the ending inventory, the lower the cost of goods sold, and the higher the reported earnings. If managers or accountants fail to write down obsolete inventory, then they overstate inventory. Department or division managers may not want to "take a hit" (reduce reported earnings) on the financial reports in the current period, so they postpone the write-off until later. In other cases, people falsify the ending inventory numbers during physical inventory counts or on audit papers.

In a shocking example of deceit, senior company officials at Miniscribe apparently broke into locked trunks containing the auditors' workpapers during the audit and inflated inventory values by approximately $1 million. In addition, employees created a computer program they called "Cook Book" to inflate inventory figures.

Overstating ending inventory will increase reported earnings in the period of overstatement but, in the absence of continuing overstatement, must result in reduced earnings reported in the next period. Refer again to the inventory equation. Higher beginning inventory increases cost of goods sold and decreases reported earnings. To continue to appear successful, the perpetrator of fraud must continue to overstate ending inventory, just to keep reported earnings from decreasing.

Example *Financial Fraud: The Overstated Inventory Problem*

Year 1: December 31

Manager thinks: "About 20 percent of my inventory is obsolete. But if I write it off this year, my profits will be lower than budget. Maybe next year, profits will be higher (or I'll have a new job somewhere else in the company)."

Year 2: December 31

> Manager thinks: "I'm still in the same job as last year and even more of my inventory is obsolete. Now I'll look really bad if I write off the inventory."

Effect on Taxes   Fraudulent financial reporting that results in higher reported earnings sometimes also overstates taxable income. If the fraud shifts income from a future period to the present period, then the overstated taxable income in the present period might be offset by lower taxable income in a future period. Nevertheless, overstating taxable income in early periods likely increases the present value of a company's tax payments. Financial fraud might not affect the total taxes paid, but it does change the timing of tax payments and, therefore, their present value.

Causes of Financial Fraud

Short-Term Orientation

Many firms use accounting numbers to grade, or evaluate, managers. Bonuses, merit pay increases, and promotions often depend on reported accounting numbers.

Why would a manager backdate sales from one year to an earlier year, which merely shifts profits but does not create them? Managers given a short-term perspective by their employment and pay arrangements will have an incentive to "manage earnings" this way. Department and division managers may believe they have an opportunity to be promoted to a new position or transferred to another part of the company if they perform well in the current year. If so, they have incentives to look good in their current year, not caring about the subsequent shortfall on their unit's reported performance.

Some companies reward managers for achieving a performance threshold, providing large and discontinuous, or lumpy, rewards for meeting specified targets. For example, a company may offer a bonus of 50 percent of salary if the manager's division achieves its target return on investment (ROI), but only 25 percent of the manager's salary if the division achieves 95 to 100 percent of the target ROI, and no bonus if the division reports an ROI less than 95 percent of the target. A manager who finds the ROI just below the threshold, say, just under 95 percent of the target ROI, has a personal financial stake in reporting ROI at the 95 percent level. The manager may hope that moving a few sales forward from next year to this year will not hurt next year's rewards as much as it helps this year's rewards.

Do Performance Evaluation Systems Create Incentives to Commit Fraud?

Management sometimes believes that high-pressure performance evaluation systems effectively motivate employees. If so, management must also realize that putting pressure on people to perform well also creates incentives to commit fraud. The pressure to perform can affect top executives as well as middle managers and employees. Top executives in a company often feel pressured to perform because of the demands of stockholders, the expectations of financial analysts, or simply their own egos.

Over the years, many commissions and congressional committees have studied financial fraud involving top management. They conclude that fraudulent financial reporting occurred because of a combination of pressures, incentives, opportunities, and environment. The forces that seemed to give rise to financial fraud are present in all companies. Fraudulent financial reporting may occur if the right mixture of forces and opportunities is present.

Experts say that fraud in financial reporting sometimes results from a manager's wish to improve a company's financial appearance to obtain a higher stock price or to escape penalty for poor performance. Examples of pressures to perform include the following:

- Unrealistic budget pressures, particularly for short-term results. These pressures occur when headquarters arbitrarily determines profit objectives and budgets without taking actual conditions into account.

- Financial pressure resulting from bonus plans that depend on short-term economic performance. This pressure is particularly acute when the bonus is a significant component of the individual's total compensation.[4]

Note the reference to companies' emphasis on short-term performance. Most cases of financial fraud involve a timing adjustment. Management will take chances on the future to make the current period look good. One department manager told us, "Of course I'm more concerned about the short run than the long run. If I don't look good now, I won't be around in the long run."

We conclude that unrealistic profit objectives in budgets can contribute to financial fraud. Top management in large and widely dispersed companies has difficulty setting reasonable expectations for its far-flung divisions. That companies decentralize their operations reflects the reality that top management of large and dispersed companies cannot involve itself in the details of local operations. Consequently, top management may mistakenly expect unrealistically good performance.

Environmental Conditions

In our opinion, the tone at the top most strongly influences fraudulent financial reporting. "The tone at the top" refers to the environment top management sets for dealing with ethical issues. No matter how extensive management's list of rules, no matter the clarity of a company code of conduct that employees must read and sign, top management's own behavior sends the most important signal about how to do things. Just looking the other way when subordinates act unethically sets a tone that encourages fraudulent reporting.

During your career, you will almost certainly sense the tone at the top in companies you work with or for. If top management looks away from unethical behavior, the chances increase that employees will commit fraud. You will less likely find financial fraud when top managers set firm guidelines and follow those guidelines themselves.

Controls to Prevent Fraud

Enough clever people working together to commit fraud will probably succeed. Companies establish **internal controls** to help prevent fraud. Internal controls are policies and procedures designed to give top management reasonable assurances that actions undertaken by employees will meet organizational goals. Internal controls help assure top management that the data it relies on for decision making do not result from fraudulent reports by lower-level employees. Because top management can override internal controls, such controls do not necessarily assure stockholders and other readers of companies' financial statements that top management reports accurately.

A fundamental principle of internal control to prevent fraud is to separate duties when a single person carrying out a series of tasks could commit fraud and take steps to hide it. For example, separation of duties in a department store requires that the person making the sale be different from the person who records it in the financial records. For the sale to be fraudulently reported, the sales clerk and the recorder would have to work together, or collude. **Collusion** is the cooperative effort of employees to commit fraud or other unethical acts.

Internal controls that separate duties make fraud more difficult because with separation of duties, fraud requires collusion. As the number of people colluding increases, so does the chance of whistle blowing to higher authorities, such as auditors, the Securities and Exchange Commission, and the media. Thus, the separation-of-duties doctrine of internal control prefers more, rather than fewer, people to handle a series of functions.

---

[4]Treadway Commission, *Report of the National Commission on Fraudulent Financial Reporting* (Washington, D.C.: National Commission on Fraudulent Financial Reporting, 1987), p. 23.

Internal Auditing

Firms hire internal auditors to help management or the board of directors or both. They often report to the audit committee of a company's board of directors. Internal auditors can both deter and detect fraud. They can deter fraud by reviewing and testing internal controls and ensuring controls are in place and working well.

Independent Auditors

Firms hire independent auditors primarily to obtain an opinion on published financial statements, not to detect fraud. Nevertheless, the presence of the independent auditors and their review of a company's internal controls help to prevent fraud. Further, independent auditors increasingly attempt to detect fraud, which should help deter it. The board of directors, management, or stockholders can also hire independent auditors specifically to conduct examinations for fraud.

Incentive Problems in International Markets

Several cultural differences among countries affect business practices. For example, in some countries, payments to government officials (for example, bribes or gifts) are an acceptable form of obtaining government contracts.

Economists argue that corruption requires three elements.

1. An individual, such as a government official, must have discretionary power to award a contract or rights (e.g., oil drilling rights or land development rights).
2. There must be economic benefits associated with such discretionary power.
3. The legal system must be unlikely to detect wrongdoing.

In 1977, Congress addressed foreign bribes paid by U.S. companies by passing the Foreign Corrupt Practices Act (FCPA), which makes it illegal for any U.S. citizen or company to make these types of payments to foreign government officials in the course of business.[5] Many other countries have restricted the payment of bribes.

The FCPA affects U.S. companies doing business in foreign countries where bribery is the norm in negotiating for government contracts. Subsidiaries of U.S. companies in foreign countries might hire native employees who might not even realize that it is illegal for U.S. companies to conduct business in this manner. For instance, recently the SEC and the U.S. Justice Department investigated allegations that officials of IBM's subsidiary in Argentina made illegal payments in order to receive a $250-million contract to modernize the National Bank of Argentina.[6] In another case, American oil companies have been charged with the payment of bribes to the president of Kazakhstan to obtain oil drilling rights.[7] So when incentives are present for managers to act aggressively in securing contracts, the incentives and the company policies must support the company upholding the act or it may be ignored.

---

[5]The act addresses questionable payments to foreign officials, record keeping, and internal accounting control. The FCPA makes it unlawful for virtually any officer, director, employee, or agent acting for any company to use the mails or interstate commerce for the purpose of paying foreign officials to obtain or retain business. "Grease payments" paid to low-level government employees to expedite routine matters are excluded. The act requires all companies registered with the SEC to make and keep accurate books and records and to devise and maintain a system of internal accounting controls adequate enough that managers of a company will know if a bribe is paid. For a discussion of economic issues about corruption, see J. D. Lyon and M. W. Maher, "The Importance of Business Risk in Setting Audit Fees," *Journal of Accounting Research,* March 2005; A. K. Jain, "Corruption, a Review," *Journal of Economic Surveys* 15, 71–121; and C. M. C. Lee and D. T. Ng, "Corruption and International Valuation: Does Virtue Pay?" Johnson School of Management, Cornell University, 2003.

[6]J. Friedland, "Kickback Allegations at IBM Argentina Trigger a Formal SEC Investigation," *Wall Street Journal,* January 18, 1996, pp. A10, A11.

[7]J. Gerth, "Bribery Inquiry Involves Kazakh Chief, and He's Unhappy," *New York Times,* December 11, 2002.

Problem 12.2 for Self-Study

Fraudulent financial reporting. Why is the "tone at the top" of a company important in preventing fraudulent financial reporting?

The solution to this self-study problem is at the end of the chapter on page 442.

The following items correspond to the learning objectives presented at the beginning of the chapter.

1. **Describe key characteristics of divisional incentive compensation plans.** Effective incentive compensation plans must induce individual behavior compatible with increasing the firm's wealth. Three common characteristics are cash bonuses and profit sharing for short-term performance, deferred compensation for long-term incentive, and special awards for particular actions or extraordinary performance.

2. **Explain how incentive plans can affect the development phase of the product life cycle.** Incentive plans based on short-term accounting performance may deter managers from investing in product development at a point in the product life cycle when the investment can do the most to ensure the most cost-effective method of production through the product's life.

3. **Compare and contrast expectancy and agency approaches to motivation.** The expectancy view of motivation recommends two things: providing desirable rewards and providing a high probability that behaving as the organization wishes will lead to the rewards. The agency view focuses on the relations between principals and agents and looks for ways to encourage agents (e.g., employees) to act in the interests of principals (e.g., managers).

4. **Describe the balanced scorecard as a way to tie performance measures to organizational goals.** The balanced scorecard is a causal model of lead and lag indicators of performance. The model is based on four perspectives: (1) learning and growth, (2) internal business and production process efficiency, (3) customer, and (4) financial.

5. **Explain the importance of performance measures for the four balanced scorecard perspectives.** One can think of performing well on learning and growth as leading to improved business processes and improved customer satisfaction, which leads to improved financial performance. There are various linkages among the four perspectives, but the point is that performing well on the three nonfinancial perspectives should lead to financial performance, or that financial performance lags nonfinancial performance.

6. **Explain what constitutes fraudulent financial reporting.** Fraudulent financial reporting results from intentional or reckless conduct, and the resulting misstatements are material to the financial statements.

7. **Define the two most common types of fraud and demonstrate their impact on financial statements.** The two most common types of fraud involve improper revenue recognition and overstating inventory. Improper revenue recognition occurs when the firm reports the profit-increasing effects of revenue in the wrong accounting period, usually early. Overstated ending inventory leads to overstated earnings, by understating cost of goods sold.

8. **Identify the incentives for committing financial fraud.** Bonuses, merit pay increases, and promotions often depend on reported accounting numbers. Managers given a short-term perspective by their employment and pay arrangements will have an incentive to "manage earnings." High-pressure performance evaluation systems not only put pressure on people to perform well but also create incentives to commit fraud.

9. **Explain how environmental conditions influence fraudulent conduct.** The tone at the top—the environment top management sets for dealing with ethical issues—most strongly influences fraudulent financial reporting. Regardless of policies and rules, looking the other way when subordinates act unethically sets a tone that encourages fraudulent reporting.

10. **Identify controls that can be instituted to prevent financial fraud.** A fundamental principle of internal control to prevent fraud separates duties where a single person carrying out a series of tasks could commit fraud and take steps to hide it. Separation of duties makes fraud more difficult because fraud then requires collusion. Internal auditors can both deter and detect fraud. The presence of independent auditors and their review of a company's internal controls help to prevent fraud.

Key Terms and Concepts

Agency cost
Agency theory
Balanced scorecard
Collusion
Expectancy theory

Extrinsic rewards
Fraudulent financial reporting
Internal controls
Intrinsic rewards

Solutions to Self-Study Problems

SUGGESTED SOLUTION TO PROBLEM 12.1 FOR SELF-STUDY

a. First, what behavior does the incentive system motivate? Second, what behavior does management desire?
b. Managers have incentives to reduce expenditures on design and development even if the expenditures would be justified in terms of future cost savings.

SUGGESTED SOLUTION TO PROBLEM 12.2 FOR SELF-STUDY

The tone at the top is important because top management influences the morale and behavior of all employees. Top management can override or circumvent an internal control system and can circumvent the formal performance evaluation and reward system, to encourage fraudulent reporting.

Questions, Exercises, Problems, and Cases

REVIEW QUESTIONS

1. Review the meaning of the concepts or terms discussed in Key Terms and Concepts.
2. What are the major characteristics of divisional incentive compensation plans?
3. Define *expectancy theory*.
4. What is an intrinsic reward? How is an intrinsic reward different from an extrinsic reward?
5. What are the four perspectives of the balanced scorecard?
6. What is fraudulent financial reporting? What are the two key concepts in the definition of fraudulent financial reporting?
7. What are common types of fraudulent financial reporting?
8. How does the separation of duties help prevent financial fraud?
9. How do internal auditors deter or detect financial fraud?

CRITICAL ANALYSIS AND DISCUSSION QUESTIONS

10. Refer to the Managerial Application "Conflicts in an Incentive Compensation Plan." What were the conflicting incentives facing the divisional controllers?
11. How could activity-based costing shift the emphasis from managing overhead to managing supplier relations?

12. Refer to the Managerial Application "Does Customer Satisfaction Pay Off?" What links between customer satisfaction and companies' financial performance did the researchers find?

13. Refer to the Managerial Application "Successfully Implementing the Balanced Scorecard: The FMC Experience." In developing the balanced scorecard, what four measures did FMC Corporation pick as particularly important for the Lithium Division? How did managers communicate the importance of meeting on-time delivery targets to employees?

14. When implementing the balanced scorecard, why do some managers use a different term to describe it?

15. How does the accounting write-off of design and development costs as current period expenses affect managers' incentives to incur these costs?

16. A large company hired your friend. She confides in you about a problem with her boss. Her boss is asking customers to sign a sales agreement just before the end of the year, which indicates a sale has been made. Her boss then tells these customers that he will give them 30 days, which is well into next year, to change their minds. If they do not change their minds, then he sends the merchandise to them. If they change their minds, her boss agrees to cancel the orders, take back the merchandise, and cancel the invoices. Her boss gives the sales agreements to the accounting department, which prepares an invoice and records the sales. One of the people in accounting keeps the invoices and shipping documents for these customers in a desk drawer either until the customers change their minds, in which case the sale is canceled, or until the merchandise is sent at the end of the 30-day waiting period.

   Your friend likes the company, and she wants to keep her job. What would you advise her to do?

17. Investigators of financial fraud cases have indicated that bonus plans based on achieving short-run financial results have been a factor in financial frauds, particularly when the bonus is a large component of an individual's compensation. Why do these bonus plans affect fraud?

18. An employee has been stealing some of the company's merchandise and selling it. Is this behavior financial fraud?

19. Suppose the employee in question **18** covers up the theft by accounting for it as spoilage. Would accounting for the stolen items as spoilage be financial fraud?

20. Suppose an accounting clerk who knows nothing about the theft in question **18** erroneously records the "lost" parts as spoilage. Would that be fraudulent financial reporting?

EXERCISES

Solutions to even-numbered exercises are at the end of the chapter after the cases.

21. **Balanced scorecard—performance measures.** Match each of the following performance measures to one or more of the four perspectives of the balanced scorecard. Note that a performance measure could measure performance for more than one perspective.

Performance Measures	Balanced Scorecard Perspectives
• Employee productivity	• Learning and growth
• Employee satisfaction	• Internal business
• Return on investment	• Customer
• Customer satisfaction	• Financial
• Employee turnover	
• On-time delivery performance from suppliers	
• Percentage of customers who are repeat customers	
• On-time delivery performance to customers	
• Product quality	

22. **Balanced scorecard—performance measures.** Match each of the following performance measures to one or more of the four perspectives of the balanced scorecard. Note that a performance measure could measure performance for more than one perspective.

Performance Measures	Balanced Scorecard Perspectives
• Throughput time	• Learning and growth
• Economic value added	• Internal business
• Employee productivity	• Customer
• Percentage of sales dollars invested in employee training	• Financial
• Ratings of supplier performance	
• Increase in market share	
• Employee retention	
• On-time delivery performance to customers	
• Product quality	

PROBLEMS

23. **Implementing the balanced scorecard.** Mary Waller, an executive in a large bank, recently attended a conference on management in the banking industry. At the conference, a manager from Citibank presented a diagram just like the one in Exhibit 12.3. Ms. Waller is intrigued by the performance measurement problems posed by the diagram. She asks, "How would you measure the performance of each step in the sequence from increased employee training to better financial results?"

    Using the balanced scorecard as a starting point, write a report to Ms. Waller that explains how to measure performance for each step in the sequence from increased employee training to better financial results.

24. **Accounting and decision making.** Salomon Company uses a cost of capital rate of 12 percent in making investment decisions. It currently is considering two mutually exclusive projects, each requiring an initial investment of $10 million. The first project has a net present value of $21 million and an internal rate of return of 20 percent. The firm will complete this project within one year. It will raise accounting income and earnings per share almost immediately thereafter. The second project has a net present value of $51 million and an internal rate of return of 30 percent. The second project requires incurring large, noncapitalizable expenses over the next few years before net cash inflows from sales revenue result. Thus accounting income and earnings per share for the next few years will not only be lower than if the first project is accepted but will also be lower than earnings currently reported.

    a. Should the short-run effects on accounting income and earnings per share influence the decision about the choice of projects? Explain.

    b. Should either of the projects be accepted? If so, which one? Why?

25. **Accounting for advertising.** Finley and Associates is a consulting firm that spends $60,000 per year advertising the company's brand names and trademarks. Gross margin on sales after taxes is up $66,000 each year because of these advertising expenditures. For the purposes of this problem, assume that the firm makes all advertising expenditures on the first day of each year and that the $66,000 extra after-tax gross margin on sales occurs on the first day of the next year. Excluding any advertising assets or profits, Finley has $200,000 of other assets that have produced an after-tax income of $20,000 per year. Finley follows a policy of declaring dividends each year equal to net income, and it has a cost of capital of 10 percent per year.

    a. Is the advertising policy a sensible one? Explain.

    b. How should accounting report the expenditures for advertising in Finley's financial statements to reflect accurately the managerial decision of advertising at the rate of $60,000 per year? In other words, how can the firm account for the advertising expenditures in such a way that the accounting rate of return for the advertising project and the rate of return on assets for the firm reflect the 10-percent return from advertising?

26. **Management incentives and accounting for research and development.** The Symantek Division produces software. It has $300,000 of total assets, earns $45,000 per year, and generates $45,000 per year of cash flow. The cost of capital is 15 percent. Each year, Symantek pays cash of $45,000 to its parent company, Microsot, Inc. Symantek's management has discovered a project requiring research and development costs now that will lead to new

products. The anticipated cash flows for this project follow: beginning of Year 1, outflow of $24,000; beginning of Years 2, 3, and 4, inflows of $10,000 each.

Assume that Microsot undertakes the project, that cash flows are as planned, and Symantek pays $45,000 to Microsot at the end of the first year and $47,000 at the end of each of the next three years.

   a. Compute Symantek's rate of return on assets for each year of the project, assuming that accounting expenses R&D expenditures as they occur. Use the year-end balance of total assets in the denominator.

   b. Compute Symantek's rate of return on assets for each year of the project, assuming that accounting capitalizes and then amortizes R&D costs on a straight-line basis over the last three years of the project. Use the year-end balance of total assets in the denominator.

   c. Compute the new project's accounting rate of return, independent of the other assets and of the income of Symantek, assuming that accounting capitalizes and then amortizes R&D costs on a straight-line basis over the entire four years of the project.

   d. How well has the management of the Symantek Division carried out its responsibility to its owners? On what basis do you make this judgment?

27. **Explain premature revenue recognition.** You have been asked to advise a business-to-business manufacturing company how to detect fraudulent financial reporting. Management does not understand how early revenue recognition by backdating invoices from next year to this year would affect financial statements. Further, management wants to know which accounts could be audited for evidence of fraud in the case of early revenue recognition.

   a. Using your own numbers, make up an example to show management the effect of early revenue recognition.

   b. Prepare a short report to management explaining the accounts that early revenue recognition would affect. Suggest some ways management could find errors in those accounts.

28. **Explain inventory overstatement.** A merchandising company has asked you to advise it on how to detect fraudulent financial reporting. Management wants your help in detecting inventory overstatement. Further, management wants to know how to find evidence of inventory overstatement.

   a. Using your own numbers, make up an example to show management the effect of overstating inventory. Show how inventory overstatement at the end of Year 1 carries through to the beginning inventory overstatement in Year 2.

   b. Prepare a brief report to management suggesting ways management could detect inventory overstatement.

29. **Top management's awareness of fraud.** The chief executive of a clothes manufacturer charged with committing financial fraud, was dismayed that the controller and other employees had committed fraud. He said the company could have taken steps to improve the situation if senior management had known the poor financial results. Financial analysts who follow the company had noted, however, that the company had marked down its clothing line in sales to retail stores such as May Department Stores and Federated Department Stores.

After the company cut prices 20 percent across the board, retail executives who were customers of the company wondered how the company could continue to be profitable. One analyst wondered how top management could not have known about the company's financial difficulties in view of the 20 percent markdown.

For your information, top management is located in New York City, and the fraud occurred at the financial offices in Wilkes-Barre, Pennsylvania. The line of reporting is as follows: The controller reports to the chief financial officer, and the chief financial officer reports to the chief executive of the company. Both the controller and chief financial officer work in Wilkes-Barre. The chief financial officer reportedly has considerable autonomy.

Write a short report indicating whether you think top management of the company is responsible for the fraud and state why (or why not).

CASES

30. **Motives and opportunities for fraud.** A report on the "income transferal" activities at the H. J. Heinz Company made the following statements. First, decentralized authority is a central principle of the company's operations. Second, the company expected its divisions to generate an annual growth in profits of approximately 10 to 12 percent per year. Third, it

was neither unusual nor undesirable for management to put pressure on the division managers and employees to produce improved results.

The report noted that putting pressure on the divisions to produce improved results coupled with the company's philosophy of autonomy, which it extended to financial and accounting controls, provided both an incentive and an opportunity for division managers to misstate financial results. The report further noted that the autonomous nature of the divisions combined with the relatively small corporate headquarters financial staff permitted a communications gap. In its simplest form, corporate management seemed to issue an order or set a standard with respect to achieving a financial result without regard to whether it was possible to achieve that result. The management of certain divisions had a feeling of "us versus them" toward corporate headquarters.

The report indicated there was an effort in certain divisions to transfer income from one fiscal period to another to provide a "financial cushion" for achieving the goal for the succeeding year. For example, divisions would overpay expenses so that they could get a credit or refund in a subsequent year. Or they would pay an expense such as insurance or advertising early, but instead of charging the amount to a prepaid expense account, they would charge the amount to expense. In good years, this practice would keep profits down and provide a cushion to meet the company's target for constantly increasing profits.

a. Using your own numbers, construct an example to demonstrate the kind of income transferal that was done at H. J. Heinz.

b. What was the motive to transfer income from one period to the other? What were the opportunities to transfer income?

c. Comment on how the communications gap and the "us versus them" attitude contributed to the fraud.

d. Refer to **c.** Have you seen communications gaps in organizations that have resulted in an "us versus them" attitude on the part of employees? If so, briefly describe the circumstances and the cause of the "us versus them" attitude. What could have been done (or could be done) to change the "us versus them" attitude in your example?

31. **Measuring managerial performance—new challenges.** Many commentators about North American business have argued that the relative deterioration in manufacturing productivity compared with that of Japanese manufacturers results from a preoccupation with short-term financial performance measures. Many firms base bonus plans for senior executives on annual accounting income. This method provides incentives to take actions that enhance short-term earnings performance but that may not serve the best long-term interests of the firm. By contrast, Japanese firms give executives incentives to ensure the long-run viability of their companies. Consequently, they are more concerned than their North American counterparts with long-run productivity, quality control, and managing the company's physical assets.

Not everyone agrees with the observation that North American business executives are preoccupied with short-term financial performance to the extent that they would take actions contrary to the best long-run economic interests of the organization just to make themselves look good on the performance measures. But suppose that an executive faces a choice between an action with a positive short-run effect on performance measures and another that has better long-run consequences for the organization but that will not affect short-run performance measures positively. We cannot fault a rational executive for taking the action that looks good in the short run. As the saying goes, "You have to look good in the short run to be around in the long run."

How would you design a control system that encourages top-level managers to be concerned about long-run productivity, quality of products, and the long-run economic well-being of the company? Assume that these managers have previously focused on maximizing quarterly and annual earnings numbers to the detriment of these other factors.

32. **Management decisions and external financial reports.** "Squeezing oranges in your idle time is not a by-product," said the Big Four partner in charge of the audit of Star Company disapprovingly. "But," replied the president of Star, "squeezing oranges is not our usual business, and your accounting plan will make us show a substantial decline in income. We all know that our decision this year to squeeze oranges was a good one that is paying off handsomely."

The argument concerned the accounting for income during the year 2002 by Star Company.

Background: The Alcoholic Control Board (ACB) of Georgia, a state not known for its production of grapes and wines, wanted to encourage the production of wine within the state. The executives of Star Company formed their company in 1995 in response to the encouragement of the ACB. The production process for wine involves aging the product. The company commenced production in 1996 but did not sell its first batch of wine until 1998. At the start of 1996, Star made a cash investment of $4,400,000 in grape-pressing equipment and a facility to house that equipment. The ACB has promised to buy Star Company's output for 10 years, starting with the first batch in 1998. Star Company decided to account for its operations by including in the cost of the wine all depreciation on the grape-pressing equipment and on the facility to house it. The firm judged the economic life of the equipment to be 10 years, the life of the contract with the ACB. Star Company reported general and administrative expenses of $100,000 per year in external financial reports for both 1996 and 1997.

Star Company's contract with the ACB promised payments of $1.8 million per year. The direct costs of labor and materials for each year's batch of wine were $130,000 each year. Accounting charges depreciation on a straight-line basis over a 10-year life. The income taxes were 40 percent of pretax income.

The wine sales began in 1998, and operations proceeded as planned. The income statements for the years 1998 through 2001 appear in Exhibit 12.5.

Management of Star Company was delighted with the offer in 2001 from a manufacturer of frozen orange juice to put its idle capacity to work. It contracted with the manufacturer to perform the services. At the end of 2002, it compiled the income statement shown in the "Management's View" column in Exhibit 12.5.

The Accounting Issue: Management of Star Company suggested that the revenues from squeezing oranges are an incremental by-product of owning the wine-making machinery. The wine-making process was undertaken on its own merits and has paid off according to schedule. The revenues from squeezing oranges are a by-product of the main purpose of the business. Ordinarily, the accounting for by-products assigns to them costs equal to their net

EXHIBIT 12.5	STAR COMPANY Income Statements (all dollar amounts in thousands)		
	1998 to 2001 **Each Year,** **Actual**	**For 2002**	
		Management's **View**	**Auditor's** **View**
Revenues			
From Wine Put into Production 2 Years Previously	$1,800	$1,800	$1,800
From Orange Juice Squeezed in Current Year	—	100[a]	100[a]
Total Revenues	$1,800	$1,900	$1,900
Cost of Goods Sold			
Direct Costs of Wine Put into Production 2 Years Previously	$ 300	$ 300	$ 300
Depreciation of Buildings and Equipment			
From 2 Years Prior, Carried in Inventory until Wine is Sold	440	440	440
From Current Year, Allocated to Orange Juice	—	100	352
Selling, General, and Administrative Expenses	130	130	130
Income Taxes at 40 Percent	372	372	271
Total Expenses	$1,242	$1,342	$1,493
Net Income	$ 558	$ 558	$ 407

[a]Manufacturer of orange juice pays out-of-pocket costs directly. These items are not shown here.

realizable value; that is, accounting assigns costs in exactly the amount that will make the sale of the by-products show neither gain nor loss. In this case, because the incremental revenue of squeezing oranges was $100,000, Star Company assigned $100,000 of the overhead to this process, reducing from $440,000 to $340,000 the overhead assigned to the main product. This will make the main product appear more profitable when it is sold.

Management of Star Company was aware that its income for 2002 would appear no different from that of the preceding year. Management knew that the benefits from squeezing oranges began to occur in 2002 but allowed the benefits to appear on the financial statements later.

The Big Four auditor who saw management's proposed income statement disapproved. The partner in charge of the audit spoke as quoted at the beginning of this case.

The auditor argued that squeezing oranges under these circumstances was not a by-product and that by-product accounting was inappropriate. Star Company must allocate the overhead costs between the two processes of grape pressing and orange squeezing according to some reasonable basis. The most reasonable basis, the auditor thought, was the time devoted to each of the processes. Because grape pressing used about 20 percent of the year, whereas orange squeezing used 80 percent of the year, the auditor assigned $352,000, or 80 percent, of the overhead costs to orange squeezing and $88,000, or 20 percent, to the wine production. Exhibit 12.5 shows the auditor's income statement in the "Auditor's View" column.

This statement upset the president of Star Company. Reported net income in 2002 is down almost 30 percent from 2001, yet things have improved. The president fears the reaction of the board of directors and the shareholders. The president wonders what has happened and what to do.

a. Assuming that the Star Company faces an after-tax cost of capital of 10 percent, did the company in fact make a good decision in 1995 to enter into an agreement with the state to produce wine? Explain.

b. Did the company in fact make a good decision in 2001 to enter into the agreement with the manufacturer of frozen orange juice?

c. Using management's view of the proper accounting practices, construct financial statements for the years 2003, 2004, and 2005, assuming that events occur as planned and in the same way as in 2002. Generalize these statements to later years.

d. Are management's statements correct given its interpretation of by-product accounting? If not, construct an income statement for 2002 that is consistent with by-product accounting.

e. Is management correct in its interpretation that the orange juice is a by-product?

f. Using the auditor's view of the situation and assuming the same facts as in part **c.**, construct income statements for the years 2003, 2004, and 2005. Generalize these statements to later years.

g. Assuming that the auditor is right, what may management of Star Company do to solve its problem?

RECOMMENDED CASES FOR CHAPTER 12.

Chadwick, Inc.: The Balanced Scorecard. Harvard Business School Case No. 196124. This case presents a relatively unsuccessful attempt to implement a balanced scorecard.

Duckworth Industries, Inc.: Incentive Compensation Programs. Harvard Business School Case No. 293091. This case evaluates various proposed incentive schemes, including one based on economic value added.

RKO Warner Video, Inc.: Incentive Compensation Plan. Harvard Business School Case No. 190067. The issues in this case include how to motivate video store managers to improve customer service and store appearance.

Montefiore Medical Center. Harvard Business School Case No. 101067. This case describes the implementation of a balanced scorecard at a large urban medical center.

Boston Medical Group. Harvard Business School Case No. 600086. This case describes the structure of a compensation plan for physicians implemented by a medical group.

Boston Lyric Opera. Harvard Business School Case No. 101111. This case describes a balanced scorecard in a nonprofit organization.

22. **Balanced scorecard—performance measures.**

Throughput time—Internal business perspective
Economic value added—Financial perspective
Employee productivity—Internal business perspective
Percentage of sales dollars invested in employee training—Learning and growth perspective
Ratings of supplier performance—Internal business perspective
Increase in market share—Customer perspective
Employee retention—Learning and growth perspective
On-time delivery performance to customers—Customer perspective
Product quality—Internal business perspective (could also be customer perspective)

chapter 13

$\mathcal{A}$llocating Costs to Responsibility Centers

Learning Objectives

1. Explain what comprises common (or indirect) costs.

2. Explain why companies allocate common costs to departments and products.

3. Describe how to allocate service department costs to production departments.

4. Explain why activity-based costing is used to allocate service department costs.

5. Identify methods of allocating marketing and administrative costs to departments.

6. Explain how to allocate joint-process costs.

7. Explain why joint-process costs are allocated.

This chapter discusses concepts and methods of assigning indirect costs, such as overhead, to departments. We call such cost assignment *cost allocation.*

Accountants distinguish between direct costs and indirect costs. (We also call indirect costs *common costs.*) A **direct cost** is one that firms can identify specifically with, or trace directly to, a particular product, department, or process. For example, direct materials and direct labor costs are direct with respect to products manufactured. A department manager's salary is a direct cost of the department, but indirect to the units the department produces.

A **common or indirect cost** results from the joint use of a facility or a service by several products, departments, or processes. For example, the cost of running an engine on a freight train for Union Pacific is common to the many cars on the train. The cost of groundskeeping at a university is common to its various schools and colleges. Many costs are common to different products manufactured. Firms allocate these common costs to develop division, department, or product cost information.

Service departments within a company offer a variety of services internally to other departments. Examples include human resources, accounting, computer support, and maintenance. Firms allocate the costs of operating these service departments to other departments, a procedure called **service department cost allocation,** for several purposes.

First and foremost, many departments consume the services provided by service departments and, therefore, should be assigned a share of the costs associated with the services consumed. It is important for each department to understand that services provided by each service department are not free! If costs of services were free to other departments, demand for services from service departments would go unchecked. Allocating service costs to other departments for services provided gives department managers incentives to control their use of support services. Service department costs are assigned to other departments to reinforce this fact.

Many companies allow departments to "shop" for services outside the company (for example, maintenance and human resources). If the services can be obtained elsewhere at a lower rate, the department may choose to use the outside service provider. This provides a clear incentive for service departments to offer services at a reasonable rate. It also provides an incentive for departments consuming the services to minimize consumption.

Service department cost allocations are made for other reasons as well. External reporting regulations—for tax and financial reporting purposes—require allocating manufacturing overhead to the units produced. This overhead often includes allocations of corporate and headquarter expenses, as discussed in the Managerial Application "Allocating Corporate Costs to Retail Stores."

Some organizations work on a cost-plus basis, particularly when working on government contracts. Companies must find a way to allocate all allowed expenses to the appropriate project to be properly reimbursed by the government.

Indirect cost allocations pervade accounting reports, both internal and external. To understand accounting reports and make appropriate interpretations, you must be familiar with the alternative allocation methods used and their effects on the resulting reports.

Managerial Application

Allocating Corporate Costs to Retail Stores

An executive of Kmart told one of the authors that "allocating corporate headquarters' costs to stores makes each store manager aware that these costs exist and must be covered by the individual stores for the company as a whole to be profitable." In view of Kmart's financial problems, we wonder whether that cost allocation procedure was sensible. Nevertheless, surveys of corporate cost allocation find that the majority of companies reported allocating common headquarters' costs to divisions (or departments) in order to give incentives to division managers to generate division profits sufficient to cover all corporate costs.

Source: Authors' research.

Cost Allocation

The following illustration demonstrates how companies allocate costs. Management could apply these methods to both manufacturing and non-manufacturing settings.

A division of First Bank has four departments. The Commercial Department and Personal Department are production departments that handle banking services for businesses (commercial) and people (personal). Computer Services and Processing are service departments. That is, they exist to provide support to the production departments. First Bank keeps records of the direct material and direct labor costs incurred in both production departments. First Bank considers all other costs associated with (but not easily traceable to) each production department to be overhead. Examples of overhead for First Bank include ATM machine maintenance and online banking technical support.

Exhibit 13.1 shows the relation among departments. Looking at Exhibit 13.1, what department would be responsible for cost allocation and for preparing accounting reports for managerial use? (Answer: Central Corporate Staff.)

Cost Allocation to Production Departments

Exhibit 13.2 shows the three steps in allocating costs. These three steps are outlined below. The ultimate goal is to assign or allocate all overhead costs to the production departments (Commercial and Personal departments in this example). Once the allocation process is complete, the service departments should have no costs remaining.

Step One: Assigning Direct Costs to Departments

First Bank will identify which costs are direct with respect to each department—that is, which costs are easily traceable to each of the four departments. Examples include salaries of managers in each department, hourly wages of department workers, and supplies used within each department. Other costs may or may not be easily traceable. If the department has its own building, rent and utilities are likely direct costs and would be assigned in this step. However, if the department is in the same building as other departments, it is more difficult to trace rent and utilities directly to the department. At this point, rent and utility costs likely become indirect costs and would be allocated as part of step two below (as is done in this example).

Exhibit 13.3 summarizes the direct and indirect overhead costs for First Bank. The direct costs assigned to departments as part of this first step include supervisor salaries for each department, labor for the computer services department, labor for the processing department, and supplies used by each department.

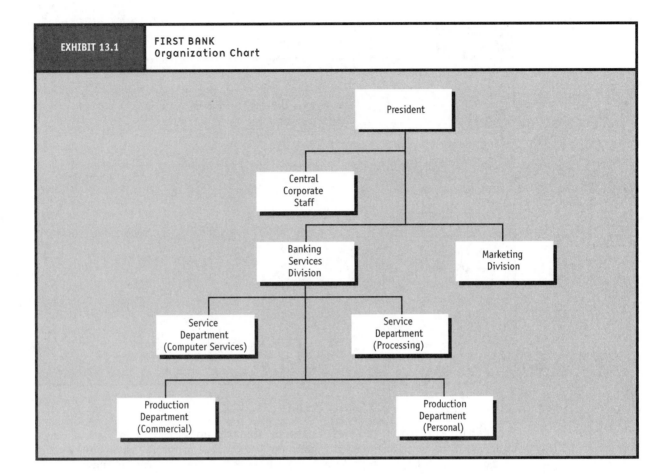

EXHIBIT 13.1 | **FIRST BANK Organization Chart**

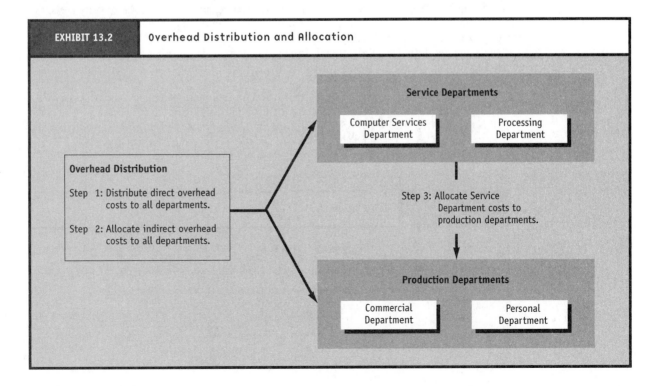

EXHIBIT 13.2 | **Overhead Distribution and Allocation**

EXHIBIT 13.3	Direct and Indirect Overhead Costs

	Total (1)	Commercial Department (2)	Personal Department (3)	Processing Department (4)	Computer Services Department (5)
Direct Costs					
Supervisor's Salary for Each Department[a]	$11,930	$3,825	$4,300	$1,260	$2,545
Labor—Computer Services[a]	6,000				6,000
Labor—Processing[a]	1,000			1,000	
Supplies Used[a]	2,750	600	900	800	450
Indirect Costs					
Payment for Security	1,000	?	?	?	?
Property Taxes	1,200	?	?	?	?
Rent and Utilities	1,440	?	?	?	?
Miscellaneous Costs	600	?	?	?	?
Total	$25,920	$?	$?	$?	$?

[a]First Bank can assign each of these items directly to a department.

Step Two: Allocating Indirect Costs to Departments

Next, First Bank allocates overhead costs that it cannot attribute directly to one of the departments. These costs include payments to an outside security agency, property taxes, rent and utilities, and miscellaneous costs. The question marks in Exhibit 13.3 show that the total indirect cost amounts in column (1) must be allocated to one or more of the four departments shown in columns (2) through (5).

At this point management of First Bank must select a cost driver for each cost. The goal is to select a cost driver (i.e., an activity or measure of an activity) that drives each cost. First Bank decided that the number of security guard visits to each department drives the security costs; the book value of assets in each department drives the property tax costs; and the square footage of floor space drives rent and utility costs. Given the insignificant amount of miscellaneous costs ($600) and the difficulty in identifying an appropriate cost driver, First Bank chose to allocate the $600 evenly among the four departments. A summary of the selected cost drivers is provided in Exhibit 13.4.

Once cost drivers are selected, First Bank's accountants must accumulate the necessary data to begin the allocation process. Exhibit 13.5 shows the cost driver data necessary to allocate indirect costs. The Solution to Self-Study Problem 13.1 (parts **a.** and **b.**) shows how to use the data in Exhibits 13.3, 13.4, and 13.5 to allocate indirect costs to the four departments.

EXHIBIT 13.4	Cost Drivers Selected

Cost	Cost Driver
Security	Number of visits made to each department
Property Taxes	Book value of equipment and inventory in each department
Rent and Utilities	Floor space each department occupies

Note: Miscellaneous costs are distributed equally over the four production and service departments because the firm has no other logical basis for an allocation.

EXHIBIT 13.5 — Cost Driver Information

Department	Number of Security Visits	Book Value of Assets	Square Feet of Floor Space
Commercial	12	$100,000	15,000
Personal	12	70,000	15,000
Processing	16	26,000	6,000
Computer Services	0	4,000	4,000
Totals	40	$200,000	40,000

Step Three: Allocating Service Department Costs to Production Departments

Once all company overhead costs are distributed to all departments (done previously in steps one and two), we can begin the final step of the process. The final step is to allocate the service department overhead costs to the production departments.

A simple and typical approach to accomplishing this cost allocation is the step method. The **step method** allocates costs in steps as follows: Begin with the service department that receives the smallest dollar amount of service from the other service departments. Allocate its cost to the other service and production departments. Next, distribute the total costs of the service department receiving the next smallest amount of service from other service departments, and so on, until all service department costs are allocated to the production departments. Once a given service department's cost has been allocated to other departments, do not allocate any costs back to that service department.

Assume the Computer Service Department provides service to the Processing Department but receives little or no service from the Processing Department. Therefore, we allocate Computer Services first, using the step method. Once again, we must select a cost driver that drives the cost associated with the Computer Services Department. First Bank management decided to use the number of computer hours required in each department as the cost driver and, therefore, as the allocation base. Computer hours used and the corresponding percentage of usage by other departments appears in Exhibit 13.6. Because the Commercial Department uses 50 percent of the computer hours, we allocate 50 percent of the computer services costs to it. In like fashion, we allocate 25 percent of the computer services costs to the Personal Department and 25 percent to the Processing Department.

Once the Computer Services Department's costs are allocated to the other three departments (as shown in the Solution to Self-Study Problem 13.1, part **c.**), the Processing Department's costs are allocated to the two production departments.

Assume the cost driver for the Processing Department's costs is the quantity of transactions by the Commercial and Personal departments. Exhibit 13.7 shows the cost driver data and corresponding percentage usage by department. Of the total transactions made by Commercial and Personal, 40 percent are for Commercial and 60 percent are for Personal. So 40 percent of the

---

EXHIBIT 13.6 — Step Method Allocation Data (Computer Services Department)

Department	Computer Hours	Percentage[a]
Commercial	400 Hours	50%
Personal	200	25
Processing	200	25
Total	800 Hours	100%

[a]50% = 400 hours/800 hours; etc.

| EXHIBIT 13.7 | Step Method Allocation Data (Processing Department) |

Department	Quantity of Transactions	Percentage[a]
Commercial	1,200	40%
Personal	1,800	60
Total	3,000	100%

[a]40% = 1,200 transactions/3,000 transactions; etc.

Processing Department's costs are allocated to the Commercial Department, and 60 percent to the Personal Department.

Problem 13.1 for Self-Study

Step method allocation. Using the data for First Bank presented in Exhibits 13.3 through 13.7, allocate overhead costs to departments as follows (assume the data are for the month of March):

a. Calculate the percentage of cost drivers used by each department (e.g., Commercial Security = 12/40 = 30%).
b. Assign the overhead to the four departments based on the percentage of cost drivers utilized.
c. Assign the service departments' costs using the step method based on computer hour usage and quantity of transactions as described in the text.

The solution to this self-study problem is at the end of the chapter on page 462.

Summary of Allocation

Firms allocate costs to departments in three steps as shown in the Solution to Problem 13.1 for Self-Study: (1) assignment of costs directly to departments for costs that are directly traceable to departments (e.g., department managers' salaries at First Bank), (2) allocation of costs not directly traceable to departments (e.g., security costs at First Bank), and (3) allocation of service department costs to the production departments.

As shown in the Solution to Problem 13.1 for Self-Study (part **c.**), the Commercial Department ultimately had $13,196 in overhead costs assigned or allocated to it, and the Personal Department had $12,724 allocated to it. The service departments correctly show $0 in overhead costs after the allocation process is complete. The Commercial and Personal departments can now begin to allocate these overhead amounts to products to compute product costs if desired.

Using Activity-Based Costing to Allocate Service Department Costs

Go back to step three of the cost allocation process (allocating service department costs to production departments). We decided in allocating computer service costs to other departments that computer hours used would be the best allocation base. However, this may not represent the best cause-and-effect relationship between resource spending (by the Computer Services Department) and resource use (by the other departments). The more closely the allocation base reflects a link between resource spending and use, the more useful allocated costs are likely to be for planning, decision making, and influencing behavior.

Applying the techniques of activity-based costing typically results in identifying more accurate cost-allocation bases (cost drivers). For example, using activity-based costing, the company has identified more accurate cost drivers for the Computer Services Department (CSD). CSD really has two segments—maintenance and technical support. Thus, CSD costs are driven by two primary factors.

First, departments that use specialized software tend to require more technical support from CSD. In fact, the Commercial Department uses more sophisticated software than the Personal Department and therefore demands more in the way of services from CSD. Technical support hours used may be the best cost driver here.

Second, the departments that use their computer equipment for longer periods tend to need more maintenance. Computer hours used may be the best cost driver here.

Instead of using one cost driver (computer hours used) to allocate CSD services, a more accurate—and therefore more equitable—approach might be to use the two cost drivers outlined above. The process of using activity-based costing to allocate costs is discussed in detail in Chapter 3. A summary of this process follows.

1. Measure each service department's resource spending by unit, batch, product, customer, or facility.
2. Identify and measure the activities demanded by other departments that require support-service spending (e.g., computer maintenance and technical support).
3. Identify appropriate cost-driver bases (e.g., computer hours used and technical support hours used) and calculate cost-driver rates.
4. Allocate service department costs based on other departments' usage of cost-driver bases.

Keep in mind that finding a cost-allocation base that approximates cause-and-effect relationships is justified if the benefits from improved decisions exceed the costs of finding and using the base. Discovering cause-and-effect relationships is often difficult and costly. As a result, many companies opt to use a system that is simpler and easier to implement (albeit less accurate) than activity-based costing.

Marketing and Administrative Costs

In allocating company costs to departments, management will often include marketing and administrative costs. Macy's department store, for example, may wish to have its customer service and billing department costs allocated to men's clothing, furnishings, teen wear, and other departments for purposes of performance evaluation. A wholesaler of Honda motorcycles may wish to allocate the costs of advertising to different territories or types of customers (such as college students). These costs are separate from the production overhead costs discussed in the previous section.

Exhibit 13.8 shows some of the bases of allocation that firms use for marketing and administrative costs. One striking aspect of the problem of such cost analysis is that firms must accumulate extensive data in addition to the regular accounting information. Looking at Exhibit 13.8,

EXHIBIT 13.8	**Allocation Bases**
For Allocation Of	**Basis**
1. Insurance	Average Value of Finished Goods
2. Storage and Building Costs	Floor Space
3. Cost of Sending Monthly Statements, Credit Investigations, etc.	Number of Customers
4. Various Joint Costs Such as Advertising and Supervision of Selling Activities	Sales, Classified by Dealers, Territories, or Products
5. Credit Investigation, Postage, Stationery, and Other Similar Expenses	Number of Orders Received
6. Handling Costs	Tonnage Handled
7. Salespersons' Expenses	Number of Salespersons' Calls
8. Order Writing and Filling	Number of Items on an Order
9. Stenographic Expense	Number of Letters Written
10. Automobile Operation, Delivery Expense, etc.	Number of Miles Operated

what would you say could be other bases for allocating salespersons' costs to a geographic territory? (Answer: miles driven or traveled, dollar value of sales, or number of units sold.)

Allocating Joint-Process Costs

Many companies, particularly those in forest products, oil and gas, and chemicals and mining, produce multiple products from a joint process. A **joint process** simultaneously converts a common input into several outcomes. For example, timber (logs) can be processed into lumber of various grades and sizes. The resulting sawdust and wood chips can be converted into paper pulp. Several different products are produced from one input (timber). The costs to operate joint processes are called **joint-process costs.** The products that result from processing a common input are called **joint products.** The difficulty for most companies is in allocating the joint-process costs to joint products so that downstream managers have product cost information available for decision making and performance evaluation.

Exhibit 13.9 is a diagram of the flow of costs incurred to process logs by Humbolt Company. These joint-process costs include materials, labor, and manufacturing overhead (totaling $360,000). As the logs are processed, two products emerge—standard lumber and specialty lumber. The stage of processing when the two products are separated is called the **splitoff point.** Exhibit 13.9 also shows the total sales value of each product for the month of July.

How will Humbolt Company allocate the $360,000 in joint-process costs to each product? The following section shows two possible approaches to allocating the joint-process costs to the products.

Joint-Process Cost Allocation Methods

The two major methods of allocating joint-process costs are (1) the net realizable value (NRV) method and (2) the physical quantities method.

Net Realizable Value (NRV) Method

The **net realizable value method** allocates joint-process costs based on the net realizable value of each product at the splitoff point. The net realizable value is the estimated sales value of each product at the splitoff point. If the joint products can be sold at the splitoff point, the market value or sales price should be used for this allocation. If the products require further processing before they are marketable, it may be necessary to estimate the net realizable value at the splitoff point by subtracting additional processing costs from the final sales value.

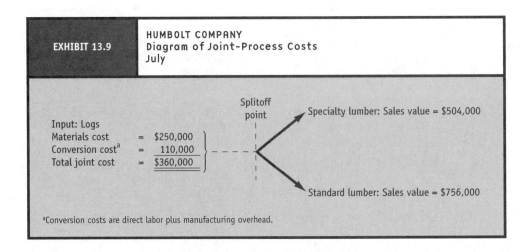

EXHIBIT 13.9	HUMBOLT COMPANY Diagram of Joint-Process Costs July

Input: Logs
Materials cost = $250,000
Conversion cost[a] = 110,000
Total joint cost = $360,000

Splitoff point

Specialty lumber: Sales value = $504,000

Standard lumber: Sales value = $756,000

[a]Conversion costs are direct labor plus manufacturing overhead.

EXHIBIT 13.10	HUMBOLT COMPANY Gross Margin Computations Using Net Realizable Value Method July			
		Specialty	Standard	Total
Sales Value		$504,000	$756,000	$1,260,000
Less Allocated Joint Costs		144,000	216,000	360,000
Gross Margin		$360,000	$540,000	$ 900,000
Gross Margin as a Percentage of Sales		71.43[a]	71.43[a]	71.43[a]

[a]71.43 = $360,000 ÷ $504,000 = $540,000 ÷ $756,000 = $900,000 ÷ $1,260,000.

From the Humbolt Company example, we know materials (logs) cost $250,000, and conversion costs are $110,000, for a total of $360,000. Specialty and standard lumber have a $1,260,000 total sales value at the splitoff point. Specialty lumber has a $504,000 sales value, or 40 percent of the total, and standard lumber has a $756,000 sales value, or 60 percent of the total. Assume no additional processing is required after the splitoff point.

The cost allocation follows the proportional distribution of net realizable values:

	Specialty Lumber	Standard Lumber	Total
Final Sales Value	$504,000	$756,000	$1,260,000
Less: Additional Processing Costs	0	0	0
Net Realizable Value at Splitoff Point	$504,000	$756,000	$1,260,000
Proportionate Share			
$504,000/$1,260,000	40%		
$756,000/$1,260,000		60%	
Allocated Joint-Process Costs			
$360,000 × 40%	$144,000		
$360,000 × 60%		$216,000	

Exhibit 13.10 shows a condensed statement of gross margins at the splitoff point. Note that the gross margin as a percentage of sales is 71.43 percent for both products. This demonstrates an important concept of the net realizable value method, that revenue dollars from any joint products are assumed to make the same percentage contribution at the splitoff point as the revenue dollars from any other joint product. The net realizable value approach implies a matching of input costs with revenues generated by each output.

Problem 13.2 for Self-Study

Net realizable value cost allocation. Creative Cookies Company purchases cocoa beans and processes them into cocoa butter, cocoa powder, and cocoa shells. The standard yield from each 100-pound sack of unprocessed cocoa beans is 20 pounds of butter, 45 pounds of powder, and 35 pounds of shells. The powder can be sold for $0.90 per pound and the butter for $1.10 per pound at the splitoff point. The shells are thrown away at no cost.

The cost of the cocoa beans is $15 per 100 pounds. It costs $37 in labor and overhead to process each 100 pounds of beans up to the splitoff point.

Compute the joint cost allocated to butter and powder produced from 100 pounds of cocoa beans using the net realizable value method.

The solution to this self-study problem is at the end of the chapter on page 463.

Physical Quantities Method

The **physical quantities method** allocates joint-process costs based on a physical measure of volume, weight, or any other common measure of physical characteristics. This method is often used when output product prices are highly volatile or when significant processing occurs between the splitoff point and the first point of marketability. This approach may also be appropriate when product prices are not set by the market—for example, with heavily regulated companies.

Returning to the Humbolt Company example, assume that market values at the splitoff point are not available for both types of lumber. However, we do know that for every $360,000 of joint costs in processing logs (the costs for July), we get 2,800 units of specialty lumber and 3,920 units of standard lumber (1 unit = 1 board foot). A total of 6,720 units are produced. Joint costs are allocated to specialty lumber by dividing specialty lumber units (2,800) by the total units (6,720) and multiplying the result by total joint costs ($360,000). Thus, $150,000 in joint costs is allocated to specialty lumber and $210,000 to standard lumber, as shown in the following:

	Specialty Lumber	Standard Lumber	Total
Output Quantities	2,800 Units	3,920 Units	6,720 Units
Allocated Joint-Process Costs			
$360,000 × (2,800/6,720)	$150,000		
$360,000 × (3,920/6,720)		$210,000	

A condensed statement of gross margins using the physical quantities method is shown in Exhibit 13.11. Note that the gross margin as a percentage of sales is 70.24 percent for specialty lumber and 72.22 percent for standard lumber.

Problem 13.3 for Self-Study

Physical quantities method. Refer to Self-Study Problem 13.2. Use the physical quantities method to allocate joint-process costs.

The solution to this self-study problem is at the end of the chapter on page 463.

EXHIBIT 13.11	HUMBOLT COMPANY Gross Margin Computations Using Physical Quantities Method July

	Specialty	Standard	Total
Sales Value	$504,000	$756,000	$1,260,000
Less Allocated Joint Costs	150,000	210,000	360,000
Gross Margin	$354,000	$546,000	$ 900,000
Gross Margin as a Percentage of Sales	70.24[a]	72.22[a]	71.43[a]

[a]70.24 = $354,000 ÷ $504,000; 72.22 = $546,000 ÷ $756,000; 71.43 = $900,000 ÷ $1,260,000.

Why Allocate Joint-Process Costs?

Why should managerial accountants and managers be concerned with allocating joint-process costs when joint-cost allocations tend to be somewhat arbitrary? Organizations allocate joint costs for many important reasons, including measuring performance, determining and responding to regulatory rate changes, estimating casualty losses, and resolving contractual interests and obligations. Manufacturing companies are required to use joint-process cost allocations for financial and tax reporting to value inventories and cost of goods sold. For example, Humbolt Company must allocate joint-process costs to its products to value inventory and measure income for reporting purposes.

Though there is no precise way of tracing joint-process costs to joint products (as ABC seeks to do in other production processes), the results of allocating joint-process costs in different ways can be very important to managers for planning, performance evaluation, and decision making.

Summary

The following items correspond to the learning objectives presented at the beginning of the chapter.

1. **Explain what comprises common (or indirect) costs.** A common, or indirect, cost results from the joint use of a facility or a service by several products, departments, or processes.
2. **Explain why companies allocate common costs to departments and products.** Firms must allocate common costs to develop product cost information for purposes of pricing and bidding, contract cost reimbursement, and motivation.
3. **Describe how to allocate service department costs to production departments.** First, assign overhead costs that are directly attributable to a service or production department. Second, allocate other overhead costs based on appropriate cost drivers. Third, allocate service department costs to production departments.
4. **Explain why activity-based costing is used to allocate service department costs.** Applying the techniques of activity-based costing typically results in identifying more accurate cost-allocation bases (cost drivers). This can lead to improved allocations of service department costs to production departments.
5. **Identify methods of allocating marketing and administrative costs to departments.** Management often applies techniques similar to those employed in allocating service department costs to allocate marketing and administrative costs for purposes of performance evaluation.
6. **Explain how to allocate joint-process costs.** Joint-process cost allocations arise from the need to assign joint-process costs to two or more products manufactured from a common input. The two methods of allocating joint-process costs are based on net realizable value or physical measures.
7. **Explain why joint-process costs are allocated.** Companies allocate joint-process costs for several reasons, including performance evaluation, reporting purposes, and establishing regulated rates.

Key Terms and Concepts

Common or indirect cost
Direct cost
Joint process
Joint-process costs
Joint products
Net realizable value method

Physical quantities method
Service department
Service department cost allocation
Splitoff point
Step method

SUGGESTED SOLUTION TO PROBLEM 13.1 FOR SELF-STUDY

a. Distribution of Various Overhead Costs for March
   (1) Security Cost

Dept.	No. of Visits	Percentage[a]	Distribution of Security Cost to Department[b]
Commercial	12	30%	$ 300
Personal	12	30	300
Processing	16	40	400
Computer Services	0	—	—
Total	40	100%	$1,000

[a]Percentage equals number of visits to each department divided by the total visits in a typical night. For Commercial, 12 visits/40 total visits = 30%.
[b]Distribution to department equals percentage times total cost. For example, for Commercial, $300 = 30% $\times$ $1,000.

   (2) Property Taxes

Dept.	Book Value of Equipment and Inventory	Percentage	Distribution of Property Taxes to Department
Commercial	$100,000	50%	$ 600
Personal	70,000	35	420
Processing	26,000	13	156
Computer Services	4,000	2	24
Total	$200,000	100%	$1,200

   (3) Rent and Utilities

Dept.	Square Feet of Floor Space	Percentage	Distribution of Rent and Utilities to Department
Commercial	$15,000	37.5%	$ 540
Personal	15,000	37.5	540
Processing	6,000	15.0	216
Computer Services	4,000	10.0	144
Total	40,000	100.0%	$1,440

b. Allocation of Overhead by Step Allocation
   Overhead Allocation Schedule for Month Ending March 31

	Total	Commercial	Personal	Processing	Computer Services	Reference[a]
Supervisors' Salaries	$11,930	$3,825	$4,300	$1,260	$2,545	*
Labor—Computer Services	6,000	—	—	—	6,000	*
Labor—Processing	1,000	—	—	1,000	—	*
Supplies Used	2,750	600	900	800	450	*
Security	1,000	300	300	400	—	(1)

(continued)

	Total	Commercial	Personal	Processing	Computer Services	Reference[a]
Property Taxes	1,200	600	420	156	24	(2)
Rent and Utilities	1,440	540	540	216	144	(3)
Miscellaneous[b]	600	150	150	150	150	
Total	$25,920	$6,015	$6,610	$3,982	$9,313	

[a]First Bank allocates each item marked with a star directly to a department. The number in parentheses refers to a section of part **a.** above.
[b]Allocated evenly to departments as indicated above.

c. Allocation of Service Department Costs to Production Departments by Step Method

	Total	Commercial	Personal	Processing	Computer Services
Total before Allocation	$25,920	$ 6,015	$ 6,610	$ 3,982	$ 9,313
		50%	25%	25%	
Computer Services to the Other Departments[a]	—	4,657	2,328	2,328	$(9,313)
	$25,920	$10,672	$ 8,938	$ 6,310	
		40%	60%		
Reallocation of Processing to Commercial and Personal[b]	—	2,524	3,786	$(6,310)	
Total Production Department Overhead Costs	$25,920	$13,196	$12,724		

[a]Percentages for these allocations are shown in Exhibit 13.6.
[b]Percentages for these allocations are shown in Exhibit 13.7.

SUGGESTED SOLUTION TO PROBLEM 13.2 FOR SELF-STUDY

The joint costs to be allocated amount to $52—the total of the $15 in direct materials costs and the $37 in conversion costs. The net realizable value for butter is $22, $1.10 per pound times 20 pounds. The net realizable value of the powder is $40.50, $.90 per pound times 45 pounds per 100 pounds of input. The allocation follows:

To cocoa butter:

$$\frac{\$22.00}{\$22.00 + \$40.50} \times \$52.00 = \$18.304$$

To cocoa powder:

$$\frac{\$40.50}{\$22.00 + \$40.50} \times \$52.00 = \$33.696$$

This results in an allocation of the total cost of $52 (= $18.304 + $33.696) to the two products.

SUGGESTED SOLUTION TO PROBLEM 13.3 FOR SELF-STUDY

Because there is a total of 65 pounds of output of major products (20 pounds of butter and 45 pounds of powder) at the splitoff point, the allocation is

To cocoa butter:

$$\frac{20}{20 + 45} \times \$52.00 = \$16.00$$

To cocoa powder:

$$\frac{45}{20 + 45} \times \$52.00 = \$36.00$$

resulting in an allocation of the total $52 to the two products.

REVIEW QUESTIONS

1. Review the meaning of the concepts or terms given in Key Terms and Concepts.
2. Distinguish between a production department and a service department.
3. Distinguish between a direct cost and an indirect cost.
4. Give the steps in the cost allocation process.
5. What is the nature of a joint-production process?
6. What is the objective of joint-cost allocation?

CRITICAL ANALYSIS AND DISCUSSION QUESTIONS

7. For each of the types of common cost in the first column, select the most appropriate allocation base from the second column:

Common Cost	Allocation Base
Building Utilities	Value of Equipment and Inventories
Payroll Accounting	Number of Units Produced
Insurance	Number of Employees
Equipment Repair	Space Occupied
Quality Control Inspection	Number of Service Calls

8. When firms allocate service department costs to production departments, why do they first accumulate these costs at the service department level rather than assigning them directly to production departments?
9. Why do firms allocate service department costs to production departments?
10. Name some of the costs and benefits of cost allocation.
11. A critic of cost allocation noted, "You can avoid arbitrary cost allocations by not allocating any costs." Comment.
12. Discuss reasons for allocating costs to departments.
13. Your division operates a joint production process. Management of the company has decided to shut down your division and liquidate all assets because the division no longer provides a competitive return. Prepare an outline of the costs and benefits (to all affected parties) of the decision to shut down and liquidate your division.
14. Consider the following conversation between a self-styled cost allocation expert and Joe, the manager of a diner.

    Expert: Joe, you said you put in these peanuts because some people ask for them, but do you realize what this rack of peanuts is costing you?

    Joe: It's not going to cost! It's going to be a profit. Sure, I had to pay $100 for a fancy rack to hold the bags, but the peanuts cost 24 cents a bag, and I sell 'em for 40 cents. Suppose I sell 50 bags a week to start. It'll take 12 weeks to cover the cost of the rack. After that I have a clear profit of 16 cents a bag. The more I sell, the more I make.

    Expert: That is an antiquated and completely unrealistic approach, Joe. Fortunately, modern accounting procedures permit a more accurate picture, which reveals the complexities involved.

    Joe: Huh?

    Expert: To be precise, those peanuts must be integrated into your entire operation and be allocated their appropriate share of business overhead. They must share a proportion of your expenditures for rent, heat, light, equipment depreciation, decorating, salaries for your waitresses, cook. . . .

    Joe: The cook? What's he got to do with the peanuts? He doesn't even know I have them.

    Expert: Look, Joe, the cook is in the kitchen, the kitchen prepares the food, the food is what brings people in here, and the people ask to buy peanuts. That's why you must charge a portion of the cook's wages, as well as a part of your own salary, to peanut sales. This sheet contains a carefully calculated cost analysis, which indicates that the peanut operation should pay exactly $2,278 per year toward these general overhead costs.

Joe: The peanuts? $2,278 a year for overhead? Nuts! The peanuts salesman said I'd make money—put 'em on the end of the counter, he said, and get 16 cents a bag profit.

Expert [with a sniff]: He's not an accountant. Do you actually know what the portion of the counter occupied by the peanut rack is worth to you?

Joe: Nothing. No stool there, just a dead spot at the end.

Expert: The modern cost picture permits no dead spots. Your counter contains 60 square feet, and your counter business grosses $60,000 a year. Consequently, the square foot of space occupied by the peanut rack is worth $1,000 per year. Since you have taken that area away from general counter use, you must charge the value of the space to the occupant.

Joe [eagerly]: Look! I have a better idea. Why don't I just throw the nuts out—put them in a trash can?

Expert: Can you afford it?

Joe: Sure. All I have is about 50 bags of peanuts—cost about 12 bucks—so I lose $100 on the rack, but I'm out of this nutty business and no more grief.

Expert [shaking head]: Joe, it isn't quite that simple. You are in the peanut business! The minute you throw those peanuts out, you are adding $2,278 of annual overhead to the rest of your operation. Joe—be realistic—can you afford to do that?

Joe [completely crushed]: It's unbelievable! Last week I was making money. Now I'm in trouble—just because I believe 50 bags of peanuts a week is easy.

Expert [with raised eyebrow]: That is the object of modern cost studies, Joe—to dispel those false illusions.

What should Joe do?

15. Three students share a house. Having better things to do than clean house, they hire someone to come in and clean once each week. How should they share the costs of the housekeeper? One simple solution is to share the cost equally. Suppose, however, that one student's bedroom is twice as large as each of the other students' bedrooms. The second student has a small bedroom and uses the house only four days per week. The third student uses the house all week, has a small bedroom, and is generally acknowledged to be the cleanest of the three. Sharing the cost equally is simple, but is it fair?

EXERCISES

Solutions to even-numbered exercises are at the end of the chapter after the cases.

16. **Allocating overhead to departments and jobs.** The accountants of Meridian Production Company, a company that makes television commercials, made the following estimates for a year:

	Filming Department	Editing Department	Printing Department
Estimated Overhead	$66,000	$100,000	$120,000
Estimated Direct Labor Time	5,500 Hours	6,250 Hours	6,000 Hours

a. Compute the overhead allocation rates for each department using direct labor hours as a basis.

b. Management wants to know how much the Toyota commercial job cost. The following table shows the materials and labor costs; you will have to add the overhead costs using direct labor hours as the allocation base.

Toyota Commercial

	Filming Department	Editing Department	Printing Department
Direct Material Cost	$1,200	—	$160
Direct Labor Cost	$3,000	$4,000	$400
Direct Labor Time	250 Hours	400 Hours	38 Hours

17. **Allocating overhead.** Cameron Company has two production departments and a maintenance department. In addition, the company keeps other costs for the general plant in a separate account. The estimated cost data for Year 1 follow:

Cost	Production Dept. 1	Production Dept. 2	Maintenance	General Plant
Direct Labor	$100,000	$ 60,000	—	—
Indirect Labor	56,000	28,000	$45,000	$40,000
Indirect Materials	18,000	14,000	1,800	16,000
Miscellaneous	6,000	10,000	3,200	10,000
	$180,000	$112,000	$50,000	$66,000
Maintenance	16,000 Hours	24,000 Hours	—	—

The general plant services the three departments in the following proportions: 50 percent (Department 1); 30 percent (Department 2); 20 percent (Maintenance). Allocate maintenance costs based on maintenance hours.

Allocate maintenance department and general plant costs to the production departments. Use the step method, starting with general plant costs.

18. **Allocating overhead to jobs.** Hamilton, Inc., uses a job system of cost accounting. The data presented here relate to operations in its plant during January.

Hamilton, Inc., has two production departments and one service department. The actual factory overhead costs during the month are $8,000. At the end of the month Mr. Hamilton allocates overhead costs as follows: Department A, $4,200; Department B, $3,200; Department C, $600. He allocates the service department (Department C) overhead of $600 as follows: two-thirds to Department A, one-third to Department B.

Mr. Hamilton applies factory overhead to jobs at the predetermined rates of 50 percent of direct labor costs in Department A and 75 percent in Department B. The firm delivers the jobs upon completion. The firm completed job nos. 789, 790, and 791 in January. Jobs 788 and 792 are still in process on January 31.

a. Complete the job production record in the following table by filling in the appropriate amounts. Be sure to show supporting calculations. (Job 788 has been done for you.)

b. For Departments A and B, compute the difference between the applied overhead using the predetermined rates and the actual overhead after allocating Department C overhead to Departments A and B.

Job Production Record

Job Order No.	Jobs in Process, Jan. 1	Direct Labor Dept. A	Direct Labor Dept. B	Direct Matl. Dept. A	Direct Matl. Dept. B	Applied Overhead Dept. A	Applied Overhead Dept. B	Total Costs	Jobs in Process, Jan. 31	Completed Jobs
788	$2,400	$ 600	$ 400	$ 500	$ 300	$300	$300	$4,800	$4,800	$
789	1,700	1,200	600	900	600					
790		1,600	800	1,100	700					
791		2,000	1,200	1,200	900					
792		2,400	1,600	1,800	800					
Totals	$4,100	$7,800	$4,600	$5,500	$3,300	$	$	$	$	$

19. **Allocating service department costs using the step method.** Gretsky Company has two service departments (maintenance and general factory administration) and two operating departments (cutting and assembly). Management has decided to allocate maintenance costs on the basis of the area in each department and general factory administration costs on the basis of labor hours the employees worked in each of their respective departments.

The following data appear in the company records for the current period:

	General Factory Administration	Maintenance	Cutting	Assembly
Area Occupied (square feet)	2,000	—	2,000	6,000
Labor Hours	—	200	400	600
Direct Labor Costs (operating departments only)			$3,000	$8,000
Service Department Direct Costs	$2,400	$4,800		

Use the step method to allocate service departments' costs to the operating departments, starting with maintenance.

20. **Using multiple cost drivers to allocate costs.** Assume Johnson Manufacturing uses three allocation bases to allocate overhead costs from departments to jobs: number of different parts, number of machine hours, and number of job setup hours. The information needed to compute the allocation rates follows:

	Department A		Department B	
	Costs	Units of Activity	Costs	Units of Activity
1. Number of Different Parts	$ 4,000	40 Parts	$ 800	10 Parts
2. Number of Machine Hours Worked	$208,000	16,000 Hours	$60,000	1,500 Hours
3. Number of Hours to Set Up Jobs	$ 24,000	300 Hours	$ 8,000	100 Hours

Job 300ZX required the following activities:

Department A: 10 parts, 1,000 machine hours, 20 setup hours.
Department B: 2 parts, 200 machine hours, 10 setup hours.

Allocate overhead costs to Job 300ZX.

21. **Allocating service department costs directly to operating departments.** Meyers Company has a commissary with two operating departments: P1, food inventory control, and P2, paper goods inventory control. It has two service departments: S1, computer services, and S2, administration, maintenance, and all other. Each department's direct costs are as follows:

P1	$90,000
P2	60,000
S1	30,000
S2	40,000

P1, P2, and S2 use S1's services as follows:

P1	10 Percent
P2	10 Percent
S2	80 Percent

P1 and P2 use S2's services as follows:

P1	37.5 Percent
P2	62.5 Percent

Allocate service department costs using the step method. Start by allocating S1 to S2, P1, and P2.

22. **Joint-process costing.** Search the Internet for an example of a company that either uses joint-process costing or provides joint-process cost consulting services. Prepare a short presentation that explains (a) the nature of the organization (industry, products, and/or services), (b) how it uses joint-process costing, and (c) how important you believe joint-process costs are to its decision making.

23. **Joint-process costing and net realizable method.** A company processes a chemical, DX-1, through a pressure treatment operation. The complete process has two outputs, L and T. The January costs to process DX-1 are $50,000 for materials and $100,000 for conversion costs. This processing results in two outputs, L and T, that sell for a total of $250,000. The sales revenue from L amounts to $200,000 of the total. Using the net realizable method, assign costs to L and T for January.

24. **Using joint-process costing to measure product costs.** The following information is for Tiger Company, which manufactures products X, Y, and Z from a joint process. Joint product costs were $63,000. Additional information follows.

| | | | If Processed Further | |
Product	Units Produced	Sales Value at Splitoff	Sales Values	Additional Costs
X	14,000	$80,000	$110,000	$18,000
Y	10,000	70,000	90,000	14,000
Z	4,000	50,000	60,000	10,000

a. Assuming that joint product costs are allocated using the physical quantities method, what were the total costs of product X (including $18,000 if processed further)?

b. Assuming the joint product costs are allocated using the net realizable value method, what were the total costs of product Y (including the $14,000 if processed further)?

PROBLEMS

25. **Allocating overhead.** The Demski Company applies manufacturing overhead to the Machining and Assembly departments. From the following data, prepare an overhead allocation schedule showing in detail the manufacturing overhead chargeable to each department. Some costs can be assigned directly (for example, indirect labor). Allocate machinery and equipment costs based on the cost of machinery and equipment, power based on horsepower rating, compensation insurance based on labor and indirect labor costs, and building-related costs based on floor space. Round all decimals to three places and all dollars to whole dollars.

DEMSKI COMPANY
Manufacturing Overhead Costs during the Month

Indirect Labor:	
Machining	$ 6,600
Assembly	3,600
Supplies Used:	
Machining	1,500
Assembly	900
Taxes (machinery and equipment, $72; building, $145)	217
Compensation Insurance	906
Power	300
Heat and Light	480
Depreciation: Building	390
Depreciation: Machinery and Equipment	360
Total	$15,253

Other Operating Data

	Floor Space (square feet)	Cost of Machinery and Equipment	Direct Labor per Month	Horsepower Rating
Department:				
Machining	4,000	$35,000	$ 2,000	120
Assembly	6,000	25,000	10,000	180
Total	10,000	$60,000	$12,000	

26. **Allocating unassigned costs to retail store departments.** The Royal Specialty Shop has two departments, Clothing and Accessories. The operating expenses for the year ending December 31 appear below.

a. Prepare a three-column statement of operating expenses with column headings: Clothing, Accessories, Total. Begin with direct departmental expenses and show a subtotal. Then continue with the allocated expenses, assigning each item to the various departments. Round all values to the nearest dollar and all percentages to one decimal place.

b. Prepare a condensed income statement with columns for Clothing, Accessories, and Total. Show the total operating expenses calculated in part **a.** as a single deduction from gross margin.

ROYAL SPECIALTY SHOP
Operating Expenses

	Clothing	Accessories	Unassigned	Total
Salaries:				
Clerks	$78,240	$69,360	—	$147,600
Others			$48,000	48,000
Supplies Used	3,800	3,200	1,400	8,400
Depreciation of Equipment	1,600	4,800	—	6,400
Advertising	3,726	8,586	3,888	16,200
Building Rent			19,000	19,000
Payroll Taxes			12,300	12,300
Workers' Compensation Insurance			2,080	2,080
Fire Insurance			1,000	1,000
Delivery Expense			1,800	1,800
Miscellaneous Expenses	1,000	800	600	2,400

ROYAL SPECIALTY SHOP
Allocation Base Activity Levels

	Clothing	Accessories	Total
Sales	$600,000	$400,000	$1,000,000
Cost of Goods Sold	$440,000	$240,000	$ 680,000
Equipment	$ 10,080	$ 24,960	$ 35,040
Inventory (average)	$100,800	$139,200	$ 240,000
Floor Space (square feet)	2,400	3,600	6,000
Number of Employees	10	15	25

ROYAL SPECIALTY SHOP
Allocation Bases

Expense	Bases of Allocation
Salaries—Other	Gross Margin
Supplies Used (unassigned)	Sales
Advertising (unassigned)	Sales
Building Rent	Floor Space
Payroll Taxes	Salaries (including both direct and other allocated salaries)
Workers' Compensation Insurance	Salaries (including both direct and other allocated salaries)
Fire Insurance	Cost of Equipment and Inventory
Delivery Expense	Sales
Miscellaneous Expenses (unassigned)	Number of Employees

27. **Allocating service department costs.** The Excel Cuisine Company has two production departments, Tubing and Packing, and two service departments, Quality Control and Maintenance. In June, the Quality Control department provided 2,000 hours of service—1,047 hours to Tubing, 255 hours to Maintenance, and 698 hours to Packing. In the same month, Maintenance provided 2,750 hours to Tubing, 1,900 hours to Packing, and 350 hours to Quality Control. Quality Control incurred costs of $100,000, and Maintenance incurred costs of $210,000.

   Use the step method to allocate service department costs sequentially based on hours of service provided. Start with Maintenance and then allocate Quality Control. Check your solution by making certain that the firm finally allocates $310,000 to the production departments.

28. **Allocating service department costs** (adapted from CPA exam). The Larson Company has three service departments (administration, maintenance, and computer support) and two production departments (creative and assembly). A summary of costs and other data for each department prior to allocation of service department costs for the year ended June 30, Year 1, follows:

	Administration	Maintenance	Computer Support	Creative	Assembly
Direct Material Costs	0	$65,000	$91,000	$3,130,000	$ 950,000
Direct Labor Costs	$90,000	$82,100	$87,000	$1,950,000	$2,050,000
Overhead Costs	$70,000	$56,100	$62,000	$1,650,000	$1,850,000
Direct Labor Hours	31,000	27,000	42,000	562,500	437,500
Number of Computers	12	8	20	280	200
Square Footage Occupied	1,750	2,000	4,800	88,000	72,000

Larson allocates the costs of the administration, maintenance, and computer support departments on the basis of direct labor hours, square footage occupied, and number of computers, respectively. Round all final calculations to the nearest dollar.

a. Assuming that Larson elects to distribute service department costs directly to production departments without interservice department cost allocation, what amount of maintenance department costs would Larson allocate to the creative department?

b. Assuming the same method of allocation as in part **a.,** what amount of administration department costs would Larson allocate to the assembly department?

c. Assuming that Larson elects to distribute service department costs to other service departments (starting with the computer support department) as well as the production departments, what amounts of computer support department costs would Larson allocate to the maintenance department? (Note: Once the firm has allocated a service department's costs, no subsequent service department costs are allocated back to it.)

d. Assuming the same method of allocation as in part **c.,** what amount of maintenance department costs would Larson allocate to the computer support department?

29. **Joint cost allocation and product profitability.** Wafers, Inc., processes silicon crystals into purified wafers and chips. Silicon crystals cost $60,000 per tank-car load. The process involves heating the crystals for 12 hours, producing 45,000 purified wafers with a market value of $20,000, and 15,000 chips with a market value of $140,000. The cost of the heat process is $25,600.

    a. If the crystal costs and the heat process costs are to be allocated on the basis of units of output, what cost is assigned to each product?

    b. If the crystal costs and the heat process costs are allocated on the basis of the net realizable value, what cost is assigned to each product?

    c. How much profit or loss does the purified wafers product provide using the data in this problem and your analysis in requirement **a.**? Is it really possible to determine which product is more profitable? Explain why or why not.

CASES

30. **Relating allocation methods to organizational characteristics for a retailer** (adapted from CMA exam). Columbia Company is a regional office supply chain with 26 independent stores. The firm holds each store responsible for its own credit and collections. The firm assigns the assistant manager in each store the responsibility for credit activities, including the collection of delinquent accounts, because the stores do not need a full-time employee assigned to credit activities. The company has experienced a sharp rise in uncollectibles the past two years. Corporate management has decided to establish a collections department in the home office that takes over the collection function companywide. The home office of Columbia Company will hire the necessary full-time personnel. The firm will base the size of this department on the historical credit activity of all the stores.

    Top management discussed the new centralized collections department at a recent management meeting. Management has had difficulty deciding on a method to assign the costs of the new department to the stores because this type of home office service is unusual. Top management is reviewing alternative methods.

    The controller favored using a predetermined rate for charging the costs to the stores. The firm would base the predetermined rate on budgeted costs. The vice-president for sales preferred an actual cost charging system.

    In addition, management also discussed the basis for the collection charges to the stores. The controller identified the following four measures of services (allocation bases) that the firm could use:

    (1) Total dollar sales.

    (2) Average number of past-due accounts.

    (3) Number of uncollectible accounts written off.

    (4) One twenty-sixth of the cost to each of the stores.

    The executive vice-president stated that he would like the accounting department to prepare a detailed analysis of the two charging methods and the four service measures (allocation bases).

    a. Evaluate the two methods identified—predetermined rate versus actual cost—that the firm could use to charge the individual stores the costs of Columbia Company's new collections department in terms of

        (1) practicality of application and ease of use.

        (2) cost control.

    Also indicate whether a centralized or decentralized organization structure would be more conducive for each charging method.

    b. For each of the four measures of services (allocation bases) the controller of Columbia Company identified:

        (1) Discuss whether using the service measure (allocation base) is appropriate in this situation.

        (2) Identify the behavioral problems, if any, that could arise as a consequence of adopting the service measure (allocation base).

31. **Allocation for economic decisions and motivation** (adapted from CMA exam). Bonn Company recently reorganized its computer and data processing system. Bonn has replaced the individual installations located within the accounting departments at its plants and subsidiaries with a single data-processing department at corporate headquarters responsible for the operations of a newly acquired large-scale computer system. The new department has

been operating for two years and regularly producing reliable and timely data for the past 12 months.

Because the department has focused its activities on converting applications to the new system and producing reports for the plant and subsidiary management, it has devoted little attention to the costs of the department. Now that the department's activities are operating relatively smoothly, company management has requested that the departmental manager recommend a cost accumulation system to facilitate cost control and the development of suitable rates to charge users for service.

For the past two years, the department has recorded costs in one account. The department has then allocated the costs to user departments on the basis of computer time used. The following schedule reports the costs and charging rate for Year 4.

Data Processing Department Costs for the Year Ended December 31, Year 4	
(1) Salaries and Benefits	$ 622,600
(2) Supplies	40,000
(3) Equipment Maintenance Contracts	15,000
(4) Insurance	25,000
(5) Heat and Air Conditioning	36,000
(6) Electricity	50,000
(7) Equipment and Furniture Depreciation	285,400
(8) Building Improvements Depreciation	10,000
(9) Building Occupancy and Security	39,300
(10) Corporate Administrative Charges	52,700
Total Costs	$1,176,000
Computer Hours for User Processing[a]	2,750
Hourly Rate ($1,176,000/2,750)	$ 428

[a]Use of available computer hours:	
Testing and Debugging Programs	250
Setup of Jobs	500
Processing Jobs	2,750
Downtime for Maintenance	750
Idle Time	742
Total Hours	4,992

The department manager recommends that the five activity centers within the department accumulate the department costs. The five activity centers are systems analysis, programming, data preparation, computer operations (processing), and administration. She then suggests that the firm allocate the costs of the administration activity to the other four activity centers before developing a separate rate for charging users for each of the first four activities.

After reviewing the details of the accounts, the manager made the following observations regarding the charges to the several subsidiary accounts within the department:

(1) Salaries and benefits—records the salary and benefit costs of all employees in the department.

(2) Supplies—records paper costs for printers and a small amount for other miscellaneous costs.

(3) Equipment maintenance contracts—records charges for maintenance contracts that cover all equipment.

(4) Insurance—records cost of insurance covering the equipment and the furniture.

(5) Heat and air conditioning—records a charge from the corporate heating and air conditioning department estimated to be the incremental costs to meet the special needs of the computer department.

(6) Electricity—records the charge for electricity based on a separate meter within the department.

(7) Equipment and furniture depreciation—records the depreciation charges for all equipment and furniture owned within the department.

(8) Building improvements depreciation—records the amortization charges for the building changes required to provide proper environmental control and electrical service for the computer equipment.

(9) Building occupancy and security—records the computer department's share of the depreciation, maintenance, heat, and security costs of the building; the firm allocates these costs to the department on the basis of square feet occupied.

(10) Corporate administrative charges—records the computer department's share of the corporate administrative costs. The firm allocates those costs to the department on the basis of number of employees in the department.

    a. For each of the ten cost items, state whether or not the firm should distribute it to the five activity centers; and for each cost item that the firm should distribute, recommend the basis on which it should be distributed. Justify your conclusion in each case.

    b. Assume that the costs of the computer operations (processing) activity will be charged to the user departments on the basis of computer hours. Using the analysis of computer utilization shown as a footnote to the department cost schedule presented in the problem, determine the total number of hours that should be employed to determine the charging rate for computer operations (processing). Justify your answer.

16. Allocating overhead to departments and jobs.

a.

	Filming Department	Editing Department	Printing Department
Labor Hours Basis	$12 per Hour	$16 per Hour	$20 per Hour

b.

	Filming Department	Editing Department	Printing Department	Total
Material	$1,200	—	$ 160	$ 1,360
Labor	3,000	$ 4,000	400	7,400
Overhead	3,000	6,400	760	10,160
Total	$7,200	$10,400	$1,320	$18,920

18. Allocating overhead to jobs.

a.

HAMILTON, INC.
Job Order Production Record
Month of January

Job Order No.	Jobs in Process, 1/1	Direct Labor Dept. A	Direct Labor Dept. B	Direct Material Dept. A	Direct Material Dept. B	Applied Overhead Dept. A[a]	Applied Overhead Dept. B[b]	Total Costs	Jobs in Process, 1/31	Completed Jobs
788	$2,400	$ 600	$ 400	$ 500	$ 300	$ 300	$ 300	$ 4,800	$ 4,800	—
789	1,700	1,200	600	900	600	600	450	6,050	—	$ 6,050
790	—	1,600	800	1,100	700	800	600	5,600	—	5,600
791	—	2,000	1,200	1,200	900	1,000	900	7,200	—	7,200
792	—	2,400	1,600	1,800	800	1,200	1,200	9,000	9,000	—
Total	$4,100	$7,800	$4,600	$5,500	$3,300	$3,900	$3,450	$32,650	$13,800	$18,850

[a]Amount = 50% of direct labor.
[b]Amount = 75% of direct labor.

b.

Overhead	Dept. A	Dept. B	Total
Applied	$3,900	$3,450	$7,350
Actual	4,600ª	3,400ᵇ	8,000
Over (Under) Applied	$ (700)	$ 50	$ (650)

ª$4,600 = $4,200 + ($\frac{2}{3}$ × $600).
ᵇ$3,400 = $3,200 + ($\frac{1}{3}$ × $600).

20. Using multiple cost drivers to allocate costs.

Step 1: Derive overhead application rates

	Department A	Department B
Number of Parts	$4,000 ÷ 40 parts = $100 per part	$800 ÷ 10 parts = $80 per part
Machine Hours	208,000 ÷ 16,000 hours = $13 per machine hour	$60,000 ÷ 1,500 hours = $40 per machine hour
Setup Hours	$24,000 ÷ 300 hours = $80 per setup hour	$8,000 ÷ 100 hours = $80 per setup hour

Step 2: Apply overhead to Job 300ZX

Department A:	($100 × 10 parts) + ($13 × 1,000 machine hours)
	+ ($80 × 20 setup hours)
	= $15,600
Department B:	($80 × 2 parts) + ($40 × 200 machine hours)
	+ ($80 × 10 setup hours)
	= $8,960
Total:	= $24,560 (= $15,600 + $8,960).

22. Joint-process costing. Solutions will vary.
24. Using joint-process costing to measure product costs.

a. Total units of X   =   14,000 units
Total units produced =   28,000 units
Joint product costs   = $63,000
    Amount allocated from joint costs:

$$\frac{14,000}{28,000} \times \$63,000 = \$31,500$$

Additional processing costs   18,000
Total costs of Product X $49,500

b. Net realizable value of Y at splitoff = $ 70,000
Total net realizable value at splitoff = $200,000
Joint product costs   = $ 63,000
    Amount allocated from joint costs:

$$\frac{70,000}{\$200,000} \times \$63,000 = \$22,050$$

Additional processing costs   14,000
Total costs allocated to Y $36,050

appendix

Compound Interest Examples and Applications

anagerial accountants and managers deal with interest calculations because expenditures for an asset most often precede the receipts for services that the asset produces. Cash received sooner has more value than cash received later. The difference in timing can affect whether or not acquiring an asset is profitable. Amounts of cash received at different times are like different commodities. Managers use interest calculations to make valid comparisons among amounts of cash their firm will pay or receive at different times.

Managers evaluate a series of cash payments over time, such as from an investment project, by finding the present value of the series of payments. The *present value* of a series of payments is a single amount of cash at the present time that is the economic equivalent of the entire series.

This appendix illustrates the use of compound interest techniques with a comprehensive series of examples that use the tables appearing after this appendix. Calculators and personal computers do the same computations if you know which buttons to push or functions to use.

Future Value

If you invest $1 today at 10 percent compounded annually, it will grow to $1.10000 at the end of 1 year, $1.21000 at the end of 2 years, $1.33100 at the end of 3 years, and so on, according to the following formula

$$F_n = P(1 + r)^n,$$

where

$$F_n = \text{accumulation or future value}$$
$$P = \text{one-time investment today}$$
$$R = \text{interest rate per period}$$
$$N = \text{number of periods from today.}$$

The amount F_n is the future value of the present payment, P, compounded at r percent per period for n periods. Table 1, following this appendix, shows the future values of P = $1 for various periods and for various interest rates.

Example 1 How much will $1,000 deposited today at 8 percent compounded annually be worth 10 years from now?

One dollar deposited today at 8 percent will grow to $2.15892; therefore, $1,000 will grow to $1,000 $\times (1.08)^{10} = \$1,000 \times 2.15892 = \$2,158.92$.

EXHIBIT A.1	Verification of Net Present Value of $10,717 Single Cash Flow of $13,500 at the End of Year 3 Discounted at 8 Percent per Year		
Year	Beginning Amount	+ Interest at 8 Percent	= Ending Amount
1	$10,717	$ 857	$11,574
2	11,574	926	12,500
3	12,500	1,000	13,500

Present Value

This section deals with the problems of calculating how much principal, P, you must invest today to have a specified amount, F_n, at the end of n periods. You know the future amount, F_n, the interest rate, r, and the number of periods, n; you want to find P. To have $1 one year from today when deposits earn 8 percent, you must invest P of $0.92593 today. That is, $F_1 = P(1.08)^1$ or $1 = 0.92593×1.08. Because $F_n = P(1 + r)^n$, dividing both sides of the equation by $(1 + r)^n$ yields

$$F_n = \frac{P}{(1 + r)^n} \text{ or } P = \frac{F_n}{(1 + r)^n} = F_n(1 + r)^{-n}$$

Table 2 following this appendix shows discount factors or, equivalently, present values of $1 for various interest (or discount) rates for various periods.

Example 2 What is the present value of $1 due 10 years from now if the interest rate (or, equivalently, the discount rate) r is 12 percent per year?

From Table 2, 12-percent column, 10-period row, the present value of $1 to be received 10 periods hence at 12 percent is $0.32197.

Example 3 You project that an investment will generate cash of $13,500 three years from today. What is the net present value today of this cash receipt if the discount rate is 8 percent per year?

One dollar received 3 years hence discounted at 8 percent has a present value of $0.79383. See Table 2, 3-period row, 8-percent column. Thus the project has a present value of $13,500 \times 0.79383 = $10,717. Exhibit A.1 shows how $10,717 grows to $13,500 in 3 years.

Changing the Compounding Period: Nominal and Effective Rates

"Twelve percent, compounded annually" represents the price for a loan; this price means interest increases, or converts to, principal once a year at the rate of 12 percent. Often, however, the price for a loan states an annual interest rate and that compounding will take place more than once a year. A savings bank may advertise that it pays interest of 6 percent, compounded quarterly. This kind of payment means that at the end of each quarter the bank credits savings accounts with interest calculated at the rate of 1.5 percent (= 6 percent/4). The investor can withdraw the interest payment or leave it on deposit to earn more interest.

If you invest $10,000 today at 12 percent compounded annually, it will grow to a future value 1 year later of $11,200. If the rate of interest is 12 percent compounded semiannually, the bank adds 6-percent interest to the principal every 6 months. At the end of the first 6 months, $10,000 will have grown to $10,600; that amount will grow to $10,600 \times 1.06 = $11,236 by the end of the year. Notice that 12 percent compounded semiannually results in the same amount as 12.36 percent compounded annually.

Suppose that the bank quotes interest as 12 percent, compounded quarterly. It will add an additional 3 percent of the principal every 3 months. By the end of the year, $10,000 will grow to $10,000 × (1.03)^4 = $10,000 × 1.12551 = $11,255. Twelve percent compounded quarterly is equivalent to 12.55 percent compounded annually. At 12 percent compounded monthly, $1 will grow to $1 × (1.01)^{12} = $1.12683, and $10,000 will grow to $11,268. Thus, 12 percent compounded monthly is equivalent to 12.68 percent compounded annually.

For a given *nominal* rate, such as the 12 percent in the preceding examples, the more often interest compounds, the higher the *effective* rate of interest paid. If a nominal rate, r, compounds m times per year, the effective rate is equal to $(1 + r/m)^m - 1$.

In practice, to solve problems that require computation of interest quoted at a nominal rate r percent per period compounded m times per period for n periods, use the tables or computer software functions for rate r/m and m × n periods. For example, 12 percent compounded quarterly for 5 years is equivalent to the rate found in the interest tables for r = 12/4 = 3 percent for m × n = 4 × 5 = 20 periods.

Example 4 What is the future value 5 years hence of $600 invested at 8 percent compounded quarterly?

Eight percent compounded four times per year for 5 years is equivalent to 2 percent per period compounded for 20 periods. Table 1 shows the value of $F_{20} = (1.02)^{20}$ to be 1.48595. Six hundred dollars, then, would grow to $600 × 1.48595 = $891.57.

Example 5 How much cash must you invest today at 12 percent compounded semiannually to have $1,000 four years from today?

Twelve percent compounded two times a year for 4 years is equivalent to 6 percent per period compounded for 8 periods. The *present value,* Table 2, of $1 received 8 periods hence at 6 percent per period is $0.62741; that is, $0.62741 invested today for 8 periods at an interest rate of 6 percent per period will grow to $1. To have $1,000 in 8 periods (4 years), you must invest $627.41 (= $1,000 × $0.62741) today.

Example 6 A local department store offers its customers credit and advertises its interest rate at 18 percent per year, compounded monthly at the rate of $1\frac{1}{2}$ percent per month. What is the effective annual interest rate?

One and one-half percent per month for 12 months is equivalent to $(1.015)^{12} - 1 = 19.562$ percent per year. See Table 1, 12-period row, $1\frac{1}{2}$-percent column, where the factor is 1.19562.

Example 7 If prices increased at the rate of 6 percent during each of two consecutive 6-month periods, how much did prices increase during the entire year?

If a price index is 100.00 at the start of the year, it will be $100.00 × (1.06)^2 = 112.36$ at the end of the year. The price change for the entire year is (112.36/100.00) − 1 = 12.36 percent.

Annuities

An *annuity* is a series of equal payments, one per equally spaced period of time. Examples of annuities include monthly rental payments, semiannual corporate bond coupon (or interest) payments, and annual payments to a lessor under a lease contract. Armed with an understanding of the tables for future and present values, you can solve any annuity problem. Annuities arise so often, however, and solving them is so tedious without special tables or computer functions that annuity problems merit special study and the use of special tables or functions.

Terminology for Annuities

Annuity terminology can be confusing because not all writers use the same terms.

An annuity with payments occurring at the end of each period is an *ordinary annuity* or an *annuity in arrears.* Semiannual corporate bonds usually promise coupon payments paid in arrears; or, equivalently, the first payment does not occur until after the bond has been outstanding for 6 months.

An annuity with payments occurring at the beginning of each period is an *annuity due* or an *annuity in advance.* Rent paid at the beginning of each month is an annuity due.

In a *deferred annuity*, the first payment occurs some time later than the end of the first period.

Annuities payments can go on forever. Such annuities are *perpetuities*. Bonds that promise payments forever are *consols*. The British and the Canadian governments have issued consols from time to time. A perpetuity can be in arrears or in advance. The two differ only in the timing of the first payment.

Annuities may confuse you. Studying them is easier with a time line such as the one shown below.

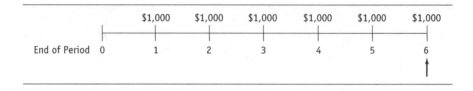

A time line marks the end of each period, numbers the periods, shows the payments the investor receives or pays, and shows the time in which the accountant wants to value the annuity. The time line above represents an ordinary annuity (in arrears) for six periods of $1,000 to be valued at the end of period 6. The end of period 0 is "now." The first payment occurs one period from now. The arrow points to the valuation date.

Ordinary Annuities (Annuities in Arrears)

The future values of ordinary annuities appear in Table 3 following this appendix.

Consider an ordinary annuity for three periods at 12 percent. The time line for the future value of such an annuity is

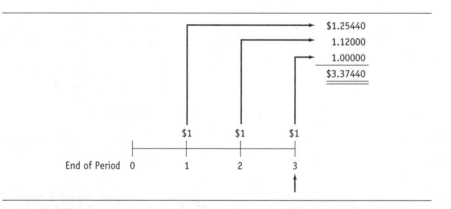

The $1 received at the end of the first period earns interest for two periods, so it is worth $1.25440 at the end of period 3 (see Table 1). The $1 received at the end of the second period grows to $1.12000 by the end of period 3, and the $1 received at the end of period 3 is, of course, worth $1.00000 at the end of period 3. The entire annuity is worth $3.37440 at the end of period 3. This amount appears in Table 3 for the future value of an ordinary annuity for three periods at 12 percent. Factors for the future value of an annuity for a particular number of periods sum the factors for the future value of $1 for each of the periods. The future value of an ordinary annuity is

$$\begin{array}{c}\text{Future Value of}\\\text{Ordinary}\\\text{Annuity}\end{array} = \begin{array}{c}\text{Periodic}\\\text{Payment}\end{array} \times \begin{array}{c}\text{Factor for}\\\text{the Future}\\\text{Value of an}\\\text{Ordinary Annuity.}\end{array}$$

Thus,

$$\$3.37440 = \$1 \times 3.37440.$$

Table 4 following this appendix shows the present value of ordinary annuities.

The time line for the present value of an ordinary annuity of $1 per period for three periods, discounted at 12 percent, is

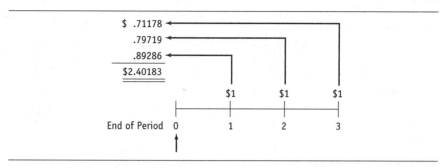

The $1 the investor receives at the end of period 1 has a present value of $0.89286, the $1 the investor receives at the end of period 2 has a present value of $0.79719, and the $1 the investor receives at the end of the third period has a present value of $0.71178. Each of these numbers comes from Table 2. The present value of the annuity equals the sum of these individual present values, $2.40183, shown in Table 4.

The present value of an ordinary annuity for n periods equals the sum of the present value of $1 received one period from now plus the present value of $1 received two periods from now, and so on until we add on the present value of $1 received n periods from now. The present value of an ordinary annuity is

$$\begin{matrix}\text{Present Value} \\ \text{of an} \\ \text{Ordinary Annuity}\end{matrix} = \begin{matrix}\text{Periodic} \\ \text{Payment}\end{matrix} \times \begin{matrix}\text{Factor for} \\ \text{the Present} \\ \text{Value of an} \\ \text{Ordinary Annuity.}\end{matrix}$$

Thus,

$$\$2.40183 = \$1 \times 2.40183.$$

Example 8   Accountants project an investment to generate $1,000 at the end of each of the next 20 years. If the interest rate is 8 percent compounded annually, what will the future value of these flows equal at the end of 20 years?

The time line for this problem is

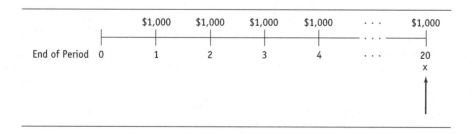

The symbol x denotes the amount you must calculate. Table 3 indicates that the factor for the future value of an annuity at 8 percent for 20 periods is 45.76196. Thus,

$$\begin{matrix}\text{Future Value of} \\ \text{Ordinary} \\ \text{Annuity}\end{matrix} = \begin{matrix}\text{Periodic} \\ \text{Payment}\end{matrix} \times \begin{matrix}\text{Factor for} \\ \text{the Future} \\ \text{Value of an} \\ \text{Ordinary Annuity}\end{matrix}$$
$$x = \$1,000 \times 45.76196$$
$$x = \$45,762.$$

The cash flows have future value $45,762.

Example 9 Parents want to accumulate a fund to send their child to college. The parents will invest a fixed amount at the end of each calendar quarter for the next 10 years. The funds will accumulate in a certificate of deposit that promises to pay 8-percent interest compounded quarterly. What amount must the parents invest to accumulate a fund of $50,000?

The time line for this problem is

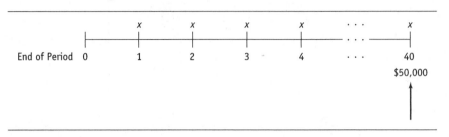

This problem resembles Example 8: Both involve periodic investments of cash that accumulate interest over time until a specific time in the future. In Example 8, you know the periodic investment and compute the future value. In Example 9, you know the future value and compute the period investment. Table 3 indicates that the future value of an annuity at 2 percent (= 8 percent per year ÷ 4 quarters per year) per period for 40 periods (= 4 quarters per year × 10 years) is 60.40198. Thus,

$$
\begin{array}{ccc}
\text{Future Value} & & \text{Factor for} \\
\text{of an} & = \text{Periodic} \times & \text{the Future} \\
\text{Ordinary Annuity} & \text{Payment} & \text{Value of an} \\
& & \text{Ordinary Annuity} \\
\$50{,}000 & = \text{x} \times & 60.40198 \\
\text{x} & = \dfrac{\$50{,}000}{60.40198} \\
\text{x} & = \$828.
\end{array}
$$

Because you want to find the periodic payment, you divide the future value amount of $50,000 by the future value factor.

Example 10 A firm borrows $30,000 from an insurance company. The loan specifies interest of 8 percent, compounded semiannually. The firm agrees to repay the loan in equal semiannual installments over the next 5 years and make the first payment 6 months from now. What is the amount of the required semiannual payment?

The time line is

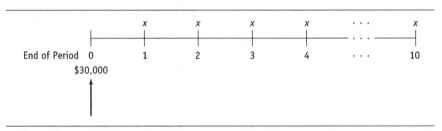

You know the present value and must compute the periodic payment. Table 4 indicates that the present value of an annuity at 4 percent (= 8 percent per year ÷ 2 semiannual periods per year) for 10 periods (= 2 periods per year × 5 years) is 8.11090. Thus,

$$
\begin{array}{ccc}
\text{Present Value} & & \text{Factor for} \\
\text{of an} & = \text{Periodic} \times & \text{the Present} \\
\text{Ordinary Annuity} & \text{Payment} & \text{Value of an} \\
& & \text{Ordinary Annuity} \\
\$30{,}000 & = \text{x} \times & 8.11090 \\
\text{x} & = \dfrac{\$30{,}000}{8.11090} \\
\text{x} & = \$3{,}699.
\end{array}
$$

	Amortization Schedule for $30,000 Mortgage, Repaid in Semiannual Installments of $3,700, Interest Rate of 8 Percent, Compounded Semiannually				
EXHIBIT A.2					

6-Month Period (1)	Mortgage Principal Start of Period (2)	Interest Expense for Period (3)	Payment (4)	Portion of Payment Reducing Principal (5)	Mortgage Principal End of Period (6)
0					$30,000
1	$30,000	$1,200	$3,700	$2,500	27,500
2	27,500	1,100	3,700	2,600	24,900
3	24,900	996	3,700	2,704	22,196
4	22,196	888	3,700	2,812	19,384
5	19,384	775	3,700	2,925	16,459
6	16,459	658	3,700	3,042	13,417
7	13,417	537	3,700	3,163	10,254
8	10,254	410	3,700	3,290	6,964
9	6,964	279	3,700	3,421	3,543
10	3,543	142	3,685	3,543	0

Column **(2)** = column **(6)** from previous period.
Column **(3)** = 0.04 × column **(2)**.
Column **(4)** is given, except row 10, where it is the amount such that column **(4)** = column **(2)** + column **(3)**.
Column **(5)** = column **(4)** − column **(3)**.
Column **(6)** = column **(2)** − column **(5)**.

Because you seek to find the periodic payment, you divide the present value amount of $30,000 by the present value factor. Exhibit A.2 shows how periodic payments of $3,700 amortize the loan. We call such a schedule an *amortization schedule.* If the periodic payments were $3,699, not $3,700, the final payment would more closely equal the amount of the preceding payments.

Example 11   A company signs a lease acquiring the right to use property for 3 years. The company promises to make lease payments of $19,709 annually at the end of this and the next 2 years. The discount, or interest, rate is 15 percent per year. What is the present value of the lease payments, which equals the equivalent cash purchase price for this property?

The time line is

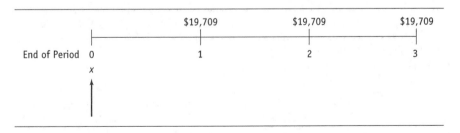

The factor from Table 4 for the present value of an annuity at 15 percent for 3 periods is 2.28323. Thus,

Present Value of an Ordinary Annuity	=	Periodic Payment	×	Factor for the Present Value of an Ordinary Annuity
x	=	$19,709	×	2.28323
x	=	$45,000.		

Managerial Application

Present Value of Cost Savings Guides Pricing Decision

Robert Mendenhall discovered a process that enables highway and road builders to reuse asphalt pavement in constructing rebuilt or new roads. He patented the process. Mendenhall's discovery promised large cost savings in road building. Mendenhall licensed his patent to CMI Corp. CMI began to produce and sell recycling plants capable of producing high-quality road surface materials from recycled asphalt.

Competitors, such as Barber-Greene (BG), approached CMI about obtaining licenses to use the patent. Management at CMI wanted some method for thinking about the license fees it might reasonably expect to collect from others' use of the patent. Management believed that the cost savings from incorporating the new process into asphalt plants justified prices at least 25 percent larger than prices for equipment using the old processes.

Data pertinent to the analysis:

- Prices for asphalt plants using the old processes averaged $735,000.
- The new recycling plants had a capacity to produce 150,000 to 300,000 tons of new road surfaces per year.
- Contractors expect the recycling plants to last for 15 to 18 years but depreciate them over 10 years on a straight-line basis for tax reporting.
- Because of air pollution problems, a contractor cannot use 100-percent recycled asphalt in producing new paving materials. Instead, the contractor must use a mixture of recycled and new, virgin asphalt. Depending on the application, the ratio of recycled to virgin asphalt ranges from 70/30 to 50/50.
- To produce a ton of paving materials from virgin asphalt costs the contractors from $14 to $17 per ton in materials and plant operating costs, not counting the cost of the plant itself.
- Various industry studies indicate a cost savings from using recycled asphalt of $0.50 to $11.40 per ton of new paving materials produced from recycled asphalt.
- The risk of the contracting process for road builders suggests a discount rate for plant acquisitions of 15 to 20 percent per year before taxes.

CMI's financial analysts constructed the analysis of two examples appearing in Exhibit A.3 to help management think about its opportunity. These examples helped management understand that cost savings justify price increases for asphalt plants of even larger than 25 percent and license fees in excess of $100,000 per plant.

Example 12   Mr. Mason is 62 years old. He wishes to invest equal amounts on his 63rd, 64th, and 65th birthdays so that starting on his 66th birthday he can withdraw $50,000 on each birthday for 10 years. His investments will earn 8 percent per year. How much should he invest on the 63rd through 65th birthdays?

The time line for this problem is

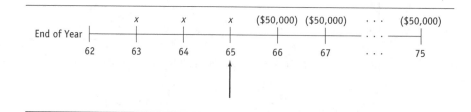

At 65, Mr. Mason needs to have accumulated a fund equal to the present value of an annuity of $50,000 per period for 10 periods, discounted at 8 percent per period. The factor from Table 4 for 8 percent and 10 periods is 6.71008. Thus,

EXHIBIT A.3	Derivation of Price Increase for Recycling Asphalt Drum Plant Justified by Cost Savings

First Illustration: Worst-case assumptions

Second Illustration: Best-case assumptions

Price (List) of New Asphalt Plant $735,000

Capacity of New Plant to Produce Output
in tons per year

   First Illustration 150,000

   Second Illustration 300,000

Life of New Asphalt Plant in Years

   First Illustration 10

   Second Illustration 15

Savings per Ton of Output Produced[a]

   First Illustration $1.50

   Second Illustration $2.50

Dollar Savings per Year

   First Illustration .... $225,000 = 150,000 tons × $1.50 per ton

   Second Illustration .... $750,000 = 300,000 tons × $2.50 per ton

Annual Discount Rate for Owner of Plant

   First Illustration 20.0%

   Second Illustration 15.0%

Present Value of Dollar Savings over Life of Plant

   First Illustration .... $943,306 = present value of $225,000 per year for
                                         10 years discounted at 20 percent per year.
                                         = $225,000 × 4.19247

   Second Illustration .... $4,385,528 = present value of $750,000 per year for
                                           15 years discounted at 15 percent per year.
                                         = $750,000 × 5.84737

Percentage Increase in Selling Price of New
Asphalt Plant Justified by Cost Savings

   First Illustration .... 128% = $943,306/$735,000

   Second Illustration .... 597% = $4,385,528/$735,000

---

[a]If each ton of output requires as much as 70 percent, or as little as 50 percent, of new material, then the savings per ton of output ranges from $1.50 (= 0.30 × $5.00) to $2.50 (= 0.50 × $5.00) per ton of output.

Present Value of an Ordinary Annuity	=	Periodic Payment	×	Factor for the Present Value of an Ordinary Annuity
x	=	$50,000	×	6.71008
x	=	$335,504.		

The time line now appears as follows:

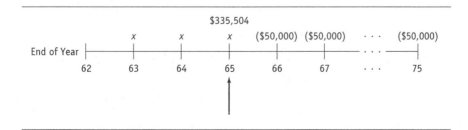

The question now becomes: How much must Mr. Mason invest on his 63rd, 64th, and 65th birthdays to accumulate a fund of $335,504 on his 65th birthday? The factor for the future value of an annuity for three periods at 8 percent is 3.24640. Thus,

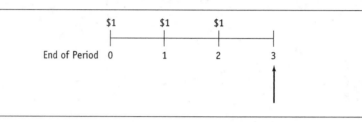

Future Value of an Ordinary Annuity = Periodic Payment × Factor for the Future Value of an Ordinary Annuity

$335,504 = x × 3.24640

$$x = \frac{\$335,504}{3.24640}$$

x = $103,346.

Annuities in Advance (Annuities Due)

The time line for the future value of a three-period annuity in advance is

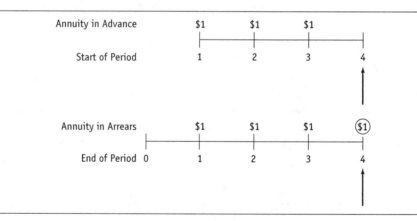

Notice that we calculated the future value for the *end* of the period in which the last payment occurs. When you have tables of ordinary annuities, tables for annuities due are unnecessary.

To see this, compare the time line for the future value of an annuity in advance for three periods with the time axis relabeled to show the start of the period and the time line for the future value of an ordinary annuity (in arrears) for four periods:

A $1 annuity in advance for n periods has a future value equal to the future value of a $1 annuity in arrears for n + 1 periods *minus* $1. The $1 circled in the time line for the annuity in arrears is the $1 that you must subtract to calculate the future value of an annuity in advance. No annuity payment occurs at the end of period 3. The note at the foot of Table 3 states: "To convert from this table to values of an annuity in advance, determine the annuity in arrears above for one more period and subtract 1.00000."

Example Problem Involving Future Value of Annuity Due

Example 13   A student plans to invest $1,000 a year at the beginning of each of the next 10 years in certificates of deposit paying interest at 12 percent per year, making the first payment today. What will be the amount of the certificates at the end of the tenth year?

The time line is

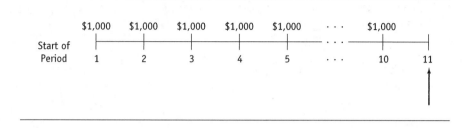

The factor for the future value of an annuity for 11 (= 10 + 1) periods is 20.65458. Because a $1,000 investment does not occur at the end of the 10th year, you subtract 1.00000 from 20.65458 to obtain the factor for the annuity in advance of 19.65458. The future value of the annuity in advance is

$$
\begin{array}{c}
\text{Future Value} \\
\text{of an} \\
\text{Annuity in Advance}
\end{array}
=
\begin{array}{c}
\text{Periodic} \\
\text{Payment}
\end{array}
\times
\begin{array}{c}
\text{Factor for} \\
\text{the Future} \\
\text{Value of an} \\
\text{Annuity in Advance}
\end{array}
$$

$$
\begin{aligned}
x &= \$1,000 \times 19.65458 \\
x &= \$19,655.
\end{aligned}
$$

Present Value of Annuity Due

The time line for the present value of an annuity in advance for three periods is

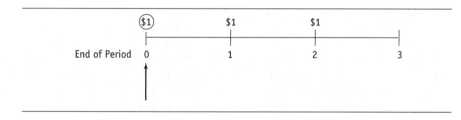

Notice that except for the first, circled payment, it looks just like the present value of an ordinary annuity for two periods. A $1 annuity in advance for n periods has a present value equal to the present value of a $1 annuity in arrears for n − 1 periods plus $1. The note at the foot of Table 4 states: "To convert from this table to values of an annuity in advance, determine the annuity in arrears above for one fewer period and add 1.00000."

Example 14   What is the present value of rents of $350 paid monthly, in advance, for 1 year when the discount rate is 1 percent per month?

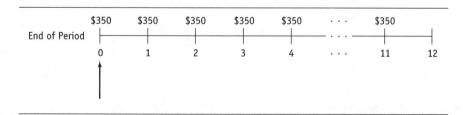

The present value of $1 per period in arrears for 11 periods at 1 percent per period is $10.36763; the present value of $1 per period in advance for 12 periods is $10.36763 + $1.00 = $11.36763, and the present value of this year's rent is $350 × 11.36763 = $3,979.

Deferred Annuities

When the first payment of an annuity occurs some time after the end of the first period, the annuity is deferred. The time line for an ordinary annuity of $1 per period for four periods deferred for two periods is

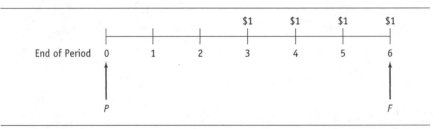

The arrow marked P shows the time of the present value calculation; the arrow marked F shows the future value calculation. The deferral does not affect the future value, which equals the future value of an ordinary annuity for four periods.

Notice that the time line for the present value looks like one for an ordinary annuity for six periods minus an ordinary annuity for two periods:

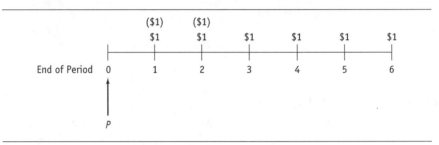

Calculate the present value of an annuity of n payments deferred for d periods by subtracting the present value of an annuity for d periods from the present value of an annuity for n + d periods.

Example 15   Refer to the data in Example 12. Recall that Mr. Mason wants to withdraw $50,000 per year on his 66th through his 75th birthdays. He wishes to invest a sufficient amount on his 63rd, 64th, and 65th birthdays to provide a fund for the later withdrawals.

The time line is

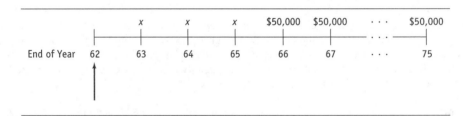

As of his 62nd birthday, the series of $50,000 payments on Mr. Mason's 66th through 75th birthdays is a deferred annuity. The interest rate is 8 percent per year.

You can find the present value using the factor for the present value of an annuity for 13 periods (10 payments deferred for three periods) of 7.90378 and subtracting the factor for the present value of an annuity for three periods of 2.57710. The net amount is 5.32668 (= 7.90378 − 2.57710). Multiplying by the $50,000 payment amount, you find the present value of the deferred annuity on Mr. Mason's 62nd birthday of $266,334 (= $50,000 × 5.32668).

Perpetuities

A periodic payment promised forever is a perpetuity. Perpetuities have no meaningful future values. They do have present values: One dollar to be received at the end of every period discounted at rate r percent has a present value of $1/r. Observe what happens in the expression for the present value of an ordinary annuity of $A per payment as n, the number of payments, approaches infinity:

$$P_A = \frac{A[1 - (1 + r)^{-n}]}{r}$$

As n approaches infinity, $(1 + r)^{-n}$ approaches zero, so that P_A approaches A(1/r). If the first payment of the perpetuity occurs now, the present value is A[1 + (1/r)].

Example 16 The Canadian government offers to pay $30 every 6 months forever in the form of a perpetual bond. What is that bond worth if the discount rate is 10 percent compounded semiannually?

Ten percent compounded semiannually is equivalent to 5 percent per 6-month period. If the first payment occurs six months from now, the present value is $30/0.05 = $600. If the first payment occurs today, the present value is $30 + $600 = $630.

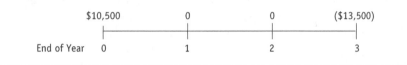

The preceding examples computed a future value or a present value given the interest rate and stated cash payment. Or they computed the required payments given their known future value or their known present value. In some calculations, we know the present or future value and the periodic payments; we must find the implicit interest rate. Assume, for example, a case in which we know that a cash investment of $10,500 will grow to $13,500 in 3 years. What is the implicit interest rate, or market rate of return, on this investment? The time line for this problem is

	$10,500	0	0	($13,500)
End of Year	0	1	2	3

The implicit interest rate is r, such that

(A.1) $$\$10,500 = \frac{\$13,500}{(1 + r)^3}$$

(A.2) $$0 = \$10,500 - \frac{\$13,500}{(1 + r)^3}$$

In other words, the present value of $13,500 discounted three periods at r percent per period is $10,500. The sum of the present values, discounted at r percent per period, of all current and future cash inflows and outflows nets to zero. In general, to find such an r requires a trial-and-error procedure.[1] We refer to that procedure as *finding the internal rate of return of a series of cash flows*. The internal rate of return of a series of cash flows is the discount rate that equates the sum of the net present value of that series of cash flows to zero. Follow these steps to find the internal rate of return:

1. Make an educated guess, called the "trial rate," at the internal rate of return. If you have no idea what to guess, try zero (or 10 percent).
2. Calculate the present value of all the cash flows (including the one at the end of year 0).
3. If the present value of the cash flows is zero, stop. The current trial rate is the internal rate of return.
4. If the amount found in step **2** is less than zero, try a larger interest rate as the trial rate and go back to step **2.**
5. If the amount found in step **2** is greater than zero, try a smaller interest rate as the new trial rate and go back to step **2.**

---

[1] In cases where r appears in only one term, as here, you can find r analytically. Here, r = ($13,500/$10,500)^{1/3} − 1 = 0.087380.

The following iterations illustrate the process for the example in Equation **A.1.**

Iteration Number	Trial Rate = r	Net Present Values: Right-Hand Side of A.2
1	0.00%	($3,000)
2	10.00	357
3	5.00	(1,162)
4	7.50	(367)
5	8.75	3

With a trial rate of 8.75 percent, the right-hand side is close enough to zero so that you can use 8.75 percent as the implicit interest rate. Continued iterations would find trial rates even closer to the true rate, which is about 8.7380 percent.

You may find calculating the internal rate of return for a series of cash flows tedious, and you should not attempt it unless you have at least a calculator. An exponential feature, the feature that allows the computation of $(1 + r)$ raised to various powers, helps.[2] Computer spreadsheets, such as Lotus 1-2-3 and Excel, have a built-in function to find the internal rate of return.

Example 17   The Alexis Company acquires a machine with a cash price of $10,500. It pays for the machine by giving a note for $12,000 promising to make payments equal to 7 percent of the face value, $840 $(= 0.07 \times \$12,000)$, at the end of each of the next 3 years and a single payment of $12,000 in 3 years. What is the implicit interest rate in the loan?

The time line for this problem is

	$10,500	($840)	($840)	($12,840)
End of Period	0	1	2	3

The implicit interest rate is r, such that[3]

$$(A.3) \qquad \$10,500 = \frac{\$840}{(1 + r)} + \frac{\$840}{(1 + r)^2} + \frac{\$840}{(1 + r)^3}.$$

The iteration process finds an internal rate of return of 12.2 percent to the nearest tenth of 1 percent:

Iteration Number	Trial Rate	Right-Hand Side of A.3
1	7.0%	$12,000
2	15.0	9,808
3	11.0	10,827
4	13.0	10,300
5	12.0	10,559
6	12.5	10,428
7	12.3	10,480
8	12.2	10,506
9	12.1	10,533

---

[2]You may use other methods to guess the trial rate that will approximate the true rate in fewer iterations than the method described here. If you want to find internal rates of return efficiently with successive trial rates, refer to a mathematical reference book to learn about the "Newton search" method, sometimes called the "method of false position."

[3]Compare this formulation to that in Equation **A.2.** Note that the left-hand side is zero in one case but not in the other. The left-hand side can be either nonzero or zero, depending on what seems convenient for the particular context.

Example 18 In some contexts, such as mortgages or leases, one knows the amount of a series of future periodic payments, which are identical in all periods, and the present value of those future payments. For example, a firm may borrow $100,000 and agree to repay the loan, in 20 payments of $11,746 each, at the end of each of the next 20 years. To calculate interest expense each period, you must find the interest rate implicit in the loan.

You have the following information:

$$\begin{array}{ccc} \text{Present Value} \\ \text{of an} & = & \text{Periodic} & \times & \text{the Present} \\ \text{Ordinary Annuity} & & \text{Payment} & & \text{Value of an} \\ & & & & \text{Ordinary Annuity} \end{array}$$

$$\$100,000 = \$11,746 \times x$$

$$x = \frac{\$100,000}{\$11,746}$$

$$x = 8.51354.$$

The factor to discount 20 payments of $11,746 to a present value of $100,000 is 8.51354. To find the interest rate implicit in the discounting, scan the 20-payment row of Table 4 to find the factor 8.51354. The interest rate at the head of the column is the implicit interest rate, approximately 10 percent in the example.

Example 19 An investment costing $11,400 today provides the following after-tax cash inflows at the ends of each of the next five periods: $5,000, $4,000, $3,000, $2,000, $1,000. What is the internal rate of return on these flows? That is, find r such that

(A.4)　　$$0 = (\$11,400) + \frac{\$5,000}{(1 + r)} + \frac{\$4,000}{(1 + r)^2} + \frac{\$3,000}{(1 + r)^3} + \frac{\$2,000}{(1 + r)^4} + \frac{\$1,000}{(1 + r)^5}.$$

Trial rates r produced the following sequences of estimates of the internal rate of return:

Iteration Number	Trial Rate	Right-Hand Side of A.4
1	0.00%	$3,600
2	10.00	692
3	15.00	(414)
4	12.50	115
5	13.50	(102)
6	13.00	6
7	13.10	(16)
8	13.01	4
9	13.01	2
10	13.03	(1)

The process of estimating goes several steps farther than necessary. To the nearest whole percentage point, the internal rate of return is 13 percent.

To the nearest one-hundredth of a percent, the internal rate of return is 13.03 percent. Further trials find an even more precise answer, $r = 13.027$ percent. Physical scientists learn early in their training not to use more significant digits in calculations than the accuracy of the measuring devices merits. Accountants, too, should not carry calculations beyond the point of accuracy. Given the likely uncertainty in the estimates of cash flows, an estimate of the internal rate of return accurate to the nearest whole percentage point will serve its intended purpose.

Compound Interest and Annuity Tables

TABLE 1   Future Value of $1

$F_n = P(1+r)^n$

r^n = interest rate; n = number of periods until valuation; $P = \$1$

Period = n	½%	1%	1½%	2%	3%	4%	5%	6%	7%	8%	10%	12%	15%	20%	25%
1	1.00500	1.01000	1.01500	1.02000	1.03000	1.04000	1.05000	1.06000	1.07000	1.08000	1.10000	1.12000	1.15000	1.20000	1.25000
2	1.01003	1.02010	1.03023	1.04040	1.06090	1.08160	1.10250	1.12360	1.14490	1.16640	1.21000	1.25440	1.32250	1.44000	1.56250
3	1.01508	1.03030	1.04568	1.06121	1.09273	1.12486	1.15763	1.19102	1.22504	1.25971	1.33100	1.40493	1.52088	1.72800	1.95313
4	1.02015	1.04060	1.06136	1.08243	1.12551	1.16986	1.21551	1.26248	1.31080	1.36049	1.46410	1.57352	1.74901	2.07360	2.44141
5	1.02525	1.05101	1.07728	1.10408	1.15927	1.21665	1.27628	1.33823	1.40255	1.46933	1.61051	1.76234	2.01136	2.48832	3.05176
6	1.03038	1.06152	1.09344	1.12616	1.19405	1.26532	1.34010	1.41852	1.50073	1.58687	1.77156	1.97382	2.31306	2.98598	3.81470
7	1.03553	1.07214	1.10984	1.14869	1.22987	1.31593	1.40710	1.50363	1.60578	1.71382	1.94872	2.21068	2.66002	3.58318	4.76837
8	1.04071	1.08286	1.12649	1.17166	1.26677	1.36857	1.47746	1.59385	1.71819	1.85093	2.14359	2.47596	3.05902	4.29982	5.96046
9	1.04591	1.09369	1.14339	1.19509	1.30477	1.42331	1.55133	1.68948	1.83846	1.99900	2.35795	2.77308	3.51788	5.15978	7.45058
10	1.05114	1.10462	1.16054	1.21899	1.34392	1.48024	1.62889	1.79085	1.96715	2.15892	2.59374	3.10585	4.04556	6.19174	9.31323
11	1.05640	1.11567	1.17795	1.24337	1.38423	1.53945	1.71034	1.89830	2.10485	2.33164	2.85312	3.47855	4.65239	7.43008	11.64153
12	1.06168	1.12683	1.19562	1.26824	1.42576	1.60103	1.79586	2.01220	2.25219	2.51817	3.13843	3.89598	5.35025	8.91610	14.55192
13	1.06699	1.13809	1.21355	1.29361	1.46853	1.66507	1.88565	2.13293	2.40985	2.71962	3.45227	4.36349	6.15279	10.69932	18.18989
14	1.07232	1.14947	1.23176	1.31948	1.51259	1.73168	1.97993	2.26090	2.57853	2.93719	3.79750	4.88711	7.07571	12.83918	22.73737
15	1.07768	1.16097	1.25023	1.34587	1.55797	1.80094	2.07893	2.39656	2.75903	3.17217	4.17725	5.47357	8.13706	15.40702	28.42171
16	1.08307	1.17258	1.26899	1.37279	1.60471	1.87298	2.18287	2.54035	2.95216	3.42594	4.59497	6.13039	9.35762	18.48843	35.52714
17	1.08849	1.18430	1.28802	1.40024	1.65285	1.94790	2.29202	2.69277	3.15882	3.70002	5.05447	6.86604	10.76126	22.18611	44.40892
18	1.09393	1.19615	1.30734	1.42825	1.70243	2.02582	2.40662	2.85434	3.37993	3.99602	5.55992	7.68997	12.37545	26.62333	55.51115
19	1.09940	1.20811	1.32695	1.45681	1.75351	2.10685	2.52695	3.02560	3.61653	4.31570	6.11591	8.61276	14.23177	31.94800	69.38894
20	1.10490	1.22019	1.34686	1.48595	1.80611	2.19112	2.65330	3.20714	3.86968	4.66096	6.72750	9.64629	16.36654	38.33760	86.73617
22	1.11597	1.24472	1.38756	1.54598	1.91610	2.36992	2.92526	3.60354	4.43040	5.43654	8.14027	12.10031	21.64475	55.20614	135.5253
24	1.12716	1.26973	1.42950	1.60844	2.03279	2.56330	3.22510	4.04893	5.07237	6.34118	9.84973	15.17863	28.62518	79.49685	211.7582
26	1.13846	1.29526	1.47271	1.67342	2.15659	2.77247	3.55567	4.54938	4.80735	7.39635	11.91818	19.04007	37.85680	114.4755	330.8722
28	1.14987	1.32129	1.51722	1.74102	2.28793	2.99870	3.92013	5.11169	6.64884	8.62711	14.42099	23.88387	50.06561	164.8447	516.9879
30	1.16140	1.34785	1.56308	1.81136	2.42726	3.24340	4.32194	5.74349	7.61226	10.06266	17.44940	29.95992	66.21177	237.3763	807.7936
32	1.17304	1.37494	1.61032	1.88454	2.57508	3.50806	4.76494	6.45339	8.71527	11.73708	21.11378	37.58173	87.56507	341.8219	1262.177
34	1.18480	1.40258	1.65900	1.96068	2.73191	3.79432	5.25335	7.25103	9.97811	13.69013	25.54767	47.14252	115.80480	492.2235	1972.152
36	1.19668	1.43077	1.70914	2.03989	2.89828	4.10393	5.79182	8.14725	11.42394	15.96817	30.91268	59.13557	153.15185	708.8019	3081.488
38	1.20668	1.45953	1.76080	2.12230	3.07478	4.43881	6.38548	9.15425	13.07927	18.62528	37.40434	74.17966	202.54332	1020.675	4814.825
40	1.22079	1.48886	1.81402	2.20804	3.26204	4.80102	7.03999	10.28572	14.97448	21.72452	45.25926	93.05097	267.86355	1469.772	7523.164
45	1.25162	1.56481	1.95421	2.43785	3.78160	5.84118	8.98501	13.76461	21.00245	31.92045	72.89048	163.9876	538.76927	3657.262	22958.87
50	1.28323	1.64463	2.10524	2.69159	4.38391	7.10668	11.46740	18.42015	29.45703	46.90161	117.3909	289.0022	1083.65744	9100.438	70064.92
100	1.64667	2.70481	4.43205	7.24465	19.21863	50.50495	131.5013	339.3021	867.7163	2199.761	13780.861	83522.27	117×10^4	828×10^5	491×10^7

TABLE 2 — Present Value of $1

$$P = F_n (1 + r)^{-n}$$

r = discount rate; n = number of periods until payment; $F_n = \$1$

Period n	½%	1%	1½%	2%	3%	4%	5%	6%	7%	8%	10%	12%	15%	20%	25%
1	.99502	.99010	.98522	.98039	.97087	.96154	.95238	.94340	.93458	.92593	.90909	.89286	.86957	.83333	.80000
2	.99007	.98030	.97066	.96117	.94260	.92456	.90703	.89000	.87344	.85734	.82645	.79719	.75614	.69444	.64000
3	.98515	.97059	.95632	.94232	.91514	.88900	.86384	.83962	.81630	.79383	.75131	.71178	.65752	.57870	.51200
4	.98025	.96098	.94218	.92385	.88849	.85480	.82270	.79209	.76290	.73503	.68301	.63552	.57175	.48225	.40960
5	.97537	.95147	.92826	.90573	.86261	.82193	.78353	.74726	.71299	.68058	.62092	.56743	.49718	.40188	.32768
6	.97052	.94205	.91454	.88797	.83748	.79031	.74622	.70496	.66634	.63017	.56447	.50663	.43233	.33490	.26214
7	.96569	.93272	.90103	.87056	.81309	.75992	.71068	.66506	.62275	.58349	.51316	.45235	.37594	.27908	.20972
8	.96089	.92348	.88771	.85349	.78941	.73069	.67684	.62741	.58201	.54027	.46651	.40388	.32690	.23257	.16777
9	.95610	.91434	.87459	.83676	.76642	.70259	.64461	.59190	.54393	.50025	.42410	.36061	.28426	.19381	.13422
10	.95135	.90529	.86167	.82035	.74409	.67556	.61391	.55839	.50835	.46319	.38554	.32197	.24718	.16151	.10737
11	.94661	.89632	.84893	.80426	.72242	.64958	.58468	.52679	.47509	.42888	.35049	.28748	.21494	.13459	.08590
12	.94191	.88745	.83639	.78849	.70138	.62460	.55684	.49697	.44401	.39711	.31863	.25668	.18691	.11216	.06872
13	.93722	.87866	.82403	.77303	.68095	.60057	.53032	.46884	.41496	.36770	.28966	.22917	.16253	.09346	.05498
14	.93256	.86996	.81185	.75788	.66112	.57748	.50507	.44230	.38782	.34046	.26333	.20462	.14133	.07789	.04398
15	.92792	.86135	.79985	.74301	.64186	.55526	.48102	.41727	.36245	.31524	.23939	.18270	.12289	.06491	.03518
16	.92330	.85282	.78803	.72845	.62317	.53391	.45811	.39365	.33873	.29189	.21763	.16312	.10686	.05409	.02815
17	.91871	.84438	.77639	.71416	.60502	.51337	.43630	.37136	.31657	.27027	.19784	.14564	.09293	.04507	.02252
18	.91414	.83602	.76491	.70016	.58739	.49363	.41552	.35034	.29586	.25025	.17986	.13004	.08081	.03756	.01801
19	.90959	.82774	.75361	.68643	.57029	.47464	.39573	.33051	.27651	.23171	.16351	.11611	.07027	.03130	.01441
20	.90506	.81954	.74247	.67297	.55368	.45639	.37689	.31180	.25842	.21455	.14864	.10367	.06110	.02608	.01153
22	.89608	.80340	.72069	.64684	.52189	.42196	.34185	.27751	.22571	.18394	.12285	.08264	.04620	.01811	.00738
24	.88719	.78757	.69954	.62172	.49193	.39012	.31007	.24698	.19715	.15770	.10153	.06588	.03493	.01258	.00472
26	.87838	.77205	.67902	.59758	.46369	.36069	.28124	.21981	.17220	.13520	.08391	.05252	.02642	.00874	.00302
28	.86966	.75684	.65910	.57437	.43708	.33348	.25509	.19563	.15040	.11591	.06934	.04187	.01997	.00607	.00193
30	.86103	.74192	.63976	.55207	.41199	.30832	.23138	.17411	.13137	.09938	.05731	.03338	.01510	.00421	.00124
32	.85248	.72730	.62099	.53063	.38834	.28506	.20987	.15496	.11474	.08520	.04736	.02661	.01142	.00293	.00079
34	.84402	.71297	.60277	.51003	.36604	.26355	.19035	.13791	.10022	.07305	.03914	.02121	.00864	.00203	.00051
36	.83564	.69892	.58509	.49022	.34503	.24367	.17266	.12274	.08754	.06262	.03235	.01691	.00653	.00141	.00032
38	.82735	.68515	.56792	.47119	.32523	.22529	.15661	.10924	.07646	.05369	.02673	.01348	.00494	.00098	.00021
40	.81914	.67165	.55126	.45289	.30656	.20829	.14205	.09722	.06678	.04603	.02209	.01075	.00373	.00068	.00013
45	.79896	.63905	.51171	.41020	.26444	.17120	.11130	.07265	.04761	.03133	.01372	.00610	.00186	.00027	.00004
50	.77929	.60804	.47500	.37153	.22811	.14071	.08720	.05429	.03395	.02132	.00852	.00346	.00092	.00011	.00001
100	.60729	.36971	.22563	.13803	.05203	.01980	.00760	.00295	.00115	.00045	.00007	.00001	.00000	.00000	.00000

TABLE 4   Present Value of Annuity of $1 in Arrears

$$P_A = \frac{1 - (1+r)^{-n}}{r} \times \$1.00$$

r = discount rate; n = number of payments

n Periods = Payments

0	$1	$1	$1	$1	$1

→ Payments in Arrears

P_A P_F

$$\left(\begin{array}{c}\text{Value in}\\\text{Table 4}\end{array}\right) = \sum \left(\begin{array}{c}\text{Individual Values}\\\text{from Table 2}\end{array}\right)$$

No. of Payments = n	½%	1%	1½%	2%	3%	4%	5%	6%	7%	8%	10%	12%	15%	20%	25%
1	.99502	.99010	.98522	.98039	.97087	.96154	.95238	.94340	.93458	.92593	.90909	.89286	.86957	.83333	.80000
2	1.98510	1.97040	1.95588	1.94156	1.91347	1.88609	1.85941	1.83339	1.80802	1.78326	1.73554	1.69005	1.62571	1.52778	1.44000
3	2.97025	2.94099	2.91220	2.88388	2.82861	2.77509	2.72325	2.67301	2.62432	2.57710	2.48685	2.40183	2.28323	2.10648	1.95200
4	3.95050	3.90197	3.85438	3.80773	3.71710	3.62990	3.54595	3.46511	3.38721	3.31213	3.16987	3.03735	2.85498	2.58873	2.36160
5	4.92587	4.85343	4.78264	4.71346	4.57971	4.45182	4.32948	4.21236	4.10020	3.99271	3.79079	3.60478	3.35216	2.99061	2.68928
6	5.89638	5.79548	5.69719	5.60143	5.41719	5.24214	5.07569	4.91732	4.76654	4.62288	4.35526	4.11141	3.78448	3.32551	2.95142
7	6.86207	6.72819	6.59821	6.47199	6.23028	6.00205	5.78637	5.58238	5.38929	5.20637	4.86842	4.56376	4.16042	3.60459	3.16114
8	7.82296	7.65168	7.48593	7.32548	7.01969	6.73274	6.46321	6.20979	5.97130	5.74664	5.33493	4.96764	4.48732	3.83716	3.32891
9	8.77906	8.56602	8.36052	8.16224	7.78611	7.43533	7.10782	6.80169	6.51523	6.24689	5.75902	5.32825	4.77158	4.03097	3.46313
10	9.73041	9.47130	9.22218	8.98259	8.53020	8.11090	7.72173	7.36009	7.02358	6.71008	6.14457	5.65022	5.01877	4.19247	3.57050
11	10.67703	10.36763	10.07112	9.78685	9.25262	8.76048	8.30641	7.88687	7.49867	7.13896	6.49506	5.93770	5.23371	4.32706	3.65640
12	11.61893	11.25508	10.90751	10.57534	9.95400	9.38507	8.86325	8.38384	7.94269	7.53608	6.81369	6.19437	5.42062	4.43922	3.72512
13	12.55615	12.13374	11.73153	11.34837	10.63496	9.98565	9.39357	8.85268	8.35765	7.90378	7.10336	6.42355	5.58315	4.53268	3.78010
14	13.48871	13.00370	12.54338	12.10625	11.29607	10.56312	9.89864	9.29498	8.74547	8.24424	7.36669	6.62817	5.72448	4.61057	3.82408
15	14.41662	13.86505	13.34323	12.84926	11.93794	11.11839	10.37966	9.71225	9.10971	8.55948	7.60608	6.81086	5.84737	4.67547	3.85926
16	15.33993	14.71787	14.13126	13.57771	12.56110	11.65230	10.83777	10.10590	9.44665	8.85137	7.82371	6.97399	5.95423	4.72956	3.88741
17	16.25863	15.56225	14.90765	14.29187	13.16612	12.16567	11.27407	10.47726	9.76322	9.12164	8.02155	7.11963	6.04716	4.77463	3.90093
18	17.17277	16.39827	15.67256	14.99203	13.75351	12.65930	11.68959	10.82760	10.05909	9.37189	8.20141	7.24967	6.12797	4.81219	3.92794
19	18.08236	17.22601	16.42617	15.67846	14.32380	13.13394	12.08532	11.15812	10.33560	9.60360	8.36492	7.36578	6.19823	4.84350	3.94235
20	18.98742	18.04555	17.16864	16.35143	14.87747	13.59033	12.46221	11.46992	10.59401	9.81815	8.51356	7.46944	6.25933	4.86958	3.95388
22	20.78406	19.66038	18.62082	17.65805	15.93692	14.45112	13.16300	12.04158	11.06124	10.20074	8.77154	7.64465	6.35866	4.90943	3.97049
24	22.56287	21.24339	20.03041	18.91393	16.93554	15.24696	13.79864	12.55036	11.46933	10.52876	8.98474	7.78432	6.43377	4.93710	3.98111
26	24.32402	22.79520	21.39863	20.12104	17.87684	15.98277	14.37519	13.00317	11.82578	10.80998	9.16095	7.89566	6.49056	4.95632	3.98791
28	26.06769	24.31644	22.72672	21.28127	18.76411	16.66306	14.89813	13.40616	12.13711	11.05108	9.30657	7.98442	6.53351	4.96967	3.99226
30	27.79405	25.80771	24.01584	22.39646	19.60044	17.29203	15.37245	13.76483	12.40904	11.25778	9.42691	8.05518	6.56598	4.97894	3.99505
32	29.50328	27.26959	25.26714	23.46833	20.38877	17.87355	15.80268	14.08404	12.64656	11.43500	9.52638	8.11159	6.59053	4.98537	3.99683
34	31.19555	28.70267	26.48173	24.49859	21.13184	18.41120	16.19290	14.36814	12.85401	11.58693	9.60857	8.15656	6.60910	4.98984	3.99797
36	32.87102	30.10751	27.66068	25.48884	21.83225	18.90828	16.54685	14.62099	13.03521	11.71719	9.67651	8.19241	6.62314	4.99295	3.99870
38	34.52985	31.48466	28.80505	26.44064	22.49246	19.36786	16.86786	14.84602	13.19347	11.82887	9.73265	8.22099	6.63375	4.99510	3.99917
40	36.17223	32.83469	29.91585	27.35548	23.11477	19.79277	17.15909	15.04630	13.33171	11.92461	9.77905	8.24378	6.64178	4.99660	3.99947
45	40.20720	36.09451	32.55234	29.49016	24.51871	20.72004	17.77407	15.45583	13.60552	12.10840	9.86281	8.28252	6.65429	4.99863	3.99983
50	44.14279	39.19612	34.99969	31.42361	25.72976	21.48218	18.25593	15.76186	13.80075	12.23348	9.91481	8.30450	6.66051	4.99945	3.99994
100	78.54264	63.02888	51.62470	43.09835	31.59891	24.50500	19.84791	16.61755	14.26925	12.49432	9.99927	8.33323	6.66666	5.00000	4.00000

Note: To convert from this table to values of an annuity in advance, determine the annuity in arrears above for one fewer period and add 1.00000.

GLOSSARY

The definitions of many words and phrases in the glossary use other glossary terms. In a given definition, we *italicize* terms that themselves (or variants thereof) appear elsewhere under their own listings. The cross-references generally take one of two forms:

1. **absorption costing.** See *full absorption costing.*
2. **ABC.** *Activity-based costing.*

Form (1) refers you to another term for discussion of this bold-faced term. Form (2) tells you that this bold-faced term is synonymous with the *italicized* term, which you can consult for discussion if necessary.

A

AAA. *American Accounting Association.*

Abacus. A scholarly journal containing articles on theoretical aspects of accounting, published by Blackwell Publishers for the Accounting Foundation of the University of Sydney.

abatement. A complete or partial cancellation of a levy imposed by a government unit.

ABC. *Activity-based costing.*

abnormal spoilage. Actual spoilage exceeding that expected when operations are normally efficient. Usual practice treats this cost as an *expense* of the period rather than as a *product cost.* Contrast with *normal spoilage.*

aboriginal cost. In public utility accounting, the *acquisition cost* of an *asset* incurred by the first *entity* devoting that asset to public use; the cost basis for most public utility regulation. If regulators used a different cost basis, then public utilities could exchange assets among themselves at ever-increasing prices in order to raise the rate base and, then, prices based on them.

absorbed overhead. *Overhead costs* allocated to individual products at some *overhead rate;* also called *applied overhead.*

absorption costing. See *full absorption costing.*

Abstracts of the EITF. See *Emerging Issues Task Force.*

Accelerated Cost Recovery System (ACRS). A form of accelerated depreciation that Congress enacted in 1981 and amended in 1986, so that now most writers refer to it as *MACRS,* or *Modified Accelerated Cost Recovery System.* The system provides percentages of the asset's cost that a firm depreciates each year for tax purposes. The percentages derive, roughly, from 150-percent *declining-balance depreciation* methods. ACRS ignores salvage value. We do not generally use these amounts for *financial accounting.*

accelerated depreciation. In calculating *depreciation* charges, any method in which the charges become progressively smaller each period. Examples are *double declining-balance depreciation* and *sum-of-the-years'-digits depreciation* methods.

acceptance. A written promise to pay; equivalent to a *promissory note.*

account. A device for representing the amount (*balance*) for any line (or a part of a line) in the *balance sheet* or *income statement.* Because income statement accounts explain the changes in the balance sheet account Retained Earnings, the definition does not require the last three words of the preceding sentence. An account is any device for accumulating additions and subtractions relating to a single *asset, liability,* or *owners' equity* item, including *revenues* and *expenses.*

account analysis method. A method of separating *fixed costs* from *variable costs* based on the analyst's judgment of whether the cost is fixed or variable. Based on their names alone, the analyst might classify *direct labor* (*materials*) *costs* as variable and *depreciation* on a factory building as fixed. In our experience, this method results in too many fixed costs and not enough variable costs—that is, analysts have insufficient information to judge management's ability to reduce costs that appear to be fixed.

account form. The form of *balance sheet* in which *assets* appear on the left and *equities* appear on the right. Contrast with *report form.* See *T-account.*

accountability center. *Responsibility center.*

accountancy. The British word for *accounting.* In the United States, it means the theory and practice of accounting.

accountant's comments. Canada: a written communication issued by a public accountant at the conclusion of a review engagement. It consists of a description of the work performed and a statement that, under the terms of the engagement, the accountant has not performed an audit and consequently expresses no opinion. (Compare *auditor's report; denial of opinion.*)

accountant's opinion. *Auditor's report.*

accountant's report. *Auditor's report.*

accounting. A system conveying information about a specific *entity.* The information is in financial terms and will appear in accounting statements only if the accountant can measure it with reasonable precision. The *AICPA* defines accounting as a service activity whose "function is to provide quantitative information, primarily financial in nature, about economic entities that is intended to be useful in making economic decisions."

accounting adjustments. *Prior-period adjustments,* changes in accounting principles accounted for on a cumulative basis, and corrections of errors. See *accounting changes.* The *FASB* indicates that it will tend to call these items "accounting adjustments," not "accounting changes," when it requires the reporting of *comprehensive income.*

Accounting and Tax Index. A publication that indexes, in detail, the accounting literature of the period. Published by UMI, a subsidiary of ProQuest Company.

accounting changes. As defined by *APB Opinion No. 20,* a change in (1) an *accounting principle* (such as a switch from *FIFO* to *LIFO* or from *sum-of-the-years'-digits depreciation* to *straight-line depreciation*), (2) an accounting estimate (such as estimated useful lives or salvage value of depreciable assets and estimates of *warranty* costs or *uncollectible accounts*), or (3) the reporting *entity*. The firm should disclose changes of type (1). It should include in reported earnings for the period of change the cumulative effect of the change on *retained earnings* at the start of the period during which it made the change. The firm should treat changes of type (2) as affecting only the period of change and, if necessary, future periods. The firm should disclose reasons for changes of type (3) in statements reporting on operations of the period of the change, and it should show the effect of the change on all other periods, for comparative purposes. In some cases (such as a change from *LIFO* to other inventory *flow assumptions* or a change in the method of accounting for long-term construction contracts), *GAAP* treat changes of type (1) like changes of type (3). That is, for these changes the firm should restate all statements shown for prior periods to show the effect of adopting the change for those periods as well. See *all-inclusive (income) concept* and *accounting errors*.

accounting conventions. Methods or procedures used in accounting. Writers tend to use this term when the method or procedure has not yet received official authoritative sanction by a pronouncement of a group such as the *APB, EITF, FASB,* or *SEC*. Contrast with *accounting principles*.

accounting cycle. The sequence of accounting procedures starting with *journal entries* for various transactions and events and ending with the *financial statements* or, perhaps, the *post-closing trial balance*.

accounting deficiency. Canada: a failure to adhere to generally accepted *accounting principles* or to disclose essential information in *financial statements*.

accounting entity. See *entity*.

accounting equation. *Assets = Equities; Assets = Liabilities + Owners' Equity.*

accounting errors. Arithmetic errors and misapplications of *accounting principles* in previously published financial statements. The firm corrects these during the current period with direct *debits* or *credits* to *retained earnings*. In this regard, the firm treats them like *prior-period adjustments,* but technically *APB Opinion No. 9* does not classify them as prior-period adjustments. See *accounting changes,* and contrast with changes in accounting estimates as described there.

accounting event. Any occurrence that is recorded in the accounting records.

Accounting Horizons. Quarterly journal of the *American Accounting Association*.

accounting methods. *Accounting principles;* procedures for carrying out accounting principles.

accounting period. The time period between consecutive *balance sheets;* the time period for which the firm prepares *financial statements* that measure *flows,* such as the *income statement* and the *statement of cash flows*. See *interim statements*.

accounting policies. *Accounting principles* adopted by a specific *entity*.

accounting principles. The methods or procedures used in accounting for events reported in the *financial statements*. We tend to use this term when the method or procedure has received official authoritative sanction from a pronouncement of a group such as the *APB, EITF, FASB,* or *SEC*. Contrast with *accounting conventions* and *conceptual framework*.

Accounting Principles Board. See *APB*.

accounting procedures. See *accounting principles*. However, this term usually refers to the methods for implementing accounting principles.

accounting rate of return. Income for a period divided by average investment during the period; based on income, rather than discounted cash flows, and hence a poor decision-making aid or tool. See *ratio*.

Accounting Research Bulletin (ARB). The name of the official pronouncements of the former *Committee on Accounting Procedure (CAP)* of the AICPA. The committee issued fifty-one bulletins between 1939 and 1959. *ARB No. 43* restated and codified the parts of the first forty-two bulletins not dealing solely with definitions.

Accounting Research Study (ARS). One of a series of studies published by the Director of Accounting Research of the *AICPA* and "designed to provide professional accountants and others interested in the development of accounting with a discussion and documentation of accounting problems." The AICPA published fifteen such studies in the period 1961–73.

Accounting Review (The Accounting Review). Scholarly publication of the *American Accounting Association*.

Accounting Series Release (ASR). See *SEC*.

accounting standards. *Accounting principles*.

Accounting Standards Executive Committee (AcSEC). The senior technical committee of the *AICPA* authorized to speak for the AICPA in the areas of *financial accounting* and reporting as well as *cost accounting*.

accounting system. The procedures for collecting and summarizing financial data in a firm.

Accounting Terminology Bulletin (ATB). One of four releases of the Committee on Terminology of the *AICPA* issued in the period 1953–57.

Accounting Trends and Techniques. An annual *AICPA* publication that surveys the reporting practices of 600 large corporations. It presents tabulations of specific practices, terminology, and disclosures along with illustrations taken from individual annual reports.

accounts payable. A *liability* representing an amount owed to a *creditor;* usually arising from the purchase of *merchandise* or materials and supplies, not necessarily due or past due; normally, a *current liability*.

accounts receivable. Claims against a *debtor;* usually arising from sales or services rendered, not necessarily due or past due; normally, a *current asset*.

accounts receivable turnover. Net sales on account divided by average accounts receivable. See *ratio*.

accretion. Occurs when a *book value* grows over time, such as a *bond* originally issued at a *discount;* the correct technical term is "accretion," not "amortization." This term also refers to an increase in economic worth through physical change caused by natural growth, usually said of a natural resource such as timber. Contrast with *appreciation*. See *amortization*.

accrual. Recognition of an *expense* (or *revenue*) and the related *liability* (or *asset*) resulting from an *accounting event,* frequently from the passage of time but not signaled by an explicit cash transaction; for example, the recognition of interest expense or revenue (or wages, salaries, or rent) at the end of a period even though the firm makes no explicit cash transaction at that time. Cash flow follows accounting recognition; contrast with *deferral.*

accrual basis of accounting. The method of recognizing *revenues* as a firm sells *goods* (or delivers them) and as it renders *services,* independent of the time when it receives cash. This system recognizes *expenses* in the period when it recognizes the related revenue, independent of the time when it pays cash. *SFAC No. 1* says, "Accrual accounting attempts to record the financial effects on an enterprise of transactions and other events and circumstances that have cash consequences for the enterprise in the periods in which those transactions, events, and circumstances occur rather than only in the periods in which cash is received or paid by the enterprise." Contrast with the *cash basis of accounting.* See *accrual* and *deferral.* We could more correctly call this "accrual/deferral" accounting.

accrue. See *accrued,* and contrast with *incur.*

accrued. Said of a *revenue* (*expense*) that the firm has earned (*recognized*) even though the related *receivable* (*payable*) has a future due date. We prefer not to use this adjective as part of an account title. Thus, we prefer to use Interest Receivable (Payable) as the account title rather than Accrued Interest Receivable (Payable). See *matching convention* and *accrual.* Contrast with *incur.*

accrued depreciation. An incorrect term for *accumulated depreciation.* Acquiring an asset with cash, capitalizing it, and then amortizing its cost over periods of use is a process of *deferral* and allocation, not of *accrual.*

accrued payable. A *payable* usually resulting from the passage of time. For example, *salaries* and *interest* accrue as time passes. See *accrued.*

accrued receivable. A *receivable* usually resulting from the passage of time. See *accrued.*

accumulated benefit obligation. See *projected benefit obligation* for definition and contrast.

accumulated depreciation. A preferred title for the asset *contra account* that shows the sum of *depreciation* charges on an asset since the time the firm acquired it. Other account titles are *allowance* for *depreciation* (acceptable term) and *reserve* for *depreciation* (unacceptable term).

accumulated other comprehensive income. *Balance sheet* amount in *owners' equity* showing the total of all *other comprehensive income* amounts from all prior periods.

accurate presentation. The qualitative accounting objective suggesting that information reported in financial statements should correspond as precisely as possible with the economic effects underlying transactions and events. See *fair presentation* and *full disclosure.*

acid test ratio. *Quick ratio.*

acquisition cost. Of an *asset,* the net *invoice* price plus all *expenditures* to place and ready the asset for its intended use. The other expenditures might include legal fees, transportation charges, and installation costs.

ACRS. *Accelerated Cost Recovery System.*

AcSEC. *Accounting Standards Executive Committee* of the *AICPA.*

activity accounting. *Responsibility accounting.*

activity-based costing (ABC). Method of assigning *indirect costs,* including non-manufacturing *overhead costs,* to products and services. ABC assumes that almost all overhead costs associate with activities within the firm and vary with respect to the *drivers* of those activities. Some practitioners suggest that ABC attempts to find the drivers for all indirect costs; these people note that in the long run, all costs are *variable,* so *fixed* indirect costs do not occur. This method first assigns costs to activities and then to products based on the products' usage of the activities.

activity-based depreciation. *Production method* (*depreciation*).

activity-based management (ABM). Analysis and management of activities required to make a product or to produce a service. ABM focuses attention to enhance activities that add value to the customer and to reduce activities that do not. Its goal is to satisfy customer needs while making smaller demands on costly resources. Some refer to this as "activity management."

activity basis. *Costs* are *variable* or *fixed* (*incremental* or *unavoidable*) with respect to some activity, such as production of units (or the undertaking of some new project). Usage calls this activity the "activity basis."

activity center. Unit of the organization that performs a set of tasks.

activity variance. *Sales volume variance.*

actual cost (basis). *Acquisition* or *historical cost.* Also contrast with *standard cost* and *normal cost.*

actual costing (system). Method of allocating costs to products using actual *direct materials,* actual *direct labor,* and actual *factory overhead.* Contrast with *normal costing* and *standard costing.*

actuarial. An adjective describing computations or analyses that involve both *compound interest* and probabilities, such as the computation of the *present value* of a life-contingent *annuity.* Some writers use the word even for computations involving only one of the two.

actuarial accrued liability. A 1981 report of the Joint Committee on Pension Terminology (of various actuarial societies) agreed to use this term rather than *prior service cost.*

ad valorem. A method of levying a tax or duty on goods by using their estimated value as the tax base.

additional paid-in capital. An alternative acceptable title for the *capital contributed in excess of par* (or *stated*) *value* account.

additional processing cost. *Costs* incurred in processing *joint products* after the *splitoff point.*

adequate disclosure. An auditing standard that, to achieve *fair presentation* of *financial statements,* requires *disclosure* of *material* items. This *auditing standard* does not, however, require publicizing all information detrimental to a company. For example, the company may face a lawsuit, and disclosure might require a *debit* to a *loss* account and a *credit* to an *estimated liability.* But the court might view the making of this entry as an admission of liability, which could adversely affect the outcome of the suit. The firm should debit expense or loss for the expected loss, as required by *SFAS No. 5,* but need not use such accurate account titles that the court can spot an admission of liability.

adjunct account. An *account* that accumulates additions to another account. For example, Premium on Bonds Payable is adjunct to the liability Bonds Payable; the effective liability is the sum of the two account balances at a given date. Contrast with *contra account.*

adjusted acquisition (historical) cost. Sometimes said of the *book value* of a *plant asset,* that is, *acquisition cost* less *accumulated depreciation.* Also, cost adjusted to a *constant-dollar* amount to reflect *general price-level changes.*

adjusted bank balance of cash. The *balance* shown on the statement from the bank plus or minus amounts, such as for unrecorded deposits or outstanding checks, to reconcile the bank's balance with the correct cash balance. See *adjusted book balance of cash.*

adjusted basis. The *basis* used to compute gain or loss on the disposition of an *asset* for tax purposes. See also *book value.*

adjusted book balance of cash. The *balance* shown in the firm's account for cash in bank plus or minus amounts, such as for *notes* collected by the bank or bank service charges, to reconcile the account balance with the correct cash balance. See *adjusted bank balance of cash.*

adjusted trial balance. *Trial balance* taken after *adjusting entries* but before *closing entries.* Contrast with *pre-* and *post-closing trial balances.* See *unadjusted trial balance* and *post-closing trial balance.* See also *work sheet.*

adjusting entry. An entry made at the end of an *accounting period* to record a *transaction* or other *accounting event* that the firm has not yet recorded or has improperly recorded during the accounting period; an entry to update the accounts. See *work sheet.*

adjustment. An *account* change produced by an *adjusting entry.* Sometimes accountants use the term to refer to the process of restating *financial statement* amounts to *constant dollars.*

administrative costs (expenses). *Costs* (*expenses*) incurred for the firm as a whole, in contrast with specific functions such as manufacturing or selling; includes items such as salaries of top executives, general office rent, legal fees, and auditing fees.

admission of partner. Occurs when a new partner joins a *partnership.* Legally, the old partnership dissolves, and a new one comes into being. In practice, however, the firm may keep the old accounting records in use, and the accounting entries reflect the manner in which the new partner joined the firm. If the new partner merely purchases the interest of another partner, the accounting changes the name for one capital account. If the new partner contributes *assets* and *liabilities* to the partnership, then the firm must recognize them. See *bonus method.*

ADR. See *asset depreciation range.*

advances from (by) customers. A preferred title for the *liability* account representing *receipts* of *cash* in advance of delivering the *goods* or rendering the *service.* After the firm delivers the goods or services, it will recognize *revenue.* Some refer to this as "deferred revenue" or "deferred income," terms likely to confuse the unwary because the item is not yet *revenue* or *income.*

advances to affiliates. *Loans* by a parent company to a *subsidiary;* frequently combined with "investment in subsidiary" as "investments and advances to subsidiary" and shown as a *noncurrent asset* on the parent's *balance sheet.* The consolidation process eliminates these advances in *consolidated financial statements.*

advances to suppliers. A preferred term for the *asset* account representing *disbursements* of cash in advance of receiving *assets* or *services.*

adverse opinion. An *auditor's report* stating that the financial statements are not fair or are not in accord with *GAAP.*

affiliated company. A company controlling or controlled by another company.

after closing. Post-closing; a *trial balance* at the end of the period, whose balances are transferred to the financial statements.

after cost. *Expenditures* to be made after *revenue* recognition. For example, *expenditures* for *repairs* under warranty are after cost. Proper recognition of after cost involves a debit to expense at the time of the sale and a credit to an *estimated liability.* When the firm discharges the liability, it debits the estimated liability and credits the assets consumed.

AG (Aktiengesellschaft). Germany: the form of a German company whose shares can trade on the stock exchange.

agency cost. The *cost* to the *principal* caused by *agents* pursuing their own interests instead of the principal's interests. Includes both the costs incurred by principals to control agents' actions and the cost to the principals if agents pursue their own interests that are not in the interest of the principals.

agency fund. An account for *assets* received by governmental units in the capacity of trustee or agent.

agency theory. A branch of economics relating the behavior of *principals* (such as owner nonmanagers or bosses) and that of their *agents* (such as nonowner managers or subordinates). The principal assigns responsibility and authority to the agent, but the agent's own risks and preferences differ from those of the principal. The principal cannot observe all activities of the agent. Both the principal and the agent must consider the differing risks and preferences in designing incentive contracts.

agent. One authorized to transact business, including executing contracts, for another.

aging accounts receivable. The process of classifying *accounts receivable* by the time elapsed since the claim came into existence for the purpose of estimating the amount of uncollectible accounts receivable as of a given date. See *sales contra, estimated uncollectibles,* and *allowance for uncollectibles.*

aging schedule. A listing of *accounts receivable,* classified by age, used in *aging accounts receivable.*

AICPA (American Institute of Certified Public Accountants). The national organization that represents *CPAs.* See *AcSEC.* It oversees the writing and grading of the Uniform CPA Examination. Each state sets its own requirements for becoming a CPA in that state. See *certified public accountant*. Web Site: http://www.aicpa.org.

all-capital earnings rate. *Rate of return on assets.*

all-current method. *Foreign currency translation* in which all *financial statement* items are translated at the *current exchange rate.*

all-inclusive (income) concept. A concept that does not distinguish between *operating* and *nonoperating revenues* and *expenses*. Thus, the only entries to retained earnings are for *net income* and *dividends*. Under this concept, the *income statement* reports all *income, gains,* and *losses;* thus, net income includes events usually reported as *prior-period adjustments* and as *corrections of errors. GAAP* do not include this concept in its pure form, but *APB Opinions No. 9* and *No. 30* move far in this direction. They do permit retained earnings entries for prior-period adjustments and correction of errors.

allocate. To divide or spread a *cost* from one *account* into several accounts, to several products or activities, or to several periods.

allocation base. The systematic method that assigns *joint costs* to *cost objectives*. For example, a firm might assign the cost of a truck to periods based on miles driven during the period; the allocation base is miles. Or the firm might assign the cost of a factory supervisor to a product based on *direct labor* hours; the allocation base is direct labor hours.

allocation of income taxes. See *deferred income tax*.

allowance. A balance sheet *contra account* generally used for *receivables* and depreciable assets. See *sales* (or *purchase*) *allowance* for another use of this term.

allowance for funds used during construction. In accounting for public utilities, a *revenue* account *credited* for *implicit interest* earnings on *shareholders' equity* balances. One principle of public utility regulation and rate setting requires that customers should pay the full costs of producing the services (e.g., electricity) that they use, nothing more and nothing less. Thus, an electric utility must capitalize into an *asset* account the full costs, but no more, of producing a new electric power-generating plant. One of the costs of building a new plant is the *interest* cost on cash tied up during construction. If *funds* are explicitly borrowed by an ordinary business, the journal entry for interest of $1,000 is typically:

Interest Expense	1,000	
Interest Payable		1,000
Interest expense for the period.		

If the firm is constructing a new plant, then another entry would be made, capitalizing interest into the plant-under-construction account:

Construction Work-in-Progress	750	
Interest Expense		750
Capitalize relevant portion of interest relating to construction work in progress into the asset account.		

The cost of the *plant asset* increases; when the firm uses the plant, it charges *depreciation*. The interest will become an expense through the depreciation process in the later periods of use, not currently as the firm pays for interest. Thus, the firm reports the full cost of the electricity generated during a given period as expense in that period. But suppose, as is common, that the electric utility does not explicitly borrow the funds but uses some of its own funds, including funds raised from equity issues as well as from debt. Even though the firm incurs no explicit interest expense or other explicit expense for capital, the funds have an *opportunity cost*. Put another way, the plant under construction will not have lower economic cost just because the firm used its own cash rather than borrowing. The public utility using its own funds, on which it would have to pay $750 of interest if it had explicitly borrowed the funds, will make the following entry:

Construction Work-in-Progress	750	
Allowance for Funds Used during Construction		750
Recognition of interest, an opportunity cost, on own funds used.		

The allowance account is a form of *revenue*, to appear on the income statement, and the firm will close it to Retained Earnings, increasing it. On the *statement of cash flows* it is an income or revenue item not producing funds, and so the firm must subtract it from net income in deriving *cash provided by operations. SFAS No. 34* specifically prohibits nonutility companies from capitalizing, into plant under construction, the opportunity cost (interest) on their own funds used.

allowance for uncollectibles (accounts receivable). A *contra account* that shows the estimated *accounts receivable* amount that the firm expects not to collect. When the firm uses such an allowance, the actual write-off of specific accounts receivable (*debit* allowance, *credit* specific customer's account) does not affect *revenue* or *expense* at the time of the write-off. The firm reduces revenue when it debits *bad debt expense* (or, our preference, a revenue contra account) and credits the allowance. The firm can base the amount of the credit to the allowance on a percentage of sales on account for a period of time or compute it from *aging accounts receivable*. This contra account enables the firm to show an estimated receivables amount that it expects to collect without identifying specific uncollectible accounts. See *allowance method*.

allowance method. A method of attempting to match all *expenses* of a transaction with their associated *revenues;* usually involves a debit to expense and a credit to an *estimated liability*, such as for estimated warranty expenditures, or a debit to a revenue (*contra*) account and a credit to an asset (*contra*) account, such as in some firms' accounting for uncollectible accounts. See *allowance for uncollectibles* for further explanation. When the firm uses the allowance method for *sales discounts*, the firm records sales at gross invoice prices (not reduced by the amounts of discounts made available).

The firm *debits* an estimate of the amount of discounts to be taken to a revenue contra account and *credits* an allowance account, shown contra to *accounts receivable*.

American Accounting Association (AAA). An organization primarily for academic accountants but open to all interested in accounting. It publishes the *Accounting Review* and several other journals.

American Institute of Certified Public Accountants. See *AICPA*.

American Stock Exchange (AMEX) (ASE). A public market where various corporate *securities* are traded.

AMEX. *American Stock Exchange.*

amortization. Strictly speaking, the process of liquidating or extinguishing ("bringing to death") a *debt* with a series of payments to the *creditor* (or to a *sinking fund*). From that usage has evolved a related use involving the accounting for the payments themselves: "amortization schedule" for a mortgage, which is a table showing the allocation between *interest* and *principal*. The term has come to mean writing off ("liquidating") the cost of an asset. In this context it means the general process of *allocating* the *acquisition cost* of an asset either to the periods of benefit as an *expense* or to *inventory* accounts as a *product cost*. This is called *depreciation* for *plant assets*, *depletion* for *wasting assets* (natural resources), and "amortization" for *intangibles*. *SFAC No. 6* refers to amortization as "the accounting process of reducing an amount by periodic payments or write-downs." The expressions "unamortized debt discount or premium" and "to amortize debt discount or premium" relate to *accruals*, not to *deferrals*. The expressions "amortization of long-term assets" and "to amortize long-term assets" refer to deferrals, not accruals. Contrast with *accretion*.

amortized cost. A measure required by *SFAS No. 115* for *held-to-maturity securities*. This amount results from applying the method described at *effective interest method*. The firm records the security at its initial cost and computes the *effective interest rate* for the security. Whenever the firm receives cash from the issuer of the security or whenever the firm reaches the end of one of its own *accounting periods* (that is, reaches the time for its own *adjusting entries*), it takes the following steps. It multiplies the amount currently recorded on the books by the effective interest rate (which remains constant over the time the firm holds the security). It debits that amount to the debt security account and credits the amount to Interest Revenue. If the firm receives cash, it debits Cash and credits the debt security account. The firm recomputes the book value of the debt security as the book value before these entries plus the increase for the interest revenue less the decrease for the cash received. The resulting amount is the amortized cost for the end of that period.

analysis of variances. See *variance analysis*.

annual report. A report prepared once a year for shareholders and other interested parties. It includes a *balance sheet*, an *income statement*, a *statement of cash flows*, a reconciliation of changes in *owners' equity* accounts, a *summary of significant accounting principles*, other explanatory *notes*, the *auditor's report*, and comments from management about the year's events. See *10-K* and *financial statements*.

annuitant. One who receives an *annuity*.

annuity. A series of payments of equal amount, usually made at equally spaced time intervals.

annuity certain. An *annuity* payable for a definite number of periods. Contrast with *contingent annuity*.

annuity due. An *annuity* whose first payment occurs at the start of period 1 (or at the end of period 0). Contrast with *annuity in arrears*.

annuity in advance. An *annuity due*.

annuity in arrears. An *ordinary annuity* whose first payment occurs at the end of the first period.

annuity method of depreciation. See *compound interest depreciation*.

antidilutive. Said of a *potentially dilutive* security that will increase *earnings per share* if its holder *exercises* it or *converts* it into common stock. In computing *primary* and *fully diluted earnings per share*, the firm must assume that holders of antidilutive securities will not exercise their options or convert securities into common shares. The opposite assumption would lead to increased reported earnings per share in a given period.

APB. Accounting Principles Board of the *AICPA*. It set *accounting principles* from 1959 through 1973, issuing 31 *APB Opinions* and 4 *APB Statements*. The *FASB* superseded it.

APB Opinion. The name for the APB pronouncements that compose much of *generally accepted accounting principles;* the APB issued 31 APB Opinions from 1962 through 1973.

APB Statement. The *APB* issued four *APB Statements* between 1962 and 1970. The *Statements* were approved by at least two-thirds of the board, but they state recommendations, not requirements. For example, *Statement No. 3* (1969) suggested the publication of *constant-dollar* financial statements but did not require them.

APBs. An abbreviation used for *APB Opinions*.

applied cost. A *cost* that a firm has *allocated* to a department, product, or activity; not necessarily based on actual costs incurred.

applied overhead. *Overhead costs* charged to departments, products, or activities. Also called *absorbed overhead*.

appraisal. In valuing an *asset* or *liability*, a process that involves expert opinion rather than evaluation of explicit market transactions.

appraisal costs. *Costs* incurred to detect individual units of products that do not conform to specifications, including end-process sampling and field-testing. Also called *detection costs*.

appraisal method of depreciation. The periodic *depreciation* charge that equals the difference between the beginning-of-period and the end-of-period appraised values of the *asset* if that difference is positive. If negative, there is no charge. Not based on *historical cost*, this method is thus not generally accepted.

appreciation. An increase in economic value caused by rising market prices for an *asset*. Contrast with *accretion*.

appropriated retained earnings. See *retained earnings, appropriated*.

appropriation. In governmental accounting, an *expenditure* authorized for a specified amount, purpose, and time.

appropriation account. In governmental accounting, an account set up to record specific authorizations to spend. The governmental unit credits this account with appropriation amounts. At the end of the period, the unit closes to (debits) this account all *expenditures* during the period and all *encumbrances* outstanding at the end of the period.

approximate net realizable value method. A method of assigning joint costs to *joint products* based on revenues minus *additional processing costs* of the end products.

ARB. *Accounting Research Bulletin.*

arbitrage. Strictly speaking, the simultaneous purchase in one market and sale in another of a *security* or commodity in hope of making a *profit* on price differences in the different markets. Often writers use this term loosely when a trader sells an item that is somewhat different from the item purchased; for example, the sale of shares of common stock and the simultaneous purchase of a *convertible bond* that is convertible into identical common shares. The trader hopes that the market will soon see that the similarities of the items should make them have equal market values. When the market values converge, the trader closes the positions and profits from the original difference in prices, less trading costs.

arbitrary. Having no causation basis. Accounting theorists and practitioners often, properly, say, "Some cost allocations are arbitrary." In that sense, the accountant does not mean that the allocations are capricious or haphazard but does mean that theory suggests no unique solution to the allocation problem at hand. Accountants require that arbitrary allocations be systematic, rational, and consistently followed over time.

arm's length. A transaction negotiated by unrelated parties, both acting in their own self-interests; the basis for a *fair market value* estimation or computation.

arrears. *Cumulative dividends* that the firm has not yet declared. See *annuity in arrears* for another context.

ARS. *Accounting Research Study.*

articles of incorporation. Document filed with state authorities by persons forming a corporation. When the state returns the document with a certificate of incorporation, the document becomes the corporation's *charter.*

articulate. The relation between any operating statement (for example, *income statement* or *statement of cash flows*) and comparative balance sheets, where the operating statement explains (or reconciles) the change in some major balance sheet category (for example, *retained earnings* or *working capital*).

ASE. *American Stock Exchange.*

ASR. *Accounting Series Release.*

assess. To value property for the purpose of property taxation; to levy a charge on the owner of property for improvements thereto, such as for sewers or sidewalks. The taxing authority computes the assessment.

assessed valuation. For real estate or other property, a dollar amount that a government uses as a basis for levying taxes. The amount need not have some relation to *market value.*

asset. *SFAC No. 6* defines assets as "probable future economic benefits obtained or controlled by a particular entity as a result of past transactions. . . . An asset has three essential characteristics: (a) it embodies a probable future benefit that involves a capacity, singly or in combination with other assets, to contribute directly or indirectly to future net cash inflows, (b) a particular entity can obtain the benefit and control others' access to it, and (c) the transaction or other event giving rise to the entity's right to or control of the benefit has already occurred." A footnote points out that "probable" means that which we can reasonably expect or believe but that is not certain or proved. You may understand condition (c) better if you think of it as requiring that a future benefit cannot be an asset if it arises from an *executory contract,* a mere exchange of promises. Receiving a purchase order from a customer provides a future benefit, but it is an executory contract, so the order cannot be an asset. An asset may be *tangible* or *intangible,* short-term (current) or long-term (noncurrent).

asset depreciation range (ADR). The range of *depreciable lives* allowed by the *Internal Revenue Service* for a specific depreciable *asset.*

asset turnover. Net sales divided by average assets. See *ratio.*

assignment of accounts receivable. Transfer of the legal ownership of an account receivable through its sale. Contrast with *pledging* accounts receivable, where the receivables serve as *collateral* for a *loan.*

ATB. *Accounting Terminology Bulletin.*

at par. A *bond* or *preferred shares* issued (or selling) at *face amount.*

attachment. The laying claim to the *assets* of a borrower (or debtor) by a lender (or creditor) when the borrower has failed to pay debts on time.

attest. An auditor's rendering of an *opinion* that the *financial statements* are fair. Common usage calls this procedure the "attest function" of the CPA. See *fair presentation.*

attestor. Typically independent *CPAs,* who *audit financial statements* prepared by management for the benefit of users. The *FASB* describes accounting's constituency as comprising preparers, attestors, and users.

attribute measured. The particular *cost* reported in the balance sheet. When making physical measurements, such as of a person, one needs to decide the units with which to measure, such as inches or centimeters or pounds or grams. One chooses the attribute height or weight independently of the measuring unit, English or metric. Conventional accounting uses *historical cost* as the attribute measured and *nominal dollars* as the measuring unit. Some theorists argue that accounting would better serve readers if it used *current cost* as the attribute measured. Others argue that accounting would better serve readers if it used *constant dollars* as the measuring unit. Some, including us, think accounting should change both the measuring unit and the attribute measured. One can measure the attribute historical cost in nominal dollars or in constant dollars. One can also measure the attribute current cost in nominal dollars or constant dollars. Choosing between the two attributes and the two measuring units implies four different accounting systems. Each of these four has its uses.

attribute(s) sampling. The use of sampling technique in which the observer assesses each item selected on the basis of whether it has a particular qualitative characteristic in order to ascertain the rate of occurrence of this characteristic in the population. See also *estimation sampling.* Compare *variables sampling.* Example of attributes sampling: take a sample population of people, note the fraction that is male (say, 40 percent), and then infer that the entire population contains 40 percent males. Example of variables sampling: take a sample population of people, observe the weight of each sample point, compute the mean of those sampled people's weights (say, 160 pounds), and then infer that the mean weight of the entire population equals 160 pounds.

audit. Systematic inspection of accounting records involving analyses, tests, and *confirmations.* See *internal audit.*

audit committee. A committee of the board of directors of a *corporation,* usually comprising outside directors, who nominate the independent auditors and discuss the auditors' work with them. If the auditors believe the shareholders should know about certain matters, the auditors, in principle, first bring these matters to the attention of the audit committee; in practice, the auditors may notify management before they notify the audit committee.

Audit Guides. See *Industry Audit Guides.*

audit program. The procedures followed by the *auditor* in carrying out the *audit.*

audit trail. A reference accompanying an entry, or *post,* to an underlying source record or document. Efficiently checking the accuracy of accounting entries requires an audit trail. See *cross-reference.*

Auditing Research Monograph. Publication series of the *AICPA.*

auditing standards. Standards promulgated by the *PCAOB* for auditors to follow in carrying out their *attest* functions. The PCAOB began operations in earnest in 2003, and initially has said that it would use the standards originally promulgated by the *AICPA,* including general standards, standards of field work, and standards of reporting. According to the AICPA, these standards "deal with the measures of the quality of the performance and the objectives to be attained" rather than with specific auditing procedures. As time passes, the PCAOB will substitute its rules for those of the AICPA.

Auditing Standards Board. *AICPA* operating committee that promulgates auditing rules. The new operations of the *PCAOB,* after 2003, render uncertain what this Board will do.

auditor. Without a modifying adjective, usually refers to an external auditor—one who checks the accuracy, fairness, and general acceptability of accounting records and statements and then *attests* to them. See *internal auditor.*

auditor's opinion. *Auditor's report.*

auditor's report. The auditor's statement of the work done and an opinion of the *financial statements.* The auditor usually gives unqualified ("clean") opinions but may qualify them, or the auditor may disclaim an opinion in the report. Often called the "accountant's report." See *adverse opinion.*

AudSEC. The former Auditing Standards Executive Committee of the *AICPA,* now functioning as the *Auditing Standards Board.*

authorized capital stock. The number of *shares* of stock that a corporation can issue; specified by the *articles of incorporation.*

available for sale, securities. *Marketable securities* a firm holds that are classified as neither *trading securities* nor *held-to-maturity* (*debt*) *securities.* This classification is important in *SFAS No. 115,* which requires the owner to carry marketable equity securities on the balance sheet at market value, not at cost. Under *SFAS No. 115,* the income statement reports *holding gains and losses* on trading securities but not on securities available for sale. The required accounting *credits* (*debits*) holding gains (losses) on securities available for sale directly to an *owners' equity* account. On sale, the firm reports realized gain or loss as the difference between the selling price and the original cost, for trading securities, and as the difference between the selling price and the book value at the beginning of the period of sale, for securities available for sale and for debt securities held to maturity. By their nature, however, the firm will only rarely sell debt securities "held to maturity."

average. The arithmetic mean of a set of numbers; obtained by summing the items and dividing by the number of items.

average collection period of receivables. See *ratio.*

average-cost flow assumption. An inventory *flow assumption* in which the cost of units equals the *weighted average* cost of the *beginning inventory* and purchases. See *inventory equation.*

average tax rate. The rate found by dividing *income tax* expense by *net income* before taxes. Contrast with *marginal tax rate* and *statutory tax rate.*

avoidable cost. A *cost* that ceases if a firm discontinues an activity; an *incremental* or *variable cost.* See *programmed cost.*

B

backflush costing. A method of *allocating indirect costs* and *overhead;* used by companies that hope to have zero or small *work-in-process inventory* at the end of the period. The method *debits* all *product costs* to *cost of goods sold* (or *finished goods inventory*) during the period. To the extent that work in process actually exists at the end of the period, the method then debits work-in-process and *credits* cost of goods sold (or finished goods inventory). This method is "backflush" in the sense that costing systems ordinarily, but not in this case, allocate first to work-in-process and then forward to cost of goods sold or to finished goods. Here, the process allocates first to cost of goods sold (or finished goods) and then, later if necessary, to work-in-process.

backlog. Orders for which a firm has insufficient *inventory* on hand for current delivery and will fill in a later period.

backlog depreciation. In *current cost accounting,* a problem arising for the *accumulated depreciation* on *plant assets.* Consider an *asset* costing $10,000 with a 10-year life depreciated with the straight-line method. Assume that a similar asset has a current cost of $10,000 at the end of the first year but $12,000 at the end of the second year. Assume that the firm bases the depreciation charge on the average current cost during the year, $10,000 for the first year and $11,000 for the second. The depreciation charge for the first year is $1,000 and for the second is $1,100 (= .10 × $11,000), so the *accumulated depreciation account* is $2,100 after two years. Note that at the end of the second year, the firm has used 20 percent of the asset's future benefits, so the accounting records based on current costs must show a *net book value* of $9,600 (= .80 × $12,000), which results only if accumulated depreciation equals $2,400, so that book value equals $9,600 (= $12,000 − $2,400). But the sum of the depreciation charges equals only $2,100 (= $1,000 + $1,100). The *journal entry* to increase the accumulated depreciation account requires a *credit* to that account of $300. The backlog depreciation question arises: what account do we debit? Some theorists would *debit* an *income* account, and others would *debit* a *balance sheet owners' equity* account without reducing current-period earnings. The answer to the question of what to debit interrelates with how the firm records the *holding gains* on the asset. When the firm debits the asset account for $2,000 to increase the recorded amount from $10,000 to $12,000, it records a holding gain of $2,000 with a credit. Many theorists believe that whatever account the firm credits for the holding gain is the same account that the firm should debit for backlog depreciation. This is sometimes called "catch-up depreciation."

bad debt. An *uncollectible account;* see *bad debt expense* and *sales contra, estimated uncollectibles.*

bad debt expense. The name for an *account debited* in both the *allowance method* for *uncollectible accounts* and the *direct write-off method.* Under the allowance method, some prefer to treat the account as a revenue contra, not as an expense, and give it an account title such as Uncollectible Accounts Adjustment.

bad debt recovery. Collection, perhaps partial, of a specific account receivable previously written off as uncollectible. If a firm uses the *allowance method,* it will usually *credit* the *allowance* account, assuming that it has correctly assessed the amount of bad debts but has merely misjudged the identity of one of the nonpaying customers. If the firm decides that its charges for bad debts have been too large, it will credit the Bad Debt Expense account. If the firm uses the *direct write-off* method, it will credit a *revenue account.*

bailout period. In a *capital budgeting* context, the total time that elapses before accumulated cash inflows from a project, including the potential *salvage value* of assets at various times, equal or exceed the accumulated cash outflows. Contrast with *payback period,* which assumes completion of the project and uses terminal salvage value. Bailout, in contrast with payback, takes into account, at least to some degree, the *present value* of the cash flows after the termination date that the analyst is considering. The potential salvage value at any time includes some estimate of the flows that can occur after that time.

balance. As a noun, the opening balance in an *account* plus the amounts of increases less the amounts of decreases. (In the absence of a modifying adjective, the term means

closing balance, in contrast to opening balance. The closing balance for a period becomes the opening balance for the next period.) As a verb, "balance" means to find the value of the arithmetic expression described above.

balance sheet. Statement of financial position that shows Total *Assets* = Total *Liabilities* + *Owners' Equity.* The *balance sheet* usually classifies Total Assets as (1) *current assets,* (2) *investments,* (3) *property, plant, and equipment,* or (4) *intangible assets.* The balance sheet accounts composing Total Liabilities usually appear under the headings Current Liabilities and Long-term Liabilities.

balance sheet account. An account that can appear on a balance sheet; a *permanent account.* Contrast with *temporary account.*

balanced scorecard. A set of performance targets, not all expressed in dollar amounts, for setting an organization's goals for its individual employees or groups or divisions. A community relations employee might, for example, set targets in terms of number of employee hours devoted to local charitable purposes.

balloon. Most *mortgage* and *installment loans* require relatively equal periodic payments. Sometimes the loan requires relatively equal periodic payments with a large final payment. Usage calls the large final payment a "balloon" payment and the loan, a "balloon" loan. Although a coupon bond meets this definition, usage seldom, if ever, applies this term to bond loans.

bank balance. The amount of the balance in a checking account shown on the *bank statement.* Compare with *adjusted bank balance of cash,* and see *bank reconciliation schedule.*

bank prime rate. See *prime rate.*

bank reconciliation schedule. A schedule that explains the difference between the book balance of the cash in a bank account and the bank's statement of that amount; takes into account the amount of items such as checks that have not cleared or deposits that have not been recorded by the bank, as well as errors made by the bank or the firm.

bank statement. A statement sent by the bank to a checking account customer showing deposits, checks cleared, and service charges for a period, usually one month.

bankrupt. Occurs when a company's *liabilities* exceed its *assets* and the firm or one of its creditors has filed a legal petition that the bankruptcy court has accepted under the bankruptcy law. A bankrupt firm is usually, but need not be, *insolvent.*

base stock method. A method of inventory valuation that assumes that a firm must keep on hand at all times a minimum normal, or base, stock of goods for effective continuity of operations. The firm values this base quantity at *acquisition cost* of the inventory on hand in the earliest period when inventory was on hand. Firms may not use this method, either for financial reporting or for tax reporting, but most theorists consider it to be the forerunner of the *LIFO* cost flow assumption.

basic accounting equation. *Accounting equation.*

basic cost-flow equation. *Cost-flow equation.*

basic earnings per share (BEPS). *Net income* to *common shareholders,* divided by the weighted average number of common shares *outstanding* during the period. Required by *SFAS No. 128* and by *IASB*. See *primary earnings per share* (*PEPS*) for contrast. Because BEPS does not deal with *common-stock equivalents*, it will almost always give a larger earnings-per-share figure than PEPS.

basis. *Acquisition cost*, or some substitute therefor, of an *asset* or *liability* used in computing gain or loss on disposition or retirement; *attribute measured*. This term appears in both *financial* and *tax reporting*, but the basis of a given item need not be the same for both purposes.

basis point. One one-hundreth (=1/100). Terminology usually quotes *interest rates* in percentage terms, such as "5.60 percent" or "5.67 percent." The difference between those two interest rates is described as "7 basis points" or seven one-hundreths of one percent. Financial writers often extend this usage to other contexts involving decimals. For example, if the mean grade point average in the class is 3.25 and a given student scores 3.30, we might say that the student scored "5 basis points" above the class average.

basket purchase. Purchase of a group of *assets* (and *liabilities*) for a single price; the acquiring firm must assign *costs* to each item so that it can record the individual items with their separate amounts in the *accounts*.

batch-level activities. Work required to ready equipment or people for a production run.

bear. One who believes that security prices will fall. A "bear market" refers to a time when stock prices are generally declining. Contrast with *bull*.

bearer bond. See *registered bond* for contrast and definition.

beginning inventory. Valuation of *inventory* on hand at the beginning of the *accounting period;* equals *ending inventory* from the preceding period.

behavioral congruence. *Goal congruence*.

benchmarking. Process of measuring a firm's performance, products, and services against standards based on best levels of performance achievable or, sometimes, achieved by other firms.

benefit element (of stock options). The amount by which the *market value* of a *share* exceeds the *exercise price* of the *stock option*.

BEPS. *Basic earnings per share*.

betterment. An *improvement*, usually *capitalized*, not *expensed*.

bid. An offer to purchase, or the amount of the offer.

big bath. A *write-off* of a substantial amount of costs previously treated as *assets;* usually occurs when a corporation drops a business line that earlier required a large investment but that proved to be unprofitable. The term is sometimes used to describe a situation in which a corporation takes a large write-off in one period in order to free later periods of gradual write-offs of those amounts. In this sense it frequently occurs when the top management of the firm changes.

Big 4 (Big 4; Final 4). The four largest U.S. *public accounting* partnerships; in alphabetical order: Deloitte & Touche (U.S. national practice of the international firm Deloitte Touche Tohmatsu); Ernst & Young; KPMG Peat Marwick; and PricewaterhouseCoopers. See *Big N*.

Big N. The largest U.S. *public accounting* partnerships. When we first prepared this glossary, there were eight such partnerships, referred to as the "Big 8." See *Big 4.* The term "Big N" came into use when various of the *Big 8* proposed to merge with each other and the ultimate number of large partnerships was in doubt, which it still is.

bill. An *invoice* of charges and *terms of sale* for *goods* and *services;* also, a piece of currency.

bill of materials. A specification of the quantities of *direct materials* that a firm expects to use to produce a given job or quantity of output.

blocked currency. Currency that the holder, by law, cannot withdraw from the issuing country or exchange for the currency of another country.

board. *Board of directors*.

board of directors. The governing body of a corporation; elected by the shareholders.

bond. A certificate to show evidence of debt. The *par value* is the *principal* or face amount of the bond payable at maturity. The *coupon rate* is the amount of the yearly payments divided by the principal amount. Coupon bonds have attached coupons that the holder can redeem at stated dates. Increasingly, firms issue not coupon bonds but registered bonds; the firm or its agent keeps track of the owners of registered bonds. Normally, bonds call for semiannual payments.

bond conversion. The act of exchanging *convertible bonds* for *preferred* or *common shares*.

bond discount. From the standpoint of the issuer of a *bond* at the issue date, the excess of the *par value* of a bond over its initial sales price and, at later dates, the excess of par over the sum of the following two amounts: initial issue price and the portion of discount already *amortized;* from the standpoint of a bondholder, the difference between par value and selling price when the bond sells below par.

bond indenture. The contract between an issuer of *bonds* and the bondholders.

bond premium. Exactly parallel to *bond discount* except that the issue price (or current selling price) exceeds *par value*.

bond ratings. Corporate and *municipal bond* issue ratings, based on the issuer's existing *debt* level, its previous record of payment, the *coupon rate* on the bonds, and the safety of the *assets* or *revenues* that are committed to paying off *principal* and *interest*. Moody's Investors Service and Standard & Poor's Corporation publish bond ratings: Moody's top rating is Aaa; Standard & Poor's is AAA.

bond redemption. Retirement of *bonds*.

bond refunding. To incur *debt*, usually through the issue of new *bonds*, intending to use the proceeds to retire an *outstanding* bond issue.

bond sinking fund. See *sinking fund*.

bond table. A table showing the current price of a *bond* as a function of the *coupon rate,* current (remaining) term *maturity,* and effective *yield to maturity* (or *effective rate*).

bonus. Premium over normal *wage* or *salary,* paid usually for meritorious performance.

bonus method. One of two methods to recognize an excess, say $10,000, when a *partnership* admits a new partner and when the new partner's capital account is to show an amount larger than the amount of *tangible* assets that he

(a) Cost-Volume-Profit Graph

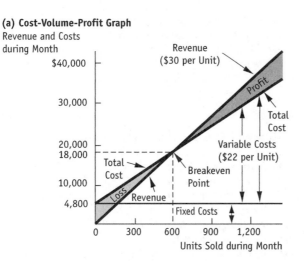

(b) Profit-Volume Graph

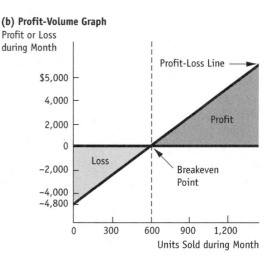

or she contributes. First, the old partners may transfer $10,000 from themselves to the new partner. This is the bonus method. Second, the partnership may recognize goodwill in the amount of $10,000, with the credit to the new partner's capital account. This is the *goodwill method*. (Notice that the new partner's percentage of total ownership differs under the two methods.) If the new partner's capital account is to show an amount smaller than the tangible assets that he or she contributed, then the old partners will receive bonus or goodwill, depending on the method.

book. As a verb, to record a transaction; as a noun, usually plural, the *journals* and *ledgers;* as an adjective, see *book value.*

book cost. *Book value.*

book inventory. An *inventory* amount that results not from physical count but from the amount of beginning inventory plus *invoice* amounts of net purchases less invoice amounts of *requisitions* or withdrawals; implies a *perpetual inventory* method.

book of original entry. *Journal.*

book value. The amount shown in the books or in the *accounts* for an *asset, liability,* or *owners' equity* item. The term is generally used to refer to the *net* amount of an *asset* or group of assets shown in the account that records the asset and reductions, such as for *amortization,* in its cost. Of a firm, it refers to the excess of total assets over total liabilities; *net assets.*

book value per share of common stock. Common *shareholders' equity* divided by the number of shares of common stock outstanding. See *ratio.*

bookkeeping. The process of analyzing and recording transactions in the accounting records.

boot. The additional cash paid (or received) along with a used item in a trade-in or *exchange* transaction for another item. See *trade-in.*

borrower. See *loan.*

bottleneck. An operation in which the work to be performed equals or exceeds the available capacity, thus holding up further operations.

branch. A sales office or other unit of an enterprise physically separated from the home office of the enterprise but

not organized as a legally separate *subsidiary.* Writers seldom use this term to refer to manufacturing units.

branch accounting. An accounting procedure that enables the firm to report the financial position and operations of each *branch* separately but later combine them for published statements.

break-even analysis. See *break-even chart.*

break-even chart. Two kinds of break-even charts appear here. The charts use the following information for one month. Revenue is $30 per unit.

Cost Classification	Variable Cost, Per Unit	Fixed Cost, Per Month
Manufacturing costs:		
Direct material	$ 4	—
Direct labor	9	—
Overhead	4	$3,060
Total manufacturing costs	$17	$3,060
Selling, general, and administrative costs	5	1,740
Total costs	$22	$4,800

The cost-volume-profit graph presents the relation between changes in volume to the amount of *profit,* or *income.* Such a graph shows total *revenue* and total *costs* for each volume level, and the user reads profit or loss at any volume directly from the chart. The profit-volume graph does not show revenues and costs but more readily indicates profit (or loss) at various output levels. Keep in mind two caveats about these graphs:

1. Although the curve depicting *variable cost* and total cost appears as a straight line for its entire length, at low or high levels of output, variable cost will probably differ from $22 per unit. The variable cost figure usually results from studies of operations at some broad central area of production, called the *relevant range.* The chart will not usually provide accurate results for low (or high) levels of activity. For this reason, the total cost and the profit-loss curves sometimes appear as dotted lines at lower (or higher) volume levels.

2. This chart, simplistically, assumes a single-product firm. For a multiproduct firm, the horizontal axis would have to be stated in dollars rather than in physical units of output. Break-even charts for multiproduct firms necessarily assume that the firm sells constant proportions of the several products, so that changes in this mixture, as well as in costs or selling prices, invalidate such a chart.

break-even point. The volume of sales required so that total *revenues* equals total *costs;* may be expressed in units (*fixed costs ÷ contribution per unit*) or in sales dollars [selling price per unit × (fixed costs ÷ contribution per unit)].

break-even time. Time required before the firm recovers the amounts it invested in developing a new product.

budget. A financial plan that a firm uses to estimate the results of future operations; frequently used to help control future operations. In governmental operations, budgets often become the law. See *standard costs* for further elaboration and contrast.

budgetary accounts. In governmental accounting, the accounts that reflect estimated operations and financial condition, as affected by estimated *revenues, appropriations,* and *encumbrances.* Contrast with *proprietary accounts,* which record the transactions.

budgetary control. Management of governmental (nongovernmental) unit in accordance with an official (approved) *budget* in order to keep total expenditures within authorized (planned) limits.

budgeted cost. See *standard costs* for definition and contrast.

budgeted statements. *Pro forma statements* prepared before the event or period occurs.

bull. One who believes that security prices will rise. A "bull market" refers to a time when stock prices are generally rising. Contrast with *bear.*

burden. See *overhead costs.*

burn rate. A new business usually begins life with cash-absorbing operating losses but with a limited amount of cash. The "burn rate" measures how long the new business can survive before operating losses must stop or the firm must receive a new infusion of cash. Writers usually express the burn rate in months.

business combination. As defined in *APB Opinion No. 16,* the bringing together into a single accounting *entity* of two or more incorporated or unincorporated businesses. The new entity will account for the *merger* either with the *purchase method* or the *pooling-of-interests method.* See *conglomerate.*

business entity. *Entity; accounting entity.*

BV (*besloten vennootschap*). Netherlands: a private limited-liability company.

bylaws. The rules adopted by the shareholders of a corporation; specify the general methods for carrying out the functions of the corporation.

by-product. A *joint product* whose sales value is so small relative to the sales value of the other joint product(s) that it does not receive normal accounting treatment. The costs assigned to by-products reduce the costs of the main prod-

uct(s). Accounting allocates by-products a share of joint costs such that the expected gain or loss at their sale is zero. Thus, by-products appear in the *accounts* at *net realizable value.*

C

C corporation. In tax terminology, a corporation paying its own income taxes. Contrast with *S corporation.*

CA. *Chartered accountant.*

call. An option to buy *shares* of a publicly traded corporation at a fixed price during a fixed time span. Contrast with *put.*

call premium. See *callable bond.*

call price. See *callable bond.*

callable bond. A *bond* for which the issuer reserves the right to pay a specific amount, the call price, to retire the obligation before its *maturity* date. If the issuer agrees to pay more than the *face amount* of the bond when called, the excess of the payment over the face amount is the "call premium."

called-up share capital. UK: *common stock* at *par value.*

Canadian Institute of Chartered Accountants. The national organization that represents *chartered accountants* in Canada. Web Site: http://www.cica.ca.

cancelable lease. See *lease.*

CAP. *Committee on Accounting Procedure.*

capacity. Stated in units of product, the amount that a firm can produce per unit of time; stated in units of input, such as *direct labor* hours, the amount of input that a firm can use in production per unit of time. A firm uses this measure of output or input in allocating *fixed costs* if the amounts producible are normal, rather than maximum, amounts.

capacity cost. A *fixed cost* incurred to provide a firm with the capacity to produce or to sell. Consists of *standby costs* and *enabling costs.* Contrast with *programmed costs.*

capacity variance. *Production volume variance.*

capital. *Owners' equity* in a business; often used, equally correctly, to mean the total assets of a business; sometimes used to mean *capital assets.* Sometimes used to mean *funds* raised. This word causes confusion in accounting and finance. Uninformed users mix up the funds (and their uses) with the sources of the funds. Consider the following transactions. A firm raises $100 cash from investors and uses the $100 to acquire *inventory* and *plant assets.* Did the investors "invest capital" of $100 or did the firm "invest capital" of $100? You will hear "invest capital" used for both sides of that transaction. Now focus on the firm that issued the shares and received the cash. Some would say the first transaction, the issue of shares, "raised capital." (If you ask of a person who answers this way, "What is the *capital,* the increase in owners' equity or the increased cash?" you will not get a clear answer, consistent across all such people.) Others would say only the second transaction, spending the cash, raised capital and only then for the plant assets, not the inventory. When a regulator focuses on a bank's capital ratios, it looks to the right-hand side of the balance sheet, not to how the firm has invested its funds. Sometimes bank regulators will take the owners' equity total and subtract from that amount the amount of intangible assets, resulting in a total with no clear conception, which they call "tangible capital." See *cost of capital* for further discussion of the confusion between the cost of raising funds and the return to, or *opportunity cost* of, investing funds. The confusion is so prevalent that we tend to avoid using the word.

capital asset. Properly used, a designation, for income tax purposes, that describes property held by a taxpayer except *cash,* inventoriable *assets,* goods held primarily for sale, most depreciable property, *real estate, receivables,* certain *intangibles,* and a few other items. Sometimes writers use this term imprecisely to describe *plant* and *equipment,* which are clearly not capital assets under the income-tax definition. Writers often use the term to refer to an *investment* in *securities.*

capital budget. Plan of proposed outlays for acquiring long-term *assets* and the means of *financing* the acquisition.

capital budgeting. The process of choosing *investment* projects for an enterprise by considering the *present value* of cash flows and deciding how to raise the funds the investment requires.

capital consumption allowance. The term used for *depreciation expense* in national income accounting and the reporting of funds in the economy.

capital contributed in excess of par (or stated) value. A preferred title for the account that shows the amount received by the issuer for *capital stock* in excess of *par (or stated)* value.

capital expenditure (outlay). An *expenditure* to acquire long-term *assets.*

capital gain. The excess of proceeds over *cost,* or other *basis,* from the sale of a *capital asset* as defined by the Internal Revenue Code. If the taxpayer has held the capital asset for a sufficiently long time before sale, then the gain is taxed at a rate lower than that used for other gains and ordinary income.

capital lease. A *lease* treated by the *lessee* as both the borrowing of funds and the acquisition of an *asset* to be *amortized.* The lessee (tenant) recognizes both the *liability* and the asset on its balance sheet. Expenses consist of *interest* on the *debt* and *amortization* of the asset. The *lessor* (landlord) treats the lease as the sale of the asset in return for a series of future cash receipts. Contrast with *operating lease.*

capital loss. A negative capital gain; see *capital gain.*

capital rationing. In a *capital budgeting* context, the imposition of constraints on the amounts of total capital expenditures in each period.

capital stock. The ownership shares of a corporation. Consists of all classes of *common* and *preferred shares.*

capital structure. The composition of a corporation's equities; the relative proportions of short-term debt, long-term debt, and *owners' equity.*

capital surplus. An inferior term for *capital contributed in excess of par (or stated) value.*

capitalization of a corporation. A term used by investment analysts to indicate *shareholders' equity* plus bonds outstanding.

capitalization of earnings. The process of estimating the *fair value* of a firm by computing the *net present value* of the predicted *net income* (not *cash flows*) of the firm for the future.

capitalization rate. An *interest rate* used to convert a series of payments or receipts or earnings into a single *present value.*

capitalize. To record an *expenditure* that may benefit a future period as an *asset* rather than to treat the expenditure as an *expense* of the period of its occurrence. Whether expenditures for advertising or for research and development should be capitalized is controversial, but *SFAS No. 2* forbids capitalizing *R&D* costs. We believe GAAP should allow firms to capitalize expenditures when they lead to future benefits and thus meet the criterion to be an asset.

carryback, carryforward, carryover. The use of losses or tax credits in one period to reduce income taxes payable in other periods. Two common kinds of carrybacks exist: for net operating losses and for *capital losses.* They apply against taxable income. In general, carrybacks are for three years, with the earliest year first. The taxpayer can carry forward operating losses for fifteen years. Corporate capital loss carryforwards are for five years. Individuals can carry forward capital losses indefinitely.

carrying cost. Costs (such as property taxes and insurance) of holding, or storing, *inventory* from the time of purchase until the time of sale or use.

carrying value (amount). *Book value.*

CASB (Cost Accounting Standards Board). A board authorized by the U.S. Congress to "promulgate cost-accounting standards designed to achieve uniformity and consistency in the cost-accounting principles followed by defense contractors and subcontractors under federal contracts." The *principles* the CASB promulgated since 1970 have considerable weight in practice wherever the *FASB* has not established a standard. Congress allowed the CASB to go out of existence in 1980 but reinstated it in 1990.

cash. Currency and coins, negotiable checks, and balances in bank accounts. For the *statement of cash flows,* "cash" also includes *marketable securities* held as *current assets.*

cash basis of accounting. In contrast to the *accrual basis of accounting,* a system of accounting in which a firm recognizes *revenues* when it receives *cash* and recognizes *expenses* as it makes *disbursements.* The firm makes no attempt to match *revenues* and *expenses* in measuring *income.* See *modified cash basis.*

cash budget. A schedule of expected cash *receipts* and *disbursements.*

cash change equation. For any *period,* the change in *cash* equals the change in *liabilities* plus the change in *owners' equity* minus the change in noncash *assets.*

cash collection basis. The *installment method* for recognizing *revenue.* Do not confuse with the *cash basis of accounting.*

cash conversion cycle. *Cash cycle.*

cash cycle. The period of time during which a firm converts *cash* into *inventories,* inventories into *accounts receivable,* and *receivables* back into cash. Sometimes called *earnings cycle.*

cash disbursements journal. A specialized *journal* used to record *expenditures* by *cash* and by *check*. If a *check register* is also used, a cash disbursements journal records only expenditures of currency and coins.

cash discount. A sales or purchase price reduction allowed for prompt payment.

cash dividend. See *dividend.*

cash equivalent. According to *SFAS No. 95,* "short-term, highly liquid investments that are both readily convertible to known amounts of cash [and] so near their maturity that they present insignificant risk of changes in value because of changes in interest rates. . . . Examples of items commonly considered to be cash equivalents are Treasury bills, commercial paper, [and] money market funds."

cash equivalent value. A term used to describe the amount for which an *asset* could be sold. Sometimes called *market value* or *fair market price (value).*

cash flow. Cash *receipts* minus *disbursements* from a given *asset,* or group of assets, for a given period. Financial analysts sometimes use this term to mean *net income + depreciation + depletion + amortization.* See also *operating cash flow* and *free cash flow.*

cash flow from operations. Receipts from customers and from investments less expenditures for inventory, labor, and services used in the usual activities of the firm, less interest expenditures. See *statement of cash flows* and *operations.* Same as *cash provided by operations.*

cash-flow hedge. A hedge of an exposure to variability in the cash flows of a recognized *asset* or *liability* or of a forecasted transaction, such as expected future foreign sales.

cash flow statement. *Statement of cash flows.*

cash provided by operations. An important subtotal in the *statement of cash flows.* This amount equals the total of revenues producing *cash* less *expenses* requiring cash. Often, the amount appears as *net income* plus expenses not requiring cash (such as depreciation charges) minus revenues not producing cash (such as revenues recognized under the *equity method* of accounting for a long-term investment). The statement of cash flows maintains the same distinctions between *continuing operations, discontinued operations,* and *income* or *loss* from *extraordinary items* as does the *income statement.*

cash receipts journal. A specialized *journal* used to record all *receipts* of *cash.*

cash (surrender) value of life insurance. An amount equal not to the face value of the policy to be paid in the event of death but to the amount that the owner could realize by immediately canceling the policy and returning it to the insurance company for cash. A firm owning a life insurance policy reports it as an asset at an amount equal to this value.

cash yield. See *yield.*

cashier's check. A bank's own *check* drawn on itself and signed by the cashier or other authorized official. It is a direct obligation of the bank. Compare with *certified check.*

catch-up depreciation. *Backlog depreciation.*

cause-and-effect analysis. An identification of potential causes of defects and taking actions to cure the problems found. To use this analysis, first define the effect and then identify the causes of the problem. The potential causes fall into four categories: human factors, methods and design factors, machine-related factors, and materials or components factors. As management identifies the prevailing causes, it develops and implements corrective measures.

CCA. *Current cost accounting; current value accounting.*

central corporate expenses. General *overhead expenses* incurred in running the corporate headquarters and related supporting activities of a corporation. Accounting treats these expenses as *period expenses.* Contrast with *manufacturing overhead. Line of business reporting* must decide how to treat these expenses—whether to allocate them to the individual segments and, if so, how to allocate them.

central processing unit (CPU). The computer system component that carries out the arithmetic, logic, and data transfer.

certificate. The document that is the physical embodiment of a *bond* or a *share of stock;* a term sometimes used for the *auditor's report.*

certificate of deposit. A form of *deposit* in a bank or thrift institution. Federal law constrains the rate of interest that banks can pay to their depositors. Current law allows banks to pay a rate higher than the one allowed on a *time deposit* if the depositor promises to leave funds on deposit for several months or more. When the bank receives such funds, it issues a certificate of deposit. The depositor can withdraw the funds before maturity by paying a penalty.

certified check. The *check* of a depositor drawn on a bank. The bank inserts the words "accepted" or "certified" on the face of the check, with the date and a signature of a bank official. The check then becomes an obligation of the bank. Compare with *cashier's check.*

certified financial statement. A financial statement attested to by an independent *auditor* who is a *CPA.*

certified internal auditor. See *CIA.*

certified management accountant. *CMA.*

certified public accountant (CPA). An accountant who has satisfied the statutory and administrative requirements of his or her jurisdiction to be registered or licensed as a public accountant. In addition to passing the Uniform CPA Examination administered by the *AICPA,* the CPA must meet certain educational, experience, and moral requirements that differ from jurisdiction to jurisdiction. The jurisdictions are the 50 states, the District of Columbia, Guam, Puerto Rico, and the Virgin Islands.

CGA (Certified General Accountant). Canada: an accountant who has satisfied the experience, education, and examination requirements of the Certified General Accountants' Association.

chain discount. A series of *discount* percentages. For example, if a chain discount of 10 and 5 percent is quoted, then the actual, or *invoice,* price is the nominal, or list, price times .90 times .95, or 85.5, percent of invoice price.

change fund. Coins and currency issued to cashiers, delivery drivers, and so on.

changes, accounting. See *accounting changes.*

changes in financial position. See *statement of cash flows.*

charge. As a noun, a *debit* to an account; as a verb, to debit.

charge off. To treat as a *loss* or *expense* an amount originally recorded as an *asset;* use of this term implies that the charge is not in accord with original expectations.

chart of accounts. A list of names and numbers, systematically organized, of *accounts.*

charter. Document issued by a state government authorizing the creation of a corporation.

chartered accountant(s) (CA). The title used in Australia, Canada, and Scotland for an accountant who has satisfied the requirements of the institute of his or her jurisdiction to be qualified to serve as a *public accountant.* In the UK other than Scotland, members use the initials ACA or FCA: *A* means Associate and *F* means Fellow; the Associate has less experience than does the Fellow. A partnership of chartered accountants signs its firm name with the letters *CA.* In Canada, each provincial institute or order has the right to administer the examination and set the standards of performance and ethics for Chartered Accountants in its province. For a number of years, however, the provincial organizations have pooled their rights to qualify new members through the Inter-provincial Education Committee, and the result is that there are nationally set and graded examinations given in English and French. Deviation from the pass/fail grade awarded by the Board of Examiners (a subcommittee of the Inter-provincial Education Committee) is rare.

check. The Federal Reserve Board defines a check as "a *draft* or order upon a bank or banking house purporting to be drawn upon a deposit of funds for the payment at all events of a certain sum of money to a certain person therein named or to him or his order or to bearer and payable instantly on demand." It must contain the phrase "pay to the order of." The amount shown on the check must be clearly readable, and the check must have the signature of the drawer. The drawer need not date the check. In the accounts, the drawer usually reduces the *balance* in the *cash account* when it issues the check, not later when the check clears the bank. See *remittance advice.*

check register. A *journal* to record *checks* issued.

CIA (Certified Internal Auditor). One who has satisfied certain requirements of the *Institute of Internal Auditors* including experience, ethics, education, and passing examinations.

CICA. *Canadian Institute of Chartered Accountants.*

CIF (cost, insurance, and freight). In contracts, a term used along with the name of a given port, such as New Orleans, to indicate that the quoted price includes insurance, handling, and freight charges up to delivery by the seller at the given port.

circulating capital. *Working capital.*

clean opinion. See *auditor's report.*

clean surplus concept. The notion that all entries to the *retained earnings* account must record *net income* and *dividends.* See *comprehensive income.* Contrast with *current operating performance concept.* This concept, with minor exceptions, now controls *GAAP.* (See *APB Opinions No. 9* and *No. 30.*)

clearing account. An account containing amounts to be transferred to another account(s) before the end of the *accounting period.* Examples are the *income summary* account (whose balance transfers to *retained earnings*) and the purchases account (whose balance transfers to *inventory* or to *cost of goods sold*).

close. As a verb, to transfer the *balance* of a *temporary* or *contra* or *adjunct account* to the main account to which it relates; for example, to transfer *revenue* and *expense* accounts directly, or through the *income summary* account, to an *owners' equity* account or to transfer *purchase discounts* to purchases.

closed account. An *account* with equal *debits* and *credits,* usually as a result of a *closing entry.* See *ruling an account.*

closing entries; closing process. The *entries* that accomplish the transfer of balances in *temporary accounts* to the related *balance sheet accounts.* See *work sheet.*

closing inventory. *Ending inventory.*

CMA (Certified Management Accountant) certificate. Awarded by the *Institute of Certified Management Accountants* of the *Institute of Management Accountants* to those who pass a set of examinations and meet certain experience and continuing-education requirements.

CoCoA. *Continuously Contemporary Accounting.*

coding of accounts. The numbering of *accounts,* as for a *chart of accounts,* that is necessary for computerized accounting.

coinsurance. Common condition of insurance policies that protect against hazards such as fire or water damage. These often specify that the owner of the property may not collect the full amount of insurance for a loss unless the insurance policy covers at least some specified "coinsurance" percentage, usually about 80 percent, of the *replacement cost* of the property. Coinsurance clauses induce the owner to carry full, or nearly full, coverage.

COLA. Cost-of-living adjustment. See *indexation.*

collateral. *Assets* pledged by a *borrower* who will surrender those assets if he or she fails to repay a *loan.*

collectible. Capable of being converted into *cash*—now if due, later otherwise.

collusion. Cooperative effort by employees to commit fraud or another unethical act.

combination. See *business combination.*

comfort letter. A letter in which an auditor conveys negative assurances as to unaudited financial statements in a prospectus or draft financial statements included in a preliminary prospectus.

commercial paper. Short-term notes issued by corporate borrowers.

commission. Employee remuneration, usually expressed as a percentage, based on an activity rate, such as sales.

committed costs. *Capacity costs.*

Committee on Accounting Procedure (CAP). Predecessor of the *APB.* The *AICPA*'s principles-promulgating body from 1939 through 1959. Its 51 pronouncements are *Accounting Research Bulletins.*

common cost. *Cost* resulting from the use of *raw materials,* a facility (for example, plant or machines), or a service (for example, fire insurance) that benefits several products or departments. A firm must allocate this cost to those products or departments. Common costs result when two or more departments produce multiple products together even though the departments could produce them separately; *joint costs* occur when two or more departments must produce multiple products together. Many writers use "common costs" and "joint costs" synonymously. See *joint cost, indirect costs, overhead,* and *sterilized allocation.*

common-dollar accounting. *Constant-dollar accounting.*

common monetary measuring unit. For U.S. corporations, the dollar. See also *stable monetary unit assumption* and *constant-dollar accounting.*

common shares. *Shares* representing the class of owners who have residual claims on the *assets* and *earnings* of a *corporation* after the firm meets all *debt* and *preferred shareholders'* claims.

common-size statement. A *percentage statement* usually based on total *assets* or *net sales* or *revenues.*

common-stock equivalent. A *security* whose primary value arises from its holder's ability to exchange it for *common shares;* includes *stock options, warrants,* and also *convertible bonds* or *convertible preferred stock* whose *effective interest rate* at the time of issue is less than two-thirds the average Aa corporate bond yield. See *bond ratings.*

companywide control. See *control system.*

comparative (financial) statements. *Financial statements* showing information for the same company for different times, usually two successive years for balance sheets and three for *income* and *cash flow statements.* Nearly all published financial statements are in this form. Contrast with *historical summary.*

compensating balance. The amount required to be left on deposit for a loan. When a bank lends funds to customers, it often requires that the customers keep on deposit in their checking accounts an amount equal to some percentage—say, 20 percent—of the loan. Such amounts effectively increase the *interest rate.* The borrower must disclose the amounts of such balances in *notes* to the *financial statements.*

completed contract method. Recognizing *revenues* and *expenses* for a job or order only when the firm finishes it, except that when the firm expects a loss on the contract, the firm must recognize all revenues and expenses in the period when the firm first foresees a loss. Accountants generally use this term only for long-term contracts. This method is otherwise equivalent to the *sales basis of revenue recognition.*

completed sales basis. See *sales basis of revenue recognition.*

compliance audit. Objectively obtaining and evaluating evidence regarding assertions, actions, and events to ascertain the degree of correspondence between them and established performance criteria.

compliance procedure. An *audit* procedure used to gain evidence as to whether the prescribed internal controls are operating effectively.

composite cost of capital. See *cost of capital.*

composite depreciation or **composite life method.** *Group depreciation* when the items are of unlike kind. The term also applies when the firm depreciates as a whole a single item (for example, a crane, which consists of separate units with differing service lives, such as the chassis, the motor, the lifting mechanism, and so on), rather than treating each of its components separately.

compound entry. A *journal entry* with more than one *debit* or more than one *credit* or both. See *trade-in transaction* for an example.

compound interest. *Interest* calculated on *principal* plus previously undistributed interest.

compound interest depreciation. A method designed to hold the *rate of return* on an asset constant. First find the *internal rate of return* on the cash inflows and outflows of the asset. The periodic depreciation charge equals the cash flow for the period less the internal rate of return multiplied by the asset's book value at the beginning of the period. When the cash flows from the asset are constant over time, usage sometimes refers to the method as the "annuity method" of depreciation.

compounding period. The time period, usually a year or a portion of a year, for which a firm calculates *interest.* At the end of the period, the borrower may pay interest to the lender or may add the interest (that is, convert it) to the principal for the next interest-earning period.

comprehensive budget. *Master budget.*

comprehensive income. Defined in *SFAC No. 3* as "the change in equity (net assets) of an entity during a period from transactions and other events and circumstances from nonowner sources. It includes all changes in equity during a period except those resulting from investments by owners and distributions to owners." In this definition, "equity" means *owners' equity* or *shareholders' equity. SFAS No. 130* requires firms to report comprehensive income as part of a statement showing *earnings* (primarily from realized transactions), comprehensive income (with additions for all other changes in owners' equity, primarily *holding gains and losses* and *foreign exchange gains and losses*), and comprehensive income plus *accounting adjustments.* The *FASB* encourages the discontinuation of the term "net income." The terms "earnings" and "comprehensive income" denote different concepts, with totals different from that of the old "net income." *SFAS No. 130* requires that the firm report comprehensive income in a format having the same prominence as other *financial statements.* We cannot predict which "income total"— earnings or comprehensive income—users of financial statements will focus on.

comptroller. Same meaning and pronunciation as *controller.*

conceptual framework. A coherent system of interrelated objectives and fundamentals, promulgated by the *FASB* primarily through its *SFAC* publications, expected to lead to consistent standards for *financial accounting* and reporting.

confidence level. The measure of probability that the actual characteristics of the population lie within the stated precision of the estimate derived from a sampling process. A sample estimate may be expressed in the following terms: "Based on the sample, we are 95 percent sure [confidence level] that the true population value is within the range of X to Y [precision]." See *precision.*

confirmation. A formal memorandum delivered by the customers or suppliers of a company to its independent *auditor* verifying the amounts shown as receivable or payable. The auditor originally sends the confirmation document to the customer. If the auditor asks that the customer return the document whether the *balance* is correct or incorrect, usage calls it a "positive confirmation." If the auditor asks that the customer return the document only if it contains an error, usage calls it a "negative confirmation."

conglomerate. *Holding company.* This term implies that the owned companies operate in dissimilar lines of business.

conservatism. A *reporting objective* that calls for anticipation of all *losses* and *expenses* but defers recognition of *gains* or *profits* until they are *realized* in *arm's-length* transactions. In the absence of certainty, report events to minimize cumulative income. Conservatism does not mean reporting low income in every *accounting period.* Over long-enough time spans, income is cash-in less cash-out. If a (conservative) reporting method shows low income in early periods, it must show higher income in some later period.

consignee. See *on consignment.*

consignment. See *on consignment.*

consignor. See *on consignment.*

consistency. Treatment of like *transactions* in the same way in consecutive periods so that financial statements will be more comparable than otherwise; the reporting policy implying that a reporting *entity,* once it adopts specified procedures, should follow them from period to period. See *accounting changes* for the treatment of inconsistencies.

consol. A *bond* that never matures; a *perpetuity* in the form of a bond; originally issued by Great Britain after the Napoleonic wars to consolidate debt issues of that period. The term arose as an abbreviation for "consolidated annuities."

consolidated financial statements. Statements that are issued by legally separate companies and that show financial position and income as they would appear if the companies were one economic *entity.*

constant dollar. A hypothetical unit of *general purchasing power,* denoted "C$" by the *FASB.*

constant-dollar accounting. Accounting that measures items in *constant dollars.* See *historical cost/constant-dollar accounting* and *current cost/nominal-dollar accounting.* Sometimes called "general price level–adjusted accounting" or "general purchasing-power accounting."

constant-dollar date. The time at which the *general purchasing power* of one *constant dollar* exactly equals the *general purchasing power* of one *nominal dollar;* that is, the date when C$1 = $1. When the constant-dollar date is midperiod, the nominal amounts of *revenues* and *expenses* spread evenly throughout the period equal their constant-dollar amounts but end-of-period *balance sheet* amounts measured in constant midperiod dollars differ from their nominal-dollar amounts. When the constant-dollar date is at the end of the period, the constant-dollar amounts equal the nominal-dollar amounts on a balance sheet for that date.

constrained share company. Canada: a public company whose *charter* specifies that people who are Canadian citizens or who are corporations resident in Canada must own a prescribed percentage of the shares.

constructive liability. *FASB*'s term for an item recorded as an accounting *liability,* which the firm has no obligation to pay but intends to pay. An example is the liability with

related *expense* that management establishes for future cash payments for severance payments for employees it intends to discharge in a restructuring.

constructive receipt. An item included in taxable income when the taxpayer can control funds whether or not it has received cash. For example, *interest* added to *principal* in a savings account is constructively received.

Consumer Price Index (CPI). A *price index* computed and issued monthly by the Bureau of Labor Statistics of the U.S. Department of Labor. The index attempts to track the price level of a group of goods and services purchased by the average consumer. The CPI is used in *constant-dollar accounting.*

contingency. A potential *liability.* If a specified event occurs, such as a firm's losing a lawsuit, it would recognize a liability. The notes disclose the contingency, but so long as it remains contingent, it does not appear in the balance sheet. *SFAS No. 5* requires treatment as a contingency until the outcome is "probable" and the amount of payment can be reasonably estimated, perhaps within a range. When the outcome becomes probable (the future event is "likely" to occur) and the firm can reasonably estimate the amount (using the lower end of a range if it can estimate only a range), then the firm recognizes a liability in the accounts, rather than just disclosing it. A *material* contingency may lead to a qualified, "*subject to*" auditor's opinion. Firms do not record *gain* contingencies in the accounts but merely disclose them in notes.

contingent annuity. An *annuity* whose number of payments depends on the outcome of an event whose timing is uncertain at the time the annuity begins; for example, an annuity payable until death of the *annuitant.* Contrast with *annuity certain.*

contingent issue (securities). Securities issuable to specific individuals at the occurrence of some event, such as the firm's attaining a specified level of earnings.

contingent liability. *Contingency.* Avoid this term because it refers to something not (yet) a *liability* on the *balance sheet.*

contingent obligation. *Contingency.*

continuing appropriation. A governmental *appropriation* automatically renewed without further legislative action until altered or revoked or expended.

continuing operations. See *income from continuing operations.*

continuity of operations. The assumption in accounting that the business *entity* will continue to operate long enough to carry out its current plans. The *going-concern assumption.*

continuous budget. A *budget* that adds a future period as the current period ends. This budget, then, always reports on the same number of periods.

continuous compounding. *Compound interest* in which the *compounding period* is every instant of time. See *e* for the computation of the equivalent annual or periodic rate.

continuous flow processing. Mass production of homogeneous products in a continuous flow. Companies manufacturing with continuous flow processes use *process costing* to account for product costs.

continuous improvement. Modern *total quality management* (*TQM*) practitioners believe that the process of seeking quality is never complete. This attitude reflects that assumption, seeking always to improve activities.

continuous inventory method. The *perpetual inventory* method.

Continuously Contemporary Accounting (CoCoA). A name coined by the Australian theorist Raymond J. Chambers to indicate a combination of *current value accounting* in which the *measuring unit* is *constant dollars* and the *attribute measured* is *exit value.*

contra account. An *account,* such as *accumulated depreciation,* that accumulates subtractions from another account, such as *machinery.* Contrast with *adjunct account.*

contributed capital. Name for the *owners' equity* account that represents amounts paid in, usually in *cash,* by owners; the sum of the balances in *capital stock* accounts plus *capital contributed in excess of par (or stated) value* accounts. Contrast with *donated capital.*

contributed surplus. An inferior term for *capital contributed in excess of par (or stated) value.*

contribution approach. *Income statement* preparation method that reports *contribution margin,* by separating *variable costs* from *fixed costs,* in order to emphasize the importance of cost-behavior patterns for purposes of planning and control.

contribution margin. *Revenue* from *sales* less all variable *expenses.* Contrast with *gross margin.*

contribution margin ratio. *Contribution margin* divided by *net sales;* usually measured from the price and cost of a single unit; sometimes measured in total for companies with multiple products.

contribution per unit. Selling price less *variable costs* per unit.

contributory. Said of a *pension plan* in which employees, as well as employers, make payments to a pension *fund.* Note that the provisions for *vesting* apply only to the employer's payments. Whatever the degree of vesting of the employer's payments, employees typically get back all their payments, with interest, in case of death or other cessation of employment before retirement.

control charts. Presentations of warning signals that help management distinguish between random or routine variations in quality and variations that it should investigate. The presentations show the results of statistical process-control measures for a sample, batch, or some other unit. These presentations depict variation in a process and its behavior over time. Management specifies an acceptable level of variation and plans to investigate the causes of deviations beyond that level.

control (controlling) account. A summary *account* with totals equal to those of entries and balances that appear in individual accounts in a *subsidiary ledger.* Accounts Receivable is a control account backed up with an account for each customer. Do not change the balance in a control account unless you make a corresponding change in one of the subsidiary accounts.

control system. A device used by top management to ensure that lower-level management carries out its plans or to safeguard assets. Control designed for a single function within the firm is "operational control"; control designed for autonomous segments that generally have responsibil-

ity for both revenues and costs is "divisional control"; control designed for activities of the firm as a whole is "companywide control." Systems designed for safeguarding *assets* are "internal control" systems.

controllable cost. A *cost* influenced by the way a firm carries out operations. For example, marketing executives control advertising costs. These costs can be *fixed* or *variable.* See *programmed costs* and managed costs.

controlled company. A company in which an individual or corporation holds a majority of the voting shares. An owner can sometimes exercise effective control even though it owns less than 50 percent of the shares.

controller. A title for the chief accountant of an organization; often spelled *comptroller.*

conversion. The act of exchanging a convertible security for another security.

conversion audit. An examination of changeover procedures, and new accounting procedures and files, that takes place when a significant change in the accounting system (e.g., a change from a manual to a computerized system or a change of computers) occurs.

conversion cost. *Direct labor* costs plus factory *overhead* costs incurred in producing a product; that is, the cost to convert raw materials to finished products. *Manufacturing cost.*

conversion period. *Compounding period;* also, period during which the holder of a *convertible bond* or *convertible preferred stock* can convert it into *common shares.*

convertible bond. A *bond* whose owner may convert it into a specified number of shares of *capital stock* during the *conversion period.*

convertible preferred stock. *Preferred shares* whose owner may convert them into a specified number of *common shares.*

cookie jar accounting. When a firm records a *loss,* such as for an *asset impairment,* it *debits* loss and *credits* an *asset account.* If management thinks the market expects a loss, then it can increase the amount of the reported loss even larger than actual. It knows that future *income* can be made to be larger by the amount of the excess loss recognized currently and management can choose the time for the future *earnings* boost. Arthur Levitt, Jr., former Chairman of the *SEC,* criticized this practice and called it "cookie jar accounting," because firms can overstate losses or expenses on one period to store, as in a jar, reportable earnings for discretionary reporting in the future.

cooperative. An incorporated organization formed for the benefit of its members (owners), who are either producers or consumers, in order to acquire for them profits or savings that otherwise accrue to middlemen. Members exercise control on the basis of one vote per member.

coproduct. A product sharing production facilities with another product. For example, if an apparel manufacturer produces shirts and jeans on the same line, these are coproducts. Distinguish coproducts from *joint products* and *by-products* that, by their very nature, a firm must produce together, such as the various grades of wood a lumber factory produces.

copyright. Exclusive right granted by the government to an individual author, composer, playwright, or the like for the life of the individual plus 50 years. If a firm receives the copyright, then the right extends 75 years after the original publication. The *economic life* of a copyright can be less than the legal life, such as, for example, the copyright of this book.

core deposit intangible. A bank borrows funds from its customers, called "depositors," who open checking and savings accounts. Those depositors can take out their funds at any time, but usually don't. The amount that depositors leave on deposit for long periods of time are called "core deposits." The bank lends those funds to other customers, called "borrowers," at *interest rates* larger than the amount it pays the depositors for the funds. (For checking accounts, the rate the bank pays depositors is often zero.) The fact that the depositors can remove their funds at any time, but, on average, leave amounts on deposit relatively permanently means that the bank can lend those funds for relatively long periods of time, usually at higher interest rates than it can charge for shorter-term loans. (See *yield curve.*) The bank's ability to borrow from some customers at a low rate and lend to other customers at a high rate creates wealth for the bank. Bankers and banking analysts call this wealth the "core deposit intangible." It represents an *asset* not recognized in the financial statements by the bank that created this wealth, although some *SEC* commissioners have expressed the thought that accounting should recognize such items as assets. When one bank buys another in a *purchase,* however, it will pay for this asset and will record it as an asset. Usually, the acquiring bank does not use the specific account title "Core Deposit Intangible," but instead uses the account title *Goodwill.*

corner. The control, of a quantity of shares or a commodity, sufficiently large that the holder can control the market price.

corporation. A legal entity authorized by a state to operate under the rules of the entity's *charter.*

correcting entry. An *adjusting entry* that properly records a previously, improperly recorded *transaction.* Do not confuse with entries that correct *accounting errors.*

correction of errors. See *accounting errors.*

cost. The sacrifice, measured by the *price* paid or to be paid, to acquire *goods* or *services.* See *acquisition cost* and *replacement cost.* Terminology often uses "cost" when referring to the valuation of a good or service acquired. When writers use the word in this sense, a cost is an *asset.* When the benefits of the acquisition (the goods or services acquired) expire, the cost becomes an *expense* or *loss.* Some writers, however, use "cost" and "expense" as synonyms. Contrast with *expense.* The word "cost" appears in more than 50 accounting terms, each with sometimes subtle distinctions in meaning. See *cost terminology* for elaboration. Clarity requires that the user include with the word "cost" an adjective or phrase to be clear about intended meaning.

cost accounting. Classifying, summarizing, recording, reporting, and allocating current or predicted *costs;* a subset of *managerial accounting.*

Cost Accounting Standards Board. See *CASB.*

cost accumulation. Bringing together, usually in a single *account,* all *costs* of a specified activity. Contrast with *cost allocation.*

cost allocation. Assigning *costs* to individual products or time periods. Contrast with *cost accumulation.*

cost-based transfer price. A *transfer price* based on *historical costs.*

cost behavior. The functional relation between changes in activity and changes in *cost;* for example: *fixed* versus *variable costs; linear* versus *curvilinear cost.*

cost/benefit criterion. Some measure of *costs* compared with some measure of *benefits* for a proposed undertaking. If the costs exceed the benefits, then the analyst judges the undertaking not worthwhile. This criterion will not yield good decisions unless the analyst estimates all costs and benefits flowing from the undertaking.

cost center. A unit of activity for which a firm accumulates *expenditures* and *expenses.*

cost driver. A factor that causes an activity's costs. See *driver* and *activity basis.*

cost driver rate. Rate at which the *cost driver* causes *costs.*

cost-effective. Among alternatives, the one whose benefit, or payoff, per unit of cost is highest; sometimes said of an action whose expected benefits exceed expected costs whether or not other alternatives exist with larger benefit-cost ratios.

cost estimation. The process of measuring the functional relation between changes in activity levels and changes in cost.

cost flow assumption. See *flow assumption.*

cost-flow equation. Beginning Balance + Transfers In = Transfers Out + Ending Balance; BB + TI = TO + EB.

cost flows. Costs passing through various classifications within an entity. See *flow of costs* for a diagram.

cost hierarchy. Categorizes costs according to whether they are *capacity, product, customer, batch,* or *unit costs.*

cost method (for investments). In accounting for an investment in the *capital stock* or *bonds* of another company, method in which the firm shows the investment at *acquisition cost* and treats only *dividends* declared or *interest receivable* as *revenue;* not allowed by *GAAP.*

cost method (for treasury stock). The method of showing *treasury stock* in a *contra account* to all other items of *shareholders' equity* in an amount equal to that paid to reacquire the stock.

cost object(ive). Any activity for which management desires a separate measurement of *costs.* Examples include departments, products, and territories.

cost of capital. *Opportunity cost* of funds invested in a business; the rate of return that rational owners require an asset to earn before they will devote that asset to a particular purpose; sometimes measured as the average annual rate that a company must pay for its *equities.* In *efficient capital markets,* this cost is the *discount rate* that equates the expected *present value* of all future cash flows to common shareholders with the market value of common stock at a given time. Analysts often measure the cost of capital by taking a *weighted average* of the firm's *debt* and various *equity securities.* We sometimes call the measurement so derived the "composite cost of capital," and some analysts confuse this measurement of the cost of capital with the cost of capital itself. For example, if the equities of a firm include substantial amounts for the *deferred income* *tax liability,* the composite cost of capital will underestimate the true cost of capital, the required rate of return on a firm's assets, because the deferred income tax liability has no explicit cost.

cost of goods manufactured. The sum of all costs allocated to products completed during a period, including materials, labor, and *overhead.*

cost of goods purchased. Net purchase price of goods acquired plus costs of storage and delivery to the place where the owner can productively use the items.

cost of goods sold. Inventoriable *costs* that firms *expense* because they sold the units; equals *beginning inventory* plus *cost of goods purchased* or *manufactured* minus *ending inventory.*

cost of sales. Generally refers to *cost of goods sold,* occasionally to *selling expenses.*

cost or market, whichever is lower. See *lower of cost or market.*

cost percentage. One less *markup percentage; cost* of *goods available for sale* divided by selling prices of goods available for sale (when FIFO is used); *cost* of *purchases* divided by selling prices of purchases (when LIFO is used). See *markup* for further detail on inclusions in the calculation of cost percentage.

cost-plus transfer pricing. Transfer price equal to the *cost* of the transferred product plus a *markup.*

cost pool. *Indirect cost pool;* groupings or aggregations of costs, usually for subsequent analysis.

cost principle. The *principle* that requires reporting *assets* at *historical* or *acquisition cost,* less accumulated *amortization.* This principle relies on the assumption that cost equals *fair market value* at the date of acquisition and that subsequent changes are not likely to be significant.

cost-recovery-first method. A method of *revenue* recognition that *credits inventory* as the firm receives cash collections and continues until the firm has collected cash equal to the sum of all costs. Only after the firm has collected cash equal to costs does it recognize *income.* A firm may not use this method in financial reporting unless the total amount of collections is highly uncertain. It is never allowed for income tax reporting. Contrast with the *installment method,* allowed for both book and tax, in which the firm credits *constant* proportions of each cash collection both to cost and to income.

cost sheet. Statement that shows all the elements composing the total cost of an item.

cost structure. For a given set of total costs, the percentages of fixed and variable costs, typically two percentages adding to 100 percent.

cost terminology. The word "cost" appears in many accounting terms. The accompanying exhibit classifies some of these terms according to the distinctions between the terms in accounting usage. Joel Dean was, to our knowledge, the first to attempt such distinctions; we have used some of his ideas here. We discuss some of the terms in more detail under their own listings.

Cost Terminology: Distinctions among Terms Containing the Word "Cost"

Terms (Synonyms Given in Parentheses)			Distinctions and Comments
			1. The following pairs of terms distinguish the basis measured in accounting.
Historical Cost (Acquisition Cost)	v.	Current Cost	A distinction used in financial accounting. Current cost can be used more specifically to mean replacement cost, net realizable value, or present value of cash flows. "Current cost" is often used narrowly to mean replacement cost.
Historical Cost (Actual Cost)	v.	Standard Cost	The distinction between historical and standard costs arises in product costing for inventory valuation. Some systems record actual costs; others record the standard costs.
			2. The following pairs of terms denote various distinctions among historical costs. For each pair of terms, the sum of the two kinds of costs equals total historical cost used in financial reporting.
Variable Cost	v.	Fixed Cost (Constant Cost)	Distinction used in breakeven analysis and in the design of cost accounting systems, particularly for product costing. See (4), below, for a further subdivision of fixed costs and (5), below, for the economic distinction between marginal and average cost closely paralleling this one.
Traceable Cost	v.	Common Cost (Joint Cost)	Distinction arises in allocating manufacturing costs to product. Common costs are allocated to product, but the allocations are more or less arbitrary. The distinction also arises in preparing segment reports and in separating manufacturing from non-manufacturing costs.
Direct Cost	v.	Indirect Cost	Distinction arises in designing cost accounting systems and in product costing. Direct costs can be traced directly to a cost object (e.g., a product, a responsibility center), whereas indirect costs cannot.

(continued on next page)

Terms (Synonyms Given in Parentheses)			Distinctions and Comments
Out-of-Pocket Cost (Outlay Cost; Cash Cost)	v.	Book Cost	Virtually all costs recorded in financial statements require a cash outlay at one time or another. The distinction here separates expenditures to occur in the future from those already made and is used in making decisions. Book costs, such as for depreciation, reduce income without requiring a future outlay of cash. The cash has already been spent. See future cost v. past cost in (5), below.
Incremental Cost (Marginal Cost; Differential Cost)	v.	Unavoidable Cost (Inescapable Cost; Sunk Cost)	Distinction used in making decisions. Incremental costs will be incurred (or saved) if a decision is made to go ahead (or to stop) some activity, but not otherwise. Unavoidable costs will be reported in financial statements whether the decision is made to go ahead or not, because cash has already been spent or committed. Not all unavoidable costs are book costs, such as, for example, a salary that is promised but not yet earned and that will be paid even if a no-go decision is made.
			The economist restricts the term *marginal cost* to the cost of producing one more unit. Thus the next unit has a marginal cost; the next week's output has an incremental cost. If a firm produces and sells a new product, the related new costs would properly be called incremental, not marginal. If a factory is closed, the costs saved are incremental, not marginal.
Escapable Cost	v.	Inescapable Cost (Unavoidable Cost)	Same distinction as incremental cost v. unavoidable cost, but this pair is used only when the decision maker is considering stopping something—ceasing to produce a product, closing a factory, or the like. See next pair.
Avoidable Cost	v.	Unavoidable Cost	A distinction sometimes used in discussing the merits of variable and absorption costing. Avoidable costs are treated as product costs and unavoidable costs are treated as period expenses under variable costing.
Controllable Cost	v.	Uncontrollable Cost	The distinction here is used in assigning responsibility and in setting bonus or incentive plans. All costs can be affected by someone in the entity; those who design incentive schemes attempt to hold a person responsible for a cost only if that person can influence the amount of the cost.
			3. In each of the following pairs, used in historical cost accounting, the word "cost" appears in one of the terms where "expense" is meant.
Expired Cost	v.	Unexpired Cost	The distinction is between expense and asset.
Product Cost	v.	Period Cost	The terms distinguish product cost from period expense. When a given asset is used, is its cost converted into work-in-process and then finished goods on the balance sheet until the goods are sold, or is it an expense shown on this period's income statement? Product costs appear on the income statement as part of cost of goods sold in the period when the goods are sold. Period expenses appear on the income statement with an appropriate caption for the item in the period when the cost is incurred or recognized.

4. The following subdivisions of fixed (historical) costs are used in analyzing operations. The relation between the components of fixed costs is as follows:

$$\underbrace{\text{Fixed Costs}} = \underbrace{\text{Capacity Costs}} + \underbrace{\text{Programmed Costs}}$$

Semifixed Costs + "Pure" Fixed Costs	Standby Costs + Enabling Costs
+ Fixed Portions of Semivariable Costs	

Terms			Distinctions and Comments
Capacity Cost (Committed Cost)	v.	Programmed Cost (Managed Cost; Discretionary Cost)	Capacity costs give a firm the capability to produce or to sell. Programmed costs, such as for advertising or research and development, may not be essential, but once a decision to incur them is made, they become fixed costs.
Standby Cost	v.	Enabling Cost	Standby costs will be incurred whether capacity, once acquired, is used or not, such as property taxes and depreciation on a factory. Enabling costs, such as for a security force, can be avoided if the capacity is unused.

(continued on next page)

Terms (Synonyms Given in Parentheses)			Distinctions and Comments
Semifixed Cost	v.	Semivariable Cost	A cost that is fixed over a wide range but that can change at various levels is a semifixed cost or "step cost." An example is the cost of rail lines from the factory to the main rail line, where fixed cost depends on whether there are one or two parallel lines but is independent of the number of trains run per day. Semivariable costs combine a strictly fixed component cost plus a variable component. Telephone charges usually have a fixed monthly component plus a charge related to usage.
			5. The following pairs of terms distinguish among economic uses or decision-making uses or regulatory uses of cost terms.
Fully Absorbed Cost	v.	Variable Cost (Direct Cost)	Fully absorbed costs refer to costs where fixed costs have been allocated to units or departments as required by generally accepted accounting principles. Variable costs, in contrast, may be more relevant for making decisions, such as setting prices.
Fully Absorbed Cost	v.	Full Cost	In full costing, all costs, manufacturing costs as well as central corporate expenses (including financing expenses), are allocated to products or divisions. In full absorption costing, only manufacturing costs are allocated to products. Only in full costing will revenues, expenses, and income summed over all products or divisions equal corporate revenues, expenses, and income.
Opportunity Cost	v.	Outlay Cost (Out-of-Pocket Cost)	Opportunity cost refers to the economic benefit forgone by using a resource for one purpose instead of for another. The outlay cost of the resource will be recorded in financial records. The distinction arises because a resource is already in the possession of the entity with a recorded historical cost. Its economic value to the firm, opportunity cost, generally differs from the historical cost; it can be either larger or smaller.
Future Cost	v.	Past Cost	Effective decision making analyzes only present and future outlay costs, or out-of-pocket costs. Opportunity costs are relevant for profit maximizing; past costs are used in financial reporting.
Short-Run Cost	v.	Long-Run Cost	Short-run costs vary as output is varied for a given configuration of plant and equipment. Long-run costs can be incurred to change that configuration. This pair of terms is the economic analog of the accounting pair, see (2) above, variable and fixed costs. The analogy is not perfect because some short-run costs are fixed, such as property taxes on the factory, from the point of view of break-even analysis.
Imputed Cost	v.	Book Cost	In a regulatory setting some costs, for example the cost of owners' equity capital, are calculated and used for various purposes; these are imputed costs. Imputed costs are not recorded in the historical costs accounting records for financial reporting. Book costs are recorded.
Average Cost	v.	Marginal Cost	The economic distinction equivalent to fully absorbed cost of product and variable cost of product. Average cost is total cost divided by number of units. Marginal cost is the cost to produce the next unit (or the last unit).
Differential Cost (Incremental Cost)	v.	Variable Cost	Whether a cost changes or remains fixed depends on the activity basis being considered. Typically, but not invariably, costs are said to be variable or with respect to an activity basis such as changes in production levels. Typically, but not invariably, costs are said to be incremental or not with respect to an activity basis such as the undertaking of some new venture. For example, consider the decision to undertake the production of food processors, rather than food blenders, which the manufacturer has been making. To produce processors requires the acquisition of a new machine tool. The cost of the new machine tool is incremental with respect to a decision to produce food processors instead of food blenders but, once acquired, becomes a fixed cost of producing food processors. If costs of direct labor hours are going to be incurred for the production of food processors or food blenders, whichever is produced (in a scenario when not both are to be produced), such costs are variable with respect to production measured in units but are not incremental with respect to the decision to produce processors rather than blenders. This distinction is often blurred in practice, so a careful understanding of the activity basis being considered is necessary to understand the concepts being used in a particular application.

cost-to-cost. The *percentage-of-completion method* in which the firm estimates the fraction of completion as the ratio of costs incurred to date divided by the total costs the firm expects to incur for the entire project.

cost-volume-profit analysis. A study of the sensitivity of *profits* to changes in units sold (or produced) or costs or prices.

cost-volume-profit graph (chart). A graph that shows the relation between *fixed costs, contribution per unit, breakeven point,* and *sales.* See *breakeven chart.*

costing. The process of calculating the cost of activities, products, or services; the British word for *cost accounting.*

counterparty. The term refers to the opposite party in a legal contract. In accounting and finance, a frequent usage arises when an entity purchases (or sells) a *derivative* financial contract, such as an *option, forward contract,* and *futures contract.*

coupon. That portion of a *bond* document redeemable at a specified date for payments. Its physical form resembles a series of tickets; each coupon has a date, and the holder either deposits it at a bank, just like a check, for collection or mails it to the issuer's agent for collection.

coupon rate. Of a *bond,* the amount of annual coupons divided by par value. Contrast with *effective rate.*

covenant. A promise with legal validity. A loan covenant specifies the terms under which the lender can force the borrower to repay funds otherwise not yet due. For example, a *bond* covenant might say that the *principal* of a bond issue falls due on December 31, 2010, unless the firm's *debt-equity ratio* falls below 40 percent, in which case the amount becomes due immediately.

CPA. See *certified public accountant.* The *AICPA* suggests that no periods appear in the abbreviation.

CPI. *Consumer price index.*

CPP. Current purchasing power; usually used, primarily in the UK, as an adjective modifying the word "accounting" to mean the accounting that produces *constant-dollar financial statements.*

Cr. Abbreviation for *credit,* always with initial capital letter. Quiz: what do you suppose *Cr.* stands for? For the answer, see *Dr.*

creative accounting. Selection of *accounting principles* and interpretation of transactions or events designed to manipulate, typically to increase but sometimes merely to smooth, reported *income from continuing operations;* one form of *fraudulent financial reporting.* Many attempts at creative accounting involve premature *revenue recognition.*

credit. As a noun, an entry on the right-hand side of an *account;* as a verb, to make an entry on the right-hand side of an account; records increases in *liabilities, owners' equity, revenues,* and *gains;* records decreases in *assets* and *expenses.* See *debit and credit conventions.* This term also refers to the ability or right to buy or borrow in return for a promise to pay later.

credit bureau. An organization that gathers and evaluates data on the ability of a person to meet financial obligations and sells this information to its clients.

credit loss. The amount of accounts receivable that the firm finds, or expects to find, *uncollectible.*

credit memorandum. A document used by a seller to inform a buyer that the seller is crediting (reducing) the buyer's account receivable because of *errors, returns,* or *allowances;* also, the document provided by a bank to a depositor to indicate that the bank is increasing the depositor's balance because of some event other than a deposit, such as the collection by the bank of the depositor's *note receivable.*

creditor. One who lends. In the UK, *account payable.*

critical path method (CPM). A method of *network analysis* in which the analyst estimates normal duration time for each activity within a project. The critical path identifies the shortest completion period based on the most time-consuming sequence of activities from the beginning to the end of the network. Compare *PERT.*

critical success factors. The important things a company must do to be successful; may vary from one company to another.

cross-reference (index). A number placed beside each *account* in a *journal entry* indicating the *ledger* account to which the record keeper posted the entry and placing in the ledger the page number of the journal where the record keeper first recorded the journal entry; used to link the *debit* and *credit* parts of an entry in the ledger accounts back to the original entry in the journal. See *audit trail.*

cross-section analysis. Analysis of *financial statements* of various firms for a single period of time; contrast with *time-series analysis,* in which analysts examine statements of a given firm for several periods of time.

Crown corporation. Canada and UK: a corporation that is ultimately accountable, through a minister of the Crown, to Parliament or a legislature for the conduct of its affairs.

cum div. (dividend). The condition of shares whose quoted market price includes a declared but unpaid dividend. This condition pertains between the declaration date of the dividend and the record date. Compare *ex div. (dividend).*

cum rights. The condition of securities whose quoted market price includes the right to purchase new securities. Compare *ex rights.*

cumulative dividend. Preferred stock *dividends* that, if not paid, accrue as a commitment that the firm must pay before it can declare dividends to common shareholders.

cumulative preferred shares. *Preferred* shares with *cumulative dividend* rights.

current assets. *Cash* and other *assets* that a firm expects to turn into cash, sell, or exchange within the normal operating cycle of the firm or one year, whichever is longer. One year is the usual period for classifying asset balances on the balance sheet. Current assets include *cash, marketable securities, receivables, inventory,* and *current prepayments.*

current cost. *Cost* stated in terms of current values (of *productive capacity*) rather than in terms of *acquisition cost.* See *net realizable value* and *current selling price.*

current cost accounting. The *FASB's* term for *financial statements* in which the *attribute measured* is *current cost.*

current cost/nominal-dollar accounting. Accounting based on *current cost* valuations measured in *nominal dollars.*

Components of *income* include an *operating margin* and *holding gains and losses.*

current exchange rate. The rate at which the holder of one unit of currency can convert it into another at the end of the *accounting period* being reported on or, for *revenues, expenses, gains,* and *losses,* the date of recognition of the transaction.

current exit value. *Exit value.*

current fund. In governmental accounting, a synonym for *general fund.*

current funds. *Cash* and other assets readily convertible into cash; in governmental accounting, funds spent for operating purposes during the current period; includes *general,* special revenue, *debt service,* and *enterprise funds.*

current (gross) margin. See *operating margin based on current costs.*

current liability. A debt or other obligation that a firm must discharge within a short time, usually the *earnings cycle* or one year, normally by expending *current assets.*

current operating performance concept. The notion that reported *income* for a period ought to reflect only ordinary, normal, and recurring operations of that period. A consequence is that *extraordinary* and nonrecurring items are entered directly in the Retained Earnings account. Contrast with *clean surplus concept.* This concept is no longer acceptable. (See *APB Opinion No. 9* and *No. 30.*)

current ratio. Sum of *current assets* divided by sum of *current liabilities.* See *ratio.*

current realizable value. *Realizable value.*

current replacement cost. Of an *asset,* the amount currently required to acquire an identical asset (in the same condition and with the same service potential) or an asset capable of rendering the same service at a current *fair market price.* If these two amounts differ, use the lower. Contrast with *reproduction cost.*

current selling price. The amount for which an *asset* could be sold as of a given time in an *arm's-length* transaction rather than in a forced sale.

current service costs. *Service costs* of a *pension plan.*

current value accounting. The form of accounting in which all assets appear at *current replacement cost* (*entry value*) or *current selling price* or *net realizable value* (*exit value*) and all *liabilities* appear at *present value.* Entry and exit values may differ from each other, so theorists have not agreed on the precise meaning of "current value accounting."

current yield. Of a *bond,* the annual amount of *coupons* divided by the current market price of the bond. Contrast with *yield to maturity.*

currently attainable standard cost. *Normal standard cost.*

curvilinear (variable) cost. A continuous, but not necessarily linear (straight-line), functional relation between activity levels and *costs.*

customer-level activities. Work performed to meet the needs of a specific customer, aggregated over all customers.

customer response time. Period that elapses from the moment a customer places an order for a product or requests service to the moment the firm delivers the product or service to the customer.

customers' ledger. The *ledger* that shows *accounts receivable* of individual customers. It is the *subsidiary ledger* for the *control account* Accounts Receivable.

cutoff rate. *Hurdle rate.*

D

data bank. An organized file of information, such as a customer name and address file, used in and kept up-to-date by a processing system.

database. A comprehensive collection of interrelated information stored together in computerized form to serve several applications.

database management system. Generalized software programs used to handle physical storage and manipulation of databases.

days of average inventory on hand. See *ratio.*

days of grace. The days allowed by law or contract for payment of a debt after its due date.

DCF. *Discounted cash flow.*

DDB. *Double declining-balance depreciation.*

debenture bond. A *bond* not secured with *collateral.*

debit. As a noun, an entry on the left-hand side of an *account;* as a verb, to make an entry on the left-hand side of an account; records increases in *assets* and *expenses;* records decreases in *liabilities, owners' equity,* and *revenues.* See *debit and credit conventions.*

debit and credit conventions. The conventional use of the *T-account* form and the rules for debit and credit in *balance sheet accounts* (see below). The equality of the two sides of the *accounting equation* results from recording equal amounts of *debits* and *credits* for each *transaction.*

Typical Asset Account

Opening Balance	
Increase	Decrease
+	−
Dr.	Cr.
Ending Balance	

Typical Liability Account

	Opening Balance
Decrease	Increase
−	+
Dr.	Cr.
	Ending Balance

Typical Owners' Equity Account

	Opening Balance
Decrease	Increase
−	+
Dr.	Cr.
	Ending Balance

Revenue and expense accounts belong to the owners' equity group. The relation and the rules for debit and credit in these accounts take the following form:

Owners' Equity

Decrease	Increase
−	+
Dr.	Cr.

Expenses		Revenues	
Dr.	Cr.	Dr.	Cr.
+	−	−	+
*			*

*Normal balance before closing

debit memorandum. A document used by a seller to inform a buyer that the seller is debiting (increasing) the amount of the buyer's *accounts receivable.* Also, the document provided by a bank to a depositor to indicate that the bank is decreasing the depositor's *balance* because of some event other than payment for a *check,* such as monthly service charges or the printing of checks.

debt. An amount owed. The general name for *notes, bonds, mortgages,* and the like that provide evidence of amounts owed and have definite payment dates.

debt capital. *Noncurrent liabilities.* See *debt financing,* and contrast with *equity financing.*

debt-equity ratio. Total *liabilities* divided by total equities. See *ratio.* Some analysts put only total shareholders' equity in the denominator. Some analysts restrict the numerator to *long-term debt.*

debt financing. *Leverage.* Raising *funds* by issuing *bonds, mortgages,* or *notes.* Contrast with *equity financing.*

debt guarantee. See *guarantee.*

debt ratio. *Debt-equity ratio.*

debt service fund. In governmental accounting, a *fund* established to account for payment of *interest* and *principal* on all general-obligation *debt* other than that payable from special *assessments.*

debt service payment. The payment required by a lending agreement, such as periodic coupon payment on a bond or installment payment on a loan or a lease payment. It is sometimes called "interest payment," but this term will mislead the unwary. Only rarely will the amount of a debt service payment equal the interest expense for the period preceding the payment. A debt service payment will always include some amount for interest, but the payment will usually differ from the interest expense.

debt service requirement. The amount of cash required for payments of *interest,* current maturities of *principal* on outstanding *debt,* and payments to *sinking funds* (corporations) or to the debt service fund (governmental).

debtor. One who borrows; in the UK, *account receivable.*

decentralized decision making. Management practice in which a firm gives a manager of a business unit responsibility for that unit's *revenues* and *costs,* freeing the manager to make decisions about prices, sources of supply, and the like, as though the unit were a separate business that the manager owns. See *responsibility accounting* and *transfer price.*

declaration date. Time when the *board of directors* declares a *dividend.*

declining-balance depreciation. The method of calculating the periodic *depreciation* charge by multiplying the *book value* at the start of the period by a constant percentage. In pure declining-balance depreciation, the constant percentage is $1 - ns/c$, where n is the *depreciable life, s* is *salvage value,* and c is *acquisition cost.* See *double declining-balance depreciation.*

deep discount bonds. Said of *bonds* selling much below (exactly how much is not clear) *par value.*

defalcation. Embezzlement.

default. Failure to pay *interest* or *principal* on a *debt* when due.

defeasance. Transaction with the economic effect of *debt retirement* that does not retire the debt. When *interest rates* increase, many firms find that the *market value* of their outstanding *debt* has dropped substantially below its *book value.* In *historical cost accounting* for debt retirements, retiring debt with a *cash* payment less than the book value of the debt results in a gain (generally, an *extraordinary item*). Many firms would like to retire the outstanding debt issues and report the gain. Two factors impede doing so: (1) the gain can be a taxable event generating adverse *income tax* consequences; and (2) the transaction costs in retiring all the debt can be large, in part because the firm cannot easily locate all the debt holders or persuade them to sell back their bonds to the issuer. The process of "defeasance" serves as the economic equivalent to retiring a debt issue while it saves the issuer from experiencing adverse tax consequences and from actually having to locate and retire the bonds. The process works as follows. The debt-issuing firm turns over to an independent trustee, such as a bank, amounts of cash or low-risk government bonds sufficient to make all debt service payments on the outstanding debt, including bond retirements, in return for the trustee's commitment to make all debt service payments. The debt issuer effectively retires the outstanding debt. It debits the liability account, credits Cash or Marketable Securities as appropriate, and credits Extraordinary Gain on Debt Retirement. The trustee can retire debt or make debt service payments, whichever it chooses. For income tax purposes, however, the firm's debt remains outstanding. The firm will have taxable interest *deductions* for its still-outstanding debt and taxable interest *revenue* on the investments held by the trustee for debt service. In law, the term "defeasance" means "a rendering null and void." This process renders the outstanding debt economically null and void, without causing a taxable event.

defensive interval. A financial *ratio* equal to the number of days of normal cash *expenditures* covered by *quick assets.* It is defined as follows:

$$\frac{\text{Quick Assets}}{(\text{All Expenses Except Amortization and Others Not Using Funds} \div 365)}$$

The denominator of the ratio is the cash expenditure per day. Analysts have found this ratio useful in predicting *bankruptcy.*

deferral. The accounting process concerned with past *cash receipts* and *payments;* in contrast to *accrual;* recognizing a liability resulting from a current cash receipt (as for magazines to be delivered) or recognizing an asset from a current cash payment (as for prepaid insurance or a long-term depreciable asset).

deferral method. See *flow-through method* (of accounting for the *investment credit*) for definition and contrast.

deferred annuity. An *annuity* whose first payment occurs sometime after the end of the first period.

deferred asset. *Deferred charge.*

deferred charge. *Expenditure* not recognized as an *expense* of the period when made but carried forward as an *asset* to be *written off* in future periods, such as for advance rent payments or insurance premiums. See *deferral.*

deferred cost. *Deferred charge.*

deferred credit. Sometimes used to indicate *advances from customers.*

deferred debit. *Deferred charge.*

deferred expense. *Deferred charge.*

deferred gross margin. *Unrealized gross margin.*

deferred income. *Advances from customers.*

deferred income tax (liability). An *indeterminate-term liability* that arises when the pretax income shown on the tax return is less than what it would have been had the firm used the same *accounting principles* and *cost basis* for *assets* and *liabilities* in tax returns as it used for financial reporting. *SFAS No. 109* requires that the firm debit income tax *expense* and credit deferred income tax with the amount of the taxes delayed by using accounting principles in tax returns different from those used in financial reports. See *temporary difference, timing difference, permanent difference,* and *installment sales.* If, as a result of temporary differences, cumulative taxable income exceeds cumulative reported income before taxes, the deferred income tax account will have a *debit* balance, which the firm will report as a *deferred charge.*

deferred revenue. Sometimes used to indicate *advances from customers.*

deferred tax. See *deferred income tax.*

deficit. A *debit balance* in the Retained Earnings account; presented on the balance sheet in a *contra account* to shareholders' equity; sometimes used to mean negative *net income* for a period.

defined-benefit plan. A *pension plan* in which the employer promises specific dollar amounts to each eligible employee; the amounts usually depend on a formula that takes into account such things as the employee's earnings, years of employment, and age. The employer adjusts its cash contributions and pension expense to *actuarial* experience in the eligible employee group and investment performance of the pension *fund.* This is sometimes called a "fixed-benefit" pension plan. Contrast with *money purchase plan.*

defined-contribution plan. A *money purchase (pension) plan* or other arrangement, based on formula or discretion, in which the employer makes cash contributions to eligible individual employee *accounts* under the terms of a written plan document. The trustee of the funds in the account manages the funds, and the employee-beneficiary receives at retirement (or at some other agreed time) the amount in the fund. The employer makes no promise about that amount. Profit-sharing pension plans are of this type.

deflation. A period of declining *general price-level changes.*

Delphi technique. Forecasting method in which members of the forecasting group prepare individual forecasts, share them anonymously with the rest of the group, and only then compare forecasts and resolve differences.

demand deposit. *Funds* in a *checking account* at a bank.

demand loan. See *term loan* for definition and contrast.

denial of opinion. Canada: the statement that an *auditor,* for reasons arising in the *audit,* is unable to express an opinion on whether the *financial statements* provide *fair presentation.*

denominator volume. Capacity measured in the number of units the firm expects to produce this period; when divided into *budgeted fixed costs,* results in fixed costs applied per unit of product.

department(al) allocation. Obtained by first accumulating *costs* in *cost pools* for each department and then, using separate rates, or sets of rates, for each department, allocating from each cost pool to products produced in that department.

dependent variable. See *regression analysis.*

depletion. Exhaustion or *amortization* of a *wasting asset* or *natural resource.* Also see *percentage depletion.*

depletion allowance. See *percentage depletion.*

deposit intangible. See *core deposit intangible.*

deposit, sinking fund. Payments made to a *sinking fund.*

deposit method (of revenue recognition). A method of *revenue* recognition that is the same as the *completed sale* or *completed contract method.* In some contexts, such as when the customer has the right to return goods for a full refund or in retail land sales, the customer must make substantial payments while still having the right to back out of the deal and receive a refund. When the seller cannot predict with reasonable precision the amount of cash it will ultimately collect and when it will receive cash, the seller must *credit* Deposits, a *liability account,* rather than *revenue.* (In this regard, the accounting differs from that in the completed contract method, in which the account credited offsets the *Work-in-Process* inventory account.) When the *sale* becomes complete, the firm credits a revenue account and *debits* the Deposits account.

deposits (by customers). A *liability* that the firm *credits* when receiving *cash* (as in a bank, or in a grocery store when the customer pays for soda-pop bottles with cash to be repaid when the customer returns the bottles) and when the firm intends to discharge the liability by returning the cash. Contrast with the liability account *Advances from Customers,* which the firm credits on receipt of cash, expecting later to discharge the liability by delivering goods or services. When the firm delivers the goods or services, it credits a *revenue* account.

deposits in transit. Deposits made by a firm but not yet reflected on the *bank statement.*

depreciable cost. That part of the *cost* of an asset, usually *acquisition cost* less *salvage value,* that the firm will charge off over the life of the asset through the process of *depreciation.*

depreciable life. For an *asset,* the time period or units of activity (such as miles driven for a truck) over which the firm allocates the *depreciable cost.* For tax returns, depreciable life may be shorter than estimated *service life.*

depreciation. *Amortization of plant assets;* the process of allocating the cost of an asset to the periods of benefit— the *depreciable life;* classified as a *production cost* or a *period expense,* depending on the asset and whether the firm uses *full absorption* or *variable costing.* Depreciation methods described in this glossary include the *annuity method, appraisal method, composite method, compound interest method, declining-balance method, production method, replacement method, retirement method, straight-line method, sinking fund method,* and *sum-of-the-years'-digits method.*

depreciation reserve. An inferior term for *accumulated depreciation.* See *reserve.* Do not confuse with a replacement *fund.*

derivative (financial instrument). A financial instrument, such as an option to purchase a share of stock, created from another, such as a share of stock; an instrument, such as a *swap,* whose value depends on the value of another asset called the "underlying"—for example, the right to receive the difference between the interest payments on a fixed-rate five-year loan for $1 million and the interest payments on a floating-rate five-year loan for $1 million. To qualify as a derivative under *FASB* rules, *SFAS No. 133,* the instrument has one or more underlyings, and one or more notional amounts or payment provisions or both, it either does not require an initial net investment or it requires one smaller than would be required for other types of contracts expected to have a similar response to changes in market factors, and its terms permit settlement for cash in lieu of physical delivery or the instrument itself trades on an exchange. See also *forward contract* and *futures contract.*

detection costs. See *appraisal costs.*

detective controls. *Internal controls* designed to detect, or maximize the chance of detection of, errors and other irregularities.

determination. See *determine.*

determine. A term often used (in our opinion, overused) by accountants and those who describe the accounting process. A leading dictionary associates the following meanings with the verb "determine": settle, decide, conclude, ascertain, cause, affect, control, impel, terminate, and decide upon. In addition, accounting writers can mean any one of the following: measure, allocate, report, calculate, compute, observe, choose, and legislate. In accounting, there are two distinct sets of meanings: those encompassed by the synonym "cause or legislate" and those encompassed by the synonym "measure." The first set of uses conveys the active notion of causing something to happen, and the second set of uses conveys the more passive notion of observing something that someone else has caused to happen. An accountant who speaks of cost or income "determination" generally means measurement or observation, not causation; management and economic conditions cause costs and income to be what they are. One who speaks of accounting principles "determination" can mean choosing or applying (as in "determining depreciation charges" from an allowable set) or causing to be acceptable (as in the *FASB*'s "determining" the accounting for *leases*). In the long run, income is cash-in less cash-out, so management and economic conditions "determine"

(cause) income to be what it is. In the short run, reported income is a function of accounting principles chosen and applied, so the accountant "determines" (measures) income. A question such as "Who determines income?" has, therefore, no unambiguous answer. The meaning of "an accountant determining acceptable accounting principles" is also vague. Does the clause mean merely choosing one principle from the set of generally acceptable principles, or does it mean using professional judgment to decide that some of the generally accepted principles are not correct under the current circumstances? We try never to use "determine" unless we mean "cause." Otherwise we use "measure," "report," "calculate," "compute," or whatever specific verb seems appropriate. We suggest that careful writers will always "determine" to use the most specific verb to convey meaning. "Determine" seldom best describes a process in which those who make decisions often differ from those who apply technique. The term *predetermined (factory) overhead rate* contains an appropriate use of the word.

development stage enterprise. As defined in *SFAS No. 7,* a firm whose planned principal *operations* have not commenced or, having commenced, have not generated significant *revenue.* The financial statements should identify such enterprises, but no special *accounting principles* apply to them.

diagnostic signal. See *warning signal* for definition and contrast.

differentiable cost. The cost increments associated with infinitesimal changes in volume. If a total cost curve is smooth (in mathematical terms, differentiable), then we say that the curve graphing the derivative of the total cost curve shows differentiable costs.

differential. An adjective used to describe the change (increase or decrease) in a *cost, expense, investment, cash flow, revenue, profit,* and the like as the firm produces or sells one or more additional (or fewer) units or undertakes (or ceases) an activity. This term has virtually the same meaning as *incremental,* but if the item declines, "decremental" better describes the change. Contrast with *marginal,* which means the change in cost or other item for a small (one unit or even less) change in number of units produced or sold.

differential analysis. Analysis of *differential costs, revenues, profits, investment, cash flow,* and the like.

differential cost. See *differential.*

differential cost analysis. See *relevant cost analysis.*

dilution. A potential reduction in *earnings per share* or *book value* per share by the potential *conversion* of securities or by the potential exercise of *warrants* or *options.*

dilutive. Said of a *security* that will reduce *earnings per share* if it is exchanged for *common shares.*

dip(ping) into LIFO layers. See *LIFO inventory layer.*

direct access. Access to computer storage where information can be located directly, regardless of its position in the storage file. Compare *sequential access.*

direct cost. Cost of *direct material* and *direct labor* incurred in producing a product. See *prime cost.* In some accounting literature, writers use this term to mean the same thing as *variable cost.*

direct costing. Another, less-preferred, term for *variable costing*.

direct-financing (capital) lease. See *sales-type (capital) lease* for definition and contrast.

direct labor (material) cost. Cost of labor (material) applied and assigned directly to a product; contrast with *indirect labor (material)*.

direct labor variance. Difference between actual and *standard direct labor* allowed.

direct method. See *statement of cash flows*.

direct posting. A method of bookkeeping in which the firm makes *entries* directly in *ledger accounts*, without using a *journal*.

direct write-off method. See *write-off method*.

disbursement. Payment by *cash* or by *check*. See *expenditure*.

DISC (domestic international sales corporation). A U.S. *corporation*, usually a *subsidiary*, whose *income* results primarily from exports. The parent firm usually defers paying *income tax* on 50 percent of a DISC's income for a long period. Generally, this results in a lower overall corporate tax for the *parent* than would otherwise be incurred.

disclaimer of opinion. An *auditor's report* stating that the auditor cannot give an opinion on the *financial statements*. Usually results from *material* restrictions on the scope of the audit or from material uncertainties, which the firm has been unable to resolve by the time of the audit, about the accounts.

disclosure. The showing of facts in *financial statements*, *notes* thereto, or the *auditor's report*.

discontinued operations. See *income from discontinued operations*.

discount. In the context of *compound interest, bonds,* and *notes,* the difference between *face amount* (or *future value*) and *present value* of a payment; in the context of *sales* and *purchases,* a reduction in price granted for prompt payment. See also *chain discount, quantity discount,* and *trade discount*.

discount factor. The reciprocal of one plus the *discount rate*. If the discount rate is 10 percent per period, the discount factor for three periods is $1/(1.10)^3 = (1.10)^{-3} = 0.75131$.

discount rate. *Interest rate* used to convert future payments to *present values*.

discounted bailout period. In a *capital budgeting* context, the total time that must elapse before discounted value of net accumulated cash flows from a project, including potential *salvage value* at various times of assets, equals or exceeds the *present value* of net accumulated cash outflows. Contrast with *discounted payback period*.

discounted cash flow (DCF). Using either the *net present value* or the *internal rate of return* in an analysis to measure the value of future expected cash *expenditures* and *receipts* at a common date. In discounted cash flow analysis, choosing the alternative with the largest *internal rate of return* may yield wrong answers given *mutually exclusive projects* with differing amounts of initial investment for two of the projects. Consider, to take an unrealistic example, a project involving an initial investment of $1, with an *IRR* of 60 percent, and another project involving an initial investment of $1 million, with an IRR of 40 percent. Under most conditions, most firms will prefer the second project to the first, but choosing the project with the larger IRR will lead to undertaking the first, not the second. Usage calls this shortcoming of choosing between alternatives based on the magnitude of the internal rate of return, rather than based on the magnitude of the *net present value* of the cash flows, the "scale effect."

discounted payback period. The shortest amount of time that must elapse before the discounted *present value* of cash inflows from a project, excluding potential *salvage value*, equals the discounted present value of the cash outflows.

discounting a note. See *note receivable discounted* and *factoring*.

discounts lapsed (lost). The sum of *discounts* offered for prompt payment that the purchaser did not take because the discount period expired. See *terms of sale*.

discovery sampling. Acceptance sampling in which the analyst accepts an entire population if and only if the sample contains no disparities.

discovery value accounting. See *reserve recognition accounting*.

discretionary cost center. See *engineered cost center* for definition and contrast.

discretionary costs. *Programmed costs*.

Discussion Memorandum. A neutral discussion of all the issues concerning an accounting problem of current concern to the *FASB*. The publication of such a document usually signals that the FASB will consider issuing an *SFAS* or *SFAC* on this particular problem. The discussion memorandum brings together material about the particular problem to facilitate interaction and comment by those interested in the matter. A public hearing follows before the FASB will issue an *Exposure Draft*.

dishonored note. A *promissory note* whose maker does not repay the loan at *maturity,* for a *term loan,* or on demand, for a *demand loan*.

disintermediation. Moving funds from one interest-earning account to another, typically one promising a higher rate. Federal law regulates the maximum *interest rate* that both banks and savings-and-loan associations can pay for *time deposits*. When free-market interest rates exceed the regulated interest ceiling for such time deposits, some depositors withdraw their funds and invest them elsewhere at a higher interest rate. This process is known as "disintermediation."

distributable income. The portion of conventional accounting net income that the firm can distribute to owners (usually in the form of *dividends*) without impairing the physical capacity of the firm to continue operations at current levels. Pretax distributable income is conventional pretax income less the excess of *current cost* of goods sold and *depreciation* charges based on the replacement cost of *productive capacity* over cost of goods sold and depreciation on an *acquisition cost basis*. Contrast with *sustainable income*. See *inventory profit*.

distributable surplus. Canada and UK: the statutory designation to describe the portion of the proceeds of the issue of shares without *par value* not allocated to share capital.

distributed processing. Processing in a computer information network in which an individual location processes data relevant to it while the operating system transmits information required elsewhere, either to the central computer or to another local computer for further processing.

distribution expense. *Expense* of selling, advertising, and delivery activities.

dividend. A distribution of assets generated from *earnings* to owners of a corporation. The firm may distribute cash (cash dividend), stock (stock dividend), property, or other securities (dividend in kind). Dividends, except stock dividends, become a legal liability of the corporation when the corporation's board declares them. Hence, the owner of stock ordinarily recognizes *revenue* when the board of the corporation declares the dividend, except for stock dividends. See also *liquidating dividend* and *stock dividend*.

dividend yield. *Dividends* declared for the year divided by market price of the stock as of the time for which the analyst computes the yield.

dividends in arrears. Dividends on *cumulative preferred stock* that the corporation's board has not yet declared in accordance with the preferred stock contract. The corporation must usually clear such arrearages before it can declare dividends on *common shares*.

dividends in kind. See *dividend*.

division. A more or less self-contained business unit that is part of a larger family of business units under common control.

division return on investment (ROI). Equals the *division* profit divided by the investment in the division.

divisional control. See *control system*.

divisional reporting. See *segment reporting*.

dollar sign rules. In accounting statements or schedules, place a dollar sign beside the first figure in each column and beside any figure below a horizontal line drawn under the preceding figure.

dollar-value LIFO method. A form of *LIFO* inventory accounting with inventory quantities (*layers*) measured in dollar, rather than physical, terms. The method adjusts for changing prices by using specific price indexes appropriate for the kinds of items in the inventory.

domestic international sales corporation. See *DISC*.

donated capital. A *shareholders' equity* account credited when the company receives gifts, such as land or buildings, without issuing shares or other owners' equity interest in return. A city might donate a plant site hoping the firm will build a factory and employ local residents. Do not confuse with *contributed capital*.

double declining-balance depreciation (DDB). *Declining-balance depreciation* in which the constant percentage used to multiply by book value in computing the depreciation charge for the year is 2/*n*, where *n* is the *depreciable life* in periods. Omit *salvage value* from the depreciable amount. Thus if the asset cost $100 and has a depreciable life of five years, the depreciation in the first year would be $40 = 2/5 × $100, in the second year would be $24 = 2/5 × ($100 − $40), and in the third year would be $14.40 = 2/5 × ($100 − $40 − $24). By the fourth year, the remaining undepreciated cost could be depreciated under the straight-line method at $10.80 = 1/2 × ($100 −

$40 − $24 − $14.40) per year for tax purposes. Note that salvage value does not affect these computations except that the method will not depreciate the book value below salvage value.

double entry. In recording transactions, a system that maintains the equality of the accounting equation or the balance sheet. Each entry results in recording equal amounts of *debits* and *credits*.

double T-account. *T-account* with an extra horizontal line showing a change in the account balance to be explained by the subsequent entries into the account.

Plant

42,000	

This account shows an increase in the asset account, plant, of $42,000 to be explained. Such accounts are useful in preparing the *statement of cash flows;* they are not a part of the formal record-keeping process.

double taxation. Occurs when the taxing authority (U.S. or state) taxes corporate income as earned (first tax) and then the same taxing authority taxes the aftertax income, distributed to owners as dividends, again as personal income tax (second tax).

doubtful accounts. *Accounts receivable* that the firm estimates to be *uncollectible*.

Dr. The abbreviation for *debit*, always with the initial capital letter. *Dr.* is a shortened form of the word *debitor*, and *Cr.* comes from the word *creditor*. In the early days of double-entry record keeping in the UK, the major asset was accounts receivable, called *creditors*, and the major liability was accounts payable, called *debitors*. Thus the *r* in *Cr.* does not refer to the *r* in *credit* but to the second *r* in *creditor*.

draft. A written order by the first party, called the drawer, instructing a second party, called the drawee (such as a bank) to pay a third party, called the payee. See also *check, cashier's check, certified check, NOW account, sight draft,* and *trade acceptance*.

drawee. See *draft*.

drawer. See *draft*.

drawing account. A *temporary account* used in *sole proprietorships* and *partnerships* to record payments to owners or partners during a period. At the end of the period, the firm closes the drawing account by crediting it and debiting the owner's or partner's share of income or, perhaps, his or her capital account.

drawings. Payments made to a *sole proprietor* or to a *partner* during a period. See *drawing account*.

driver, cost driver. A cause of costs incurred. Examples include processing orders, issuing an engineering change order, changing the production schedule, and stopping production to change machine settings. The notion arises primarily in product costing, particularly *activity-based costing*.

drop ship(ment). Occurs when a distributor asks a manufacturer to send an order directly to the customer (ordinarily a manufacturer sends goods to a distributor, who sends the goods to its customer). Usage calls the shipment a "drop shipment" and refers to the goods as "drop shipped."

dry-hole accounting. See *reserve recognition accounting* for definition and contrast.

dual-transactions assumption (fiction). Occurs when an analyst, in understanding cash flows, views transactions not involving *cash* as though the firm first generated cash and then used it. For example, the analyst might view the issue of *capital stock* in return for the *asset* land as though the firm issued stock for *cash* and then used cash to acquire the land. Other examples of transactions that could involve the dual-transaction assumption are the issue of a *mortgage* in return for a noncurrent asset and the issue of stock to bondholders on *conversion* of their *convertible bonds.*

dual transfer prices. Occurs when the *transfer price charged* to the buying *division* differs from that *credited* to the selling division. Such prices make sense when the selling division has excess capacity and, as usual, the *fair market value* exceeds the *incremental cost* to produce the goods or services being transferred.

duality. The *double entry* record-keeping axiom that every *transaction* must result in equal *debit* and *credit* amounts.

dumping. A foreign firm's selling a good or service in the United States at a price below market price at home or, in some contexts, below some measure of cost (which concept is not clearly defined). The practice is illegal in the United States if it harms (or threatens to harm) a U.S. industry.

E

e. The base of natural logarithms; 2.71828. . . . If *interest* compounds continuously during a period at stated rate of *r* per period, then the effective *interest rate* is equivalent to interest compounded once per period at rate *i* where $i = e^r - 1$. Tables of e^r are widely available. If 12 percent annual interest compounds continuously, the effective annual rate is $e^{.12} - 1 = 12.75$ percent. Interest compounded continuously at rate *r* for *d* days is $e^{rd/365} - 1$. For example, interest compounded for 92 days at 12 percent is $e^{.12 \times 92/365} - 1 = 3.07$ percent.

earn-out. For two merging firms, an agreement in which the amount paid by the acquiring firm to the acquired firm's shareholders depends on the future earnings of the acquired firm or, perhaps, of the *consolidated entity.*

earned surplus. A term that writers once used, but no longer use, for *retained earnings.*

earnings. A term with no precise meaning but used to mean *income* or sometimes *profit.* The *FASB*, in requiring that firms report *comprehensive income,* encouraged firms to use the term "earnings" for the total formerly reported as *net income.* Firms will likely only slowly change from using the term "net income" to the term "earnings."

earnings, retained. See *retained earnings.*

earnings cycle. The period of time, or the series of transactions, during which a given firm converts *cash* into *goods* and *services,* then sells goods and services to customers, and finally collects cash from customers. *Cash cycle.*

earnings per share (of common stock). *Net income* to common shareholders (net income minus *preferred dividends*) divided by the average number of *common shares* outstanding; see also *primary earnings per share* and *fully diluted earnings per share.* See *ratio.*

earnings per share (of preferred stock). *Net income* divided by the average number of *preferred shares* outstanding during the period. This ratio indicates how well income covers (or protects) the preferred dividends; it does not indicate a legal share of *earnings.* See *ratio.*

earnings statement. *Income statement.*

easement. The acquired right or privilege of one person to use, or have access to, certain property of another. For example, a public utility's right to lay pipes or lines under the property of another and to service those facilities.

EBIT. *Earnings* before *income taxes;* acronym used by analysts.

EBITDA. *Earnings* before *income taxes, depreciation,* and *amortization;* acronym used by analysts to focus on a particular measure of *cash flow* used in valuation. This is not the same as, but is similar in concept to, *cash flow from operations.* Some analysts exclude *nonrecurring* items from this total.

economic consequences. The *FASB* says that in setting *accounting principles,* it should take into account the real effects on various participants in the business world. It calls these effects "economic consequences."

economic depreciation. Decline in *current cost* (or *fair value*) of an *asset* during a period.

economic entity. See *entity.*

economic life. The time span over which the firm expects to receive the benefits of an *asset.* The economic life of a *patent, copyright,* or *franchise* may be less than the legal life. *Service life.*

economic order quantity (EOQ). In mathematical *inventory* analysis, the optimal amount of stock to order when demand reduces inventory to a level called the "reorder point." If *A* represents the *incremental cost* of placing a single order, *D* represents the total demand for a period of time in units, and *H* represents the incremental holding cost during the period per unit of inventory, then the economic order quantity is $EOQ = \sqrt{2AD/H}$. Usage sometimes calls *EOQ* the "optimal lot size."

economic transfer pricing rule. Transfer at the *differential outlay cost* to the selling division (typically *variable costs*), plus the *opportunity cost* to the company of making the internal transfers ($0 if the seller has idle capacity, or selling price minus variable costs if the seller is operating at capacity).

economic value added (EVA®). The amount of earnings generated above the cost of funds invested to generate those earnings. To calculate economic value added, find the difference between the net after-tax operating profit and the product of the weighted-average cost of capital multiplied by the investment in the economic unit.

ED. *Exposure Draft.*

EDGAR. Electronic Data, Gathering, Analysis, and Retrieval system; rules and systems adopted by the *SEC* in 1993 to ensure that all the paperwork involved in the filings submitted by more than 15,000 public companies is electronically submitted.

EDP. *Electronic data processing.*

effective interest method. In computing *interest expense* (or *revenue*), a systematic method that makes the interest expense (revenue) for each period divided by the amount of the net *liability* (*asset*) at the beginning of the period equal to the *yield rate* on the liability (asset) at the time of issue (acquisition). Interest for a period is the yield rate (at time of issue) multiplied by the net liability (asset) at the start of the period. The *amortization* of discount or premium is the *plug* to give equal *debits* and *credits*. (Interest expense is a debit, and the amount of debt service payment is a credit.)

effective (interest) rate. Of a liability such as a bond, the *internal rate of return* or *yield to maturity* at the time of issue. Contrast with *coupon rate*. If the borrower issues the bond for a price below *par,* the effective rate is higher than the coupon rate; if it issues the bond for a price greater than par, the effective rate is lower than the coupon rate. In the context of *compound interest,* the effective rate occurs when the *compounding period* on a *loan* differs from one year, such as a nominal interest rate of 12 percent compounded monthly. The effective interest is the single rate that one could use at the end of the year to multiply the *principal* at the beginning of the year and give the same amount as results from compounding interest each period during the year. For example, if 12 percent per year compounds monthly, the effective annual interest rate is 12.683 percent. That is, if you compound $100 each month at 1 percent per month, the $100 will grow to $112.68 at the end of the year. In general, if the nominal rate of *r* percent per year compounds *m* times per year, then the effective rate is $(1 + r/m)^m - 1$.

efficiency variance. A term used for the *quantity variance* for materials or labor or *variable overhead* in a *standard costing system*.

efficient capital market. A market in which security prices reflect all available information and react nearly instantaneously and in an unbiased fashion to new information.

efficient market hypothesis. The finance supposition that security prices trade in *efficient capital markets*.

EITF. *Emerging Issues Task Force.*

electronic data processing. Performing computations and other data-organizing steps in a computer, in contrast to doing these steps by hand or with mechanical calculators.

eligible. Under income tax legislation, a term that restricts or otherwise alters the meaning of another tax or accounting term, generally to signify that the related assets or operations may receive a specified tax treatment.

eliminations. In preparing *consolidated statements, work sheet* entries made to avoid duplicating the amounts of *assets, liabilities, owners' equity, revenues,* and *expenses* of the consolidated *entity* when the firm sums the accounts of the *parent* and *subsidiaries.*

Emerging Issues Task Force (EITF). A group convened by the *FASB* to deal more rapidly with accounting issues than the FASB's due-process procedures can allow. The task force comprises about 20 members from public account-ing, industry, and several trade associations. It meets every six weeks. Several FASB board members usually attend and participate. The chief accountant of the *SEC* has indicated that the SEC will require that published financial statements follow guidelines set by a consensus of the EITF. The EITF requires that nearly all its members agree on a position before that position receives the label of "consensus." Such positions appear in *Abstracts of the EITF,* published by the FASB. Since 1984, the EITF has become one of the promulgators of *GAAP.*

employee stock option. See *stock option.*

Employee Stock Ownership Trust (or Plan). See *ESOT.*

employer, employee payroll taxes. See *payroll taxes.*

enabling costs. A type of *capacity cost* that a firm will stop incurring if it shuts down operations completely but will incur in full if it carries out operations at any level. Examples include costs of a security force or of a quality-control inspector for an assembly line. Contrast with *standby costs.*

encumbrance. In governmental accounting, an anticipated *expenditure* or *funds* restricted for an anticipated expenditure, such as for outstanding purchase orders. *Appropriations* less expenditures less outstanding encumbrances yields unencumbered balance.

ending inventory. The *cost* of *inventory* on hand at the end of the *accounting period;* often called "closing inventory." Ending inventory from the end of one period becomes the *beginning inventory* for the next period.

endorsee. See *endorser.*

endorsement. See *draft.* The *payee* signs the draft and transfers it to a fourth party, such as the payee's bank.

endorser. A *note* or *draft payee,* who signs the note after writing "Pay to the order of X," transfers the note to person X, and presumably receives some benefit, such as cash, in return. Usage refers to person X as the "endorsee." The endorsee then has the rights of the payee and may in turn become an endorser by endorsing the note to another endorsee.

engineered cost center. Responsibility center with sufficiently well-established relations between inputs and outputs that the analyst, given data on inputs, can predict the outputs or, conversely, given the outputs, can estimate the amounts of inputs that the process should have used. Consider the relation between pounds of flour (input) and loaves of bread (output). Contrast discretionary cost center, where such relations are so imprecise that analysts have no reliable way to relate inputs to outputs. Consider the relation between advertising the corporate logo or trademark (input) and future revenues (output).

engineering method (of cost estimation). To estimate unit cost of product from study of the materials, labor, and *overhead* components of the production process.

enterprise. Any business organization, usually defining the accounting *entity.*

enterprise fund. A *fund* that a governmental unit establishes to account for acquisition, operation, and maintenance of governmental services that the government intends to be self-supporting from user charges, such as for water or airports and some toll roads.

entity. A person, *partnership, corporation,* or other organization. The *accounting entity* that issues accounting statements may not be the same as the entity defined by law. For example, a *sole proprietorship* is an accounting entity, but the individual's combined business and personal assets are the legal entity in most jurisdictions. Several affiliated corporations may be separate legal entities but issue *consolidated financial statements* for the group of companies operating as a single economic entity.

entity theory. The corporation view that emphasizes the form of the *accounting equation* that says *assets = equities.* Contrast with *proprietorship theory.* The entity theory focuses less on the distinction between *liabilities* and *shareholders' equity* than does the proprietorship theory. The entity theory views all equities as coming to the corporation from outsiders who have claims of differing legal standings. The entity theory implies using a *multiple-step* income statement.

entry value. The *current cost* of acquiring an asset or service at a *fair market price. Replacement cost.*

EOQ. *Economic order quantity.*

EPS. *Earnings per share.*

EPVI. *Excess present value index.*

equalization reserve. An inferior title for the allowance or *estimated liability* account when the firm uses the *allowance method* for such things as maintenance expenses. Periodically, the accountant will debit maintenance *expense* and credit the allowance. As the firm makes *expenditures* for maintenance, it will debit the allowance and credit cash or the other asset used in maintenance.

equities. *Liabilities* plus *owners' equity.* See *equity.*

equity. A claim to *assets;* a source of assets. *SFAC No. 3* defines equity as "the residual interest in the assets of an entity that remains after deducting its liabilities." Thus, many knowledgeable people use "equity" to exclude liabilities and count only owners' equities. We prefer to use the term to mean all liabilities plus all owners' equity because there is no other single word that serves this useful purpose. We fight a losing battle.

equity financing. Raising *funds* by issuing *capital stock.* Contrast with *debt financing.*

equity method. In accounting for an *investment* in the stock of another company, a method that debits the proportionate share of the earnings of the other company to the investment account and credits that amount to a *revenue* account as earned. When the investor receives *dividends,* it debits *cash* and credits the investment account. An investor who owns sufficient shares of stock of an unconsolidated company to exercise significant control over the actions of that company must use the equity method. It is one of the few instances in which the firm recognizes revenue without an increase in *working capital.*

equity ratio. *Shareholders' equity* divided by total *assets.* See *ratio.*

equivalent production. *Equivalent units.*

equivalent units (of work). The number of units of completed output that would require the same costs that a firm would actually incur for the production of completed and partially completed units during a period. For example, if at the beginning of a period the firm starts 100 units and

by the end of the period has incurred costs for each of these equal to 75 percent of total costs to complete the units, then the equivalent units of work for the period would be 75. This is used primarily in *process costing* calculations to measure in uniform terms the output of a continuous process.

ERISA (Employee Retirement Income Security Act of 1974). The federal law that sets most *pension plan* requirements.

error accounting. See *accounting errors.*

escalator clause. Inserted in a purchase or rental contract, a clause that permits, under specified conditions, upward adjustments of price.

escapable cost. *Avoidable cost.*

ESOP (Employee Stock Ownership Plan). See *ESOT.*

ESOT (Employee Stock Ownership Trust). A trust *fund* that is created by a corporate employer and that can provide certain tax benefits to the corporation while providing for employee stock ownership. The corporate employer can contribute up to 25 percent of its payroll per year to the trust. The corporation may deduct the amount of the contribution from otherwise taxable income for federal *income tax* purposes. The trustee of the assets must use them for the benefit of employees—for example, to fund death or retirement benefits. The assets of the trust are usually the *common shares,* sometimes nonvoting, of the corporate employer. For an example of the potential *tax shelter,* consider the case of a corporation with $1 million of *debt* outstanding, which it wants to retire, and an annual payroll of $2 million. The corporation sells $1 million of common stock to the ESOT. The ESOT borrows $1 million with the loan guaranteed by, and therefore a *contingency* of, the corporation. The corporation uses the $1 million proceeds of the stock issue to retire its outstanding debt. (The debt of the corporation has been replaced with the debt of the ESOT.) The corporation can contribute $500,000 (= .25 × $2 million payroll) to the ESOT each year and treat the contribution as a deduction for tax purposes. After a little more than two years, the ESOT has received sufficient funds to retire its loan. The corporation has effectively repaid its original $1 million debt with pretax dollars. Assuming an income tax rate of 40 percent, it has saved $400,000 (= .40 × $1 million) of aftertax dollars *if* the $500,000 expense for the contribution to the ESOT for the pension benefits of employees would have been made, in one form or another, anyway. Observe that the corporation could use the proceeds ($1 million in the example) of the stock issued to the ESOT for any of several different purposes: financing expansion, replacing plant assets, or acquiring another company. Basically this same form of pretax-dollar financing through pensions is available with almost any corporate pension plan, with one important exception. The trustees of an ordinary pension trust must invest the assets prudently, and if they do not, they are personally liable to the employees. Current judgment about prudent investment requires diversification—trustees should invest pension trust assets in a wide variety of investment opportunities. (The trustee may not ordinarily invest more than 10 percent of a pension trust's assets in the parent's common stock.) Thus the ordinary pension trust cannot, in practice, invest all, or even most, of its assets in the parent corporation's stock. This constraint does not apply to the investments of an ESOT. The trustee may invest all ESOT assets in the parent company's stock. The ESOT also provides a means for closely held corporations to achieve wider ownership of shares without *going public*. The laws enabling ESOTs provide for the independent professional appraisal of shares not traded in public markets and for transactions between the corporation and the ESOT or between the ESOT and the employees to be based on the appraised values of the shares.

estate planning. The arrangement of an individual's affairs to facilitate the passage of assets to beneficiaries and to minimize taxes at death.

estimated expenses. See *after cost*.

estimated liability. The preferred terminology for estimated costs the firm will incur for such uncertain things as repairs under *warranty*. An estimated liability appears on the *balance sheet*. Contrast with *contingency*.

estimated revenue. A term used in governmental accounting to designate revenue expected to accrue during a period independent of whether the government will collect it during the period. The governmental unit usually establishes a *budgetary account* at the beginning of the budget period.

estimated salvage value. Synonymous with *salvage value* of an *asset* before its retirement.

estimates, changes in. See *accounting changes*.

estimation sampling. The use of sampling technique in which the sampler infers a qualitative (e.g., fraction female) or quantitative (e.g., mean weight) characteristic of the population from the occurrence of that characteristic in the sample drawn. See *attribute(s) sampling; variables sampling*.

EURL (entreprise unipersonnelle à responsabilité limitée). France: similar to *SARL* but having only one shareholder.

ex div. (dividend). Said of *shares* whose market price quoted in the market has been reduced by a *dividend* already declared but not yet paid. The *corporation* will send the dividend to the person who owned the share on the *record date*. One who buys the share ex dividend will not receive the dividend although the corporation has not yet paid it.

ex rights. The condition of securities whose quoted market price no longer includes the right to purchase new securities, such rights having expired or been retained by the seller. Compare *cum rights*.

except for. Qualification in *auditor's report,* usually caused by a change, approved by the auditor, from one acceptable accounting principle or procedure to another.

excess present value. In a *capital budgeting* context, *present value* (of anticipated net cash inflows minus cash outflows including initial cash outflow) for a project. The analyst uses the *cost of capital* as the *discount rate*.

excess present value index. *Present value* of future *cash* inflows divided by initial cash outlay.

exchange. The generic term for a transaction (or, more technically, a reciprocal transfer) between one entity and another; in another context, the name for a market, such as the New York Stock Exchange.

exchange gain or loss. The phrase used by the *FASB* for *foreign exchange gain or loss*.

exchange rate. The *price* of one country's currency in terms of another country's currency. For example, the British pound sterling might be worth US$1.60 at a given time. The exchange rate would be stated as "one pound is worth one dollar and sixty cents" or "one dollar is worth £.625" (= £1/$1.60).

excise tax. Tax on the manufacture, sale, or consumption of a commodity.

executory contract. A mere exchange of promises; an agreement providing for payment by a payor to a payee on the performance of an act or service by the payee, such as a labor contract. Accounting does not recognize benefits arising from executory contracts as *assets,* nor does it recognize obligations arising from such contracts as *liabilities*. See *partially executory contract*.

exemption. A term used for various amounts subtracted from gross income in computing taxable income. Usage does not call all such subtractions "exemptions." See *tax deduction*.

exercise. Occurs when owners of an *option* or *warrant* purchase the security that the option entitles them to purchase.

exercise price. See *option*.

exit value. The proceeds that would be received if assets were disposed of in an *arm's-length transaction. Current selling price; net realizable value*.

expectancy theory. The notion that people act in ways to obtain rewards and prevent penalties.

expected value. The mean or arithmetic *average* of a statistical distribution or series of numbers.

expected value of (perfect) information. Expected *net benefits* from an undertaking with (perfect) information minus expected net benefits of the undertaking without (perfect) information.

expendable fund. In governmental accounting, a *fund* whose resources, *principal,* and earnings the governmental unit may distribute.

expenditure. Payment of *cash* for goods or services received. Payment may occur at the time the purchaser receives the goods or services or at a later time. Virtually synonymous with *disbursement* except that disbursement is a broader term and includes all payments for goods or services. Contrast with *expense*.

expense. As a noun, a decrease in *owners' equity* accompanying the decrease in *net assets* caused by selling goods or rendering services or by the passage of time; a "gone" (net) asset; an expired cost. Measure expense as the *cost* of the (net) assets used. Do not confuse with *expenditure* or *disbursement,* which may occur before, when, or after the firm recognizes the related expense. Use the word "cost" to refer to an item that still has service potential and is an asset. Use the word "expense" after the firm has used the asset's service potential. As a verb, "expense" means to designate an expenditure—past, current, or future—as a current expense.

expense account. An *account* to accumulate *expenses; closed* to *retained earnings* at the end of the accounting period; a *temporary owners' equity* account; also used to describe a listing of expenses that an employee submits to the employer for reimbursement.

experience rating. A term used in insurance, particularly unemployment insurance, to denote changes from ordinary rates to reflect extraordinarily large or small amounts of claims over time by the insured.

expired cost. An *expense* or a *loss.*

Exposure Draft (ED). A preliminary statement of the *FASB* (or the *APB* between 1962 and 1973) showing the contents of a pronouncement being considered for enactment by the board.

external failure costs. Costs that a firm *incurs* when it detects nonconforming products and services after delivering them to customers, including warranty repairs, product liability, marketing costs, and *sales allowances.*

external reporting. Reporting to shareholders and the public, as opposed to internal reporting for management's benefit. See *financial accounting,* and contrast with *managerial accounting.*

extraordinary item. A *material expense* or *revenue* item characterized both by its unusual nature and by its infrequency of occurrence; appears along with its income tax effects separately from ordinary income and *income from discontinued operations* on the *income statement.* Accountants would probably classify a *loss* from an earthquake as an extraordinary item. Accountants treat gain (or loss) on the retirement of *bonds* as an extraordinary item under the terms of *SFAS No. 4.*

extrinsic rewards. Rewards that come from outside the individual, such as rewards from a teacher, a parent, an organization, or a spouse; they include grades, money, praise, and prizes. Contrast with *intrinsic rewards.*

F

face amount (value). The nominal amount due at *maturity* from a *bond* or *note* not including the contractual periodic payment that may also come due on the same date. Good usage calls the corresponding amount of a stock certificate the *par* or *stated value,* whichever applies.

facility-level activities. Work that supports the entire organization. Examples include top management, human resources, and research and development.

factoring. The process of buying *notes* or *accounts receivable* at a *discount* from the holder owed the debt; from the holder's point of view, the selling of such notes or accounts. When the transaction involves a single note, usage calls the process "discounting a note."

factory. Used synonymously with *manufacturing* as an adjective.

factory burden. *Manufacturing overhead.*

factory cost. *Manufacturing cost.*

factory expense. *Manufacturing overhead. Expense* is a poor term in this context because the item is a *product cost.*

factory overhead. Usually an item of *manufacturing cost* other than *direct labor* or *direct materials.*

fair market price (value). See *fair value.*

fair presentation (fairness). One of the qualitative standards of financial reporting. When the *auditor's report* says that the *financial statements* "present fairly . . . ," the auditor means that the accounting alternatives used by the entity all comply with *GAAP.* In recent years, however, courts have ruled that conformity with *generally accepted accounting principles* may be insufficient grounds for an opinion that the statements are fair. *SAS No. 5* requires that the auditor judge the accounting principles used in the statements to be "appropriate in the circumstances" before attesting to fair presentation.

fair value, fair market price (value). Price (value) negotiated at *arm's length* between a willing buyer and a willing seller, each acting rationally in his or her own self-interest. The accountant may estimate this amount in the absence of a monetary transaction. This is sometimes measured as the present value of expected cash flows.

fair-value hedge. A hedge of an exposure to changes in the *fair value* of a recognized *asset* or *liability* or of an unrecognized firm commitment.

FASAC. *Financial Accounting Standards Advisory Council.*

FASB (Financial Accounting Standards Board). An independent board responsible, since 1973, for establishing *generally accepted accounting principles.* Its official pronouncements are *Statements of Financial Accounting Concepts (SFAC), Statements of Financial Accounting Standards (SFAS),* and *FASB Interpretations.* See also *Discussion Memorandum* and *Technical Bulletin.* Web site: http://www.fasb.org.

FASB Interpretation. An official *FASB* statement interpreting the meaning of *Accounting Research Bulletins, APB Opinions,* and *Statements of Financial Accounting Standards.*

FASB Technical Bulletin. See *Technical Bulletin.*

favorable variance. An excess of actual *revenues* over expected revenues; an excess of *standard cost* over actual cost.

federal income tax. *Income tax* levied by the U.S. government on individuals and corporations.

Federal Insurance Contributions Act. See *FICA.*

Federal Unemployment Tax Act. See *FUTA.*

feedback. The process of informing employees about how their actual performance compares with the expected or desired level of performance, in the hope that the information will reinforce desired behavior and reduce unproductive behavior.

FEI. *Financial Executives Institute.*

FICA (Federal Insurance Contributions Act). The law that sets *Social Security taxes* and benefits.

fiduciary. Someone responsible for the custody or administration of property belonging to another; for example, an executor (of an estate), agent, receiver (in *bankruptcy*), or trustee (of a trust).

FIFO (first-in, first-out). The *inventory flow assumption* that firms use to compute *ending inventory* cost from most recent purchases and *cost of goods sold* from oldest purchases including beginning inventory. FIFO describes cost flow from the viewpoint of the income statement. From the balance sheet perspective, *LISH* (last-in, still-here) describes this same cost flow. Contrast with *LIFO.*

finance. As a verb, to supply with *funds* through the *issue* of stocks, bonds, notes, or mortgages or through the retention of earnings.

financial accounting. The accounting for *assets, equities, revenues,* and *expenses* of a business; primarily concerned with the historical reporting, to external users, of the *financial position* and operations of an *entity* on a regular, periodic basis. Contrast with *managerial accounting.*

Financial Accounting Foundation. The independent foundation (committee), governed by a board of trustees, that raises funds to support the *FASB* and *GASB.*

Financial Accounting Standards Advisory Council (FASAC). A committee of academics, preparers, attestors, and users giving advice to the *FASB* on matters of strategy and emerging issues. The council spends much of each meeting learning about current developments in standard-setting from the FASB staff.

Financial Accounting Standards Board. *FASB.*

Financial Executives Institute (FEI). An organization of financial executives, such as chief accountants, *controllers,* and treasurers, of large businesses. In recent years, the FEI has been a critic of the FASB because it views many of the FASB requirements as burdensome while not *cost-effective.*

financial expense. An *expense* incurred in raising or managing *funds.*

financial flexibility. As defined by *SFAC No. 5,* "the ability of an entity to take effective actions to alter amounts and timing of cash flows so it can respond to unexpected needs and opportunities."

financial forecast. See *financial projection* for definition and contrast.

financial instrument. The *FASB* defines this term as follows: "Cash, evidence of an ownership interest in an entity, or a contract that both:

[a] imposes on one entity a contractual obligation (1) to deliver cash or another financial instrument to a second entity or (2) to exchange financial instruments on potentially unfavorable terms with the second entity, and

[b] conveys to that second entity a contractual right (1) to receive cash or another financial instrument from the first entity or (2) to exchange other financial instruments on potentially favorable terms with the first entity."

financial leverage. See *leverage.*

financial model. Model, typically expressed with arithmetic relations, that allows an organization to test the interaction of economic variables in a variety of settings.

financial position (condition). Statement of the *assets* and *equities* of a firm; displayed as a *balance sheet.*

financial projection. An estimate of *financial position,* results of *operations,* and changes in cash flows for one or more future periods based on a set of assumptions. If the assumptions do not represent the most likely outcomes, then auditors call the estimate a "projection." If the assumptions represent the most probable outcomes, then auditors call the estimate a "forecast." "Most probable" means that management has evaluated the assumptions and that they are management's judgment of the most likely set of conditions and most likely outcomes.

financial ratio. See *ratio.*

financial reporting objectives. Broad objectives that are intended to guide the development of specific *accounting standards;* set out by *FASB SFAC No. 1.*

Financial Reporting Release. Series of releases, issued by the SEC since 1982; replaces the *Accounting Series Release.* See *SEC.*

financial statements. The *balance sheet, income statement, statement of retained earnings, statement of cash flows,* statement of changes in *owners' equity accounts,* statement of *comprehensive income,* and *notes* thereto.

financial structure. *Capital structure.*

financial vice-president. Person in charge of the entire accounting and finance function; typically one of the three most influential people in the company.

financial year. Australia and UK: term for *fiscal year.*

financing activities. Obtaining resources from (a) owners and providing them with a return on and a return of their *investment* and (b) *creditors* and repaying amounts borrowed (or otherwise settling the obligation). See *statement of cash flows.*

financing lease. *Capital lease.*

finished goods (inventory account). Manufactured product ready for sale; a *current asset* (inventory) account.

firm. Informally, any business entity. (Strictly speaking, a firm is a *partnership.*)

firm commitment. The *FASB,* in *SFAS No. 133,* defines this as "an agreement with an unrelated party, binding on both parties and usually legally enforceable," which requires that the firm promise to pay a specified amount of a currency and that the firm has sufficient disincentives for nonpayment that the firm will probably make the payment. A firm commitment resembles a *liability,* but it is an *executory contract,* so is not a liability. *SFAS No. 133* allows the firm to recognize certain financial *hedges* in the balance sheet if they hedge firm commitments. The *FASB* first used the term in *SFAS No. 52* and *No. 80* but made the term more definite and more important in *SFAS No. 133.* This is an early, perhaps the first, step in changing the recognition criteria for assets and liabilities to exclude the test that the future benefit (asset) or obligation (liability) not arise from an executory contract.

first-in, first-out. See *FIFO.*

fiscal year. A period of 12 consecutive months chosen by a business as the *accounting period* for *annual reports,* not necessarily a *natural business year* or a calendar year.

FISH. An acronym, conceived by George H. Sorter, for *first-in, still-here.* FISH is the same cost flow assumption as *LIFO.* Many readers of accounting statements find it easier to think about inventory questions in terms of items still on hand. Think of LIFO in connection with *cost of goods sold* but of FISH in connection with *ending inventory.* See *LISH.*

fixed assets. *Plant assets.*

fixed assets turnover. *Sales* divided by average total *fixed assets.*

fixed benefit plan. A *defined-benefit plan.*

fixed budget. A plan that provides for specified amounts of *expenditures* and *receipts* that do not vary with activity levels; sometimes called a "static budget." Contrast with *flexible budget.*

fixed charges earned (coverage) ratio. *Income* before *interest expense* and *income tax expense* divided by interest expense.

fixed cost (expense). An *expenditure* or *expense* that does not vary with volume of activity, at least in the short run. See *capacity costs*, which include *enabling costs* and *standby costs*, and *programmed costs* for various subdivisions of fixed costs. See *cost terminology*.

fixed cost price variance (spending variance). The difference between actual and *budgeted fixed costs*.

fixed interval sampling. A method of choosing a sample: the analyst selects the first item from the population randomly, drawing the remaining sample items at equally spaced intervals.

fixed liability. *Long-term* liability.

fixed manufacturing overhead applied. The portion of *fixed manufacturing overhead cost* allocated to units produced during a period.

fixed overhead variance. Difference between *actual fixed manufacturing costs* and fixed manufacturing costs applied to production in a *standard costing system*.

flexible budget. *Budget* that projects receipts and expenditures as a function of activity levels. Contrast with *fixed budget*.

flexible budget allowance. With respect to manufacturing overhead, the total cost that a firm should have incurred at the level of activity actually experienced during the period.

float. *Checks* whose amounts the bank has *added* to the depositor's bank account but whose amounts the bank has not yet reduced from the *drawer's* bank account.

flow. The change in the amount of an item over time. Contrast with *stock*.

flow assumption. An assumption used when the firm makes a *withdrawal* from *inventory*. The firm must compute the cost of the withdrawal by a flow assumption if the firm does not use the *specific identification* method. The usual flow assumptions are *FIFO, LIFO,* and *weighted average*.

flow of costs. *Costs* passing through various classifications within an *entity* engaging, at least in part, in manufacturing activities. See the accompanying diagram for a summary of *product* and *period cost* flows.

flow-through method. Accounting for the *investment credit* to show all income statement benefits of the credit in the year of acquisition rather than spreading them over the life of the asset acquired (called the "deferral method"). The *APB* preferred the deferral method in *Opinion No. 2* (1962) but accepted the flow-through method in *Opinion*

Flow of Costs (and Sales Revenue)

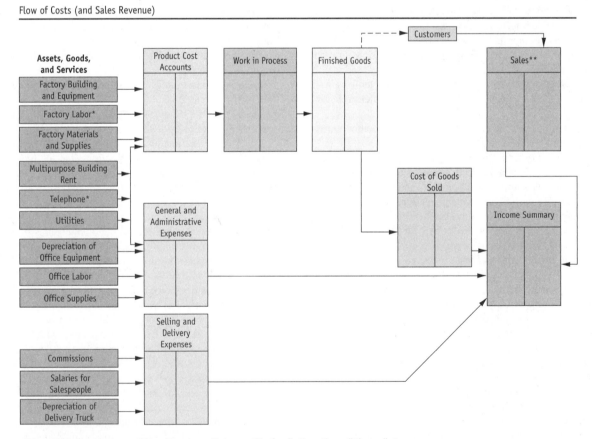

*The credit in the entry to record these items is usually to a payable; for all others, the credit is usually to an asset, or to an asset contra account.

**When the firm records sales to customers, it credits the Sales account. The debit is usually to Cash or Accounts Receivable.

No. 4 (1964). The term also applies to *depreciation* accounting in which the firm uses the *straight-line method* for financial reporting and an *accelerated depreciation* method for tax reporting. Followers of the flow-through method would not recognize a *deferred tax liability. APB Opinion No. 11* prohibits the use of the flow-through approach in financial reporting, although some regulatory commissions have used it.

FOB. Free on board some location (for example, FOB shipping point, FOB destination). The *invoice* price includes delivery at seller's expense to that location. Title to goods usually passes from seller to buyer at the FOB location.

folio. A page number or other identifying reference used in posting to indicate the source of entry.

footing. Adding a column of figures.

footnotes. More detailed information than that provided in the *income statement, balance sheet, statement of retained earnings,* and *statement of cash flows.* These are an integral part of the statements, and the *auditor's report* covers them. They are sometimes called "notes."

forecast. See *financial projection* for definition and contrast.

foreclosure. Occurs when a lender takes possession of property for his or her own use or sale after the borrower fails to make a required payment on a *mortgage.* Assume that the lender sells the property but that the proceeds of the sale are too small to cover the outstanding balance on the loan at the time of foreclosure. Under the terms of most mortgages, the lender becomes an unsecured creditor of the borrower for the still-unrecovered balance of the loan.

foreign currency. For *financial statements* prepared in a given currency, any other currency.

foreign currency translation. Reporting in the currency used in financial statements the amounts denominated or measured in a different currency.

foreign exchange gain or loss. Gain or loss from holding *net* foreign *monetary items* during a period when the *exchange rate* changes.

foreign sales corporation. See *FSC.*

forfeited share. A share to which a subscriber has lost title because of nonpayment of a *call.*

Form 10-K. See *10-K.*

Form 20-F. See *20-F.*

forward contract. An agreement to purchase or sell a specific commodity or financial instrument for a specified price, the *forward price,* at a specified date. Contrast with *futures contract.* Typically, forward contracts are not traded on organized exchanges (unlike *futures contract*), so the parties to the agreement sacrifice liquidity but gain flexibility in setting contract quantities, qualities, and settlement dates.

forward-exchange contract. An agreement to exchange at a specified future date currencies of different countries at a specified rate called the "forward rate."

forward price. The price of a commodity for delivery at a specified future date; in contrast to the "spot price," the price of that commodity on the day of the price quotation.

franchise. A privilege granted or sold, such as to use a name or to sell products or services.

fraudulent conveyance. A transfer of goods or cash that a court finds illegal. *Creditors* of a *bankrupt* firm usually receive less than the firm owed them. For example, a creditor of a bankrupt firm might collect from the trustee of the bankrupt firm only $.60 for every dollar the bankrupt firm owed. Creditors, anticipating bankruptcy, sometimes attempt to persuade the firm to pay the debt in full before the firm declares bankruptcy, reducing the net assets available to other creditors. Bankruptcy laws have rules forbidding such transfers from a near-bankrupt firm to some of its creditors. Such a transfer is called a "fraudulent conveyance." Courts sometimes ask accountants to judge whether a firm had liabilities exceeding assets even before the firm went into bankruptcy. When the court can find that economic bankruptcy occurred before legal bankruptcy, it will declare transfers of assets to creditors after economic bankruptcy to be fraudulent conveyances and have the assets returned to the trustees (or to a legal entity called the "bankrupt's estate") for redistribution to all creditors.

fraudulent financial reporting. Intentional or reckless conduct that results in materially misleading *financial statements.* See *creative accounting.*

free cash flow. This term has no standard meaning. Some financial statement analysts use it to mean *cash flow from operations + interest expense + income tax expense.* Others mean the excess of cash flow from operations over cash flow for investing. Usage varies so much that you should ascertain the meaning intended in context by this phrase.

free on board. *FOB.*

freight-in. The *cost* of freight or shipping incurred in acquiring *inventory,* preferably treated as a part of the cost of *inventory;* often shown temporarily in an *adjunct account* that the acquirer closes at the end of the period with other purchase accounts to the inventory account.

freight-out. The *cost* of freight or shipping incurred in selling *inventory,* treated by the seller as a selling *expense* in the period of sale.

FSC (foreign sales corporation). A foreign *corporation* engaging in certain export activities, some of whose *income* the United States exempts from federal *income tax.* A U.S. corporation need pay no income taxes on *dividends* distributed by an FSC out of *earnings* attributable to certain foreign income.

full absorption costing. The *costing* method that assigns all types of manufacturing costs (*direct material, direct labor, fixed* and *variable overhead*) to units produced; required by *GAAP;* also called "absorption costing." Contrast with *variable costing.*

full costing, full costs. The total cost of producing and selling a unit; often used in *long-term* profitability and pricing decisions. Full cost per unit equals *full absorption cost* per unit plus *marketing, administrative, interest,* and other *central corporate expenses,* per unit. The sum of full costs for all units equals total costs of the firm.

full disclosure. The reporting policy requiring that all significant or *material* information appear in the financial statements. See *fair presentation.*

fully diluted earnings per share. For *common stock,* smallest *earnings per share* figure that one can obtain by computing an earnings per share for all possible combinations of assumed *exercise* or *conversion* of *potentially dilutive securities*. This figure must appear on the *income statement* if it is less than 97 percent of earnings available to common shareholders divided by the average number of common shares outstanding during the period.

fully vested. Said of a *pension plan* when an employee (or his or her estate) has rights to all the benefits purchased with the employer's contributions to the plan even if the employee does not work for this employer at the time of death or retirement.

function. In governmental accounting, said of a group of related activities for accomplishing a service or regulatory program for which the governmental unit has responsibility; in mathematics, a rule for associating a number, called the dependent variable, with another number (or numbers), called independent variable(s).

functional classification. *Income statement* reporting form that classifies *expenses* by function, that is, cost of goods sold, administrative expenses, financing expenses, selling expenses. Contrast with *natural classification*.

functional currency. Currency in which an entity carries out its principal economic activity.

fund. An *asset* or group of assets set aside for a specific purpose. See also *fund accounting*.

fund accounting. The accounting for resources, obligations, and *capital* balances, usually of a not-for-profit or governmental *entity*, which the entity has segregated into *accounts* representing logical groupings based on legal, donor, or administrative restrictions or requirements. The groupings are "funds." The accounts of each fund are *self-balancing*, and from them one can prepare a *balance sheet* and an operating statement for each fund. See *fund* and *fund balance*.

fund balance. In governmental accounting, the excess of assets of a *fund* over its liabilities and reserves; the not-for-profit equivalent of *owners' equity*.

funded. Said of a *pension plan* or other obligation when the firm has set aside *funds* for meeting the obligation when it comes due. The federal law for pension plans requires that the firm fund all *normal costs* when it recognizes them as expenses. In addition, the firm must fund *prior service cost* of pension plans over 30 or over 40 years, depending on the circumstances.

funding. Replacing *short-term* liabilities with *long-term* debt.

funds. Generally *working capital;* current assets less current liabilities; sometimes used to refer to *cash* or to cash and *marketable securities*.

funds provided by operations. See *cash provided by operations*.

funds statement. An informal name often used for the *statement of cash flows*.

funny money. Said of securities, such as *convertible preferred stock, convertible bonds, options,* and *warrants,* that have aspects of *common shares* but that did not reduce reported *earnings per share* before the issuance of *APB Opinion No. 9* in 1966 and *No. 15* in 1969.

FUTA (Federal Unemployment Tax Act). Provides for taxes to be collected at the federal level, to help subsidize the individual states' administration of their unemployment compensation programs.

future value. Value at a specified future date of a sum increased at a specified *interest rate*.

futures contract. An agreement to purchase or sell a specific commodity or financial instrument for a specified price, at a specific future time or during a specified future period. Contrast with *forward contract*. When traded on an organized exchange, the exchange sets the minimum contract size and expiration date(s). The exchange requires that the holder of the contract settle in cash each day the fluctuations in the value of the contract. That is, each day, the exchange marks the contract to market value, called the "(daily) settlement price." A contract holder who has lost during the day must put up more cash, and a holder who has gained receives cash.

G

GAAP. *Generally accepted accounting principles;* a plural noun. In the UK and elsewhere, this means "generally accepted accounting practices."

GAAS. *Generally accepted auditing standards;* a plural noun. Do not confuse with *GAS*.

gain. In *financial accounting* contexts, the increase in *owners' equity* caused by a transaction that is not part of a firm's typical, day-to-day operations and not part of owners' *investment* or *withdrawals*. Accounting distinguishes the meaning of the term "gain" (or *loss*) from that of related terms. First, gains (and losses) generally refer to nonoperating, incidental, peripheral, or nonroutine transactions: gain on sale of land in contrast to *gross margin* on *sale* of *inventory*. Second, gains and losses are *net* concepts, not gross concepts: gain or loss results from subtracting some measure of *cost* from the measure of inflow. *Revenues* and *expenses,* on the other hand, are gross concepts; their difference is a net concept. Gain is nonroutine and net, *profit* or *margin* is routine and net; revenue from *continuing operations* is routine and gross; revenue from *discontinued operations* is nonroutine and gross. Loss is net but can be either routine ("loss on sale of inventory") or not ("loss on disposal of segment of business").

In *managerial accounting* and lay contexts, the difference between some measure of *revenue* or *receipts* or *proceeds* and some measure of costs, such as direct costs or variable costs or fully absorbed costs or full costs (see *cost terminology*). Because the word can have so many different meanings, careful writers should be explicit to designate one.

gain contingency. See *contingency*.

GAS. *Goods available for sale*. Do not confuse with *GAAS*.

GASB (Governmental Accounting Standards Board). An independent body responsible, since 1984, for establishing accounting standards for state and local government units. It is part of the *Financial Accounting Foundation,* parallel to the *FASB,* and currently consists of five members.

GbR (Gesellschaft des bürgerlichen Rechtes). Germany: a *partnership* whose members agree to share in specific aspects of their own separate business pursuits, such as an office. This partnership has no legal form and is not a separate accounting *entity*.

GDP Implicit Price Deflator (index). A *price index* issued quarterly by the Office of Business Economics of the U.S. Department of Commerce. This index attempts to trace the price level of all *goods and services* composing the *gross domestic product.* Contrast with *Consumer Price Index.*

gearing. UK: *financial leverage.*

gearing adjustment. A *revenue* representing part of a *holding gain.* Consider a firm that has part of its assets financed by *noncurrent liabilities* and that has experienced *holding gains* on its *assets* during a period. All the increase in wealth caused by the holding gains belongs to the owners; none typically belongs to the lenders. Some British accounting authorities believe that published *income statements* should show part of the holding gain in *income* for the period. The part they would report in income is the fraction of the gain equal to the fraction that debt composes of total financing; for example, if debt equals 40 percent of total equities and the holding gain equals $100 for the period, the amount to appear in income for the period would be $40. Usage calls that part the "gearing adjustment."

general debt. A governmental unit's debt legally payable from general revenues and backed by the full faith and credit of the governmental unit.

general expenses. *Operating expenses* other than those specifically identified as cost of goods sold, selling, and administration.

general fixed asset (group of accounts). Accounts showing a governmental unit's long-term assets that are not accounted for in *enterprise, trust,* or intragovernmental service funds.

general fund. A nonprofit entity's assets and liabilities not specifically earmarked for other purposes; the primary operating fund of a governmental unit.

general journal. The formal record in which the firm records transactions, or summaries of similar transactions, in *journal entry* form as they occur. Use of the adjective "general" usually implies that the journal has only two columns for cash amounts or that the firm also uses various *special journals,* such as a *check register* or *sales journal.*

general ledger. The name for the formal *ledger* containing all the financial statement accounts. It has equal debits and credits, as evidenced by the *trial balance.* Some of the accounts in the general ledger may be *control accounts,* supported by details contained in *subsidiary ledgers.*

general partner. *Partnership* member who is personally liable for all debts of the partnership; contrast with *limited partner.*

general price index. A measure of the aggregate prices of a wide range of goods and services in the economy at one time relative to the prices during a base period. See *Consumer Price Index* and *GDP Implicit Price Deflator.* Contrast with *specific price index.*

general price level–adjusted statements. See *constant-dollar accounting.*

general price-level changes. Changes in the aggregate prices of a wide range of goods and services in the economy. These price measurements result from using a *general price index.* Contrast with *specific price changes.*

general purchasing power. The command of the dollar over a wide range of goods and services in the economy. The general purchasing power of the dollar is inversely related to changes in a general price index. See *general price index.*

general purchasing-power accounting. See *constant-dollar accounting.*

generally accepted accounting principles (GAAP). As previously defined by the *CAP, APB,* and now the *FASB,* the conventions, rules, and procedures necessary to define accepted accounting practice at a particular time; includes both broad guidelines and relatively detailed practices and procedures. In the United States the FASB defines GAAP to include accounting pronouncements of the *SEC* and other government agencies as well as a variety of authoritative sources, such as this book.

generally accepted auditing standards (GAAS). The *PCAOB* has explicitly stated that it began compiling its auditing promulgations with GAAS, as issued by the *AICPA,* but "a reference to generally accepted auditing standards in auditors' reports is no longer appropriate or necessary." The phrase has referred to the standards, as opposed to particular procedures, that the AICPA promulgated (in *Statements on Auditing Standards*) and that concern "the auditor's professional quantities" and "the judgment exercised by him in the performance of his examination and in his report." Currently, there have been ten such standards: three general ones (concerned with proficiency, independence, and degree of care to be exercised), three standards of field work, and four standards of reporting. The first standard of reporting requires that the *auditor's report* state whether the firm prepared the *financial statements* in accordance with *generally accepted accounting principles.* Thus, before the PCAOB became the auditing rulemaker, the typical auditor's report says that the auditor conducted the examination in accordance with generally accepted auditing standards and that the firm prepared the statements in accordance with generally accepted accounting principles. The report will not refer to the standards of the Public Company Accounting Oversight Board (United States). See *auditor's report.*

geographic segment. A single operation or a group of operations that are located in a particular geographic area and that generate revenue, incur costs, and have assets used in or associated with generating such revenue.

G4+1. A group concerned with unifying accounting standards across countries. It originally comprised the *FASB,* *CICA* (Canada), the Accounting Standards Board (UK), and the Australian Accounting Standards Board, plus the *IASB.* Hence, the name: a group of four national standard-setters plus the *IASB.* The group now includes participants from New Zealand.

GIE (groupement d'intérêt économique). France: a joint venture, normally used for exports and research-and-development pooling.

GmbH (Gesellschaft mit beschränkter Haftung). Germany: a private company with an unlimited number of shareholders. Transfer of ownership can take place only with the consent of other shareholders. Contrast with *AG.*

goal congruence. The idea that all members of an organization have incentives to perform for a common interest, such as *shareholder* wealth maximization for a *corporation*.

going-concern assumption. For accounting purposes, accountants' assumption that a business will remain in operation long enough to carry out all its current plans. This assumption partially justifies the *acquisition cost* basis, rather than a *liquidation* or *exit value* basis, of accounting.

going public. Said of a business when its *shares* become widely traded rather than being closely held by relatively few shareholders; issuing shares to the general investing public.

goods. Items of merchandise, supplies, raw materials, or finished goods. Sometimes the meaning of "goods" is extended to include all *tangible* items, as in the phrase "goods and services."

goods available for sale. The sum of *beginning inventory* plus all acquisitions of merchandise or finished goods during an *accounting period*.

goods-in-process. *Work-in-process*.

goodwill. The excess of cost of an acquired firm (or operating unit) over the current *fair market value* of the separately identifiable *net assets* of the acquired unit. Before the acquiring firm can recognize goodwill, it must assign a fair market value to all identifiable assets, even when not recorded on the books of the acquired unit. For example, if a firm has developed a *patent* that does not appear on its books because of *SFAS No. 2*, if another company acquires the firm, the acquirer will recognize the patent at an amount equal to its estimated fair market value. The acquirer will compute the amount of goodwill only after assigning values to all assets it can identify. Informally, the term indicates the value of good customer relations, high employee morale, a well-respected business name, and so on, all of which the firm or analyst expects to result in greater-than-normal earning power.

goodwill method. A method of accounting for the *admission* of a new partner to a *partnership* when the new partner will receive a portion of capital different from the value of the *tangible* assets contributed as a fraction of tangible assets of the partnership. See *bonus method* for a description and contrast.

Governmental Accounting Standards Advisory Council. A group that consults with the *GASB* on agenda, technical issues, and the assignment of priorities to projects. It comprises more than a dozen members representing various areas of expertise.

Governmental Accounting Standards Board. *GASB*.

GPL (general price level). Usually used as an adjective modifying the word "accounting" to mean *constant-dollar accounting*.

GPLA (general price level–adjusted accounting). *Constant-dollar accounting*.

GPP (general purchasing power). Usually used as an adjective modifying the word "accounting" to mean *constant-dollar accounting*.

graded vesting. Said of a *pension plan* in which not all employees currently have fully *vested* benefits. By law, the benefits must vest according to one of several formulas as time passes.

grandfather clause. An exemption in new accounting *pronouncements* exempting transactions that occurred before a given date from the new accounting treatment. For example, *APB Opinion No. 17,* adopted in 1970, exempted *goodwill* acquired before 1970 from required *amortization*. The term "grandfather" appears in the title to *SFAS No. 10*.

gross. Not adjusted or reduced by deductions or subtractions. Contrast with *net,* and see *gain* for a description of how the difference between net and gross affects usage of the terms *revenue, gain, expense,* and *loss*.

gross domestic product (GDP). The market value of all goods and services produced by capital or labor within a country, regardless of who owns the capital or of the nationality of the labor; most widely used measure of production within a country. Contrast with gross national product (GNP), which measures the market value of all goods and services produced with capital owned by, and labor services supplied by, the residents of that country regardless of where they work or where they own capital. In the United States in recent years, the difference between GDP and GNP equals about two-tenths of 1 percent of GDP.

gross margin. *Net sales* minus *cost of goods sold*.

gross margin percent. $100 \times (1 - cost\ of\ goods\ sold/net\ sales) = 100 \times (gross\ margin/net\ sales)$.

gross national product (GNP). See *gross domestic product* for definition and contrast.

gross price method (of recording purchase or sales discounts). The firm records the *purchase* (or *sale*) at the *invoice price,* not deducting the amounts of *discounts* available. Later, it uses a *contra* account to purchases (or sales) to record the amounts of discounts taken. Since information on discounts lapsed will not emerge from this system, most firms should prefer the *net price method* of recording purchase discounts.

gross profit. *Gross margin*.

gross profit method. A method of estimating *ending inventory* amounts. First, the firm measures *cost of goods sold* as some fraction of sales; then, it uses the *inventory equation* to value *ending inventory*.

gross profit ratio. *Gross margin* divided by *net sales*.

gross sales. All *sales* at *invoice* prices, not reduced by *discounts, allowances, returns,* or other adjustments.

group depreciation. In calculating *depreciation* charges, a method that combines similar assets rather than depreciating them separately. It does not recognize gain or loss on retirement of items from the group until the firm sells or retires the last item in the group. See *composite life method*.

Group of 4 Plus 1. See *G4+1*.

guarantee. A promise to answer for payment of debt or performance of some obligation if the person liable for the debt or obligation fails to perform. A guarantee is a *contingency* of the *entity* making the promise. Often, writers use the words "guarantee" and "warranty" to mean the same thing. In precise usage, however, "guarantee" means some person's promise to perform a contractual obligation such as to pay a sum of cash, whereas "warranty" refers to promises about pieces of machinery or other products. See *warranty.*

H

half-year convention. In *tax accounting* under *ACRS,* and sometimes in *financial accounting,* an assumption that the firm acquired *depreciable assets* at midyear of the year of acquisition. When the firm uses this convention, it computes the *depreciation charge* for the year as one-half the charge that it would have used if it had acquired the assets at the beginning of the year.

hardware. The physical equipment or devices forming a computer and peripheral equipment.

hash total. Used to establish accuracy of data processing; a control that takes the sum of data items not normally added together (e.g., the sum of a list of part numbers) and subsequently compares that sum with a computer-generated total of the same values. If the two sums are identical, then the analyst takes some comfort that the two lists are identical.

Hasselback. An annual directory of accounting faculty at colleges and universities; gives information about the faculty's training and fields of specialization. James R. Hasselback, of Florida State University, has compiled the directory since the 1970s; Prentice-Hall distributes it. Online, you can find it at the Rutgers University accounting Web site: http://www.rutgers.edu/Accounting/.

health-care benefits obligation. At any time, the present value of the non-pension benefits promised by an employer to employees during their retirement years.

hedge. To reduce, perhaps cancel altogether, one risk the entity already bears, by purchasing a security or other financial instrument. For example, a farmer growing corn runs the risk that corn prices may decline before the corn matures and can be brought to market. Such a farmer can arrange to sell the corn now for future delivery, hedging the risk of corn price changes. A firm may have a *receivable* denominated in German marks due in six months. It runs the risk that the exchange rate between the dollar and the mark will change and the firm will receive a smaller number of dollars in the future than it would receive from the same number of marks received today. Such a firm may hedge its exposure to risk of changes in the exchange rate between dollars and German marks in a variety of ways.

held-to-maturity securities. *Marketable debt securities* that a firm expects to, and has the ability to, hold to *maturity;* a classification important in *SFAS No. 115,* which generally requires the owner to carry marketable securities on the balance sheet at market value, not at cost. Under *SFAS No. 115,* the firm may show held-to-maturity debt securities at *amortized cost.* If the firm lacks either the expectation or the intent to hold the debt security to its maturity, then the firm will show that security at market value as a security *available for sale.*

hidden reserve. An amount by which a firm has understated *owners' equity,* perhaps deliberately. The understatement arises from an undervaluation of *assets* or overvaluation of *liabilities.* By undervaluing assets on this period's *balance sheet,* the firm can overstate *net income* in some future period by disposing of the asset: actual *revenues* less artificially low cost of assets sold yields artificially high net income. No *account* in the *ledger* has this title.

hire-purchase agreement (contract). UK: a *lease* containing a purchase *option.*

historical cost. *Acquisition cost; original cost; a sunk cost.*

historical cost/constant-dollar accounting. Accounting based on *historical cost* valuations measured in *constant dollars.* The method restates *nonmonetary items* to reflect changes in the *general purchasing power* of the dollar since the time the firm acquired specific *assets* or incurred specific *liabilities.* The method recognizes a *gain* or *loss* on *monetary items* as the firm holds them over time periods when the general purchasing power of the dollar changes.

historical exchange rate. The rate at which one currency converts into another at the date a transaction took place. Contrast with *current exchange rate.*

historical summary. A part of the *annual report* that shows items, such as *net income, revenues, expenses, asset* and *equity* totals, *earnings per share,* and the like, for five or ten periods including the current one. Usually not as much detail appears in the historical summary as in *comparative statements,* which typically report as much detail for the two preceding years as for the current year. Annual reports may contain both comparative statements and a historical summary.

historical valuation. Showing balance sheet amounts at acquisition cost, sometimes reduced for *accumulated amortization;* sometimes reduced to *lower of cost or market.*

holdback. Under the terms of a contract, a portion of the progress payments that the customer need not pay until the contractor has fulfilled the contract or satisfied financial obligations to subcontractors.

holding company. A company that confines its activities to owning *stock* in, and supervising management of, other companies. A holding company usually owns a controlling interest in—that is, more than 50 percent of the voting stock of—the companies whose stock it holds. Contrast with *mutual fund.* See *conglomerate.* In British usage, the term refers to any company with controlling interest in another company.

holding gain or loss. Difference between end-of-period price and beginning-of-period price of an asset held during the period. The financial statements ordinarily do not separately report realized holding gains and losses. Income does not usually report unrealized gains at all, except on *trading securities.* See *lower of cost or market.* See *inventory profit* for further refinement, including *gains* on *assets* sold during the period.

holding gain or loss net of inflation. Increase or decrease in the *current cost* of an asset while it is held; measured in units of *constant dollars.*

horizontal analysis. *Time-series analysis.*

horizontal integration. An organization's extension of activity in the same general line of business or its expansion into supplementary, complementary, or compatible products. Compare *vertical integration*.

house account. An account with a customer who does not pay sales commissions.

human resource accounting. A term used to describe a variety of proposals that seek to report the importance of human resources—knowledgeable, trained, and loyal employees—in a company's earning process and total assets.

hurdle rate. Required rate of return in a *discounted cash flow* analysis.

hybrid security. *Security,* such as a *convertible bond,* containing elements of both *debt* and *owners' equity*.

hypothecation. The *pledging* of property, without transfer of title or possession, to secure a loan.

I

IAA. *Interamerican Accounting Association.*

IASB. *International Accounting Standards Board.*

ICMA (Institute of Certified Management Accountants). See *CMA* and *Institute of Management Accountants*.

ideal standard costs. *Standard costs* set equal to those that a firm would incur under the best-possible conditions.

IIA. *Institute of Internal Auditors.*

IMA. *Institute of Management Accountants.*

impairment. Reduction in *market value* of an *asset.* When the firm has information indicating that its long-lived *assets,* such as *plant,* identifiable *intangibles,* and *goodwill,* have declined in *market value* or will provide a smaller future benefit than originally anticipated, it tests to see if the decline in value is so drastic that the expected future cash flows from the asset have declined below *book value.* If then-current book value exceeds the sum of expected cash flows, an asset impairment has occurred. At the time the firm judges that an impairment has occurred, the firm writes down the book value of the asset to its then-current *fair value,* which is the market value of the asset or, if the firm cannot assess the market value, the expected *net present value* of the future cash flows.

impairment loss. See *impairment.* This term refers to the amount by which the firm writes down the asset.

implicit interest. *Interest* not paid or received. See *interest, imputed.* All transactions involving the deferred payment or receipt of cash involve interest, whether explicitly stated or not. The implicit interest on a single-payment *note* equals the difference between the amount collected at maturity and the amount lent at the start of the loan. One can compute the implicit *interest rate* per year for loans with a single cash inflow and a single cash outflow from the following equation:

$$\left[\frac{\text{Cash Received at Maturity}}{\text{Cash Lent}} \right]^{(1/t)} - 1$$

where t is the term of the loan in years; t need not be an integer.

imprest fund. *Petty cash fund.*

improvement. An *expenditure* to extend the useful life of an *asset* or to improve its performance (rate of output, cost) over that of the original asset; sometimes called "betterment." The firm capitalizes such expenditures as part of the asset's cost. Contrast with *maintenance* and *repair*.

imputed cost. A cost that does not appear in accounting records, such as the *interest* that a firm could earn on cash spent to acquire inventories rather than, say, government bonds. Or, consider a firm that owns the buildings it occupies. This firm has an imputed cost for rent in an amount equal to what it would have to pay to use similar buildings owned by another or equal to the amount it could collect from someone renting the premises from the firm. *Opportunity cost*.

imputed interest. See *interest, imputed*.

in the black (red). Operating at a profit (loss).

in-process R&D. When one firm acquires another, the acquired firm will often have *research and development* activities under way that, following *GAAP,* it has *expensed.* The acquiring firm will pay for these activities to the extent they have value and will then, following GAAP, write off the activities. For each dollar of in-process R&D the acquiring firm identifies and immediately *expenses,* it will have one less dollar of *goodwill* or other assets to *amortize.* Some acquirers have overstated the valuations of acquired in-process R&D in order to increase immediate *write-offs* and subsequent, recurring *income*.

incentive compatible compensation. Said of a compensation plan that induces managers to act for the interests of owners while acting also in their own interests. For example, consider that a time of rising prices and increasing inventories when using a *LIFO* cost flow assumption implies paying lower *income taxes* than using *FIFO.* A bonus scheme for managers based on accounting *net income* is not incentive-compatible because owners likely benefit more under LIFO, whereas managers benefit more if they report using FIFO. See *LIFO conformity rule* and *goal congruence*.

income. *Excess of revenues* and *gains* over *expenses* and *losses* for a period; *net income.* The term is sometimes used with an appropriate modifier to refer to the various intermediate amounts shown in a *multiple-step income statement* or to refer to revenues, as in "rental income." See *comprehensive income*.

income accounts. *Revenue* and *expense accounts*.

income before taxes. On the *income statement,* the difference between all *revenues* and *expenses* except *income tax* expense. Contrast with *net income*.

income determination. See *determine*.

income distribution account. *Temporary account* sometimes debited when the firm declares *dividends;* closed to *retained earnings*.

income from continuing operations. As defined by *APB Opinion No. 30,* all *revenues* less all *expenses* except for the following: results of operations (including *income tax* effects) that a firm has discontinued or will discontinue; *gains* or *losses,* including income tax effects, on disposal of segments of the business; gains or losses, including income tax effects, from *extraordinary items;* and the cumulative effect of *accounting changes.*

income from discontinued operations. *Income,* net of tax effects, from parts of the business that the firm has discontinued during the period or will discontinue in the near future. Accountants report such items on separate lines of the *income statement,* after *income from continuing operations* but before *extraordinary items.*

income (revenue) bond. See *special revenue debt.*

income smoothing. A method of timing business *transactions* or choosing *accounting principles* so that the firm reports smaller variations in *income* from year to year than it otherwise would. Although some managements set income smoothing as an objective, no standard-setter does.

income statement. The statement of *revenues, expenses, gains,* and *losses* for the period, ending with *net income* for the period. Accountants usually show the *earnings-per-share* amount on the income statement; the *reconciliation* of beginning and ending balances of *retained earnings* may also appear in a combined statement of income and retained earnings. See *income from continuing operations, income from discontinued operations, extraordinary items, multiple-step,* and *single-step.*

income summary. In problem solving, an *account* that serves as a surrogate for the *income statement.* In using an income summary, close all *revenue* accounts to the Income Summary as *credits* and all *expense* accounts as *debits.* The *balance* in the account, after you make all these *closing entries,* represents income or loss for the period. Then, close the income summary balance to retained earnings.

income tax. An annual tax levied by the federal and other governments on the income of an entity.

income tax allocation. See *deferred income tax (liability)* and *tax allocation: intra-statement.*

incremental. An adjective used to describe the increase in *cost, expense, investment, cash flow, revenue, profit,* and the like if the firm produces or sells one or more units or if it undertakes an activity. See *differential.*

incremental analysis. Analysis to estimate the change in *cost, expense, investment, cash flow, revenue, profit,* and the like caused by some change in a causal variable, such as units produced.

incremental cost. See *incremental.*

incur. Said of an obligation of a firm, whether or not that obligation is *accrued.* For example, a firm incurs interest expense on a loan as time passes but accrues that interest only on payment dates or when it makes an *adjusting entry.*

indenture. See *bond indenture.*

independence. The mental attitude required of the *CPA* in performing the *attest* function. It implies that the CPA is impartial and that the members of the auditing CPA firm own no stock in the corporation being audited.

independent accountant. The *CPA* who performs the *attest* function for a firm.

independent variable. See *regression analysis.*

indeterminate-term liability. A *liability* lacking the criterion of being due at a definite time. This term is our own coinage to encompass the *minority interest.*

indexation. An attempt by lawmakers or parties to a contract to cope with the effects of *inflation.* Amounts fixed in law or contracts are "indexed" when these amounts change as a given measure of price changes. For example, a so-called escalator clause (COLA—cost of living allowance or adjustment) in a labor contract might provide that hourly wages will be increased as the *Consumer Price Index* increases. Many economists have suggested the indexation of numbers fixed in the *income tax* laws. If, for example, the personal *exemption* is $2,500 at the start of the period, if prices rise by 10 percent during the period, and if the personal exemption is indexed, then the personal exemption would automatically rise to $2,750 (= $2,500 + .10 × $2,500) at the end of the period.

indirect cost pool. Any grouping of individual costs that a firm does not identify with a *cost objective.*

indirect costs. Production costs not easily associated with the production of specific goods and services; *overhead costs.* Accountants may *allocate* them on some *arbitrary* basis to specific products or departments.

indirect labor (material) cost. An *indirect cost* for labor (material), such as for supervisors (supplies).

indirect method. See *statement of cash flows.*

individual proprietorship. *Sole proprietorship.*

Industry Audit Guides. A series of *AICPA* publications providing specific accounting and *auditing principles* for specialized situations. Audit guides have been issued covering government contractors, state and local government units, investment companies, finance companies, brokers and dealers in securities, and many other subjects.

inescapable cost. A *cost* that the firm or manager cannot avoid (see *avoidable*) because of an action. For example, if management shuts down two operating rooms in a hospital but still must employ security guards in unreduced numbers, the security costs are "inescapable" with respect to the decision to close the operating rooms.

inflation. A time of generally rising prices.

inflation accounting. Strictly speaking, *constant-dollar accounting.* Some writers incorrectly use the term to mean *current cost accounting.*

information circular. Canada: a document, accompanying the notice of a shareholders' meeting, prepared in connection with the solicitation of proxies by or on behalf of the management of the corporation. It contains information concerning the people making the solicitation, election of directors, appointment of auditors, and other matters to be acted on at the meeting.

information system. A system, sometimes formal and sometimes informal, for collecting, processing, and communicating data that are useful for the managerial functions of decision making, planning, and control and for financial reporting under the *attest* requirement.

inherent interest rate. *Implicit interest* rate.

initial cash flows. *Cash flows* associated with the beginning of an investment project. Often include *asset,* freight, and installation costs, reduced by cash proceeds from disposing of existing assets made redundant or unnecessary by the new project, and *income tax* effect of *gain (loss)* on disposal of existing assets.

insolvent. Unable to pay debts when due; said of a company even though *assets* exceed *liabilities.*

installment. Partial payment of a debt or partial collection of a receivable, usually according to a contract.

installment contracts receivable. The name used for *accounts receivable* when the firm uses the *installment method* of recognizing revenue. Its *contra account, unrealized gross margin,* appears on the balance sheet as a subtraction from the amount receivable.

installment sales. Sales on account when the buyer promises to pay in several separate payments, called *installments.* The seller may, but need not, account for such sales using the *installment method.* If the seller accounts for installment sales with the sales *basis of revenue recognition* for financial reporting but with the installment method for income tax returns, then it will have *deferred income tax* (*liability*).

installment (sales) method. Recognizing *revenue* and *expense* (or *gross margin*) from a sales transaction in proportion to the fraction of the selling price collected during a period; allowed by the *IRS* for income tax reporting but acceptable in *GAAP* (*APB Opinion No. 10*) only when the firm cannot estimate cash collections with reasonable precision. See *realized* (and *unrealized*) *gross margin.*

Institute of Certified Management Accountants (ICMA). See *CMA* and *Institute of Management Accountants.*

Institute of Internal Auditors (IIA). The national association of accountants who are engaged in internal auditing and are employed by business firms; administers a comprehensive professional examination. Those who pass the exam qualify to be designated *CIA* (Certified Internal Auditor).

Institute of Management Accountants (IMA). Formerly, the National Association of Accountants, NAA; a society open to those engaged in management accounting; parent organization of the *ICMA,* which oversees the *CMA* program.

insurance. A contract for reimbursement of specific losses; purchased with insurance premiums. "Self-insurance" is not insurance but is merely the noninsured's willingness to assume the risk of incurring losses while saving the premium.

intangible asset. A nonphysical right that gives a firm an exclusive or preferred position in the marketplace. Examples are *copyright, patent, trademark, goodwill, organization costs, capitalized* advertising cost, computer programs, licenses for any of the preceding, government licenses (e.g., broadcasting or the right to sell liquor), *leases,* franchises, mailing lists, exploration permits, import and export permits, construction permits, and marketing quotas. Invariably, accountants define "intangible" using a "for example" list, as we have just done, because accounting has been unable to devise a definition of "intangible" that will include items such as those listed above but exclude stock and bond certificates. Accountants classify these items as tangibles, even though they give their holders a preferred position in receiving dividends and interest payments.

Interamerican Accounting Association (IAA). An organization, headquartered in Miami, devoted to facilitating interaction between accounting practitioners in the Americas.

intercompany elimination. See *eliminations.*

intercompany profit. Profit within an organization. If one *affiliated company* sells to another, and the goods remain in the second company's *inventory* at the end of the period, then the first company has not yet realized a *profit* by a sale to an outsider. The profit is "intercompany profit," and the accountant eliminates it from net *income* when preparing *consolidated income statements* or when the firm uses the *equity method.*

intercompany transaction. *Transaction* between a *parent company* and a *subsidiary* or between subsidiaries in a *consolidated entity;* the accountant must eliminate the effects of such a transaction when preparing *consolidated financial statements.* See *intercompany profit.*

intercorporate investment. Occurs when a given *corporation* owns *shares* or *debt* issued by another.

interdepartment monitoring. An *internal control* device. The advantage of allocating *service department costs* to *production departments* stems from the incentives that this gives those charged with the costs to control the costs incurred in the service department. That process of having one group monitor the performance of another is interdepartment monitoring.

interest. The charge or cost for using cash, usually borrowed funds. Interest on one's own cash used is an *opportunity cost, imputed interest.* The amount of interest for a loan is the total amount paid by a borrower to a lender less the amount paid by the lender to the borrower. Accounting seeks to allocate that interest over the time of the loan so that the interest rate (= interest charge/amount borrowed) stays constant each period. See *interest rate* for discussion of the quoted amount. See *effective interest rate* and *nominal interest rate.*

interest, imputed. The difference between the face amount and the present value of a promise. If a borrower merely promises to pay a single amount, sometime later than the present, then the face amount the borrower will repay at *maturity* will exceed the present value (computed at a *fair market* interest rate, called the "imputed interest rate") of the promise. See also *imputed cost.*

interest factor. One plus the *interest* rate.

interest method. See *effective interest method.*

interest rate. A basis used for computing the cost of borrowing funds; usually expressed as a ratio between the number of currency units (e.g., dollars) charged for a period of time and the number of currency units borrowed for that same period of time. When the writers and speakers do not state a period, they almost always mean a period of one year. See *interest, simple interest, compound interest, effective* (*interest*) *rate,* and *nominal interest rate.*

interest rate swap. See *swap.*

interfund accounts. In governmental accounting, the accounts that show transactions between funds, especially interfund receivables and payables.

interim statements. Statements issued for periods less than the regular, annual *accounting period.* The *SEC* requires most corporations to issue interim statements on a quarterly basis. In preparing interim reports, a problem arises that the accountant can resolve only by understanding whether interim reports should report on the interim period (1) as a self-contained accounting period or (2) as an integral part of the year so that analysts can make forecasts of annual performance. For example, assume that at the end of the first quarter, a retailer has dipped into old LIFO layers, depleting its *inventory,* so that it computes *LIFO cost of goods sold* artificially low and *net income* artificially high, relative to the amounts the firm would have computed if it had made the "normal" purchases, equal to or greater than sales. The retailer expects to purchase inventory sufficiently large so that when it computes cost of goods sold for the year, there will be no *dips into old LIFO layers* and income will not be artificially high. The first approach will compute the quarterly income from low cost of goods sold using data for the dips that have actually occurred by the end of the quarter. The second approach will compute quarterly income from cost of goods sold assuming that purchases were equal to "normal" amounts and that the firm did not dip into old LIFO layers. *APB Opinion No. 28* and the *SEC* require that interim reports be constructed largely to satisfy the second purpose.

internal audit, internal auditor. An *audit* conducted by the firm's own employees, called "internal auditors," to ascertain whether the firm's *internal control* procedures work as planned. Contrast with an external audit conducted by a *CPA.*

internal controls. Policies and procedures designed to provide management with reasonable assurances that employees behave in a way that enables the firm to meet its organizational goals. See *control system.*

internal failure costs. *Costs incurred* when a firm detects nonconforming products and services before delivering them to customers; these include scrap, rework, and retesting.

internal rate of return (IRR). The discount rate that equates the net *present value* of a stream of cash outflows and inflows to zero.

internal reporting. Reporting for management's use in planning and control. Contrast with *external reporting* for financial statement users.

Internal Revenue Service (IRS). Agency of the U.S. Treasury Department responsible for administering the Internal Revenue Code and collecting income and certain other taxes.

International Accounting Standards Board (IASB). An organization that promotes the international harmonization of accounting standards. Web site: http://www.iasb.org.uk.

International Organization of Securities Commissions. *IOSCO.*

interperiod tax allocation. See *deferred income tax* (liability).

interpolation. The estimation of an unknown number intermediate between two (or more) known numbers.

Interpretations. See *FASB Interpretation.*

intrastatement tax allocation. See *tax allocation: intrastatement.*

intrinsic rewards. Rewards that come from within the individual, such as the satisfaction from studying hard, providing help to someone in need, or doing a good job. Contrast with *extrinsic rewards.*

inventoriable costs. *Costs* incurred that the firm adds to the cost of manufactured products; *product costs* (*assets*) as opposed to *period expenses.*

inventory. As a noun, the *balance* in an asset *account,* such as raw materials, supplies, work-in-process, and finished goods; as a verb, to calculate the *cost* of goods on hand at a given time or to count items on hand physically.

inventory equation. *Beginning inventory* + net additions − withdrawals = *ending inventory.* Ordinarily, additions are net purchases, and withdrawals are *cost of goods sold.* Notice that ending inventory, appearing on the balance sheet, and cost of goods sold, appearing on the income statement, must add to a fixed sum. The larger is one; the smaller must be the other. In valuing inventories, the firm usually knows beginning inventory and net purchases. Some inventory methods (for example, some applications of the *retail inventory method*) measure costs of goods sold and use the equation to find the cost of ending inventory. Most methods measure cost of ending inventory and use the equation to find the cost of goods sold (withdrawals). In *current cost* (in contrast to *historical cost*) *accounting,* additions (in the equation) include holding gains, whether realized or not. Thus the current cost inventory equation is as follows: Beginning Inventory (at Current Cost) + Purchases (where Current Cost is Historical Cost) + Holding Gains (whether Realized or Not) − Ending Inventory (at Current Cost) = Cost of Goods Sold (Current Cost).

inventory holding gains. See *inventory profit.*

inventory layer. See *LIFO inventory layer.*

inventory profit. A term with several possible meanings. Consider the data in the accompanying illustration (next page). The firm uses a *FIFO cost flow assumption* and derives its *historical cost* data. The assumed *current cost* data resemble those that the FASB suggested in *SFAS No. 89.* The term *income from continuing operations* refers to revenues less expenses based on current, rather than historical, costs. To that subtotal, add realized holding gains to arrive at realized (conventional) income. To that, add unrealized holding gains to arrive at economic income. The term "inventory profit" often refers (for example, in some *SEC* releases) to the realized holding gain, $110 in the illustration. The amount of inventory profit will usually be material when the firm uses FIFO and when prices rise. Other analysts, including us, prefer to use the term "inventory profit" to refer to the total *holding gain,* $300 (= $110 + $190, both realized and unrealized), but writers use this meaning less often. In periods of rising prices and increasing inventories, the realized holding gains under a FIFO cost flow assumption will exceed those under LIFO. In the illustration, for example, assume under LIFO that the historical cost of goods sold is $4,800, that historical LIFO cost of beginning inventory is $600, and that historical LIFO cost of ending inventory is $800. Then income from continuing operations, based on current costs, remains $350 (= $5,200 − $4,850), realized holding gains are $50 (= $4,850 − $4,800), realized income is $400 (= $350 + $50), the unrealized holding gain for the year is $250 [= ($1,550 − $800) − ($1,100 − $600)], and economic income is $650 (= $350 + $50 + $250). The cost flow assumption has only one real effect on this series of calculations: the split of the total holding gain into realized and unrealized portions. Thus, economic

Inventory Profit Illustration

	(Historical) Acquisition Cost Assuming FIFO	Current Cost
ASSUMED DATA		
Inventory, 1/1	$ 900	$1,100
Inventory, 12/31	1,160	1,550
Cost of Goods Sold for the Year	4,740	4,850
Sales for the Year	$5,200	$5,200
INCOME STATEMENT FOR THE YEAR		
Sales	$5,200	$5,200
Cost of Goods Sold	4,740	4,850
(1) Income from Continuing Operations		$ 350
Realized Holding Gains		110[a]
(2) Realized Income = Conventional Net Income (under FIFO)	$ 460	$ 460
Unrealized Holding Gain		190[b]
(3) Economic Income		$ 650

[a]Realized holding gain during a period is current cost of goods sold less historical cost of goods sold; for the year the realized holding gain under FIFO is $110 = $4,850 − $4,740. Some refer to this as "inventory profit."

[b]The total unrealized holding gain at any time is current cost of inventory on hand at that time less historical cost of that inventory. The unrealized holding gain during a period is unrealized holding gain at the end of the period less the unrealized holding gain prior to this year: $200 = $1,100 − $900. Unrealized holding gain during the year = ($1,550 − $1,160) − ($1,100 − $900) = $390 − $200 = $190.

income does not depend on the cost flow assumption. Holding gains total $300 in the illustration. The choice of cost flow assumption determines the portion reported as realized.

inventory turnover. Number of times the firm sells the average *inventory* during a period; *cost of goods sold* for a period divided by average inventory for the period. See *ratio*.

inventory valuation allowance. A preferred term for the difference between the *FIFO* (or *current cost*) of *inventory* and its *LIFO* valuation. Many in business refer to this as the "LIFO reserve." See *reserve* for an explanation of why we dislike that term.

invested capital. *Contributed capital*.

investee. A company in which another entity, the "investor," owns stock.

investing activities. Acquiring and selling *securities* or productive *assets* expected to produce *revenue* over several *periods*.

investment. An *expenditure* to acquire property or other *assets* in order to produce *revenue*; the asset so acquired; hence a *current* expenditure made in anticipation of future income; said of other companies' *securities* held for the long term and appearing in a separate section of the *balance sheet*; in this context, contrast with *marketable securities*.

investment center. A *responsibility center*, with control over *revenues, costs*, and *assets*.

investment credit. A reduction in income tax liability sometimes granted by the federal government to firms that buy new equipment. This item is a credit in that the taxpayer deducts it from the tax bill, not from pretax income. The tax credit has been a given percentage of the purchase price of the assets purchased. The government has changed the actual rules and rates over the years. As of 1999, there is no investment credit. See *flow-through method* and *carryforward*.

investment decision. The decision whether to undertake an action involving production of goods or services; contrast with financing decision.

investment tax credit. *Investment credit*.

investment turnover ratio. A term that means the same thing as *total assets turnover ratio*.

investments. A balance sheet heading for tangible assets held for periods longer than the operating cycle and not used in revenue production (assets not meeting the definitions of *current assets* or *property, plant, and equipment*).

invoice. A document showing the details of a sale or purchase *transaction*.

IOSCO (International Organization of Securities Commissions). The name, since 1983, of a confederation of regulators of securities and futures markets. Members come from over 80 countries. The IOSCO encourages the *IASB* to eliminate accounting alternatives and to ensure that accounting standards are detailed and complete, with adequate disclosure requirements, and that financial statements are user-friendly.

I.O.U. An informal document acknowledging a debt, setting out the amount of the debt and signed by the debtor.

IRR. *Internal rate of return*.

IRS. *Internal Revenue Service*.

isoprofit line. On a graph showing feasible production possibilities of two products that require the use of the same, limited resources, a line showing all feasible production possibility combinations with the same *profit* or, perhaps, *contribution margin*.

issue. A corporation exchange of its stock (or *bonds*) for cash or other *assets*. Terminology says the corporation "issues," not "sells," that stock (or bonds). Also used in the context of withdrawing supplies or materials from inventory for use in operations and of drawing a *check*.

issued shares. Those shares of *authorized capital stock* that a *corporation* has distributed to the shareholders. See *issue*. Shares of *treasury stock* are legally issued but are not *outstanding* for the purpose of voting, *dividend declarations*, and *earnings-per-share* calculations.

J

JIT. See *just-in-time inventory*.

job cost sheet. A schedule showing actual or budgeted inputs for a special order.

job development credit. The name used for the *investment credit* in the 1971 tax law, since repealed, on this subject.

job(-order) costing. Accumulation of *costs* for a particular identifiable batch of product, known as a job, as it moves through production.

jobs. Customized products.

joint cost. Cost of simultaneously producing or otherwise acquiring two or more products, called joint products, that a firm must, by the nature of the process, produce or acquire together, such as the cost of beef and hides of cattle. Generally, accounting allocates the joint costs of production to the individual products in proportion to their respective sales value (or, sometimes and usually not preferred, their respective physical quantities) at the *split-off* point. Other examples include *central corporate expenses* and *overhead* of a department when it manufactures several products. See *common cost* and *sterilized allocation.*

joint cost allocation. See *joint cost.*

joint process. A process that converts a common input into several outputs.

joint product. One of two or more outputs with significant value that a firm must produce or acquire simultaneously. See *by-product* and *joint cost.*

journal. The place where the firm records transactions as they occur; the book of original entry.

journal entry. A dated *journal* recording, showing the accounts affected, of equal *debits* and *credits,* with an explanation of the *transaction,* if necessary.

Journal of Accountancy. A monthly publication of the *AICPA.*

Journal of Accounting and Economics. Scholarly journal published by the William E. Simon Graduate School of Business Administration of the University of Rochester.

Journal of Accounting Research. Scholarly journal containing articles on theoretical and empirical aspects of accounting; published by the Graduate School of Business of the University of Chicago.

journal voucher. A *voucher* documenting (and sometimes authorizing) a *transaction,* leading to an entry in the *journal.*

journalize. To make an entry in a *journal.*

judgment(al) sampling. A method of choosing a sample in which the analyst subjectively selects items for examination, in contrast to selecting them by statistical methods. Compare *random sampling.*

junk bond. A low-rated *bond* that lacks the merit and characteristics of an investment-grade bond. It offers high yields, typically in excess of 15 percent per year, but also possesses high risk of default. Sometimes writers, less pejoratively, call these "high-yield bonds." No clear line separates junk from nonjunk bonds.

just-in-time inventory (production) (JIT). In managing *inventory* for manufacturing, system in which a firm purchases or manufactures each component just before the firm uses it. Contrast with systems in which firms acquire or manufacture many parts in advance of needs. JIT systems have much smaller carrying costs for inventory, ideally none, but run higher risks of incurring *stockout* costs.

K

k. Two to the tenth power (2^{10} or 1,024), when referring to computer storage capacity. The one-letter abbreviation derives from the first letter of the prefix "kilo-" (which means 1,000 in decimal notation).

Kaizen costing. A management concept that seeks continuous improvements, likely occurring in small incremental amounts, by refinements of all components of a production process.

KG (Kommanditgesellschaft). Germany: similar to a general partnership (*OHG*) except that some of its members may limit their liability. One of the partners must be a *general partner* with unlimited liability.

kiting. A term with slightly different meanings in banking and auditing contexts. In both, however, it refers to the wrongful practice of taking advantage of the *float,* the time that elapses between the deposit of a *check* in one bank and its collection at another. In the banking context, an individual deposits in Bank A a check written on Bank B. He (or she) then writes checks against the deposit created in Bank A. Several days later, he deposits in Bank B a check written on Bank A, to cover the original check written on Bank B. Still later, he deposits in Bank A a check written on Bank B. The process of covering the deposit in Bank A with a check written on Bank B and vice versa continues until the person can arrange an actual deposit of cash. In the auditing context, kiting refers to a form of *window dressing* in which the firm makes the amount of the account Cash in Bank appear larger than it actually is by depositing in Bank A a check written on Bank B without recording the check written on Bank B in the *check register* until after the close of the *accounting period.*

know-how. Technical or business information that is of the type defined under *trade secret* but that a firm does not maintain as a secret. The rules of accounting for this *asset* are the same as for other *intangibles.*

L

labor efficiency variance. Measures labor productivity by multiplying the *standard* labor price times the difference between the standard labor hours and the actual labor hours.

labor price (or wage) variance. Measures the difference between the actual and *standard* labor prices (wage rates).

labor variances. The *price* (or *rate*) and *quantity* (or *usage*) *variances* for *direct labor* inputs in a *standard costing system.*

laid-down cost. Canada and UK: the sum of all direct costs incurred for procurement of goods up to the time of physical receipt, such as invoice cost plus customs and excise duties, freight, and cartage.

land. An *asset* shown at *acquisition cost* plus the *cost* of any nondepreciable *improvements;* in accounting, implies use as a plant or office site rather than as a *natural resource,* such as timberland or farmland.

lapping (accounts receivable). The theft, by an employee, of cash sent in by a customer to discharge the latter's *payable*. The employee conceals the theft from the first customer by using cash received from a second customer. The employee conceals the theft from the second customer by using cash received from a third customer, and so on. The process continues until the thief returns the funds or can make the theft permanent by creating a fictitious *expense* or receivable write-off or until someone discovers the fraud.

lapse. To expire; said of, for example, an insurance policy or discounts that are made available for prompt payment and that the purchaser does not take.

last-in, first-out. See *LIFO*.

layer. See *LIFO inventory layer*.

lead time. The time that elapses between placing an order and receiving the *goods* or *services* ordered.

learning curve. A mathematical expression of the phenomenon that incremental unit costs to produce decrease as managers and labor gain experience from practice.

lease. A contract calling for the lessee (user) to pay the lessor (owner) for the use of an asset. A cancelable lease allows the lessee to cancel at any time. A noncancelable lease requires payments from the lessee for the life of the lease and usually shares many of the economic characteristics of *debt financing*. Most long-term noncancelable leases meet the usual criteria for classifying them as *liabilities,* and GAAP require the firm to show them as liabilities. *SFAS No. 13* and the *SEC* require disclosure, in notes to the financial statements, of the commitments for long-term noncancelable leases. See *capital lease* and *operating lease*.

leasehold. The *asset* representing the right of the lessee to use leased property. See *lease* and *leasehold improvement*.

leasehold improvement. An *improvement* to leased property. The firm should *amortize* it over the *service life* or the life of the lease, whichever is shorter.

least and latest rule. Paying the least amount of taxes as late as possible within the law to minimize the *present value* of tax payments for a given set of operations. Sensible taxpayers will follow this rule. When a taxpayer knows that tax rates will increase later, the taxpayer may reduce the present value of the tax burden by paying smaller taxes sooner. Each set of circumstances requires its own computations.

ledger. A book of accounts; book of final entry. See *general ledger* and *subsidiary ledger*. Contrast with *journal*.

legal capital. The amount of *contributed capital* that, according to state law, the firm must keep permanently in the firm as protection for creditors.

legal entity. See *entity*.

lender. See *loan*.

lessee. See *lease*.

lessor. See *lease*.

letter stock. Privately placed *common shares;* so called because the *SEC* requires the purchaser to sign a letter of intent not to resell the shares.

leverage. More than proportional result from extra effort or financing. Some measure of output increases faster than the measure of input. "Operating leverage" refers to the tendency of *net income* to rise at a faster rate than sales in the presence of *fixed costs*. A doubling of sales, for example, usually implies a more than doubling of net income. "Financial leverage" (or "capital leverage") refers to an increase in rate of return larger than the increase in explicit financing costs—the increased rate of return on *owners' equity* (see *ratio*) when an *investment* earns a return larger than the after-tax *interest rate* paid for *debt* financing. Because the interest charges on debt usually do not change, any *incremental* income benefits owners and none benefits debtors. When writers use the term "leverage" without a qualifying adjective, the term usually refers to financial leverage, the use of *long-term* debt in securing *funds* for the *entity*.

leveraged lease. A special form of lease involving three parties: a *lender,* a *lessor,* and a *lessee*. The lender, such as a bank or insurance company, lends a portion, say 80 percent, of the cash required for acquiring the *asset*. The lessor puts up the remainder, 20 percent, of the cash required. The lessor acquires the asset with the cash, using the asset as security for the loan, and leases it to the lessee on a *noncancelable* basis. The lessee makes periodic lease payments to the lessor, who in turn makes payments on the loan to the lender. Typically, the lessor has no obligation for the debt to the lender other than transferring a portion of the receipts from the lessee. If the lessee should default on the required lease payments, then the lender can repossess the leased asset. The lessor usually has the right to benefit from the tax deductions for *depreciation* on the asset, for *interest expense* on the loan from the lender, and for any *investment credit*. The lease is leveraged in the sense that the lessor, who takes most of the risks and enjoys most of the rewards of ownership, usually borrows most of the funds needed to acquire the asset. See *leverage*.

liability. An obligation to pay a definite (or reasonably definite) amount at a definite (or reasonably definite) time in return for a past or current benefit (that is, the obligation arises from a transaction that is not an *executory contract*); a probable future sacrifice of economic benefits arising from present obligations of a particular *entity* to *transfer assets* or to provide services to other entities in the future as a result of past *transactions* or events. *SFAC No. 6* says that "probable" refers to that which we can reasonably expect or believe but that is neither certain nor proved. A liability has three essential characteristics: (1) the obligation to transfer assets or services has a specified or knowable date, (2) the entity has little or no discretion to avoid the transfer, and (3) the event causing the obligation has already happened, that is, it is not executory.

lien. The right of person A to satisfy a claim against person B by holding B's property as security or by seizing B's property.

life annuity. A *contingent annuity* in which payments cease at the death of a specified person(s), usually the *annuitant(s)*.

LIFO (last-in, first-out). An *inventory* flow assumption in which the *cost of goods sold* equals the cost of the most recently acquired units and a firm computes the *ending inventory cost* from the costs of the oldest units. In periods of rising prices and increasing inventories, LIFO leads to higher reported expenses and therefore lower reported income and lower balance sheet inventories than does FIFO. Contrast with *FIFO*. See *FISH* and *inventory profit*.

LIFO conformity rule. The *IRS* rule requiring that companies that use a *LIFO cost flow assumption* for *income taxes* must also use LIFO in computing *income* reported in *financial statements* and forbidding the disclosure of pro forma results from using any other cost flow assumption.

LIFO, dollar-value method. See *dollar-value LIFO method*.

LIFO inventory layer. A portion of LIFO inventory cost on the *balance sheet*. The *ending inventory* in physical quantity will usually exceed the *beginning inventory*. The *LIFO cost flow assumption* assigns to this increase in physical quantities a cost computed from the prices of the earliest purchases during the year. The LIFO inventory then consists of layers, sometimes called "slices," which typically consist of relatively small amounts of physical quantities from each of the past years when purchases in physical units exceeded sales in units. Each layer carries the prices from near the beginning of the period when the firm acquired it. The earliest layers will typically (in periods of rising prices) have prices much less than current prices. If inventory quantities should decline in a subsequent period—a "dip into old LIFO layers"—the latest layers enter cost of goods sold first.

LIFO reserve. *Unrealized holding gain* in *ending inventory*: current or *FIFO historical* cost of ending inventory less LIFO *historical cost*. A better term for this concept is "excess of current cost over LIFO historical cost." See *reserve*.

limited liability. The legal concept that shareholders of corporations are not personally liable for debts of the company.

limited partner. A *partnership* member who is not personally liable for debts of the partnership. Every partnership must have at least one *general partner*, who is fully liable.

line-of-business reporting. See *segment reporting*.

line of credit. An agreement with a bank or set of banks for short-term borrowings on demand.

linear programming. A mathematical tool for finding profit-maximizing (or cost-minimizing) combinations of products to produce when a firm has several products that it can produce but faces linear constraints on the resources available in the production processes or on maximum and minimum production requirements.

liquid. Said of a business with a substantial amount (the amount is unspecified) of *working capital*, especially *quick assets*.

liquid assets. *Cash, current marketable securities,* and sometimes, *current receivables*.

liquidating dividend. A *dividend* that a firm declares in the winding up of a business to distribute its assets to the shareholders. Usually the recipient treats this as a return of *investment*, not as *revenue*.

liquidation. Payment of a debt; sale of assets in closing down a business or a segment thereof.

liquidation value per share. The amount each *share* of stock will receive if the *board* dissolves a corporation; for

preferred stock with a liquidation preference, a stated amount per share.

liquidity. Refers to the availability of *cash,* or near-cash resources, for meeting a firm's obligations.

LISH. An acronym, conceived by George H. Sorter, for *last-in, still-here*. LISH is the same cost flow assumption as *FIFO*. Many readers of accounting statements find it easier to think about inventory questions in terms of items still on hand. Think of FIFO in connection with *cost of goods sold* but of LISH in connection with *ending inventory*. See *FISH*.

list price. The published or nominally quoted price for goods.

list price method. See *trade-in transaction*.

loan. An arrangement in which the owner of property, called the lender, allows someone else, called the borrower, the use of the property for a period of time, which the agreement setting up the loan usually specifies. The borrower promises to return the property to the lender and, often, to make a payment for the use of the property. This term is generally used when the property is *cash* and the payment for its use is *interest*.

LOCOM. *Lower of cost or market*.

long-lived (term) asset. An asset whose benefits the firm expects to receive over several years; a *noncurrent* asset, usually includes *investments, plant assets,* and *intangibles*.

long run. Period of time long enough to allow management to change total productive capacity, as opposed to the *short run*.

long-term (construction) contract accounting. The *percentage-of-completion method* of *revenue* recognition; sometimes used to mean the *completed contract method*.

long-term debt ratio. *Noncurrent liabilities* divided by total *assets*.

long-term liability (debt). *Noncurrent liability*.

long-term, long-run. A term denoting a time or time periods in the future. How far in the future depends on context. For some securities traders, "long-term" can mean anything beyond the next hour or two. For most managers, it means anything beyond the next year or two. For government policymakers, it can mean anything beyond the next decade or two. For geologists, it can mean millions of years.

long-term solvency risk. The risk that a firm will not have sufficient *cash* to pay its *debts* sometime in the *long run*.

loophole. Imprecise term meaning a technicality allowing a taxpayer (or *financial statements*) to circumvent the intent, without violating the letter, of the law (or *GAAP*).

loss. Excess of *cost* over net proceeds for a single transaction; negative *income* for a period; a cost expiration that produced no *revenue*. See *gain* for a discussion of related and contrasting terms and how to distinguish loss from *expense*.

loss contingency. See *contingency*.

lower of cost or market (LOCOM). A basis for valuation of *inventory*. This basis sets inventory value at the lower of *acquisition cost* or *current replacement cost* (market), subject to the following constraints. First, the market value of an item used in the computation cannot exceed its *net realizable value*—an amount equal to selling price less reasonable costs to complete production and to sell the item. Second, the market value of an item used in the computation cannot be less than the net realizable value minus the normal *profit* ordinarily realized on disposition of completed items of this type. The basis chooses the lower-of-cost-or-market valuation as the lower of acquisition *cost* or replacement cost (*market*) subject to the upper and lower bounds on replacement cost established in the first two steps. Thus,

Market Value = Midvalue of (Replacement Cost, Net Realizable Value, Net Realizable Value Less Normal Profit Margin)

Lower of Cost or Market Valuation = Minimum (Acquisition Cost, Market Value)

The accompanying exhibit illustrates the calculation of the lower-of-cost-or-market valuation for four inventory items. Notice that each of the four possible outcomes occurs once in measuring lower of cost or market. Item 1 uses acquisition cost; item 2 uses net realizable value; item 3 uses replacement cost; and item 4 uses net realizable value less normal profit margin.

	Item			
	1	2	3	4
Calculation of Market Value				
(a) Replacement Cost	$92	$96	$92	$96
(b) Net Realizable Value	95	95	95	95
(c) Net Realizable Value Less Normal Profit Margin [= (b) − $9]	86	86	86	86
(d) Market = Midvalue [(a), (b), (c)]	92	95	92	95
Calculation of Lower of Cost or Market				
(e) Acquisition Cost	90	97	96	90
(f) Market [= (d)]	92	95	92	95
(g) Lower of Cost or Market = Minimum [(e), (f)]	90	95	92	90

A taxpayer may not use the lower-of-cost-or-market basis for inventory on tax returns in combination with a *LIFO cost flow assumption*. In the context of inventory, once the firm writes down the asset, it establishes a new "original cost" basis and ignores subsequent increases in market value in the accounts.

The firm may apply lower of cost or market to individual items of inventory or to groups (usually called *pools*) of items. The smaller the group, the more *conservative* the resulting valuation.

Omit hyphens when you use the term as a noun, but use them when you use the term as an adjectival phrase.

Ltd., Limited. UK: a private limited corporation. The name of a private limited company must include the word "Limited" or its abbreviation "Ltd."

lump-sum acquisition. *Basket purchase.*

M

MACRS. *Modified Accelerated Cost Recovery System.* See *Accelerated Cost Recovery System.* Since 1986, MACRS has been the accelerated depreciation method required for U.S. income tax purposes.

maintenance. *Expenditures* undertaken to preserve an *asset*'s service potential for its originally intended life. These expenditures are *period expenses* or *product costs.* Contrast with *improvement,* and see *repair.*

make-or-buy decision. A managerial decision about whether the firm should produce a product internally or purchase it from others. Proper make-or-buy decisions in the short run result only when a firm considers *incremental costs* in the analysis.

maker (of note) (of check). One who signs a *note* to borrow; one who signs a *check;* in the latter context, synonymous with "drawer." See *draft.*

management. Executive authority that operates a business.

management accounting. See *managerial accounting.*

Management Accounting. Monthly publication of the *IMA.*

management audit. An audit conducted to ascertain whether a firm or one of its operating units properly carries out its objectives, policies, and procedures; generally applies only to activities for which accountants can specify qualitative standards. See *audit* and *internal audit.*

management by exception. A principle of management in which managers focus attention on performance only if it differs significantly from that expected.

management by objective (MBO). A management approach designed to focus on the definition and attainment of overall and individual objectives with the participation of all levels of management.

management information system (MIS). A system designed to provide all levels of management with timely and reliable information required for planning, control, and evaluation of performance.

management's discussion and analysis (MD&A). A discussion of management's views of the company's performance; required by the *SEC* to be included in the *10-K* and in the *annual report* to shareholders. The information typically contains discussion of such items as liquidity, results of *operations, segments,* and the effects of *inflation.*

managerial (management) accounting. Reporting designed to enhance the ability of management to do its job of decision making, planning, and control. Contrast with *financial accounting.*

manufacturing cost. Cost of producing goods, usually in a factory.

manufacturing expense. An imprecise, and generally incorrect, alternative title for *manufacturing overhead.* The term is generally incorrect because these costs are usually *product costs,* not expenses.

manufacturing overhead. General manufacturing *costs* that are not directly associated with identifiable units of product and that the firm incurs in providing a capacity to carry on productive activities. Accounting treats *fixed* manufacturing overhead cost as a *product cost* under *full absorption costing* but as an *expense* of the period under *variable costing.*

margin. *Revenue* less specified expenses. See *contribution margin, gross margin,* and *current margin.*

margin of safety. Excess of actual, or budgeted, sales over *breakeven* sales; usually expressed in dollars but may be expressed in units of product.

marginal cost. The *incremental cost* or *differential cost* of the last unit added to production or the first unit subtracted from production. See *cost terminology* and *differential* for contrast.

marginal costing. *Variable costing.*

marginal revenue. The increment in *revenue* from the sale of one additional unit of product.

marginal tax rate. The amount, expressed as a percentage, by which income taxes increase when taxable income increases by one dollar. Contrast with *average tax rate.*

markdown. See *markup* for definition and contrast.

markdown cancellation. See *markup* for definition and contrast.

market-based transfer price. A *transfer price* based on external market data rather than internal company data.

market price. See *fair value.*

market rate. The rate of *interest* a company must pay to borrow *funds* currently. See *effective rate.*

market value. *Fair market value.*

marketable equity securities. *Marketable securities* representing *owners' equity* interest in other companies, rather than *loans* to them.

marketable securities. Other companies' *stocks* and *bonds* held that can be readily sold on stock exchanges or over-the-counter markets and that the company plans to sell as cash is needed; classified as *current assets* and as part of "cash" in preparing the *statement of cash flows.* If the firm holds these same securities for *long-term* purposes, it will classify them as *noncurrent assets. SFAS No. 115* requires that all marketable equity and all debt securities (except those debt securities the holder has the ability and intent to hold to maturity) appear at market value on the balance sheet. The firm reports changes in market value in income for *trading securities* but debits holding losses (or credits holding gains) directly to owners' equity accounts for *securities available for sale.*

marketing costs. Costs incurred to sell; includes locating customers, persuading them to buy, delivering the goods or services, and collecting the sales proceeds.

markon. See *markup* for definition and contrast.

markup. The difference between the original selling price of items acquired for *inventory* and the cost. Precise usage calls this "markon," although many businesspeople use the term "markup." Because of confusion of this use of "markup" with its precise definition (see below), terminology sometimes uses "original markup." If the originally established retail price increases, the precise term for the amount of price increase is "markup," although terminology sometimes uses "additional markup." If a firm reduces selling price, terminology uses the terms "markdown" and "markup cancellation." "Markup cancellation" refers to reduction in price following "additional markups" and can, by definition, be no more than the amount of the additional markup; "cancellation of additional markup," although not used, is descriptive. "Mark-down" refers to price reductions from the original retail price. A price increase after a markdown is a "markdown cancellation." If original cost is $12 and original selling price is $20, then markon (original markup) is $8; if the firm later increases the price to $24, the $4 increase is markup (additional markup); if the firm later lowers the price to $21, the $3 reduction is markup cancellation; if the firm further lowers the price to $17, the $4 reduction comprises $1 markup cancellation and $3 markdown; if the firm later increases the price to $22, the $5 increase comprises $3 of markdown cancellation and $2 of markup (additional markup). Accountants track markup cancellations and markdowns separately because they deduct the former (but not the latter) in computing the selling prices of goods available for sale for the denominator of the *cost percentage* used in the conventional *retail inventory method.*

markup cancellation. See *markup* for definition and contrast.

markup percentage. *Markup* divided by (acquisition cost plus *markup*).

master budget. A *budget* projecting all *financial statements* and their components.

matching convention; matching principle. The concept of recognizing cost expirations (*expenses*) in the same accounting period during which the firm recognizes related *revenues;* combining or simultaneously recognizing the revenues and expenses that jointly result from the same *transactions* or other events.

material. As an adjective, it means relatively important, capable of influencing a decision (see *materiality*); as a noun, *raw material.*

materiality. The concept that accounting should disclose separately only those events that are relatively important (no operable definition yet exists) for the business or for understanding its statements. *SFAC No. 2* suggests that accounting information is material if "the judgment of a reasonable person relying on the information would have been changed or influenced by the omission or misstatement."

materials efficiency variance. Measures materials waste by multiplying the *standard* materials price times the difference between the standard materials quantity used and the actual materials quantity used.

materials price variance. Measures the difference between the actual and *standard* materials prices.

materials variances. *Price* and *quantity variances* for *direct materials* in *standard costing systems;* difference between actual cost and standard cost.

matrix. A rectangular array of numbers or mathematical symbols.

matrix inverse. For a given square *matrix* $\mathbf{A}$, the matrix, $\mathbf{A}^{-1}$ such that $\mathbf{A}\mathbf{A}^{-1} = \mathbf{A}^{-1}\mathbf{A} = \mathbf{I}$, the identity matrix. Not all square matrices have inverses. Those that do not are "singular"; those that do are nonsingular.

maturity. The date at which an obligation, such as the *principal* of a *bond* or a *note,* becomes due.

maturity value. The amount expected to be collected when a loan reaches *maturity.* Depending on the context, the amount may be *principal* or principal and *interest.*

MBO. *Management by objective.*

MD&A. *Management's discussion and analysis* section of the *annual report.*

measuring unit. See *attribute measured* for definition and contrast.

merchandise. *Finished goods* bought by a retailer or wholesaler for resale; contrast with finished goods of a manufacturing business.

merchandise costs. Costs incurred to sell a product, such as commissions and advertising.

merchandise turnover. *Inventory turnover* for merchandise. See *ratio.*

merchandising business. As opposed to a manufacturing or service business, one that purchases (rather than manufactures) *finished goods* for resale.

merger. The joining of two or more businesses into a single *economic entity.* See *holding company.*

minority interest. A *balance sheet account* on *consolidated statements* showing the *equity* in a less-than-100-percent-owned *subsidiary* company; equity allocable to those who are not part of the controlling (majority) interest; may be classified either as shareholders' equity or as a liability of *indeterminate term* on the consolidated balance sheet. The *income statement* must subtract the minority interest in the current period's income of the less-than-100-percent-owned subsidiary to arrive at consolidated *net income* for the period.

minority investment. A holding of less than 50 percent of the *voting stock* in another corporation; accounted for with the *equity method* when the investor owns sufficient shares that it can exercise "significant influence" and as *marketable securities* otherwise. See *mutual fund.*

minutes book. A record of all actions authorized at corporate *board of directors* or shareholders' meetings.

MIS. *Management information system.*

mix variance. One of the *manufacturing variances.* Many *standard cost* systems specify combinations of inputs—for example, labor of a certain skill and materials of a certain quality grade. Sometimes combinations of inputs used differ from those contemplated by the standard. The mix variance attempts to report the cost difference caused by those changes in the combination of inputs.

mixed cost. A *semifixed* or a *semivariable* cost.

Modified Accelerated Cost Recovery System (MACRS). Name used for the *Accelerated Cost Recovery System,* originally passed by Congress in 1981 and amended by Congress in 1986.

modified cash basis. The *cash basis of accounting* with long-term assets accounted for using the *accrual basis of accounting.* Most users of the term "cash basis of accounting" actually mean "modified cash basis."

monetary assets and liabilities. See *monetary items.*

monetary gain or loss. The firm's *gain* or *loss* in *general purchasing power* as a result of its holding *monetary assets* or liabilities during a period when the *general purchasing power of the dollar* changes; explicitly reported in *constant-dollar accounting.* During periods of *inflation,* holders of net monetary assets lose, and holders of net monetary liabilities gain, general purchasing power. During periods of *deflation,* holders of net monetary assets

gain, and holders of net monetary liabilities lose, general purchasing power.

monetary items. Amounts fixed in terms of dollars by statute or contract; *cash, accounts receivable, accounts payable,* and *debt.* The distinction between monetary and nonmonetary items is important for *constant-dollar accounting* and for *foreign exchange gain or loss* computations. In the foreign exchange context, account amounts denominated in dollars are not monetary items, whereas amounts denominated in any other currency are monetary.

monetary-nonmonetary method. *Foreign currency translation* that translates all *monetary items* at the *current exchange rate* and translates all *nonmonetary items* at the *historical rate.*

money. A word seldom used with precision in accounting, at least in part because economists have not yet agreed on its definition. Economists use the term to refer to both a medium of exchange and a store of value. See *cash* and *monetary items.* Consider a different set of issues concerning the phrase, "making money." Lay terminology uses this to mean "earning income" whether, as a result, the firm increased its cash balances or other net assets. The user does not typically mean that the firm has increased cash equal to the amount of net income, although the unaware listeners often think the phrase means this. Given that usage equates "making money" with "earning income," in this sense "money" has a credit balance not a debit balance. Since cash typically has a debit balance, the phrase "making money" is even more troublesome. Consider the following language from the U.S. statutes on forfeitures required of some who commit illegal acts: "... the amount of money acquired through illegal transactions ..." Does the law mean the cash left over after the lawbreaker has completed the illegal transactions, the income earned from the transactions, or something else? Sometimes "making money" means avoiding a cost, not recognized in financial accounting.

Consider the following sets of questions and see how you have to think to decide whether, in a given question, "money" refers to a debit or a credit. Assume I start with $10 in cash.

1. I took a cab and it cost $10; I spent money. Did the cabbie make money? Does the cabbie have money?
2. I decided to walk, so I didn't spend $10. Did I make money?
3. I canceled the trip. Did I make money?

"Money" sometimes refers to debits and sometimes to credits; "making money" sometimes means earning accounting income and sometimes avoiding a cost, not reported in accounting, so careful writing about accounting avoids the word.

money purchase plan. A *pension plan* in which the employer contributes a specified amount of cash each year to each employee's pension fund; sometimes called a *defined-contribution plan;* contrast with *defined-benefit plan.* The plan does not specify the benefits ultimately received by the employee, since these benefits depend on the rate of return on the cash invested. As of the mid-

1990s, most corporate pension plans were defined-benefit plans because both the law and *generally accepted accounting principles* for pensions made defined-benefit plans more attractive than money purchase plans. *ERISA* makes money purchase plans relatively more attractive than they had been. We expect the relative number of money purchase plans to continue to increase.

mortality table. Data of life expectancies or probabilities of death for persons of specified age and sex.

mortgage. A claim given by the borrower (mortgagor) to the lender (mortgagee) against the borrower's property in return for a loan.

moving average. An *average* computed on observations over time. As a new observation becomes available, analysts drop the oldest one so that they always compute the average for the same number of observations and use only the most recent ones.

moving average method. *Weighted-average inventory method.*

multiple-step. Said of an *income statement* that shows various subtotals of *expenses* and *losses* subtracted from *revenues* to show intermediate items such as *operating income,* income of the enterprise (operating income plus *interest* income), income to investors (income of the enterprise less *income taxes*), net income to shareholders (income to investors less interest charges), and income retained (net income to shareholders less dividends). See *entity theory.*

municipal bond. A *bond* issued by a village, town, or city. *Interest* on such bonds is generally exempt from federal *income taxes* and from some state income taxes. Because bonds issued by state and county governments often have these characteristics, terminology often calls such bonds "municipals" as well. These are also sometimes called "tax-exempts."

mutual fund. An investment company that issues its own stock to the public and uses the proceeds to invest in securities of other companies. A mutual fund usually owns less than 5 or 10 percent of the stock of any one company and accounts for its investments using current *market values.* Contrast with *holding company.*

mutually exclusive (investment) projects. Competing investment projects in which accepting one project eliminates the possibility of undertaking the remaining projects.

N

NAARS. *National Automated Accounting Research System.*

NASDAQ (National Association of Securities Dealers Automated Quotation System). A computerized system to provide brokers and dealers with price quotations for securities traded *over the counter* as well as for some *NYSE* securities.

National Association of Accountants (NAA). Former name for the *Institute of Management Accountants* (*IMA*).

National Automated Accounting Research System (NAARS). A computer-based information-retrieval system containing, among other things, the complete text of most public corporate annual reports and *Forms 10-K.* Users may access the system through the *AICPA.*

natural business year. A 12-month period chosen as the reporting period so that the end of the period coincides with a low point in activity or inventories. See *ratio* for a discussion of analyses of financial statements of companies using a natural business year.

natural classification. *Income statement* reporting form that classifies *expenses* by nature of items acquired, that is, materials, wages, salaries, insurance, and taxes, as well as depreciation. Contrast with *functional classification.*

natural resources. Timberland, oil and gas wells, ore deposits, and other products of nature that have economic value. Terminology uses the term *depletion* to refer to the process of *amortizing* the cost of natural resources. Natural resources are "nonrenewable" (for example, oil, coal, gas, ore deposits) or "renewable" (timberland, sod fields); terminology often calls the former "wasting assets." See also *reserve recognition accounting* and *percentage depletion.*

negative confirmation. See *confirmation.*

negative goodwill. See *goodwill.* When a firm acquires another company, and the *fair market value* of the *net assets* acquired exceeds the purchase price, *APB Opinion No. 16* requires that the acquiring company reduce the valuation of noncurrent assets (except *investments* in *marketable securities*) until the purchase price equals the adjusted valuation of the fair market value of net assets acquired. If, after the acquiring company reduces the valuation of noncurrent assets to zero, the valuation of the remaining net assets acquired still exceeds the purchase price, then the difference appears as a credit balance on the balance sheet as negative goodwill. For negative goodwill to exist, someone must be willing to sell a company for less than the fair market value of net current assets and marketable securities. Because such bargain purchases are rare, one seldom sees negative goodwill in the financial statements. When it does appear, it generally signals unrecorded obligations, such as a contingency related to a pending lawsuit.

negotiable. Legally capable of being transferred by *endorsement.* Usually said of *checks* and *notes* and sometimes of *stocks* and *bearer bonds.*

negotiated transfer price. A *transfer price* set jointly by the buying and the selling divisions.

net. Reduced by all relevant deductions.

net assets. Total *assets* minus total *liabilities;* equals the amount of *owners' equity.* Often, we find it useful to split the balance sheet into two parts: owners' equity and all the rest. The "rest" is total assets less total liabilities. To take an example, consider one definition of *revenue:* the increase in owners' equity accompanying the net assets increase caused by selling goods or rendering services. An alternative, more cumbersome way to say the same thing is: the increase in owners' equity accompanying the assets increase or the liabilities decrease, or both, caused by selling goods or rendering services. Consider the definition of *goodwill:* the excess of purchase price over the fair market value of identifiable net assets acquired in a purchase transaction. Without the phrase "net assets," the definition might be as follows: the excess of purchase price over the fair market value of identifiable assets reduced by the fair market value of identifiable liabilities acquired in a purchase transaction.

net bank position. From a firm's point of view, *cash* in a specific bank less *loans* payable to that bank.

net book value. *Book value.*

net current asset value (per share). *Working capital* divided by the number of common shares outstanding. Some analysts think that when a common share trades in the market for an amount less than net current asset value, the shares are undervalued and investors should purchase them. We find this view naive because it ignores, generally, the efficiency of capital markets and, specifically, unrecorded obligations, such as for executory contracts and contingencies, not currently reported as *liabilities* in the *balance sheet* under *GAAP.*

net current assets. *Working capital = current assets − current liabilities.*

net income. The excess of all *revenues* and *gains* for a period over all *expenses* and *losses* of the period. The *FASB* is proposing to discontinue use of this term and substitute *earnings.* See *comprehensive income.*

net loss. The excess of all *expenses* and *losses* for a period over all *revenues* and *gains* of the period; negative *net income.*

net markup. In the context of *retail inventory methods, markups* less markup cancellations; a figure that usually ignores *markdowns* and markdown cancellations.

net of tax method. A nonsanctioned method for dealing with the problem of *income tax allocation;* described in *APB Opinion No. 11.* The method subtracts deferred tax items from specific *asset* amounts rather than showing them as a deferred credit or *liability.*

net of tax reporting. Reporting, such as for *income from discontinued operations, extraordinary items,* and *prior-period adjustments,* in which the firm adjusts the amounts presented in the *financial statements* for all income tax effects. For example, if an extraordinary loss amounted to $10,000, and the marginal tax rate was 40 percent, then the extraordinary item would appear "net of taxes" as a $6,000 loss. Hence, not all a firm's income taxes necessarily appear on one line of the income statement. The reporting allocates the total taxes among *income from continuing operations, income from discontinued operations, extraordinary items,* cumulative effects of *accounting changes,* and *prior-period adjustments.*

net operating profit. *Income from continuing operations.*

net present value. Discounted or *present value* of all cash inflows and outflows of a project or of an *investment* at a given *discount rate.*

net price method (of recording purchase or sales discounts). Method that records a *purchase* (or *sale*) at its *invoice* price less all *discounts* made available, under the assumption that the firm will take nearly all discounts offered. The purchaser debits, to an *expense* account, discounts lapsed through failure to pay promptly. For purchases, management usually prefers to know about the amount of discounts lost because of inefficient operations,

not the amounts taken, so that most managers prefer the net price method to the *gross price method.*

net realizable (sales) value. Current selling price less reasonable costs to complete production and to sell the item. Also, a method for *allocating joint costs* in proportion to *realizable values* of the joint products. For example, joint products A and B together cost $100; A sells for $60, whereas B sells for $90. Then a firm would allocate to A ($60/$150) × $100 = .40 × $100 = $40 of cost while it would allocate to B ($90/$150) × $100 = $60 of cost.

net sales. Sales (at gross invoice amount) less *returns, allowances,* freight paid for customers, and *discounts* taken.

net working capital. *Working capital;* the term "net" is redundant in accounting. Financial analysts sometimes mean *current assets* when they speak of working capital, so for them the "net" is not redundant.

net worth. A misleading term with the same meaning as *owners' equity.* Avoid using this term; accounting valuations at *historical cost* do not show economic worth.

network analysis. A project planning and scheduling method, usually displayed in a diagram, that enables management to identify the interrelated sequences that it must accomplish to complete the project.

new product development time. The period between a firm's first consideration of a product and delivery of it to the customer.

New York Stock Exchange (NYSE). A public market in which those who own seats (a seat is the right to participate) trade various corporate *securities.*

next-in, first-out. See *NIFO.*

NIFO (next-in, first-out). A *cost flow assumption,* one not allowed by *GAAP.* In making decisions, many managers consider *replacement costs* (rather than *historical costs*) and refer to them as NIFO costs.

no par. Said of *stock* without a *par value.*

nominal accounts. *Temporary accounts,* such as *revenue* and *expense* accounts; contrast with *balance sheet accounts.* The firm *closes* all nominal accounts at the end of each *accounting period.*

nominal amount (value). An amount stated in dollars, in contrast to an amount stated in *constant dollars.* Contrast with *real amount (value).*

nominal dollars. The measuring unit giving no consideration to differences in the *general purchasing power of the dollar* over time. The face amount of currency or coin, a *bond,* an *invoice,* or a *receivable* is a nominal-dollar amount. When the analyst adjusts that amount for changes in *general purchasing power,* it becomes a *constant-dollar* amount.

nominal interest rate. A rate specified on a *debt* instrument; usually differs from the market or *effective rate;* also, a rate of *interest* quoted for a year. If the interest compounds more often than annually, then the *effective interest rate* exceeds the nominal rate.

noncancelable. See *lease.*

nonconsolidated subsidiary. An *intercorporate investment* in which the parent owns more than 50 percent of the shares of the *subsidiary* but accounts for the investment with the *cost method.*

noncontributory. Said of a *pension plan* in which only the employer makes payments to a pension *fund.* Contrast with *contributory.*

noncontrollable cost. A cost that a particular manager cannot *control.*

noncurrent. Of a *liability,* due in more than one year (or more than one *operating cycle*); of an *asset,* the firm will enjoy the future benefit in more than one year (or more than one operating cycle).

nonexpendable fund. A governmental fund whose *principal,* and sometimes earnings, the entity may not spend.

noninterest-bearing note. A *note* that does not specify explicit interest. The *face value* of such a note will exceed its *present value* at any time before *maturity* value so long as *interest rates* are positive. *APB Opinion No. 21* requires that firms report the present value, not face value, of long-term noninterest-bearing notes as the *asset* or *liability* amount in financial statements. For this purpose, the firm uses the *historical interest rate.* See *interest, imputed.*

non-manufacturing costs. All *costs* incurred other than those necessary to produce goods. Typically, only manufacturing firms use this designation.

nonmonetary items. All items that are not monetary. See *monetary items.*

nonoperating. In the *income statement* context, said of *revenues* and *expenses* arising from *transactions* incidental to the company's main line(s) of business; in the *statement of cash flows* context, said of all financing and investing sources or uses of cash in contrast to cash provided by operations. See *operations.*

nonprofit corporation. An incorporated *entity,* such as a hospital, with owners who do not share in the earnings. It usually emphasizes providing services rather than maximizing income.

nonrecurring. Said of an event that is not expected to happen often for a given firm. *APB Opinion No. 30* requires firms to disclose separately the effects of such events as part of *ordinary* items unless the event is also unusual. See *extraordinary* item.

non–value-added activity. An activity that causes costs without increasing a product's or service's value to the customer.

normal cost. Former name for *service cost* in accounting for pensions and other postemployment benefits.

normal costing. Method of charging costs to products using actual *direct materials,* actual *direct labor,* and predetermined *factory overhead* rates.

normal costing system. *Costing* based on *actual material* and *labor* costs but using *predetermined overhead* rates per unit of some *activity* basis (such as *direct labor hours* or machine hours) to apply overhead to production. Management decides the rate to charge to production for overhead at the start of the period. At the end of the period the accounting multiplies this rate by the actual number of units of the base activity (such as actual direct labor hours worked or actual machine hours used during the period) to apply overhead to production.

normal spoilage. Costs incurred because of ordinary amounts of spoilage. Accounting prorates such costs to units produced as *product costs.* Contrast with *abnormal spoilage.*

normal standard cost, normal standards. The *cost* a firm expects to incur under reasonably efficient operating conditions with adequate provision for an average amount of rework, spoilage, and the like.

normal volume. The level of production that will, over a time span, usually one year, satisfy purchasers' demands and provide for reasonable *inventory* levels.

note. An unconditional written promise by the maker (borrower) to pay a certain amount on demand or at a certain future time.

note receivable discounted. A *note* assigned by the holder to another. The new holder of the note typically pays the old holder an amount less than the *face value* of the note, hence the word "discounted." If the old holder assigns the note to the new holder with recourse, the old holder has a *contingent liability* until the maker of the note pays the debt. See *factoring.*

notes. Some use this word instead of *footnotes* when referring to the detailed information included by management as an integral part of the *financial statements* and covered by the *auditor's report.*

NOW (negotiable order of withdrawal) account. Negotiable order of withdrawal. A *savings account* whose owner can draw an order to pay, much like a *check* but technically not a check, and give it to others, who can redeem the order at the savings institution.

number of days sales in inventory (or receivables). Days of average inventory on hand (or average collection period for receivables). See *ratio.*

NV (naamloze vennootschap). Netherlands: a public limited liability company.

NYSE. *New York Stock Exchange.*

O

OASD(H)I. *Old Age, Survivors, Disability, and (Hospital) Insurance.*

objective. See *reporting objectives* and *objectivity.*

objective function. In *linear programming,* the name of the profit (or cost) criterion the analyst wants to maximize (or minimize).

objectivity. The reporting policy implying that the firm will not give formal recognition to an event in financial statements until the firm can measure the magnitude of the events with reasonable accuracy and check that amount with independent verification.

obsolescence. An asset's *market value* decline caused by improved alternatives becoming available that will be more *cost-effective.* The decline in market value does not relate to physical changes in the asset itself. For example, computers become obsolete long before they wear out. See *partial obsolescence.*

Occupational Safety and Health Act. *OSHA.*

off-balance-sheet financing. A description often used for an obligation that meets all the tests to be classified a liability except that the obligation arises from an *executory contract* and, hence, is not a *liability*. Consider the following example. Miller Corporation desires to acquire land costing $25 million, on which it will build a shopping center. It could borrow the $25 million from its bank, paying interest at 12 percent, and buy the land outright from the seller. If so, both an asset and a liability will appear on the balance sheet. Instead, it borrows $5 million and purchases for $5 million from the seller an *option* to buy the land from the seller at any time within the next six years for a price of $20 million. The option costs Miller Corporation $5 million immediately and provides for continuing "option" payments of $2.4 million per year, which precisely equal Miller Corporation's borrowing rate multiplied by the remaining purchase price of the land: $2.4 million = .12 × $20 million. Although Miller Corporation need not continue payments and can let the option lapse at any time, it also has an obligation to begin developing on the site immediately. Because Miller Corporation has invested a substantial sum in the option, will invest more, and will begin immediately developing the land, Miller Corporation will almost certainly exercise its option before expiration. The seller of the land can take the option contract to the bank and borrow $20 million, paying interest at Miller Corporation's borrowing rate, 12 percent per year. The continuing option payments from Miller Corporation will be sufficient to enable the seller to make its payments to the bank. *Generally accepted accounting principles* view Miller Corporation as having acquired an option for $5 million rather than having acquired land costing $25 million in return for $25 million of debt. The firm will not recognize debt on the balance sheet until it borrows more funds to exercise the option.

off-balance-sheet risk. A contract that exposes an entity to the possibility of loss but that does not appear in the financial statements. For example, a *forward-exchange contract* generally does not appear on the balance sheet because it is an *executory contract*. The contract may reduce or increase the entity's exposure to foreign-exchange risk (the chance of loss due to unfavorable changes in the foreign-exchange rate). It may also expose the entity to credit risk (the chance of loss that occurs when the *counterparty* to the contract cannot fulfill the contract terms). *SFAS No. 105* requires entities to describe contracts with off-balance-sheet risk.

OHG (Offene Handelsgesellschaft). Germany: a general *partnership*. The partners have unlimited *liability*.

Old Age, Survivors, Disability, and (Hospital) Insurance, or OASD(H)I. The technical name for social security under the Federal Insurance Contributions Act (*FICA*).

on consignment. Said of goods delivered by the owner (the consignor) to another (the consignee) to be sold by the consignee. The arrangement entitles the owner either to the return of the property or to payment of a specified amount. The goods are *assets* of the consignor. Such arrangements provide the consignor with better protection than an outright *sale on account* to the consignee in case the consignee becomes bankrupt. In event of *bankruptcy,* the ordinary seller, holding an account receivable, has no special claim to the return of the goods, whereas a consignor can reclaim the goods without going through bank-

ruptcy proceedings, from which the consignor might recover only a fraction of the amounts owed to it.

on (open) account. Said of a *purchase* (or *sale*) when the seller expects payment sometime after delivery and the purchaser does not give a *note* evidencing the *debt*. The purchaser has generally signed an agreement sometime in the past promising to pay for such purchases according to an agreed time schedule. When the firm sells (purchases) on open account, it *debits* (*credits*) *Accounts Receivable* (*Payable*).

one-line consolidation. Said of an *intercorporate investment* accounted for with the *equity method*. With this method, the *income* and *balance sheet* total *assets* and *equities* amounts are identical to those that would appear if the parent consolidated the investee firm, even though the income from the investment appears on a single line of the income statement and the net investment appears on a single line in the Assets section of the balance sheet.

one-write system. A system of bookkeeping that produces several records, including original documents, in one operation by the use of reproductive paper and equipment that provides for the proper alignment of the documents.

on-time performance. The firm delivers the product or service at the time scheduled for delivery.

open account. Any *account* with a nonzero *debit* or *credit* balance. See *on (open) account.*

operating. An adjective used to refer to *revenue* and *expense* items relating to the company's main line(s) of business. See *operations.*

operating accounts. *Revenue, expense,* and *production cost accounts.* Contrast with *balance sheet accounts.*

operating activities. For purposes of the *statement of cash flows,* all *transactions* and *events* that are neither *financing activities* nor *investing activities.* See *operations.*

operating budget. A formal *budget* for the *operating cycle* or for a year.

operating cash flow. *Cash flow from operations.* Financial statement analysts sometimes use this term to mean *cash flow from operations – capital expenditures – dividends.* This usage leads to such ambiguity that the reader should always confirm the definition that the writer uses before drawing inferences from the reported data.

operating cycle. *Earnings cycle.*

operating expenses. *Expenses* incurred in the course of *ordinary* activities of an *entity;* frequently, a classification including only *selling, general,* and *administrative expenses,* thereby excluding *cost of goods sold, interest,* and *income tax* expenses. See *operations.*

operating lease. A *lease* accounted for by the *lessee* without showing an *asset* for the lease rights (*leasehold*) or a liability for the lease payment obligations. The lessee reports only rental payments during the period, as *expenses* of the period. The asset remains on the lessor's *books,* where rental collections appear as *revenues.* Contrast with *capital lease.*

operating leverage. Usually said of a firm with a large proportion of *fixed costs* in its *total costs.* Consider a book publisher or a railroad: such a firm has large costs to produce the first unit of service; then, the *incremental costs* of producing another book or transporting another freight car are much less than the *average cost,* so the *gross margin* on the sale of the subsequent units is relatively large. Contrast this situation with that, for example, of a grocery store, where the *contribution margin* equals less than 5 percent of the selling price. For firms with equal profitability, however defined, we say that the one with the larger percentage increase in income from a given percentage increase in dollar sales has the larger operating leverage. See *leverage* for contrast of this term with "financial leverage." See *cost terminology* for definitions of terms involving the word "cost."

operating margin. *Revenues* from *sales* minus *cost of goods sold* and *operating expenses.*

operating margin based on current costs. *Revenues* from *sales* minus *current cost* of goods sold; a measure of operating efficiency that does not depend on the *cost flow assumption* for *inventory;* sometimes called "current (gross) margin." See *inventory profit* for illustrative computations.

operating ratio. See *ratio.*

operational control. See *control system.*

operational measures of time. Indicators of the speed and reliability with which organizations supply products and services to customers. Companies generally use two operational measures of time: *customer response time* and *on-time performance.*

operations. A word not precisely defined in *accounting.* Generally, analysts distinguish operating activities (producing and selling *goods* or *services*) from financing activities (raising funds) and *investing activities.* Acquiring goods on account and then paying for them one month later, though generally classified as an operating activity, has the characteristics of a financing activity. Or consider the transaction of selling plant assets for a price in excess of book value. On the *income statement,* the gain appears as part of income from operations ("continuing operations" or "discontinued" operations, depending on the circumstances), but the *statement of cash flows* reports all the funds received below the Cash from Operations section, as a nonoperating source of cash, "disposition of noncurrent assets." In income tax accounting, an "operating loss" results whenever deductions exceed taxable revenues.

opinion. The *auditor's report* containing an attestation or lack thereof; also, *APB Opinion.*

opinion paragraph. Section of *auditor's report,* generally following the *scope paragraph* and giving the auditor's conclusion that the *financial statements* are (rarely, are not) in accordance with *GAAP* and present fairly the *financial position,* changes in financial position, and the results of *operations.*

opportunity cost. The *present value* of the *income* (or *costs*) that a firm could earn (or save) from using an *asset* in its best alternative use to the one under consideration.

opportunity cost of capital. *Cost of capital.*

option. The legal right to buy or sell something during a specified period at a specified price, called the *exercise* price. If the right exists during a specified time interval, it is known as an "American option." If it exists for only one specific day, it is known as a "European option." Do not confuse employee stock options with *put* and *call* options, traded in various public markets.

ordinary annuity. An *annuity in arrears.*

ordinary income. For income tax purposes, reportable *income* not qualifying as *capital gains.*

organization costs. The *costs* incurred in planning and establishing an *entity;* example of an *intangible* asset. The firm must treat these costs as *expenses* of the period, even though the *expenditures* clearly provide future benefits and meet the test to be *assets.*

organization goals. Broad objectives for an organization established by management.

original cost. *Acquisition cost;* in public utility accounting, the acquisition cost of the *entity* first devoting the *asset* to public use. See *aboriginal cost.*

original entry. Entry in a *journal.*

OSHA (Occupational Safety and Health Act). The federal law that governs working conditions in commerce and industry.

other comprehensive income. According to the *FASB, comprehensive income* items that are not themselves part of earnings. See *comprehensive income.* To define comprehensive income does not convey its essence. To understand comprehensive income, you need to understand how it differs from *earnings* (or *net income*), the concept measured in the *earnings* (*income*) *statement.* The term *earnings* (or *net income*) refers to the sum of all components of comprehensive income *minus* the components of other comprehensive income.

outlay. The amount of an *expenditure.*

outlier. Said of an observation (or data point) that appears to differ significantly in some regard from other observations (or data points) of supposedly the same phenomenon; in a *regression analysis,* often used to describe an observation that falls far from the fitted regression equation (in two dimensions, line).

out-of-pocket. Said of an *expenditure* usually paid for with cash; an *incremental* cost.

out-of-stock cost. The estimated decrease in future *profit* as a result of losing customers because a firm has insufficient quantities of *inventory* currently on hand to meet customers' demands.

output. Physical quantity or monetary measurement of *goods* and *services* produced.

outside director. A corporate board of directors member who is not a company officer and does not participate in the corporation's day-to-day management.

outstanding. Unpaid or uncollected; when said of *stock,* refers to the shares issued less *treasury stock;* when said of *checks,* refers to a check issued that did not clear the *drawer*'s bank prior to the *bank statement* date.

over-and-short. Title for an *expense account* used to account for small differences between book balances of cash and actual cash and vouchers or receipts in *petty cash* or *change funds.*

overapplied (overabsorbed) overhead. Costs applied, or *charged,* to product and exceeding actual *overhead costs* during the period; a *credit balance* in an overhead account after overhead is assigned to product.

overdraft. A *check* written on a checking account that contains funds less than the amount of the check.

overhead costs. Any *cost* not directly associated with the production or sale of identifiable goods and services;

sometimes called "burden" or "indirect costs" and, in the UK, "oncosts"; frequently limited to manufacturing overhead. See *central corporate expenses* and *manufacturing overhead.*

overhead rate. Standard, or other predetermined rate, at which a firm applies *overhead costs* to products or to services.

over-the-counter. Said of a *security* traded in a negotiated transaction, as on *NASDAQ,* rather than in an auctioned one on an organized stock exchange, such as the *New York Stock Exchange.*

owners' equity. *Proprietorship; assets* minus *liabilities; paid-in capital* plus *retained earnings* of a corporation; partners' capital accounts in a *partnership;* owner's capital account in a *sole proprietorship.*

P

paid-in capital. Sum of balances in *capital stock* and *capital contributed in excess of par (or stated) value* accounts; same as *contributed capital* (minus *donated capital*). Some use the term to mean only *capital contributed in excess of par (or stated) value.*

paid-in surplus. See *surplus.*

P&L. Profit-and-loss statement; *income statement.*

paper profit. A *gain* not yet realized through a *transaction;* an *unrealized holding gain.*

par. See *at par* and *face amount.*

par value. *Face amount* of a *security.*

par value method. In accounting for *treasury stock,* method that *debits* a common stock account with the *par value* of the shares required and allocates the remaining debits between the *Additional Paid-in Capital* and *Retained Earnings* accounts. Contrast with *cost method.*

parent company. Company owning more than 50 percent of the voting shares of another company, called the *subsidiary.*

Pareto chart. A graph of a skewed statistical distribution. In many business settings, a relatively small percentage of the potential population causes a relatively large percentage of the business activity. For example, some businesses find that the top 20 percent of the customers buy 80 percent of the goods sold. Or, the top 10 percent of products account for 60 percent of the revenues or 70 percent of the profits. The statistical distribution known as the Pareto distribution has this property of skewness, so a graph of a phenomenon with such skewness has come to be known as a Pareto chart, even if the underlying data do not actually well fit the Pareto distribution. Practitioners of *total quality management* find that in many businesses, a small number of processes account for a large fraction of the quality problems, so they advocate charting potential problems and actual occurrences of problems to identify the relatively small number of sources of trouble. They call such a chart a "Pareto chart."

partial obsolescence. One cause of decline in *market value* of an *asset.* As technology improves, the economic value of existing *assets* declines. In many cases, however, it will not pay a firm to replace the existing asset with a new one, even though it would acquire the new type rather than the old if it did make a new acquisition currently. In these cases, the accountant should theoretically recognize a loss from partial obsolescence from the firm's owning an old, out-of-date asset, but *GAAP* do not permit recognition of partial obsolescence until the sum of future cash flows from the asset total less than book value; see *impairment.* The firm will carry the old asset at *cost* less *accumulated depreciation* until the firm retires it from service so long as the *undiscounted* future *cash flows* from the asset exceed its book value. Thus management that uses an asset subject to partial obsolescence reports results inferior to those reported by a similar management that uses a new asset. See *obsolescence.*

partially executory contract. *Executory contract* in which one or both parties have done something other than merely promise.

partially funded. Said of a *pension plan* in which the firm has not funded all earned benefits. See *funded* for funding requirements.

partially vested. Said of a *pension plan* in which not all employee benefits have *vested.* See *graded vesting.*

participating dividend. *Dividend* paid to preferred shareholders in addition to the minimum preferred dividends when the *preferred stock* contract provides for such sharing in earnings. Usually the contract specifies that dividends on *common shares* must reach a specified level before the preferred shares receive the participating dividend.

participating preferred stock. *Preferred stock* with rights to *participating dividends.*

participative budgeting. Using input from lower- and middle-management employees in setting goals.

partner's drawing. A payment made to a partner and debited against his or her share of income or capital. The name of a *temporary account,* closed to the partner's capital account, to record the debits when the partner receives such payments.

partnership. Contractual arrangement between individuals to share resources and operations in a jointly run business. See *general* and *limited partner* and *Uniform Partnership Act.*

patent. A right granted for up to 20 years by the federal government to exclude others from manufacturing, using, or selling a claimed design, product, or plant (e.g., a new breed of rose) or from using a claimed process or method of manufacture; an *asset* if the firm acquires it by purchase. If the firm develops it internally, current *GAAP* require the firm to *expense* the development costs when incurred.

payable. Unpaid but not necessarily due or past due.

pay-as-you-go. Said of an *income tax* scheme in which the taxpayer makes periodic payments of income taxes during the period when it earns the income to be taxed; in contrast to a scheme in which the taxpayer owes no payments until the end of, or after, the period when it earned the income being taxed (called PAYE—pay-as-you-earn—in the UK). The phrase is sometimes used to describe an *unfunded pension plan,* or retirement benefit plan, in which the firm makes payments to pension plan beneficiaries from general corporate funds, not from cash previously contributed to a fund. Under this method, the firm debits expense as it makes payments, not as it incurs the obligations. This is not acceptable as a method of accounting for pension plans, under *SFAS No. 87,* or as a method of *funding,* under *ERISA.*

payback period. Amount of time that must elapse before the cash inflows from a project equal the cash outflows.

payback reciprocal. One divided by the *payback period.* This number approximates the *internal rate of return* on a project when the project life exceeds twice the payback period and the cash inflows are identical in every period after the initial period.

PAYE (pay-as-you-earn). See *pay-as-you-go* for contrast.

payee. The person or entity who receives a cash payment or who will receive the stated amount of cash on a *check.* See *draft.*

payout ratio. *Common stock dividends* declared for a year divided by net *income* to common stock for the year; a term used by financial analysts. Contrast with *dividend yield.*

payroll taxes. Taxes levied because the taxpayer pays salaries or wages; for example, *FICA* and unemployment compensation insurance taxes. Typically, the employer pays a portion and withholds part of the employee's wages.

P/E ratio. *Price-earnings ratio.*

Pension Benefit Guarantee Corporation (PBGC). A federal corporation established under *ERISA* to guarantee basic pension benefits in covered pension plans by administering terminated pension plans and placing *liens* on corporate assets for certain unfunded pension liabilities.

pension fund. *Fund,* the assets of which the trustee will pay to retired ex-employees, usually as a *life annuity;* generally held by an independent trustee and thus not an *asset* of the employer.

pension plan. Details or provisions of employer's contract with employees for paying retirement *annuities* or other benefits. See *funded, vested, service cost, prior service cost, money purchase plan,* and *defined-benefit plan.*

per books. An expression used to refer to the *book value* of an item at a specific time.

percent. Any number, expressed as a decimal, multiplied by 100.

percentage depletion (allowance). Deductible *expense* allowed in some cases by the federal *income tax* regulations; computed as a percentage of gross income from a *natural resource* independent of the unamortized cost of the *asset.* Because the amount of the total deductions for tax purposes usually exceeds the cost of the asset being *depleted,* many people think the deduction is an unfair tax advantage or *loophole.*

percentage-of-completion method. Recognizing *revenues* and *expenses* on a job, order, or contract (1) in proportion to the *costs* incurred for the period divided by total costs expected to be incurred for the job or order ("cost to cost") or (2) in proportion to engineers' or architects' estimates of the incremental degree of completion of the job, order, or contract during the period. Contrast with *completed contract method.*

percentage of sales method. Measuring *bad debt expense* as a fraction of *sales revenue.* When the firm uses this

method, it must periodically check the adequacy of the *allowance for uncollectibles* by *aging accounts receivable.* See *allowance method* for contrast.

percentage statement. A statement containing, in addition to (or instead of) dollar amounts, ratios of dollar amounts to some base. In a percentage *income statement,* the base is usually either *net sales* or total *revenues,* and in a percentage *balance sheet,* the base is usually total *assets.*

period. *Accounting period.*

period cost. An inferior term for *period expense.*

period expense (charge). *Expenditure,* usually based on the passage of time, charged to operations of the accounting period rather than *capitalized* as an asset. Contrast with *product cost.*

periodic cash flows. *Cash flows* that occur during the life of an investment project. Often include *receipts* from *sales,* *expenditures* for *fixed* and *variable production costs,* and savings of fixed and variable production costs, to name a few. They do not include noncash items, such as *financial accounting depreciation* charges or *allocated* items of *overhead* not requiring *differential* cash expenditures.

periodic inventory. In recording *inventory,* a method that uses data on beginning inventory, additions to inventories, and ending inventory to find the cost of withdrawals from inventory. Contrast with *perpetual inventory.*

periodic procedures. The process of making *adjusting entries* and *closing entries* and preparing the *financial statements,* usually by use of *trial balances* and *work sheets.*

permanent account. An account that appears on the *balance sheet.* Contrast with *temporary account.*

permanent difference. Difference between reported income and taxable income that will never reverse and, hence, requires no entry in the *deferred income tax* (*liability*) account; for example, nontaxable state and municipal *bond* interest that will appear on the financial statements. Contrast with *temporary difference.* See *deferred income tax liability.*

permanent file. The file of working papers that are prepared by a public accountant and that contain the information required for reference in successive professional engagements for a particular organization, as distinguished from working papers applicable only to a particular engagement.

perpetual annuity. *Perpetuity.*

perpetual inventory. *Inventory* quantity and amount records that the firm changes and makes current with each physical addition to or withdrawal from the stock of goods; an inventory so recorded. The records will show the physical quantities and, frequently, the dollar valuations that should be on hand at any time. Because the firm explicitly computes *cost of goods sold,* it can use the *inventory equation* to compute an amount for what *ending inventory* should be. It can then compare the computed amount of ending inventory with the actual amount of ending inventory as a *control* device to measure the amount of *shrinkages.* Contrast with *periodic inventory.*

perpetuity. An *annuity* whose payments continue forever. The *present value* of a perpetuity in *arrears* is p/r where p is the periodic payment and r is the *interest rate* per period. If a perpetuity promises $100 each year, in arrears, forever and the interest rate is 8 percent per year, then the perpetuity has a value of $1,250 = $100/.08.

perpetuity (with) growth model. See *perpetuity*. A *perpetuity* whose cash flows grow at the rate *g* per period and thus has *present value* of $1/(r - g)$. Some call this the "Gordon Growth Model" because Myron Gordon wrote about applications of this formula and its variants in the 1950s. John Burr Williams wrote about them in the 1930s.

personal account. *Drawing account.*

PERT (Program Evaluation and Review Technique). A method of *network analysis* in which the analyst makes three time estimates for each activity—the optimistic time, the most likely time, and the pessimistic time—and gives an expected completion date for the project within a probability range.

petty cash fund. Currency and coins maintained for expenditures that the firm makes with cash on hand.

physical units method. A method of allocating a *joint cost* to the *joint products* based on a physical measure of the joint products; for example, allocating the cost of a cow to sirloin steak and to hamburger, based on the weight of the meat. This method usually provides nonsensical (see *sterilized allocation*) results unless the physical units of the joint products tend to have the same value.

physical verification. *Verification,* by an *auditor,* performed by actually inspecting items in *inventory, plant assets,* and the like, in contrast to merely checking the written records. The auditor may use statistical sampling procedures.

planning and control process. General name for the management techniques comprising the setting of organizational goals and *strategic plans, capital budgeting, operations* budgeting, comparison of plans with actual results, performance evaluation and corrective action, and revisions of goals, plans, and budgets.

plant. *Plant assets.*

plant asset turnover. Number of dollars of *sales* generated per dollar of *plant assets;* equal to sales divided by average *plant assets.*

plant assets. *Assets* used in the revenue-production process. Plant assets include buildings, machinery, equipment, land, and natural resources. The phrase "property, plant, and equipment" (though often appearing on *balance sheets*) is therefore a redundancy. In this context, "plant" used alone means buildings.

plantwide allocation method. A method for *allocating overhead costs* to product. First, use one *cost pool* for the entire plant. Then, allocate all costs from that pool to products using a single overhead *allocation* rate, or one set of rates, for all the products of the plant, independent of the number of departments in the plant.

PLC (public limited company). UK: a publicly held *corporation.* Contrast with *Ltd.*

pledging. The borrower assigns *assets* as security or *collateral* for repayment of a loan.

pledging of receivables. The process of using expected collections on *accounts receivable* as *collateral* for a loan. The borrower remains responsible for collecting the receivable but promises to use the proceeds for repaying the debt.

plow back. To retain *assets* generated by earnings for continued investment in the business.

plug. Process for finding an unknown amount. For any *account,* beginning balance + additions − deductions = ending balance; if you know any three of the four items, you can find the fourth with simple arithmetic, called "plugging." In making a *journal entry,* often you know all *debits* and all but one of the *credits* (or vice versa). Because *double-entry* bookkeeping requires equal debits and credits, you can compute the unknown quantity by subtracting the sum of the known credits from the sum of all the debits (or vice versa), also called "plugging." Accountants often call the unknown the "plug." For example, in amortizing a *discount* on *bonds payable* with the *straight-line depreciation* method, *interest expense* is a plug: interest expense = interest payable + *discount amortization.* See *trade-in transaction* for an example. The term sometimes has a bad connotation for accountants because plugging can occur in a slightly different context. During the process of preparing a *preclosing trial balance* (or *balance sheet*), often the sum of the debits does not equal the sum of the credits. Rather than find the error, some accountants are tempted to force equality by changing one of the amounts, with a plugged debit or credit to an account such as Other Expenses. No harm results from this procedure if the amount of the error is small compared with asset totals, since spending tens or hundreds of dollars in a bookkeeper's or accountant's time to find an error of a few dollars will not be *cost-effective.* Still, most accounting teachers rightly disallow this use of plugging because exercises and problems set for students provide enough information not to require it.

point of sale. The time, not the location, at which a *sale* occurs.

pooling-of-interests method. Accounting for a *business combination* by adding together the *book value* of the *assets* and *equities* of the combined firms; generally leads to a higher reported *net income* for the combined firms than results when the firm accounts for the business combination as a purchase because the *market values* of the merged assets generally exceed their book values. *GAAP* no longer allows this treatment in the U.S. Contrast with *purchase method.* Called *uniting-of-interests method* by the *IASB* and allowed by it under some conditions.

population. The entire set of numbers or items from which the analyst samples or performs some other analysis.

positive confirmation. See *confirmation.*

post. To record entries in an *account* to a *ledger,* usually as transfers from a *journal.*

post-closing trial balance. *Trial balance* taken after the accountant has *closed* all *temporary accounts.*

post-statement events. Events that have *material* impact and that occur between the end of the *accounting period* and the formal publication of the *financial statements.* Even though the events occur after the end of the period being reported on, the firm must disclose such events in notes if the auditor is to give a *clean opinion.*

potentially dilutive. A *security* that its holder may convert into, or exchange for, common stock and thereby reduce reported *earnings per share; options, warrants, convertible bonds,* and *convertible preferred stock.*

PPB. *Program budgeting.* The second "P" stands for "plan."

practical capacity. Maximum level at which a plant or department can operate efficiently.

precision. The degree of accuracy for an estimate derived from a sampling process, usually expressed as a range of values around the estimate. The analyst might express a sample estimate in the following terms: "Based on the sample, we are 95 percent sure [confidence level] that the true population value is within the range of X to Y [precision]." See *confidence level.*

preclosing trial balance. *Trial balance* taken at the end of the period before *closing entries;* in this sense, an *adjusted trial balance;* sometimes taken before *adjusting entries* and then synonymous with *unadjusted trial balance.*

predatory prices. Setting prices below some measure of cost in an effort to drive out competitors with the hope of recouping losses later by charging monopoly prices. Illegal in the United States if the prices set are below long-run variable costs. We know of no empirical evidence that firms are successful at recoupment.

predetermined (factory) overhead rate. Rate used in applying *overhead costs* to products or departments developed at the start of a period. Compute the rate as estimated overhead cost divided by the estimated number of units of the overhead allocation base (or *denominator volume*) activity. See *normal costing.*

preemptive right. The privilege of a *shareholder* to maintain a proportionate share of ownership by purchasing a proportionate share of any new stock issues. Most state corporation laws allow corporations to pay shareholders to waive their preemptive rights or state that preemptive rights exist only if the *corporation charter* explicitly grants them. In practice, then, preemptive rights are the exception rather than the rule.

preference as to assets. The rights of *preferred shareholders* to receive certain payments before common shareholders receive payments in case the board dissolves the corporation.

preferred shares. *Capital stock* with a claim to *income* or *assets* after *bondholders* but before *common shares. Dividends* on preferred shares are *income distributions,* not *expenses.* See *cumulative preferred stock.*

premium. The excess of issue (or market) price over *par value.* For a different context, see *insurance.*

premium on capital stock. Alternative but inferior title for *capital contributed in excess of par (or stated) value.*

prepaid expense. An *expenditure* that leads to a *deferred charge* or *prepayment.* Strictly speaking, this is a contradiction in terms because an *expense* is a gone asset, and this title refers to past *expenditures,* such as for rent or insurance premiums, that still have future benefits and thus are *assets.* We try to avoid this term and use "prepayment" instead.

prepaid income. An inferior alternative title for *advances from customers.* Do not call an item *revenue* or *income* until the firm earns it by delivering goods or rendering services.

prepayments. *Deferred charges; assets* representing *expenditures* for future benefits. Rent and insurance premiums paid in advance are usually current prepayments.

present value. Value today (or at some specific date) of an amount or amounts to be paid or received later (or at other, different dates), discounted at some *interest* or *discount rate;* an amount that, if invested today at the specified rate, will grow to the amount to be paid or received in the future.

prevention costs. *Costs incurred* to prevent defects in the products or services they produce, including procurement inspection, processing control (inspection), design, quality training, and machine inspection.

price. The quantity of one *good* or *service,* usually *cash,* asked in return for a unit of another good or service. See *fair value.*

price-earnings (P/E) ratio. At a given time, the market value of a company's *common share,* per share, divided by the *earnings per* common *share* for the past year. The analyst usually bases the denominator on *income from continuing operations* or, if the analyst thinks the current figure for that amount does not represent a usual situation—such as when the number is negative or, if positive, close to zero—on some estimate of the number. See *ratio.*

price index. A series of numbers, one for each period, that purports to represent some *average* of prices for a series of periods, relative to a base period.

price level. The number from a *price index* series for a given period or date.

price level–adjusted statements. *Financial statements* expressed in terms of dollars of uniform purchasing power. The statements restate *nonmonetary* items to reflect changes in general *price levels* since the time the firm acquired specific *assets* and incurred *liabilities.* The statements recognize a *gain* or *loss* on *monetary items* as the firm holds them over time periods when the general *price level* changes. Conventional financial statements show *historical costs* and ignore differences in purchasing power in different periods.

price variance. In accounting for *standard costs,* an amount equal to (actual cost per unit – standard cost per unit) times actual quantity.

primary earnings per share (PEPS). Net *income* to common shareholders plus *interest* (net of tax effects) or *dividends* paid on *common-stock equivalents* divided by (weighted average of common shares outstanding plus the net increase in the number of common shares that would become *outstanding* if the holders of all common stock equivalents were to exchange them for common shares with cash proceeds, if any, used to retire common shares). As of 1997 and *SFAS No. 128,* replaced with *basic earnings per share.*

prime cost. Sum of *direct materials* plus *direct labor* costs assigned to product.

prime rate. The loan rate charged by commercial banks to their creditworthy customers. Some customers pay even less than the prime rate and others, more. The *Federal Reserve Bulletin* is the authoritative source of information about historical prime rates.

principal. An amount on which *interest* accrues, either as *expense* (for the borrower) or as *revenue* (for the lender); the *face amount* of a *loan;* also, the absent owner (principal) who hires the manager (agent) in a "principal-agent" relationship.

principle. See *generally accepted accounting principles.*

prior-period adjustment. A *debit* or *credit* that is made directly to *retained earnings* (and that does not affect *income* for the period) to adjust earnings as calculated for prior periods. Such adjustments are now rare. Theory suggests that accounting should correct for errors in accounting estimates (such as the *depreciable life* or *salvage value* of an asset) by adjusting retained earnings so that statements for future periods will show correct amounts. But *GAAP* require that corrections of such estimates flow through current, and perhaps future, *income statements.* See *accounting changes* and *accounting errors.*

prior service cost. *Present value* at a given time of a *pension plan*'s retroactive *benefits.* "Unrecognized prior service cost" refers to that portion of prior service cost not yet *debited* to *expense.* See *actuarial accrued liability* and *funded.* Contrast with *normal cost.*

pro forma statements. Hypothetical statements; financial statements as they would appear if some event, such as a *merger* or increased production and sales, had occurred or were to occur; sometimes spelled as one word, "proforma."

probable. In many of its definitions, the *FASB* uses the term "probable." See, for example, *asset, firm commitment, liability.* A survey of practicing accountants revealed that the average of the probabilities that those surveyed had in mind when they used the term "probable" was 85 percent. Some accountants think that any event whose outcome is greater than 50 percent should be called "probable." The FASB uses the phrase "more likely than not" when it means greater than 50 percent.

proceeds. The *funds* received from the disposition of assets or from the issue of securities.

process costing. A method of *cost accounting* based on average costs (total cost divided by the *equivalent units* of work done in a period); typically used for assembly lines or for products that the firm produces in a series of steps that are more continuous than discrete.

product. *Goods* or *services* produced.

product cost. Any *manufacturing cost* that the firm can—or, in some contexts, should—debit to an *inventory* account. See *flow of costs,* for example. Contrast with *period expenses.*

product-level activities. Work that supports a particular product or service line. Examples include design work, supervision, and advertising that are specific to each type of product or service.

product life cycle. Time span between initial concept (typically starting with research and development) of a good or service and the time when the firm ceases to support customers who have purchased the good or service.

production cost. *Manufacturing cost.*

production cost account. A *temporary account* for accumulating *manufacturing costs* during a period.

production cycle efficiency. Measures the efficiency of the production cycle by computing the ratio of the time spent processing a unit divided by the *production cycle time.* The higher the percentage, the less the time and costs spent on *non–value-added activities,* such as moving and storage.

production cycle time. The total time to produce a unit. Includes processing, moving, storing, and inspecting.

production department. A department producing salable *goods* or *services;* contrast with *service department.*

production method (depreciation). One form of *straight-line depreciation.* The firm assigns to the depreciable asset (e.g., a truck) a *depreciable life* measured not in elapsed time but in units of output (e.g., miles) or perhaps in units of time of expected use. Then the *depreciation* charge for a period is a portion of depreciable cost equal to a fraction computed as the actual output produced during the period divided by the expected total output to be produced over the life of the asset. This method is sometimes called the "units-of-production (or output) method."

production method (revenue recognition). *Percentage-of-completion method* for recognizing *revenue.*

production volume variance. Standard fixed *overhead* rate per unit of normal *capacity* (or base activity) times (units of base activity budgeted or planned for a period minus actual units of base activity worked or assigned to product during the period); often called a "volume variance."

productive capacity. One *attribute measured* for *assets.* The *current cost* of *long-term assets* means the cost of reproducing the productive capacity (for example, the ability to manufacture one million units a year), not the cost of reproducing the actual physical assets currently used (see *reproduction cost*). *Replacement cost* of productive capacity will be the same as reproduction cost of assets only in the unusual case when no technological improvement in production processes has occurred and the relative prices of goods and services used in production have remained approximately the same as when the firm acquired the currently used goods and services.

profit. Excess of *revenues* over *expenses* for a *transaction;* sometimes used synonymously with *net income* for the period.

profit and loss account. UK: *retained earnings.*

profit-and-loss sharing ratio. The fraction of *net income* or loss allocable to a partner in a *partnership;* need not be the same fraction as the partner's share of capital.

profit-and-loss statement. *Income statement.*

profit center. A *responsibility center* for which a firm accumulates both *revenues* and *expenses.* Contrast with *cost center.*

profit margin. *Sales* minus all *expenses.*

profit margin percentage. *Profit margin* divided by *net sales.*

profit maximization. The doctrine that the firm should account for a given set of operations so as to make reported *net income* as large as possible; contrast with *conservatism.* This concept in accounting differs from the profit-maximizing concept in economics, which states that the firm should manage operations to maximize the present value of the firm's wealth, generally by equating *marginal costs* and *marginal revenues.*

profit plan. The *income statement* portion of a *master budget.*

profit-sharing plan. A *defined-contribution plan* in which the employer contributes amounts based on *net income*.

profit variance analysis. Analysis of the causes of the difference between budgeted profit in the *master budget* and the profits earned.

profit-volume analysis (equation). Analysis of effects, on *profits,* caused by changes in volume or *contribution margin* per unit or *fixed costs*. See *break-even chart*.

profit-volume graph. See *break-even chart*.

profit-volume ratio. *Net income* divided by net sales in dollars.

profitability. Some measure of the firm's ability to earn *income* relative to the size of the firm or its *revenues*.

profitability accounting. *Responsibility accounting*.

program budgeting (PPB). Specification and analysis of inputs, outputs, costs, and alternatives that link plans to *budgets*.

programmed cost. A *fixed cost* not essential for carrying out operations. For example, a firm can control costs for research and development and advertising designed to generate new business, but once it commits to incur them, they become fixed costs. These costs are sometimes called managed costs or *discretionary costs*. Contrast with *capacity costs*.

progressive tax. Tax for which the rate increases as the taxed base, such as income, increases. Contrast with *regressive tax*.

project financing arrangement. As defined by *SFAS No. 47,* the financing of an investment project in which the lender looks principally to the *cash flows* and *earnings* of the project as the source of funds for repayment and to the *assets* of the project as *collateral* for the loan. The general *credit* of the project entity usually does not affect the terms of the financing either because the borrowing entity is a *corporation* without other assets or because the financing provides that the lender has no direct *recourse* to the entity's owners.

projected benefit obligation. The *actuarial present value* at a given date of all pension benefits attributed by a *defined-benefit pension* formula to employee service rendered before that date. The analyst measures the obligation using assumptions as to future compensation levels if the formula incorporates future compensation, as happens, for example, when the plan bases the eventual pension benefit on wages of the last several years of employees' work lives. Contrast to "accumulated benefit obligation," where the analyst measures the obligation using employee compensation levels at the time of the measurement date.

projected financial statement. *Pro forma* financial statement.

projection. See *financial projection* for definition and contrast.

promissory note. An unconditional written promise to pay a specified sum of cash on demand or at a specified date.

proof of journal. The process of checking the arithmetic accuracy of *journal entries* by testing for the equality of all *debits* and all *credits* since the last previous proof.

property dividend. A *dividend in kind*.

property, plant, and equipment. See *plant assets*.

proportionate consolidation. Canada: a presentation of the *financial statements* of any investor-investment relationship, whereby the investor's pro rata share of each *asset,* *liability, income* item, and *expense* item appears in the *financial statements* of the investor under the various *balance sheet* and *income statement* headings.

proprietary accounts. See *budgetary accounts* for definition and contrast in the context of governmental accounting.

proprietorship. *Assets* minus *liabilities* of an *entity;* equals *contributed capital* plus *retained earnings*.

proprietorship theory. The corporation view that emphasizes the form of the *accounting equation* that says *assets – liabilities = owners' equity;* contrast with *entity theory*. The major implication of a choice between these theories deals with the treatment of *subsidiaries*. For example, the proprietorship theory views *minority interest* as an *indeterminate-term liability*. The proprietorship theory implies using a *single-step income statement*.

prorate. To *allocate* in proportion to some base; for example, to allocate *service department* costs in proportion to hours of service used by the benefited department or to allocate *manufacturing variances* to product sold and to product added to *ending inventory*.

prorating variances. See *prorate*.

prospectus. Formal written document describing *securities* a firm will issue. See *proxy*.

protest fee. Fee charged by banks or other financial agencies when the bank cannot collect items (such as *checks*) presented for collection.

provision. Part of an *account* title. Often the firm must recognize an *expense* even though it cannot be sure of the exact amount. The entry for the estimated expense, such as for *income taxes* or expected costs under *warranty,* is as follows:

Expense (Estimated)	X	
Liability (Estimated)		X

American terminology often uses "provision" in the expense account title of the above entry. Thus, Provision for Income Taxes means the estimate of income tax expense. (British terminology uses "provision" in the title for the estimated liability of the above entry, so that Provision for Income Taxes is a *balance sheet account*.)

proxy. Written authorization given by one person to another so that the second person can act for the first, such as to vote shares of stock; of particular significance to accountants because the *SEC* presumes that management distributes financial information along with its proxy solicitations.

public accountant. Generally, this term is synonymous with *certified public accountant*. Some jurisdictions, however, license individuals who are not CPAs as public accountants.

public accounting. That portion of accounting primarily involving the *attest* function, culminating in the *auditor's report*.

PuPU. Acronym for *pu*rchasing *p*ower *u*nit; conceived by John C. Burton, former chief accountant of the *SEC*. Those who think that *constant-dollar accounting* is not particularly useful poke fun at it by calling it "PuPU accounting."

purchase allowance. A reduction in sales *invoice price* usually granted because the purchaser received *goods* not exactly as ordered. The purchaser does not return the goods but agrees to keep them for a price lower than originally agreed upon.

purchase discount. A reduction in purchase *invoice price* granted for prompt payment. See *sales discount* and *terms of sale.*

purchase investigation. An investigation of the financial affairs of a company for the purpose of disclosing matters that may influence the terms or conclusion of a potential acquisition.

purchase method. Accounting for a *business combination* by adding the acquired company's assets at the price paid for them to the acquiring company's assets. Contrast with *pooling-of-interests method.* The firm adds the acquired assets to the books at current values rather than original costs; the subsequent *amortization expenses* usually exceed those (and reported income is smaller than that) for the same business combination accounted for as a pooling of interests. *GAAP* in the U.S. require that the acquirer use the purchase method but other countries still allow the pooling-of-interests method.

purchase order. Document issued by a buyer authorizing a seller to deliver goods, with the buyer to make payment later.

purchasing power gain or loss. *Monetary gain or loss.*

push-down accounting. An accounting method used in some *purchase transactions.* Assume that Company A purchases substantially all the *common shares* of Company B but that Company B must still issue its own *financial statements.* The question arises, shall Company B change the *basis* for its *assets* and *equities* on its own books to the same updated amounts at which they appear on Company A's *consolidated financial statements*? Company B uses "push-down accounting" when it shows the new asset and equity bases reflecting Company A's purchase, because the method "pushes down" the new bases from Company A (where *GAAP* require them) to Company B (where the new bases would not appear in *historical cost accounting*). Since 1983, the *SEC* has required push-down accounting under some circumstances.

put. An option to sell *shares* of a publicly traded corporation at a fixed price during a fixed time span. Contrast with *call.*

Q

qualified report (opinion). *Auditor's report* containing a statement that the auditor was unable to complete a satisfactory examination of all things considered relevant or that the auditor has doubts about the financial impact of some *material* item reported in the financial statements. See *except for* and *subject to.*

quality. In modern usage, a product or service has quality to the extent it conforms to specifications or provides customers the characteristics promised them.

quality of earnings. A phrase with no single, agreed-upon meaning. Some who use the phrase use it with different meanings on different occasions. "Quality of earnings" has an accounting aspect and a business cycle aspect.

In its accounting aspect, managers have choices in measuring and reporting *earnings.* This discretion can involve any of the following: selecting *accounting principles* or standards when *GAAP* allow a choice; making estimates in the application of accounting principles; and timing transactions to allow recognizing *nonrecurring* items in earnings. In some instances the range of choices has a large impact on reported earnings and in others, small. (1) Some use the phrase "quality of earnings" to mean the degree to which management can affect reported income by its choices of accounting estimates even though the choices recur every period. These users judge, for example, insurance companies to have low-quality earnings. Insurance company management must reestimate its liabilities for future payments to the insured each period, thereby having an opportunity to report periodic earnings within a wide range. (2) Others use the phrase to mean the degree to which management actually takes advantage of its flexibility. For them, an insurance company that does not vary its methods and estimating techniques, even though it has the opportunity to do so, has high-quality earnings. (3) Some have in mind the proximity in time between *revenue* recognition and cash collection. For them, the smaller the time delay, the higher will be the quality. (4) Still others use the phrase to mean the degree to which managers who have a choice among the items with large influence on earnings choose the ones that result in income measures that are more likely to recur. For them, the more likely an item of earnings is to recur, the higher will be its quality. Often these last two groups trade off with each other. Consider a dealer leasing a car on a long-term *lease,* receiving monthly collections. The dealer who uses *sales-type lease* accounting scores low on proximity of revenue recognition (all at the time of signing the lease) to cash collection but highlights the non-repetitive nature of the transaction. The leasing dealer who uses *operating lease* accounting has perfectly matching revenue recognition and cash collection, but the *recurring* nature of the revenue gives a misleading picture of a repetitive transaction. The phrase "item of earnings" in (4) is ambiguous. The writer could mean the underlying economic event (which occurs when the lease for the car is signed) or the revenue recognition (which occurs every time the dealer using operating lease accounting receives cash). Hence, you should try to understand what other speakers and writers mean by "quality of earnings" when you interpret what they say and write. Some who refer to "earnings quality" suspect that managers will usually make choices that enhance current earnings and present the firm in the best light, independent of the ability of the firm to generate similar earnings in the future.

In the business cycle aspect, management's action often has no impact on the stability and recurrence of earnings. Compare a company that sells consumer products and likely has sales repeating every week with a construction company that builds to order. Companies in noncyclical businesses, such as some public utilities, likely have more stable earnings than ones in cyclical businesses, such as steel. Some use "quality of earnings" to refer to the stability and recurrence of basic revenue-generating activities.

Those who use the phrase this way rarely associate earnings quality with accounting issues.

quality of financial position. Because of the *articulation* of the *income statement* with the *balance sheet,* the factors that imply a high (or low) *quality of earnings* also affect the balance sheet. Users of this phrase have in mind the same accounting issues as they have in mind when they use the phrase "quality of earnings."

quantitative performance measure. A measure of output based on an objectively observable quantity, such as units produced or *direct costs* incurred, rather than on an unobservable quantity or a quantity observable only nonobjectively, like quality of service provided.

quantity discount. A reduction in purchase price as quantity purchased increases. The Robinson-Patman Act constrains the amount of the discount. Do not confuse with *purchase discount.*

quantity variance. *Efficiency variance;* in *standard cost* systems, the standard price per unit times (actual quantity used minus standard quantity that should be used).

quasi-reorganization. A *reorganization* in which no new company emerges or no court has intervened, as would happen in *bankruptcy.* The primary purpose is to rid the balance sheet of a *deficit* (negative *retained earnings*) and give the firm a "fresh start."

quick assets. *Assets* readily convertible into *cash;* includes cash, current marketable securities, and current receivables.

quick ratio. Sum of (cash, current marketable securities, and current receivables) divided by *current liabilities;* often called the "acid test ratio." The analyst may exclude some nonliquid receivables from the numerator. See *ratio.*

R

R^2. The proportion of the statistical variance of a *dependent variable* explained by the equation fit to *independent variable(s)* in a *regression analysis.*

Railroad Accounting Principles Board (RAPB). A board brought into existence by the Staggers Rail Act of 1980 to advise the Interstate Commerce Commission on accounting matters affecting railroads. The RAPB was the only cost-accounting body authorized by the government during the decade of the 1980s (because Congress ceased funding the CASB during the 1980s). The RAPB incorporated the pronouncements of the CASB and became the government's authority on cost accounting principles.

R&D. See *research and development.*

random number sampling. For choosing a sample, a method in which the analyst selects items from the *population* by using a random number table or generator.

random sampling. For choosing a sample, a method in which all items in the population have an equal chance of being selected. Compare *judgment(al) sampling.*

RAPB. *Railroad Accounting Principles Board.*

rate of return on assets. *Return on assets.*

rate of return on common stock equity. See *ratio.*

rate of return on shareholders' (owners') equity. See *ratio.*

rate of return (on total capital). See *ratio* and *return on assets.*

rate variance. *Price variance,* usually for *direct labor costs.*

ratio. The number resulting when one number divides another. Analysts generally use ratios to assess aspects of profitability, solvency, and liquidity. The commonly used financial ratios fall into three categories: (1) those that summarize some aspect of *operations* for a period, usually a year, (2) those that summarize some aspect of *financial position* at a given moment—the moment for which a *balance sheet* reports, and (3) those that relate some aspect of operations to some aspect of financial position. Exhibit 5.11 lists the most common financial ratios and shows separately both the numerator and the denominator for each ratio.

For all ratios that require an average balance during the period, the analyst often derives the average as one half the sum of the beginning and the ending balances. Sophisticated analysts recognize, however, that particularly when companies use a fiscal year different from the calendar year, this averaging of beginning and ending balances may mislead. Consider, for example, the rate of *return on assets* of Sears, Roebuck & Company, whose fiscal year ends on January 31. Sears chooses a January 31 closing date at least in part because inventories are at a low level and are therefore easy to count—it has sold the Christmas merchandise, and the Easter merchandise has not yet all arrived. Furthermore, by January 31, Sears has collected for most Christmas sales, so receivable amounts are not unusually large. Thus at January 31, the amount of total assets is lower than at many other times during the year. Consequently, the denominator of the rate of return on assets, total assets, for Sears more likely represents the smallest amount of total assets on hand during the year rather than the average amount. The return on assets rate for Sears and other companies that choose a fiscal year-end to coincide with low points in the inventory cycle is likely to exceed the ratio measured with a more accurate estimate of the average amounts of total assets.

raw material. Goods purchased for use in manufacturing a product.

reacquired stock. *Treasury shares.*

real accounts. *Balance sheet accounts,* as opposed to *nominal accounts.* See *permanent account.*

real amount (value). An amount stated in *constant dollars.* For example, if the firm sells an investment costing $100 for $130 after a period of 10 percent general *inflation,* the *nominal amount* of *gain* is $30 (= $130 − $100) but the real amount of gain is C$20 (= $130 − 1.10 × $100), where "C$" denotes constant dollars of purchasing power on the date of sale.

real estate. *Land* and its *improvements,* such as landscaping and roads, but not buildings.

real interest rate. Interest rate reflecting the productivity of capital, not including a premium for inflation anticipated over the life of the loan.

realizable value. *Fair value* or, sometimes, *net realizable (sales) value.*

realization convention. The accounting practice of delaying the recognition of *gains* and *losses* from changes in the market price of *assets* until the firm sells the assets. However, the firm recognizes unrealized losses on *inventory* (or *marketable securities* classified as *trading securities*) prior to sale when the firm uses the *lower-of-cost-or-market* valuation basis for inventory (or the *fair value* basis for marketable securities).

realize. To convert into *funds;* when applied to a *gain* or *loss,* implies that an *arm's-length transaction* has taken place. Contrast with *recognize;* the firm may recognize a loss (as, for example, on *marketable equity securities*) in the financial statements even though it has not yet realized the loss via a transaction.

realized gain (or loss) on marketable equity securities. An income statement account title for the difference between the proceeds of disposition and the *original cost* of *marketable equity securities.*

realized holding gain. See *inventory profit* for definition and an example.

rearrangement costs. Costs of reinstalling assets, perhaps in a different location. The firm may, but need not, *capitalize* them as part of the assets cost, just as is done with original installation cost. The firm will *expense* these costs if they merely maintain the asset's future benefits at their originally intended level before the relocation.

recapitalization. *Reorganization.*

recapture. Name for one kind of tax payment. Various provisions of the *income tax* rules require a refund by the taxpayer (recapture by the government) of various tax advantages under certain conditions. For example, the taxpayer must repay tax savings provided by *accelerated depreciation* if the taxpayer prematurely retires the item providing the tax savings.

receipt. Acquisition of *cash.*

receivable. Any *collectible,* whether or not it is currently due.

receivable turnover. See *ratio.*

reciprocal holdings. Company A owns stock of Company B, and Company B owns stock of Company A; or Company B owns stock of Company C, which owns stock of Company A.

recognize. To enter a transaction in the accounts; not synonymous with *realize.*

reconciliation. A calculation that shows how one balance or figure derives from another, such as a reconciliation of retained earnings or a *bank reconciliation schedule.* See *articulate.*

record date. The date at which the firm pays *dividends* on payment date to those who own the stock.

recourse. The rights of the lender if a borrower does not repay as promised. A recourse loan gives the lender the right to take any of the borrower's assets not exempted from such taking by the contract. See also *note receivable discounted.*

recovery of unrealized loss on trading securities. An *income statement account title* for the *gain* during the current period on *trading securities.*

recurring. Occurring again; occurring repetitively; in accounting, an adjective often used in describing *revenue* or *earnings.* In some contexts, the term "recurring revenue" is ambiguous. Consider a construction contractor

who accounts for a single long-term project with the *installment method,* with revenue recognized at the time of each cash collection from the customer. The recognized revenue is recurring, but the transaction leading to the revenue is not. See *quality of earnings.*

redemption. Retirement by the issuer, usually by a purchase or *call,* of *stocks* or *bonds.*

redemption premium. *Call premium.*

redemption value. The price a corporation will pay to retire *bonds* or *preferred stock* if it calls them before *maturity.*

refinancing. An adjustment in the *capital structure* of a corporation, involving changes in the nature and amounts of the various classes of *debt* and, in some cases, *capital* as well as other components of *shareholders' equity. Asset* carrying values in the accounts remain unchanged.

refunding bond issue. Said of a *bond* issue whose proceeds the firm uses to retire bonds already *outstanding.*

register. A collection of consecutive entries, or other information, in chronological order, such as a check register or an insurance register that lists all insurance policies owned. If the firm records entries in the register, it can serve as a *journal.*

registered bond. A bond for which the issuer will pay the *principal* and *interest,* if registered as to interest, to the owner listed on the books of the issuer; as opposed to a bearer bond, in which the issuer must pay the possessor of the bond.

registrar. An *agent,* usually a bank or trust company, appointed by a corporation to keep track of the names of shareholders and distributions to them.

registration statement. Required by the Securities Act of 1933, statement of most companies that want to have owners of their securities trade the securities in public markets. The statement discloses financial data and other items of interest to potential investors.

regression analysis. A method of *cost estimation* based on statistical techniques for fitting a line (or its equivalent in higher mathematical dimensions) to an observed series of data points, usually by minimizing the sum of squared deviations of the observed data from the fitted line. Common usage calls the cost that the analysis explains the "dependent variable"; it calls the variable(s) we use to estimate cost behavior "independent variable(s)." If we use more than one independent variable, the term for the analysis is "multiple regression analysis." See R^2, *standard error,* and *t-value.*

regressive tax. Tax for which the rate decreases as the taxed base, such as income, increases. Contrast with *progressive tax.*

Regulation S-K. The *SEC*'s standardization of nonfinancial statement disclosure requirements for documents filed with the SEC.

Regulation S-T. The *SEC*'s regulations specifying formats for electronic filing and the *EDGAR* system.

Regulation S-X. The *SEC*'s principal accounting regulation, which specifies the form and content of financial reports to the SEC.

rehabilitation. The improving of a used *asset* via an extensive repair. Ordinary *repairs* and *maintenance* restore or maintain expected *service potential* of an asset, and the firm treats them as *expenses*. A rehabilitation improves the asset beyond its current service potential, enhancing the service potential to a significantly higher level than before the rehabilitation. Once rehabilitated, the asset may be better, but need not be, than it was when new. The firm will *capitalize expenditures* for rehabilitation, like those for *betterments* and *improvements*.

reinvestment rate. In a *capital budgeting* context, the rate at which the firm invests cash inflows from a project occurring before the project's completion. Once the analyst assumes such a rate, no project can ever have multiple *internal rates of return*.

relative performance evaluation. Setting performance targets and, sometimes, compensation in relation to the performance of others, perhaps in different firms or divisions, who face a similar environment.

relative sales value method. See *net realizable (sales) value*.

relevant cost. Cost used by an analyst in making a decision. *Incremental cost; opportunity cost*.

relevant cost analysis. Identifies the *costs* (or *revenues*) relevant to the decision to be made. A cost or revenue is relevant only if an amount differs between alternatives. Also called *differential cost analysis*.

relevant range. Activity levels over which costs are linear or for which *flexible budget* estimates and *break-even charts* will remain valid.

remit earnings. An expression likely to confuse a reader without a firm understanding of accounting basics. A firm generates *net assets* by earning *income* and retains net assets if it does not declare *dividends* in the amount of net income. When a firm declares dividends and pays the cash (or other net assets), some writers would say the firm "remits earnings." We think the student learns better by conceiving earnings as a *credit balance*. When a firm pays dividends it sends net assets, things with debit balances, not something with a credit balance, to the recipient. When writers say firms "remit earnings," they mean the firms send assets (or net assets) that previous earnings have generated and reduce *retained earnings*.

remittance advice. Information on a *check stub*, or on a document attached to a check by the *drawer*, that tells the *payee* why a payment is being made.

rent. A charge for use of land, buildings, or other assets.

reorganization. In the *capital structure* of a corporation, a major change that leads to changes in the rights, interests, and implied ownership of the various security owners; usually results from a *merger* or an agreement by senior security holders to take action to forestall *bankruptcy*.

repair. An *expenditure* to restore an *asset*'s service potential after damage or after prolonged use. In the second sense, after prolonged use, the difference between repairs and maintenance is one of degree and not of kind. A repair is treated as an *expense* of the period when incurred. Because the firm treats repairs and maintenance similarly in this regard, the distinction is not important. A repair helps to maintain capacity at the levels planned when the firm acquired the *asset*. Contrast with *improvement*.

replacement cost. For an asset, the current *fair market price* to purchase another, similar asset (with the same future benefit or service potential). *Current cost*. See *reproduc-*

tion cost and *productive capacity*. See also *distributable income* and *inventory profit*.

replacement cost method of depreciation. Method in which the analyst augments the original-cost *depreciation* charge with an amount based on a portion of the difference between the *current replacement cost* of the asset and its *original cost*.

replacement system of depreciation. See *retirement method of depreciation* for definition and contrast.

report. *Financial statement; auditor's report*.

report form. *Balance sheet* form that typically shows *assets* minus *liabilities* as one total. Then, below that total appears the components of *owners' equity* summing to the same total. Often, the top section shows *current assets* less *current liabilities* before *noncurrent* assets less noncurrent liabilities. Contrast with *account form*.

reporting objectives (policies). The general purposes for which the firm prepares *financial statements*. The *FASB* has discussed these in *SFAC No. 1*.

representative item sampling. Sampling in which the analyst believes the sample selected is typical of the entire population from which it comes. Compare *specific item sampling*.

reproduction cost. The *cost* necessary to acquire an *asset* similar in all physical respects to another asset for which the analyst requires a *current value*. See *replacement cost* and *productive capacity* for contrast.

required rate of return (RRR). *Cost of capital*.

requisition. A formal written order or request, such as for withdrawal of supplies from the storeroom.

resale value. *Exit value; net realizable value*.

research and development (R&D). A form of economic activity with special accounting rules. Firms engage in research in hopes of discovering new knowledge that will create a new product, process, or service or of improving a present product, process, or service. Development translates research findings or other knowledge into a new or improved product, process, or service. *SFAS No. 2* requires that firms expense costs of such activities as incurred on the grounds that the future benefits are too uncertain to warrant *capitalization* as an *asset*. This treatment seems questionable to us because we wonder why firms would continue to undertake R&D if there was no expectation of future benefit; if future benefits exist, then R&D *costs* should be assets that appear, like other assets, at *historical cost*.

reserve. The worst word in accounting because almost everyone not trained in accounting, and some who are, misunderstands it. The common confusion is that "reserves" represent a pool of *cash* or other *assets* available when the firm needs them. Wrong. Cash always has a *debit balance*. Reserves always have a *credit* balance. When properly used in accounting, "reserves" refer to an account that appropriates *retained earnings* and restricts dividend declarations. Appropriating retained earnings is itself a poor and vanishing practice, so the word should seldom appear in accounting. In addition, "reserve" was used in the past to indicate an asset *contra account* (for example, "reserve for depreciation") or an *estimated liability* (for example, "reserve for warranty costs"). In any case, reserve accounts have *credit* balances and are not pools of *funds*, as the unwary reader might infer. If a company has set aside a pool of *cash* (or *marketable securities*) to serve some specific purpose such as paying for a new factory, then it will call that cash a *fund*. No other word in accounting causes so much misunderstanding by nonexperts as well as by "experts" who should know better. A leading unabridged dictionary defines "reserve" as "cash, or assets readily convertible into cash, held aside, as by a corporation, bank, state or national government, etc. to meet expected or unexpected demands." This definition is absolutely wrong in accounting. Reserves are not funds. For example, the firm creates a contingency fund of $10,000 by depositing cash in a fund and makes the following entry:

Dr. Contingency Fund	10,000	
Cr. Cash		10,000

The following entry may accompany the previous entry, if the firm wants to appropriate retained earnings:

Dr. Retained Earnings	10,000	
Cr. Reserve for Contingencies		10,000

The transaction leading to the first entry has economic significance. The second entry has little economic impact for most firms. The problem with the word "reserve" arises because the firm can make the second entry without the first—a company can create a reserve, that is, appropriate retained earnings, without creating a fund. The problem results, at least in part, from the fact that in common usage, "reserve" means a pool of assets, as in the phrase "oil reserves." The *Internal Revenue Service* does not help in dispelling confusion about the term "reserves." The federal *income tax* return for corporations uses the title "Reserve for Bad Debts" to mean "Allowance for Uncollectible Accounts" and speaks of the "Reserve Method" in referring to the *allowance method* for estimating *revenue* or *income* reductions from estimated *uncollectibles*.

reserve recognition accounting (RRA). One form of *accounting* for natural resources. In exploration for natural resources, the problem arises of how to treat the expenditures for exploration, both before the firm knows the outcome of the efforts and after it knows the outcome. Suppose that the firm spends $10 million to drill 10 holes ($1 million each) and that nine of them are dry whereas one is a gusher containing oil with a *net realizable value* of $40 million. Dry hole, or *successful efforts,* accounting would expense $9 million and *capitalize* $1 million, which the firm will *deplete* as it lifts the oil from the ground. *SFAS No. 19,* now suspended, required *successful efforts costing.* Full costing would expense nothing but would capitalize the $10 million of drilling costs that the firm will deplete as it lifts the oil from the single productive well. Reserve recognition accounting would capitalize $40 million, which the firm will deplete as it lifts the oil, with a $30 million *credit* to *income* or *contributed capital.* The

balance sheet shows the *net realizable value* of proven oil and gas reserves. The *income statement* has three sorts of items: (1) current income resulting from production or "lifting profit," which is the *revenue* from sales of oil and gas less the expense based on the current valuation amount at which these items have appeared on the balance sheet, (2) profit or loss from exploration efforts in which the current value of new discoveries is revenue and all the exploration cost is expense, and (3) gain or loss on changes in current value during the year, which accountants in other contexts call a *holding gain or loss.*

reset bond. A bond, typically a *junk bond,* that specifies that periodically the issuer will reset the coupon rate so that the bond sells at *par* in the market. Investment bankers created this type of instrument to help ensure the purchasers of such bonds of getting a fair rate of return, given the riskiness of the issuer. If the issuer gets into financial trouble, its bonds will trade for less than par in the market. The issuer of a reset bond promises to raise the interest rate and preserve the value of the bond. Ironically, the reset feature has often had just the opposite effect. The default risk of many issuers of reset bonds has deteriorated so much that the bonds have dropped to less than 50 percent of par. To raise the value to par, the issuer would have to raise the interest rate to more than 25 percent per year. That rate is so large that issuers have declared bankruptcy rather than attempt to make the new large interest payments; this then reduces the market value of the bonds rather than increases them.

residual income. In an external reporting context, a term that refers to *net income* to *common shares* (= net income less *preferred stock dividends*). In *managerial accounting,* this term refers to the excess of income for a *division* or *segment* of a company over the product of the *cost of capital* for the company multiplied by the average amount of capital invested in the division during the period over which the division earned the income.

residual security. A *potentially dilutive security.* Options, warrants, convertible bonds, and convertible preferred stock.

residual value. At any time, the estimated or actual *net realizable value* (that is, proceeds less removal costs) of an *asset,* usually a depreciable *plant asset.* In the context of depreciation accounting, this term is equivalent to *salvage value* and is preferred to *scrap value* because the firm need not scrap the asset. It is sometimes used to mean net *book value.* In the context of a *noncancelable* lease, it is the estimated value of the leased asset at the end of the lease period. See *lease.*

resources supplied. *Expenditures* made for an activity.

resources used. *Cost driver* rate times cost driver volume.

responsibility accounting. Accounting for a business by considering various units as separate entities, or *profit centers,* giving management of each unit responsibility for the unit's *revenues* and *expenses.* See *transfer price.*

responsibility center. An organization part or *segment* that top management holds accountable for a specified set of activities. Also called "accountability center." See *cost center, investment center, profit center,* and *revenue center.*

restricted assets. Governmental resources restricted by legal or contractual requirements for a specific purpose.

restricted retained earnings. That part of *retained earnings* not legally available for *dividends*. See *retained earnings, appropriated*. Bond indentures and other loan contracts can curtail the legal ability of the corporation to declare dividends without formally requiring a retained earnings appropriation, but the firm must disclose such restrictions.

retail inventory method. Ascertaining cost amounts of *ending inventory* as follows (assuming *FIFO*): cost of ending inventory = (selling price of *goods available for sale* − sales) × *cost percentage*. The analyst then computes cost of goods sold from the inventory equation; costs of beginning inventory, purchases, and ending inventory are all known. (When the firm uses *LIFO,* the method resembles the *dollar-value LIFO method.*) See *markup*.

retail terminology. See *markup*.

retained earnings. Net *income* over the life of a corporation less all *dividends* (including capitalization through *stock dividends*); *owners' equity* less *contributed capital*.

retained earnings, appropriated. An *account* set up by crediting it and debiting *retained earnings;* used to indicate that a portion of retained earnings is not available for dividends. The practice of appropriating retained earnings is misleading unless the firm marks all capital with its use, which is not practicable, nor sensible, since capital is fungible—all the *equities* jointly fund all the *assets*. The use of formal retained earnings appropriations is declining.

retained earnings statement. A *reconciliation* of the beginning and the ending balances in the *retained earnings account;* required by *generally accepted accounting principles* whenever the firm presents *comparative balance sheets* and an *income statement*. This reconciliation can appear in a separate statement, in a combined statement of income and retained earnings, or in the balance sheet.

retirement method of depreciation. A method in which the firm records no entry for *depreciation expense* until it retires an *asset* from service. Then, it makes an entry *debiting* depreciation expense and *crediting* the asset account for the cost of the asset retired. If the retired asset has a *salvage value,* the firm reduces the amount of the debit to depreciation expense by the amount of salvage value with a corresponding debit to cash, receivables, or salvaged materials. The "replacement system of depreciation" is similar, except that the debit to depreciation expense equals the cost of the new asset less the salvage value, if any, of the old asset. Some public utilities used these methods. For example, if the firm acquired ten telephone poles in Year 1 for $60 each and replaces them in Year 10 for $100 each when the salvage value of the old poles is $5 each, the accounting would be as follows:

Retirement Method

Plant Assets	600	
Cash		600
To acquire assets in Year 1.		
Depreciation Expense	550	
Salvage Receivable	50	
Plant Assets		600

(continued)

To record retirement and depreciation in Year 10.

Plant Assets	1,000	
Cash		1,000

To record acquisition of new assets in Year 10.

Replacement Method

Plant Assets	600	
Cash		600
To acquire assets in Year 1.		
Depreciation Expense	950	
Salvage Receivable	50	
Cash		1,000

To record depreciation on old asset in amount quantified by net cost of replacement asset in Year 10.

The retirement method is like *FIFO* in that it records the cost of the first assets as depreciation and puts the cost of the second assets on the balance sheet. The replacement method is like *LIFO* in that it records the cost of the second assets as depreciation expense and leaves the cost of the first assets on the *balance sheet.*

retirement plan. *Pension plan.*

retroactive benefits. In initiating or amending a *defined-benefit pension plan,* benefits that the benefit formula attributes to employee services rendered in periods prior to the initiation or amendment. See *prior service costs.*

return. A schedule of information required by governmental bodies, such as the tax return required by the *Internal Revenue Service;* also the physical return of merchandise. See also *return on investment.*

return on assets (ROA). *Net income* plus after-tax *interest charges* plus *minority interest* in income divided by average total *assets;* perhaps the single most useful ratio for assessing management's overall operating performance. Most financial economists would subtract average noninterest-bearing *liabilities* from the denominator. Economists realize that when liabilities do not provide for explicit interest charges, the creditor adjusts the terms of contract, such as setting a higher selling price or lower discount, to those who do not pay cash immediately. (To take an extreme example, consider how much higher salary a worker who receives a salary once per year, rather than once per month, would demand.) This ratio requires in the numerator the income amount before the firm accrues any charges to suppliers of funds. We cannot measure the interest charges implicit in the noninterest-bearing liabilities because they cause items such as cost of goods sold and salary expense to be somewhat larger, since the interest is implicit. Subtracting their amounts from the denominator adjusts for their implicit cost. Such subtraction assumes that assets financed with noninterest-bearing liabilities have the same rate of return as all the other assets.

return on investment (ROI), return on capital. *Income* (before distributions to suppliers of capital) for a period; as a rate, this amount divided by average total assets. The analyst should add back *interest,* net of tax effects, to *net income* for the numerator. See *ratio.*

revenue. The *owners' equity* increase accompanying the *net assets* increase caused by selling goods or rendering services; in short, a service rendered; *sales* of products, merchandise, and services and earnings from *interest, dividends, rents,* and the like. Measure revenue as the expected *net present value* of the net assets the firm will receive. Do not confuse with *receipt* of *funds,* which may occur before, when, or after revenue is recognized. Contrast with *gain* and *income.* See also *holding gain.* Some writers use the term *gross income* synonymously with *revenue;* avoid such usage.

revenue center. Within a firm, a *responsibility center* that has control only over revenues generated. Contrast with *cost center.* See *profit center.*

revenue expenditure. A term sometimes used to mean an *expense,* in contrast to a capital *expenditure* to acquire an *asset* or to discharge a *liability.* Avoid using this term; use *period expense* instead.

revenue received in advance. An inferior term for *advances from customers.*

reversal (reversing) entry. An *entry* in which all *debits* and *credits* are the credits and debits, respectively, of another entry, and in the same amounts. The accountant usually records a reversal entry on the first day of an *accounting period* to reverse a previous *adjusting entry,* usually an *accrual.* The purpose of such entries is to make the bookkeeper's tasks easier. Suppose that the firm pays salaries every other Friday, with paychecks compensating employees for the two weeks just ended. Total salaries accrue at the rate of $5,000 per five-day workweek. The bookkeeper is accustomed to making the following entry every other Friday:

(1) Salary Expense	10,000	
Cash		10,000
To record salary expense and salary payments.		

If the firm delivers paychecks to employees on Friday, November 25, then the *adjusting entry* made on November 30 (or perhaps later) to record accrued salaries for November 28, 29, and 30 would be as follows:

(2) Salary Expense	3,000	
Salaries Payable		3,000
To charge November operations with all salaries earned in November.		

The firm would close the Salary Expense account as part of the November 30 closing entries. On the next payday, December 9, the salary entry would be as follows:

(3) Salary Expense	7,000	
Salaries Payable	3,000	
Cash		10,000
To record salary payments split between expense for December (seven days) and liability carried over from November.		

To make entry (3), the bookkeeper must look back into the records to see how much of the debit is to Salaries Payable accrued from the previous month in order to split the total debits between December expense and the liability carried over from November. Notice that this entry forces the bookkeeper both (a) to refer to balances in old accounts and (b) to make an entry different from the one customarily made, entry (1). The reversing entry, made just after the books have been closed for the second quarter, makes the salary entry for December 9 the same as that made on all other Friday paydays. The reversing entry merely *reverses* the adjusting entry (2):

(4) Salaries Payable	3,000	
Salary Expense		3,000
To reverse the adjusting entry.		

This entry results in a zero balance in the Salaries Payable account and a credit balance in the Salary Expense account. If the firm makes entry (4) just after it closes the books for November, then the entry on December 9 will be the customary entry (1). Entries (4) and (1) together have exactly the same effect as entry (3).

The procedure for using reversal entries is as follows: the firm makes the required adjustment to record an accrual (*payable* or *receivable*) at the end of an *accounting period;* it makes the closing entry as usual; as of the first day of the following period, it makes an entry reversing the adjusting entry; when the firm makes (or receives) a payment, it records the entry as though it had not recorded an adjusting entry at the end of the preceding period. Whether a firm uses reversal entries affects the record-keeping procedures but not the financial statements.

This term is also used to describe the entry reversing an incorrect entry before recording the correct entry.

reverse stock split. A stock split in which the firm decreases the number of shares *outstanding.* See *stock split.*

revolving fund. A fund whose amounts the firm continually spends and replenishes; for example, a *petty cash fund.*

revolving loan. A *loan* that both the borrower and the lender expect to renew at *maturity.*

right. The privilege to subscribe to new *stock* issues or to purchase stock. Usually, securities called *warrants* contain the rights, and the owner of the warrants may sell them. See also *preemptive right.*

risk. A measure of the variability of the *return on investment.* For a given expected amount of return, most people prefer less risk to more risk. Therefore, in rational markets, investments with more risk usually promise, or investors expect to receive, a higher rate of return than investments with lower risk. Most people use "risk" and "uncertainty" as synonyms. In technical language, however, these terms have different meanings. We use "risk" when we know the probabilities attached to the various outcomes, such as the probabilities of heads or tails in the flip of a fair coin. "Uncertainty" refers to an event for which we can only estimate the probabilities of the outcomes, such as winning or losing a lawsuit.

risk-adjusted discount rate. Rate used in discounting cash flows for projects more or less risky than the firm's average. In a *capital budgeting* context, a decision analyst compares projects by comparing their net *present values* for a given *interest* rate, usually the cost of capital. If the analyst considers a given project's outcome to be much more or much less risky than the normal undertakings of the company, then the analyst will use a larger interest rate (if the project is riskier) or a smaller interest rate (if less risky) in discounting, and the rate used is "risk-adjusted."

risk-free rate. An interest rate reflecting only the pure interest rate plus an amount to compensate for inflation anticipated over the life of a loan, excluding a premium for the risk of default by the borrower. Financial economists usually measure the risk-free rate in the United States from U.S. government securities, such as Treasury bills and notes.

risk premium. Extra compensation paid to employees or extra *interest* paid to lenders, over amounts usually considered normal, in return for their undertaking to engage in activities riskier than normal.

ROA. *Return on assets.*

ROI. *Return on investment;* usually used to refer to a single project and expressed as a ratio: *income* divided by average *cost* of *assets* devoted to the project.

royalty. Compensation for the use of property, usually a patent, copyrighted material, or natural resources. The amount is often expressed as a percentage of receipts from using the property or as an amount per unit produced.

RRA. *Reserve recognition accounting.*

RRR. Required rate of return. See *cost of capital.*

rule of 69. Rule stating that an amount of cash invested at *r* percent per period will double in $69/r + .35$ periods. This approximation is accurate to one-tenth of a period for interest rates between 1/4 and 100 percent per period. For example, at 10 percent per period, the rule says that a given sum will double in $69/10 + .35 = 7.25$ periods. At 10 percent per period, a given sum actually doubles in $7.27+$ periods.

rule of 72. Rule stating that an amount of cash invested at *r* percent per period will double in $72/r$ periods. A reasonable approximation for interest rates between 4 and 10 percent but not nearly as accurate as the *rule of 69* for interest rates outside that range. For example, at 10 percent per period, the rule says that a given sum will double in $72/10 = 7.2$ periods.

rule of 78. The rule followed by many finance companies for allocating earnings on *loans* among the months of a year on the sum-of-the-months'-digits basis when the borrower makes equal monthly payments to the lender. The sum of the digits from 1 through 12 is 78, so the rule allocates 12/78 of the year's earnings to the first month, 11/78 to the second month, and so on. This approximation allocates more of the early payments to interest and less to principal than does the correct, compound-interest method. Hence, lenders still use this method even though present-day computers can make the compound-interest computation as easily as they can carry out the approximation. See *sum-of-the-years'-digits depreciation.*

ruling (and balancing) an account. The process of summarizing a series of entries in an *account* by computing a new *balance* and drawing double lines to indicate that the new balance summarizes the information above the double lines. An illustration appears below. The steps are as follows: (1) Compute the sum of all *debit* entries including opening debit balance, if any—$1,464.16. (2) Compute the sum of all credit entries including opening credit balance, if any—$413.57. (3) If the amount in (1) exceeds the amount in (2), then write the excess as a credit with a checkmark—$1,464.16 − $413.57 = $1,050.59. (4) Add both debit and credit columns, which should both now sum to the same amount, and show that identical total at the foot of both columns. (5) Draw double lines under those numbers and write the excess of debits over credits as the new debit balance with a checkmark. (6) If the amount in (2) exceeds the amount in (1), then write the excess as a debit with a checkmark. (7) Do steps (4) and (5) except that the excess becomes the new credit balance. (8) If the amount in (1) equals the amount in (2), then the balance is zero, and only the totals with the double lines beneath them need appear.

Rutgers Accounting Web site. See http://www.rutgers.edu/Accounting/ for a useful compendium of accounting information.

An Open Account, Ruled and Balanced
(Steps indicated in parentheses correspond to steps described in "ruling an account.")

	Date 2004	Explanation	Ref.	Debit (1)	Date 2004	Explanation	Ref.	Credit (2)	
	Jan. 2	Balance	√	100.00					
	Jan. 13		VR	121.37	Sept. 15		J	.42	
	Mar. 20		VR	56.42	Nov. 12		J	413.15	
	June 5		J	1,138.09	Dec. 31	Balance	√	1,050.59	(3)
	Aug. 18		J	1.21					
	Nov. 20		VR	38.43					
	Dec. 7		VR	8.64					
(4)	2005			1,464.16	2005			1,464.16	(4)
(5)	Jan. 1	Balance	√	1,050.59					

S

S corporation. A corporation taxed like a *partnership*. Corporation (or partnership) agreements allocate the periodic *income* to the individual shareholders (or partners) who report these amounts on their individual *income tax* returns. Contrast with *C corporation*.

SA (société anonyme). France: A *corporation*.

SAB. *Staff Accounting Bulletin* of the *SEC*.

safe-harbor lease. A form of *tax-transfer lease*.

safety stock. Extra items of *inventory* kept on hand to protect against running out.

salary. Compensation earned by managers, administrators, and professionals, not based on an hourly rate. Contrast with *wage*.

sale. A *revenue* transaction in which the firm delivers *goods* or *services* to a customer in return for cash or a contractual obligation to pay.

sale and leaseback. A *financing* transaction in which the firm sells improved property but takes it back for use on a long-term *lease*. Such transactions often have advantageous *income tax* effects but usually have no effect on *financial statement income*.

sales activity variance. *Sales volume variance*.

sales allowance. A sales *invoice* price reduction that a seller grants to a buyer because the seller delivered *goods* different from, perhaps because of damage, those the buyer ordered. The seller often accumulates amounts of such adjustments in a temporary *revenue contra account* having this, or a similar, title. See *sales discount*.

sales basis of revenue recognition. Recognition of *revenue* not when a firm produces goods or when it receives orders but only when it has completed the sale by delivering the goods or services and has received cash or a claim to cash. Most firms recognize revenue on this basis. Compare with the *percentage-of-completion method* and the *installment method*. This is identical with the *completed contract method*, but the latter term ordinarily applies only to *long-term* construction projects.

sales contra, estimated uncollectibles. A title for the contra-revenue account to recognize estimated reductions in income caused by *accounts receivable* that will not be collected. See *bad debt expense, allowance for uncollectibles,* and *allowance method*.

sales discount. A sales *invoice* price reduction usually offered for prompt payment. See *terms of sale* and *2/10, n/30*.

sales return. The physical return of merchandise. The seller often accumulates amounts of such returns in a temporary *revenue contra account*.

sales-type (capital) lease. A form of *lease*. See *capital lease*. When a manufacturer (or other firm) that ordinarily sells goods enters a capital lease as *lessor,* the lease is a "sales-type lease." When a financial firm, such as a bank or insurance company or leasing company, acquires the asset from the manufacturer and then enters a capital lease as lessor, the lease is a "direct-financing-type lease." The manufacturer recognizes its ordinary profit (sales price less *cost of goods sold,* where sales price is the *present value* of the contractual lease payments plus any down payment) on executing the sales-type capital lease, but the financial firm does not recognize profit on executing a capital lease of the direct-financing type.

sales value method. *Relative sales value method.* See *net realizable value method*.

sales volume variance. Budgeted *contribution margin* per unit times (planned sales volume minus actual sales volume).

salvage value. Actual or estimated selling price, net of removal or disposal costs, of a used *plant asset* that the firm expects to sell or otherwise retire. See *residual value*.

SAR. *Summary annual report*.

SARL (société à responsabilité limitée). France: a *corporation* with limited liability and a life of no more than 99 years; must have at least two and no more than 50 *shareholders*.

SAS. *Statement on Auditing Standards* of the *AICPA*.

scale effect. See *discounted cash flow*.

scatter diagram. A graphic representation of the relation between two or more variables within a population.

schedule. A supporting set of calculations, with explanations, that show how to derive figures in a *financial statement* or tax return.

scientific method. *Effective interest method* of *amortizing bond discount* or *premium*.

scrap value. *Salvage value* assuming the owner intends to junk the item. A *net realizable value*. *Residual value*.

SEC (Securities and Exchange Commission). An agency authorized by the U.S. Congress to regulate, among other things, the financial reporting practices of most public corporations. The SEC has indicated that it will usually allow the *FASB* to set accounting principles, but it often requires more disclosure than the FASB requires. The SEC states its accounting requirements in its *Accounting Series Releases (ASR), Financial Reporting Releases, Accounting and Auditing Enforcement Releases, Staff Accounting Bulletins* (these are, strictly speaking, interpretations by the accounting staff, not rules of the commissioners themselves), and *Regulations S-X*. See also *registration statement, 10-K,* and *20-F*.

secret reserve. *Hidden reserve*.

Securities and Exchange Commission. *SEC*.

security. Document that indicates ownership, such as a *share* of *stock*, or indebtedness, such as a *bond*, or potential ownership, such as an *option* or *warrant*.

security available for sale. According to *SFAS No. 115* (1993), a *debt* or *equity security* that is not a *trading security*, or a debt security that is not a *security held to maturity*.

security held to maturity. According to *SFAS No. 115* (1993), a *debt security* the holder has both the ability and the intent to hold to *maturity;* valued in the *balance sheet* at amortized acquisition cost: the book value of the security at the end of each period is the book value at the beginning of the period multiplied by the historical *yield* on the security (measured as of the time of purchase) less any cash the holder receives at the end of this period from the security.

segment (of a business). As defined by *APB Opinion No. 30,* "a component of an *entity* whose activities represent a separate major line of business or class of customer. . . . [It may be] a *subsidiary,* a *division,* or a department, . . . provided that its *assets,* results of *operations,* and activities can be clearly distinguished, physically and operationally for financial reporting purposes, from the other assets, results of operations, and activities of the entity." In *SFAS No. 14,* a segment is defined as a "component of an enterprise engaged in promoting a product or service or a group of related products and services primarily to unaffiliated customers . . . for a profit." *SFAS No. 131* defines operating segments using the "management approach" as components of the enterprise engaging in revenue- and expense-generating business activities "whose operating results are regularly reviewed by the enterprise's chief operating decision maker to make decisions about resources . . . and asset performance."

segment reporting. Reporting of *sales, income,* and *assets* by *segments of a business,* usually classified by nature of products sold but sometimes by geographical area where the firm produces or sells goods or by type of customers; sometimes called "line of business reporting." The accounting for segment income does not allocate *central corporate expenses* to the segments.

self-balancing. A set of records with equal *debits* and *credits* such as the *ledger* (but not individual accounts), the *balance sheet,* and a *fund* in nonprofit accounting.

self-check(ing) digit. A digit forming part of an account or code number, normally the last digit of the number, which is mathematically derived from the other numbers of the code and is used to detect errors in transcribing the code number. For example, assume the last digit of the account number is the remainder after summing the preceding digits and dividing that sum by nine. Suppose the computer encounters the account numbers 7027261-7 and 9445229-7. The program can tell that something has gone wrong with the encoding of the second account number because the sum of the first seven digits is 35, whose remainder on division by 9 is 8, not 7. The first account number does not show such an error because the sum of the first seven digits is 25, whose remainder on division by 9 is, indeed, 7. The first account number may be in error, but the second surely is.

self-insurance. See *insurance.*

self-sustaining foreign operation. A foreign operation both financially and operationally independent of the reporting enterprise (owner) so that the owner's exposure to exchange-rate changes results only from the owner's net investment in the foreign entity.

selling and administrative expenses. *Expenses* not specifically identifiable with, or assigned to, production.

semifixed costs. *Costs* that increase with activity as a step function.

semivariable costs. *Costs* that increase strictly linearly with activity but that are positive at zero activity level. Royalty fees of 2 percent of sales are variable; royalty fees of $1,000 per year plus 2 percent of sales are semivariable.

senior securities. *Bonds* as opposed to *preferred stock; preferred stock* as opposed to *common stock.* The firm must meet the senior security claim against *earnings* or *assets* before meeting the claims of less-senior securities.

sensitivity analysis. A study of how the outcome of a decision-making process changes as one or more of the assumptions change.

sequential access. Computer-storage access in which the analyst can locate information only by a sequential search of the storage file. Compare *direct access.*

serial bonds. An *issue* of *bonds* that mature in part at one date, another part on another date, and so on. The various maturity dates usually occur at equally spaced intervals. Contrast with *term bonds.*

service basis of depreciation. *Production method.*

service bureau. A commercial data-processing center providing service to various customers.

service cost, (current) service cost. *Pension plan expenses incurred* during an *accounting period* for employment services performed during that period. Contrast with *prior service cost.* See *funded.*

service department. A department, such as the personnel or computer department, that provides services to other departments rather than direct work on a salable product. Contrast with *production department.* A firm must allocate costs of service departments whose services benefit manufacturing operations to *product costs* under *full absorption costing.*

service department cost allocation. A procedure in which firms *allocate* the *costs* of operating service departments to other departments.

service life. Period of expected usefulness of an asset; may differ from *depreciable life* for *income tax* purposes.

service potential. The future benefits that cause an item to be classified as an *asset.* Without service potential, an item has no future benefits, and accounting will not classify the item as an asset. *SFAC No. 6* suggests that the primary characteristic of service potential is the ability to generate future net cash inflows.

services. Useful work done by a person, a machine, or an organization. See *goods.*

setup. The time or costs required to prepare production equipment for doing a job.

SFAC. *Statement of Financial Accounting Concepts* of the *FASB.*

SFAS. *Statement of Financial Accounting Standards.* See *FASB.*

shadow price. An opportunity cost. A *linear programming* analysis provides as one of its outputs the potential value of having available more of the scarce resources that constrain the production process, for example, the value of having more time available on a machine tool critical to the production of two products. Common terminology refers to this value as the "shadow price" or the "dual value" of the scarce resource.

share. A unit of *stock* representing ownership in a corporation.

share premium. UK: *additional paid-in capital* or *capital contributed in excess of par* (or *stated*) *value.*

shareholders' equity. *Proprietorship* or *owners' equity* of a corporation. Because *stock* means inventory in Australia, the UK, and Canada, their writers use the term "shareholders' equity" rather than the term "stockholders' equity."

short run. Period of time long enough to allow management to change the level of production or other activity within the constraints of current total productive capacity, as opposed to the *long run.*

short-term. Current; ordinarily, due within one year.

short-term liquidity risk. The risk that an *entity* will not have enough *cash* in the *short run* to pay its *debts*.

short-term operating budget. Management's quantitative action plan for the coming year.

shrinkage. An excess of *inventory* shown on the *books* over actual physical quantities on hand; can result from theft or shoplifting as well as from evaporation or general wear and tear. Some accountants, in an attempt to downplay their own errors, use the term to mean record-keeping mistakes that they later must correct, with some embarrassment, and that result in material changes in reported income. One should not use the term "shrinkage" for the correction of mistakes because adequate terminology exists for describing mistakes.

shutdown cost. Those fixed costs that the firm continues to incur after it has ceased production; the costs of closing down a particular production facility.

sight draft. A demand for payment drawn by Person A to whom Person B owes cash. Person A presents the *draft* to Person B's (the debtor's) bank in expectation that Person B will authorize his or her bank to disburse the funds. Sellers often use such drafts when selling goods to a new customer in a different city. The seller is uncertain whether the buyer will pay the bill. The seller sends the *bill* of lading, or other evidence of ownership of the goods, along with a sight draft to the buyer's bank. Before the warehouse holding the goods can release them to the buyer, the buyer must instruct its bank to honor the sight draft by withdrawing funds from the buyer's account. Once the bank honors the sight draft, it hands to the buyer the bill of lading or other document evidencing ownership, and the goods become the property of the buyer.

significant influence. A firm will use the *equity method* of accounting for its *investment* in another when it has significant influence over the *investee company*. GAAP do not define this term, but give examples of it: representation on the *board of directors,* participation in policy making processes, *material* intercompany transactions, interchange of managerial personnel, and technological dependency. Ultimately, the accountant must judge whether the investor's influence is significant.

simple interest. *Interest* calculated on *principal* where interest earned during periods before maturity of the loan does not increase the principal amount earning interest for the subsequent periods and the lender cannot withdraw the funds before maturity. Interest = principal × interest rate × time, where the rate is a rate per period (typically a year) and time is expressed in units of that period. For example, if the *rate* is annual and the time is two months, then in the formula, use 2/12 for *time.* Simple interest is seldom used in economic calculations except for periods of less than one year and then only for computational convenience. Contrast with *compound interest.*

single-entry accounting. Accounting that is neither *self-balancing* nor *articulated.* That is, it does not rely on equal *debits* and *credits.* The firm makes no *journal entries* and must *plug* to derive *owners' equity* for the *balance sheet.*

single proprietorship. *Sole proprietorship.*

single-step. Said of an *income statement* in which *ordinary revenue* and *gain* items appear first, with their total. Then come all ordinary *expenses* and *losses,* with their total. The difference between these two totals, plus the effect of *income from discontinued operations* and *extraordinary items,* appears as *net income.* Contrast with *multiple-step* and see *proprietorship theory.*

sinking fund. *Assets* and their earnings earmarked for the retirement of bonds or other long-term obligations. Earnings of sinking fund investments become taxable income of the company.

sinking fund method of depreciation. Method in which the periodic charge is an equal amount each period so that the *future value* of the charges, considered as an *annuity,* will accumulate at the end of the depreciable life to an amount equal to the *acquisition cost* of the asset. The firm does not necessarily, or even usually, accumulate a *fund* of cash. Firms rarely use this method.

skeleton account. *T-account.*

slide. The name of the error made by a bookkeeper in recording the digits of a number correctly with the decimal point misplaced; for example, recording $123.40 as $1,234.00 or as $12.34. If the only errors in a *trial balance* result from one or more slides, then the difference between the sum of the *debits* and the sum of the *credits* will be divisible by nine. Not all such differences divisible by nine result from slides. See *transposition error.*

SMAC (Society of Management Accountants of Canada). The national association of accountants whose provincial associations engage in industrial and governmental accounting. The association undertakes research and administers an educational program and comprehensive examinations; those who pass qualify to be designated CMA (Certified Management Accountants), formerly called RIA (Registered Industrial Accountant).

SNC (société en nom collectif). France: a *partnership.*

soak-up method. The *equity method.*

Social Security taxes. Taxes levied by the federal government on both employers and employees to provide *funds* to pay retired persons (or their survivors) who are entitled to receive such payments, either because they paid Social Security taxes themselves or because Congress has declared them eligible. Unlike a *pension plan,* the Social Security system does not collect funds and invest them for many years. The tax collections in a given year pay primarily for benefits distributed that year. At any given time the system has a multitrillion-dollar unfunded obligation to current workers for their eventual retirement benefits. See *Old Age, Survivors, Disability, and (Hospital) Insurance.*

software. The programming aids, such as compilers, sort and report programs, and generators, that extend the capabilities of and simplify the use of the computer, as well as certain operating systems and other control programs. Compare *hardware.*

sole proprietorship. A firm in which all *owners' equity* belongs to one person.

solvent. Able to meet debts when due.

SOP. *Statement of Position* (of the *AcSEC* of the *AICPA*).

sound value. A phrase used mainly in appraisals of *fixed assets* to mean *fair market price* (*value*) or *replacement cost* in present condition.

source of funds. Any *transaction* that increases *cash* and *marketable securities* held as *current assets*.

sources and uses statement. *Statement of cash flows.*

SOYD. *Sum-of-the-years'-digits depreciation.*

SP (société en participation). France: a silent *partnership* in which the managing partner acts for the partnership as an individual in transacting with others who need not know that the person represents a partnership.

special assessment. A compulsory levy made by a governmental unit on property to pay the costs of a specific improvement or service presumed not to benefit the general public but only the owners of the property so assessed; accounted for in a special assessment fund.

special journal. A *journal,* such as a sales journal or cash disbursements journal, to record *transactions* of a similar nature that occur frequently.

special purpose entity (vehicle); SPE (SPV). A term unknown by laypeople until the Enron shambles of 2001. A legal entity—corporation or partnership or trust—with substantial owners' equity provided by investors other than the firm organizing the SPE. The independent owners must have significant risks and rewards of ownership. A parent firm, such as Enron, establishes the SPE to transfer assets and debt off its balance sheet. Some of Enron's SPEs appear not to have satisfied all the *GAAP* tests to be kept off the balance sheet. Many SPEs have a legitimate purpose. Consider, for example, a firm that wishes to sell its accounts receivable. It sells the receivables to a corporation in which others have provided owners' equity funding. The corporation runs the risks (or will reap the rewards) of collecting less (or more) from the receivables than the organizers of the SPE forecast.

special revenue debt. A governmental unit's debt backed only by revenues from specific sources, such as tolls from a bridge.

specific identification method. Method for valuing *ending inventory* and *cost of goods sold* by identifying actual units sold and remaining in inventory and summing the actual costs of those individual units; usually used for items with large unit values, such as precious jewelry, automobiles, and fur coats.

specific item sampling. Sampling in which the analyst selects particular items because of their nature, value, or method of recording. Compare *representative item sampling.*

specific price changes. Changes in the market prices of specific *goods* and *services.* Contrast with *general price-level changes.*

specific price index. A measure of the price of a specific good or service, or a small group of similar goods or services, at one time relative to the price during a base period. Contrast with *general price index.* See *dollar-value LIFO method.*

spending variance. In *standard cost systems,* the *rate* or *price variance* for *overhead costs.*

split. *Stock split.* Sometimes called "split-up."

splitoff point. In accumulating and allocating costs for *joint products,* the point at which all costs are no longer *joint costs* but at which an analyst can identify costs associated with individual products or perhaps with a smaller number of *joint products.*

spoilage. See *abnormal spoilage* and *normal spoilage.*

spot price. The price of a commodity for delivery on the day of the price quotation. See *forward price* for contrast.

spreadsheet. For many years, a term that referred specifically to a *work sheet* organized like a *matrix* that provides a two-way classification of accounting data. The rows and columns both have labels, which are *account* titles. An entry in a row represents a *debit,* whereas an entry in a column represents a *credit.* Thus, the number "100" in the "cash" row and the "accounts receivable" column records an entry debiting cash and crediting accounts receivable for $100. A given row total indicates all debit entries to the account represented by that row, and a given column total indicates the sum of all credit entries to the account represented by the column. Since personal-computer software has become widespread, this term has come to refer to any file created by programs such as Lotus 1-2-3® and Microsoft Excel®. Such files have rows and columns, but they need not represent debits and credits. Moreover, they can have more than two dimensions.

squeeze. A term sometimes used for *plug.*

SSARS. *Statement on Standards for Accounting and Review Services.*

stabilized accounting. *Constant-dollar accounting.*

stable monetary unit assumption. In spite of *inflation,* which appears to be a way of life, the assumption that underlies historical cost/nominal-dollar accounting—namely that one can meaningfully add together current dollars and dollars of previous years. The assumption gives no specific recognition to changing values of the dollar in the usual *financial statements.* See *constant-dollar accounting.*

Staff Accounting Bulletin. An interpretation issued by the staff of the Chief Accountant of the *SEC* "suggesting" how the accountants should apply various *Accounting Series Releases* in practice. The suggestions are part of *GAAP.*

stakeholder. An individual or group, such as employees, suppliers, customers, and shareholders, who have an interest in the corporation's activities and outcomes.

standard cost. Anticipated *cost* of producing a unit of output; a predetermined cost to be assigned to products produced. Standard cost implies a norm—what costs should be. Budgeted cost implies a forecast—something likely, but not necessarily, a "should," as implied by a norm. Firms use standard costs as the benchmark for gauging good and bad performance. Although a firm may similarly use a budget, it need not. A budget may be a planning document, subject to changes whenever plans change, whereas standard costs usually change annually or when technology significantly changes or when costs of labor and materials significantly change.

standard costing. *Costing* based on *standard costs.*

standard costing system. *Product costing* using *standard costs* rather than actual costs. The firm may use either *full absorption* or *variable costing* principles.

standard error (of regression coefficients). A measure of the uncertainty about the magnitude of the estimated parameters of an equation fit with a *regression analysis*.

standard manufacturing overhead. *Overhead costs* expected to be incurred per unit of time and per unit produced.

standard price (rate). Unit price established for materials or labor used in *standard cost systems*.

standard quantity allowed. The direct material or direct labor (inputs) quantity that production should have used if it had produced the units of output in accordance with preset *standards*.

standby costs. A type of *capacity cost*, such as property taxes, incurred even if a firm shuts down operations completely. Contrast with *enabling costs*.

stated capital. Amount of capital contributed by shareholders; sometimes used to mean *legal capital*.

stated value. A term sometimes used for the *face amount of capital stock*, when the *board* has not designated a *par value*. Where there is stated value per share, capital *contributed in excess of stated value* may come into being.

statement of affairs. A *balance sheet* showing immediate *liquidation* amounts rather than *historical costs,* usually prepared when *insolvency* or *bankruptcy* is imminent. Such a statement specifically does not use the *going-concern assumption*.

statement of cash flows. A schedule of *cash receipts* and *payments,* classified by *investing, financing,* and *operating activities;* required by the *FASB* for all for-profit companies. Companies may report operating activities with either the direct method (which shows only receipts and payments of cash) or the indirect method (which starts with *net income* and shows adjustments for *revenues* not currently producing cash and for *expenses* not currently using cash). "Cash" includes cash equivalents such as Treasury bills, commercial paper, and *marketable securities* held as *current assets*. This is sometimes called the "funds statement." Before 1987, the FASB required the presentation of a similar statement called the *statement of changes in financial position,* which tended to emphasize *working capital,* not cash.

statement of changes in financial position. As defined by *APB Opinion No. 19,* a statement that explains the changes in *working capital* (or cash) balances during a period and shows the changes in the working capital (or cash) accounts themselves. The *statement of cash flows* has replaced this statement.

statement of charge and discharge. A financial statement, showing *net assets* or *income,* drawn up by an executor or administrator, to account for receipts and dispositions of cash or other assets in an estate or trust.

Statement of Financial Accounting Concepts (SFAC). One of a series of *FASB* publications in its *conceptual framework* for *financial accounting* and reporting. Such statements set forth objectives and fundamentals to be the basis for specific financial accounting and reporting standards.

Statement of Financial Accounting Standards (SFAS). See *FASB*.

statement of financial position. *Balance sheet*.

Statement of Position (SOP). A recommendation, on an emerging accounting problem, issued by the *AcSEC* of the *AICPA*. The AICPA's Code of Professional Ethics specifically states that *CPAs* need not treat *SOPs* as they do rules from the *FASB,* but a CPA would be wary of departing from the recommendations of an *SOP*.

statement of retained earnings (income). A statement that reconciles the beginning-of-period and the end-of-period balances in the *retained earnings* account. It shows the effects of *earnings, dividend declarations,* and *prior-period adjustments*.

statement of significant accounting policies (principles). A summary of the significant *accounting principles* used in compiling an *annual report;* required by *APB Opinion No. 22.* This summary may be a separate exhibit or the first *note* to the financial statements.

Statement on Auditing Standards (SAS). A series addressing specific auditing standards and procedures. *No. 1* (1973) of this series codifies all statements on auditing standards previously promulgated by the *AICPA*.

Statement on Standards for Accounting and Review Services (SSARS). Pronouncements issued by the *AICPA* on unaudited *financial statements* and unaudited financial information of nonpublic entities.

static budget. *Fixed budget*. Budget developed for a set level of the driving variable, such as production or sales, which the analyst does not change if the actual level deviates from the level set at the outset of the analysis.

status quo. Events or cost incurrences that will happen or that a firm expects to happen in the absence of taking some contemplated action.

statutory tax rate. The tax rate specified in the *income tax law* for each type of income (for example, *ordinary income, capital gain or loss*).

step allocation method. *Step-down method*.

step cost. *Semifixed cost*.

step-down method. In *allocating service department* costs, a method that starts by allocating one service department's costs to *production departments* and to all other service departments. Then the firm allocates a second service department's costs, including costs allocated from the first, to production departments and to all other service departments except the first one. In this fashion, a firm may allocate all service departments' costs, including previous allocations, to production departments and to those service departments whose costs it has not yet allocated.

step method. *Step-down method*.

step(ped) cost. *Semifixed cost*.

sterilized allocation. Desirable characteristics of cost allocation methods. Optimal decisions result from considering *incremental costs* only. Optimal decisions never require *allocations* of *joint* or *common costs*. A "sterilized allocation" causes the optimal decision choice not to differ from the one that occurs when the accountant does not allocate joint or common costs "sterilized" with respect to that decision. Arthur L. Thomas first used the term in this context. Because *absorption costing* requires that product costs absorb all manufacturing costs and because some allocations can lead to bad decisions, Thomas (and we) advocate that the analyst choose a sterilized allocation scheme that will not alter the otherwise optimal decision. No single allocation scheme is always sterilized with respect to all decisions. Thus, Thomas (and we) advocate that decisions be made on the basis of incremental costs before any allocations.

stewardship. Principle by which management is accountable for an *entity*'s resources, for their efficient use, and for protecting them from adverse impact. Some theorists believe that accounting has as a primary goal aiding users of *financial statements* in their assessment of management's performance in stewardship.

stock. A measure of the amount of something on hand at a specific time. In this sense, contrast with *flow.* See *inventory* and *capital stock.*

stock appreciation rights. An employer's promise to pay to the employee an amount of *cash* on a certain future date, with the amount of cash being the difference between the *market value* of a specified number of *shares* of *stock* in the employer's company on the given future date and some base price set on the date the rights are granted. Firms sometimes use this form of compensation because changes in tax laws in recent years have made *stock options* relatively less attractive. *GAAP* compute compensation based on the difference between the market value of the shares and the base price set at the time of the grant.

stock dividend. A so-called *dividend* in which the firm distributes additional *shares* of *capital stock* without cash payments to existing shareholders. It results in a *debit* to *retained earnings* in the amount of the market value of the shares issued and a *credit* to *capital stock* accounts. Firms ordinarily use stock dividends to indicate that they have permanently reinvested earnings in the business. Contrast with a *stock split,* which requires no entry in the capital stock accounts other than a notation that the *par* or *stated value* per share has changed.

stock option. The right to purchase or sell a specified number of shares of *stock* for a specified price at specified times. Employee stock options are purchase rights granted by a corporation to employees, a form of compensation. Traded stock options are *derivative* securities, rights created and traded by investors, independent of the corporation whose stock is optioned. Contrast with *warrant.*

stock right. See *right.*

stock split(-up). Increase in the number of common shares outstanding resulting from the issuance of additional shares to existing shareholders without additional capital contributions by them. Does not increase the total *value* (or *stated value*) of *common shares* outstanding because the *board* reduces the par (or stated) value per share in inverse proportion. A three-for-one stock split reduces par (or stated) value per share to one-third of its former amount. A stock split usually implies a distribution that increases the number of shares outstanding by 20 percent or more. Compare with *stock dividend.*

stock subscriptions. See *subscription* and *subscribed stock.*

stock warrant. See *warrant.*

stockholders' equity. See *shareholders' equity.*

stockout. Occurs when a firm needs a unit of *inventory* to use in production or to sell to a customer but has none available.

stockout costs. *Contribution margin* or other measure of *profits* not earned because a seller has run out of *inventory*

and cannot fill a customer's order. A firm may incur an extra cost because of delay in filling an order.

stores. *Raw materials,* parts, and supplies.

straight-debt value. An estimate of the *market value* of a *convertible bond* if the bond did not contain a conversion privilege.

straight-line depreciation. Method in which, if the *depreciable life* is n periods, the periodic *depreciation* charge is 1/n of the *depreciable cost;* results in equal periodic charges. Accountants sometimes call it "straight-time depreciation."

strategic plan. A statement of the method for achieving an organization's goals.

stratified sampling. In choosing a *sample,* a method in which the investigator first divides the entire *population* into relatively homogeneous subgroups (strata) and then selects random samples from these subgroups.

street security. A stock certificate in immediately transferable form, most commonly because the issuing firm has registered it in the name of the broker, who has endorsed it with "payee" left blank.

Subchapter S corporation. A firm legally organized as a *corporation* but taxed as if it were a *partnership.* Tax terminology calls the corporations paying their own income taxes *C corporations.*

subject to. In an *auditor's report,* qualifications usually caused by a *material* uncertainty in the valuation of an item, such as future promised payments from a foreign government or outcome of pending litigation.

subordinated. *Debt* whose claim on income or assets has lower priority than claims of other debt.

subscribed stock. A *shareholders' equity* account showing the capital that the firm will receive as soon as the share-purchaser pays the subscription price. A subscription is a legal contract, so once the share-purchaser signs it, the firm makes an entry *debiting* an *owners' equity contra account* and *crediting* subscribed stock.

subscription. Agreement to buy a *security* or to purchase periodicals, such as magazines.

subsequent events. *Poststatement events.*

subsidiary. A company in which another company owns more than 50 percent of the voting shares.

subsidiary ledger. The *ledger* that contains the detailed accounts whose total appears in a *controlling account* of the *general ledger.*

subsidiary (ledger) accounts. The *accounts* in a *subsidiary ledger.*

successful efforts costing. In petroleum accounting, the *capitalization* of the drilling costs of only those wells that contain gas or oil. See *reserve recognition accounting* for an example.

summary annual report (SAR). Condensed financial statements distributed in lieu of the usual *annual report.* Since 1987, the *SEC* has allowed firms to include such statements in the annual report to shareholders as long as the firm includes full, detailed statements in SEC filings and in *proxy* materials sent to shareholders.

summary of significant accounting principles. *Statement of significant accounting policies (principles).*

sum-of-the-years'-digits depreciation (SYD, SOYD). An *accelerated depreciation* method for · an asset with *depreciable life* of n years where the charge in period i ($i = 1, \ldots, n$) is the fraction $(n + 1 - i)/[n(n + 1)/2]$ of the *depreciable cost*. If an asset has a depreciable cost of $15,000 and a five-year depreciable life, for example, the depreciation charges would be $5,000 (= 5/15 × $15,000) in the first year, $4,000 in the second, $3,000 in the third, $2,000 in the fourth, and $1,000 in the fifth. The name derives from the fact that the denominator in the fraction is the sum of the digits 1 through n.

sunk cost. Past *costs* that current and future decisions cannot affect and, hence, that are irrelevant for decision making aside from *income tax* effects. Contrast with *incremental costs* and *imputed costs*. For example, the *acquisition cost* of machinery is irrelevant to a decision of whether to scrap the machinery. The current *exit value* of the machinery is the *opportunity cost* of continuing to own it, and the cost of, say, the electricity to run the machinery is an incremental cost of its operation. Sunk costs become relevant for decision making when the analysis requires taking *income taxes* (*gain* or *loss* on disposal of asset) into account, since the cash payment for income taxes depends on the tax basis of the asset. Avoid this term in careful writing because it is ambiguous. Consider, for example, a machine costing $100,000 with current *salvage value* of $20,000. Some (including us) would say that $100,000 (the *gross* amount) is "sunk"; others would say that only $80,000 (the *net* amount) is "sunk."

supplementary statements (schedules). Statements (schedules) in addition to the four basic *financial statements* (*balance sheet, income statement, statement of cash flows,* and the *statement of retained earnings*).

surplus. A word once used but now considered poor terminology; prefaced by "earned" to mean *retained earnings* and prefaced by "capital" to mean *capital contributed in excess of par* (*or stated*) *value*.

surplus reserves. *Appropriated retained earnings*. A phrase with nothing to recommend it: of all the words in accounting, *reserve* is the most objectionable, and *surplus* is the second-most objectionable.

suspense account. A *temporary account* used to record part of a transaction before final analysis of that transaction. For example, if a business regularly classifies all sales into a dozen or more different categories but wants to deposit the proceeds of cash sales every day, it may credit a sales suspense account pending detailed classification of all sales into Durable Goods Sales, Women's Clothing Sales, Men's Clothing Sales, Housewares Sales, and so on.

sustainable income. The part of *distributable income* (computed from *current cost* data) that the firm can expect to earn in the next accounting period if it continues operations at the same levels as were maintained during the current period. *Income from discontinued operations,* for example, may be distributable but not sustainable.

swap. A currency swap is a financial instrument in which the holder promises to pay to (or receive from) the *counterparty* the difference between *debt* denominated in one currency (such as U.S. dollars) and the payments on debt denominated in another currency (such as German marks). An interest-rate swap typically obligates the party and counterparty to exchange the difference between fixed- and floating-rate interest payments on otherwise similar loans.

S-X. See *Regulation S-X*.

SYD. *Sum-of-the-years'-digits depreciation.*

T

T-account. Account form shaped like the letter T with the title above the horizontal line. *Debits* appear on the left of the vertical line, *credits* on the right.

take-home pay. The amount of a paycheck; earned wages or *salary* reduced by deductions for *income taxes, Social Security taxes,* contributions to fringe-benefit plans, union dues, and so on. Take-home pay might be as little as half of earned compensation.

take-or-pay contract. As defined by *SFAS No. 47,* a purchaser-seller agreement that provides for the purchaser to pay specified amounts periodically in return for products or services. The purchaser must make specified minimum payments even if it does not take delivery of the contracted products or services.

taking a bath. To incur a large loss. See *big bath*.

tangible. Having physical form. Accounting has never satisfactorily defined the distinction between tangible and intangible assets. Typically, accountants define intangibles by giving an exhaustive list, and everything not on the list is defined as tangible. See *intangible asset* for such a list.

target cost. *Standard cost*. Sometimes, target price less expected profit margin.

target price. Selling price based on customers' value in use of a good or service, constrained by competitors' prices of similar items.

tax. A nonpenal, but compulsory, charge levied by a government on income, consumption, wealth, or other basis, for the benefit of all those governed. The term does not include fines or specific charges for benefits accruing only to those paying the charges, such as licenses, permits, special assessments, admission fees, and tolls.

tax allocation: interperiod. See *deferred income tax liability*.

tax allocation: intrastatement. The showing of *income tax* effects on *extraordinary items, income from discontinued operations,* and *prior-period adjustments,* along with these items, separately from income taxes on other income. See *net-of-tax reporting*.

tax avoidance. See *tax shelter* and *loophole*.

tax basis of assets and liabilities. A concept important for applying *SFAS No. 109* on *deferred income taxes*. Two *assets* will generally have different *book values* if the firm paid different amounts for them, *amortizes* them on a different schedule, or both. Similarly a single asset will generally have a book value different from what it will have for tax purposes if the firm recorded different *acquisition* amounts for the asset for book and for tax purposes, amortizes it differently for book and for tax purposes, or both. The difference between financial book value and income tax basis becomes important in computing deferred income tax amounts. The adjusted cost in the financial records is the "book basis," and the adjusted amount in the tax records is the "tax basis." Differences between book and tax basis can arise for *liabilities* as well as for assets.

tax credit. A subtraction from taxes otherwise payable. Contrast with *tax deduction.*

tax deduction. A subtraction from *revenues* and *gains* to arrive at taxable income. Tax deductions differ technically from tax *exemptions,* but both reduce gross income in computing taxable income. Both differ from *tax credits,* which reduce the computed tax itself in computing taxes payable. If the tax rate is the fraction *t* of pretax income, then a *tax credit* of $1 is worth $1/*t* of tax deductions. Deductions appear on tax returns, *expenses* appear on *income statements.*

tax evasion. The fraudulent understatement of taxable revenues or overstatement of deductions and expenses or both. Contrast with *tax shelter* and *loophole.*

tax-exempts. See *municipal bonds.*

tax shelter. The legal avoidance of, or reduction in, *income taxes* resulting from a careful reading of the complex income-tax regulations and the subsequent rearrangement of financial affairs to take advantage of the regulations. Often writers use the term pejoratively, but the courts have long held that a taxpayer has no obligation to pay taxes any larger than the legal minimum. If the public concludes that a given tax shelter is "unfair," then Congress can change, and has changed, the laws and regulations. The term is sometimes used to refer to the investment that permits tax avoidance. See *loophole.*

tax shield. The amount of an *expense,* such as *depreciation,* that reduces taxable income but does not require *working capital.* Sometimes this term includes expenses that reduce taxable income and use working capital. A depreciation deduction (or *R&D expense* in the expanded sense) of $10,000 provides a tax shield of $3,700 when the marginal tax rate is 37 percent.

taxable income. *Income* computed according to *IRS* regulations and subject to *income taxes.* Contrast with income, *net income, income before taxes* (in the *income statement*), and *comprehensive income* (a *financial reporting* concept). Use the term "pretax income" to refer to income before taxes on the income statement in financial reports.

tax-transfer lease. One form of *capital lease.* Congress has in the past provided business with an incentive to invest in qualifying *plant and equipment* by granting an *investment credit,* which, though it occurs as a reduction in *income taxes* otherwise payable, effectively reduces the purchase price of the assets. Similarly, Congress continues to grant an incentive to acquire such assets by allowing the *Modified Accelerated Cost Recovery System (MACRS,* form of unusually *accelerated depreciation*). Accelerated depreciation for tax purposes allows a reduction of taxes paid in the early years of an asset's life, providing the firm with an increased *net present value* of *cash flows.* The *IRS* administers both of these incentives through the income tax laws, rather than paying an outright cash payment. A business with no taxable income in many cases had difficulty reaping the benefits of the investment credit or of accelerated depreciation because Congress had not provided for tax refunds to those who acquire qualifying assets but who have no taxable income. In principle, a

company without taxable income could lease from another firm with taxable income an asset that it would otherwise purchase. The second firm acquires the asset, gets the tax-reduction benefits from the acquisition, and becomes a lessor, leasing the asset (presumably at a lower price reflecting its own costs lowered by the tax reductions) to the unprofitable company. Before 1981, tax laws discouraged such leases. That is, although firms could enter into such leases, they could not legally transfer the tax benefits. Under certain restrictive conditions, the tax law now allows a profitable firm to earn tax credits and take deductions while leasing to the firm without tax liability in such leases. These are sometimes called "safe-harbor leases."

Technical Bulletin. The *FASB* has authorized its staff to issue bulletins to provide guidance on financial accounting and reporting problems. Although the FASB does not formally approve the contents of the bulletins, their contents are part of *GAAP.*

technology. The sum of a firm's technical *trade secrets* and *know-how,* as distinct from its *patents.*

temporary account. *Account* that does not appear on the *balance sheet; revenue* and *expense* accounts, their *adjuncts* and *contras, production cost accounts, dividend distribution accounts,* and purchases-related accounts (which close to the various inventories); sometimes called a *nominal account.*

temporary difference. According to the *SFAS No. 109* (1992) definition: "A difference between the tax basis of an asset or liability and its reported amount in the financial statements that will result in taxable or deductible amounts in future years." Temporary differences include *timing differences* and differences between *taxable income* and pretax income caused by different cost bases for assets. For example, a plant asset might have a cost of $10,000 for financial reporting but a basis of $7,000 for income tax purposes. This temporary difference might arise because the firm has used an accelerated depreciation method for tax but straight-line for book, or the firm may have purchased the asset in a transaction in which the fair value of the asset exceeded its tax basis. Both situations create a temporary difference.

temporary investments. Investments in *marketable securities* that the owner intends to sell within a short time, usually one year, and hence classifies as *current assets.*

10-K. The name of the annual report that the *SEC* requires of nearly all publicly held corporations.

term bonds. A *bond issue* whose component bonds all mature at the same time. Contrast with *serial bonds.*

term loan. A loan with a *maturity* date, as opposed to a demand loan, which is due whenever the lender requests payment. In practice, bankers and auditors use this phrase only for loans for a year or more.

term structure. A phrase with different meanings in *accounting* and *financial economics.* In accounting, it refers to the pattern of times that must elapse before *assets* turn into, or produce, *cash* and the pattern of times that must elapse before *liabilities* require cash. In financial economics, the phrase refers to the pattern of interest rates as a function of the time that elapses for loans to come due. For example, if six-month loans cost 6 percent per year and 10-year loans cost 9 percent per year, this is called a "normal" term structure because the longer-term loan carries a higher rate. If the six-month loan costs 9 percent per year and the 10-year loan costs 6 percent per year, the term structure is said to be "inverted." See *yield curve.*

terminal cash flows. *Cash flows* that occur at the end of an *investment* project. Often include proceeds of *salvage* of equipment and tax on *gain (loss)* on disposal.

terms of sale. The conditions governing payment for a sale. For example, the terms *2/10, n(et)/30* mean that if the purchaser makes payment within 10 days of the invoice date, it can take a *discount* of 2 percent from *invoice* price; the purchaser must pay the invoice amount, in any event, within 30 days, or it becomes overdue.

theory of constraints (TOC). Concept of improving operations by identifying and reducing bottlenecks in process flows.

thin capitalization. A state of having a high *debt-equity ratio.* Under *income tax* legislation, the term has a special meaning.

throughput contract. As defined by *SFAS No. 47,* an agreement that is signed by a shipper (processor) and by the owner of a transportation facility (such as an oil or natural gas pipeline or a ship) or a manufacturing facility and that provides for the shipper (processor) to pay specified amounts periodically in return for the transportation (processing) of a product. The shipper (processor) must make cash payments even if it does not ship (process) the contracted quantities.

throughput contribution. Sales dollars minus the sum of all short-run variable costs.

tickler file. A collection of *vouchers* or other memoranda arranged chronologically to remind the person in charge of certain duties to make payments (or to do other tasks) as scheduled.

time-adjusted rate of return. *Internal rate of return.*

time cost. *Period cost.*

time deposit. Cash in bank earning interest. Contrast with *demand deposit.*

time value element (of stock options). All else equal, the longer one has to exercise an *option,* the more valuable that option. This term refers to the part of an option's value on a date caused by the option's not expiring until sometime after that date. All else equal, the more volatile the *market price* of the *security* receivable on exercise, the more valuable is this element.

time-series analysis. See *cross-section analysis* for definition and contrast.

times-interest (charges) earned. Ratio of pretax *income* plus *interest* charges to interest charges. See *ratio.*

timing difference. The major type of *temporary difference* between taxable *income* and pretax income reported to shareholders; reverses in a subsequent period and requires an entry in the *deferred income tax* account; for example, the use of *accelerated depreciation* for tax returns and *straight-line depreciation* for financial reporting. Contrast with *permanent difference.*

Toronto Stock Exchange (TSE). A public market where various corporate securities trade.

total assets turnover. *Sales* divided by average total *assets.*

total quality management (TQM). Concept of organizing a company to excel in all its activities in order to increase the quality of products and services.

traceable cost. A *cost* that a firm can identify with or assign to a specific product. Contrast with a *joint cost.*

trade acceptance. A *draft* that a seller presents for signature (acceptance) to the buyer at the time it sells goods. The draft then becomes the equivalent of a *note receivable* of the seller and a *note payable* of the buyer.

trade credit. Occurs when one business allows another to buy from it in return for a promise to pay later. Contrast with "consumer credit," which occurs when a business extends a retail customer the privilege of paying later.

trade discount. A *list price discount* offered to all customers of a given type. Contrast with a *discount* offered for prompt payment and with *quantity discount.*

trade-in. Acquiring a new *asset* in *exchange* for a used one and perhaps additional cash. See *boot* and *trade-in transaction.*

trade-in transaction. The accounting for a *trade-in;* depends on whether the firm receives an asset "similar" to (and used in the same line of business as) the asset traded in and whether the accounting is for *financial statements* or for *income tax* returns. Assume that an old asset cost $5,000, has $3,000 of *accumulated depreciation* (after recording depreciation to the date of the trade-in), and hence has a *book value* of $2,000. The old asset appears to have a market value of $1,500, according to price quotations in used asset markets. The firm trades in the old asset on a new asset with a list price of $10,000. The firm gives up the old asset and $5,500 cash (*boot*) for the new asset. The generic entry for the trade-in transaction is as follows:

New Asset	A		
Accumulated Depreciation (Old Asset)	3,000		
Adjustment on Exchange of Asset	B	or	B
Old Asset			5,000
Cash			5,500

(1) The *list price* method of accounting for trade-ins rests on the assumption that the list price of the new asset closely approximates its market value. The firm records the new asset at its list price (A = $10,000 in the example); B is a *plug* (= $2,500 credit in the example). If B requires a *debit* plug, the Adjustment on Exchange of Asset is a *loss;* if B requires a *credit* plug (as in the example), the adjustment is a *gain.*

(2) Another theoretically sound method of accounting for trade-ins rests on the assumption that the price quotation from used-asset markets gives a market value of the old asset that is a more reliable measure than the market value of the new asset determined by list price. This method uses the *fair market price (value)* of the old asset, $1,500 in the example, to determine B (= $2,000 book value − $1,500 assumed proceeds on disposition = $500

debit or loss). The *exchange* results in a loss if the book value of the old asset exceeds its market value and in a gain if the market value exceeds the book value. The firm records the new asset on the books by plugging for A (= $7,000 in the example).

(3) For income tax reporting, the taxpayer must recognize neither gain nor loss on the trade-in. Thus the taxpayer records the new asset for tax purposes by assuming B is zero and plugging for A (= $7,500 in the example). In practice, firms that want to recognize the loss currently will sell the old asset directly, rather than trading it in, and acquire the new asset entirely for cash.

(4) *Generally accepted accounting principles* (*APB Opinion No. 29*) require a variant of these methods. The basic method is (1) or (2), depending on whether the list price of the new asset (1) or the quotation of the old asset's market value (2) provides the more reliable indication of market value. If the basic method requires a debit entry, or loss, for the Adjustment on Exchange of Asset, then the firm records the trade-in as in (1) or (2) and recognizes the full amount of the loss currently. If, however, the basic method requires a credit entry, or gain, for the Adjustment on Exchange of Asset, then the firm recognizes the gain currently if the old asset and the new asset are not "similar." If the assets are similar and the party trading in receives no cash, then it recognizes no gain and the treatment resembles that in (3); that is B = 0, plug for A. If the assets are similar and the firm trading in receives cash—a rare case—then it recognizes a portion of the gain currently. The portion of the gain recognized currently is the fraction cash received/fair market value of total consideration received. (When the firm uses the list price method, (1), it assumes that the market value of the old asset is the list price of the new asset plus the amount of cash received by the party trading in.)

A summary of the results of applying *GAAP* to the example follows.

More Reliable Information as to Fair Market Value	Old Asset Compared with New Asset	
	Similar	Not Similar
New Asset List	A = $7,500	A = $10,000
Price	B = 0	B = 2,500 gain
Old Asset Market	A = $7,000	A = $ 7,000
Price	B = 500 loss	B = 500 loss

trade payables (receivables). *Payables* (*receivables*) arising in the ordinary course of business transactions. Most *accounts payable* (*receivable*) are of this kind.

trade secret. Technical or business information such as formulas, recipes, computer programs, and marketing data not generally known by competitors and maintained by the firm as a secret; theoretically capable of having an indefinite, finite life. A famous example is the secret process for Coca-Cola® (a registered *trademark* of the company). Compare with *know-how*. The firm will capitalize this intangible asset only if purchased and then will amortize it over a period not to exceed 40 years. If the firm develops the intangible internally, the firm will *expense* the costs as incurred and show no asset.

trademark. A distinctive word or symbol that is affixed to a product, its package, or its dispenser and that uniquely identifies the firm's products and services. See *trademark right.*

trademark right. The right to exclude competitors in sales or advertising from using words or symbols that are so similar to the firm's *trademarks* as possibly to confuse consumers. Trademark rights last as long as the firm continues to use the trademarks in question. In the United States, trademark rights arise from use and not from government registration. They therefore have a legal life independent of the life of a registration. Registrations last 20 years, and the holder may renew them as long as the holder uses the trademark. Although a trademark right might have an indefinite life, *GAAP* require amortization over some estimate of its life, not to exceed 40 years. Under *SFAS No. 2*, the firm must *expense* internally developed trademark rights.

trading on the equity. Said of a firm engaging in *debt financing;* frequently said of a firm doing so to a degree considered abnormal for a firm of its kind. *Leverage.*

trading securities. *Marketable securities* that a firm holds and expects to sell within a relatively short time; a classification important in *SFAS No. 115,* which requires the owner to carry marketable equity securities on the *balance sheet* at market value, not at cost. Contrast with *available for sale, securities* and *held-to-maturity securities.* Under *SFAS No. 115,* the balance sheet reports trading securities at market value on the balance sheet date, and the income statement reports *holding gains and losses* on trading securities. When the firm sells the securities, it reports realized gain or loss as the difference between the selling price and the market value at the last balance sheet date.

transaction. A *transfer* (of more than promises—see *executory contract*) between the accounting *entity* and another party or parties.

transfer. Under *SFAC No. 6,* consists of two types: "reciprocal" and "nonreciprocal." In a reciprocal transfer, or "exchange," the entity both receives and sacrifices. In a nonreciprocal transfer, the entity sacrifices but does not receive (examples include gifts, distributions to owners) or receives but does not sacrifice (investment by owner in entity). *SFAC No. 6* suggests that the term "internal transfer" is self-contradictory and that writers should use the term "internal event" instead.

transfer agent. Usually a bank or trust company designated by a corporation to make legal transfers of *stock* (*bonds*) and, perhaps, to pay *dividends* (*coupons*).

transfer price. A substitute for a *market,* or *arm's-length, price* used in *profit,* or *responsibility center, accounting* when one segment of the business "sells" to another segment. Incentives of profit center managers will not coincide with the best interests of the entire business unless a firm sets transfer prices properly.

transfer-pricing problem. The problem of setting *transfer prices* so that both buyer and seller have *goal congruence* with respect to the parent organization's goals.

translation adjustment. The effect of *exchange-rate* changes caused by converting the value of a net investment denominated in a *foreign currency* to the entity's reporting currency. *SFAS No. 52* requires firms to translate their net investment in relatively self-contained foreign operations at the *balance sheet* date. Year-to-year changes in value caused by exchange-rate changes accumulate in an *owners' equity* account, sometimes called the "cumulative translation adjustment."

translation gain (or loss). *Foreign exchange gain (or loss).*

transportation-in. *Freight-in.*

transposition error. An error in record keeping resulting from reversing the order of digits in a number, such as recording "32" for "23." If the only errors in a *trial balance* result from one or more transposition errors, then the difference between the sum of the *debits* and the sum of the *credits* will be divisible by nine. Not all such differences result from transposition errors. See *slide.*

treasurer. The financial officer responsible for managing cash and raising funds.

treasury bond. A bond issued by a corporation and then reacquired. Such bonds are treated as retired when reacquired, and an *extraordinary gain or loss* on reacquisition is recognized. This term also refers to a *bond* issued by the U.S. Treasury Department.

treasury shares. *Capital stock* issued and then reacquired by the corporation. Such reacquisitions result in a reduction of *shareholders' equity* and usually appear on the balance sheet as contra to shareholders' equity. Accounting recognizes neither *gain* nor *loss* on transactions involving treasury stock. The accounting debits (if positive) or credits (if negative) any difference between the amounts paid and received for treasury stock transactions to *additional paid-in capital.* See *cost method* and *par value method.*

treasury stock. *Treasury shares.*

trend analysis. Investigation of sales or other economic trends. Can range from a simple visual extrapolation of points on a graph to a sophisticated computerized time series analysis.

trial balance. A two-column listing of *account balances.* The left-hand column shows all accounts with *debit* balances and their total. The right-hand column shows all accounts with *credit* balances and their total. The two totals should be equal. Accountants compute trial balances as a partial check of the arithmetic accuracy of the entries previously made. See *adjusted, preclosing, post-closing, unadjusted trial balance, plug, slide,* and *transposition error.*

troubled debt restructuring. As defined in *SFAS No. 15,* a concession (changing of the terms of a *debt*) that is granted by a *creditor* for economic or legal reasons related to the *debtor's* financial difficulty and that the creditor would not otherwise consider.

TSE. *Toronto Stock Exchange.*

t-statistic. For an estimated *regression* coefficient, the estimated coefficient divided by the *standard error* of the estimate.

turnover. The number of times that *assets,* such as *inventory* or *accounts receivable,* are replaced on average during the period. Accounts receivable turnover, for example, is total sales on account for a period divided by the average accounts receivable balance for the period. See *ratio.* In the UK, "turnover" means *sales.*

turnover of plant and equipment. See *ratio.*

t-value. In *regression analysis,* the ratio of an estimated regression coefficient divided by its *standard error.*

20-F. Form required by the *SEC* for foreign companies issuing or trading their securities in the United States. This form reconciles the foreign accounting amounts resulting from using foreign *GAAP* to amounts resulting from using U.S. GAAP.

two T-account method. A method for computing either (1) *foreign-exchange gains and losses* or (2) *monetary gains* or *losses* for *constant-dollar accounting statements.* The left-hand *T-account* shows actual net balances of *monetary items,* and the right-hand T-account shows implied (common) dollar amounts.

2/10, n(et)/30. See *terms of sale.*

U

unadjusted trial balance. *Trial balance* taken before the accountant makes *adjusting* and *closing entries* at the end of the period.

unappropriated retained earnings. *Retained earnings* not appropriated and therefore against which the *board* can declare *dividends* in the absence of retained earnings restrictions. See *restricted retained earnings.*

unavoidable cost. A *cost* that is not an *avoidable cost.*

uncertainty. See *risk* for definition and contrast.

uncollectible account. An *account receivable* that the *debtor* will not pay. If the firm uses the preferable *allowance method,* the entry on judging a specific account to be uncollectible *debits* the allowance for uncollectible accounts and *credits* the specific account receivable. See *bad debt expense* and *sales contra, estimated uncollectibles.*

unconsolidated subsidiary. A *subsidiary* not consolidated and, hence, not accounted for in the *equity method.*

uncontrollable cost. The opposite of *controllable cost.*

underapplied (underabsorbed) overhead. An excess of actual *overhead costs* for a period over costs applied, or charged, to products produced during the period; a *debit balance* remaining in an overhead account after the accounting assigns overhead to product.

underlying document. The record, memorandum, *voucher,* or other signal that is the authority for making an *entry* into a *journal.*

underwriter. One who agrees to purchase an entire *security issue* for a specified price, usually for resale to others.

undistributed earnings. *Retained earnings.* Typically, this term refers to that amount retained for a given year.

unearned income (revenue). *Advances from customers;* strictly speaking, a contradiction in terms because the terms "income" and "revenue" mean earned.

unemployment tax. See *FUTA.*

unencumbered appropriation. In governmental accounting, portion of an *appropriation* not yet spent or encumbered.

unexpired cost. An *asset.*

unfavorable variance. In *standard cost* accounting, an excess of expected revenue over actual revenue or an excess of actual cost over standard cost.

unfunded. Not *funded.* An obligation or *liability,* usually for *pension costs,* exists, but no *funds* have been set aside to discharge the obligation or liability.

Uniform Partnership Act. A model law, enacted by many states, to govern the relations between partners when the *partnership* agreement fails to specify the agreed-upon treatment.

unissued capital stock. *Stock* authorized but not yet issued.

uniting-of-interests method. The IASB's term for the *pooling-of-interests method.* The IASB allows uniting of interests only when the merging firms are roughly equal in size and the shareholders retain substantially the same, relative to each other, voting rights and interests in the combined entity after the combination as before.

unit-level activities. Work that converts resources into individual products. Examples include *direct materials, direct labor,* and energy to run the machines.

units-of-production method. The *production method of depreciation.*

unlimited liability. The legal obligation of *general partners* or the sole proprietor for all debts of the *partnership* or *sole proprietorship.*

unqualified opinion. See *auditor's report.*

unrealized appreciation. An *unrealized holding gain;* frequently used in the context of *marketable securities.*

unrealized gain (loss) on marketable securities. An *income statement account* title for the amount of *gain (loss)* during the current period on the portfolio of *marketable securities* held as *trading securities. SFAS No. 115* requires the firm to recognize, in the income statement, gains and losses caused by changes in market values, even though the firm has not yet *realized* them.

unrealized gross margin (profit). A *contra account* to *installment accounts receivable* used with the *installment method* of revenue recognition; shows the amount of profit that the firm will eventually realize when it collects the receivable. Some accountants show this account as a *liability.*

unrealized holding gain. See *inventory profit* for the definition and an example.

unrecovered cost. *Book value* of an *asset.*

unused capacity. The difference between resources supplied and resources used.

usage variance. *Efficiency variance.*

use of funds. Any transaction that reduces funds (however "funds" is defined).

useful life. *Service life.*

V

valuation account. A *contra account* or *adjunct account.* When the firm reports *accounts receivable* at expected collectible amounts, it will credit any expected uncollectible amounts to the *allowance for uncollectibles,* a valuation account. In this way, the firm can show both the gross receivables amount and the amount it expects to collect. *SFAC No. 6* says a valuation account is "a separate item that reduces and increases the carrying amount" of an asset (or liability). The accounts are part of the related assets (or liabilities) and are not assets (or liabilities) in their own right.

value. Monetary worth. This term is usually so vague that you should not use it without a modifying adjective unless most people would agree on the amount. Do not confuse with cost. See *fair market price (value), entry value,* and *exit value.*

value added. *Cost* of a product or *work-in-process* minus the cost of the material purchased for the product or work-in-process.

value-added activity. Any activity that increases the usefulness to a customer of a product or service.

value chain. The set of business functions that increase the usefulness to the customer of a product or service; typically including research and development, design of products and services, production, marketing, distribution, and customer service.

value engineering. An evaluation of the activities in the value chain to reduce costs.

value variance. *Price variance.*

variable annuity. An *annuity* whose periodic payments depend on some uncertain outcome, such as stock market prices.

variable budget. *Flexible budget.*

variable costing. In allocating costs, a method that assigns only *variable manufacturing costs* to products and treats *fixed manufacturing costs* as *period expenses.* Contrast with *full absorption costing.*

variable costs. *Costs* that change as activity levels change. Strictly speaking, variable costs are zero when the activity level is zero. See *semivariable costs.* In accounting, this term most often means the sum of *direct costs* and variable *overhead.*

variable overhead efficiency variance. The difference between the *actual* and *standard cost driver* volume times the standard *cost driver rate.*

variable overhead price variance. The difference between the *actual* and *standard cost driver* rate times the actual *cost driver* volume.

variable overhead variance. Difference between actual and *standard variable overhead costs.*

variable rate debt. *Debt* whose interest rate results from the periodic application of a formula, such as "three-month LIBOR [London Interbank Offered Rate] plus 1 percent [one hundred basis points] set on the 8th day of each February, May, August, and November."

variables sampling. The use of a sampling technique in which the sampler infers a particular quantitative characteristic of an entire population from a sample (e.g., mean amount of accounts receivable). See also *estimation sampling.* See *attribute(s) sampling* for contrast and further examples.

variance. Difference between actual and *standard costs* or between *budgeted* and actual *expenditures* or, sometimes, *expenses*. The word has completely different meanings in accounting and in statistics, where it means a measure of dispersion of a distribution.

variance analysis. *Variance investigation.* This term's meaning differs in statistics.

variance investigation. A step in managerial control processes. *Standard costing systems* produce *variance* numbers of various sorts. These numbers seldom exactly equal zero. Management must decide when a variance differs sufficiently from zero to study its cause. This term refers both to the decision about when to study the cause and to the study itself.

variation analysis. Analysis of the causes of changes in financial statement items of interest such as *net income* or *gross margin*.

VAT (Value-added tax). A tax levied on the market value of a firm's outputs less the market value of its purchased inputs.

vendor. A seller; sometimes spelled "vender."

verifiable. A qualitative *objective* of financial reporting specifying that accountants can trace items in *financial statements* back to *underlying documents*—supporting *invoices,* canceled *checks,* and other physical pieces of evidence.

verification. The auditor's act of reviewing or checking items in *financial statements* by tracing back to *underlying documents*—supporting *invoices,* canceled *checks,* and other business documents—or sending out *confirmations* to be returned. Compare with *physical verification.*

vertical analysis. Analysis of the financial statements of a single firm or across several firms for a particular time, as opposed to *horizontal* or *time-series analysis,* in which the analyst compares items over time for a single firm or across firms.

vertical integration. The extension of activity by an organization into business directly related to the production or distribution of the organization's end products. Although a firm may sell products to others at various stages, a vertically integrated firm devotes the substantial portion of the output at each stage to the production of the next stage or to end products. Compare *horizontal integration.*

vested. An employee's *pension plan* benefits that are not contingent on the employee's continuing to work for the employer.

visual curve fitting method. One crude form of cost *estimation.* Sometimes, when a firm needs only rough approximations of the amounts of *fixed* and *variable costs,* management need not perform a formal *regression analysis* but can plot the data and draw a line that seems to fit the data. Then it can use the parameters of that line for the rough approximations.

volume variance. *Production volume variance;* less often, used to mean *sales volume variance.*

voucher. A document that signals recognition of a *liability* and authorizes the disbursement of cash; sometimes used to refer to the written evidence documenting an *accounting entry,* as in the term *journal voucher.*

voucher system. In controlling *cash,* a method that requires someone in the firm to authorize each *check* with an approved *voucher.* The firm makes no *disbursements* of currency or coins except from *petty cash funds.*

vouching. The function performed by an *auditor* to ascertain that underlying data or documents support a *journal entry.*

W

wage. Compensation of employees based on time worked or output of product for manual labor. But see *take-home pay.*

warning signal. Tool used to identify quality-control problems; only signals a problem. Contrast with *diagnostic signal,* which both signals a problem and suggests its cause.

warrant. A certificate entitling the owner to buy a specified number of shares at a specified time(s) for a specified price; differs from a *stock option* only in that the firm grants options to employees and issues warrants to the public. See *right.*

warranty. A promise by a seller to correct deficiencies in products sold. When the seller gives warranties, proper accounting practice recognizes an estimate of warranty *expense* and an *estimated liability* at the time of sale. See *guarantee* for contrast in proper usage.

wash sale. The sale and purchase of the same or similar *asset* within a short time period. For *income tax* purposes, the taxpayer may not recognize *losses* on a sale of stock if the taxpayer purchases equivalent stock within 30 days before or after the date of sale.

waste. Material that is a residue from manufacturing operations and that has no sale value. Frequently, this has negative value because a firm must incur additional costs for disposal.

wasting asset. A *natural resource* that has a limited *useful life* and, hence, is subject to *amortization,* called *depletion.* Examples are timberland, oil and gas wells, and ore deposits.

watered stock. Shares issued for *assets* with *fair market price (value)* less than *par* or *stated value.* The firm records the assets on the books at the overstated values. In the law, for shares to be considered watered, the *board of directors* must have acted in bad faith or fraudulently in issuing the shares under these circumstances. The term originated from a former practice of cattle owners who fed cattle ("stock") large quantities of salt to make them thirsty. The cattle then drank much water before their owner took them to market. The owners did this to make the cattle appear heavier and more valuable than otherwise.

weighted average. An average computed by counting each occurrence of each value, not merely a single occurrence of each value. For example, if a firm purchases one unit for $1 and two units for $2 each, then the simple average of the purchase prices is $1.50, but the weighted average price per unit is $5/3 = $1.67. Contrast with *moving average*.

weighted-average cost of capital. Measured as the *weighted average* of the after-tax *cost* of *long-term debt* and the cost of *equity*.

weighted-average inventory method. Valuing either *withdrawals* or *ending inventory* at the *weighted-average* purchase price of all units on hand at the time of withdrawal or of computation of ending inventory. The firm uses the *inventory equation* to calculate the other quantity. If a firm uses the *perpetual inventory* method, accountants often call it the *moving average method*.

where-got, where-gone statement. A term allegedly used in the 1920s by W. M. Cole for a statement much like the *statement of cash flows*. Noted accounting historian S. Zeff reports that Cole actually used the term "where-got-gone" statement.

wind up. To bring to an end, such as the life of a corporation. The *board* winds up the life of a corporation by following the winding-up provisions of applicable statutes, by surrendering the charter, or by following *bankruptcy* proceedings. See also *liquidation*.

window dressing. The attempt to make financial statements show *operating* results, or a *financial position*, more favorable than they would otherwise show.

with recourse. See *note receivable discounted*.

withdrawals. *Assets* distributed to an owner. *Partner's drawings*. See *inventory equation* for another context.

withholding. Deductions that are taken from *salaries* or *wages*, usually for *income taxes*, and that the employer remits, in the employee's name, to the taxing authority.

without recourse. See *note receivable discounted*.

work sheet (program). (1) A computer program designed to combine explanations and calculations. This type of program helps in preparing *financial statements* and *schedules*. (2) A tabular schedule for convenient summary of *adjusting* and *closing entries*. The work sheet usually begins with an *unadjusted trial balance*. Adjusting entries appear in the next two columns, one for *debits* and one for *credits*. The work sheet carries the horizontal sum of each line to the right into either the *income statement* or the *balance sheet* column, as appropriate. The *plug* to equate the income statement column totals is, if a debit, the *income* or, if a credit, a *loss* for the period. That income will close *retained earnings* on the balance sheet. The income statement credit columns are the *revenues* for the period, and the debit columns are the *expenses* (and revenue contras) that appear on the income statement. "Work sheet" also refers to *schedules* for ascertaining other items that appear on the *financial statements* and that require adjustment or compilation.

working capital. *Current assets* minus *current liabilities*; sometimes called "net working capital" or "net current assets."

work(ing) papers. The schedules and analyses prepared by the *auditor* in carrying out investigations before issuing an *opinion* on *financial statements*.

work-in-process (inventory account). Partially completed product; appears on the balance sheet as *inventory*.

worth. *Value*. See *net worth*.

worth-debt ratio. Reciprocal of the *debt-equity ratio*. See *ratio*.

write down. To *write off*, except that the firm does not charge all the *asset*'s cost to *expense* or *loss;* generally used for nonrecurring items.

write off. To *charge* an *asset* to *expense* or *loss;* that is, to *debit* expense (or loss) and *credit* the asset.

write-off method. For treating *uncollectible accounts*, a method that *debits bad debt expense* and *credits* accounts receivable of specific customers as the firm identifies specific accounts as uncollectible. The firm cannot use this method when it can estimate uncollectible amounts and they are significant. See *bad debt expense, sales contra, estimated uncollectibles,* and the *allowance method* for contrast.

write up. To increase the recorded *cost* of an *asset* with no corresponding *disbursement* of *funds;* that is, to *debit* asset and *credit* revenue or, perhaps, *owners' equity;* seldom done in the United States because currently accepted accounting principles await actual transactions before recording asset increases. An exception occurs in accounting for *marketable equity securities*.

Y

yield. *Internal rate of return* of a stream of cash flows. Cash yield is *cash flow* divided by *book value*. See also *dividend yield*.

yield curve. The relation between *interest rates* and the term to maturity of loans. Ordinarily, longer-term loans have higher interest rates than shorter-term loans. This is called a "normal" yield curve. Sometimes long-term and short-term rates are approximately the same—a "flat" yield curve. Sometimes short-term loans have a higher rate than long-term ones—an "inverted" yield curve. *Term structure* of interest rates.

yield to maturity. At a given time, the *internal rate of return* of a series of cash flows; usually said of a *bond;* sometimes called the "effective rate."

yield variance. Measures the input-output relation while holding the standard mix of inputs constant: (standard price multiplied by actual amount of input used in the standard mix) − (standard price multiplied by standard quantity allowed for the actual output). It is the part of the *efficiency variance* not called the *mix variance*.

Z

zero-base(d) budgeting (ZBB). One philosophy for setting budgets. In preparing an ordinary *budget* for the next period, a manager starts with the budget for the current period and makes adjustments as seem necessary because of changed conditions for the next period. Since most managers like to increase the scope of the activities managed and since most prices increase most of the time, amounts in budgets prepared in the ordinary, incremental way seem to increase period after period. The authority approving the budget assumes that managers will carry out operations in the same way as in the past and that next period's expenditures will have to be at least as large as those of the current period. Thus, this authority tends to study only the increments to the current period's budget. In ZBB, the authority questions the process for carrying out a program and the entire budget for the next period. The authority studies every dollar in the budget, not just the dollars incremental to the previous period's amounts.

The advocates of ZBB claim that in this way, (1) management will more likely delete programs or divisions of marginal benefit to the business or governmental unit, rather than continuing with costs at least as large as the present ones, and (2) management may discover and implement alternative, more cost-effective ways of carrying out programs. ZBB implies questioning the existence of programs and the fundamental nature of the way that firms carry them out, not merely the amounts used to fund them. Experts appear to divide evenly as to whether the middle word should be "base" or "based."

Index

TABLE 3 Future Value of Annuity of $1 in Arrears

$$F_A = \frac{(1+r)^n - 1}{r}$$

r = interest rate; n = number of payments

No. of Payments = n	½%	1%	1½%	2%	3%	4%	5%	6%	7%	8%	10%	12%	15%	20%	25%
1	1.00000	1.00000	1.00000	1.00000	1.00000	1.00000	1.00000	1.00000	1.00000	1.00000	1.00000	1.00000	1.00000	1.00000	1.00000
2	2.00500	2.01000	2.01500	2.02000	2.03000	2.04000	2.05000	2.06000	2.07000	2.08000	2.10000	2.12000	2.15000	2.20000	2.25000
3	3.01503	3.03010	3.04523	3.06040	3.09090	3.12160	3.15250	3.18360	3.21490	3.24640	3.31000	3.37440	3.47250	3.64000	3.81250
4	4.03010	4.06040	4.09090	4.12160	4.18363	4.24646	4.31013	4.37462	4.43994	4.50611	4.64100	4.77933	4.99338	5.36800	5.76563
5	5.05025	5.10101	5.15227	5.20404	5.30914	5.41632	5.52563	5.63709	5.75074	5.86660	6.10510	6.35285	6.74238	7.44160	8.20703
6	6.07550	6.15202	6.22955	6.30812	6.46841	6.63298	6.80191	6.97532	7.15329	7.33593	7.71561	8.11519	8.75374	9.92992	11.25879
7	7.10588	7.21354	7.32299	7.43428	7.66246	7.89829	8.14201	8.39384	8.65402	8.92280	9.48717	10.08901	11.06680	12.91590	15.07349
8	8.14141	8.28567	8.43284	8.58297	8.89234	9.21423	9.54911	9.89747	10.25980	10.63663	11.43589	12.29969	13.72682	16.49908	19.84186
9	9.18212	9.36853	9.55933	9.75463	10.15911	10.58280	11.02656	11.49132	11.97799	12.48756	13.57948	14.77566	16.78584	20.79890	25.80232
10	10.22803	10.46221	10.70272	10.94972	11.46388	12.00611	12.57789	13.18079	13.81645	14.48656	15.93742	17.54874	20.30372	25.95868	33.25290
11	11.27917	11.56683	11.86326	12.16872	12.80780	13.48635	14.20679	14.97164	15.78360	16.64549	18.53117	20.65458	24.34928	32.15042	42.56613
12	12.33556	12.68250	13.04121	13.41209	14.19203	15.02581	15.91713	16.86994	17.88845	18.97713	21.38428	24.13313	29.00167	39.58050	54.20766
13	13.39724	13.80933	14.23683	14.68033	15.61779	16.62684	17.71298	18.88214	20.14064	21.49530	24.52271	28.02911	34.35192	48.49660	68.75958
14	14.46423	14.94742	15.45038	15.97394	17.08632	18.29191	19.59863	21.01507	22.55049	24.21492	27.97498	32.39260	40.50471	59.19592	86.94947
15	15.53655	16.09690	16.68214	17.29342	18.59891	20.02359	21.57856	23.27597	25.12902	27.15211	31.77248	37.27971	47.58041	72.03511	109.6868
16	16.61423	17.25786	17.93237	18.63929	20.15688	21.82453	23.65749	25.67253	27.88805	30.32438	35.94973	42.75328	55.71747	87.44213	138.1085
17	17.69730	18.43044	19.20136	20.01207	21.76159	23.69751	25.84037	28.21288	30.84022	33.75023	40.54470	48.88367	65.07509	105.9306	173.6357
18	18.78579	19.61475	20.48938	21.41231	23.41444	25.64541	28.13238	30.90565	33.99903	37.45024	45.59917	55.74971	75.83636	128.1167	218.0446
19	19.87972	20.81090	21.79672	22.84056	25.11687	27.67123	30.53900	33.75999	37.37896	41.44626	51.15909	63.43968	88.21181	154.7400	273.5558
20	20.97912	22.01900	23.12367	24.87037	26.87037	29.77808	33.06595	36.78559	40.99549	45.76196	57.27500	72.05244	102.44358	186.6880	342.9447
22	23.19443	24.47159	25.83758	27.29898	30.53678	34.24797	38.50521	43.39229	49.00574	55.45676	71.40275	92.50258	137.63164	271.0307	538.1011
24	25.43196	26.97346	28.63352	30.42186	34.42647	39.08260	44.50200	50.81558	58.17667	66.76476	88.49733	118.15524	184.16784	392.4842	843.0329
26	27.69191	29.52563	31.51397	33.67091	38.55304	44.31174	51.11345	59.15638	68.67647	79.95442	109.18177	150.33393	245.71197	567.3773	1319.489
28	29.97452	32.12910	34.48148	37.05121	42.93092	49.96758	58.40258	68.52811	80.69769	95.33883	134.20994	190.69889	327.10408	819.2233	2063.952
30	32.28002	34.78489	37.53868	40.56808	47.57542	56.08494	66.43885	79.05819	94.46079	113.28321	164.49402	241.33268	434.74515	1181.881	3227.174
32	34.60862	37.49407	40.68829	44.22703	52.50276	62.70147	75.29883	90.88978	110.21815	134.21354	201.13777	304.84772	577.10046	1704.109	5044.710
34	36.96058	40.25770	43.93309	48.03380	57.73018	69.85791	85.06696	104.18375	128.25876	158.62667	245.47670	384.52098	765.36535	2456.118	7884.609
36	39.33610	43.07688	47.27597	51.99437	63.27594	77.59831	95.83632	119.12087	148.91346	187.10215	299.12681	484.46312	1014.34568	3539.009	12321.95
38	41.73545	45.95272	50.71989	56.11494	69.15945	85.97034	107.70955	135.90421	172.56102	220.31595	364.04343	609.83053	1343.62216	5098.373	19255.30
40	44.15885	48.88637	54.26789	60.40198	75.40126	95.02552	120.79977	154.76197	199.63511	259.05652	442.59556	767.09142	1779.09031	7343.858	30088.66
45	50.32416	56.48107	63.61420	71.89271	92.71986	121.0294	159.7002	212.7435	285.7493	386.5056	718.9048	1358.230	3585.12846	18281.31	91831.50
50	56.64516	64.46318	73.68283	84.57940	112.7969	152.6671	209.3480	290.3359	406.5289	573.7702	1163.909	2400.018	7217.71628	45497.19	280255.7
100	129.33370	170.4814	228.8030	312.2323	607.2877	1237.624	2610.025	5638.368	12381.66	27484.52	137796.1	696010.5	783 × 10⁴	414 × 10⁵	196 × 10⁸

Note: To convert from this table to values of an annuity in advance, determine the annuity in arrears above for one more period and subtract 1.00000.

which equals the budgeted contribution margin per unit times the difference between budgeted and actual sales volume. Recall that each unit sold generates $6.00 of revenue, each unit has a budgeted (or standard) variable manufacturing cost of $3.67, a budgeted shipping cost of $0.02 per unit, and a budgeted sales commission of $0.12 (= 2 percent × $6.00). Thus the contribution margin expected from each unit is $2.19 (= $6.00 − $3.67 − $0.02 − $0.12).

Why is the *standard* variable cost used to compute the contribution margin instead of the *actual* cost? Recall that we are calculating the effect of sales *volume* alone. By using standard variable cost in computing contribution margins, we avoid mixing cost variances, discussed later in this chapter, with the effect of sales volume.

Marketing also may be responsible for the sales price variance. Note that the increase in sales commission (2 percent of $8,000 = $160), a result of the higher-than-budgeted selling price, partially offsets the favorable sales price variance of $8,000.

Investigation of the $1,440 (unfavorable) variable marketing cost variance should start with sales commissions. Did the firm inappropriately pay commissions—for example, on sales that customers returned? Did the commission rate exceed the 2 percent budgeted? Did the sales staff earn commissions in previous periods reported in the current period? Managers would ask similar questions about shipping costs. Did rates increase, for example?

The accounting staff usually ascertains whether variances result from bookkeeping adjustments or errors, whereas marketing managers investigate marketing activities that may have caused the variances.

Fixed marketing costs are often discretionary. A favorable variance does not necessarily mean good performance. For example, the $1,000 favorable variance at Victoria's Gourmet Coffee could mean the company advertised less than intended, which could have a negative effect on future sales.

Administration

The accounting process assigns a $200 favorable variance to administration. Administrative variances are often the hardest to manage because they are not engineered; that is, no well-defined causal relation exists between administrative input and administrative output.

Management usually budgets administrative costs with discretion, placing a ceiling on costs for a particular set of tasks. For example, suppose an organization's corporate internal audit staff received a budget of $2,000,000 for 40 people's salaries and an additional $400,000 for travel, supplies, and other costs. The internal audit department may not spend more than those limits without obtaining approvals, which would normally come from top executives (for example, the company president) or the board of directors.

Although discretionary budgets can provide a ceiling for expenditure, they do not provide a norm like a flexible manufacturing cost budget. If you cannot measure output, then you cannot measure the input-output relation, which makes ascertaining the "proper" levels of costs difficult. You should take these difficulties into account when you evaluate an administrative cost variance or any other discretionary cost variance.

Problem 10.1 for Self-Study

Preparing the profit variance analysis. Computer Supply, Inc., budgeted production and sales of 40,000 laptop computer cases for the month of April at a selling price of $11 each. The company actually sold 50,000 cases for $10 each. The company budgeted the following costs:

Budget	
Standard Variable Manufacturing Costs per Unit	$4.00
Fixed Manufacturing Overhead for the Month	$80,000
Marketing and Administrative Costs:	
Variable (per unit)	$1.00
Fixed (monthly budget)	$100,000